PATTERNS OF
EXPOSITION
Eighteenth Edition

Robert A. Schwegler
University of Rhode Island

PEARSON
Longman

New York   San Francisco   Boston
London   Toronto   Sydney   Tokyo   Singapore   Madrid
Mexico City   Munich   Paris   Capetown   Hong Kong   Montreal

Publisher: Joseph Opiela
Senior Marketing Manager: Sandra McGuire
Senior Supplements Editor: Donna Campion
Production Manager: Denise Phillip
Project Coordination, Text Design, and Electronic Page Makeup:
    WestWords Inc.
Cover Designer/Manager: Wendy Ann Fredericks
Cover Art: © Nic Miller, Digital Vision/Getty Images, Inc.
Senior Manufacturing Buyer: Alfred C. Dorsey
Printer and Binder: R. R. Donnelley and Sons
Cover Printer: Phoenix Graphics Services

Library of Congress Cataloging-in-Publication Data

Patterns of exposition / [edited by] Robert A. Schwegler.-- 18th ed.
    p. cm.
  Includes index.
  ISBN 0-321-40921-3
  1. College readers. 2. Exposition (Rhetoric) 3. English language--Rhetoric.
I. Schwegler, Robert A.
  PE1417.P3954 2006
  808'.0427--dc22
                        2005038062

Please visit us at http://www.ablongman.com

ISBN 0–321–40921–3

1 2 3 4 5 6 7 8 9 10—DOC—09   08   07   06

Contents

Thematic Contents

Morals, Crime, and Punishment

Growing Up/Getting Old

Differences

Families and Children

Society and Social Change

Media

Essay Pairs

To the Instructor

Instructors familiar with *Patterns of Exposition* will notice that it retains the substantially expanded discussions of rhetorical patterns, student essay examples, and extensively revised chapters on reading and writing that were well received in the preceding edition. And it continues the tradition of providing many new and interesting readings. The discussions of patterns of exposition and argument and the essays illustrating these strategies demonstrate the ways rhetorical patterns enable writers and readers to explore, understand, and take a stand on questions of culture, identity, and value in college communities, in the workplace, and in society at large.

Chapter 1, "Reading as a Writer," introduces students to reading strategies especially useful for the essays in this text, for academic reading in general, and for turning reading into writing. Brent Staples's essay, "Just Walk on By," appears early in the chapter and introduces students to the kinds of readings they will encounter in the text and to ways they can use reading as a springboard to writing. The chapter pays particular attention to critical reading and reading for technique as well as reading for understanding. It introduces students to concrete reading strategies for use in composition courses, in other college courses, and beyond.

Chapter 2, "Ways of Writing," introduces students to the composing process and to a variety of useful techniques for discovering ideas and information, planning an essay, developing a thesis, drafting, and revising. The chapter also provides numerous student examples, including a student essay in draft and revised form. Our emphasis here and elsewhere in the text is on the practical: concrete writing strategies, specific suggestions, and concise illustrations.

Each chapter covering a pattern of exposition (or argument) begins with a discussion of the roles the particular pattern can play for writers and readers. The discussions provide a definition of the pattern; a paragraph example taken from the work of an accomplished, professional writer; a discussion of the various uses of the pattern

("Why Use . . . ?); suggestions for designing essays that employ the pattern ("Choosing a Strategy"); and techniques for developing the content of an essay as well as individual paragraphs and sentences ("Developing. . . .").

The first few essay selections in each chapter illustrate some of the many roles a pattern can play in organizing thought and expression within an essay or the roles a pattern can play in working with other rhetorical patterns to create an organized, purposeful, effective exposition (or argument).

Each chapter concludes with a cluster of essays focusing on "Issues and Ideas" of contemporary and (perhaps) enduring significance. The primary goal of these clusters is not simply to encourage students to think and write about the specific themes and issues, but to help students develop an awareness of rhetorical strategies as a critical tool for understanding differing perspectives and to demonstrate the variety of purposes a strategy can serve. It is precisely the broad similarity in subject matter and strategy among the essays in a cluster that serves to highlight for students the important differences and the varied models for expression the selections provide.

The questions at the end of each selection highlight important issues of meaning, technique, and style that help develop students' abilities as readers and the range of options available to them as they write. "Read to Write" activities follow the questions. The first activity in each set, labeled "Collaborating," offers students a chance to work with their classmates to develop ideas, essay plans, brief essays, and, occasionally, a collaboratively written essay. The second activity, labeled "Considering Audience," directs students' attention to readers' expectations and audience constraints. Some of the activities ask them to consider the likely reactions of readers to the essay presented in the text; other activities call for speculation about readers' reactions to different writing strategies. The third activity, "Developing an Essay," helps students view the sample essay in the text as a broad model for their own work—a model that they are encouraged to alter and develop in a fashion appropriate to their own perspectives and purposes. These activities provide practice in linking reading to writing—one of the primary focuses of the book as a whole. The "Writing Suggestions" at the end of each chapter include collaborative activities and offer further avenues for students to follow from reading into writing.

In choosing new essays and retaining those from previous editions, I have looked first for selections that are well written and insightful and that reward careful (re)reading, and then for selections that can serve as useful models for thought, organization, and expression. I have also drawn on suggestions from the text's instructor-users and have reviewed the responses of students. Although obviously I am unable to comply with all requests, I have seriously considered and fully appreciated all of them, and I have incorporated many suggestions into this new edition. I have responded, as well, to requests for added essays in some of the most heavily used chapters of the book.

The wealth of excellent and recent nonfiction writing reflecting the perspectives of many different cultural and social groups has made it possible for me to choose selections reflecting the intellectual ferment and challenge of our times. In drawing on this diversity, I have not tried to represent every identity in an unimaginative and rigid fashion but have instead tried to use it to create an exciting mixture of perspectives and backgrounds designed to encourage varied, engaged responses from students.

Because so many instructors find it useful, I continue to retain the table of contents listing pairs of essays. Each pair provides contrasts (or similarities) in theme, approach, and style that are worth studying. The essay pairs can form the focus of class discussion or writing assignments.

The "Further Readings: Combining Patterns" chapter provides contemporary selections to provoke discussion. The pieces also suggest some intriguing combinations of patterns and goals for writing essays that can be pursued in the hands of skilled and daring writers. The essays in this section can be used on their own or with the other chapters of the book.

Throughout *Patterns of Exposition*, Eighteenth Edition, I have tried to make possible the convenient use of all materials in whatever ways instructors think best for their own classes. With a few exceptions, only complete essays or freestanding units of larger works have been included. With their inevitable overlap of patterns, they are more complicated than excerpts illustrating single principles, but they are also more realistic examples of exposition and more useful for other classroom purposes. Versatility has been an important criterion in choosing materials.

Fifty-two of the selections best liked in previous editions have been retained. Seventeen selections are new, and all but a few of these are anthologized for the first time.

The arrangement of essays is but one of the many workable orders; instructors can easily develop another if they so desire. The thematic table of contents and the table of essay pairs also suggest a variety of arrangements.

I have tried to vary the study questions—and undoubtedly have included far more than any one teacher will want—from the purely objective to those calling for some serious self-examination by students. (The Instructor's Manual supplements these materials.)

"A Guide to Terms," at the end of the book, briefly discusses matters from *Abstract* to *Unity* and refers whenever possible to the essays themselves for illustrations. Its location is designed to permit unity and easy access, and there are cross-references to it in the study questions following each selection.

In all respects—size, content, arrangement, format—I have tried to keep *Patterns of Exposition* uncluttered and easy to use.

ACKNOWLEDGMENTS

This edition of *Patterns of Exposition* is a truly collaborative effort, and I want to acknowledge and thank my collaborator: Nancy Newman Schwegler. I have benefitted immensely from her insights and efforts. Working with her has been a pleasure as well as a learning experience for me. Nancy Newman Schwegler has contributed much to prior editions of the text, but until recently I have not had a chance to acknowledge her contributions in a way they certainly deserve. Her insight, taste, and intelligence have helped make this book a continued success for instructors and students.

I would also like to thank Brian and Tara Schwegler for their advice on current social developments and cultural trends; Christopher Schwegler for tolerating this all; and Ashley Marie Schwegler for putting up with two authors in the house and making our lives a lot sunnier. And I want to thank Nancy Newman Schwegler for her love and support.

In addition, special thanks are due to the many users of this text and to the reviewers for this revision: Diann L. Baecker, Virginia State University; Jacqueline A. Blackwell, Thomas Nelson Community College Ellen Clay, Vermont State College; Huey Crisp, University of Arkansas at Little Rock; Lawrence J. Epstein, Suffolk County Community College; Richard D. Greenwood, Montgomery County Community College; Arden Jensen, Lee University; Robert Koch, St. Louis Community College; and Jane Waitkus, Pensylvania State University, Hazleton.

Robert A. Schwegler

1
Reading as a Writer

Reading and writing work together. Good writers draw ideas and information from their reading. They use reading to help understand an audience's likely reactions. They read to discover techniques of expression. They use critical reading as a springboard for their own writing. You can read for all of these purposes—understanding, critical response, and discovery of technique—or for only a few, depending on your goals as a writer. This book assumes that much of your attention will be devoted to two important purposes for writing, **exposition** and **argument.**

You encounter **expository writing** every day in many forms, including essays, magazine articles, reports, memos, newspaper reports, and nonfiction books. It brings facts and insights, helping writers and readers share experiences and understanding. You encounter **argumentative writing** in editorials and opinion essays, reports and proposals, policy statements and investigative reporting, and academic or professional articles. It focuses on differences but also provides reasons to agree with the writer's perspective.

To develop your skills as a reader and writer of expository and argumentative texts, you need to pay attention to three ways of approaching a text: reading for understanding, critical reading, and reading for technique. No matter what your approach, however, you need to pay attention to the elements of the **reading process: previewing, reading,** and **reviewing.**

THE READING PROCESS

If you plunge right into reading, moving quickly through an article, essay, or book and then put it aside, you are missing important opportunities. Effective readers treat reading as a process consisting of **previewing, reading,** and **reviewing.** They develop techniques for each of these stages of the reading process.

You can develop your ability to read critically and actively by employing strategies like those outlined in the following pages and applying them as you read the selections in this book (and on other occasions, too).

Previewing Strategies

Previewing means "reading before you start reading." Newspapers provide headlines to tell you what to expect in an article. Books and articles have titles. Authors and editors often provide brief summaries at the beginning of a chapter or in a table of contents. Magazine editors often take key statements from an article and reprint them in large type within boxes where readers can see them as they flip through the pages. Paying attention to these features is important because the knowledge and expectation you bring to a text can affect how well you understand it and determine what you are able to draw from it. For example, reading an expository or argumentative essay without some idea of where it is going or what the writer intends is like following a complicated set of plans without any idea of what you are building.

Moreover, you can more readily understand the reasoning or information in an essay and evaluate the author's arguments and point of view when you already know something about the topic or issue. Previewing helps you bring to mind what you already know about a subject before you begin a careful reading of an essay. It helps you develop reasonable expectations for understanding and evaluating the paths an essay takes.

Strategy: Look for help from the editor or writer. Writers and editors often provide you with considerable help for previewing because they recognize its importance. The titles they choose are a good place to start. While some may be imaginative but not particularly helpful, others will tell you much about a work's contents and organization, as does the title of Don Aslett's book, *How*

Do I Clean the Moosehead? And 99 More Tough Questions About Housecleaning.

A table of contents provides detailed information about the coverage and purpose of a work and perhaps even a summary of individual sections of the work. The table of contents for this book, for example, offers brief summaries of the essay selections, identifying the general topic of each and the writer's perspective. Here, for instance, is the entry for Catherine Seipp's essay, "Meet Today's Dad."

> A conservative writer takes a satiric look at "Today's Dad," contrasting the contemporary version with "Yesterday's Dad" and finding the traditional model (and traditional values) superior in a number of ways.

Once you know that Seipp writes from the perspective of the cultural and political right (the selection comes from the conservative website *National Review Online*), you can read her essay (pp. 189–193) with a greater appreciation of the origin and consequences of her ideas.

If an article or book does not have a table of contents, skim the text looking for headings and subheadings that reveal the writer's plan and the topics being discussed.

If an editor highlights important passages in an essay or article, pay attention to them. Here are three passages from an magazine article entitled "What Makes Sammy Walk?" that the editor chose to reprint in large type in the middle of a page.

> Less than 70 percent of U.S. men are now full-time year-round workers.
>
> "You don't have a social life," Dave's daughter says, "and you don't do anything."
>
> "I just put in a proposal to cut my hours to thirty-two a week and take a 20 percent pay cut," says a woman. "It's been accepted. I'm so happy."

Strategy: Look for help from the context. The kind of magazine, scholarly journal, or newspaper in which an essay appears can tell you important things about its outlook. Some publications have a reputation for publishing articles with a particular social, cultural, or political point of view. Look for any statements of the periodical's editorial outlook. Pay attention to the magazine's title and to the titles of the other articles it contains.

For books, look at the back cover or dust jacket. They may provide a brief summary of the contents or the writer's outlook. They may also offer quotations from reviewers that highlight a book's main points.

Strategy: Practice your previewing skills. Use some or all of the techniques discussed in the preceding paragraphs to preview the essay that follows, Brent Staples's "Just Walk on By" (pp. 5–9).

BRENT STAPLES

BRENT STAPLES was born in 1951 in Chester, Pennsylvania. He received his B.A. in 1973 from Widener University and his Ph.D. (in psychology) in 1982 from the University of Chicago. He is a member of the *New York Times* editorial board, writing on matters of culture and society. He was formerly a reporter for the *Chicago Sun Times* and an editor of the *New York Times Book Review.* Staples is the author of *Parallel Time* (1994), a memoir.

Just Walk on By

The power of examples to enable a reader to see through someone else's eyes is evident in this selection. Though many of the examples in the essay draw on a reader's sympathy, their main purpose appears to be explanatory; hence, the author accompanies them with detailed discussions. The result is a piece that is both enlightening and moving.

My first victim was a woman—white, well dressed, probably in her early twenties. I came upon her late one evening on a deserted street in Hyde Park, a relatively affluent neighborhood in an otherwise mean, impoverished section of Chicago. As I swung onto the avenue behind her, there seemed to be a discreet, uninflammatory distance between us. Not so. She cast back a worried glance. To her, the youngish black man—a broad six feet two inches with a beard and billowing hair, both hands shoved into the pockets of a bulky military jacket—seemed menacingly close. After a few more quick glimpses, she picked up her pace and was soon running in earnest. Within seconds she disappeared into a cross street.

That was more than a decade ago. I was 22 years old, a graduate student newly arrived at the University of Chicago. It was in the echo of that terrified woman's footfalls that I first began to know the unwieldy inheritance I'd come into—the ability to alter public space in ugly ways. It was clear that she thought herself the quarry of a mugger, a rapist, or worse. Suffering a bout of insomnia, however, I was stalking sleep, not defenseless wayfarers. As a softy who is scarcely able to take a knife to a raw chicken—let alone hold it to a person's throat—I was surprised, embarrassed, and dismayed all at once. Her flight made me feel like an accomplice in tyranny. It also made it clear that I was indistinguishable from the muggers who occasionally

seeped into the area from the surrounding ghetto. That first encounter, and those that followed, signified that a vast, unnerving gulf
lay between nighttime pedestrians—particularly women—and me.
And I soon gathered that being perceived as dangerous is a hazard in
itself. I only needed to turn a corner into a dicey situation, or crowd
some frightened, armed person in a foyer somewhere, or make an er-
rant move after being pulled over by a policeman. Where fear and
weapons meet—and they often do in urban America—there is always the possibility of death.

In the first year, my first away from my hometown, I was to become thoroughly familiar with the language of fear. At dark, shad-
owy intersections in Chicago, I could cross in front of a car stopped
at a traffic light and elicit the *thunk, thunk, thunk, thunk* of the
driver—black, white, male, or female—hammering down the door
locks. On less traveled streets after dark, I grew accustomed to but
never comfortable with people who crossed to the other side of the
street rather than pass me. Then there were the standard unpleas-
antries with police, doormen, bouncers, cab drivers, and others
whose business it is to screen out troublesome individuals *before*
there is any nastiness.

I moved to New York nearly two years ago and I have remained
an avid night walker. In central Manhattan, the near-constant crowd
cover minimized tense one-on-one street encounters. Elsewhere—
visiting friends in SoHo, where sidewalks are narrow and tightly
spaced buildings shut out the sky—things can get very taut indeed.

Black men have a firm place in New York mugging literature.
Norman Podhoretz in his famed (or infamous) 1963 essay, "My
Negro Problem—And Ours," recalls growing up in terror of black
males; they "were tougher than we were, more ruthless," he
writes—and as an adult on the Upper West Side of Manhattan, he
continues, he cannot constrain his nervousness when he meets black
men on certain streets. Similarly, a decade later, the essayist and
novelist Edward Hoagland extols a New York where once "Negro
bitterness bore down mainly on other Negroes." Where some see
mere panhandlers, Hoagland sees "a mugger who is clearly screwing
up his nerve to do more than just *ask* for money." But Hoagland has
"the New Yorker's quick-hunch posture for broken-field maneuver-
ing," and the bad guy swerves away.

I often witness that "hunch posture," from women after dark on
the warrenlike streets of Brooklyn where I live. They seem to set
their faces on neutral and, with their purse straps strung across their
chests bandolier style, they forge ahead as though bracing them-

selves against being tackled. I understand, of course, that the danger they perceive is not a hallucination. Women are particularly vulnerable to street violence, and young black males are drastically over-represented among the perpetrators of that violence. Yet these truths are no solace against the kind of alienation that comes of being ever the suspect, against being set apart, a fearsome entity with whom pedestrians avoid making eye contact.

It is not altogether clear to me how I reached the ripe old age of 22 without being conscious of the lethality nighttime pedestrians attributed to me. Perhaps it was because in Chester, Pennsylvania, the small, angry industrial town where I came of age in the 1960s, I was scarcely noticeable against a backdrop of gang warfare, street knifing, and murders. I grew up one of the good boys, had perhaps a half-dozen fist fights. In retrospect, my shyness of combat has clear sources. 7

Many things go into the making of a young thug. One of those things is the consummation of the male romance with the power to intimidate. An infant discovers that random flailings send the baby bottle flying out of the crib and crashing to the floor. Delighted, the joyful babe repeats those motions again and again, seeking to duplicate the feat. Just so, I recall the points at which some of my boyhood friends were finally seduced by the perception of themselves as tough guys. When a mark cowered and surrendered his money without resistance, myth and reality merged—and paid off. It is, after all, only manly to embrace the power to frighten and intimidate. We, as men, are not supposed to give an inch of our lane on the highway; we are to seize the fighter's edge in work and in play and even in love; we are to be valiant in the face of hostile forces. 8

Unfortunately, poor and powerless young men seem to take all this nonsense literally. As a boy, I saw countless tough guys locked away; I have since buried several. They were babies, really—a teenage cousin, a brother of 22, a childhood friend in his mid-twenties—all gone down in episodes of bravado played out in the streets. I came to doubt the virtues of intimidation early on. I chose, perhaps even unconsciously, to remain a shadow—timid, but a survivor. 9

The fearsomeness mistakenly attributed to me in public places often has a perilous flavor. The most frightening of these confusions occurred in the late 1970s and early 1980s when I worked as a journalist in Chicago. One day, rushing into the office of a magazine I was writing for, with a deadline story in hand, I was mistaken for a 10 burglar. The office manager called security and, with an ad hoc posse, pursued me through the labyrinthine halls, nearly to my editor's door. I had no way of proving who I was. I could only move briskly toward the company of someone who knew me.

Another time I was on assignment for a local paper and killing   11
time before an interview. I entered a jewelry store on the city's affluent Near North Side. The proprietor excused herself and returned with an enormous red Doberman pinscher straining at the end of a leash. She stood, the dog extended toward me, silent to my questions, her eyes bulging nearly out of her head. I took a cursory look around, nodded, and bade her good night. Relatively speaking, however, I never fared as badly as another black male journalist. He went to nearby Waukegan, Illinois, a couple of summers ago to work on a story about a murderer who was born there. Mistaking the reporter for the killer, police hauled him from his car at gunpoint and but for his press credentials would probably have tried to book him. Such episodes are not uncommon. Black men trade tales like this all the time.

In "My Negro Problem—And Ours," Podhoretz writes that the   12
hatred he feels for blacks makes itself known to him through a variety of avenues—one being his discomfort with that "special brand of paranoid touchiness" to which he says blacks are prone. No doubt he is speaking here of black men. In time, I learned to smother the rage I felt at so often being taken for a criminal. Not to do so would surely have led to madness—via that special "paranoid touchiness" that so annoyed Podhoretz at the time he wrote the essay.

I began to take precautions to make myself less threatening. I   13
move about with care, particularly late in the evening. I give a wide berth to nervous people on subway platforms during the wee hours, particularly when I have exchanged business clothes for jeans. If I happen to be entering a building behind some people who appear skittish, I may walk by, letting them clear the lobby before I return, so as not to seem to be following them. I have been calm and extremely congenial on those rare occasions when I've been pulled over by the police.

And on late-evening constitutionals along streets less traveled   14
by, I employ what has proved to be an excellent tension-reducing measure: I whistle melodies from Beethoven and Vivaldi and the more popular classical composers. Even steely New Yorkers hunching toward nighttime destinations seem to relax, and occasionally they even join in the tune. Virtually everybody seems to sense that a mugger wouldn't be warbling bright, sunny selections

from Vivaldi's *Four Seasons*. It is my equivalent of the cowbell that hikers wear when they know they are in bear country.

READING STRATEGIES

The reading strategies you employ should vary according to your goals for reading: to understand, to respond critically, or to understand writing techniques. These goals can overlap, of course, but whenever you try to do too many things as you read, your effectiveness at each task suffers. For this reason, you may often need to read a selection more than once, concentrating on a different goal each time. The strategies on the following pages should help enrich your reading experience.

Reading for Understanding

When you read for understanding, you focus on ideas and information. You try to identify the main idea (**thesis**) and the line of reasoning that supports it. You explore meanings and values. Keep these questions in mind as you read for understanding.

- What is this selection about?
- What does this selection mean?
- What is this selection's purpose?
- How is the main idea developed or supported?

What is this selection about? Some essays focus on one topic throughout. Other essays, just as effective, discuss several related topics, such as the effect of television on attitudes towards violence and its consequences for family life. Brent Staples's essay, "Just Walk on By," presents a variety of examples and brief incidents, but they all illustrate how people reacted to the author's presence.

As a reader, you need to be able to identify the topic or related topics around which an essay is constructed. Avoid the temptation to pay attention only to ideas and information that interest you. You risk misunderstanding the real focus of the essay if you give selective attention to the elements that interest you.

Strategy: Look for cues. Writers frequently use a title, headings in the text, or direct statements as cues identifying an essay's topic or focus.

> **Title:** "Women, Men, and the Media"
> **Heading:** "Stereotypical Portrayals of Men and Women"

> **Direct Statements:** "But in what ways are our behaviors, especially those of children, shaped by the inaccurate and over-simplified portraits of men and women that populate the mass media?"

Strategy: Make a list of topics. Review what you have read and make a list of the topics or important ideas discussed in the essay. If the elements in your list fit clearly within a broader topic, state it; or if they do not, try stating their relationship in a way that identifies the essay's focus.

> local restaurants replaced by fast food
> small shops replaced by malls
> family farms turn into agribusinesses
> hardware stores replaced by home building centers
> small towns replaced by sprawling suburbs

> **Overall Topic:** change from small, individualized social organizations to large, more impersonal ones

Strategy: Look for repetition. Identify words, ideas, or subjects that appear repeatedly in the text. Such repetitions provide evidence of an essay's focus and may even be intentional signals provided by the writer. In "Just Walk on By," for example, Brent Staples uses words like "softy," "embarrassed," and "frightening" to refer to himself, his feelings, and his reaction to the incidents he describes. He uses a contrasting set of words like "fearsomeness," "dangerous," and "terror" to describe people's (mistaken) reactions to him and to other young black men like him.

What does this selection mean? Expository writing offers conclusions and insights. Argumentative writing offers opinions or proposes a course of action. Much of the value of these kinds of writing lies in the insights, ideas, and opinions conveyed: What the writing means.

Sometimes direct statements announce the meaning(s) of an essay, as when Brent Staples in "Just Walk on By" says that "the fearsomeness mistakenly attributed to me in public places often has a perilous flavor." Often, however, conclusions are presented less directly or even implied, requiring you to provide an answer to the question, "What does it mean?" Good writing generally offers more than one insight or conclusion, typically a main point and several related points. Identifying the main point is an important step for any reader trying to understand an essay.

*Mis*understanding is always possible, however. Some of an essay's conclusions may be relatively difficult to understand. Some may be implied rather than stated directly. Some may seem very important to you because you find them particularly interesting, even though their role in the essay may not be that significant.

Strategy: Highlight direct statements. While you read or when you have finished reading an essay, try highlighting, underlining, or otherwise making note of conclusions, generalizations, or opinions stated directly to readers. These can include statements (or restatements) of an essay's main idea or *thesis* like the following.

"Taboos, big or small, are always about having to respect somebody's (often irrational) boundary—or else."

—Michael Ventura
"Don't Even Think About It!"

"I am a peace-loving woman. But several events in the past 10 years have convinced me I'm safer when I carry a pistol."

—Linda Hasselstrom
"A Peaceful Woman Explains Why She Carries a Pistol"

They can also include headings in the text, topic sentences in paragraphs, or other statements that receive special emphasis.

For many essays, a list of such statements would provide a rough but revealing outline of the writer's exploration of a subject or of the chain of argument supporting a thesis. Here is the list Shauna Benoit compiled from her reading of Cullen Murphy's essay, "Hello, Darkness" (pp. 327–332). Note how the list clarifies the way the writer has arranged the essay.

"The average American a hundred years ago was able to sleep 20 percent longer than the average American today."
"Other evidence seems to indicate that the rate of sleep loss is in fact accelerating."
"We are laboring under a large and increasingly burdensome 'sleep deficit'. . . ."
"Many commentators would blame it on what might be called the AWOL factor—that is, the American Way of Life. We are by nature a busy and ambitious people whom tectonic social forces . . . have turned into a race of laboratory rats on a treadmill going nowhere ever faster."

> "Yet electricity's ubiquitous and seemingly most innocuous use—to power the common light bulb—could not help exacting a price in sleep."
>
> "Whatever it is that we wish or are made to do—pursue leisure, earn a living—there are simply far more usable hours now in which to do it."

Strategy: Look for repetition and emphasis. Look for words, phrases, details, and ideas that the writer repeats throughout a text. They are cues to ideas or issues that receive special emphasis within the text—even if not all the repetition was consciously intended by the writer. Repetitions can help you interpret the meanings and values around which an essay has been constructed and can also act as evidence for your conclusions about the essay.

Strategy: Pause and summarize. As you read an essay you will likely pause at a number of "resting places," between sections or paragraphs, for example. When you pause, take a moment to summarize what the essay has already said and to predict what it will say next. Glance back over the essay for evidence to support your interpretation, then read ahead to test the accuracy of your predictions as well as your understanding of the essay's meanings and values.

What is this selection's purpose? Expository and argumentative writing each have general purposes: expository—to explain and explore; and argumentative—to convince and persuade. To understand an individual essay, you need to recognize its more specific purpose(s), however.

By taking purpose into account as you read, you can more easily grasp an essay's meaning and evaluate its likely effect on readers. Sometimes, writers state their purpose directly; at other times, you will need to pay attention to repeated phrases and ideas in a text to understand its purpose. Remember, too, that essays often have secondary purposes as well as primary ones.

How is the main idea developed or supported? Once you have identified the main idea (thesis) and related ideas in an essay, you can pay attention to the distinction between them and the examples, information, and discussions that develop or support them. To do so, try keeping two questions in mind as you read: How is the main idea developed or supported? How adequate is the development/support?

Writers will often make your job easier by using familiar words or phrases to signal supporting details, discussions, or examples. Here are a few of the most familiar.

for example	supports	in the case of
for instance	explains	sheds light on
contributes to	because	illustrates
justifies	as a consequence	explains

In "Just Walk on By," for example, Brent Staples uses phrases like "in my first year," "that was more than a decade ago," "I often witness," and "another time" to emphasize that the examples he presents show an enduring pattern of mistaken reactions to him—simply because of his age and race.

Reading Critically

Critical reading questions and challenges a text. It treats the text as a starting point, not the final word on a subject or issue. Critical reading helps you develop your own ideas and conclusions. It helps you evaluate the ideas and information in a text. Critical reading suggests ways to draw on reading for your own writing. Developing a habit of critical reading is an important part of developing your ability as a writer.

Above all, critical reading is active reading. It calls for activity on your part—jotting down ideas and responses, evaluating conclusions and information, speculating about consequences, or making notes for an essay of your own. At times, of course, you may wish to read simply to gather ideas and information. But even when you do, critical reading habits can come to your aid by prompting you to consider just how reliable a text's information and ideas are.

Strategy: Keeping a reading journal. A **reading journal** is a notebook, folder, or computer file in which you keep your responses to reading: notes, questions, ideas, criticisms, and the like. Turning the fleeting ideas, questions, and responses that occur to you as you read into sentences in a journal helps you remember them. It gives you a chance to consider them at greater length and makes them available for later use, perhaps in an essay of your own.

You can organize entries in a reading journal according to the particular selection, allotting a few pages to each article, chapter, or book, for example. Or you can organize the journal by categories, such as "Responses (and Objections) to Readings About New Roles for Men and Women" or "Quotations and Information for Use in My 'Dangers of Dieting' Paper."

Are you looking for topics and issues to address in your own writing? Make notes about interesting or controversial topics you encounter in reading, particularly those about which you have strong feelings or a distinct point of view or those that the author treats superficially, leaving you an opportunity to provide a detailed treatment of your own. Are you looking for conclusions or perspectives that differ from yours? Summarize or quote any that you encounter and explore them in writing along with your own point of view so you can discover ways to incorporate both in an essay of your own.

Strategy: Create marginal notes. Marginal notes are the scribbles, jottings, abbreviations, and other annotations you make in the margins of a book or magazine. Typically, you make such annotations when something you read prompts a strong response that you can record in brief form. You may wish to use marginal notes to record agreements or disagreements with what the writer says, to highlight passages or techniques you admire, or to note important ideas and information.

Your marginal notes are most likely to be of use to you when they indicate ways to turn the text or your response to it into material for your own writing, as with the following.

> No! Putting attractive people in an ad is not necessarily a way of using sex to sell.
> People can be attractive without being sexy, for example.
> And the people belong in the ad because they show how the product works. (They wear safety goggles, for example.)
> Would it be better to have ugly people? Or just plain-looking people? I bet audiences would be critical of that approach, too.

To make your marginal annotations as useful as possible, try to give some variety to your responses. Consider making comments in categories like these.

> Interpretations of what the author is trying to say
> Questions you wish the author had answered
> Objections to the author's conclusions
> Counterarguments the writer fails to mention

Notes on passages you find confusing

Evaluations of the writer's conclusions or techniques of expression.

Strategy: Identify opportunities for writing. By responding to your reading with questions like the following, you can identify opportunities for your own writing.

1. What topics or issues does the writer address satisfactorily and completely? What questions are left unanswered, problems left unsolved, or issues left unresolved?
2. Does the writer present a balanced perspective in offering conclusions or are important explanations and points of view left unconsidered?
3. Does the writer reason fairly and provide adequate support for conclusions? Or is the writing clearly biased, omitting evidence or misrepresenting facts and distorting others' positions?
4. Are there other kinds of information and experiences or different ideas and approaches that might lead to conclusions differing from those offered by the writer?

Strategy: Evaluate a source's reliability and usefulness. Evaluating the trustworthiness of a source and identifying its strengths and limitations are important parts of critical reading. To read critically and evaluate a source, ask questions like these.

1. What conclusions or generalizations does the source offer? Are they supported adequately or do they go beyond the facts presented in the text? Are they consistent with my knowledge of the topic?
2. What is the reputation of the author, the publisher, or the publication in which the text appeared? Is the reputation one of thoroughness and balance or of bias and carelessness? How does this piece of writing compare with others on the topic?
3. Are there any obvious errors? Which parts of the discussion are detailed and well documented?
4. Does the text acknowledge and document its own sources? Does it appear to treat others' opinions fairly, presenting them in clear summaries or through quotations?

Strategy: Evaluate electronic sources with special care. Electronic sources such as Web pages and discussion groups pose some special problems—and opportunities. These sites can be rich and provocative sources of ideas and details. At the same time, electronic sites are often produced by individuals or organizations whose trustworthiness or bias are difficult to determine—unlike those for sources in scholarly journals, well-known magazines, or books from reputable publishers. Use questions like these to evaluate electronic sources.

1. Who is responsible for the site? Are there any obvious signs of bias or distortion, such as highly selective information or exaggerated language and points of view? In what ways does the site serve the interests of the person or organization that produced it, and how might this affect its reliability?
2. Are sources for information indicated clearly, or are details, examples, and ideas presented without attribution or documentation? Is information presented clearly and carefully? Are ideas and opinions explained thoroughly? Are alternate points of view acknowledged and discussed?

Reading for Technique

Reading for technique helps you identify and understand writing strategies you can adapt for your own work. Patterns of organization, ways to explore ideas, strategies for presenting supporting details, and ways to use words and sentences—reading for technique brings all of these to your attention.

The questions on "Expository (or Argumentative) Techniques" and "Diction and Vocabulary" following each selection in this book focus on technique. They help you develop your ability to analyze the techniques writers employ. They also suggest ways various techniques help writers achieve a range of purposes.

Strategy: Pay attention to expository (and argumentative) patterns. Writers use expository and argumentative patterns in varied ways: alone or in combination, for whole essays or sections of essays. The introductions to Chapters 3–13 in this book discuss patterns and their uses. The following questions can also help you identify patterns and the roles they play.

Questions	Pattern
Does the essay use examples and illustrations to illustrate a generality? Does the writer use examples to help readers understand the topic and his or her conclusions? Does the essay	Example (Chapter 3)

use examples to illustrate and
support a thesis?

Does the essay present ideas or information in categories? Are the categories arranged to explain or support the writer's conclusions?	Classification (Chapter 4)
Does the essay discuss differences or similarities among concepts, activities, outlooks, situations, or subjects? Are contrasts or similarities used to make a point or support a thesis?	Comparison and Contrast (Chapter 5)
Does the essay highlight surprising similarities between one subject and another, seemingly very different subjects? Does it use the similarities to illustrate or explain issues, processes, objects, or concepts?	Analogy (Chapter 6)
Does the essay explain how something works or how it can be done? Does it use the explanation to support conclusions or a thesis?	Process Analysis (Chapter 7)
Does the essay tell why something happened and what is likely to happen in the future? Is the discussion of causes and effects organized to explain or to support the author's opinion?	Cause and Effect (Chapter 8)
Does the writer offer an extended definition or a number of definitions? Are they arranged to support or lead up to the writer's conclusions? Does the writer use definitions to present an issue and develop reasons for agreeing with his or her opinion?	Definition (Chapter 9)
Does the essay discuss the features (physical, emotional, etc.) of the subject? Is this discussion arranged to support the essay's conclusions or to develop support for the writer's stand on an issue?	Description (Chapter 10)

Does the essay explain what happened? To whom? When? Where? Is the story arranged to make a point or provide an explanation? To support an opinion?	Narration (Chapter 11)
Does the writer reason from facts or events to arrive at a generalization or move from a generalization to interpret facts and events?	Induction and Deduction (Chapter 12)
Does the writer offer an opinion (an argumentative thesis or proposition)? Does the writer provide evidence to support the opinion and persuade readers to agree with it?	Argument (Chapter 13)

Strategy: Turn to "A Guide to Terms." "A Guide to Terms" at the end of this book (pp. 657–676) contains entries for important writing techniques, from subjects such as essay introductions and closings to creating emphasis and using the correct choice of words ("Diction") or sentence structure ("Syntax"). Before reading a selection in this book or elsewhere, turn to the Guide, choose an entry that interests you, and then read with attention to the technique described in the entry.

REVIEWING

The questions you ask while reading, your pauses to summarize and understand, your marginal notes and journal entries, your evaluations and responses—all these should come to mind when you have finished reading an essay and begin to review it. You may find the following framework helpful for review: Meanings and Values, Expository (or Argumentative) Techniques, Diction and Vocabulary, and Reading to Write. Questions and activities to lead you through these areas of review follow the selections in the text.

When you focus on meanings and values, you look back at the different topics covered in a text and the writer's conclusions about them. You ask if the topics are linked by a focus on a primary concern and if the various conclusions or interpretations are unified by a single perspective or thesis. You also consider the values and value judgments advanced in the essay.

When you focus on expository or argumentative techniques, you pay attention to overall patterns of organization and development (see pp. 16–18), to opening and closing strategies, to paragraph and sentence techniques, to the use of detail and kinds of support—in short, to the many different strategies a writer employs, except for those dealing primarily with words and groups of words.

In focusing on diction and vocabulary, you look at the words an author has chosen, the patterns of word choice (or diction), the way the diction supports the writer's purposes, and any words you need to look up in order to understand the text.

Finally, when you focus on reading to write, you look at the ways you can use the essay as a springboard for collaborating with other writers, for considering possible audiences, and for developing an essay of your own.

2
Ways of Writing

Confident writers know that the path to an effective essay calls for more than stringing loosely related ideas and information together. Their confidence comes in part from their understanding of the importance of each of the stages of the composing process: discovering, drafting, revising, editing, and proofreading.

They also know there is no single formula for all writing tasks, so they try to develop a variety of techniques. Making choices among strategies means paying attention to the needs of potential readers and the demands of a particular writing task, as well as the subject matter and purposes for writing.

Viewed from a distance, the stages of the writing process look regular and orderly: Discovering, Planning, Drafting, Revising, Editing, and Proofreading. Viewed from inside, however, the lines between these activities often blur: writers often discover worthwhile new ideas as they draft and revise or amend an essay's plan in response to further insight or reader's responses.

In your own writing you need to maintain an awareness of the stages of the writing process while remaining flexible in response to the demands of your writing task, audience, and purpose.

GETTING STARTED

Most writing begins with an assignment or invitation: an essay for a college course, a report at work, or a call for submissions to a local newspaper, for example. Your success as a writer depends to a great extent on your ability to analyze and respond. At the same time, good writing is frequently self-sponsored, growing from a writer's experiences and feelings and taking initial shape in the writer's journal or personal writing. Some of the best writers are those able to

21

blend an understanding of task and audience with the impulse toward personal expression.

Look for the Assignment's Focus and Purpose—Nouns

When your writing begins with an assignment, make sure you have the exact wording—along with any explanatory comments from the person making the assignment.

Sometimes an assignment will announce a topic clearly. Often, however, assignments use nouns and noun phrases to introduce the various elements of the topic. Consider underlining any direct statements and associated nouns and noun phrases in your assignment. Then, draw on them as you write out the topic focus of the assignment. Rachel Baez underlined terms in the following assignment, then summarized it for herself.

> Many of the <u>studies</u> we have read about <u>violent behavior among teens</u> point to the influence of <u>violent scenes on television and in movies.</u> In the <u>interviews</u> we read, however, teenagers themselves point to <u>different causes</u>: social pressures, the personalities of individuals, drug and alcohol use, or a "desire for excitement and adventure." Analyze the differences among these explanations, tell which you find most convincing, and support your conclusions.

What do I see as the focus of this assignment? Two sets of explanations, one set in the studies and one set in the interviews.

Look for Purposes and Patterns in an Assignment—Verbs

The verbs and verb phrases in an assignment set goals (purposes) for your writing and may even suggest patterns for organizing and developing an essay. Verbs like *inform, explain, analyze, discuss,* and *show* suggest that your purpose will be *expository:* helping readers understand ideas, events, and information and offering carefully reasoned and supported conclusions about a subject. Words like *argue, persuade,* and *evaluate* suggest that your purpose will be argumentative: presenting reasoned arguments and supporting evidence designed to convince readers to share your opinion on an issue.

Underline such words in your assignment and write a purpose statement for your task, including information about the topic. When she went back to her assignment, here are the action words Rachel Baez underlined and the purpose statement she prepared.

Many of the studies we have read about violent behavior among teens point to the influence of violent scenes on television and in movies. In the interviews we read, however, teenagers themselves point to different causes: social pressures, the personalities of individuals, drug and alcohol use, or a "desire for excitement and adventure." Analyze the differences among these explanations, tell which you find most convincing, and support your conclusions.

What are my purposes for this assignment? To give specific information about the differences, to offer my conclusion about the causes, and to give reasons and information that will help readers understand why my conclusions are reasonable.

Verbs and other words in the assignment may suggest (or require) patterns of exposition (or argument) for you to employ in all or part of an essay, alone or in combination with other patterns. Look for words like the following (or their synonyms) and consult the appropriate chapters in this book for ideas on using these patterns:

> *illustrate* or provide *examples* (Chapter 3)
> *classify* or *classification* (Chapter 4)
> *compare* and *contrast* (Chapter 5)
> create an *analogy* (Chapter 6)
> analyze or explain a *process* or *process analysis* (Chapter 7)
> analyze *cause* and *effect* (Chapter 8)
> *define* or provide a *definition* (Chapter 9)
> *describe* or create a *description* (Chapter 10)
> *narrate* or use *narration* (Chapter 11)
> reason *inductively* and *deductively* or use *induction* and *deduction* (Chapter 12)
> *argue* or present an *argument* (Chapter 13)

Use these words, combined with information about your topic and purpose, to create a *design statement* for your writing, as did Rachel Baez.

I plan to begin with a section contrasting the sets of explanations for violent behavior among teens and indicating the specific differences. Then I will state clearly those I find convincing: media influence, social pressures, and the personalities of individuals. Finally, I will present examples and reasons why I think these are probably the most important causes for violent behavior.

Keep a Writing Journal

A *writing journal* (or *academic journal*) is a place (often a notebook or a computer file) in which you jot down ideas and discoveries, try out different perspectives on a topic, prepare rough drafts of paragraphs or essays, and note responses to readings or observations. Journals are not diaries: journals are starting places for public writing while diaries are places to record and keep your private observations.

This passage from Scott Giglio's journal, made in response to an article in his local newspaper, illustrates some of the ways journals can provide an imaginative start for the essay-writing process while at the same time be hard for anyone but the author to read.

> Article in PrJo 6/10/05 "Hispanics losing ground in strong economy" hadn't thought about this. Why? I figured unemployment was down etc. and that most people were either doing well or things getting better for them so what abt. Hispanics? Article claims—uh, where is it—Census Bureau claims Hispanic families income down 5.1% rest up 2.7 (can get rest of stats from article if impt. cut it out of paper) Ok Ok why happening and why important is this something to argue about or can I use it as part of paper on how people just seem to be same but lead diff. lives?? A campaign issue or do people vote on personality rather than how things are going?

Ask Questions to Develop a Topic

Once you have a topic in mind, you can begin envisioning how to develop it into an essay. Many writers use groups of questions to identify aspects of a subject likely to interest readers, to develop perspectives and insights worth sharing, or to clarify their purposes for writing. Questions can also suggest possible designs for an essay.

Focusing questions help you identify goals or main ideas for your writing and may suggest general ways to divide a topic into parts and organize an essay around key points. They may even point toward a thesis around which you can build an essay (see pp. 27–28).

Here are some focusing questions that ask you to consider both your perspective on a topic and your readers' likely responses.

- What parts of this subject or ways of looking at it interest me the most? Is the subject as a whole interesting or does some part of it or specific way of looking at it seem more intriguing?
- What aspect of the subject is most likely to interest readers?
- What would I most like to learn about this subject? Would readers like to learn the same thing?

- What feelings about the subject do I want to share with readers? What knowledge, opinions, or insights do I want to share?
- How is my perspective different from the ones readers will likely bring with them?
- What are two (three? four?) fresh, unusual, unsettling, or controversial insights I have to share? Why may some readers have trouble understanding or accepting them?

PLANNING

Planning before you draft an essay does not mean deciding ahead of time the exact order in which you will present each detail or idea. It does not mean determining at the start the precise conclusions you will offer and support in each paragraph.

For most writers, writing is itself a form of discovery. The very act of putting sentences and paragraphs together brings ideas and information into often unanticipated relationships that create fresh perspectives worth sharing with readers.

But a lack of planning can be harmful to the quality of an essay or report and frustrating to you as the writer. If you begin writing without any plan, you are probably dooming yourself to false starts and long periods of inactivity when you try to decide what to say next—or whether to scrap the whole draft and start over.

How can you know when to begin planning? Sometimes your exploration of a topic suggests a clear pattern and direction for your writing. Sometimes your **discovering** activities (pp. 24–26) suggest a point or **thesis** as a focus. And still other times, you have gathered so many ideas, opinions, and details that you need to move ahead before you are overwhelmed. All these are good times to begin planning.

Cluster and Diagram

Both clustering and diagramming (creating tree diagrams) lead to conceptual maps that group ideas to help you see relationships and develop focal points for your writing.

In **clustering** you develop ideas related to a central topic and link the ideas with lines to display how they are associated. Clustering encourages the interconnection of ideas. You may begin by developing a single idea into several seemingly unconnected nodes, but on further reflection recognize some connections you hadn't yet considered.

Begin by writing a concept, idea, or topic in the center of a page, and circle it. Then randomly jot down associations with the central idea, circling them and connecting them with lines to the center, like the spokes of a wheel. As you continue to generate ideas around the central focus, think about the interconnections among subsidiary ideas, and draw lines to show those.

You can also create clusters in cycles, each subsidiary idea becoming the central focus on a new page. You'll soon find that some clusters begin petering out once you've exhausted your fund of knowledge. Stand back and assess what you have. Is there enough to go on, without further consideration? If so, you may be ready to start some harder, more critical consideration of your paper's direction. If not, perhaps further strategies will open up additional ideas.

Tree diagrams resemble clusters, but their branches tend to be a little more linear, with few interconnections. Tree diagrams rely on the notion of subordination: each larger branch can lead to smaller and smaller branches. For this reason, tree diagramming can provide a useful way to visualize the components of your paper. You can even revise a tree diagram into a sort of preliminary outline (see p. 29) to use when deciding what to place in each paragraph of your paper.

Use Patterns of Exposition and Argument

As you become familiar with the patterns of exposition (and argument) discussed in the text, you can use them to develop a plan for an essay, using them either alone or in combination. One way to do this is to treat the patterns like questions.

- Can I develop my essay through examples that illustrate a generality or by examining the categories into which the ideas and information fall (Example, Chapter 3; Classification, Chapter 4)?
- Can I look at similarities and differences or at the surprising similarities between seemingly very different subjects (Comparison and Contrast, Chapter 5; Analogy, Chapter 6)?
- Should I write about how my subject works or can be done, or about how it happened and what is likely to occur in the future (Process Analysis, Chapter 7; Cause and Effect, Chapter 8)?
- Should I define my subject, or describe it in detail (Definition, Chapter 9; Description, Chapter 10)?
- Should I talk about what happened, or should I reason from facts a conclusion and use the conclusion to arrive at further interpretations (Narration, Chapter 11; Induction and Deduction, Chapter 12)?

- Should I argue for a proposition and provide evidence to convince readers (Argument, Chapter 13)?

Develop a Thesis

Perhaps the most important and useful planning technique involves focusing on what you want to say and do. In a finished essay, a **thesis statement** creates focus by announcing your main idea(s) to readers and helping organize supporting ideas, evidence, and discussions. An effective thesis statement is specific and limited; it announces and highlights the main idea without getting bogged down in details.

> **Specific:** A good community exercise program makes provisions for four kinds of exercisers: people dedicated to fitness, people wanting to become fit, people struggling with health problems, and children building a base for a healthy lifestyle.
>
> **Vague:** A community exercise program is good when it has room for people who want to exercise for all sorts of different reasons.

> **Limited:** Extensive use of fossil fuels and widespread changes in agriculture have had significant effects on our climate in the last 75 years.
>
> **Too Broad:** The last several centuries have seen massive changes in industrial production, in the use of fossil fuels, in transportation, in the development of cities, in agriculture, and in many other areas that have had an impact on our climate.

> **Direct:** Despite all their protests to the contrary, people tend to value appearance, likelihood of success, and similarity of background in choosing a mate.
>
> **Bogged:** People may say they look for spiritual qualities rather than looks in choosing a mate, yet research points out that they are more likely to be influenced by some traditional factors, and these are likely to include how a person looks, whether or not a person is likely to succeed financially or in social terms, and the extent to which the people's families, experiences, and social class are similar.

But effective thesis statements seldom start out specific, limited, and direct. They begin as **tentative thesis statements** that provide a focus for planning. As you draft and revise, they become clearer and more sharply focused, eventually taking final form in a finished essay.

Here are some techniques for developing a tentative thesis statement as part of your planning.

List Your Conclusions and Evidence

Create a list of possible conclusions and evidence you wish to offer in an essay. Then sum them up in **generalization,** which highlights the main idea linking them all.

> **Support:** Fashions in children's toys change quickly—sometimes several times a year.
>
> **Support:** Toy manufacturers must make product decisions a year before the toys appear in stores, so they need to predict trends a year ahead.
>
> **Support:** Bringing a new toy to market can cost millions of dollars.
>
> **Support:** Most new toys are not successes; many make very little money.
>
> **Support:** There are many well-managed and imaginative companies competing for business in the toy market.
>
> **Generalization (Tentative Thesis):** Manufacturing children's toys is a risky business.

Create a Tentative Purpose Statement

Try writing yourself a note stating your potential topic along with your conclusions and possible goals for writing. To remain flexible and open to new ideas, you might begin your statement with a phrase like "I'd like to. . . ." or "I'm planning to. . . ."

> I'm planning to explain the reasons why many college students lose their motivation to work hard at their studies.
>
> —Bippin Kumar

> I'd like to tell what it felt like to be forced to leave my homeland, Haiti, so that my readers can understand why to leave something you love is to die a little.
>
> —Fredza Léger

Create a Rough Purpose/Thesis Outline

When you have in mind the various ideas and details you wish to present in an essay, create a **purpose/thesis outline** arranging the ideas and details in groups by clustering the details and summing up your conclusions and purpose for each section of an essay.

Here is Bippin Kumar's purpose outline for a paper exploring the reasons why college students may lose the motivation necessary to succeed at their studies.

1. Get readers' attention by mentioning the *bad habits* most of us have and that we may be able to correct on our own. (minor causes of the problem)

   lack of sleep

   disorganization

   distractions (television, etc.)

2. Show how we are often responsible because of the choices we make and explain that we need to make wiser choices. (more serious causes)

   sports and other extracurricular activities

   friends and socializing

   Greek life

   letting ourselves get frustrated and angry over daily hassles (bookstores, commuting)

3. Conclude with problems that we can't avoid and that may require special planning or counseling to overcome. (more serious causes)

   work

   financial stresses

   family demands or problems

   lack of necessary skills

DRAFTING

Drafting involves a good deal more than setting pen to paper or fingers to keyboard and letting the words flow according to your plan. It means paying attention to the way each section of an essay relates to the other sections and to the central theme. It means making sure you begin and end the essay in ways that are clear, helpful, and interesting to readers. And it means making sure each section and each paragraph present sufficient, detailed information so that readers can understand your subject and have reasons to agree with your explanations and conclusions.

Drafting does not mean getting everything right the first time. Such a goal is likely to prove both exhausting and impossible to achieve. A much better goal is to draft with the most important features of an essay in mind and to work quickly enough so that you have sufficient time to revise later and then pay attention to details.

Keep Your Plan in Mind

As you draft, therefore, make sure that you introduce readers to your topic, indicate its importance, generate interest in it, and suggest the direction your essay will take. The essays in this collection can provide you with models of successful strategies for the beginnings of essays, and the *Introductions* entry in the Guide to Terms (at the back of the text, pp. 666–667) offers a detailed list of opening strategies. The Guide also provides advice about another important feature that should be a focus during drafting—your essay's conclusion.

Keep in mind the various sections you have planned for your essay, or keep at hand a copy of any planning strategies you have used, especially those that identify the planned parts of your essay, their general content, and their purposes.

Keep Your Focus in Mind

Most likely, you will also alter, revise, or change the main point (theme or thesis) of your essay as you write, and such changes often make for a better essay. By the time your essay is complete, moreover, you will also have to decide whether to announce your main point directly to readers in a concise **thesis statement** (see below), to present it less directly in a series of statements in the body of the essay, or to imply it through the details and arrangement of the paper. No matter which strategy you choose, you should have a relatively clear idea of your thesis before you begin drafting. Try stating your thesis to yourself in a tentative form. You can do this in several ways:

- Start with a phrase like "I want my readers to understand. . . ." or "The point of the whole essay is. . . ."
- Make up a title that embodies your main idea.

- Send an imaginary note to your readers: "By the time you are finished with this essay, I hope you will see (or agree with me) that. . . ."

If you want to share your knowledge of bicycling as a sport, for instance, you might try one or more of these thesis-building strategies, as in the following examples.

1. The point of the whole essay is that people can choose what kind of bicycle riders they want to be—recreational, competitive, or cross-country.
2. What Kind of Bicycle Rider Do You Want to Be?
3. By the time you finish this essay, I hope you will be able to choose the kind of bicycle riding—recreational, competitive, or cross-country—that is best for you.

A tentative thesis statement can guide your drafting by reminding you of your essay's main point. You can create a **tentative thesis statement** by summing up in a sentence or two your main point, the conclusion you plan to draw from the information and ideas you will present, or the proposition for which you plan to argue. You may eventually use a revised form of the tentative thesis statement in your completed essay as a way of announcing clearly to readers the main idea behind your writing.

For example, when Ken Chin was preparing a paper on different meanings of the phrase "recent immigrant," he used the following tentative thesis statement: "For some people, *recent immigrant* means a threat to their jobs or more strain on the resources of schools and social service agencies. For others it means fresh ideas and a broadening of our culture and outlook." In his final paper he used this thesis statement: "For some, *recent immigrant* means *cheap labor* or *higher taxes;* for others, it means *fresh ideas* and *a richer, more diverse culture.*"

Pay Attention to Sections

As you write, include statements that alert readers to the various sections, along with transitions marking the movement from one section to the next (or from paragraph to paragraph). Make sure, too, that in making shifts in time, place, ideas, and content you do not confuse readers, but instead give them adequate indication of the shifts. Remember to provide readers with concrete, specific details and evidence that will give them the information they need about your topic, or the support necessary to make your explanations or arguments convincing.

Pay attention to the arrangement of your essay, especially to the patterns of exposition or argument you are employing. In any essay that classifies, for example, don't provide a detailed treatment of one category in the classification but skimpy treatment of the others—unless you have a special reason for doing so. Let your readers know, directly or indirectly, whatever pattern(s) you are employing. This will make them aware of your essay's design and will help to guide their attention to the key points you cover. Make every effort to stick to your main idea (perhaps using your tentative thesis statement as a guide), and check to see that the parts of the essay are clearly related to and support the main idea. If you have trouble developing a section because you need more information, or because you can't express ideas as clearly as you want, make a note of the things that need to be done and then move on.

REVISING

When you shift your focus to revising, you pay special attention to the success with which your draft essay embodies your intentions and meets your readers' likely expectations. You examine the draft to see if it does a good job presenting insights, reasoning, and details. You look at the draft from a reader's perspective to see if the discussions are clear and informative, the reasoning is logical, and the examples and supporting details are related to the central theme.

Read for Revision

Revision starts with rereading—looking over your draft with a dual perspective: as an author and as a member of your potential audience. As you read for revision, keep track of the places that need more work and make note of the directions your rewriting might take. Most writers find it hard to read for revision directly from a computer screen, and they print a hard copy of their drafts for this purpose.

Whether you are working with a handwritten text, a typed copy, or a print from a word processor, you may find reading for revision most effective if you do it with a pencil or pen in hand to record your reactions and plans for revision.

Reading for revision can be even more effective when another writer does it for you (and you return the favor). Remember, collaborative readings of this sort are best done in a cooperative, rather than harshly critical, atmosphere. Your job and that of your reader(s) is to identify strengths as well as weaknesses and to suggest (if possible) ways to turn weaknesses into strong points. (For more about collaborative revising and editing, see pp. 38–39.)

Whether you are reading your own work or someone else's, you may find these symbols useful shortcuts for making marginal comments to guide revision.

Reader Response Symbols

?	Could you explain this a bit more? I can't really understand this.
Add?	I would like to know more about this. I think you could use more detail here.
Leave out?	This information or this passage may not be necessary. You have already said this.
Missing?	Did you leave something out? I think there is a gap in the information, explanation, or argument here.
Confusing?	I have trouble following this explanation/argument. The information here is presented in a confusing manner.
Reorganize?	I think this section (or paper) would be more effective if you presented it in a different order.
Interesting, Good, Effective, etc.	Your writing really works here. I like it.

You may be tempted to revise as you read, and for sentences or paragraphs that need a quick fix, this approach is often adequate. In most cases, however, your revisions need to go beyond tinkering with words and sentences if they are to lead to real improvement. You will need to pay attention to the overall focus, to the need for additional paragraphs presenting detailed evidence, and to the arrangement of the steps in an explanation or argument. To see the need for such large-scale changes, you need to read the draft paying attention to the essay as a whole, something you cannot do if you stop frequently to rework the parts. In addition, it makes little sense to correct the flaws in a sentence if you realize later on that the entire paragraph ought to be dropped.

Read with Questions

One good way to read for revision is to prepare questions that will focus your attention as you read—questions appropriate for your topic, your purposes, your pattern(s) of exposition or argument, and your intended readers. You may wish to direct attention to those features you worked on while drafting (introductions or transitions, for example). You may wish to use questions that reflect the specific topic or purposes of your essay or that reflect the probable outlook of your intended readers. Make notes in the margins of your draft or on a separate sheet of paper (or computer file). Don't keep too many questions in mind as you read; instead, reread as many times as necessary, each time with a different set of questions. Following are some possible questions to help you evaluate your draft.

Questions for Revision

General
>   Does my essay have a clear topic and focus?
>   Does it stick to the topic and focus throughout?
>   How have I signaled the topic and focus to readers?
>   Is the essay divided into parts? What are they?
>   Are the parts clearly identified for readers?

Thesis and theme
>   Does the essay have a thesis statement? Is it clearly stated?
>   Is the thesis statement in the best possible location?
>   Should the thesis statement be more (or less) specific?
>   Are all the different parts of the essay clearly related to the thesis statement or the central theme?
>   In what ways have I reminded readers of the thesis or theme in the course of the essay? Do I need to remind them more often or in other ways?

Introductions and conclusions

> Does my introduction make the topic clear? Does it interest readers in what I will have to say?
>
> Does my introduction give readers some indication of the arrangement of the essay and its purpose(s)?
>
> Does the conclusion help tie together the main points of the essay or remind readers of the significance of the information and ideas I have presented?
>
> Does my conclusion have a clear purpose or have I ended the essay without any clear strategy?

Information and ideas

> Have I presented enough information and enough details so that readers will feel they have learned something worthwhile about the topic?
>
> At what specific places would the essay be improved if I added more information?
>
> What information can be cut because it is repetitive, uninteresting, or unrelated to the topic or theme of the essay?
>
> Is my information fresh and worth sharing? Do I need to do more thinking or research so that the content of my essay is worth sharing?
>
> Do the examples and details I present support my conclusions in a convincing way? Do I need to explain them more fully?
>
> Would more research or thinking enable me to offer better support? What kinds of support would readers find helpful?
>
> Have I learned something new or worthwhile about my topic and communicated it to readers?

Sentences and paragraphs

> Have I divided the essay into paragraphs that help readers identify shifts in topic, stages in an explanation, steps in a line of reasoning, key ideas, or important segments of information?
>
> Does each paragraph make its topic or purpose clear to readers?
>
> Which short paragraphs need greater development through the addition of details or explanations?
>
> Which long paragraphs could be trimmed or divided?
>
> Do the sentences reflect what I want to say? Which sentences could be clearer?
>
> Are the sentences varied in length? Do they provide appropriate emphasis to key ideas?

Can I word the explanations or arguments more clearly?
Can I use more vivid and concrete language?
Would the paper benefit from more complicated or imaginative language? From simpler, more direct wording?

Readers' perspective
In what ways are my readers likely to view this topic or argument? Have I taken their perspectives into account?
What do I want my readers to learn from this essay? What opinion do I want them to share? What do I want them to do?
Have I considered what my readers are likely to know or believe and how this will shape their response to my purpose(s) for writing?

Sample Student Essay

Here is the draft of an essay Sarah Lake produced in response to an assignment asking her to write about a community of some sort, taking the perspective of an outsider trying to understand how the community works and what kinds of relationships people in the community form. The marginal comments on the paper are notes she has addressed to the classmates (peer readers) who will be responding to her paper with revision suggestions.

Welcome to the Gym!

As I stepped up to the door to the field house I saw myself in the reflection from the door. I had chosen mesh shorts, a white v-neck T-shirt, and tattered old sneakers in hope to "fit in" with the crowd. Luckily, I still possess the Ram sticker on the back of my I.D. I was all set. I was in. A cheery eyed student asked for my I.D., and pointed me towards the training room. So far, so good, I thought. My only hopes were that the gym was going to be a great place.

I've tried to make this interesting. Is it?

This is the community I studied. Is my purpose clear?

The smell was rather distinct; one part sweat, one part machine oil, and one part cleaner, or maybe it was the chlorine coming from the pool. Surprisingly, it was a rather welcoming smell. The kind of smell that says "Come on in, have fun, workout, sweat, be hot and sticky and smelly, it's O.K." I liked what it had to say, so I continued on, farther into the training room. As I stepped inside to the training room, heavy breathing and strenuous shouts of "One!, Two!, Three!" could be heard. The shouting seemed common, and went unnoticed by regulars. Weightlifters, mostly men, would grunt, scream, moan, and sometimes yell in agony as they tried to lift weights two, three times the weight they could handle. Their heads turned a tomato red and looked as if they were about to explode. Their veins, like thick rope, popped through the skin on their necks, arms, and legs. Due to the fact that I'm not a weightlifter or a man, I surely don't understand the meaning behind this behavior. It looked rather painful and it wasn't very flattering to them, but it was entertaining.

I added a lot of detail. Does it work?

   I squirmed my way through the machines, and people, and found myself a spot on one of the stair masters. I curiously stared at the screen in front of me. Blinking letters zoomed across the screen reading enter your weight and then press enter. Enter my weight? That's a lot to ask of a girl. I thought about it, and even considered lying to the machine, but reality set in, I realized it was just a machine. Why lie to a machine? I punched in my weight, and continued to answer the questions the screen produced.

   As I started my workout, I began to gaze around and inspect everyone's interaction with each other. "Rules of the Gym" were listed on the wall and were followed by everyone. Everyone respected everyone and everything. On the other hand rules for socializing weren't posted, but underlying rules seemed to be understood. Socializing while working out or better yet, while in motion was not encouraged. Talking only took place while one was motionless or waiting for a machine. It seemed as if it took so much concentration to work out that no one could even talk while doing so. I, on the other hand, couldn't wait to talk when I got finished. I felt like I had

I think my punctuation and grammar got a bit out of control at times in this draft. Help!

gone through withdrawal. I needed some sort of outlet to make the time go by and my workout faster so I turned from people behavior watching to people's attire watching.

Gym attire was rather diverse. Some wore the typical workout uniform, which consisted of tight spandex. It included tops, tops over tops, bottoms, bottoms over bottoms, etc., etc. Others wore outfits very similar to my own which was very comforting. My favorite outfit (I'm being sarcastic) was on a young woman, about 21, who turned more heads in twenty minutes than Cindy Crawford has in her whole career. It consisted of, from top to bottom: a bright pink scrunchie (one of those cloth elastics), a black headband, a bright pink jog bra, black lycra spandex, covered by a workout g-string, also bright pink in color. As I worked my eyes down to her legs and then to her feet I noticed she had boxing sneakers on. The ones NIKE made in the eighties with the high laces. Smashing, was the only word to describe her ensemble.

Is this too much detail?

Peer Response

Before you revise (or in between successive drafts), getting a look at your work through another's eyes can help you spot strengths and weaknesses and identify steps you can take to improve your essay. To do this, ask a person or a group of people to read and comment on the strengths and weaknesses of your draft essay. Ask them, too, to suggest ways the writing might be improved. Their comments are most likely to be useful if you ask them to respond to specific questions (like those in the list on pp. 34–36) and to make concrete suggestions for improvement.

Here are some comments Tonya Williams and Dave Cisneros made on Sarah Lake's essay.

Does this essay have a clear and interesting thesis statement or generalization?

TONYA: I don't see any thesis statement. The assignment asked us to make a generalization about the community. What is yours?

DAVE: In the planning materials you shared with us, you talked about the reasons people were exercising. Could you add a generalization about the motivations of people in this community?

Does this essay provide detailed examples that support or explain the essay's thesis statement or generalization?

TONYA: I like some of the pictures of gym life that you provide, but I don't see how they fit with any kind of generalization. The last example probably talks too much about clothes.

DAVE: I suggest cutting the last paragraph. It doesn't fit with the rest of the paper.

Are the sentences clear and effective? How might they be improved?

TONYA: A lot of the sentences begin with "I," so the paper seems to focus on you rather than the community you are exploring.

DAVE: I like the way you write. I think your sentences are easy to read in general. At times, though, the paper seems a bit informal. I'm not sure whether the writing is too informal in style or whether you are focusing more on your personal feelings than on the kinds of observations and conclusions you are trying to explain.

Are there any places the grammar and spelling might be improved?

TONYA: I think you have some grammar problems, especially fragments and run-ons. I put a question mark next to these on the paper.

DAVE: I noticed a few spelling problems and other small errors. I tried to mark them, but I may have missed a few.

EDITING AND FINAL REVISION

After you have carefully rewritten your essay at least one time and perhaps several, you can focus on editing and on the final revision. In creating your finished paper, pay special attention to matters such as the style and clarity of sentences and paragraphs as well as correctness in grammar and usage. Before you hand in your final draft, carefully correct any typographical errors along with any mistakes in spelling or expression that remain.

Here is the final version of Sarah Lake's paper, including some revision that she made during a last reading and some editing before she typed the final copy. In revising, Sarah took into account the comments of her classmates and those her instructor wrote on a copy of her draft. In addition, she went back to her planning document for ideas she left out of the draft, and she developed these ideas at some length in the revised version of the paper. The comments in the margin of the paper below have been added to highlight features of the essay.

Welcome to the Gym:
A Community of Worriers

As I stepped up to the door of the field house, I saw my reflection in the glass, and I started worrying. I had chosen mesh shorts, a white V-necked T-shirt, and tattered old sneakers in hopes of fitting in with the community I planned to observe: people exercising for fitness inside the gym. I was worrying about how well I would fit in. After my visit, I realized I fit in quite well. Not only had I dressed appropriately, but I was also worried, and worrying about appearance seemed to be one trait everybody at the gym shared. <u>It seems to be the attribute that defines this community and ties its members together.</u>

> Moves from personal experience to the conclusion that will be explored in the essay.

> Thesis statement

As I stepped inside the training room I heard heavy breathing and strenuous shouts of "One! Two! Three!" Weightlifters, mostly men, were grunting, screaming, moaning, and yelling in agony as they tried to lift weights two, three times more than they could handle. Their heads turned tomato red, and they looked as if they were about to explode. I'm neither a man nor a weightlifter, and I had no idea why they were trying to overexert themselves, or so it seemed to me.

> Paragraph presents observations

When I spoke with several of the weightlifters, they admitted that for many people who spend time lifting weights, appearance is a primary concern. They claimed that many male weightlifters begin exercising because they feel inferior about their physical appear-

> Evidence supports overall thesis

ance or because they want to get that "He-man" or "Caveman" look that they consider an ideal for men. Though the men I talked to said that they, personally, weren't that anxious about the way they looked, they also admitted that they felt that potential dates pay more attention to a man who has "bulked up." I asked why they felt it was important to have a muscular and masculine appearance in today's society, especially when a lot of people (women especially) talk about the need for men to be "sensitive." I was surprised by the answers because they seemed to reveal worry and insecurity—which was surprising coming from a group of very well-muscled college men. The weightlifters said they thought sensitivity was a good thing, and they claimed to work toward it in their relationships. They also said that sensitivity grows out of self-confidence, and that for men self-confidence often comes through physical fitness and athletic ability.

Observations likely to surprise and intrigue reader

Though the weightlifters seemed sincere, as a woman I felt rather awed by their appearance and kept waiting for one of them to knock one of the female ex-ercisers over the head and drag her back to his cave. This thought made me shift my attention to the women, most of whom were working on machines like Stair Masters, stationary bicycles, or Nautilus. To enter into the women's part of this community, I squirmed my way through the machines and people, and I found a spot on one of the Stair Masters. I stared curiously at the screen in front of me. Blinking letters zoomed across the screen asking me to enter my weight. "Enter my weight," I thought. "That's a lot to ask of a girl." I even thought about lying, but then I got embar-rassed about lying to a machine. Later, when I shared this worry with some of the women at the gym, I real-ized they shared my apprehension and a lot of my other worries.

Transition to second set of observations

Personal experience supports thesis

Observations act as evidence for thesis

Like the men, the women shared many concerns about their appearance, especially about their

attractiveness and about the relationship of appearance to self-confidence. They spoke of how the
Baywatch girls are the ideals of appearance for
women in our society, and of how they felt a need to
compete with the "Barbies" of this world, even
though such an appearance is unrealistic for the average woman. They also talked about having a kind of
balance scale in their heads. As their weight increases,
they feel less attractive, and as their weight decreases,
they feel more attractive. They pointed out how magazines, TV programs, and movies seem to equate thin-
ness with attractiveness and link attractiveness to
self-confidence. Though they admitted that working
women with responsibilities as wives and mothers
might not have time or energy to work out in a gym,
they worried about how their self-confidence might
suffer if they didn't have the opportunity to exercise
to control their weight.

Summarizes interviews

    After my time on the Stair Master came to an end
and I had finished talking to the members of the gym
community, I left, feeling as though I fit in. I was a wor-
rier and I had dressed like many of the women. On my
way out, however, I passed a woman dressed in a daring pink and black outfit who began turning heads as
soon as she walked in the door. I started worrying
again, and I knew the people in the gym were now worrying even more about their looks.

Conclusion echoes main point

3

Illustrating Ideas by Use of *Example*

The use of examples to illustrate an idea under discussion is the most common, and frequently the most efficient, pattern of exposition. It is a method we use almost instinctively; for instance, instead of talking in generalities about the qualities of a good city manager, we cite Angela Lopes as an example. We may go further and illustrate her virtues as a manager by a specific account of her handling a crucial situation during the last power shortage or hurricane. In this way, we put our abstract ideas into concrete form— making them clearer and more convincing. As readers, we look for examples as well, often responding to general statements with a silently voiced question, "For instance?" and expecting the writer to provide us with appropriate specifics.

Examples can be short or long: a brief illustration within a sentence or a fully developed instance filling a paragraph or more. They can appear singly, or they can work together in clusters, as in the following paragraph where brief examples serve to make a generalization vivid and convincing.

> *There were many superstitions regarding food.* Dropping a fork meant that company would be coming. If we were to take a second helping of potatoes while we still had some left on our plate, someone always predicted that a person more hungry than we were would drop in during the day. Every housewife believed that food from a tin can had to be removed immediately after opening, or it would become deadly poison within a few seconds. My mother always ran across the room to dump the contents immediately.
>
> —Lewis Hill, "Black Cats and Horse Hairs"

43

Generality

> Example 1
> Example 2
> Example 3
> Example 4

Whether making an explanation clear, a generality more convincing, or an argument more persuasive, examples work in the same way. They make the general more specific, the abstract more concrete, and in so doing they illustrate a sound principle of writing.

WHY USE EXAMPLES?

Examples clarify by showing readers what a general statement means in terms of individual events, people, or ideas. By pointing out students who use "lucky" pens to take a test, lawyers who wear "special" ties or shoes to a big day in court, and engineers who begin a new project with a special breakfast, a writer can aid understanding of the statement, "Even educated people often make superstition part of their everyday lives."

On the other hand, lack of clear illustrations may leave readers with only a hazy conception of the points the writer has tried to make. Even worse, readers may try to supply examples from their own knowledge or experience, leading them to an impression different from that intended by the author. Since writers are the ones trying to communicate, clarity is primarily their responsibility.

Not only do good examples put into clear form what otherwise might remain vague and abstract, but they also serve to make generalizations and conclusions convincing. Not every generality requires supporting examples, of course. An audience with even a passing familiarity with films probably does not need extended examples to understand and accept the statement, "Action films are characterized by physical violence, explosions, chase scenes, and broadly drawn characters." Conclusions about unfamiliar or complicated subjects, technical discussions, and perspectives that may be difficult for readers to share initially usually call for examples. College instructors, for instance, will usually look for examples to render an interpretation convincing; business and public audiences will search reports and memorandums for examples that make the writer's judgments plausible.

With something specific for readers to visualize, a statement becomes more convincing—but convincing within certain limitations.

If you use the Volvo as an example of Swedish manufacturing, the reader is probably aware that this car may not be entirely typical. For ordinary purposes of explanation, the Volvo example could make its point convincingly enough. In supporting an argument, however, you need either to choose an example that is clearly typical or to present several examples to show that you have represented the situation fairly.

CHOOSING A STRATEGY

As a writer, you need to recognize not only places where individual examples can aid your writing but also occasions when your ideas might be most effectively presented through the use of examples as the primary strategy for an essay. If you have a fresh, unusual, or surprising conclusion to offer readers, consider using examples in a **thesis-and-support strategy.** Announce your thesis (perspective, interpretation) to readers, then offer evidence of its reasonableness in the form of varied, carefully developed examples, as illustrated in the following plan for an essay.

Tentative Thesis	Modern technology offers many new creative outlets for writers, musicians, and artists.
Supporting Point	Cable television has multiplied the opportunities for creative work by increasing greatly the number of television programs.
	Example: It provides more work for scriptwriters of all kinds: dramatic, documentary, news, sports, and comedy.
	Example: It creates more opportunities for actors, cinematographers, and directors.
	Example: It produces more programs calling for original music, art, and graphics.
Supporting Point	Software development calls for creative artists as well as software engineers.
	Example: Games require scriptwriters, artistic designers, graphic artists, and composers (for music to accompany the action).
	Example: Office programs require graphic design; home and landscape design programs

involve artistic and graphic design; educational software calls for writers and designers (sometimes even music).

Supporting Point   Personal computers and the Internet provide the means to create and distribute works of art without significant financial resources.

> **Example:** Composers and performers can create musical works without hiring performers or renting a studio and distribute their work on the World Wide Web.

> **Example:** Desktop publishing allows writers to create printed copies of their novels, essays, and other writing without the expense or difficulty of working with publishers and printers.

> **Example:** Design programs and drawing/painting programs let visual artists create without having to maintain a studio or buy expensive materials, and the World Wide Web gives them a way to advertise and distribute their work.

If an extended, especially detailed example covers all aspects of your topic that need explaining or provides a particularly appropriate instance of your main idea, consider using a **representative example strategy.** A representative example needs to be interesting in itself because it will serve as the main focus of the writing, preceded or followed (or both) by the main idea it illustrates.

In this chapter, Andy Rooney's "In and of Ourselves We Trust" (pp. 55–56) provides a particularly successful instance of a representative example (stopping at a red light when no one is around) followed by the writer's conclusion that "the whole structure of our society depends on mutual trust, not distrust."

CHOOSING EXAMPLES

Successful writers select and use example cautiously, keeping in mind their readers and their own specific purposes for communicating. To be effective, an example must be pertinent to the chief qualities of the generality it illustrates. In writing about horror films, for instance, you might offer this interpretation: "The films generally have contemporary settings, yet most reinforce traditional, even old-fashioned, roles for both men and women." To be pertinent, examples would need to address the various elements of this thesis, including the contrast between the contemporary setting and the old-fashioned values, the roles of both men and women, and exceptions to the conclusion (the interpretation applies to "most" horror films, but not all).

Examples should be representative as well, presenting in a fair manner the range of situations, people, or ideas to which a generality applies. In discussing a new approach to education, you should be ready to consider it in terms of urban and rural as well as suburban communities. Your interpretation of a play, film, novel, or recording should take into account the work as a whole, not simply those parts corresponding most directly to your thesis. If you wish readers to adopt your perspective, you should choose examples that represent any important differences among their outlooks, often the product of differences in background, gender, ethnicity, or education.

It is possible to provide too many examples and make them too long, but for most writers, the opposite is usually the problem. We frequently underestimate the number of examples needed because we pay attention only to those that come to mind most readily. Almost any part of a subject can provide potential examples, however. With your generality or thesis in mind, look for representative events, situations, quotations, or people; typical attitudes, opinions, or ideas; and characteristic physical and emotional details. Make a conscious effort to draw examples from a variety of sources.

- *Your Experiences:* Draw on your involvement with the topic. For an essay on work, draw on jobs you have held. For an essay on sports, think of your experiences (pleasant and unpleasant) as an athlete or spectator. For a report on health care, begin with your own broken bones, doctor's appointments, sessions in the dentist's chair, and trips to the hospital either as patient or visitor.
- *Your Reading:* Add to your knowledge of a topic by searching a library catalog or using an Internet search engine. Choose articles and reports that expand your understanding and suggest the ways others may respond to your conclusions. Draw examples (including statistics) from your reading, being careful to acknowledge your sources.
- *Other People:* Think about other people whose experiences are consistent with your conclusions: the neighbor whose job history reflects a changing view of loyalty to an employer or your cousin

whose reliance on the Internet for shopping illustrates changing patterns of consumption.

- *One from a Group:* When your thesis or generalization applies to a wide variety of people, situations, organizations, or experiences, you may be tempted to provide numerous examples as a way of representing the group as a whole but instead end up with a cluster of indistinct, ineffective illustrations. Instead, consider focusing on one or two members of the group and presenting them in extended detail that explains and supports your conclusions. To illustrate the features of science fiction movies, for example, turn to one or two films likely to be familiar to your readers.

There is no set length for effective examples. They can be as short as a few words or as long as several paragraphs in length, depending on the purpose they serve. For a thesis-and-support essay, however, a paragraph of four to six sentences provides a good measure.

Each paragraph supporting your main idea should provide several brief examples (as in the sample paragraph on p. 43) or several sentences presenting the example and discussing it in detail. Writers often overestimate how much their readers know about a subject and offer examples lacking in important ideas and information, as in the following student example from a paper for a course on public health policy.

> Nonprescription drugs are still drugs and can be dangerous if misused. Many people make themselves ill by doubling or tripling the dosage of nonprescription drugs in order to get a greater effect.

When her instructor and fellow students pointed out the lack of information in this paragraph, the writer realized that she could have included examples of the toxic effects of high dosages of aspirin and other painkillers, of allergic reactions to excessive intake of vitamin and mineral supplements, and of physical damage that can result from overuse of digestive remedies—examples her readers would have found informative and useful.

Remember, a good example must be either instantly obvious to readers or fully developed so that they learn exactly what it illustrates, and how. Sometimes, however, illustration may be provided best by something other than a real-life example—a fictional anecdote, an analogy, or perhaps a parable that demonstrates the general idea. Here even greater care is needed to be sure these examples are both precise and clear.

Student Essay

If you looked back over the events in your life, how would you interpret them? Would you be able to state the perspective or idea that ties them together? The generality that runs through them? How would you select and present examples to illustrate the generality and help readers understand and share your perspective?

Adrian Boykin's experiences as a stutterer and his struggles to deal with the impediment shaped many of the events in his life, and he is able to share an understanding of his experiences and his perspective through carefully selected examples in the essay that follows.

Overcoming an Impediment: A Rite of Passage
Adrian Boykin

"Sp, sp, sp, sp spit it out already Adrian!" These were among the insults I received from classmates throughout elementary and junior high school. Inheriting the stuttering, dominantly linked phenotype from my father's side of my family has affected my speech, and in turn my relationships, since I first began to speak.

Dramatic opening

Thesis statement

Starting when I was only eight years old and in the third grade, I took speech lessons at school in an attempt to overcome a speech impediment. The trait dates back to my great grandfather. In the last four generations, many Boykin men have expressed a stutter, while others, such as my younger brother, have not. Throughout childhood I often encountered a block in my speech at the first word of each sentence when beginning to speak. From third grade through my freshman year in high school, I participated in monthly, one-on-one speech classes. Through my working diligently with a speech specialist, I have, for the most part, been able to overcome this genetic defect successfully and speak without impediment.

Short examples of how his family has been affected

As a stutterer, it is difficult to explain to a nonstutterer why we sometimes just can't get the words out. Speaking in a casual one-on-one situation has never been a problem for me. Only in stressful situations

Background explanation of stuttering

where a large group of people were gathered, or in a setting where everyone is attempting to speak, did my speech impediment become evident. At these times I would compare the first word of my sentence to ice cream that has been in the freezer for a month on the coldest setting. No matter how hard you try to get a full scoop out of the container, only small tastes of the ice cream will come out. Unfortunately, for the stutterer, that small, unfulfilling taste of ice cream is the first syllable of the stutterer's first word. Repeatedly.

Uses an analogy to explain—see Chapter 4

The problems I encountered with speech never rivaled what my dad experienced growing up. Unable to answer the telephone, speak in class, or even speak without incessant stuttering at the dinner table, my father attended a summer camp in Michigan for three months each summer, four summers in a row, with the hopes of correcting his impediment. Today, though he still often stutters momentarily at the beginning of his sentences, he is a successful custom furniture designer and businessman. About ten years ago, still having difficulty speaking in front of groups, Dad completed the Toastmasters speaking course. Because his speech impediment hindered his social development for so many years and in so many ways, he was determined to never let my impediment hold me back socially.

Examples of how his father's life was affected

Because children are often cruel, I was picked on many times by my peers in elementary and junior high school for stuttering. Friends often made fun of me by imitating the stutter I had at the beginning of my sentences. Furthermore, I grew up watching television shows such as In Living Color and movies such as Harlem Nights and Billy Madison, which depict people with speech impediments as being stupid outcasts or class clowns. Looking back at these television shows and movies, I sometimes ask myself why dehumanization of stutterers is tolerated by the public. Racist stabs at minorities are viewed as disgusting and intolerable by the masses, but attacks and mockery aimed at stutterers are seen as hilarious.

Short examples of how stuttering made him feel in elementary school and junior high school

Fortunately, my speech impediment was never something that hindered me from experiencing all the things that other students with normal speech experienced. Because my father knew firsthand what it was like to have a speech impediment, he made sure that I was given therapy to correct my stutter. My father first sent me to a speech therapist affiliated with my elementary school in Denver. Only eight years old, I saw speech therapy as a fun way to get out of class and meet another boy, Michael, who also had a "block in his throat." Attending therapy with another child helped me get away from the feeling that I was alone in my speech problem. During speech class, though, I really never concentrated on Michael. What I remember is my therapist, Mrs. Rainart. "Wow," I always thought, "she is the nicest lady, and pretty too!" This was better than playing with G. I. Joes! By fifth grade, the main reason I liked going to therapy was because I liked seeing her.

Fifth grade was a time of physical change and of change in how I looked at the girls. Mrs. Rainart's milky white teeth and spiral, burgundy-colored hair made speech therapy more than tolerable for me. You know how elementary school children all have a crush on a teacher at one time or another? I guess that teacher was Mrs. Rainart for me.

My mother got a job in Boulder with Celestial Seasonings Tea Company when I was eleven. As a result we moved to a house in a suburb called Broomfield, wherein my father promptly found me another speech therapist in Boulder. The change in scenery made me nervous. Entering Birch Elementary School, I had to make all new friends. Fortunately, everyone at Birch was really nice. My confidence was soaring, and I was convinced that I no longer needed to go to some stupid speech class.

Then came my worst-ever stuttering experience. For my seventh-grade birthday, my parents let me have a party for both my boyfriends and my girlfriends. The

Extended example

Elementary school— relationships with another stutterer and with therapist

Extended example

Begins to develop new kinds of relationships— successfully

Extended example

night started well, with my friends and I boogying down to the latest Michael Jackson album. I was wearing my nicest polyester shirt to go with my loafers and tight Wranglers. My parents interrupted our disco party for cake, ice cream, and presents.

With the speech impediment seemingly gone, I started socializing with the group while I was opening my gifts. My girlfriend, Emily, gave me the coolest Michael Jordan poster. I began to tell Emily how much I appreciated her gift, when out of nowhere, a heavy encompassing piece of cake got stuck in my throat, and I could only stutter to Emily. I ran to the sink to get water when I realized it wasn't the cake that wasn't letting me speak, but that frickin' stutter. Trying to regain my composure, I went back into the family room and said to Emily, "Th, th, th, th." Once more, I tried to thank Emily, "Th, th, th, th."

Junior high school stuttering undermines relationships

Embarrassed, I could not speak, but only heard the laughter of ten wild seventh graders reverberating throughout the room. My good friend Shawn, always quick-witted, decided to slash open my wound a little further and promptly pour a tablespoon of salt on it. He said clearly and loudly, "Dang, Adrian speaks about as well as a cat barks."

More than anything, my stuttering as a child pushed me to aspire to excel socially. Throughout high school, I struggled to become a class leader whom others admired as someone who would express the concerns and wants of the school and group.

High school stuttering pushes him to excel

At the end of my junior year, my speech impediment was rarely noticeable. Furthermore, I wanted to prove to myself that I could speak in the most pressure-packed situations without a problem. Thus, I decided to run for senior class vice president. I gave my election speech in front of my senior class of about 300 and Broomfield High School's faculty. Approaching the podium, I was nervous, but confident in my speech. Usually having difficulties with my first word, I concentrated on my therapy tactics. "Keep it slow in the first

Extended example

Meets and overcomes challenges

Develops new relationships and self-confidence

word," I reminded myself. "Breathe deeply and imagine being in a one-on-one conversation." The sweat flowing in large beads down my back, I delivered a strong, stutter-free, three-minute speech. The crowd could not concentrate on my impediment because there was none. My classmates were forced to concentrate on the content of my speech. The next day I was given word of my election as class vice president.

During my senior year I realized that I was no longer getting any comments about my speech. I also started using my techniques learned from seven years of speech therapy without thinking about them. I had not been in a dusty brown, eight-by-twelve cubicle for three years. Even better, there was no reason for me to ever foresee going back. My father and I sat down and discussed our impediment from time to time, but his assistance was all I would need.

No longer needs speech therapy

By the time I graduated from high school, I had overcome the biggest fear of my speech impediment. Speaking in front of large groups was no longer a time where my speech impediment would reveal itself. As the senior class vice president, I was responsible for giving the closing address at graduation, probably the most high-pressure speech of all. For three weeks I rehearsed my graduation speech.

Extended example

On his own—biggest challenge

The biggest speech of my life was delivered on June 3, 1995, in front of 2,000 friends, classmates, faculty, and family. The football stadium stands were packed like a Mexican piñata for a Cinco de Mayo celebration. Over 2,000 were in attendance, all to hear my closing address. Walking into the stadium, I looked at the happy but tightly squeezed crowd and realized that this was going to be a special moment in my eighteen-year-old life. More than the high school graduation that the class of 1995 was celebrating, I was celebrating my ability to speak in front of crowds.

For the following two hours I tried listening intently to all of the other speeches. I found myself getting very nervous, but my stutter did not once come to my mind as being a problem. I was only nervous because I was soon going to be on the biggest stage I had ever been on before. Principal Martin gave a short address after we received our diplomas. He then said, "Ladies and gentlemen, the closing address will be given by Class of 1995 Vice President Adrian Boykin."

I looked to the crowd, started slowly, and let my voice flow continuously and smoothly, similar to an eagle soaring through the sky. As I concluded, I looked into the dots of faces in the crowd and my eyes met my father's.

Throwing my graduation cap into the still, windless sky, I celebrated a rite of passage.

Builds to climax emphasizing his victory over the impediment and the barriers it creates

ANDY ROONEY

ANDREW A. ROONEY was born in 1920 in Albany, New York. Drafted into the army while still a student at Colgate University, he served in the European theater of operations as a *Stars and Stripes* reporter. After the war Rooney began what has been a prolific and illustrious career as a writer-producer for various television networks—chiefly for CBS—and has won numerous awards, including the Writers Guild Award for Best Script of the Year (six times—more than any other writer in the history of the medium) and three National Academy Emmy awards. The author of a number of magazine articles in publications like *Esquire, Harper's,* and *Playboy,* Rooney is nonetheless probably most familiar for his regular appearances as a commentator on the television program *60 Minutes.* Rooney also writes a syndicated column, which appears in more than 250 newspapers, and has lectured on documentary writing at various universities. His most recent books are *Pieces of My Mind* (1984), *Word for Word* (1986), *Not That You Asked. . . .* (1989), *Sweet and Sour* (1992), *My War* (1995), *Common Nonsense* (2002), and *Years of Minutes* (2003). He now lives in Rowayton, Connecticut.

In and of Ourselves We Trust

"In and of Ourselves We Trust" was one of Rooney's syndicated columns. Rooney's piece uses one simple example to illustrate a generality. He draws from it a far-reaching set of conclusions: that we have a "contract" with each other to stop for red lights—and further, that our whole system of trust depends on everyone doing the right thing.

L ast night I was driving from Harrisburg to Lewisburg, Pa., a dis-   1
tance of about 80 miles. It was late, I was late, and if anyone asked me how fast I was driving, I'd have to plead the Fifth Amendment to avoid self-incrimination.

At one point along an open highway, I came to a crossroads   2
with a traffic light. I was alone on the road by now, but as I approached the light, it turned red, and I braked to a halt. I looked left, right, and behind me. Nothing. Not a car, no suggestion of headlights, but there I sat, waiting for the light to change, the only human being, for at least a mile in any direction.

I started wondering why I refused to run the light. I was not   3
afraid of being arrested, because there was obviously no cop anywhere

around and there certainly would have been no danger in going through it.

Much later that night, after I'd met with a group in Lewisburg   4
and had climbed into bed near midnight, the question of why I'd stopped for that light came back to me. I think I stopped because it's part of a contract we all have with each other. It's not only the law, but it's an agreement we have, and we trust each other to honor it: We don't go through red lights. Like most of us, I'm more apt to be restrained from doing something bad by the social convention that disapproves of it than by any law against it.

It's amazing that we ever trust each other to do the right thing,   5
isn't it? And we do, too. Trust is our first inclination. We have to make a deliberate decision to mistrust someone or to be suspicious or skeptical.

It's a darn good thing, too, because the whole structure of our   6
society depends on mutual trust, not distrust. This whole thing we have going for us would fall apart if we didn't trust each other most of the time. In Italy they have an awful time getting any money for the government because many people just plain don't pay their income tax. Here, the Internal Revenue Service makes some gestures toward enforcing the law, but mostly they just have to trust that we'll pay what we owe. There has often been talk of a tax revolt in this country, most recently among unemployed auto workers in Michigan, and our government pretty much admits that if there were a widespread tax revolt here, they wouldn't be able to do any thing about it.

We do what we say we'll do. We show up when we say we'll   7
show up.

I was so proud of myself for stopping for that red light. And   8
inasmuch as no one would ever have known what a good person I was on the road from Harrisburg to Lewisburg, I had to tell someone.

MEANINGS AND VALUES

1. Explain the concept of a "contract we all have with each other" (Par. 4). How is the "agreement" achieved (Par. 4)?

2. Why do you suppose exceeding the speed limit (Par. 1) would not also be included in the "contract"? Or is there some other reason for Rooney's apparent inconsistency?

3. Explain the significance of the title of this selection.

EXPOSITORY TECHNIQUES

1. How does the example of the red light "work" for readers? How does an analysis of this example help us better understand each other?

2. What other uses of example do you find in the selection?

3. What, if anything, do the brief examples in Paragraph 6 add to this piece? (See "Guide to Terms": *Evaluation*.)

DICTION AND VOCABULARY

1. Does it seem to you that the diction and vocabulary levels of this selection are appropriate for the purpose intended? Why or why not? (Guide: *Diction*.)

2. Could this be classified as a formal essay? Why or why not? (Guide: *Essay*.)

3. Rooney uses the word "trust" six times in Paragraphs 4–6. How effective is the repetition of such a word? Why might Rooney have chosen this strategy?

READ TO WRITE

1. **Collaborating:** Working in groups of three, list several examples that could help convey a main idea similar to the generality Rooney advances in his essay. Then, together, write a brief essay using these examples and employing a casual tone of voice similar to Rooney's.

2. **Considering Audience:** Andy Rooney often appears on television as an oral commentator on events and social behavior. The style of this essay is more similar in some ways to spoken language than written language. How effective is this style for the essay's audience? Why is it or isn't it effective? Rewrite Rooney's essay in a more formal style and analyze the effectiveness of your new version.

3. **Developing an Essay:** Choose an experience that revealed to you something about your personal characteristics, the traits of family or friends, or the "character" of a larger cultural or social group to which you belong. Using Rooney's essay as a model, use this experience as an example to illustrate a generality about your subject, and draw also on briefer examples in the course of your essay.

(NOTE: Suggestions for topics requiring development by use of EXAMPLE are on pp. 90–91 at the end of this chapter.)

BARRY SCHWARTZ

BARRY SCHWARTZ is Dorwin Cartwright Professor of Social Theory and Social Action at Swarthmore College, where he teaches courses in psychology and economics. He received his B.A. from New York University and his Ph.D. from the University of Pennsylvania. His articles have appeared in numerous scholarly journals, magazines, and newspapers, including *American Psychologist, Society, Academe, Behaviorism, Scientific American, USA Today, Chronicle of Higher Education, New York Times,* and *Philadelphia Inquirer.* Among his books are *The Paradox of Choice: Why More Is Less* (2004), *The Battle for Human Nature: Science, Morality, and Modern Life* (1986), *Learning and Memory* (1991) (coauthor), and *Behaviorism, Science, and Human Nature* (1982).

When It's All Too Much

Most of us might readily accept the generalization that having many choices is a good thing. We might be able to provide many examples to support this conclusion. Barry Schwartz's essay moves in the opposite direction. Schwartz points out that having many choices can be a significant problem, and he offers detailed examples to explain his outlook. This selection from *The Paradox of Choice* was published as a magazine article.

One day I went to the GAP to buy a pair of jeans. A salesperson   1
asked if she could help. "I want a pair of jeans—32–28," I said. "Do you want them slim fit, easy fit, relaxed fit, baggy or extra-baggy?" she replied. "Do you want them stone-washed, acid-washed or distressed? Do you want them button-fly or zipper-fly? Do you want them faded or regular?"

I was stunned. A moment or two later, I sputtered out some-   2
thing like, "I just want regular jeans. You know, the kind that used to be the only kind."

She pointed me in the right direction. The trouble was that with   3
all these options available to me now, I was no longer sure that "regular" jeans were what I wanted. Perhaps the easy fit or the relaxed fit would be more comfortable. So I tried on all the pants and scrutinized myself in a mirror. Whereas very little was riding on my decision, I was now convinced that one of these options had to be right for me, and I was determined to figure it out.

The jeans I chose turned out to be just fine, but it occurred to me   4
that buying a pair of pants should not be a daylong project.

Purchasing jeans was once a five-minute affair; now it was a complex decision.

Buying jeans is a trivial matter, but it is an example of a much 5 larger issue. When people have no choice, life can be almost unbearable. As the number of choices increases, the autonomy, control and liberation this variety brings can be powerful and positive.

But if the number of choices keeps growing, negative effects 6 start to appear. As choices grow further, the negatives can escalate until we become overloaded. At this point, choice no longer liberates us; it might even be said to tyrannize.

The Explosion Of Choices

Modern life has provided a huge array of products to choose from. 7 Just walk into any large supermarket or drugstore looking for hair-care products, and you'll likely be confronted with more than 360 types of shampoo, conditioner and mousse. Need a painkiller? There are 80 options. How about tooth-paste? You have 40 types to pick from.

In addition, we now have to make choices in areas of life in 8 which we used to have few or no options. We have to decide which telephone service providers and retirement pension plans are the best for us. Modern cosmetic surgery allows us to change virtually any aspect of our appearance. An explosion of tolerance for "alternative" lifestyles has given us real choices about whether to be monogamous, whether (and when) to marry, whether (and when) to have kids and even whether to have intimate relations with partners of the same or the opposite sex (or both).

More Choices . . . More Happiness?

It seems a simple matter of logic that increased choice improves 9 well-being. But, in fact, the opposite is true. Respected social scientists such as psychologist David G. Myers and political scientist Robert E. Lane tell us that increased choice and increased affluence have, in fact, been accompanied by decreased well-being.

The American "happiness quotient" has been going gently but 10 consistently downhill for more than a generation. In the last 30 years—a time of great prosperity—the proportion of the population describing itself as "very happy" has declined. The decline was about 5%. This might not seem like much, but 5% translates into about 14 million Americans.

Not only that, but today, as a society, more Americans than ever   11
are clinically depressed. By some estimates (for example, those of
psychologist Martin Seligman in his book *Learned Optimism*), depression in the year 2000 was about 10 times as likely as it was in 1900.

Of course, no one believes that a single factor explains this. But   12
accumulating evidence from psychological research indicates that
the explosion of choice plays an important role. It seems that as we
become freer to pursue and do whatever we want, we get less and
less happy.

The More We Have, The More We Want

Increases in our expectations are partly to blame. The more we are   13
allowed to be the masters of our fates, the more we expect to be. We
believe we should be able to find work that is exciting, socially valuable and remunerative. We expect spouses who are sexually, emotionally and intellectually stimulating. Our children should be
beautiful, smart, affectionate, obedient and independent. And
everything we buy is supposed to be the best of its kind.

With all the choices available, we may believe we should never   14
have to settle for things that are just "good enough." Those who accept only the best, I call maximizers. In my research, I've found that
maximizers are less happy, less optimistic and more depressed. At
the very least, maximizing behavior can lead to dissatisfaction—
and, sometimes, paralysis.

I have a friend who makes going out to dinner a nightmare. He   15
struggles to select a dish and changes his mind repeatedly as his
companions sit and stew. And I see my students agonize about
which of many paths to follow when they graduate. Many of them
are looking for jobs that will give them everything, and they expect
to find them.

Only Ourselves To Blame

We are told we are now in the driver's seat when it comes to what   16
happens in our lives. If we fail, it's our own fault. This might sound
only fair, but the pressure we are put under can be enormous—
especially in crucial areas of our lives such as medical care.

For example, people in one study were asked whether, if they   17
got cancer, they would want to be in charge of their treatment decisions; 65% said yes. Unless, however, they actually had cancer. Then
only 12% said yes. People with cancer have experienced the awe-

some psychological consequences of being responsible for a life-and-death decision, and they don't want that responsibility.

Unattainable expectations, plus a tendency to blame ourselves   18
for our failures, make a lethal combination.

This is the paradox: Here we are, living at the pinnacle of human   19
possibility, awash in material abundance. We get what we say we
want, only to discover that it doesn't satisfy us. The success of 21st-
century life turns out to be bittersweet. And I believe that a significant contributing factor is the overabundance of choice.

MEANINGS AND VALUES

1. What is the expository purpose of this selection? Does the selection
   have any argumentative purpose as well? If so, explain which purpose you think is most important in the selection, and tell why you
   think so. (See "Guide to Terms": *Purpose*.)

2. The body of this selection contains a number of subheadings. Discuss
   how these are linked to the overall theme (or thesis) of the essay. Can
   the essay be considered unified? Why, or why not? (Guide: *Unity*.)

3. Why is being a "maximizer" not an especially good trait? (See Paragraphs 14–15.)

EXPOSITORY TECHNIQUES

1. Which paragraph first announces the thesis of this essay? (Is the thesis stated in a single sentence or more than one? If it is stated in more
   than one sentence, why do you think the writer chose this strategy? Is
   it effective? Why, or why not? (Guide: *Evaluation*.)

2. Can the example used to open the essay be considered an extended
   example? Why, or why not? What specific words or phrases does the
   writer employ to link this opening example to the paragraph containing the thesis of the essay? How, if at all, does this link indicate the
   main expository pattern of the selection?

3. What examples and generalizations characterize each of these clusters of paragraphs: 7–8, 9–12, 13–15, and 16–19?

4. Identify the transitional words and phrases the writer uses to link the
   paragraphs and ideas within each of the clusters identified in question 3. (Guide: *Transition*.)

Diction and Vocabulary

1. What words in Paragraph 7 suggest that the writer views the variety of choices negatively? (Guide: *Diction*.)

2. What words in Paragraph 8 suggest that the writer considers the options as forced choices that do not necessarily make life better than it was at an earlier time? (Guide: *Diction*.) Discuss whether the phrase "explosion of tolerance" has negative or positive connotations? (Guide: *Connotation and Denotation*.)

3. If you do not know the meaning of some of the following words, look them up in a dictionary: scrutinized (Par. 3); autonomy (5); tyrannize (6); affluence (9); quotient (10); paradox (19).

Read to Write

1. **Collaborating:** Some of Schwartz's examples are brief, such as the mention of kinds of toothpaste or hair products in Paragraph 7. Working in a group, take three brief examples from the text and expand them by making a long list of more specific instances or illustrations. You may wish to alter the examples somewhat, listing types of painkillers, greeting cards, or candy rather than toothpaste, for example.

2. **Considering Audience:** Schwartz suggests that we might be better off with fewer options. Write a brief description of three situations (relatively unimportant, somewhat important, and very important) in which fewer options might be an improvement. (Or write about situations in which you think the opposite is true: more options would be better.) Poll some of your friends or fellow students to find out whether or not they agree with your conclusions and ask them to explain the reasoning behind their agreement or lack of agreement. Report the responses and reasons in a short paper, indicating also whether you think most readers are likely to agree with either you or the people you have polled.

3. **Developing an Essay:** Follow Schwartz's lead in using a series of examples to explain a generality about ways we commonly respond to choices we regularly encounter. Consider including some examples from your own behavior, including ones in which you poke fun at yourself or criticize your own actions.

(NOTE: Suggestions for topics requiring development by use of EXAMPLE are on pp. 90–91 at the end of this chapter.)

ATUL GAWANDE

ATUL GAWANDE teaches in the Department of Health Policy and Management at the Harvard School of Public Health and is assistant professor of surgery at the Harvard Medical School. He received his B.A. from Stanford University (1987), an M.A. from Oxford University (1989), and his M.D. from Harvard Medical School (1995). Gawande writes the "Notes of a Surgeon" column for the *New England Journal of Medicine* and is a staff writer for the *New Yorker* magazine. He publishes regularly in medical journals, and his book, *Complications: A Surgeon's Notes on an Imperfect Science,* appeared in 2003.

Full Moon Friday the Thirteenth

In this essay from *Complications,* Atul Gawande uses examples to view a puzzling phenomenon from a variety of perspectives. His examples may change your outlook, confirm it, or leave you just as uncertain as he seems to be at the end of the essay.

Jack Nicklaus would not play a round of golf without three pennies in his pocket. Michael Jordan always had to wear University of North Carolina boxer shorts under his Chicago Bulls uniform. And Duke Ellington would not play a show, or allow his band members to play a show, wearing anything yellow. For people who have to perform for a living, superstitions seem almost *de rigueur.* Baseball players, for example, are notoriously superstitious. Wade Boggs, the Boston Red Sox's former star third baseman, famously insisted on eating chicken before every game. Tommy Lasorda, on the other hand, when he was managing the Los Angeles Dodgers, always ate linguine—with either red clam sauce if his team was facing a right-handed pitcher, or white if up against a lefty. Even in this crowd, however, the New York Met's pitcher Turk Wendell seems unusual. For luck during games, he used to wear an animal-fang necklace, refuse to wear socks, never step on the foul line, and brush his teeth between innings. When he signed his contact for the 1999 season, he insisted that his salary be $1,200,000.99. "Hey, I just like the number ninety-nine," he told the press.

    I have yet to know, however, any doctors with such superstitions. Doctors tend to have a fierce commitment to the rational—surgeons especially. For one of the main satisfactions of science, and operating on people in particular, is the success of logical planning and thinking. If there is a credo in practical medicine, it is that the important thing is to be sensible. And we who are in it are usually uncomfortable, if not outright contemptuous, of the mystical. At the most, you might find a surgeon with a favorite pair of operating shoes or a quirky way of dressing a wound after closing up. And even then we are always careful to account for our idiosyncrasies with at least a plausible-sounding explanation: "Other shoes aren't as comfortable," the surgeon might say, or, "That dressing tape causes blisters" (though no one else seems to have trouble with it). As a rule, you will not find doctors saying that, actually, we just think a thing is unlucky.

So it struck me as odd to find, one afternoon when I and my fel-   3
low surgical residents sat around a table divvying up the next month's schedule of nights on emergency room duty, that no one was volunteering to take Friday the thirteenth. We were taking turns making picks, and for the first few rounds, everything seemed normal. We left all the Fridays alone, weekend nights not being popular. But as the nights remaining dwindled to just a few, it became apparent that that one Friday was being conspicuously bypassed. C'mon, I thought, this is ridiculous. So when my turn came up again, I put my name down for duty that night. "Rest up," one resident said. "You're going to be in for a busy night." I laughed and dismissed the idea.

Looking at my calendar a few days later, however, I noticed   4
that the moon would also be full that Friday night. Then someone mentioned that a lunar eclipse would be occurring then, too. And for a moment—only a moment, mind you—I felt my confidence slip. Perhaps I really would be in for a miserable night, I began to think. But being a sober and well-trained doctor, I did not let myself succumb to such thoughts so easily. Surely, I thought, the evidence is against such preposterousness. And then, just to confirm it, I went to the library to check.

I managed to find exactly one scientific study assessing whether   5
or not luck actually does go bad on Friday the thirteenth. (I'm not sure which is more surprising: that people have in fact researched this question, or that I could only find one such example. This is, after all, a world with studies on almost anything you could think of. Once, poking around the library, I even found a report on how saliva distributes around the mouth when chewing gum.) The 1993 study, published in the *British Medical Journal,* compared hospital admissions for traffic accidents on a Friday the thirteenth with those

on a Friday the sixth in a community outside London. Despite a lower highway traffic volume on the thirteenth than on the sixth, admissions for traffic accident victims increased 52 percent on the thirteenth. "Friday the thirteenth is unlucky for some," the authors concluded. "Staying at home is recommended." How you escape the bad luck at home they didn't explain.

Still, I told myself, you really can't make much of one study of one Friday the thirteenth in one town. Random variation could easily have accounted for the increase in crashes. You would need to see consistently bad results across a number of studies to be convinced. And that has yet to be shown.   6

By contrast, one thing that has been shown is that human beings commonly imagine patters (whether good or bad) where really there are none. It's just how our brains work. Even totally random patterns will often appear non-random to us. The statistician William Feller described one now classic example. During the Germans' intensive bombing of South London in the Second World War, a few areas were hit many times over while others were not hit at all. The places that were not hit seemed to have been deliberately spared, and people concluded that those places were where the Germans had their spies. When Feller analyzed the statistics of the bomb hits, however, he found that the distribution was purely random.   7

This propensity to see nonexistent patterns has been called the Texas-sharpshooter fallacy. Like a Texas sharpshooter who shoots at the side of a barn and then draws a bull's-eye around the bullet holes, we tend to notice unusual occurrences first—four bad things happening on one day, for example—and then define a pattern around them. It seems to me we could just as well have feared Thursday the thirteenth, or Friday the fifth, as Friday the thirteenth. Nonetheless, phobia about Friday the thirteenth is widespread. Based on surveys, Donald Dossey, a North Carolina behavioral scientist, estimates that between seventeen million and twenty-one million Americans suffer mild to severe anxiety or change their activities because of *paraskevidekatriaphobia* (which is Greek for "fear of Friday the thirteenth"). They perform rituals before leaving the house, call in sick to work, or postpone flights or major purchases, causing businesses to lose seven hundred and fifty million dollars annually.   8

Superstitions about the moon appear to be taken even more seriously. A 1995 poll found that 43 percent of Americans believed that the moon alters individual behavior. And, interestingly, mental health professionals were more likely to believe it than people in other lines of work. The full moon has been thought to be linked to   9 madness for centuries—hence the term "lunatic"—and in disparate civilizations across the world. Certainly, the idea of lunar human cycles seems more plausible than a Friday-the-thirteenth effect. Scientists once dismissed the idea of biological cycles, but now widely accept that seasons can affect mood and behavior and that we all have "circadian rhythms" in which time of day affects body temperature, alertness, memory, and mood.

In a computer search, I managed to find some one hundred   10
studies that attempted to identify "circalunidian" cycles. The most intriguing one I looked up was a five-year study of self-poisoning at a hospital in New South Wales, Australia, published in the *Medical Journal of Australia*. From 1988 to 1993, the hospital admitted 2,215 patients for overdosing on drugs or poisoning themselves with toxic substances. The researchers checked to see whether peaks in such events occurred not just according to the phase of the moon but also according to one's zodiac sign or numerological reading (as "calculated according to the formulas contained in *Zolar's Encyclopedia of Ancient and Forbidden Knowledge*," the authors reported). To no one's surprise, self-poisoning rates were not affected by whether a patient was born a Virgo or a Libra. Nor did Zolar's "Name Number," "Month Number," or "Birth Path Number" for a person make any difference. However, women (but not men) were about 25 percent *less* likely to overdose around the time of a full moon than around a new moon.

Strangely enough, this decrease in self-poisonings actually cor-   11
related with the results of other studies. If any link between psychology and the full moon exists, it would seem to be protective. The authors of a 1996 study of ten years of suicides in the Dordogne region of France concluded, in charmingly ungrammatical English, that "the French dies less in Full Moon, and more in New Moon period." Studies in Cuyahoga County, Ohio, and Dade County, Florida, also found a drop in suicides at the full moon. These studies didn't quite clinch the full moon's happy effect, however. Far more studies failed to find any lunar correlation with suicide.

As for other forms of craziness, the moon seems to play no role.   12
Researchers have reviewed logs for calls to police stations, consultations to psychiatrists, homicides, and other records of our daily burden of madness—including, I noticed, emergency room visits. They found no consistent relationship, one way or another, with the moon.

Reassured by this, I was finally able to leave the library con-   13
vinced that neither the full moon nor the inauspicious date threatened my night on call. A couple of weeks later the appointed

evening arrived. I walked into the ER at 6 P.M. sharp to take over from the daytime resident. To my dismay, he was already swamped with patients for me to see. Then, just as soon as I began to get caught up, a fresh trauma came in—a pale and bloodied twenty-eight-year-old knocked unconscious in a high-speed head-on collision. The police and paramedics said he had been stalking his girlfriend with a gun in hand. The cops then arrived and he fled in his car, leading them on a chase that ended in the massive crash.

The rest of the night went no better. I was, as we say, "slammed"—running hard, unable to get two minutes to sit down, hardly able to keep the patients straight.   14

"It's a full moon Friday the thirteenth," a nurse explained.   15

I was about to say that, actually, the studies show no connection. But my pager went off before I could get the words out of my mouth. I had a new trauma coming in.   16

MEANINGS AND VALUES

1. In your own words, state the generalization that is illustrated by the brief examples in the opening paragraph of the essay.

2. a. What generalization begins the second paragraph?

   b. To what extent, if at all, do the examples in the paragraph undermine the generalization?

3. What "odd" (Par. 3) phenomenon does the writer decide to investigate? How do Paragraphs 1 and 2 prepare readers for the writer's evaluation of the phenomenon as "odd" and "ridiculous" (Par. 3)?

4. What reasons does the writer give for deciding to investigate the phenomenon?

EXPOSITORY TECHNIQUES

1. a. What extended example makes up the bulk of the essay?

   b. How would you describe the purpose of this example within the essay as a whole? (See "Guide to Terms": *Purpose*.)

2. In which paragraphs does the writer explain reasons for not believing in the truth of "full moon Friday the thirteenth"?

3. In which paragraphs does the writer present and explain reasons for taking "full moon Friday the thirteenth" seriously, or at least somewhat seriously?

4.   a. Explain the ways in which the concluding paragraph of the essay (Par. 16) might be considered the writer's conclusion about "full moon Friday the thirteenth."

b. What strategy does the writer employ to conclude the essay? (Guide: *Closings.*)

DICTION AND VOCABULARY

1.   What words does the writer include in Paragraph 2 that emphasize how highly-educated and (generally) rational surgeons are? (Guide: *Diction.*)

2.   What words in Paragraph 3 emphasize the informal nature of the meeting? (Guide: *Diction.*)

3.   How does the writer use words at the beginning of sentences in Paragraph 4 to indicate his growing uncertainty? (Guide *Diction, Transitions.*)

4.   In what ways can the phrase "Texas-sharpshooter" be considered ironic? (Guide: *Irony.*)

5.   If you do not know the meaning of some of the following words, look them up in the dictionary: *de rigueur* (Par. 1); contemptuous, mystical, idiosyncracies (Par. 2); phobia (8); correlation (11); trauma (13).

READ TO WRITE

1.   **Collaborating:** Beliefs about happenings on the full moon or Friday the thirteenth are widespread. Working in a group, discuss how Gawande's essay might be expanded to groups of people other than surgeons. To do so, create a list of three examples of other groups of people likely to be skeptical of either set of beliefs and three examples that support the sets of beliefs.

2.   **Considering Audience:** Many people display contradictory behaviors toward common sets of beliefs, regarding them both as worthy of respect and as misleading superstitions. Astrology, good luck charms, ways to avoid misfortune, and love potions (or foods) are among the subjects that draw forth contradictory attitudes. Choose one of these or a similar subject and explain briefly the contradictory perspectives readers are likely to bring to an essay exploring the subject.

3.   **Developing an Essay:** Follow Gawande's example, and create an essay that explores differing reactions to a set of common beliefs. You may wish to add to the variety of attitudes that Gawande explores. Here are some perspectives that may serve as starting points: absolute skepticism, complete belief, cautious acceptance, ambivalence, open-mindedness, confusion, suspicion, curiosity, slight uncertainty, and complete neutrality.

(NOTE: Suggestions for topics requiring development by use of EXAMPLE are on pp. 90–91 at the end of this chapter.)

MARY KARR

Mary Karr's highly praised memoir of her Texas childhood and unusual family, *The Liar's Club,* was first published in 1995. It won a PEN Prize and is frequently cited as among the best of the many moving and insightful accounts of growing up that have appeared in recent years. Her memoir of teenage years, *Cherry* (2000) has also been widely praised. Karr, who teaches creative writing at Syracuse University, has also published several volumes of poetry, including *Abacus* (1987) and *The Devil's Tour* (1993).

Dysfunctional Nation

To make the point that her dysfunctional family was far from unique, Karr draws examples from the many stories of other families she heard on a tour to promote her memoir. She suggests, in addition, that growing up in such a setting may not prevent a person from achieving a healthy identity and sense of self as an adult.

When I set out on a book tour to promote the memoir about my less-than-perfect Texas clan, I did so with soul-sucking dread. Surely we'd be held up as grotesques, my beloveds and I. Instead, I shoved into bookstores where sometimes hundreds of people stood claiming to identify with my story, which fact stunned me. 1

For one thing, my artist mother had been married seven times, twice to my Texas oil-worker daddy, who was Nos. 5 and 7. Both of my parents drank hard enough to hit some jackpots. Both were well armed. (The tile man who came to redo my mother's kitchen last spring pried more than one .22 slug from the wall.) 2

Yet in towns across this country I sat at various bookstore tables till near closing and heard people posit that reading about my tribe brought not slack-jawed horror, but recognition. Maybe these peoples' family lives differed from mine in terms of surface pyrotechnics—houses set afire and fortunes squandered. But the feelings didn't. After eight weeks of travel, I ginned up this working definition for a dysfunctional family: any family with more than one person in it. 3

Even the most perfect-looking clan seemed to suffer a rough patch. "I'm from one of these Donna Reed households you always wanted to belong to," said the elegant woman in Chicago. But her doctor daddy got saddled with a wicked malpractice suit, a few more martinis than usual got poured from his silver shaker every night. Rumor was he took up with his nurse. 4

What happened? "We worked it out. It passed." But not before   5
his Cadillac plowed over her bicycle one drunken night and her
mother threatened divorce. Like me, she'd lain awake listening to
her parents storm around in the masks of monsters and felt the
metaphorical foundations of her house tremble, hopeless to prop it
all up.

Not all folks reported such rough times as mere blips on the   6
family time line. In fact, I met dozens of people from way more
chaotic households than mine. One guy's drug-dealer parents allegedly dragged him across several borders with bags of heroin
taped under his Doctor Denton sleeper. Another woman had, at
age 5, watched her alcoholic mother stick her head in a noose and
step off a kitchen stool while the girl fought to shield her toddler
brother's eyes. Surely many don't survive such childhoods intact
(or they don't go to book signings because they're too busy being
serial killers). But the myth that such a childhood condemns you to
a life curled up in the back ward of a mental institution dissolved
for me. On the surface, people seemed to have got over their troubled upbringings.

The female therapist in a Portland bookstore talked specifically   7
about the power of narrative in her life. She'd been raised by a
chronic schizophrenic. On a given day, her school clothes were selected by God himself talking to her mother through scalp implants.
The girl got good at worming her way into the homes of neighbors
and any halfway decent teacher. In college, she fought depression
with counseling she continued for nearly 10 years.

At 50, happily married, she wore a Burberry raincoat and toted   8
a briefcase of fine leather. She showed no visible signs of trauma.
The real miracle? She was in fairly close touch with her mother,
whose psychosis had diminished with new medications.

In part, this woman claimed to have survived through stories.   9
Traditional therapy, of course, starts with retelling family dramas.
Talk about it, in the old wisdom, and the hurt eventually recedes.
From narratives about her childhood, a self eventually emerged.
Her tendency otherwise would have been to lop herself off from her
own past, to make a false self for navigating the world. But false
selves rarely withstand the real blows life delivers, hence, her need
for stories, her own and other peoples'.

In our longing for some assurance that we're behaving O.K. in-   10
side fairly isolated families, personal experience has assumed some
new power. Just as the novel form once took up experiences of urban, industrialized society that weren't being handled in epic poems

or epistles, so memoir—with its single, intensely personal voice—wrestles subjects in a way readers of late find compelling. The good ones I've read confirm my experience in a flawed family. They reassure the same way belonging to a community reassures.

My bookstore chats did the same. On the road, I came to believe   11
that our families are working, albeit in new forms. People go on birthing babies and burying dead and loving those with whom they've shared deeply wretched patches of history. We do this partly by telling stories, in voices that seek neither to deny family struggles nor to make demons of our beloveds.

MEANINGS AND VALUES

1. What conclusion about families does Karr offer in Paragraph 3? What examples does she provide to illustrate and support this generality?

2. Does Karr believe our identities and well being are primarily determined by our family backgrounds? If so, where in the essay does she make this point? If not, what else does she believe shapes who we are?

EXPOSITORY TECHNIQUES

1. Explain how the statement, "On the surface, people seemed to have got over their troubled upbringings" (Par. 6), serves both to separate the two halves of the essay and to link them (see "Guide to Terms": *Transition*) . In what ways does the second half of the essay answer questions suggested by the statement?

2. In what specific ways does the example in the second half of the essay (Pars. 7–9) and the way it is presented differ from the examples in the first half? How much space does the writer devote to presenting the later example and how much to commenting on and interpreting it?

3. What strategy does the writer employ to conclude the essay? (Guide: *Closings.*)

DICTION AND VOCABULARY

1. Karr uses a number of vivid phrases in the course of the essay: "soul-sucking dread" (Par. 1); "drank hard enough to hit some jackpots" (2); "in the masks of monsters" and "the metaphorical foundations of her house" (5). Tell what each of these phrases means and what it contributes to the essay's effectiveness.

2.   If you do not know the meaning of any of the following words, look them up in a dictionary: memoir, grotesques (Par. 1); pyrotechnics, squandered, ginned, dysfunctional (3); trauma, psychosis (8); epistles (10); albeit (11).

READ TO WRITE

1.   **Collaborating:** Karr's essay touches on a variety of subjects, including storytelling, alcoholism, and family relationships. Make a list of all the subjects she mentions, and then choose two that you find most interesting. Then for each subject, make a list of topics or issues you might wish to explore in an essay of your own. Share your list with a group of classmates, asking them to identify topics they find most intriguing. Do the same for their lists, and, as a group, decide which topics are the most compelling and why.

2.   **Considering Audience:** Other than the ones Karr discusses, what situations, relationships, or social forces make it hard for people to establish healthy identities? How many of these is the average person likely to encounter in his or her life? How many are they likely to know about from other people's experiences? How do people learn about such matters if not from their own experiences? Prepare a short essay discussing why readers in general would be likely to be comfortable or uncomfortable with an essay that presents examples of each type of negative situation, relationship, or social force. Include an explanation of why different groups of readers might react in different ways.

3.   **Developing an Essay:** Karr begins her essay by describing a situation that surprised her by turning out to be the opposite of what she expected. Use this strategy to begin an essay of your own, and then go on to explore what you learned through the experience (just as Karr does).

(NOTE: Suggestions for topics requiring development by use of EXAMPLE are on pp. 90–91 at the end of this chapter.)

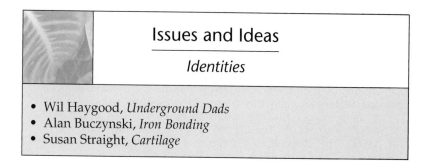

Issues and Ideas

Identities

- Wil Haygood, *Underground Dads*
- Alan Buczynski, *Iron Bonding*
- Susan Straight, *Cartilage*

Discovering (or constructing) our identities—the attitudes, feelings, and ways of behaving that make us individuals—is an ongoing job for most people. Personal identity is a favorite topic for writers, too, because it plays an important role in determining what we believe and how we act.

Though they may agree on its importance, writers are just as likely to disagree about the meaning of "identity" and to argue over whether each of us has one true identity or many different ones. For some, identity is the sum of what we are as individuals, the product of our unique experiences and personal outlooks. For others, it is part of the "character" we share with people who are shaped by similar social and cultural forces. For still others, an identity is a role we construct for ourselves and play in specific settings or for particular purposes, and we are likely to have more than one identity.

The first three essays in this chapter (by Andy Rooney, Barry Schwartz, and Mary Karr) alert readers to some of the perspectives that shape our lives. The three essays that follow (by Wil Haygood, Alan Buczynski, and Susan Straight) offer generalities and examples that focus more specifically on the various ways we discover, construct, use, and struggle with our various identities.

WIL HAYGOOD

> After graduating from college, Wil Haygood began his career as a writer with the *Charlestown Gazette* and the *Pittsburgh Post-Gazette*. He then spent seventeen years with the *Boston Globe* as a staff writer and currently writes for the Style section of the *Washington Post*. His four nonfiction books are *Two on the River* (1987), *King of Cats: The Life and Times of Adam Clayton Powell, Jr.* (1993), *The Haygoods of Columbus: A Love Story* (1997), and *In Black and White: The Life of Sammy Davis, Jr.* (2003).

Underground Dads

> Parents generally play key roles in shaping our identities, but what happens to someone who has not one parent or two, but a number of people who fill the role? Using as examples the men who acted as "underground fathers" for him, Haygood explains how unconventional parenting of the kind he experienced as a boy can be loving, supportive, and successful. This essay first appeared in the *New York Times Magazine*.

For years, while growing up, I shamelessly told my playmates that I didn't have a father. In my neighborhood, where men went to work with lunch pails, my friends thought there was a gaping hole in my household. My father never came to the park with me to toss a softball, never came to see me in any of my school plays. I'd explain to friends, with the simplicity of explaining to someone that there are, in some woods, no deer, that I just had no father. My friends looked at me and squinted. My mother and father had divorced shortly after my birth. As the years rolled by, however, I did not have the chance to turn into the pitiful little black boy who had been abandoned by his father. There was a reason: other men showed up. They were warm, honest (at least as far as my eyes could see) and big-hearted. They were the good black men in the shadows, the men who taught me right from wrong, who taught me how to behave, who told me, by their very actions, that they expected me to do good things in life.

There are heartbreaking statistics tossed about regarding single-parent black households these days, about children growing up fatherless. Those statistics must be considered. But how do you count the other men, the ones who show up—with perfect timing, with a kind of soft-stepping loveliness—to give a hand, to take a boy to watch airplanes lift off, to show a young boy the beauty of planting tomatoes in the ground and to tell a child that all of life is not misery?

In my life, there was Jerry, who hauled junk. He had a lean body and a sweet smile. He walked like a cowboy, all bowlegged, swinging his shoulders. It was almost a strut. The sound of his pickup truck rumbling down our alley in Columbus, Ohio, could raise me from sleep.   3

When he wasn't hauling junk, Jerry fixed things. More than once, he fixed my red bicycle. The gears were always slipping; the chain could turn into a tangled mess. Hearing pain in my voice, Jerry would instruct me to leave my bike on our front porch. In our neighborhood, in the 60's, no one would steal your bike from your porch. Jerry promised me he'd pick it up, and he always did. He never lied to me, and he cautioned me not to tell lies. He was, off and on, my mother's boyfriend. At raucous family gatherings, he'd pull me aside and explain to me the importance of honesty, of doing what one promised to do.   4

And there was Jimmy, my grandfather, who all his life paid his bills the day they arrived: that was a mighty lesson in itself—it taught me a work ethic. He held two jobs, and there were times when he allowed me to accompany him on his night job, when he cleaned a Greek restaurant on the north side of Columbus. Often he'd mop the place twice, as if trying to win some award. He frightened me too. It was not because he was mean. It was because he had exacting standards, and there were times when I didn't measure up to those standards. He didn't like shortcutters. His instructions, on anything, were to be carried out to the letter. He believed in independence, doing as much for yourself as you possibly could. It should not have surprised me when, one morning while having stomach pains, he chose not to wait for a taxi and instead walked the mile to the local hospital, where he died a week later of stomach cancer.   5

My uncles provided plenty of good background music when I was coming of age. Uncle Henry took me fishing. He'd phone the night before. "Be ready. Seven o'clock." I'd trail him through woods—as a son does a father—until we found our fishing hole. We'd sit for hours. He taught me patience and an appreciation of the outdoors, of nature. He talked, incessantly, of family—his family, my family, the family of friends. The man had a reverence for family. I knew to listen.   6

I think these underground fathers simply appear, decade to decade, flowing through the generations. Hardly everywhere, and hardly, to be sure, in enough places, but there. As mystical, sometimes, as fate when fate is sweet.   7

Sometimes I think that all these men who have swept in and out   8
of my life still couldn't replace a good, warm father. But inasmuch
as I've never known a good, warm father, the men who entered my
life, who taught me right from wrong, who did things they were not
asked to do, have become unforgettable. I know of the cold statistics
out there. And yet, the mountain of father-son literature does not
haunt me. I've known good black men.

MEANINGS AND VALUES

1. What are some of the important things that fathers are supposed to
    teach their sons? Why in Paragraph 1 does Haygood compare a boy
    without a father to woods without deer?

2. Twice in the essay Haygood mentions "good black men." Why do
    you think he makes race an issue with this reference?

3. In the beginning of Paragraph 2, Haygood speaks of "heartbreaking
    statistics tossed about regarding single-parent households. . . ." He
    says that these figures must be considered, yet he goes on to talk
    about households such as his, where "good black men" have helped
    raise children. Why does he mention such statistics if he does not
    plan to focus on them in the essay?

EXPOSITORY TECHNIQUES

1. What examples does the author present of fatherly acts he experi-
    enced while growing up?

2. Would the examples of fatherly acts be sufficient to convince most
    readers that the writer should not be pitied for the lack of a father in
    his home? (See "Guide to Terms": *Evaluation.*)

3. Why does Haygood list several men who had an effect on his life and
    attitudes? Would his essay have been more effective if he had built it
    around one representative example of an influential man?

DICTION AND VOCABULARY

1. Why does the writer use the words "gaping hole" to describe his
    friends' image of his household? Is this a figure of speech? (Guide:
    Figures of Speech.)

2. How does the word "shamelessly" (Par. 1) help define the image of
    himself the writer presents to readers? What other words and
    phrases does he employ to shape his audience's responses to himself?

READ TO WRITE

1. **Collaborating:** Prepare a list of men (not including your biological or adoptive father) who have had a profound impact on your life. Note also their relationship to you. Share your list with two other students in your class. Compare the roles that these men have had in shaping you into an adult. Write a two-page essay analyzing the similarities and differences between the adult males in your life and those in the lives of your classmates.

2. **Considering Audience:** Haygood's essay may strike chords in readers who have been raised without a father at home. However, even readers who have had fathers in their daily lives are likely to respond strongly to this essay. Why would both groups of readers understand the points Haygood makes? What similarities exist between children raised with fathers as a daily presence and those without? What are important differences, if any? Consider the varied ways in which readers might react to this essay based on their upbringing. Prepare a short essay explaining the different reactions readers might have to Haygood's essay.

3. **Developing an Essay:** Haygood mentions his mother briefly in Paragraph 1 of his essay; however, he does not discuss her effect on his life or the expectations he held for her. Make a list of the traditional "teaching" responsibilities of mothers and of fathers. Using these responsibilities as examples, prepare an essay supporting or refuting the notion that one person can take on the roles of both parents.

(NOTE: Suggestions for topics requiring development by use of EXAMPLE are on pp. 90–91 at the end of this chapter.)

ALAN BUCZYNSKI

> ALAN BUCZYNSKI is a construction worker and a writer who lives in the Detroit area.

Iron Bonding

> Newspaper columns, magazine articles, and everyday conversations are often filled with generalities about the different ways men and women behave. This essay looks at the emotional life of men, offering a working person's perspective rather than that of the intellectuals and professional people often associated with the "men's movement." The essay first appeared in the *New York Times Magazine*.

"I just don't get it." We were up on the iron, about 120 feet, waiting 1 for the gang below to swing up another beam. Sweat from under Ron's hard hat dripped on the beam we were sitting on and evaporated immediately, like water thrown on a sauna stove. We were talking about the "men's movement" and "wildman weekends."

"I mean," he continued, "if they want to get dirty and sweat and 2 cuss and pound on things, why don't they just get real jobs and get paid for it?" Below, the crane growled, the next piece lifting skyward.

I replied: "Nah, Ron, that isn't the point. They don't want to 3 sweat every day, just sometimes."

He said: "Man, if you only sweat when you want to, I don't call 4 that real sweatin."

Although my degree is in English, I am an ironworker by trade; 5 my girlfriend, Patti, is a graduate student in English literature. Like a tennis ball volleyed by two players with distinctly different styles, I am bounced between blue-collar maulers and precise academicians. My conversations range from fishing to Foucault, derricks to deconstruction. There is very little overlap, but when it does occur it is generally the academics who are curious about the working life.

Patti and I were at a dinner party. The question of communica- 6 tion between men had arisen. Becky, the host, is a persistent interrogator: "What do you and Ron talk about?"

I said, "Well, we talk about work, drinking, ah, women." 7

Becky asked, "Do you guys ever say, 'I love you' to each other?" 8
This smelled mightily of Robert Bly and the men's movement.

I replied: "Certainly. All the time." 9

I am still dissatisfied with this answer. Not because it was a lie,   10
but because it was perceived as one.

The notion prevails that men's emotional communication skills   11
are less advanced than that of chimpanzees, that we can no more
communicate with one another than can earthworms.

Ironworkers as a group may well validate this theory. We are   12
not a very articulate bunch. Most of us have only a basic education.
Construction sites are extremely noisy, and much of our communication takes place via hand signals. There is little premium placed
on words that don't stem from our own jargon. Conversations can
be blunt.

Bly's approach, of adapting a fable for instruction, may instinc-   13
tively mimic the way men communicate. Ironworkers are otherwise
very direct, yet when emotional issues arise we speak to one another
in allegory and parable. One of my co-workers, Cliff, is a good sto-
ryteller, with an understated delivery: "The old man got home one
night, drunk, real messed up and got to roughhousing with the cat.
Old Smoke, well she laid into him, scratched him good. Out comes
the shotgun. The old man loads up, chases Smoke into the front yard
and blam! Off goes the gun. My Mom and my sisters and me we're
all screamin'. Smoke comes walkin' in the side door. Seems the old
man blew away the wrong cat, the neighbor's Siamese. Red lights
were flashin' against the house, fur was splattered all over the lawn,
the cops cuffed my old man and he's hollerin' and man, I'll tell you,
I was cryin'."

Now, we didn't all get up from our beers and go over and hug   14
him. This was a story, not therapy. Cliff is amiable, but tough, more
inclined to solving any perceived injustices with his fists than verbal
banter, but I don't need to see him cry to know that he can. He has
before, and he can tell a story about it without shame, without any
disclaimers about being "just a kid," and that's enough for me.

Ron and I have worked together for nine years and are as close as   15
29 is to 30. We have worked through heat and cold and seen each
other injured in the stupidest of accidents. One February we were
working inside a plant, erecting steel with a little crane; it was near the
end of the day, and I was tired. I hooked onto a piece and, while still
holding the load cable, signaled the operator "up." My thumb was
promptly sucked into the sheave of the crane. I screamed, and the operator came down on the load, releasing my thumb. It hurt. A lot.
Water started leaking from my eyes. The gang gathered around while
Ron tugged gently at my work glove, everyone curious whether my
thumb would come off with the glove or stay on my hand.

"O.K., man, relax, just relax," Ron said. "See if you can move   16
it." Ron held my hand. The thumb had a neat crease right down the
center, lengthwise. All the capillaries on one side had burst and
were turning remarkable colors. My new thumbnail was on back order and would arrive in about five months. I wiggled the thumb, an
eighth of an inch, a quarter, a half.

"You're O.K., man, it's still yours and it ain't broke. Let's go   17
back to work."

Afterwards, in the bar, while I wrapped my hand around a cold   18
beer to keep the swelling and pain down, Ron hoisted his bottle in a
toast: "That," he said, "was the best scream I ever heard, real authentic, like you were in actual pain, like you were really *scared*."

If this wasn't exactly Wind in His Hair howling eternal friend-   19
ship for Dances with Wolves, I still understood what Ron was saying. It's more like a 7-year-old boy putting a frog down the back of a
little girl's dress because he has a crush on her. It's a backward way
of showing affection, of saying "I love you," but it's the only way we
know. We should have outgrown it, and hordes of men are now
paying thousands of dollars to sweat and stink and pound and
grieve together to try and do just that. Maybe it works, maybe it
doesn't. But no matter how cryptic, how Byzantine, how weird and
weary the way it travels, the message still manages to get through.

MEANINGS AND VALUES

1. According to the writer, how do men communicate with each other
   on emotional matters?

2. Buczynski concludes that "no matter how cryptic, how Byzantine,
   how weird and weary the way it travels, the message still manages to
   get through" (Par. 19). Does he convince you that this generality is
   well-founded? Why or why not?

EXPOSITORY TECHNIQUES

1. Identify those places in the essay where the generality being illustrated is stated more or less directly. Would presenting the generality
   as a thesis statement in the opening paragraphs make the essay more
   effective? (See "Guide to Terms": *Thesis; Evaluation*.)

2. What strategy does the writer use in Paragraphs 1–10 to open the essay? (Guide: *Introduction*.)

3. Identify the main examples Buczynski uses and then discuss the effectiveness of each. (Guide: *Evaluation.*)

DICTION AND VOCABULARY

1. Discuss how the simile in the third sentence of the opening paragraph, "like water thrown on a sauna stove," heightens the contrast between iron workers and people involved in the "men's movement." (Guide: *Figures of Speech.*)

2. Explain how the word choice in Paragraph 5 emphasizes contrasts between academics and blue-collar workers. (Guide: *Diction; Emphasis.*)

3. If you do not know the meaning of any of the following words, look them up in a dictionary: maulers (Par. 5); interrogator (6); articulate (12); allegory, parable (13); disclaimers (14).

READ TO WRITE

1. **Collaborating:** Working in a small group, discuss the roles of stories, especially allegories or parables, in communicating emotions within your college environment. How do you, as college students, share emotions? Can you think of particular stories that helped you share such feelings? Has there been a significant event on campus that has generated such stories? Write a list of such events and stories that might be good examples for use in an expository essay about communicating.

2. **Considering Audience:** How do the communication and self-disclosure examples help this writer to establish an identity? Does the reader need some prior understanding of "blue-collar" workers to understand Buczynski's piece? With what other examples of male camaraderie and emotion sharing are Americans familiar? How about examples of female identity building and emotion sharing?

3. **Developing an Essay:** Using "Iron Bonding" as a model, use examples to create an essay explaining the communication strategies of a particular group of people with which you are familiar.

(NOTE: Suggestions for topics requring development by use of EXAMPLE follow.)

SUSAN STRAIGHT

Susan Straight was born in Riverside, California, in 1960, and she continues to live there. She attended Riverside Community College, the University of Southern California, and the University of Massachusetts—Amherst, from which she received an M.F.A. in 1984. She is currently Professor of Creative Writing at the University of California-Riverside. She is the author of five novels. The most recent, *Highwire Moon* (2001), was a finalist for the National Book Award and received the Commonwealth of California Gold Medal for Fiction. Her other books include *Aquaboogie* (1990), *I Been in Sorrow's Kitchen and Licked Out All the Pots* (1993), *Blacker Than a Thousand Midnights* (1995), and *The Gettin' Place* (1996). Her essays have appeared in many publications, including the *New York Times, Harper's,* and *Salon.* Her short stories have appeared in *Zoetrope, TriQuarterly, Story, North American Review, Ploughshare,* and the *Ontario Review.*

Cartilage

The examples in this essay focus on the blended (or shared) identities of the writer's circle of friends and her community. At the same time, they present and explore a broader insight into the ways ethnicity and race contribute to the blended identities that often characterize contemporary society and culture. This selection was first published in a collection of essays by contemporary writers entitled *Some of My Best Friends: Writings on Interracial Friendships.*

"Girl, we can't have the Disco Ball on Saturday before Labor 1 Day," I said. "Won't we all be cooking for The Hole?" When everyone looked at me, I added, "We're the old folks now. Right?"

We are in our early and late forties, and our children and 2 grandchildren milled about outside the community room at the park where we'd gathered to make our plans. Most of us have lived here, in Riverside, California, for all our lives, have known one another since we were children or teens or just-married, and all the women around the table started laughing when I showed my palms to the sky in question of our status. My friend Revia said, "Since last year we are."

Last Labor Day, we realized that all the aunts and uncles and el- 3 ders who used to have holiday celebrations in someone's driveway or yard had passed on or moved away to quieter places. So we took over, barbecuing and cooking side dishes and bringing tables and chairs to this park, to a sunken spot we call The Hole because it's down the slope of an arroyo and shaded by huge pecan trees.

In the seventies, many white people in this city used to be afraid   4
to drive past this park because black teenagers sometimes threw rocks at pale faces in luxury cars. But now, the neighborhood known as the Eastside, where my husband and many of my friends grew up, is shifting from African-American to Mexican-born, and the whole city is as integrated as our old neighborhoods always were.

Today, the familiar faces I have known nearly all my life, de-   5
scended from men and women born in Louisiana, Oklahoma, Mississippi, and Georgia, are all around me at this table as we plan fund-raisers for a group formed to keep the old neighborhood alive through dinners and talent shows and community projects.

And me, always the only white person in the room, with blond   6
hair, blue eyes, and black-rimmed glasses instead of the granny specs some of the women in this room teased me for when we were in junior high.

Back then, when I met my future husband, his skin red-brown   7
as palm bark, his natural wide enough to frame my face when we stood in front of a mirror, a few of these women gave me a hard time, and I knew to expect it. I knew what they thought of white girls.

In junior high and then high school, I'd watched closely the   8
chameleonlike shifts in clothes, voice, hair, and attitude as people decided how they would transform themselves into who they thought they wanted to be. A few white girls considered them-selves Chicanas, and matched their friends' wire-thin eyebrows, dark lipstick, and babydoll tanks covered with flannel Pendletons. A few black girls were cheerleaders and looked exactly like their white counterparts, with tight ponytails and great posture and matching overalls. A few Chicano guys were black gangsters, and one black guy from my old neighborhood was a vato. Stoners and cholos and letterman jocks—all had uniforms, theme songs, and secret code words sprinkled in their conversations. They all had their territories on campus, too—the hill, the arcade, the brick wall, and the parking lot.

The white girls who wanted to be black, before the nineties   9
when the word "wigger" came into play, worked very hard, but as I watched, I had the feeling they were going about it all wrong.

They talked as if born in Mississippi. They cornrowed their   10
brown or red hair, and their scalps shone white as mother-of-pearl in the gaps. They snapped their fingers and sat at the right table, but

they were never quite comfortable there, because most of the black girls didn't trust them at all.

For good reason. When one of the white girls, upper-middle class, not from my mixed neighborhood or from the Eastside, decided she really wanted to be homecoming queen her senior year, she went right out and got a blond escort from the crosstown rival and wealthier high school. Her hair blow-dried straight, her lipstick pink, she was transformed back into her true self. And she got her butt kicked. Her transformation and betrayal were so obvious and egregious she became legend: to do what she did was called "pulling a Sheila." 11

Even then, knowing I'd probably marry my boyfriend, I watched. I was so pale, so blond, and I wished I at least had black hair, darker eyebrows. But having had girlfriends since junior high who'd taught me how to dance in the gym and during PE, who sat patiently with me during class and braided hair and told stories, I thought my caution and observance might help when I knew nothing of my physical appearance would. 12

He was sixteen, I was fifteen, and on Labor Day in 1976, he brought me to his parents' house, where—no pressure—everyone gathered in the driveway and the living room. About a hundred people, all staring at the little blond girl with a halter dress and nervous smile. One of those white girls, I knew they were thinking. 13

The aunts, eight of them, stared me down in the living room, but nodded and shook my hand. But his sister and cousins and stepsister and other girls were in the dining room, girls my age who didn't trust me for a minute. They cut their eyes my way, muttered things not quite under their breaths, and elbowed me out of the way after refusing my hand. They sucked their teeth instead, along with a few female neighbors who raised their eyebrows and said, "Mmm, mmm, mmm. What does he think he's doing?" 14

And what did I think I was doing? How could they not think I was pulling a Sheila? I headed for the kitchen out of instinct. I knew what to do. 15

My mother is Swiss. I am the oldest of all her children, birth and foster, and I have been cooking and cleaning since I was seven. When my future husband introduced me to his mother, holding court at the stove where she fed not only her own six kids but half the neighborhood, she looked into my face and said graciously, "Let's get you a plate." 16

I said, "Can I help you with the dishes?" 17

She stood near me at the Formica counters and stove the same 18
color as my mother's. I exclaimed over the barbecue and helped her
cut the ham and asked how she made monkey bread, her famous
circle of rolls. At Thanksgiving, then Christmas, and on Super Bowl
Sunday (a family holiday with the same importance as the others), I
washed dishes and stayed in the kitchen with the women, who followed my future mother-in-law's noddings and finally accepted me,
after a period of intense observation.

And my own mother, who stands four-eleven, looked up at the 19
tall brown boy who came to pick me up and said, "You're on the
basketball team?" Anyone who played a sport, and was of reasonable height, was fine with her. He didn't drink, smoke, or do anything to hurt his basketball career, and our first dates consisted of
shooting hoops at the playground and then playing tennis at the
university courts.

She accepted him without reservation. During our senior year, 20
she came to his basketball games, knitting in the stands a few rows
below his father, who sat with cronies in trench coats to conceal their
flasks, shouting, "Fall, ball!" whenever his son lofted a shot.

During all those years, I did listen to the same music, and we 21
danced the same dances, and used the same secret code words of the
neighborhood. How could we have talked otherwise? But I never
cornrowed my hair or pretended that I was not half Swiss. I was always too skinny. I still am.

I have been an honorary Eastsider for twenty-five years now. 22
We all wear jeans or comfortable pants to our many gatherings, and
even though I have been divorced for five years, my daughters and I
are expected at each and every event. Most of the time, we all wear
our hair in buns, because we are at that stage in our lives. We are
kind of tired, and we've been cooking all day.

We sit around the table today: Doris and Revia, whose mother 23
was born in Louisiana but has lived at the end of this block for forty-
five years. Revia's daughters and nieces, who all call me Auntie. My
sister-in-law Tina, and my brother-in-law's girlfriend Shirley, whose
father was born in the South and whose mother was born in Mexico.
Her tamales and temper are legendary, and though they never married, my children call her Auntie.

The Aunties. That's what we are now, and we have earned the 24
status. We bring one another food when someone is sick or someone
has died. We sit companionably and holler at the kids to keep it
down.

We direct the younger girls not to walk too far from where we   25
are in the park. And I laugh inside when I watch the rare white teen,
girl or boy, try to navigate the hundred-plus people of Labor Day or
August Family Reunion. They have the right jackets, carry the
proper CDs, and have cornrows or tattoos.

But they don't have stretch marks, knife cuts from dissembling   26
hams and chicken, laugh lines and frown marks from our children
and spouses, sore backs from carrying wet laundry, and sore feet
from carrying babies and pacing sidelines and grocery lines.

"How did we get to be the old folks?" Shirley asked, laughing   27
and yet a deep furrow between her brows. We were watching
teenagers gather around the table in The Hole, irritating us with
their loudness and greedy helpings, just the way we used to get on
the aunts' nerves.

I shrugged, and Revia did, too.   28

"'Cause nobody else stepped in."   29

On Labor Day, our knees met in a companionable semicircle, a   30
crescent grin of white plastic chairs arranged on the slope of the depression under the pecan trees, where we can keep an eye on the
food. We are in charge. We brought macaroni and cheese, pineap-
ple upside-down cake, potato salads, and string beans with ham
hocks. I brought rice and blackeyed peas and hot sausage, my dish,
the one people ask if I am bringing. Along with the scars, you'd better have a dish.

I am still blond and small, and my women friends and sister-in-   31
law and relatives are not, but our arms rest alongside one another's
on the chairs' plastic smoothness, and they are all alike. Sun-
marked, softer than when we were young, our knuckles bigger, our
fingers sore. We talk about our hurts. My feet, Shirley's wrists,
Doris's back, and Revia's migraines.

A white family shows up, friends of someone's, and their   32
teenage boy stares at me when introductions are made. He has on
the right football jersey, the right haircut, the right tattoos. I nod at
him, and we watch him get a plate of food with our nephews. He
says, "This looks really good. Thank you."

From our vantage point, we raise our brows and smile.   33

My house is a mile-and-a-half from the park, not on the   34
Eastside. Half of us don't live in the neighborhood anymore, but we
gather there and our hearts remain there.

My three daughters have lived in the same house for fourteen   35
years, and they have friends from our neigborhood. Half Mexican,
half white. Half Salvadoran, half Polish. Half Saudi, half black.

My girls are Swiss, French, African, Creek, Cherokee, and Irish. 36
They don't judge their friends, or themselves, by music or clothes or
hairstyles. They listen to Nickelback and Lenny Kravitz and Santana
and the Dixie Chicks. They roll their eyes at their father and me
when we play the Bar-Kays and Parliament. They roll their eyes at
white teens who cruise by our house in expensive trucks, blaring
Jay-Z and Snoop Dogg and shouting, "What up, dog?"

They suck their teeth and say, "Not you," and in their tone, I 37
hear the voices of their actual ancestors and their mother's friends,
the women who sit in the circle with me. We know it's all about the
scars and pain, the food and laughs, the secret code you can only
understand when you've bumped elbows while standing at the
stove, when you've sat by the hospital bed while someone you
loved was fading away—places where it doesn't matter what you
wear or listen to or how your hair looks. It matters that your knees
touch while you wait.

MEANINGS AND VALUES

1. Where in the essay does the writer state a generalization that the examples illustrate and explore? In your own words, state the essay's
   broader, implied generalization about the roles of race and ethnicity
   in the construction of contemporary identities.

2. *Cartilage* refers to strong, elastic connective tissue in humans and
   other mammals. In what ways is this term an appropriate (or inappropriate) title for the essay?

3. What differences between her adolescent experiences and those of
   contemporary adolescents does the writer highlight? What similarities does she point out?

EXPOSITORY TECHNIQUES

1. Where in the essay does the writer present extended examples?
   Where does she present briefer examples? Which examples, if any,
   seem to fall between brief and extended in length?

2. Choose two examples you consider particularly effective, and explain what you think makes them so effective. (See "Guide to
   Terms": *Evaluation.*) Do you think other readers are likely to agree
   with your evaluation? Why, or why not?

3. What narrative does the writer present at the beginning of the essay and at the end? Discuss the ways in which this narrative acts as an example illustrating the main themes of the essay. Explain how it acts as a "frame" for other examples in the selection.

Diction and Vocabulary

1. Where in the essay does the writer use words or phrases from language other than English? Make a list of these words and phrases, and provide a definition or synonym for each terms whose meaning you understand.

2. Is it necessary to understand the meaning of the terms you listed for question 1 in order to understand the passages in which they appear? Why, or why not? (Provide specific examples to support your answer.)

3. What, if anything, do the terms from other languages contribute to the effectiveness of the essay? What do slang expressions contribute? (Guide: *Colloquial Expressions.*)

Read to Write

1. **Collaborating:** Consider the challenges to building a secure identity that you and your friends faced in high school as well as the strategies you used to develop your identity. Working with a group of fellow students, prepare a list of these challenges and strategies and compare them to the challenges and strategies described in Straight's essay. Are there similarities? Do some experiences seem to cross social, cultural, and economic boundaries to become universal to teens in North America? Which seem unique to particular groups? After you have completed the list as a group, write a short essay of your own on the topic of establishing a personal identity during high school, discussing the challenges you faced and the strategies you employed. Or write an essay exploring the contrasts you discovered among your experiences and those of your classmates.

2. **Considering Audience:** Think about the different groups of people that might read this essay. How do you think teens would react to it? Would they identify with the examples? Would their responses vary according to the neighborhoods where they lived, their ages, the schools they attended, or their ethnic and cultural backgrounds? Would the examples in this piece be effective for a 60-year-old reader, for example? Why, or why not? Are the experieces of such a reader in any way similar to those described in the essay? Put yourself in the role of various readers by writing three 1-paragraph responses to the essay: one from the perspecive of an 18-year-old from a rural community, one from the perspective of a 50-year-old raised in the suburbs, and one from the perspective of a 50-year-old living and raised in a large city.

3.   **Developing an Essay:** Write an essay describing the culture of your neighborhood. Be sure to provide examples of the different types of people you knew and the different groups of friends that lived there. What did you need to "fit in" the neighborhood? Were there different "requirements" for each group?

(NOTE: Suggestions for topics requiring development by use of EXAMPLE are on pp. 90–91 at the end of this chapter.)

Writing Suggestions for Chapter 3

EXAMPLE

Use one of the following statements or another suggested by them as your central theme. Develop it into a unified composition, using examples from history, current events, or personal experience to illustrate your ideas. Be sure to have your reader-audience clearly in mind, as well as your specific purpose for the communication.

1. Successful businesses keep employees at their highest level of competence.

2. In an age of working mothers, fathers spend considerable time and effort helping raise the children.

3. Family life can create considerable stress.

4. Laws holding parents responsible for their children's crimes would (or would not) result in serious injustices.

5. Letting people decide for themselves which laws to obey and which to ignore would result in anarchy.

6. Many people find horror movies entertaining.

7. Service professions are often personally rewarding.

8. Religion in the United States is not dying.

9. Democracy is not always the best form of government.

10. A successful career is worth the sacrifices it requires.

11. "An ounce of prevention is worth a pound of cure."

12. The general quality of television commercials may be improving (or deteriorating).

13. An expensive car can be a poor investment.

14. "Some books are to be tasted; others swallowed; and some few to be chewed *and* digested." (Francis Bacon, English scientist-author, 1561–1626)

15. Most people are superstitious in one way or another.

16. Relationships within the family are much more important than relationships outside the family.

COLLABORATIVE EXERCISE

Working in a group, begin with the statement "Many people find horror movies entertaining," and ask each person to identify two examples to illustrate and support the generality advanced in the statement. (This task will probably require each group member to do some research.) After the examples have been collected, group members should present them, and the group as a whole should vote for those that best illustrate the generality. Each group member should then create a short essay using the examples to explain and support the statement. (Statements 7, 10, 12, and 13 also lend themselves well to this activity.)

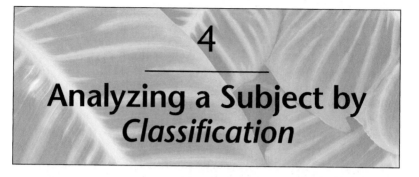

4

Analyzing a Subject by *Classification*

People naturally like to sort and classify things. A young child, moving into a new dresser of her own, will put handkerchiefs together, socks and underwear in separate stacks, and hair clips in a pretty holder for the dresser top. Another young child may classify animals as those with legs, those with wings, and those with neither. As they get older, they may find schoolteachers have ways of classifying *them*, not only into reading or math groups, but periodically on the basis of "A," "B," or "C" papers. On errands to the grocery store, they discover macaroni in the same department as spaghetti, pork chops somewhere near the ham, and apples just down from the miniature carrots (themselves part of larger groups like "carrots" and "root vegetables"). In reading the local newspaper, they observe that its staff has done some classifying for them, putting most of the comics together and seldom mixing sports stories with news of social affairs and marriage announcements (classifications based in turn on traditional categories of behavior). Eventually, they find courses neatly classified in college catalogs, and they know enough not to look for biology courses under "Social Science" or "Arts and Letters."

Classification also helps writers and readers sort through and understand detailed information or ideas. It groups people, ideas, objects, experiences, or concepts according to shared qualities and helps point out patterns of relationships among them. For example, if you were writing an article to help people understand their personal characteristics, you might draw on the ancient Indian concept of "ayurveda," as does the author of the following paragraph.

The three ayurvedic types (or doshas) are vata, pitta, and kapha. Vatas (space and air) are creative, thin people with light bones and dark hair and eyes who are light sleepers, dislike routine, and tend toward fear and anxiety when they're under stress. Pittas (fire and water) are medium built, light-eyed, oily-skinned people who enjoy routine, make good leaders and initiators, are opinionated, and tend toward anger and frustration when they're under stress. Kaphas (water and earth) are amply built, thick-skinned and thick-haired people who are good at running projects, love leisure, sleep soundly, and tend to avoid difficult situations.

—Lynette Lamb, "Living the Ayurvedic Way"

WHY USE CLASSIFICATION?

A classification creates groups on the basis of shared characteristics. It is a useful strategy when you are dealing with facts, events, or ideas whose differences are worth detailed examination. Many subjects that you may need to write and think about will remain a hodgepodge of facts and opinions unless you can find some system of analyzing the material, dividing the subject into categories, and classifying individual elements into those categories. The two patterns, **division** and **classification,** or *dividing* and *grouping,* move in different directions, at least to begin with. But when put in use for analysis and understanding, the two processes become inevitable companions that lead to a system of classification you can employ in your writing.

Expository writing both explains and informs, and classification is a pattern that enables writers to bring clarity to discussions of complicated subjects. Exercise programs, undergraduate majors, investment strategies, personal computers, ways to prepare for tests, even used cars—all these come in various types that are worth understanding. So, too, do other possible subjects for writing: behavior patterns; literary or anthropological theories; careers in engineering, business, or communications; management techniques; or environmental policies.

When readers encounter a classification, however, they expect more than a simple identification of categories. They look for an explanation of the qualities that distinguish each category and an explanation of the overall arrangement of the categories. In short, they expect the writer to provide a conclusion—a thesis—about the categories themselves, perhaps an explanation of why the subject falls into a particular set of categories or what implications the pattern of sorting has. A conclusion helps readers decide what to do with the information being presented; it helps them choose among alternatives, understand the specific uses of each set of policies or products; or grasp the implications of different psychological perspectives and social groupings.

CHOOSING A STRATEGY

If you choose to employ classification as a strategy for sharing information and ideas, your readers will expect you to take them into account from the beginning. They will want to know what information you are going to present and why it is important to them. They will expect you to make clear the purpose for your classification and the main idea or thesis tying it together.

From the start, therefore, you need to focus clearly on a **principle of classification,** that is, the quality that members of each group share and what distinguishes them from the members of other groups. The simplest classifications form two groups, those with a particular quality and those without it: vegetarians and meat-eaters, closed-end mutual funds and open-ended funds, introverts and extroverts, environmentally sensitive policies and environmentally destructive policies. But such simple classifications often break down, usually because the differences among groups are matters of degree or level (varying levels of environmental sensitivity; different degrees of strictness in adhering to a vegetarian diet) and not absolute.

In creating a classification, then, you should choose a strategy that reflects your purpose for writing while allowing you to maintain clear and logical distinctions among the categories. If your purpose is to help people understand the dietary options available to them—vegan, ovo-lacto-vegetarian, avoidance of all meat except fish, and meat eating, for example—then your categories should be built around the kinds of food that people choose to include or avoid in their diet. In addition, the principle of classification should be consistent throughout the categories and complete with respect to the subject being investigated.

It would not be logical to divide movies into categories such as action films, science fiction films, romantic films, political films, serious films, and entertaining films because the principles of classification are not consistent and the categories therefore overlap: romantic films can be serious, entertaining, or both, for example. Likewise, it would not make sense to limit discussion of religious practices in North America to those of Christians, Jews, and

Moslems because to do so would exclude, for example, the many people who identify themselves as Buddhists and Hindus. A more limited system might be appropriate, however, when discussing the religious backgrounds of residents in a particular region (southwest Louisiana, rural Mexico) or from a particular cultural or ethnic group (Hungarians, Native Americans in Alaska or northern Canada). Although your classification system need not be exhaustive, it should at the same time not omit significant numbers of whatever behaviors, people, or ideas you are planning to discuss.

In many cases, the pattern of classification you choose will also serve to organize your writing, as the following tentative plan for an essay illustrates.

Tentative Thesis
> People who love sports but have only limited athletic talent need not give up their dreams of a career in professional sports because being a player is only one of many career paths.

Category
> Name: administrators. Definition: people involved in management of sports teams. Members: managers, coaches, public relations specialists, personnel managers.

Category
> Name: medical staff. Definition: people concerned with physical and mental health of athletes. Members: trainers, team doctors, sports psychologists.

Category
> Name: facilities staff. Definition: people who create and maintain sports facilities. Members: sports architects and designers, engineers, groundskeepers, facilities managers.

Category
> Name: equipment specialists. Definition: people who design, manufacture, and sell sports equipment. Members: designers, testers, advertisers, manufacturing engineers, sales representatives.

A plan like this could logically include players' agents and legal representatives, people who work in financing sports, and people who arrange travel for sports teams. But although this would be a logical classification, it would be far too detailed for most readers. You should therefore limit the number of categories you present in an essay to avoid overwhelming and confusing your readers, but make sure you do not leave out any that are essential to the subject. Four categories of sports-related jobs should be enough to support and explain the writer's thesis (though some mention of sports broadcasting might be appropriate because most readers will expect discussion of the category). A brief mention of the other kinds of jobs, perhaps near the essay's conclusion, would help complete the classification without overburdening readers with detail.

Any plan like this seems almost absurdly obvious, of course— *after* the planning is done. It appears less obvious, however, to inexperienced writers who are dealing with a jumble of information they must explain to someone else. This is when writers should be aware of the patterns at their disposal, and one of the most useful of these, alone or combined with others, is classification.

DEVELOPING CATEGORIES

At the center of any essay employing classification are the paragraphs that present, explain, and illustrate categories. There is no single strategy for presenting categories, and the way you approach the task should vary according to your subject and purpose for writing. Nonetheless, many writers find the following techniques useful for alerting readers to the structure of an essay, structuring the presentation of categories, and making sure they present each category with enough explanatory detail.

- *Use Transitions:* You can make effective use of transitional terms to signal the beginning of a new category.

type	sort	trait	segment
category	kind	species	characteristic
class	aspect	element	component
part	subcategory	subset	group

- *Name the Categories:* To help identify categories and also help readers remember them, try giving each a name when you explain it. The names can be purely descriptive ("supporters/opponents/compromisers of the policy") or they can be somewhat imaginative ("lookers/browsers/testers/buyers").
- *Provide Detailed Examples:* To help readers visualize and understand each category, consider providing at least one extended example or a cluster of shorter ones. By making the examples

detailed and specific, you help explain the categories while making them more memorable.

- *Explain:* Remind readers of the principle of classification, of the qualities that characterize a category, and of the ways it differs from other categories. Let them know, too, how the categories are related: Do they represent differing or contradictory approaches to a problem? Are they different products with similar functions? Will readers be faced with sharply differing options or a gradual range of choices?

Here is how one student, Hung Bui, put these techniques to work in a paragraph.

> Cigarettes play an even larger role in the lives of the next group, habitual smokers. They cannot quit as readily as the casual smoker can because of one key factor: habit. When the phone rings, they quickly grab an ashtray and cigarettes and chat. When having a cup of coffee in the morning, they simply must have a cigarette because "the coffee won't taste as good without it." And always, without fail, a good meal is followed by a good cigarette. Habitual smokers also smoke on a regular basis—a pack or two a day, never more, never less. They become irritated when they discover they are down to their last cigarette and rush to buy another pack. They also play games by buying only packs instead of cartons, rationalizing that because cigarettes aren't always on hand, they can't be smoking too much. They are constantly trying to cut down and tell everyone so, but never actually do, because in reality, smoking is an essential part of their lives.

Student Essay

Whenever you are learning, you do so in stages, from beginner, to novice, to (perhaps) expert. Heather Farnum applied these stages to a task she knew well (playing the piano) and came up with a system of classification that readers can apply to musicians in general and extend to other learners as well.

Piano Recitals

by Heather Farnum

Last night while I was sitting at the piano and relaxing by playing some old recital pieces, memories of playing in piano recitals as a child and high school student came flooding back to me. I remember looking at each pianist intently, watching how she or he presented

Begins with anecdote introducing the topic and creating interest

a piece, and imagining myself sitting at the piano and playing in a similar way. I watched how each presented a selection—whether or not the person gave feeling to the music and was comfortable with playing it. Most of all, I watched how the pianist interpreted a piece, for there are several quite different ways to interpret the same selection for an audience.

Novice pianists, intermediate pianists, and top-class pianists all approach the job of interpretation in different and characteristic ways. You can help me explain these differences if you will imagine a stage in a brightly lit church hall or school auditorium. Stretched across the stage is a grand piano, set up so the audience of parents, friends, and fellow students can see the recitalist. **Thesis statement**

The first person to walk tentatively across the stage to polite applause is a novice pianist. Like all novices, this one either rushes through the piece or plays much too slowly. He bobs his head up and down trying to maintain the tempo, messes up notes, and plays too loudly or too softly, but seldom in between. **Category 1 example**

The best example of a novice pianist I can recall is Stephany Cody, a girl of about 7. For her first recital, Stephany played "Twinkle, Twinkle, Little Star" as loudly as she could, bobbing her head throughout the familiar piece. Every time she reached the "twinkle, twinkle, little star" she speeded up because she knew that part best. However, when she reached "up above the sky so gray," she slowed way down as she struggled through the less familiar notes. **Another example (detailed)**

Next across the stage is an intermediate pianist. Sitting down, she strives for a professional look in form and stature. Unlike the novice pianist, she has control over dynamics, yet she is more tense because she is more aware of the things she needs to do and the things that can go wrong. **Category 2 example**

John Cody (Stephany's ten-year-old brother) comes to my mind as an image of the intermediate pianist. For one of his recitals, John played a piece called "Festival of Arragon." He sat down at the piano with a serious **Another example (detailed)** disposition, like a professional. When he began playing, however, his form fell apart. His shoulders sagged and he held his head at an awkward angle because he was paying more attention to the correct tempo and the correct shade of loudness or softness than to the image he was presenting of himself and the music.

Last across the stage is an advanced pianist. She (or he) sits in a relaxed yet formal manner at the piano. When she plays, the dynamics and shades of sound are balanced and put the piece on display rather than the pianist. The tempo is even and steady, and the audience senses a performer in control with a strong stage presence.

Category 3 example

My piano teacher, Ann Fitch, remains in my mind as an image of the advanced pianist. Whenever she sits at the piano, she is calm and relaxed; her disposition alone makes the audience feel relaxed and at ease—ready for the piece to begin. She plays with tempos and rhythms that are steady and gradual. Most of all, however, she makes the audience members feel they are living the music.

Another example (detailed)

An advanced pianist like Ann goes even further with her performance. She plays with a mood and a stage presence that enable listeners to share the pianist's emotions. A top-flight pianist can convey feelings of love, romance, anger, sadness, depression, and excitement and arrange them in ways that guide listeners to the heart of the music without overwhelming them. Finally, if advanced pianists have a secret, it is that they keep four questions always in mind:

Example continues

1. What is the tempo I want to follow for this piece?
2. What mood do I wish to present?
3. What emotions do I want to convey?
4. How can I play so that the audience can live the piece of music at the same time I do?

In place of a conventional conclusion—a list of things all pianists should keep in mind

JUDITH STONE

JUDITH STONE has been a regular contributor to a number of magazines, including *Discover*. Her writings have been collected in *Light Matters: Essays in Science from Gravity to Levity* (1991). As the title suggests, Stone writes about science and scientific matters with both wit and detailed knowledge.

Personal Beast

From the play on words in its title through the rest of its many puns and humorous images, this essay looks critically and understandingly at our often exaggerated and absurd affection for pets—and the status they can confer on their owners. The essay first appeared as a column in *Discover* magazine.

For the past several millennia, dogs have pretty much had the   1
Man's Best Friend market cornered. Lately, however, thanks to a sort of demographic Darwinism, several strong contenders for the title are nipping at the heels of the chosen species.

The dog emerged as protopet in Mesopotamia, where our no-   2
madic ancestors first began living in villages about 12,000 to 14,000 years ago. (And if you think it's hard to paper-train a puppy, imagine having to use stone tablets.)

"Domestication was an urban event," explains Alan Beck,   3
Ph.D., Director of the University of Pennsylvania's Center for the Interaction of Animals and Society. "The garbage generated by these new high-density human communities probably attracted wolf packs; villagers may have bred the pups into pets with the idea of making peace with the pack. These domesticated creatures could bark a warning when nondomestic animals came around, and also help with trash control. And perhaps one of the earliest reasons for breeding pets was for companionship; the desire to nurture is part of human culture." (Those days, when Hector was a pup, probably marked the first time in history that a human being uttered the words, "Aw, Ma, can't I keep it?")

Now a new kind of urbanization is creating a new kind of pet.   4
People are choosing animals that better fit a busier life and a smaller dwelling. Is there room for Fido in Mondo Condo, a world of two-income families with less time but more discretionary income? Folks

want pets that are small and independent, pets that offer them a way to announce their individuality in a crowded, standardized world. Miniaturization, convenience, chic—the pet of the nineties has many of the same fine qualities as an under-the-counter microwave or a car phone. Here, hot off the Ark Nouveau, are the exotic animals that busy Americans simply must have.

Some of you may be seeking a companion that's low-maintenance, 5 affectionate, cute (though swaybacked and paunchy), and perfectly content curled up in front of the TV, pigging out on junk food. (Yeah, yeah, I know—you're already married to it. You're a scream, honestly.) I mean the Vietnamese pot-bellied pig, the nation's top-selling Asian import. A black, beagle-sized porker that's also called a Chinese house pig, it looks like a cross between a hog, a honey bear, and a hand puppet.

"If you can keep a poodle, you can keep one of these pigs," 6 says Fredericka Wagner, co-owner, with husband Bob, of Flying W Farms in Piketon, Ohio, which sends more of the little piggies to market than anyone in the country. "They're very appealing. Full grown, they weigh up to 45 or 50 pounds and stand about 12 to 13 inches high. They graze instead of root. Ordinary pigs have a long, straight snout; this one has a short, pushed-in, wrinkly nose. Its little ears stick straight up like a bat's and it has a straight tail that it wags like a dog's. It barks, too, and it can learn tricks—to come when it's called, sit up and beg, or roll over and play dead hog instead of dead dog." And it's easier to house-break than a cat, Wagner says. Her three little pigs, Choo-Choo, Matilda, and Hamlet, like to sit around with the family and watch movies on TV (presumably *Porky's I* through *III*), and they enjoy supplementing their diet of Purina Pig Chow with candy, brownies, peanuts, and potato chips.

When the pigs arrived two years ago from Vietnam (by way of 7 Sweden and Canada, after three years of red tape), the Wagners already ran a midget menagerie, selling impossibly cute 18-inch miniature sheep (perfect for baby sweaters, easy to count for insomniacs), pygmy goats, miniature donkeys, and championship miniature Arabian horses. (Apparently there are no bonsai bovines, or the Wagners would have them.) "Miniature horses are bred down from larger horses—anything from huge Belgian draft horses to Shetland ponies—a process that can take a century," Wagner says. "In our experience, to reduce a horse from 48 inches to 34 inches takes six generations—about twenty years. You can do it in only three generations if you have a 30-inch stallion, but you'd have to dig a hole to put the mare in."

Wagner first heard about the pigs from a friend in California; reportedly they'd been imported by Vietnam veterans who recalled the friendly critters from their tours of duty. Though Wagner was instantly attracted to them, she wasn't sure she'd get the business off the ground. But the swine flew. "We can't keep up with the demand," she says. "In the first eighteen months we sold a hundred pigs." Wagner is boarish on pot-bellied pigs as an investment. "Not even the stock market will pay you back as fast as these pigs will. I've had several retired people buy them to supplement their income. They breed at six months [the pigs, not the retirees] and it takes three weeks, three months, and three days for them to have babies. By the time your gilt is a year old—a gilt is a pregnant sow—she's given you her first litter of pigs and you have your investment back three times over." Since you can only have gilt by association, those who want to breed pigs must buy an unrelated pair for $2,500. "We expect that to go up to $3,000, because the demand is so great," says Wagner, in hog heaven. "We've sold them to everyone from poets to princes—we shipped some overseas to a Saudi Arabian prince. Stephanie Zimbalist, the actress, has one." 8

Stephanie Zimbalist! A recommendation, indeed. But what about having the same pet as *Michael Jackson?* For part of his personal zoo (boa, deer, chimp/valet, glove, and, nearly, the Elephant Man), Jackson has chosen a taller order of hip creature, the llama. His is one of about 15,000 in the country. "But in years to come, we'll see more and more of them in the average home," says Florence Dicks, owner of the Llonesome Llama Ranch in Sumner, Washington. "They're great hiking companions, their wool is increasingly in demand, and they make wonderful pets. They've been part of domestic life in South America for centuries. I think of them as one of life's necessities." 9

Dicks, who runs Llama Lluvs Unltd., the world's only Llamagram delivery service, notes that the recent lifting of a government ban on imports will increase the llama population; most American-born llamas are descended from a single herd owned by William Randolph Hearst. 10

"They're very gentle," Dicks says. "Many of my fifteen llamas lived in the house for their first year. They're easier to house-train than a cat." (You know how all weird meat is described as "sort of like chicken"? Apparently all weird pets are easier to housebreak 11 than a cat.) Dicks explains, in more detail than necessary, that llamas are what's called communal voiders—a great name for a rock band. Spread some llama droppings where you want them to go, and, in the comradely way of communal voiders everywhere, they will use that spot forever after. "We've shared our bathroom with llamas for five years, and they've never had an accident," Dicks says. Okay, they squeeze the toothpaste from the top, but nobody's perfect.

"I train my llamas to hum—that's the noise they make—when   12
they want to go outside," Dicks reports. "They communicate by tone variance. If they're relaxed, there's a musical quality to the hum. If they're stressed, you can hear the anxiety. I have a llama who hums with a rising inflection when he's curious."

Full-grown llamas can stand over six feet tall and weigh up to   13
500 pounds. A male costs between $1,500 and $15,000. (And at a recent auction, a male said to have outstanding stud qualities—he always sends a thank-you note—fetched $100,000.) A gelded male will set you back $700 or $800, a female about $8,000. The only bad thing about llamas, Dicks says, is that you have to clip their toenails every three or four months. Which doesn't sound like a big deal if you're already sharing a bathroom.

But more and more of us have life-styles and living spaces—to   14
use a pair of expressions even more nauseating than the word *pus*—that can't accommodate a dog, let alone a llama. I know I barely have room in my apartment for a pet peeve. Hence the proliferation among city dwellers of ferrets, dwarf rabbits, and birds. According to the American Veterinary Medical Association, birds are the fastest growing pet category. Their numbers increased 24 percent between 1983 and 1987, from 10.3 million to 12.8 million. Talking birds, like Amazon parrots, are especially sought after, reports veterinarian Katherine Quesenberry, head of the exotic pet service of the Animal Medical Center of New York. (And I guess if you crossed these South American birds with llamas, you'd get Fernando Llamas six-foot communal voiders that squawk, "You look *mahv*elous." Cheep gag.)

The ferret, a more personable cousin of the weasel, has been   15
bred in captivity for a century, mostly for lab research. But its popularity as a pet has steadily risen over the last decade. Says Tina Ellenbogen, a Seattle veterinarian and information services director for the Delta Society, a national organization dedicated to the study of human-animal bonding, "People become attached to ferrets because they have a lot of personality. They're small, clean, and amusing." (It's sometimes hard to tell when people are talking about

ferrets and when they're talking about Dudley Moore.) You can walk them on a harness or let them play on a ferrets wheel. They're easily litter-trained, says Ellenbogen—easier than a cat, I imagine—and statistically less likely to bite than a dog is. Males are unpleasant if you don't remove their stink glands, and females are sexually insatiable until you have them fixed, but hey.

Maybe you're a person who doesn't understand all the sound and furry over mammals. Maybe you'd rather see something in cold blood.   16

The reptile of the hour is the African Old World chameleon. "Having one is like owning a dinosaur!" says Gary Bagnall, head of California Zoological Supplies, one of the five largest reptile distributors in the country. "They look truly prehistoric. Their eyes move independently and they have 10-inch tongues with stickum at the end for catching insects. The base color is green, but they can blend into their surroundings by changing to yellow, orange, white, black, brown, and sometimes blue." The 6- to 10-inch chameleons start at $35; a foot-long variety, called Miller's chameleon, goes for $1,000. "We get only about four of them a year," Bagnall says. "There's a waiting list."   17

The nation's most sought-after amphibian, according to Bagnall, is the poison arrow frog, a tiny (less than an inch long), jewel-like native of South America that comes in orange and black, yellow and black, or blue. The really great thing about the poison arrow frog is that if you boil up about fifty of them, you get enough of the toxin they secrete to brew a dandy blowdart dip guaranteed to make hunting small jungle mammals a breeze.   18

Alive, the frogs, which cost from $35 to $200, require a lot of attention, Bagnall warns. "They can't take extremes in temperature or dryness, and their diet is restricted to very small insects. In fact, you have to raise fruit flies for them." Most of us don't have time to raise fruit flies for our families, let alone for a pet. But, paradoxically, though exotic pet owners are getting busier, they're also getting savvier and more dedicated.   19

"The whole pet industry has changed," says Bagnall. "Exotic pet owners can't afford to be ignorant, because they're paying more." Making a fatal mistake with a $3,500 miniature ram and ewe is a whole different thing from accidentally offing a twenty-five-cent baby turtle. (I'd like to take this opportunity to make a public confession. I'm sorry, Shelly. I was only seven, and I didn't know that painting your back with nail polish would kill you. Forgive me, too, for digging you up two weeks after the funeral, but I was curious to   20 see if the rumors I'd heard about deterioration were true. You didn't disappoint.) Continues Bagnall, "I can't speak for birds and mammals, but the prices of even standard, bread-and-butter reptiles—boas, garter snakes, pythons—have tripled over the last three years because of government regulation of imports." But the high prices seem to add to the mystique, he says. "Reptiles attract people who want something not everybody has. Also, if you're allergic to fur, they're a nice alternative." (And probably a certain percentage of newly minted MBAs are even now saying to their mentors, "Rep *ties?* I thought you said 'invest in some rep*tiles!*'") Bagnall adds that poison arrow frogs and Old World chameleons are especially popular now because they've only recently appeared in zoos. "And if a reptile shows up in a movie, its popularity increases tenfold, like the Burmese python in *Raiders of the Lost Ark.*"

Yes, it's a cachet as cachet can world. Perhaps all human   21
progress stems from the tension between two basic drives: to have just what everyone else has and to have what no one has. Covet your neighbor's ass? Get yourself a miniature one and watch him mewl with envy. But be careful: Once an odd animal enters the mainstream, those on the cutting edge of the pet thing have to push for a new personal beast. "Pygmy goats used to be really rare," Fredericka Wagner says with a sigh. "Now everyone has them." (Haven't you noticed that the first question you're asked at the best restaurants these days is "May I check your goat?")

The proliferation of peculiar pets may necessitate a revamping   22
of terminology, says veterinarian Quesenberry. "The term *exotics* is no longer valid. We're talking about animals that haven't historically been domesticated, but they're not wild anymore, either, because they're being bred in captivity and exposed to humans from an early age. Somebody has suggested using the term *special species* for these animals, and reserving the term exotics for the zoo stuff."

If you're not ready to pay big bucks for little pigs, you'll be   23
happy to know that the classic exotic pet, the simple yet eloquent sea monkey, retails for just $3.99. Remember sea monkeys? When some of us were kids, during what scientists call the Late Cleaver-Brady Epoch, sea monkeys were advertised in the backs of magazines, usually between the Mark Eden Bust Developer and the Can You Draw This Elf School of Art. A smiling, bikini-clad creature with the head of a monkey and the body of a seahorse promised the requisite hours of fun for kids from eight to—if I recall the stats correctly—eighty. Remember your disappointment when the "monkeys" turned out to be brine shrimp, so infinitesimal that they could only be clearly seen with the enclosed magnifying glass? Remember how

not one of them wore a bathing suit? Well, for the same low price, a new generation of kids can learn a powerful lesson about the true nature of existence (sometimes when you expect a bikini-clad aquatic primate, you get a bunch of stupid, skinny-dipping germs). And sea monkeys are easier to house-train than cats.

MEANINGS AND VALUES

1. In your own words, tell what Stone considers the main qualities of the pet of the 1990s. Explain the differences she sees between contemporary pets (and owners) and those of the past.

2. Identify the categories Stone presents in this essay. Are there any subcategories? If so, what are they? Do any of the categories overlap? If so, is the overlap confusing?

3. If you believe this essay has a serious purpose, tell what it is.

EXPOSITORY TECHNIQUES

1. Can the second sentence in this essay be considered a thesis statement? If so, why? (See "Guide to Terms": *Thesis.*) Are there any other sentences that might be considered additional thesis statements or repetitions and developments of the second sentence? Identify any such sentences and discuss their role in the essay.

2. Why does the author choose to begin the essay by discussing dogs? Would the essay have been more effective had she begun with a discussion of cats or of some other familiar kind of pet? (Guide: *Evaluation.*)

3. Discuss the role of the comments within the parentheses in Paragraph 20. Explain the ways these comments are similar to or different from other parenthetical comments in the essay.

DICTION AND VOCABULARY

1. What does "Mondo Condo" (Par. 4) mean, and for what purpose does the writer use the phrase?

2. Identify the source of each of the following allusions, and discuss what each means: Hector (Par. 3); Ark Nouveau (4); swine flew (8); in cold blood (16). (Guide: *Figures of Speech.*)

3. How does the word choice in the last sentence of Paragraph 5 emphasize the meaning and create a pattern of sound? (Guide: *Emphasis; Diction.*)

4. If you do not know the meaning of some of the following words, look them up in the dictionary: nomadic (Par. 2); discretionary (4); voiders (11); variance (12); gelded (13); insatiable (15); cachet (21).

READ TO WRITE

1.   **Collaborating:** Working with a group of fellow students, list several categories of dogs (or some other animal). Subdivide these categories if you can. Then, as a group, write down what you consider the stereotypical characteristics of people who own the different kinds of animals you classified. Develop all or most of these categories of people and animals into a short essay of your own, and compare your essay with those written by the others in your group.

2.   **Considering Audience:** Are readers who do not own pets likely to find much in this essay to interest them? What other subjects can be sorted into categories that a wide range of readers are likely to find interesting? Make a list of such subjects, and be ready to explain what kinds of readers are likely to find each subject interesting or uninteresting. To what extent does the presentation rather than the subject determine readers' interest? Why?

3.   **Developing an Essay:** Taking Stone's essay as a model, classify the contemporary versions of some activity or object (other than pet owning and pets) that has been around in different forms for a long time. Following Stone's lead, show how the modern versions reflect changes in attitude and fashion.

(NOTE: Suggestions for topics requiring development by use of CLASSIFICATION are on pp. 147–148 at the end of this chapter.)

ALISSA QUART

ALISSA QUART attended Brown University and the Columbia
University School of Journalism. Her articles have appeared in nu-
merous periodicals, including the *New York Times, The Nation, Elle,
Film Comment,* and *Salon.* Her book, *Branded: The Buying and
Selling of Teenagers* was published in 2003.

Cinema of the In-Crowd

This selection from *Branded* uses classification (and numerous examples) to look at a perennial favorite of filmgoers: the teenage
film. Any classification of this sort is a look backward at films that
have already appeared in theaters, of course. At the same time,
thinking about films in this way helps us to understand new films
as they are created. It even encourages us to create new categories.

I was thirteen when I first understood what a teen film was.
Knowledge arrived in the form of *The Breakfast Club.*   1

The characters include an indulged clotheshorse, a driven nerd,   2
a vacant jock, a splenetic stoner, and an attention-deprived Goth. It
was 1985, and the film was the *Ulysses* of its director, that maestro of
puberty John Hughes, taking place as it did during a day of detention in the school library. At first the film's kids are mere types. The
jock eats six turkey sandwiches for lunch, the nerd toadies up to the
supervising teacher. The stoner sneers at the princess for being a virgin, bringing her own sushi, and having a drunk, rich mother. The
jock accuses the loser of lying about his abuse—that his father burns
the stoner with lit cigarettes.

But suddenly the quintet comes together, dancing, implausi-   3
bly, to new wave music that emanates from an invisible stereo.
Limbered up, they tell all. The nerd (Anthony Michael Hall) announces that he brought a gun to school to off himself—he was
failing shop and thus screwing up his GPA. The jock (Emilio
Estevez) lets it be known that he taped a geek's "buns together,"
imagining that doing so would finally convince his macho father
he was a real man.

The nerd, lean with a scraggly mop of blonde hair and buggy   4
eyes, recognizes that his day of inclusion and quasi-Method acting
will end as soon as detention does. Near tears, as if recalling his

grade-grubbing harridan mom waiting for him at home, the nerd announces that they will all "become their parents": "It's unavoidable. . . . It just happens." "When you grow up, your heart dies," answers the Goth (Ally Sheedy), glittery-eyed and black-clad, excited by her own bleakness.

At thirteen, I suspected my heart would die also, sooner rather   5 than later. It's embarrassing to admit now, but the film spoke to me. Sure, it's overacted and broad, like a summer-stock theater production. But it also has the ring of a diary entry, of what life is really like when our parents or teachers leave the room. Raging against high school cliques and hierarchies, it puts forth an appealingly sappy proposition: that all strata of kids should unite against two common enemies, their parents and a future of soulless-ness.

BRINGING IT ON

Fifteen years later, few popular teen films would depict such mo-   6 ments of veracity, or have responsible, liberal reflexes to guide them. Teen blockbusters—among them *Clueless, Bring It On, She's All That, Legally Blonde,* and *Varsity Blues*—had become the stories of insiders: sports stars, beauties, rich kids, and cheerleaders. These kids live in the blondest, richest suburbs, suburbs without seasons. The characters have abs so hard and defined they seem to have replaced personalities. It's difficult to feel affection for these studs and sylphs and even harder to pity them. . . . After visiting this cinematic life-world, one misses John Hughes. In fact, Hughes seems the apotheosis of teen film integrity.

The new films' fascination with the high school in-crowd   7 echoes the marketing recommendations of Teenage Research Unlimited, a youth marketing agency whose clients include Sony and Coca-Cola. TRU's goal is to snag the shoppers of the in-crowd, called channelers or influencers—"the cream of the crop," those "that know their status and revel in it," as the TRU spokesman has said. "If you can attract them, you have scored. The biggest kiss of death is for you to be a cool brand in the mind of the conformers." The taste of the popular kids will reverberate downward.

In *Varsity Blues,* the hero is an influencer, a star quarterback   8 (James Van Der Beek, formerly of *Dawson's Creek*). At the center of *She's All That* is an influencer, the senior class president and soccer star played by the canine-ishly handsome Freddie Prinze Jr. The heroine of *Legally Blonde* is a Bel Airhead beauty queen named Elle Woods. Elle, played by Reese Witherspoon, is the best-loved, pettiest, blondest sorority girl at California University (this invented institution of higher learning happens to be an allusion to the college in the teen television show *Beverly Hills 90210*). When Elle goes to Harvard Law School, however, she is an outcast—because of the very qualities that made her so popular at CU. But she regains her influencer status at Harvard by applying her CU sensibility to a major law case. Her master stroke: keeping secret the shameful liposuction of her legal client, an aerobics instructor.

In *Bring It On*, the heroine is not just a cheerleader but a cheer- 9
leading *captain*, Torrance, played by Kirsten Dunst. Torrance struggles to keep her kingdom of cruel, anorexic simps happy—the resulting cheer-meets and cheer-offs are suffused with dialogue so excessively acid it resembles exchanges between drag queens in a mock cat fight. When one of the cheerleaders asks the team's hired choreographer why everyone has to go on a diet, he replies, "Because we're cheerleaders. We throw people in the air. And fat people don't go as high." When Torrance smiles winsomely at her crush while he watches her do her routine from the bleachers, her teammates are quick to judge. "You were having cheer-sex with him!" they say, aghast.

As a viewer shaped by an earlier teen film era, in which most 10
films carried a whiff of after-school-special decency, I figured I knew what was coming in *Bring It On*. I expected Torrance to learn a lesson of some sort by the film's close, presumably some humanist nostrum about how girls of normal body mass are people, too. No such primer is doled out. Torrance doesn't muse about why she relies on pep and looks to get by but continues to let them work for her. (As for the film's box office, *Bring It On* appeals not just to lascivious boys but also to the prurient-older-man rental market; and no wonder, given the lithe teenagers performing deep splits and high kicks, their bodies encased in super-tight shirts, jog bras, colored panties, and even sudsy wet bikinis, the latter in the name of a car wash for, um, charity). *Bring It On's* screen teens are more often than not what critic Pauline Kael termed "un-people." *Most* of the kids in teen films are. Where in a former era the pubescent stars might have evinced personal fragility, they are now brittle and paper-thin. Where they once were confronted with real-life difficulties, they now have contests, social machinations, and makeovers.

The in-crowd wasn't always given the benefit of the doubt. 11
Once, the in-crowd were ice princesses and authoritarian despots: the girls in 1989's *Heathers* or the malevolent pranksters who think drenching a freak in pig's blood is funny, pace *Carrie*. In the former,

the film's entirely unpleasant torturers, the all-named-Heather clones with upturned noses and flowing manes, answer the question "Why are you such a megabitch?" with the riposte "Because I can be." One of the Heathers demands that Veronica (played by a still *compos mentis* Winona Ryder) hold their hair while they vomit and that she join them in tormenting her former grade-geek friends. So when Veronica's gun-toting hipster boyfriend J. D. (Christian Slater) poisons one of the Heathers, our heroine's joining an offing of the gorgeous tyrants is something of a no-brainer. J. D. puts kitchen pipe cleanser into a hangover cure, and then Veronica willingly forges that Heather's suicide note. The two repeat the murder routine with two more of the school's vicious snobs. One can't help but notice that the dying villains of *Heathers* are boys and girls who would now be the heroes of teen films. In fact, the popular kids' brand consciousness—Veronica curses them as "Swatch dogs and Diet Coke heads"—is part of their villainy. Viewers are asked to hate these iniquitous snots to the extent that they might think the popular teens *do* deserve death by industrial-strength drain cleaner rather than sympathy or worship.

And, of course, the outsiders that do exist in the films today are never as radically kooky as Ally Sheedy's character in *The Breakfast Club,* who shakes a head full of dandruff on her own drawing of a wintry landscape to make snow. If they start out disaffected and shunned, like the heroine of *She's All That,* for instance, we can be assured their marginality is only momentary—a quick costume change will seamlessly transform them into insiders in Act II. 12

The move toward the in-crowd emerges from an ever-increasing need to appeal to huge audiences. With films opening on twice as many screens as they did twenty years ago, expensive television ad campaigns and an aversion to risk have become the norm. Films are no longer allowed to accrue audiences slowly; for the most part, if they don't open with a bang, they die. And studios have decreed that teens in particular must be herded into the theaters on opening weekend or else. The twelve-to-twenty-four-year-old niche may constitute only 18 percent of the public, but it makes up 37 percent of the film-going public. This is also the demographic that buys tie-ins: Studios are increasingly engaging in a "synergetic" cross-marketing agenda by hawking soundtracks and other products. With so much of a sales burden now riding on teen cinema, it's not a surprise that films have shrugged off their loser characters; after all, outcasts are less likely to sell clothes or music than their popular peers. 13

DON'T YOU FORGET ABOUT ME:
A SHORT HISTORY LESSON

Of course, even the original teen pix were mostly market-savvy en-   14
terprises. The genre emerged from the film studios of the 1950s,
when the industry discovered it had a young, eager audience willing to spend. Teen rock-and-roll films came to the fore, Elvis flicks
and Frankie Avalon beach-and-bikini movies. For the first time,
adults were offering adolescents a pop mirror of themselves on a
mass scale.

Over the years, the teen pix genre morphed into the teen sex ex-   15
ploitation film, the likes of *Animal House, Porky's, Porky's Revenge,*
and *Risky Business.* These films featured boys humiliating one another in the quest for "pussy" and trying to trip up fatuous authority
figures on their way to the whorehouse. And the films did very well
at the box office, setting the standard for the caricatured teen films
that we have today. *Porky's* raked in $21 million in its first twelve
days, and $105 million at the box office total, breaking box-office
records in 1982. Its franchise prospered still more from the rise of the
video rental (*Porky's 3* bombed in theaters, but it rose from the ashes
as a home video). The *Porky's* movies centered on sex-mad Floridian
high school students peeping at girls in shower stalls and bopping
one another with a giant inflated condom. After *Porky's,* filmmakers suddenly knew how to strike gold: They made popular
films quickly and cheaply without the aid of stars or sets or well-
established directors or scriptwriters; films whose plots could be
described entirely by a movie poster.

Back in the 1950s, however, a more well-meaning model vied   16
with the fun-in-the-sun teen pic for supremacy, the teen angst
movie. The prime example was the 1955 classic *Rebel Without a
Cause,* followed by other social-realist youth-gone-bad films such as
Blackboard Jungle. They spoke to the extremity of adolescent desires
and violence, but also to adult fears of teenagers. In the lush *Rebel,*
police officers act as psychologists to the burgeoning "juvie" population. In the 1950s, a period of relatively luxurious living, the
youth-in-trouble was the counterpoint to the young consumer built
for records, beaches, and stupid glee. As cultural theorist Dick
Hebdige writes, "The two image clusters, the bleak portrayal of
juvenile offenders and the exuberant cameos of teenage life reverberate, alternate and sometimes they get crossed."

Rebel-informed films continued to appear through the 1980s,   17
which in retrospect looks like a golden age for teen films. Teen films

in the 1980s were often about kids living violently in the inner city, or simply living in comfortable towns on the wrong side of the tracks (a favorite theme of John Hughes). This strain included *Fast Times at Ridgemont High, Pretty in Pink, The Breakfast Club, Heathers,* and *Say Anything . . .*, and ended with *Boyz N the Hood.* They did well at the box office: *Pretty in Pink* helped its studio, Paramount, get to the box office pinnacle in 1986. Despite the shiny clean appearances of these films' screen teens and the randy humor around their edges, the films were dedicated to themes other than which team would win at the football game or the cheer meet. Molly Ringwald in *Pretty in Pink* or Mary Stuart Masterson in *Some Kind of Wonderful* or John Cusack in *Say Anything . . .* were quasi outsiders. They were poorer than their peers, and sometimes seemingly parent-free, but also wittier and attractively subversive. At the end of the films, their triumphs were on their own terms, understood as testaments to the victory of personality and grit.

The teen film golden age also included stylish versions of teen   18
novels by S. E. Hinton, most notably Francis Ford Coppola's *The Outsiders* and *Rumble Fish.* The central characters were juvenile delinquents, isolated lost boys (played by Matt Dillon, who handled this job in film after film in the 1980s) who found comfort only in other boys who had fallen off the grid. Coppola shot his teen films through colored filters and at oblique angles or in glowering black and white, underlining the teens' anomie (and perhaps also the director's frustration with making mere teen pix). At any rate, the teen films of the 1980s borrowed somewhat from the personal dystopias of early–1970s "New Hollywood," films such as *Taxi Driver, Nashville,* and *Five Easy Pieces*—what the essayist Robert Kolker famously dubbed "a cinema of loneliness." Now, teen pix steal their visual vocabulary from commercials and MTV.

In the teen-angst films of 1980s, the characters were capable of   19
vulnerability, and vulnerability's flip side, defiance, which found its best expression in *The Breakfast Club.* A letter from the film's nerd that amounted to a Bill of Rights for white upper-middle-class adolescents reads:

> Dear Mr. Vernon,
> We accept the fact that we had to sacrifice a whole Saturday in detention for whatever it was we did wrong. . . . You see us as you want to see us: in the simplest terms and the most convenient definitions. You see us as a brain, an athlete, a basket case, a princess, and a criminal. Correct? That's the way we saw each other at 7 o'clock this morning. We were brainwashed.

Surprisingly, given the greed underwriting the 1980s, con- 20
sumerism wasn't a big part of the teen movies of that age: Films
such as *Porky's* were exploitative about sex, not money. *"Risky
Business* aside, many of the eighties teen flicks expressed a yearning
for a pluralistic school yard where wealth was no longer an impediment to the interaction of previously segregated social strata, where
the jock could lie down with the geek and where the punkette could
break bread with the princess," writes Jonathan Bernstein in *Pretty
in Pink: The Golden Age of Teenage Movies.* Despite a penchant for too-
obvious poignancies, the best 1980s teen films regularly depicted
kids who rejected the established order.

The teen angst genre lives on today only in its most diminished 21
form, in a take off of the very worst scene in *The Breakfast Club.* In
that episode, the princess (Molly Ringwald) transforms kohl-rim-
eyed Ally Sheedy. Using a normal amount of eyeliner, a headband,
and a white blouse, the princess turns the freak from an androgy-
nous ball of drama into a dull but pretty girl. That moment gave
birth to one of the biggest teen film genres of our period, the makeover movie.

SCENES FROM A MALL

In 1995, director Amy Heckerling, who made *Fast Times at* 22
Ridgemont High, came out with *Clueless,* which draws on *The
Breakfast Club's* makeover scene for its major subplot. *Clueless* was
the first and best film of the new branded teen wave. (It was also a
big box office success, which clued in studios that girls would spend
to see themselves on screen.) The film set in place not only the
genre's exaltation of high-end goods and opulence but also the
genre's dependence on sharp-edged satire camouflaging an ardor
for consumption.

Clueless's heroine Cher Horowitz is a Beverly Hills shopaholic: 23
babelicious, surfacey, and affluent, played with good humor by the
sunflower-like then-teen Alicia Silverstone, formerly jailbait in
Aerosmith music videos of the early 1990s. Her upper lip is perpetu-
ally curved skyward as if there's something amusing on the horizon.

Cher is so fashion-mad that she uses a computer to tell her 24
when her clothes match. Her nonvirtual fashion "project" is making
over the new kid, a working-class stoner named Tai, played by
Brittany Murphy. Cher is like one of the TRU channelers, introducing labels and cell phones to the conformers and the losers in her
class. Most of her "work" with Tai occurs at the mall.

In the ten years since *Fast Times at Ridgemont High,* the meaning   25
of the mall had changed dramatically for Heckerling and her teens.
The Sherman Oaks Mall in *Fast Times* is strange to the movie's characters: a giddily forbidding fortress of mirrored walls, a place where
one practices a future of wasting one's life in dead-end jobs or being
hit on by older men. We understand that in the mall the nubile but
naive waitress played by Jennifer Jason Leigh is inevitably quarry
for predatory guys, and we aren't surprised when the circumstances
lead ineluctably to first sex—and first abortion. In fact, the manic,
estranged atmosphere of the film's mall breeds abuses of power in
general, as when a teen wiseguy, lording his illegal access, scalps
concert tickets to younger kids. In *Clueless,* by contrast, the mall is
the film's safe space, homier than Cher's own home, a huge and remote white manse. Malls are "a way of homecoming to a self that
has been lost," as one theorist wrote in the book *Lifestyle Shopping:
The Subject of Consumption.*

The pivot between the depressing and heroic views of the mall   26
can be found in a late 1980s film, *Bill & Ted's Excellent Adventure,*
whose two eponymous Cali mess-ups retrieve Socrates and a host of
other historical figures and bring these great personages back to the
future in a phone booth; first, there's a stop at the mall before Bill
and Ted drag their finds to high school, where the resurrected figures will act as their hosts' living history class presentation. Genghis
Khan, Beethoven, and Joan of Arc set loose in the shopping center
simply don't *get* that it's a place for shopping. Beethoven plays all
the keyboards in the music shop. Genghis Khan swings bats and destroys a sporting-goods store. Joan of Arc leads a chaotic medieval-
style aerobics class. Their antics underline the oddness of the mall
and also that *Bill & Ted* is anything but one of the in-crowd teen
movies. In fact, it's a high school loser's ultimate fantasy—passing
history class (and passing life) thanks to the genial, dopey openness
that would, in real life, probably pave a kid's self-destruction.

Bill and Ted's failure-as-success life plan wouldn't be permitted   27
in today's teen cinema. In the six years between *Bill & Ted* and
Clueless, all losers were sent to the margins. The winners were the
ones sent to the mall. The mall would become, in fact, the ideal stage
for the makeover film, which is all about normalizing social outcasts, turning them into influencers, and carrying them from the
lowest high school social rung to the top. As Cher works to raise
Tai's social profile, she acts as both stylist and publicist. She creates
photo opportunities in which Tai will look "classic"—posing with a
flower, paired off with a popular boy. And sure enough, Tai be-

comes a well-liked fashionista Frankenstein, so much so that she nearly supplants her doctor-creator.

She's All That is another makeover movie out to teach kids the importance of having fancy clothes and wearing good makeup. Zach (Freddie Prinze Jr.), a boy who looks good in sportswear, gets dumped by his girlfriend and then makes a bet with his jock friends: He can turn a loser into his prom queen in six weeks. Laney (Rachael Leigh Cook), the lucky loser, soon metamorphoses from an alienated artiste into a pert drone. The filmmakers, well aware of the new law of teen films that says all main characters must be style influencers, create Zach's sister (Anna Paquin), younger but more worldly, to make Laney over. A new look, an attitude adjustment, and Laney quickly goes from bespectacled neo-hippie to homecoming queen nominee in a short skirt. By the film's end, Laney even draws a parallel between herself and another branded film babe when she tells Zach that she feels "like Julia Roberts in *Pretty Woman.*" Clearly, the transformation recalls Liza Doolittle and *The Breakfast Club's* infamous scene. (Critic Owen Gleiberman noted this connection in his 1999 review of the film in *Entertainment Weekly:* "*She's All That* is like a feature-length extension of Sheedy's transformation.") 28

The instant transformations promised by the makeover film seem very much a Generation Y phenomenon, an obvious way to speak to kids who have been taught to believe that respect and a new self are merely a new slip dress or new lip gloss away. But the makeover genre does have deeper roots. For one, it bastardizes the cinematic tradition of the "hidden" celebrity. As cinema scholar Stanley Cavell writes in *Contesting Tears: The Hollywood Melodrama of the Unknown Woman,* it was common in the films of the 1930s and 1940s for stars' faces to be "first shown hidden, or marred . . . perhaps simply as in the plainness of youth or of some other restricted office, and later revealed in the astonishment of its familiar power." 29

For Cavell, these films of physical reinvention are not just gaudy baubles describing the wish to be beautiful or to possess beautiful people; they are also morality plays that show an audience its beloved icons gone ugly and damaged. When the icon reverts, over the course of the film, to his or her naturally beautiful self, that transformation illustrates "the courage to become who you are," writes Cavell. Perhaps the most famous of these metamorphoses occurred in 1942's *Now, Voyager.* In that film Bette Davis plays the fat, beetle-browed Aunt Charlotte, but then she sloughs off her dominating mother. She transforms into the Bette Davis we know and 30 love—a graceful beauty in the white, wide-brimmed hat, ready for an ocean voyage.

The transformations of *Clueless* and *She's All That* don't illus-   31
trate courage. Rather, they show girls willing to be tampered with by stylists. These girls believed that their stylists had a better grasp of what it means to look like a teenager than teenagers do themselves. The makeover movies claim that the girls being powdered and primped and branded are becoming their "true" selves. But the alchemized girls of the makeover film are in fact testifying to the power of constructed and artificial selves. Although the films give lip service to the notion that girls can find the courage to be themselves, they are in effect encouraging their audiences to be someone else, someone more suave, someone with straightened hair and designer clothes and overclass mannerisms. The real mission of the makeover films is to get across to their teen and tween viewers a limited notion of success. Anyone can turn into a popular girl or a prom queen, the films say. All it takes is a full commitment to beauty conventions and the high school brand economy.

MEANINGS AND VALUES

1.   Identify each of the categories of films discussed in this selection.

2.   What different sets of categories does the writer introduce in the course of this essay?

3.   According to the writer, what are then main differences between the films of the 1980s and more recent films?

4.   What elements of the film *Bring It On* does the writer find objectionable?

EXPOSITORY TECHNIQUES

1.   What techniques does the author use to announce the categories in the essay to readers?

2.   Identify the strategy the author uses to begin this selection, and explain how it is connected to the rest of the discussion. (See "Guide to Terms": *Introductions*.)

3.   The writer spends considerable time discussing the role played by Ally Sheedy in *The Breakfast Club*. What role does this extended discussion play in the essay?

4. The discussion in Paragraphs 14–31 follows a rough chronological order in presenting different categories of films (along with illustrations of each category). It is also arranged to convey the author's interpretation of the way the films and their themes have developed. What themes does the author highlight in the way the films have developed over the decades?

DICTION AND VOCABULARY

1. Identify particular words or groups of words the author uses in Paragraphs 9–10 to highlight what she considers objectionable features of *Bring It On*. (Guide: *Diction*.)

2. Identify those words or groups of words the author uses to convey and emphasize her evaluation of *Heathers*. (Guide: *Diction, Emphasis*.)

3. If you do not know the meaning of some of these words, look them up in a dictionary: splenetic, toadies (Par. 2); implausibly, emanates (3); harridan (4); sappy (5); veracity, apotheosis (6); reverberate (7); aghast (9); nostrum, lascivious, prurient, lithe (10); despots, malevolent, riposte, iniquitous (11); disaffected, marginality (12); constitute (13); exuberant, cameos (16); anomie, dystopias (18); pluralistic, impediment, strata (20); nubile (25); metamorphoses, artiste, drone (28); icon (30).

READ TO WRITE

1. **Collaborating:** Working with a group of writers, make a list of types of films, recordings, television shows or other components of popular culture that you feel can be understood and explained through classification. Then identify one or more sets of categories that help understand your subject. Finally, make a list of the sets of categories and each subcategory you might decide to include in an essay.

2. **Considering Audience:** Take the topic and categories you identified in question 1, above, and still working in a group, create four possible thesis statements, one each for each of these potential audiences: people from 18–25, 26–40, 41–60, and 61 or older.

3. **Developing an Essay:** Choose one of the audiences from question 2, above, and create an essay of your own using either the possible thesis statement you developed in a group or one you developed on your own.

(NOTE: Suggestions for topics requiring development by analysis of DEFINITION are on pp. 147–148 at the end of this chapter.)

MICHAEL VENTURA

> MICHAEL VENTURA worked as an editor for the *Austin Sun* and the *Los Angeles Weekly* (which he cofounded). He has been a columnist for the *Austin Chronicle* and the *Los Angeles Village View*. His books include *The Mollyhawk Poems* (1977); *Night Time, Losing Time* (1989); and *The Zoo Where You're Fed to God* (1994). His most recent book is a novel, *The Death of Frank Sinatra* (2000).

Don't Even Think About It!

> In this essay, Michael Ventura explains how taboos, which many readers might associate with primitive societies or superstitions, help shape the things we do in our daily lives. By showing how many different kinds of taboos we routinely observe (more categories than readers usually encounter in an essay), Ventura demonstrates their prevalence and importance. The concrete examples that Ventura provides help keep the numerous categories from seeming overwhelming and abstract. The illustrations also help readers recognize taboos in their own behavior.

Taboos come in all sizes. Big taboos: when I was a kid in the Italian neighborhoods of Brooklyn, to insult someone's mother meant a brutal fight—the kind of fight no one interferes with until one of the combatants goes down and stays down. Little taboos: until the sixties, it was an insult to use someone's first name without asking or being offered permission. Personal taboos: Cyrano de Bergerac would not tolerate the mention of his enormous nose. Taboos peculiar to one city: in Brooklyn (again), when the Dodgers were still at Ebbets Field, if you rooted for the Yankees you kept it to yourself unless you wanted a brawl. Taboos, big or small, are always about having to respect somebody's (often irrational) boundary—or else.

There are taboos shared within one family: my father did not feel free to speak to us of his grandmother's suicide until his father died. Taboos within intellectual elites: try putting a serious metaphysical or spiritual slant on a "think-piece" (as we call them in the trade) written for the *New York Times,* the *Washington Post,* or most big name magazines—it won't be printed. Taboos in the corporate and legal worlds: if you're male, you had best wear suits of somber colors, or you're not likely to be taken seriously; if you're female, you have to strike a very uneasy balance between the attractive and the prim, and even then you might not be taken seriously. Cultural

1

2

taboos: in the Jim Crow days in the South, a black man who spoke with familiarity to a white woman might be beaten, driven out of town, or (as was not uncommon) lynched.

Unclassifiable taboos: in Afghanistan, as I write this, it is a sin— 3
punishable by beatings and imprisonment—to fly a kite. Sexual taboos: there are few communities on this planet where two men can walk down a street holding hands without being harassed or even arrested; in Afghanistan (a great place for taboos these days) the Taliban would stone them to death. Gender taboos: how many American corporations (or institutions of any kind) promote women to power? National taboos: until the seventies, a divorced person could not run for major public office in America (it wasn't until 1981 that our first and only divorced president, Ronald Reagan, took office); today, no professed atheist would dare try for the presidency. And most readers of this article probably approve, as I do, of this comparatively recent taboo: even the most rabid bigot must avoid saying "nigger," "spic," or "kike" during, say, a job interview—and the most macho sexist must avoid words like "broad."

Notice that nearly all of our taboos, big and small, public and in- 4
timate, involve silence—keeping one's silence, or paying a price for not keeping it. Yet keeping silent has its own price: for then silence begins to fill the heart, until silence becomes the heart—a heart swelling with restraint until it bursts in frustration, anger, even madness.

The taboos hardest on the soul are those which fester in our 5
intimacies—taboos known only to the people involved, taboos that can make us feel alone even with those to whom we're closest. One of the deep pains of marriage—one that also plagues brothers and sisters, parents and children, even close friends—is that as we grow more intimate, certain silences often become more necessary. We discover taboo areas, both in ourselves and in the other, that cannot be transgressed without paying an awful price. If we speak of them, we may endanger the relationship; but if we do not speak, if we do not violate the taboo, the relationship may become static and tense, until the silence takes on a life of its own. Such silences are corrosive. They eat at the innards of intimacy until, often, the silence itself causes the very rupture or break-up that we've tried to avoid by keeping silent.

The Cannibal in Us All

You may measure how many taboos constrict you, how many taboos 6
you've surrendered to—at home, at parties, at work, with your lover or your family—by how much of yourself you must suppress. You

may measure your life, in these realms, by what you cannot say, do, admit—cannot and must not, and for no better reason than that your actions or words would disrupt your established order. By this measure, most of us are living within as complex and strictured a system of taboos as the aborigines who gave us the word in the first place. You can see how fitting it is that the word "taboo" comes from a part of the world where cannibalism is said to be practiced to this day: the islands off eastern Australia—Polynesia, New Zealand, Melanesia. Until 1777, when Captain James Cook published an account of his first world voyage, Europe and colonial America had many taboos but no word that precisely meant taboo. Cook introduced this useful word to the West. Its instant popularity, quick assimilation into most European languages, and constant usage since, are testimony to how much of our lives the word describes. Before the word came to us, we'd ostracized, coerced, exiled, tormented, and murdered each other for myriad infractions (as we still do), but we never had a satisfying, precise word for our reasons.

We needed cannibals to give us a word to describe our behavior, so how "civilized" are we, really? We do things differently from those cannibals, on the surface, but is the nature of what we do all that different? We don't cook each other for ceremonial dinners, at least not physically (though therapists can testify that our ceremonial seasons, like Christmas and Thanksgiving, draw lots of business—something's cooking). But we stockpile weapons that can cook the entire world, and we organize our national priorities around their "necessity," and it's a national political taboo to seriously cut spending for those planet-cookers. If that's "progress," it's lost on me. In China it's taboo to be a Christian, in Israel it's taboo to be a Moslem, in Syria it's taboo to be a Jew, in much of the United States it's still taboo to be an atheist, while in American academia it's taboo to be deeply religious. Our headlines are full of this stuff. So it's hardly surprising that a cannibal's word still describes much of our behavior. 7

I'm not denying the necessity of every society to set limits and invent taboos (some rational, some not) simply in order to get on with the day—and to try to contain the constant, crazy, never-to-be-escaped longings that blossom in our sleep and distract or compel us while awake. Such longings are why even a comparatively tiny desert tribe like the ancient Hebrews needed commandments and laws against coveting each other's wives, stealing, killing, committing incest. That the tribe hadn't seen violent, sexy movies, hadn't listened to rock 'n' roll, hadn't been bombarded with ads featuring 8 half-naked models, and hadn't watched too much TV. They didn't need to. Like us, they had their hearts, desires, and dreams to instruct them how to be very, very naughty. The taboo underlying all others is that we must not live by the dictates of our irrational hearts—as though we haven't forgiven each other, or ourselves, for having hearts.

If there's a taboo against something, it's usually because a con- 9
siderable number of people desire to do it. The very taboos that we employ to protect us from each other and ourselves, are a map of our secret natures. When you know a culture's taboos (or an individual's, or a family's) you know its secrets—you know what it really wants.

Favorite Taboos

It's hard to keep a human being from his or her desire, taboo or not. 10
We've always been very clever, very resourceful, when it comes to sneaking around our taboos. The Aztecs killed virgins and called it religion. The Europeans enslaved blacks and called it economics. Americans tease each other sexually and call it fashion.

If we can't kill and screw and steal and betray to our heart's de- 11
sire, and, in general, violate every taboo in sight—well, we can at least watch other people do it. Or read about it. Or listen to it. As we have done, since ancient times, through every form of religion and entertainment. The appeal of taboos and our inability to escape our longing for transgression (whether or not we ourselves transgress) are why so many people who call themselves honest and law-abiding spend so much time with movies, operas, soaps, garish trials, novels, songs, Biblical tales, tribal myths, folk stories, and Shakespeare—virtually all of which, both the great and the trivial, are about those who dare to violate taboos. It's a little unsettling when you think about it: the very stuff we say we most object to is the fundamental material of what we call culture.

That's one reason that fundamentalists of all religions are so 12
hostile to the arts. But fundamentalists partake of taboos in the sneakiest fashion of all. Senator Jesse Helms led the fight against the National Endowment for the Arts because he couldn't get the (vastly overrated) homosexual art of Robert Mapplethorpe or the most extreme performance artists out of his mind—he didn't and doesn't want to. He, like all fundamentalists, will vigorously oppose such art and all it stands for until he dies, because his very opposition gives him permission to concentrate on taboo acts. The Taliban of

Afghanistan will ride around in jeeps toting guns, searching out any woman who dares show an inch of facial skin or wear white socks (Taliban boys consider white socks provocative), and when they find such a woman they'll jail and beat her—because their so-called righteousness gives them permission to obsess on their taboos. Pat Robertson and his ilk will fuss and rage about any moral "deviation," any taboo violation they can find, because that's the only way they can give themselves permission to entertain the taboos. They get to not have their taboo cake, yet eat it too.

We are all guilty of this to some extent. Why else have outlaws   13
from Antigone to Robin Hood to Jesse James to John Gotti become folk heroes? Oedipus killed his father and slept with his mother, and we've been performing that play for 2500 years because he is the ultimate violator of our deepest taboos. Aristotle said we watch such plays for "catharsis," to purge our desires and fears in a moment of revelation. Baloney. Ideas like "catharsis" are an intellectual game, to glossy-up our sins. What's closer to the truth is that we need Oedipus to stand in for us. We can't have changed much in 2500 years, if we still keep him alive in our hearts to enact our darkest taboos for us. Clearly, the very survival of Oedipus as an instantly recognizable name tells us that we still want to kill our fathers and screw our mothers (or vice versa).

A Country of Broken Taboos

Taboos are a special paradox for Americans. However much we   14
may long for tradition and order, our longings are subverted by the inescapable fact that our country was founded upon a break with tradition and a challenge to order—which is to say, the United States was founded upon the violation of taboos. Specifically, this country was founded upon the violation of Europe's most suffocating taboo: its feudal suppression (still enforced in 1776, when America declared its independence) of the voices of the common people. We were the first nation on earth to write into law that any human being has the right to say anything, and that even the government is (theoretically) not allowed to silence you.

At the time, Europe was a continent of state-enforced religions,   15
where royalty's word was law and all other words could be crushed by law. (Again: taboo was a matter of enforced silence.) We were the first nation to postulate verbal freedom for everyone. All our other freedoms depend upon verbal freedom; no matter how badly and how often we've failed that ideal, it still remains our ideal.

Once we broke Europe's verbal taboos, it was only a matter of   16
time before other traditional taboos fell too. As the writer Albert
Murray has put it, Americans could not afford piety in their new
homeland: "You can't be over respectful of established forms; you're
trying to get through the wilderness of Kentucky." Thus, from the
moment the Pilgrims landed, our famous puritanism faced an inherent contradiction. How could we domesticate the wilderness of this
continent; how could peasants and rejects and "commoners" form a
strong and viable nation; how could we develop all the new social
forms and technologies necessary to blend all the disparate peoples
who came here—without violating those same Puritan taboos which
are so ingrained, to this day, in our national character?

It can't be over-emphasized that America's fundamental stance   17
against both the taboos of Europe and the taboos of our own
Puritans, was our insistence upon freedom of speech. America led
the attack against silence. And it is through that freedom, the freedom to break the silence, that we've destroyed so many other
taboos. Especially during the last 40 years, we've broken the silence
that surrounded ancient taboos of enormous significance. Incest,
child abuse, wife-battering, homosexuality, and some (by no means
all) forms of racial and gender oppression, are not merely spoken of,
and spoken against, they're shouted about from the rooftops. Many
breathe easier because of this inevitable result of free speech. In certain sections of our large cities, for the first time in modern history,
gay people can live openly and without fear. The feminist movement has made previously forbidden or hidden behaviors both
speakable and doable. The National Organization of Women can rail
against the Promise Keepers all they want (and they have some
good reasons), but when you get a million working-class guys crying and hugging in public, the stoic mask of the American male has
definitely cracked. And I'm old enough to remember when it was
shocking for women to speak about wanting a career. Now virtually
all affluent young women are expected to want a career.

Fifty years ago, not one important world or national leader was   18
black. Now there are more people of color in positions of influence
than ever. Bad marriages can be dissolved without social stigma.
Children born out of wedlock are not damned as "bastards" for something that wasn't their fault. And those of us who've experienced incest and abuse have finally found a voice, and through our voices
we've achieved a certain amount of liberation from shame and pain.

These boons are rooted in our decidedly un-Puritan freedom of   19
speech. But we left those Puritans behind a long time ago—for the

breaking of silence is the fundamental political basis of our nation, and no taboo is safe when people have the right to speak.

Keeper of Your Silence

In the process, though, we've lost the sanctity of silence. We've lost   20
the sense of dark but sacred power inherent in sex, in nature, even in crime. Perhaps that is the price of our new freedoms.

It's also true that by breaking the silence we've thrown our-   21
selves into a state of society's structure. Without them, that structure has undeniably weakened. We are faced with shoring up the weakened parts, inventing new ways of being together that have pattern and order—for we cannot live without some pattern and order—but aren't so restrictive. Without sexual taboos, for instance, what are the social boundaries between men and women? When are they breached? What is offensive? Nobody's sure. Everybody's making mistakes. This is so excruciating that many are nostalgic for some of the old taboos. But once a taboo is broken, then for good or ill it's very hard, perhaps impossible, to reinstate it.

But there is another, subtler confusion: yes, enormous taboos   22
have fallen, but many taboos, equally important, remain. And, both as individuals and as a society, we're strained enough, confused enough, by the results of doing away with so many taboos in so short a time, that maybe we're not terribly eager for our remaining taboos to fall. We may sincerely desire that, but maybe we're tired, fed up, scared. Many people would rather our taboos remain intact for a couple of generations while we get our act together again, and perhaps they have a point. But the price of taboos remains what it's always been: silence and constriction.

What do we see, when we pass each other on the street, but many   23
faces molded by the price paid for keeping the silences of the taboos that remain—spirits confined within their own, and their society's, silences? Even this brief essay on our public and intimate strictures is enough to demonstrate that we are still a primitive race, bounded by fear and prejudice, with taboos looming in every direction—no matter how much we like to brag and/or bitch that modern life is liberating us from all the old boundaries. The word taboo still says much more about us than most prefer to admit.

What is the keeper of your silence? The answer to that question   24
is your own guide to your personal taboos. How must you confine yourself in order to get through your day at the job, or to be acceptable in your social circle? The answer to that is your map of your so-

ciety's taboos. What makes you most afraid to speak? What desire, what word, what possibility, freezes and fevers you at the same time, making any sincere communication out of the question? What makes you vanish into your secret? That's your taboo, baby. You're still in the room, maybe even still smiling, still talking, but not really—what's really happened is that you've vanished down some hole in yourself, and you'll stay there until you're sure the threat to your taboo is gone and it's safe to come out again. If, that is, you've ever come out in the first place. Some never have.

What utterance, what hint, what insinuation, can quiet a room   25
of family or friends? What makes people change the subject? What makes those at a dinner party dismiss a remark as though it wasn't said, or dismiss a person as though he or she wasn't really there? We've all seen conversations suddenly go dead, and just as suddenly divert around a particular person or subject, leaving them behind in the dead space, because something has been said or implied that skirts a silently shared taboo. If that happens to you often, don't kid yourself that you're living in a "free" society. Because you're only as free as your freedom from taboos—not on some grand abstract level, but in your day-to-day life.

It is probably inherent in the human condition that there are no   26
"last" taboos. Or perhaps it just feels that way because we have such a long way to go. But at least we can know where to look; right in front of our eyes, in the recesses of our speechlessness, in the depths of our silences. And there is nothing for it but to confront the keepers of our silence. Either that, or to submit to being lost, as most of us silently are, without admitting it to each other or to ourselves—lost in a maze of taboos.

MEANINGS AND VALUES

1. Ventura says, "Taboos, big or small, are always about having to respect somebody's (often irrational) boundary—or else" (Par. 1). Do you agree with this definition of the word "taboo"? Why, or why not? Why do you think that we must honor other people's boundaries? What does "or else" mean?

2. Explain the connection that Ventura makes in Paragraph 5 between silence and taboos. How does silence impact us personally and in relationships?

3. Why does much of our popular culture violate many societal taboos? How do the media encourage this?

EXPOSITORY TECHNIQUES

1. Ventura places taboos into many categories. Some are broad (e.g., "big taboos" and "little taboos") while others are very specific (i.e., "corporate taboos" and "language taboos"). Does he deliberately give equal standing to specific taboos? If so, why?

2. Beginning in Paragraph 14, Ventura explains how enforced silence led to a whole series of taboos. What are some of the subcategories of taboos that disappeared with the American practice of free speech, and what connection does Ventura make between these subcategories and Americans' willingness to talk?

DICTION AND VOCABULARY

1. Ventura uses the expression "social stigma" in Paragraph 18 in conjunction with dissolved marriages. He uses the words "shame" and "pain" connected to incest and abuse. Why does he use such words when he is comparing American society before its willingness to speak openly with contemporary, more open American society? (See "Guide to Terms": *Diction.*)

2. Why does Ventura provide us with the etymology (history) of the word "taboo" and an explanation of its assimilation into languages (Par. 6)?

3. If you do not know the meaning of some of the following words, look them up in a dictionary: assimilation, ostracized, coerced (Par. 6); garish (10); catharsis (13); piety, disparate (16); stoic (17).

READ TO WRITE

1. **Collaborating:** Ventura makes clear his opinion that taboos, though a reflection of human nature, are dangerous to society because they cause us to be silent about many horrible things that may be happening in our lives. Can you think of cases in which silence and taboos might be positive? In a small group, create a list of such instances, and as a team prepare a short essay classifying and explaining these taboos.

2. **Considering Audience:** Society's taboos about premarital and extramarital sex are less strong now than they were in the first half of the twentieth century. Other taboos have changed as well. Consider an audience reading this essay in the 1960s. What parts of the discussion and examples might have worked well for most readers at the time? What taboos were probably no longer as forceful for these readers as they might have been for readers earlier in the century? Prepare an essay examining how one or more taboos changed during the course of the century.

3. **Developing an Essay:** Look over one or more editions of a local newspaper. Identify and list some issues or behaviors that the articles

treat as taboos. Separate the items in the list into categories. Adding further examples from your experience and knowledge, develop the list into an essay on the way newspapers and similar media such as magazines reinforce or undermine taboos. You might also examine the various kinds of news programs on television (both "hard" and "soft" news) and write about the way they treat taboos.

(NOTE: Suggestions for topics requiring development by use of CLASSIFICATION are on pp. 147–148 at the end of this chapter.)

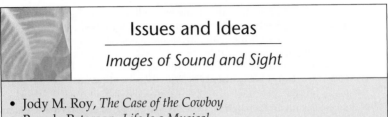

Issues and Ideas

Images of Sound and Sight

- Jody M. Roy, *The Case of the Cowboy*
- Brenda Peterson, *Life Is a Musical*

Every day on television, in films, through songs, in magazine articles, and in countless other places we encounter images of people like us and also images of people whose lives are unfamiliar to us except as we encounter them through these images. Because images have the power to shape perceptions, relationships, and values, we need to recognize they can sometimes represent accurately and yet sometimes simplify and distort.

But what is an image? This is an easy question to answer for visual media like films, television, advertisements, and posters. It is a representation of a person's actions, attitudes, character traits, and relationships. The image can represent the person as an individual or as a typical member of a group. When the image is constructed simply from the traits of a group (often negative traits), we can refer to it as a stereotype. Negative (and often hurtful) stereotypes are quite familiar: the bimbo, the less-than-intelligent "jock," the absent-minded professor, or the violent gang member.

People frequently share traits with other members of a group, of course, but a stereotype erases individual differences. When all we know about a group comes from stereotypic images, especially negative ones, we need to be aware of the limitations of our understanding and look for more accurate images. Jody Roy's goal in "The Case of the Cowboy" is in part to alert us to the need for more realistic images and to the unfortunate effects of inaccurate ones, both of individuals and of the society at large.

The images we receive through music, literature, and other forms of reading can be a bit harder to describe. In representing relationships, feelings, and values, these media present us with definitions of appropriate (or inappropriate) behavior and attitudes. These, in turn, can shape our perceptions, self-understanding, values, and relationships. Many of the images we receive through music can be positive and useful, as Brenda Peterson points out in "Life Is a Musical."

Images are not simply given to us by others. We can create them as well, especially in this age of recorders, cameras, and computers. Brenda Peterson's discussion of the way her family uses music to create and maintain its identity and the ways she integrates collections of songs into her own life are particularly interesting illustrations of how we can create images of ourselves (and others)—images that may act as creative responses to those thrust upon us every day.

JODY M. ROY

JODY M. ROY teaches speech communication at Ripon College. She received her B.A. from Illinois College and her Ph.D. from Indiana University. In 2002, she published *Love to Hate: America's Obsession with Hatred and Violence*. In this book, she looks at the ways the habits of our daily lives and popular culture reinforce violent attitudes and acts.

The Case of the Cowboy

In this selection from *Love to Hate*, Jody Roy looks at the images of cowboys and bad guys we encounter in films, on television, and throughout popular culture. Though most of us view cowboys as admirable, or "cool," and as models for behavior, the values they represent are often, according to Roy, far from admirable.

The image appears slowly over the horizon. With the sun blazing   1
in the background, we see him only in silhouette. The Stetson-style hat, cocked to the side. The broad shoulders and lean waist. The holster and guns draping loosely over sauntering hips that seem to keep time to some inaudible tune. And, finally, as he emerges fully, the trademark boots, the subtle clinking of the spurs.

There he is. Wyatt Earp, Doc Holiday, Clint Eastwood, and John   2
Wayne rolled into one. One tiny six-year-old hero of the backyard frontier, that is. For much of the twentieth century, American boys have preoccupied themselves with dreams and games involving cowboys. Pint-sized "pardners" have roamed summertime streets and ruled recess for decades. Late October normally brings a small herd of would-be cowboys to the costume shops. Those same tykes inundate Santa with requests for child-size chaps, hats, holsters, and guns.

Young boys' quests for cowboy paraphernalia are themselves   3
part of our popular culture. For example, the very funny movie, *A Christmas Story*, revolves around one boy's yuletide campaign for a particular type of pellet gun endorsed by his favorite movie-star cowboy. He leaves notes and clippings about the gun around the house, mentions it often in conversations with his parents, even features it in an essay for school. Yet every time he raises the subject, some adult warns he'll put his eye out and dashes his dreams of being fully outfitted like his hero.

While we adults have an almost automatic response to a pellet   4
gun—"you'll put your eye out"—we rarely if ever offer children
cautions about the larger issue: the very nature of the cowboy icon.
It is after all the adoration of such icons in movies, books, and television that fosters in children the desire for toy guns. As such, we need
to consider the messages behind the symbol or, in this case, the cowboy behind the gun, in order to understand both the positive and the
potentially negative sides of this enduring icon of American popular
culture.

First, and perhaps most fundamentally, the cowboy icon has   5
two basic incarnations: the cowboy hero and the cowboy villain.
Cowboy heroes often appear in roles such as sheriff, leader of a cattle drive, or what I'll call a "wandering hero," such as the Lone
Ranger, who appears much like a frontier Superman wherever and
whenever help is needed. Writers and producers most commonly
place cowboy heroes in conflict either with "Indians" or with the
cowboy villain. In contrast to the other classic bad guys of the
Western genre, cowboy villains pose a special challenge because
they are essentially the alter ego of the cowboy hero; the cowboy villain shares the hero's skill with a gun, his horse-riding maneuvers,
and his knowledge of the land. What distinguishes the two, of
course, is character: the cowboy hero is essentially good, while the
cowboy villain is essentially evil.

Even if we assume that our cultural icon of the cowboy only in-   6
volves the cowboy hero—an assumption I suspect may not be as
safe today as it was in the 1950s—we still find ourselves with a complex icon capable of sending mixed messages about hatred and violence. Among the issues surrounding the cowboy that merit some
consideration are: the actual profile of the cowboy and thus the connotation of "us" offered to those who identify with the character; the
absolutism that seems a central feature of almost all stories starring
the cowboy; the tendency of the cowboy to dehumanize his enemies;
and, ultimately, what such features of the icon say about the cowboy's fitness as a traditional role model for "cool."

I would like to begin with a basic consideration of the profile of   7
the cowboy icon. What does he look like? How does he react in various situations? Who are his friends, his enemies, his family? How
does he accomplish his goals?

Although I have never in fact tried the following experiment,   8
I'm quite sure I know what results it would produce. Enter any
classroom, office, factory lunchroom, shopping mall, or bar in
America and ask every person you meet to describe a cowboy. I can

almost guarantee that the first word out of each person's mouth would be "He. . . ." Now, I admit it seems rather obvious that a cowBOY would normally be considered a male. But let's stop and consider the issue a bit more carefully. While males surely were responsible for most of the sheriffing, cattle driving, Indian skirmish-waging, and wild-horse corraling on the American frontier in the nineteenth century, they were not there alone. Hidden in the annals of history are the women—the settlers, farmers, teachers, nurses, business speculators, missionaries, and, in a few cases, gunslinging Annie Oakley types. Also buried in the past are the other men of the American West—the doctors, lawyers, farmers, ranchers, preachers, investors, and carpenters to name just a few. The American frontier was a complex social environment in which the cowboy was but one character type.

Yet only the cowboy has been elevated to the status of cultural   9
icon. Several features of his profile lend him a compelling air. First, and perhaps most basically, the cowboy's physique and physical prowess are at the very pinnacle of American ideals for men. While the typical working cowboy in 1875 may have had a potbelly overhanging his gunbelt and, after a few weeks on the hot and dusty trail, a scent worse than that of a skunk, the cowboy *icon* has been portrayed almost universally in literature and movies as a ruggedly handsome, physically appealing character. Classic twentieth-century leading men such as John Wayne and Clint Eastwood have shaped our notions of how cowboys looked in the past.

The uniformity of advertising appeals based on the cowboy   10
suggests how very clear the image of the cowboy is in our minds. For example, several popular brands of men's cologne center their advertising campaigns around the cowboy and the implicit argument that men who wear the colognes will be appealing in the same way that the cowboy is appealing. But let's stop and think about that for a moment. Realistically, what would an actual cowboy have smelled like—on the trail, in temperatures hovering over ninety degrees, for weeks on end, with a bunch of cattle and a horse, and his last bath—taken in community bath water at Miss Beverly's Saloon—a distant memory? Is this a scent one would really want to pay money for? I doubt it. But we don't see the model dressed like a cowboy holding a lasso in one hand and the cologne bottle in the other and think of an actual cowboy; rather, we think of the cowboy icon who, apparently, smells like pine trees, citrus, and a tiny bit of synthetic musk.

The cowboy icon, then, is a sanitized version of reality, an im-   11
age born of early "cowboys" such as Roy Rogers, then reborn in all the other ruggedly handsome men who have enacted the icon, from

the Duke to the Marlboro Man. From the amalgam of their physiques and mannerism emerges the profile of the cowboy icon: tall, lean, and muscular, with a strong jaw and piercing eyes. His age varies, but he is never so young as to be naïve nor so old that we even for a second would question his virility. He is male, always and absolutely, rigidly upholding social conventions about masculinity in all his actions and, in turn, reinforcing those conventions for those who watch him.

Ironically, the cowboy's traditional masculinity, though perhaps the critical centering element of his character, almost never leads him into the most traditional male social roles of husband and father. Rather, the cowboy usually is depicted alone, though not obviously lonely. We rarely see the cowboy with close friends. We rarely see his family of origin. We rarely see him take a wife and start a family of his own. To the extent that the cowboy involves himself with women, he most often carries on some sort of informal dalliance with a woman who, in the era of actual cowboys, would have been socially taboo. But the cowboy does not care: he loves the prostitute with the "heart of gold," just not enough to make an "honest woman" out of her in most stories. The cowboy is not the marrying kind. He is unsettled and unsettling. No woman can tame him. He is like the wild stallion—untamed, free, strong, proud.   12

And here we find the essential "coolness" of the cowboy icon. He is cool in the way the stallion is cool—he is a force of nature society may sometimes think it has tamed but, in fact, never will. His innate wildness and the fact that he alone controls the wildness inside himself are the grounds of his claim to "cool." His knowledge of these traits allows him to slowly, confidently walk down the dusty street, knowing he could be shot at any moment, because he trusts that he will somehow sense an opponent's movement in time to spin, draw, and shoot to kill in the knick of time. His self-knowledge guides his hand to his hat as he cockily tips it to a local lady, making her blush because they both know she will think of him that night as she lies in bed with her portly, timid husband. Thus it is the coolness of the cowboy that raises him to the status of icon, for without his cool he would be just another smelly guy on a horse, riding quickly toward home so his wife does not get angry that he is late for dinner.   13

With this general profile of the cowboy icon in mind, I want to investigate what this "cool" character tells us about hatred. First, in the literature and movies where we find him, the cowboy icon lives in a world of absolutes. The cowboy hero, though sometimes shown to have a dark side in his own personality, ultimately makes the commitment to fight for the side of "good." The cowboy hero   14 literally dons his white hat as a symbol of his status as our hero. As such, he plays the sympathetic character in narratives; when we cheer him on we are cheering for all of "us" and reinforcing our shared value commitments. In consequence, those the cowboy battles are not simply "other" or "them" but necessarily become a "bad" other because they are pitted in conflict with *our* hero. In the basic plot lines of cowboy narratives characterization is overt, even stereotypical; there is little room for complex and ambiguous morality.

Yet, within the seemingly crystal-clear morality tales pitting   15
good against evil, a truly ambiguous message is often to be found: in a society that claims it believes hatred is bad, one of our foremost popular culture icons, the cowboy hero, is quite often saying that hate is cool. As I [have] discussed . . . absolutist thinking patterns themselves can easily be warped into the dangerous form of "us versus them" thinking that lies at the very heart of most hatred. In stories involving the cowboy icon some elements of "us" and "them" are required simply to allow the plotlines to advance because stories need some form of tension to develop. However, normal conceptions of us and them cross into the potentially dangerous arena of us versus them when the cowboy's enemies are defined solely by their other-ness and not by any clearly explained evil motivations. For example, stories of the cowboy icon convey us versus them patterns when the "Indian" is delivered up as the enemy simply because he is Indian. When the cowboy opposes others simply because they are not "us," with no reason or motivation given, the cowboy icon is sending audiences a message: that cool guys hate people who are not part of their group.

In addition to being defined as bad because they are not part of   16
the cowboy's group, the enemies of the cowboy in literature and the movies are very often victims of various dehumanization strategies. Perhaps no bad guy in American popular culture has been dehumanized quite so fully or so frequently as the "Indian." No doubt racist in origin, portrayals of Native American characters as savage, animalistic, and thus essentially subhuman typify most stories involving the cowboy hero. The dehumanization of the Indian is, of course, a critical mechanism in the stories involving cowboys: for if the cowboy is good and he kills the Indian, then the Indian must be very bad. Dehumanization strategies encourage us to view the Indian as negative and thus enable us to view his death at the hands of the cowboy as justified. In this way, then, cowboy stories employ dehumanization strategies in the same ways governments do in times of war: as a means to rally us so solidly against an enemy that we do not question killing the enemy as a moral good.

Even when the Indian is moved out of the role of bad guy and   17
into the role of sidekick, he is often still shown in negative ways. Take,
for instance, Tonto, the sidekick of the Lone Ranger and perhaps the
most well-known Native American character in American popular
culture. While a good guy shown to be both compassionate to those in
need and loyal to the cowboy hero, Tonto nevertheless always is displayed as somewhat uncivilized (by the Lone Ranger's standards) because he resists the white man's style of dress and norms of behavior.
His character never fully develops: he is only the sum of his interactions with the Lone Ranger and other whites. We never really learn
about Tonto's family, his tribe, his ideas and values. Tonto inhabits
what is called a satellite role: he revolves around the lead character
and has no real existence outside of that character's perspective.

This could of course simply be written off by saying that Tonto   18
is treated rather poorly in the Lone Ranger tales because they are the
Lone Ranger tales, not the Tonto tales. While that is true—stories by
their very nature must focus in on a lead in order to develop—it
nevertheless misses the more fundamental point: there never have
been lead roles for the Tontos in the stories that comprise American
popular culture because the us associated with the cowboy icon
does not include Indians, or women, or dentists, or any of the other
roles people fill in order to keep our society functioning. Only cowboys refuse such roles and stay truly "free." As such, by the logic of
the cowboy stories themselves, only cowboys are fully human in our
popular tales of the Old West.

What then do we learn from our hero, the cowboy icon, about   19
what it means to be "cool"? First, we learn that coolness involves an
aura of wildness, a sense of independence in the extreme that elevates him above others but also isolates him and detaches him from
others. Second, we learn that it is cool to see the world in absolute
terms and, as a result, participate in us versus them thinking patterns. Finally, we learn that it is cool to dehumanize those who are
different not only when "they" are the enemy, but even when "they"
approach "us" in such tangential roles as sidekicks.

The question then becomes, is the cowboy icon evil? I don't think   20
so. But is the cowboy icon as good a social role model as we were
raised to believe? I don't think that either. Rather, my examination of
the cowboy icon suggests that the icon itself and the stories involving
the icon that have featured so prominently in American popular
culture for decades send mixed, even contradictory messages about
hatred. On the one hand, our frontier hero defends us, leads us,
and embodies such central American values as independence and
self-reliance. On the other hand, however, the cowboy also tends to

partake in absolutist and dehumanizing thinking patterns and to exist in a state of at least partial detachment from society. The cowboy icon, then, symbolizes not just independence but indifference, not just toughness but in some cases intolerance. He straddles the line between coolness of self and coldness to others and thus embodies the flirtation with hatred that runs parallel to our culture's commitment to compassion.

MEANINGS AND VALUES

1. What are the two kinds of cowboys Roy discusses in this selection? What kind of character other than cowboys does she discuss at length?

2. Summarize the differences between actual cowboys and the cowboy as "cultural icon" (see especially Paragraphs 9–12).

3. a. What does the writer seem to mean when she refers to the cowboy as a "cultural icon" (Pars. 9–11)?

   b. Explain the following statement: "There have never been lead roles for the Tontos in the stories that comprise American popular culture because the us associated with the cowboy icon does not include Indians, or women, or dentists, or any of the other roles people fill in order to keep our society functioning" (Par. 18).

4. How would you characterize the overall tone of this essay? (See "Guide to Terms": *Style/Tone.*)

5. In the concluding paragraph, the writer identifies mixed messages she believes are embodied in the cowboy icon. State these messages in your own words.

EXPOSITORY TECHNIQUES

1. Does Roy offer a clear definition of each category she discusses? If not, how might the categories be introduced and defined more clearly?

2. Are the categories in this essay distinct or is there some overlapping? If the categories overlap, does the author acknowledge this? Where?

3. In Paragraph 6, the writer summarizes a set of "issues" associated with the image of the cowboy and its effect on us. Does this set of issues serve to organize the rest of the essay? If so, which paragraphs are associated with each issue? If not, what organization does the rest of the essay follow?

4. Would this essay be more effective if it had fewer examples? A greater number? Explain. (Guide: *Evaluation.*) Evaluate the examples in the following paragraphs for clarity and effectiveness: 5, 9–13, and 17.

5.   What example does the author use to open the selection? Where does she explain its relationship to the rest of the selection? To what extent does Paragraph 20 echo or expand on the discussion in Paragraph 4?

DICTION AND VOCABULARY

1.   Examine the diction in Paragraphs 9–11 and discuss how the writer uses it to emphasis the contrast between the cowboy as an icon or ideal type and actual cowboys (Guide: *Diction; Emphasis*). Tell what use she makes of specific rather than general terms in these paragraphs (Guide: *Specific/General*).

2.   If you do not know the meaning of some of the following words, look them up in a dictionary: icon (Par. 4); incarnations, alter ego (5); absolutism (6); annals (8); prowess (9); amalgam (11); dalliance (12); innate, portly (13); overt, stereotypical (14).

READ TO WRITE

1.   **Collaborating:** Films and television programs frequently follow stereotypes in their treatment of various ethnic and social groups (such as African Americans or people in their twenties) or in the representation of groups united by beliefs or behaviors (religious conservatives or athletes, for example). Working with a group of classmates, list groups of people you often encounter that are represented by stereotypical characters on film or television. Then, in an essay of your own, arrange and discuss the different groups based on the way they are represented.

2.   **Considering Audience:** Readers today might be familiar with images of groups of people defined by gender or ethnic and racial background that differ from traditional images—that is, the images of groups of people presented in contemporary video games. For example, in many video games, women battle aggressively with men. Prepare a short discussion of the treatment of such groups in contemporary video games.

3.   **Developing an Essay:** As Roy's essay suggests, racial and ethnic minority groups are often subject to negative stereotyping. Immigrant groups often receive similar treatment. Draw on your own knowledge or experience for examples of this practice or on research into racial and ethnic minority or immigrant groups that were once treated as outsiders though they are now considered part of mainstream society. Using the information you have gathered, write an essay of your own, classifying the ways such groups are or have been treated.

(NOTE: Suggestions for topics requiring development by use of CLASSIFICATION are on pp. 147–148 at the end of this section.)

BRENDA PETERSON

BRENDA PETERSON, a novelist and essayist, was born in 1950 in a forest ranger station in the Sierra Nevada Mountains. As a child she lived in many different places, especially in the Southeast. Currently, she lives in Seattle. Peterson received a B.A. in 1972 from the University of California-Davis. From 1972 to 1976 she worked as an editorial assistant at the *New Yorker* magazine. She has taught creative writing at Arizona State University and now works as an environmental writer. Her novels include *River of Light* (1978), *Becoming the Enemy* (1988), and *Duck and Cover* (1991). Her essays have been collected in *Living by Water: Essays on Life, Land and Spirit* (1990); *Nature and Other Mothers* (1992); and *Sister Stories: Taking the Journey Together* (1996).

Life Is a Musical

In this essay, Peterson offers several closely related classifications as a way of exploring the ways music can (and ought to) enrich and heal our emotional lives. This essay was first published in *Nature and Other Mothers.*

When the day is too gray, when the typewriter is too loud, after   1
a lovers' quarrel, when a sister calls with another family horror story, when the phone never stops and those unanswered messages blink on my machine like angry, red eyes—I tune out my life and turn up the music. Not my favorite public radio station but my own personal frequency—I have my own soul's station. It is somewhere on the dial between Mozart's *Magic Flute,* the gospel-stomping tiger growl of Miss Aretha Franklin, Motown's deep dance 'n' strut, and the singing story of Broadway musicals.

Whether Katie Webster's Swamp Boogie Queen singing "Try a   2
Little Tenderness," or a South American samba, whether it's the Persuasions crooning "Let It Be" or that throbbing baritone solo "Other Pleasures" from *Aspects of Love,* my musical solace is so complete it surrounds me in a mellifluous bubble like a placenta of sound. To paraphrase the visionary Stevie Wonder, I have learned to survive by making sound tracks in my own particular key of life.

For years now I've made what I call "tapes against terror" to   3
hide me away from the noisy yak and call of the outside world. These homemade productions are dubbed Mermaid Music; sometimes I send them to friends for birthdays and feel the pleasure of

playing personal disc jockey to accompany their lives too. Among my siblings, we now exchange music tapes instead of letters. It is particularly gratifying to hear my nieces and nephews singing along to my tapes, as another generation inherits our family frequency.

I trace making my musical escapes to a childhood of moving   4
around. As we packed the cardboard boxes with our every belonging—sometimes we hadn't even bothered to unpack our dresses from those convenient hanging garment containers provided by the last moving company—the singing began. From every corner of the emptying house, we'd hear the harmonies: my father a walking bass as he heaved-ho in the basement; my mother's soprano sometimes shrill and sharp as the breaking glass in the kitchen; my little brother between pure falsetto and a tenor so perfect we knew he'd stopped packing his room simply to sing; my sisters and I weaving between soprano and first and second alto from our bedrooms as we traded and swapped possessions for our next life. At last gathered in the clean, white space that was once our house, we'd hold hands and sing "Auld Lang Syne." Piling into the station wagon, with the cat in a wooden box with slats for air holes, Mother would shift into a rousing hymn, "We'll Leave It All Behind," or sometimes, if she was mutinously happy to hightail it out of some small "burg" as she called them, she'd lead us into "Shuffle Off to Buffalo," substituting wherever we were moving for the last word. "Chattanooga Choo Choo" and "California, Here We Come" were her standard favorites for leave-taking. If, as we drove past our schools and our friends' houses for the last time, the harmonies in the backseat faltered, Mother might remind us that choirs of angels never stayed long in one place singing because the whole world needed music. Father might suggest some slower songs, as long as they weren't sad.

In all the shifting landscapes and faces of my childhood, what   5
stays the same is the music. First, there was my mother's music, which seems now to have entered effortlessly into her children's minds as if we were tiny tape recorders: the mild, sweetly suave Mills Brothers, Mitch Miller's upbeat swing, the close sibling harmonies of the Andrews Sisters, and always the church music, the heartfelt Sunday singing, which is the only thing I ever miss since leaving that tight fellowship of Southern Baptist believers.

Ever since I can remember—certainly I have flashes of being   6
bounced around in the floating dark of my mother's womb as she tap-danced on the church organ pedals, sang at the top of her voice, and boogied across the keys—there has been this music. It is the

only counterpoint to, the only salvation from a sermon that para-
lyzes the soul into submitting to a jealous God. From the beginning,
music was an alternative to that hellfire terror. I can still hear it: a
preacher's voice, first a boom, then a purr that raises into a hiss and
howl to summon that holy hurricane of fire and brimstone. But after
enduring the scourge of sins, there came the choir. Cooing and
shushing, mercy at last fell upon those of us left on an Earth that this
God had long ago abandoned. Listening to the full-bodied harmonies, I could close my eyes and heretically wonder, Wasn't
Heaven still here?

   Yessss, hallelujah, still here. . . . Hush, can't you hear? the choir   7
murmured like so many mammies' lullabies. Then silence as a small
woman stepped forward, her rapt vibrato shimmering like humid
heat lightning right before rain. Or a baritone dropping his woes
and his dulcet voice low as a cello, caressing a whole congregation.
If we were blessed that Sunday, there might be a shorter sermon and
a "songfest" with harmonies we could hear in our heads, syncopat-
ing, counterpointing in a lovely braid of bright sound that beckoned
us. *Sing now, brothers and sisters.* And we were many voices making
one song. The fundamental fear was gone; weren't we already angels in Heaven?

   Now that I am forty and have been what my family pityingly   8
refers to as "settled-down" for ten years, now that I am so far back-
slid from the fellowship of the Southern Baptist believers, now that I
no longer even make top ten on my mother's prayer list, now that
the terror of Hell has been replaced by the terror of living, I still find
myself calling upon my homemade choirs to accompany me in my
car, to surround my study or kitchen and sing back the demons of
daily life. Sometimes I've even caught myself slipping another tape
against terror into the stereo and singing a distracted riff of my
mother's favorite, "We'll Leave It All Behind."

   During the recent holy war between the United States and Iraq,   9
with the apocalyptic rhetoric about "Satan" and "infidels" eerily
reminiscent of southern revivals—Mermaid Music was working
long hours to meet my own and my friends' wartime demands. To
offset NPR's daily interviews with military experts commenting on
the allied video-war air strikes with the zealous aplomb of sports-
casters, I'd surrender to the tender tenor of Aaron Neville singing
"With God on Our Side" or "Will the Circle Be Unbroken?" As I
drove along freeways where phosphorescent orange bumper stickers shouted USA KICKS BUTT! or OPERATION DESERT STORM, as if it were a
souvenir banner of a hot vacation spot, I wondered that there was

no music for the Gulf War. Where were the songs like "My Buddy" or "It's a Long Way to Tipperary"?

During the last days of the war, I relied upon Bach's Violin 10
Concerto in D Minor, the fierce longing of Jacqueline DePres's cello, Fauré's Requiem and, as always, Mozart. On a particularly bad day, between the Pentagon press conferences—men with pointers, target maps, smart-bomb videos, and a doublespeak war doggerel that called bombing "servicing a target"—I made a beeline to my public library and checked out every musical from *Oklahoma* to *Miss Saigon*. I made a tape entitled "Life Is a Musical" and divided it into three sections: (1) Love Found in Strange Places, (2) Love Lost Everywhere, and (3) Love Returns. It was astonishing how songs from vastly different time periods and places segued together. My favorite storyline riff is "Empty Chairs at Empty Tables," from *Les Misérables* to "The American Dream" from *Miss Saigon* to "Carefully Taught" from *South Pacific* to "Don't Cry for Me, Argentina," from *Evita* to "Bring Him Home" from *Les Misérables*. When I sent copies out to a select group of musicals-loving friends, it was as if we were all together at a candlelight mass or cross-continent communion, trying to imagine a war where no bombs fell.

Playing my own tapes against terror is a way to document and 11
summon back the necessities that mothered them. For example, "My Funny Valentine," with its Billie Holiday/Sarah Vaughan/Ella Fitzgerald/Alberta Hunter blues and ebullience is still a favorite, long after that lover has gone. Upon hearing that an old friend had bone cancer, I made him a tape called "Music to Heal By," which included the Delta Rhythm Boys' version of "Dry Bones." My friend wrote to say it was the first time he'd laughed in a long time. Now he's making his own tapes. After a writer friend of mine drank herself to death, I felt so bereft—since, after all, we'd planned to retire to the Black Hole Nursing Home for Wayward Writers together—that I made a tape called "The Ten Commandments of Love, or Southern Baptists Beware!" It's every song I ever slow-danced to or memorized in the sweaty backseat of a borrowed car as my date and I broke Sunday school rules on Saturday night. Declared by my siblings and southern pals to have gone into "metal" (their word for platinum or gold), it includes Etta James's soaring "At Last," Sam Cooke's silky "Wonderful World," and a steamy duet of "634–5789" with Robert Cray and Tina Turner. It's a great tape for getting in the mood.

Since ancient times, the Chinese have believed that certain 12
sounds can balance and heal. In acupressure, for example, each organ has a sound. Listening to a healthy heart, an astute healer can

hear laughter or, if there is disease, wind. The gallbladder shouts; the stomach speaks in a singsong, sometimes overly sympathetic voice; and the kidney, ever the perfectionist, groans. Sighs can be a sign of liver ailments, and the pitch of a person's voice can tell a story of that body's health just as well as a tongue. In some Taoist practices to enhance longevity, re-creating the sounds of certain organs can strengthen and tone them. For example, the *whuuuh whu- uuh* sound of the kidney can revitalize the adrenals, fortifying the immune system. If one cannot take time to sing in the key of every organ, I'd suggest Chinese wind chimes like the ones that grace my back porch. When a strong salt wind blows off the beach, my chimes, which are perfectly pitched to a five-element Chinese scale, play an impromptu arpeggio—a momentary transport to some monastic garden, a Shangri-la of sound. Scientific studies report that the actual sound of nature resonates at the level of eight hertz; by comparison, a refrigerator reverberates at eighty hertz. Is it any wonder some of us need to return to a musical womb to retreat from such technological onslaughts to our nervous systems?

In fact, our time in the womb is not at all quiet; it is a noisy   13 symphony of voices, lower-tract rumbles, whirrings like waterfalls, and white noise. One of my friends found that if she played a tape of the roar of her sturdy Kirby vacuum cleaner, the sound immediately put her boisterous newborn twins to sleep. I have another friend whose entire house is wall-to-wall egg cartons, which absorb sound as well as enhance his audiophilic tendencies. I've visited houses that sound like living inside an aquarium, where pleasant underwater burbles from elaborate tropical fish tanks drown out the world. I've also entered homes where cuckoo clocks, grandfather chimes, and deep gongs count the hours so that I felt I was inside a ticking time bomb. Consciously or unconsciously we all make sound tracks to underscore our lives.

Mermaid Music has allowed me to enter a reverie of song, a   14 backstage "smaller-than-life" sojourn away from all the stresses. Right now I'm at work on two dance tapes for a summer roll-up-the-rug party. Entitled "Bop till You Drop" and "Bad Girls," the tapes defy all hearers not to kick up their heels with such all-time hits as "Heat Wave" and "I Heard It Through the Grapevine," as well as the ever-popular "R-E-S-P-E-C-T." Of course, I've had request for sequels and am at work on "Life Is a Musical II" divided into (1) "Falling," (2) "Feeling," and (3) "Forever Ruined/Recovery." It flows from "People Will Say We're in Love" to "Happy Talk" to "Just You Wait, Henry Higgins!"

My siblings say I should sell my tapes against terror on late-   15
night TV in the company of such classics as Veg-O-Matics and "Elvis
Lives" medleys. The idea fills me with horror. After all, there are
copyright violations cops who come like revenuers in the dark of the
night to bust local moonshiners and music makers. I'd rather stay
strictly small-time and nonprofit, like that long-ago lullaby service I
had in college, a trio of nannies against nightmares. But if anyone
out there in music land is making his or her own tapes against terror, I'd be open to an exchange. After all, it's better than bombs
through the mail or collecting baseball cards.

So tune in, and maybe we'll find ourselves on the same fre-   16
quency. On this lifelong Freeway of Love, I just want to be an Earth
Angel with my Magic Flute. Because after all, Everybody Plays the
Fool and Ain't Nobody's Business If I Do.

MEANINGS AND VALUES

1. In a paragraph of your own, summarize what this essay has to say
   about music, human emotions, and the relationship between them.

2. What subject or subjects is Peterson classifying in this essay?

3. Explain what the writer means by the phrase "my soul's station"
   (Par. 1).

EXPOSITORY TECHNIQUES

1. Which paragraph announces the purpose and theme of the essay?
   (See "Guide to Terms": *Purpose; Unity.*) Can this essay be said to have
   a thesis statement? If so, where is it? (Guide: *Thesis.*)

2. What pattern other than classification does the writer employ in
   Paragraph 4? (Hint: see Chapter 8.)

3. What different subjects does Peterson classify in this essay? How, if
   at all, does the writer keep these different classifications from overlapping in a confusing manner? Would this essay be more effective if
   the writer had concentrated on only one or two of the classifications?
   Explain. (Guide: *Evaluation.*)

4. What is the function of the clauses that open the first sentence in the
   essay? (Guide: *Syntax; Introductions.*)

DICTION AND VOCABULARY

1. Identify the extended comparison in Paragraph 12 and explain its relation to the central theme of the essay. (Guide: *Figures of Speech; Unity.*)

2. Identify those paragraphs in the essay that begin with transition words indicating that they will further develop the topic or ideas of the preceding paragraph. Discuss whether the transition words serve effectively to link paragraphs and ideas within the essay. (Guide: *Transition.*)

3. If you do not know the meaning of some of the following words, look them up in the dictionary: solace, mellifluous, placenta (Par. 2); falsetto (4); suave (5); heretically (6); dulcet (7); riff (8); eerily, zealous, aplomb (9); segued (10); ebullience (11); astute (12); audiophilic (13).

READ TO WRITE

1. **Collaborating:** Working in a group, list several types or categories of music. Then list the types of experiences, moods, or activities each group member associates with the different types of music. Note any similarities or patterns the group observes in the relationship between the kinds of music and the responses or uses of the music. Collectively plan an essay explaining the kinds of music and the typical responses to them. Consider drawing on this plan for an essay of your own.

2. **Considering Audience:** How effective are Peterson's examples for a young adult audience today? For an audience in some other age group? Write an essay on a plan similar to Peterson's but using musical examples directed at a particular age or cultural group with which you are familiar.

3. **Developing an Essay:** Drawing strategies from Peterson's essay, prepare an essay of your own, classifying tastes in art, movies, sports, or some other area of cultural or social activity. Try to explain why differences in people's tastes can be understood on the basis of differences in character, background, or some other factor.

(NOTE: Suggestions for topics requiring development by use of CLASSIFICATION follow.)

Writing Suggestions for Chapter 4

CLASSIFICATION

Use division and classification (into at least three categories) as your basic method of analyzing one of the following subjects from an interesting point of view. (Your instructor may have good reason to place limitations on your choice of subject.) Narrow the topic as necessary to enable you to do a thorough job.

1. College students

2. College teachers

3. Athletes

4. Coaches

5. Salespeople

6. Hunters (or fishers)

7. Parents

8. Drug users

9. Police officers

10. Summer (or part-time) jobs

11. Sailing vessels

12. Game show hosts

13. Friends

14. Careers

15. Horses (or other animals)

16. Television programs

17. Motivations for study

18. Methods of studying for exams

19. Lies

20. Selling techniques

21. Tastes in clothes

22. Contemporary music or films

23. Love

24. Ways to spend money

25. Attitudes toward life

26. Fast foods (or junk foods)

27. Smokers

28. Investments

29. Actors

30. Books or magazines

COLLABORATIVE EXERCISES

1. Working in a group, prepare a classification essay on college life using numbers 1–4 in the preceding exercise as the major sections for your classification. Assign group members to divide each of the four sections into two or three subcategories and to prepare a section of an essay explaining these subcategories. Then prepare a collaboratively written essay linking each section with clear transitions and unifying the whole with a central idea on which all members of the group agree. (See "Guide to Terms": *Unity.*)

2. As a group, create three or more categories from the subject "careers" (see number 14). Have each member of the group research one of the types of careers and then create a collaboratively written essay with an appropriate introduction, conclusion, thesis, and transitions.

5

Explaining by Means of *Comparison* and *Contrast*

One of the first expository methods we used as children was **comparison,** noticing similarities of objects, qualities, and actions, or **contrast,** noticing their differences. We compared the color of the new puppies with that of their mother, contrasted a parent's height with our own. Then the process became more complicated. Now we employ it frequently in college essay examinations or term papers when we compare or contrast forms of government, reproductive systems of animals, or ethical philosophies of humans. In the business or professional world, we prepare important reports based on comparison and contrast—between kinds of equipment for purchase, the personnel policies of different departments, or precedents in legal matters. Nearly all people use the process of comparison (meaning both *comparing* and *contrasting*) many times a day—in choosing a head of lettuce, in deciding what to wear to school, in selecting a house, or a friend, or a religion.

In expository writing, brief comparisons—a sentence or two—may serve to alert readers to similarities or highlight differences. Longer comparisons need to do more; they need to explore the subject and convey the writer's perspective. For a longer comparison or contrast that explains or explores ideas, you need an ordered plan to avoid having a mere list of characteristics or a frustrating jumble of similarities and differences. You also need to give attention to all the important points of similarity (or difference). The following paragraph accomplishes all these things.

> We really are terribly confused about our relationship with nature.
> On the one hand, we like to live in houses that are tidy and clean, and

if nature should be rude enough to enter—in the form of a bat in the attic, or a mouse in the kitchen, or a cockroach crawling along the skirting boards—we stalk it with the blood-lust of a tabby cat; we resort to chemical warfare. In fact, we judge people harshly if their house is full of dust and dirt. And yet, on the other hand, we just as obsessively bring nature indoors. We touch a switch and light floods the room. We turn a dial and suddenly it feels like summer or winter. We live in a perpetual breeze or bake of our devising. We buy posters and calendars with photographs of nature. We hang paintings of landscapes on our walls. We scent everything that touches our lives. We fill our houses with flowers and pets. We try hard to remove ourselves from all the dramas and sensations of nature, and yet without them we feel lost and disconnected. So, subconsciously, we bring them right back indoors again. Then we obsessively visit nature—we go swimming, jogging, or cross-country skiing, we take strolls in a park. Confusing, isn't it?

—Diane Ackerman, *Deep Play*

WHY USE COMPARISON?

Highlighting similarities and differences is the most obvious use for comparison, but merely a starting point for effective writing. Whenever you employ the pattern, therefore, make sure you give it a worthwhile purpose. You can contrast llamas with potbellied pigs, for example, but your efforts will likely seem silly or trivial unless tied to some larger goal, as in the case of Judith Stone's essay, "Personal Beast" (Ch. 4), in which she contrasts their relatively suitability as pets.

The question of purpose is especially important in a formal, full-scale analysis by comparison and contrast where the pattern lends shape to an entire essay. Sometimes the purpose may be merely to reveal *surprising or frequently overlooked likenesses and differences*, with the goal of adding to readers' knowledge, satisfying their curiosity, or developing their self-awareness. For example, an essay on generational differences over responsibility for housework might explain that younger people are more likely to share the work of cooking and cleaning, but that all generations seem to be maintaining traditional gender differences in the responsibility of home maintenance. Mark Twain, in the selection "Two Ways of Seeing a River" (pp. 160–163), contrasts his view of the Mississippi as a young man with his perspective as an experienced river pilot. In doing so, he helps readers understand how radically experience and changes in attitude can affect our perceptions of the external world—even making the same stretch of scenery appear a different place.

The aim may be to show *the superiority* of one thing over another. Or it may be to *explain* and *evaluate,* as in a discussion of alternatives or of differing points of view on an issue. For instance, you might examine competing proposals for an antismoking campaign, one designed by teenagers and the other by advertising professionals, evaluating the strengths and limitations of each.

The purpose could be to explain the *unfamiliar* (wedding customs in Ethiopia) by comparing it to the *familiar* (wedding customs in Kansas). Or it could be to support and explore a thesis, as is the case with several of the essays in this chapter. Alice Walker ("Am I Blue?" pp. 176–182), for example, uses comparison to advance the thesis that animals have emotional lives similar to those of humans. Catherine Seipp ("Meet Today's Dad," pp. 189–193) uses contrast between "Today's Dad" and "Yesterday's Dad" to explain why she believes the current version is "a model to avoid."

CHOOSING A STRATEGY

To take a comparison beyond the obvious and develop knowledge and insight worth sharing with readers, you need to begin by identifying **points of comparison** (or **points of contrast**), both major and minor. Some important points of comparison will be apparent to you (and your readers) from the outset, and therefore should be part of your analysis. Others will be less apparent, though not necessarily less important. Including them will enable you to provide a fresh or more thorough perspective, adding to your reader's understanding. Consider using the following questions to identify and explore points of comparison, adapted, of course, to the particular demands of your subjects.

What are the similar (or different) **physical aspects** (shape, color, size, texture, movement) of the subjects you are analyzing?

> **Parts and Processes** (elements and their relationships, methods of operation, instructions)?
> **Benefits** (individual, social, political, environmental)?
> **Problems** (dangers, difficulties, limitations)?
> **Costs** (financial, emotional, political)?
> **Uses** (personal, social, environmental; to provide benefits, to create relationships, to accomplish a particular goal)?

As you develop responses to questions like these, keep in mind that you are trying to develop fresh insights both for yourself and your readers. Consider using questions like these to help you develop such a perspective.

What similarities (or differences) are readers likely to consider. . . .

Intriguing or surprising?

Useful or worth learning about?

Quite different from what they expected before they began reading?

Significant enough to make them more likely to consider different opinions on an issue or approaches to a problem?

Important enough to guide their choice among alternative policies, products, or conclusions?

The points of comparison you choose, along with your tentative thesis, your purpose for writing, and the complexity of your materials, will usually suggest an arrangement for your writing. The number of subjects making up any comparison (two or more) and the likelihood that you will be exploring multiple points of comparison along with their supporting details mean that you should plan the organization of an essay carefully and remember to make this arrangement clear to readers.

One of the two basic methods of comparison is to present all the information on the two (or more) subjects, one at a time, and to summarize by combining their most important similarities and differences. Here is a subject-by-subject plan for an essay.

Subject-by-Subject Pattern

Introduction

Subjects: Bella Costa Medical Center (curing illness) and Foothills Regional Health Complex (creating wellness)

Tentative Thesis: Today's health care dilemmas have gone beyond choices among insurance plans to choices between two very different kinds of medical treatment: one focused on curing illness (represented by Bella Costa M.C.), the other focused on creating wellness (represented by Foothills R.H.C.).

Subject 1: Bella Costa Medical Center

Feature 1: Traditional medicine—curing illness

Feature 2: Large hospital, newest equipment

Feature 3: Large staff of physicians
Feature 4: Emphasis on drugs, surgery, physical therapy

Subject 2: Foothills Regional Health Complex
Feature 1: Preventive medicine—creating wellness
Feature 2: Small hospital, limited facilities, local clinics
Feature 3: Some physicians, other staff including nutri-
tionists, exercise specialists, and alternative therapists
Feature 4: Emphasis on diet, exercise, alternative therapies
(acupuncture, holistic medicine), healthy lifestyle

Conclusion (summary): Summarize reasons for choosing either
one and suggest that personal preferences may play an important role.

This method may be desirable if there are few points to compare, or if the individual points are less important than the overall
picture they present.

However, if there are several points of comparison to be considered, or if the points are of individual importance, alternation of the
material would be a better arrangement.

Point-by-Point Pattern

Subjects: *The Mummy* (1932) starring Boris Karloff
The Mummy (1999) starring Brendan Fraser

Tentative Thesis: The original version of *The Mummy* (1932)
takes itself and the horror movie form seriously and provides an often scary portrait of evil. The remake (1999)
takes itself only half-seriously and gently pokes fun at the
conventions of the horror movie, so it is only occasionally
scary and conveys no sense of evil.

Subject 1: Original version of *The Mummy*
Feature 1 (acting): Boris Karloff, serious acting style, dramatic scenes and speeches
Feature 2 (script): Provides motivation for characters, emphasizes force of evil desires
Feature 3 (special effects): Support story line, emphasize
unnatural desires and presence of evil

Subject 2: Remake of *The Mummy*
Feature 1 (acting): Brendan Fraser, comic or ironic acting
style, action scenes and physical comedy
Feature 2 (script): Little motivation for characters, highlights stereotypes and conventions of horror movies

Feature 3 (special effects): Call attention to themselves, emphasize unreal and exaggerated elements of horror stories

Conclusion (summary):
Original and remake show changing attitudes toward the horror movie as a portrait of evil.

Often the subject matter or the purpose itself will suggest a more casual treatment, or some combination or variation of the two basic methods. We might present the complete information on the first subject, then summarize it point by point within the complete information on the second. And although expository comparisons and contrasts are frequently handled together, it is sometimes best to present all similarities first, then all differences—or vice versa, depending on the emphasis desired. In any basic use of comparison, the important thing is to have a plan that suits the purpose and material, thoughtfully worked out in advance.

DEVELOPING COMPARISONS

In writing an essay using comparison as a primary pattern of exposition, keep these two important tasks in mind: 1) take care that your comparisons are logical and arranged in a manner that will be clear to your readers, and 2) provide detailed explanations of the similarities and differences in order to support your conclusions.

Above all, your comparison needs to be *logical.* A logical comparison or contrast can be made only between subjects of the same general type. (Analogy, a special form of comparison used for another purpose, is discussed in the next chapter.) For example, contrasting modern medicine (prescription drugs, surgery) and traditional medicine (herbal remedies, acupuncture) could be useful or meaningful, but little would be gained by contrasting surgery and carpentry.

Transition words and phrases are a big help with both logic and the arrangement of an essay, reminding you of an essay's plan as you write and signaling the arrangement to readers. Some transition words identify the elements of a subject, some indicate logical relationships or highlight the place of a paragraph in the overall organization, and some identify conclusions and supporting detail.

Elements of a Subject: trait, characteristic, element, part, segment, unit, feature

Logical Relationships and Arrangement: in comparison, in contrast, on the other side, on the other hand, likewise, moreover, similarly, in the same (or different) manner, in addition, then, further, yet, but, however, nonetheless, first, second, third, although, still

Conclusions and Supporting Detail: in conclusion, to sum up, finally, for example, for instance

Paragraphs are especially important in writing that compares or contrasts. Typically, they are devoted to one of the major steps in the exposition, often to one of the main points of comparison. In focusing on points of similarity or dissimilarity, be thorough. Provide facts, concrete details, and examples. Consider those that support your conclusions or recommendations as well as those that provide contrary evidence. Remember, too, that effective comparisons serve a purpose, so include details that support your overall thesis and further the purpose for which you are writing.

Student Essay

In the following essay, Amy Bell uses comparison as a pattern of thinking: a way to raise questions about and explore her topic. She inquires into the "truthfulness" of two pieces of writing that claim to be portrayals of events that really happened, and in so doing she raises questions about what really constitutes "truth" in writing. Amy uses comparison effectively in her own writing both as a way of representing her thinking and as a way of helping readers understand the many detailed similarities and differences she analyzes.

Perception of Truth
by Amy Bell

"The following motion picture is based on a true story." How many times have you seen this on the movie screen and thought, "Yeah, right, 'true' story my foot"? We all know that the movie producers/directors take huge liberties with the facts and portray events differently from the way they actually occurred. The same is true in non-fiction writing. Each author chooses what information to give to the reader and what information to withhold. In doing this the "truth" is blurred and the

Focuses on general topic/issue to be explored

author's personal bias emerges. Truman Capote and Norman Mailer are both hailed as authors who succeeded in writing "true-story" novels. In describing Norman Mailer's <u>The Executioner's Song</u>, critics have said he is "our greatest chronicler" and "the best journalist in the country" (Mailer cover). Critics have described Truman Capote's <u>In Cold Blood</u> as a "superbly written 'true account'" and "the best documentary of an American crime" (Capote cover). All of these book reviews imply that Mailer and Capote gave only the truth in their books. However, this is not possible. Mailer's and Capote's personal opinions also must be in these novels. So which novel is more truthful? This question cannot be answered. How can we ever know what information these authors changed or what information they left out completely? However, it is possible to show which novel creates a greater impression of truth. Truman Capote's novel, <u>In Cold Blood</u>, seems more truthful than Mailer's <u>The Executioner's Song</u>. The impression of truth in these novels was partly created by the way in which each author portrayed the murderer in his story.

> *Focuses on specific topic of essay*

> *Purpose of essay—to be accomplished by comparing and contrasting*

> *Thesis statement*

> *General plan for essay—compare the works*

Norman Mailer and Truman Capote both had unlimited access to the facts about the murderers, Gary Gilmore and Perry Smith [respectively]. In researching Gilmore, Mailer collected interview manuscripts, court records, and documents. He also conducted nearly 300 interviews, which added up to a manuscript of 15,000 pages (Mailer 1020). Capote also collected numerous official records and conducted interviews (Capote acknowledgments page). Capote and Mailer used carefully selected bits of truth from this multitude of information to portray their murderers differently.

> *Background— both Mailer and Capote*

One obvious way in which Mailer and Capote described the murderers was to directly quote them. Norman Mailer put a numerous amount of quotations from Gilmore in his novel. Nearly forty letters written by Gilmore to his girlfriend Nicole were printed in the book. Mailer also included a great deal of interviews between Gilmore and his two lawyers. A lot of "truth" is

> *Feature 1: Quotations*
>
> *Discussion of Mailer*

divulged because so much personal information about Gilmore is given. However, for the reader this truth becomes blurred because of Gilmore's contradicting feelings and intense emotions. For instance, in one letter Gilmore writes to Nicole he says, "I saw a simple, quiet Truth, a profound, deep, and personal Truth of beauty and love" (qtd. in Mailer 345). It would seem that through these words the reader might see who the "true" Gary is. However, in the next letter the reader is bombarded with ". . . these chickens——t pricks. Give a motherf——er a little authority and they think they have to start taking privileges away from people . . . bunch of slack-jawed . . . gurgling . . . punks" (Mailer 348). Gilmore's variety of raving emotions weaves in and out of the letters in the book, leaving the reader wary of believing anything Gilmore says. Norman Mailer gives us too much information from an unreliable Gilmore, and in doing so there seems to be less truth.

Supporting details

Interpretation of details

Capote also quotes his murderer, Perry Smith; however, he uses fewer, carefully selected quotations. Capote only uses enough quotations to give an ample description of Smith. This creates less confusion for the reader about Smith. Smith could have been just as confusing to understand as Gilmore was; after all, Smith did kill four people without knowing why he did it. For example, Capote includes a few carefully selected quotations to describe Smith's childhood. Smith is describing the brutality of the nuns in an orphanage he lived in as a child: "She woke me up. She had a flashlight, and she hit me with it. Hit me and hit me. And when the flashlight broke, she went on hitting me in the dark" (qtd. in Capote 93). This well-chosen quotation gives the reader an understanding of Smith's childhood and gives a glimpse into the mind of Smith. Capote tells the reader who Smith is, instead of the reader having to figure out who Smith is by sorting through hundreds of Smith's thoughts. Capote gives us what he thinks the truth about Smith is, and he does it in such a way that the reader is compelled to believe it.

Feature 1: Quotations

Discussion of Capote

Supporting details

Interpretation of details

One way to make a story more believable and truthful is to give equal weight to everyone's side of the story. Mailer thoroughly gives Gilmore's side of the story; however, the stories of the victims are hardly mentioned. In chapters twelve and fifteen of part four, Mailer gives a basic description of the lives of the Bushnells and the Jensens. He only devotes about twenty pages out of 1,000 pages to these people. Also, Mailer's description of these people is not an intimate one. He gives an overview of their lives in a distant, journalistic style. Mailer writes, "It was at Utah State that Colleen was introduced to her future husband, Max Jensen" (Mailer 212). This is simply a description, and the voices and feelings of Max and Colleen are not seen.

> Feature 2: Equal weight in presentation
>
> Discussion of Mailer
>
> Conclusion followed by supporting details

Capote, on the other hand, gives an equal amount of time to everyone's side of the story. In the first chapter, "Last to See Them Alive," Capote describes the Clutter family while also describing Dick [Smith's accomplice] and Perry [Smith]. Capote shows each member of the Clutter family, their relationships with each other and with the community. Capote includes a lot of dialogue between members of the family, so that the reader can see the murder victims as real people. The following is a conversation between Nancy Clutter and her brother, Kenyon. [Nancy speaks first.]

> Feature 2: Equal weight in presentation
>
> Discussion of Capote
>
> Conclusion followed by supporting details

"I keep smelling cigarette smoke."

"On your breath?" inquired Kenyon.

"No funny one. Yours." (Capote 19)

In this interplay between brother and sister the reader can relate to the Clutters as human beings and not just as murder victims. Capote gives an in-depth, intimate description of every person's side of the story. For the reader this creates a perception that Capote was less biased, and therefore the story seems truthful.

> Interpretation of details

Using basic logic, it would seem that Mailer probably wrote down more "truth" in a 1,000-page book than Capote wrote in a meager 350-page book. However, the amount of truth and the perception of truth are two very different things. Truman Capote's In Cold Blood

> Summary conclusion: Capote seems more truthful

gives a greater perception of truth than Norman Mailer's <u>The Executioner's Song</u>. Then again, this statement is merely my opinion. As the author of this essay, I selected only the "appropriate" bits of information from these two novels to give my reader(s) my perception of what "truth" is.

Works Cited

Capote, Truman. <u>In Cold Blood</u>. New York: Modern Library, 1965.

Mailer, Norman. <u>The Executioner's Song</u>. New York: Warner, 1979.

MARK TWAIN

MARK TWAIN was the pen name of Samuel Clemens (1835–1910).
He was born in Missouri and became the first author of importance
to emerge from "beyond the Mississippi." Although best known for
bringing humor, realism, and Western local color to American fiction, Mark Twain wanted to be remembered as a philosopher and
social critic. Still widely read, in most languages and in all parts of
the world, are his numerous short stories (his "tall tales," in particular), autobiographical accounts, and novels, especially *Adventures of
Huckleberry Finn* (1884). Ernest Hemingway called the last "the best
book we've had," an appraisal with which many critics agree.

Two Ways of Seeing a River

"Two Ways of Seeing a River" (editor's title) is from Mark Twain's
"Old Times on the Mississippi," which was later expanded and published in book form as *Life on the Mississippi* (1883). It is autobiographical. The prose of this selection is vivid, as is all of Mark
Twain's writing, but considerably more reflective in tone than most.

Now when I had mastered the language of this water and had   1
come to know every trifling feature that bordered the great
river as familiarly as I knew the letters of the alphabet, I had made a
valuable acquisition. But I had lost something, too. I had lost something which could never be restored to me while I lived. All the
grace, the beauty, the poetry, had gone out of the majestic river! I
still kept in mind a certain wonderful sunset which I witnessed
when steamboating was new to me. A broad expanse of the river
was turned to blood; in the middle distance the red hue brightened
into gold, through which a solitary log came floating, black and conspicuous; in one place a long, slanting mark lay sparkling upon the
water; in another the surface was broken by boiling, tumbling rings
that were as many-tinted as an opal; where the ruddy flush was
faintest was a smooth spot that was covered with graceful circles
and radiating lines, ever so delicately traced; the shore on our left
was densely wooded, and the somber shadow that fell from this forest was broken in one place by a long, ruffled trail that shone like silver; and high above the forest wall a clean-stemmed dead tree
waved a single leafy bough that glowed like a flame in the unob-
structed splendor that was flowing from the sun. There were graceful curves, reflected images, woody heights, soft distances, and over

the whole scene, far and near, the dissolving lights drifted steadily, enriching it every passing moment with new marvels of coloring.

I stood like one bewitched. I drank it in, in a speechless rapture. The world was new to me and I had never seen anything like this at home. But as I have said, a day came when I began to cease from noting the glories and the charms which the moon and the sun and the twilight wrought upon the river's face; another day came when I ceased altogether to note them. Then, if that sunset scene had been repeated, I should have looked upon it without rapture and should have commented upon it inwardly after this fashion: "This sun means that we are going to have wind tomorrow; that floating log means that the river is rising, small thanks to it; that slanting mark on the water refers to a bluff reef which is going to kill somebody's steamboat one of these nights, if it keeps on stretching out like that; those tumbling 'boils' show a dissolving bar and a changing channel there; the lines and circles in the slick water over yonder are a warning that that troublesome place is shoaling up dangerously; that silver streak in the shadow of the forest is the 'break' from a new snag and he has located himself in the very best place he could have found to fish for steamboats; that tall dead tree, with a single living branch, is not going to last long, and then how is a body ever going to get through this blind place at night without the friendly old landmark?"

No, the romance and beauty were all gone from the river. All the value any feature of it had for me now was the amount of usefulness it could furnish toward compassing the safe piloting of a steamboat. Since those days, I have pitied doctors from my heart. What does the lovely flush in a beauty's cheek mean to a doctor but a "break" that ripples above some deadly disease? Are not all her visible charms sown thick with what are to him the signs and symbols of hidden decay? Does he ever see her beauty at all, or doesn't he simply view her professionally and comment upon her unwholesome condition all to himself? And doesn't he sometimes wonder whether he has gained most or lost most by learning his trade?

MEANINGS AND VALUES

1. What is the point of view in Paragraph 1? (See "Guide to Terms": *Point of View.*) Where, and how, does it change in Paragraph 2? Why is the shift important to the author's contrast?

2. Show how the noticeable change of tone between Paragraphs 1 and 2 is related to the change in point of view. (Guide: *Style/Tone.*)

Specifically, what changes in style accompany the shift in tone and attitude? How effectively do they all relate to the central theme itself? (Remember that such effects seldom just "happen"; the writer *makes* them happen.)

3. Is the first paragraph primarily objective or subjective? (Guide: *Objective/Subjective.*) How about the latter part of Paragraph 2? Are your answers related to point of view? If so, how?

4. Do you think the last sentence refers only to doctors? Why, or why not?

EXPOSITORY TECHNIQUES

1. Where do you find a second comparison or contrast? Which is it? Is the comparison/contrast made within itself, with something external, or both? Explain.

2. Is the second comparison/contrast closely enough related to the major contrast to justify its use? Why, or why not?

3. In developing the numerous points of the major contrast, would an alternating, point-to-point system have been better? Why, or why not? Show how the author uses organization within the groups to assist in the overall contrast.

4. What is the most noteworthy feature of syntax in Paragraphs 1 and 2? (Guide: *Syntax.*) How effectively does it perform the function intended?

5. What is gained by the apparently deliberate decision to use rhetorical questions only toward the end? (Guide: *Rhetorical Questions.*)

DICTION AND VOCABULARY

1. In what ways do the word choices in Paragraph 1 differ from those in Paragraph 2? (Guide: *Diction.*)

2. Compare the quality of metaphors in the quotation of Paragraph 2 with the quality of those preceding it. (Guide: *Figures of Speech.*) Is the difference justified? Why, or why not?

READ TO WRITE

1. **Collaborate:** We spend much of our lives preparing for work, working, and thinking about work. As Twain's essay points out, moreover, work shapes the way we perceive things and respond to them. Work can therefore be an excellent source of writing topics that are interesting to both writers and readers. Working in a group, add five more questions about work to the following list, and then use it to help generate possible topics for an essay: How do specific kinds of work shape perceptions and values? Are people's outlooks likely to vary according to the kinds of jobs they hold (or want to hold)? How

do my work habits, preferences, or experiences set me apart from others (or bring me closer)?

2.   **Considering Audience:** Would readers of Twain's era, used to traveling by steamboat, horse-drawn carriage, steam-powered trains, and horseback, respond differently than readers of today to this essay? Write a brief essay of your own (1–3 paragraphs) explaining why readers might or might not respond differently. In doing so, consider the ways in which modern means of transportation affect our perceptions and values.

3.   **Developing an Essay:** Twain's essay not only describes two scenes but also explains what changes in outlook and experience make them seem different. Prepare an essay of your own with a similar purpose. Choose a scene or event that you have observed more than once and from differing perspectives. Explain to readers the ways in which the scene appeared different and what it was about your perceptions that accounted for the difference.

(NOTE: Suggestions for topics requiring development by use of COMPARISON and CONTRAST are on pp. 202–203, at the end of this chapter.)

BRUCE CATTON

BRUCE CATTON (1899–1978) was a Civil War specialist whose early career included reporting for various newspapers. In 1954 he received both the Pulitzer Prize for historical work and the National Book Award. He served as director of information for the United States Department of Commerce and wrote many books, including *Mr. Lincoln's Army* (1951), *Glory Road* (1952), *A Stillness at Appomattox* (1953), *The Hallowed Ground* (1956), *America Goes to War* (1958), *The Coming Fury* (1961), *Terrible Swift Sword* (1963), *Never Call Retreat* (1966), *Waiting for the Morning Train: An American Boyhood* (1972), and *Gettysburg: The Final Fury* (1974). For five years, Catton edited *American Heritage*.

Grant and Lee: A Study in Contrasts

"Grant and Lee: A Study in Contrasts" was written as a chapter of *The American Story,* a collection of essays by noted historians. In this study, as in most of his other writing, Catton does more than recount the facts of history: he shows the significance within them. It is a carefully constructed essay, using contrast and comparison as the entire framework for his explanation.

When Ulysses S. Grant and Robert E. Lee met in the parlor of a modest house at Appomattox Court House, Virginia, on April 9, 1865, to work out the terms for the surrender of Lee's Army of Northern Virginia, a great chapter in American life came to a close, and a great new chapter began.   1

These men were bringing the Civil War to its virtual finish. To be sure, other armies had yet to surrender, and for a few days the fugitive Confederate government would struggle desperately and vainly, trying to find some way to go on living now that its chief support was gone. But in effect it was all over when Grant and Lee signed the papers. And the little room where they wrote out the terms was the scene of one of the most poignant, dramatic contrasts in American history.   2

They were two strong men these oddly different generals, and they represented the strengths of two conflicting currents that, through them, had come into final collision.   3

Back of Robert E. Lee was the notion that the old aristocratic concept might somehow survive and be dominant in American life.   4

Lee was tidewater Virginia, and in his background were family,   5
culture, and tradition . . . the age of chivalry transplanted to a New
World which was making its own legends and its own myths. He
embodied a way of life that had come down through the age of
knighthood and the English country squire. America was a land that
was beginning all over again, dedicated to nothing much more complicated than the rather hazy belief that all men had equal rights and
should have an equal chance in the world. In such a land Lee stood
for the feeling that it was somehow of advantage to human society
to have a pronounced inequality in the social structure. There
should be a leisure class, backed by ownership of land; in turn, society itself should be keyed to the land as the chief source of wealth
and influence. It would bring forth (according to this ideal) a class of
men with a strong sense of obligation to the community; men who
lived not to gain advantage for themselves, but to meet the solemn
obligations which had been laid on them by the very fact that they
were privileged. From them the country would get its leadership; to
them it could look for the higher values—of thought, of conduct, or
personal deportment—to give it strength and virtue.

Lee embodied the noblest element of this aristocratic ideal.   6
Through him, the landed nobility justified itself. For four years, the
Southern states had fought a desperate war to uphold the ideals for
which Lee stood. In the end, it almost seemed as if the Confederacy
fought for Lee; as if he himself was the Confederacy . . . the best thing
that the way of life for which the Confederacy stood could ever have
to offer. He had passed into legend before Appomattox. Thousands
of tired, underfed, poorly clothed Confederate soldiers, long since
past the simple enthusiasm of the early days of the struggle, somehow considered Lee the symbol of everything for which they had
been willing to die. But they could not quite put this feeling into
words. If the Lost Cause, sanctified by so much heroism and so many
deaths, had a living justification, its justification was General Lee.

Grant, the son of a tanner on the Western frontier, was every-   7
thing Lee was not. He had come up the hard way and embodied
nothing in particular except the eternal toughness and sinewy fiber
of the men who grew up beyond the mountains. He was one of a
body of men who owed reverence and obeisance to no one, who
were self-reliant to a fault, who cared hardly anything for the past
but who had a sharp eye for the future.

These frontier men were the precise opposites of the tidewater   8
aristocrats. Back of them, in the great surge that had taken people
over the Alleghenies and into the opening Western country, there

was a deep, implicit dissatisfaction with a past that had settled into grooves. They stood for democracy, not from any reasoned conclusion about the proper ordering of human society, but simply because they had grown up in the middle of democracy and knew how it worked. Their society might have privileges, but they would be privileges each man had won for himself. Forms and patterns meant nothing. No man was born to anything, except perhaps to a chance to show how far he could rise. Life was competition.

Yet along with this feeling had come a deep sense of belonging   9
to a national community. The Westerner who developed a farm, opened a shop, or set up in business as a trader could hope to prosper only as his own community prospered—and his community ran from the Atlantic to the Pacific and from Canada down to Mexico. If the land was settled, with towns and highways and accessible markets, he could better himself. He saw his fate in terms of the nation's own destiny. As its horizons expanded, so did his. He had, in other words, an acute dollars-and-cents stake in the continued growth and development of his country.

And that, perhaps, is where the contrast between Grant and Lee   10
becomes most striking. The Virginia aristocrat, inevitably, saw himself in relation to his own region. He lived in a static society which could endure almost anything except change. Instinctively, his first loyalty would go to the locality in which that society existed. He would fight to the limit of endurance to defend it, because in defending it he was defending everything that gave his own life its deepest meaning.

The Westerner, on the other hand, would fight with an equal   11
tenacity for the broader concept of society. He fought so because everything he lived by was tied to growth, expansion, and a constantly widening horizon. What he lived by would survive or fall with the nation itself. He could not possibly stand by unmoved in the face of an attempt to destroy the Union. He would combat it with everything he had, because he could only see it as an effort to cut the ground out from under his feet.

So Grant and Lee were in complete contrast, representing two   12
diametrically opposed elements in American life. Grant was the modern man emerging; beyond him, ready to come on the stage, was the great age of steel and machinery, of crowded cities and a restless burgeoning vitality. Lee might have ridden down from the old age of chivalry, lance in hand, silken banner fluttering over his head. Each man was the perfect champion of his cause, drawing both his strengths and his weaknesses from the people he led.

Yet it was not all contrast, after all. Different as they were—in 13
background, in personality, in underlying aspiration—these two
great soldiers had much in common. Under everything else, they
were marvelous fighters. Furthermore, their fighting qualities were
really very much alike.

Each man had, to begin with, the great virtue of utter tenacity 14
and fidelity. Grant fought his way down the Mississippi Valley in
spite of acute personal discouragement and profound military
handicaps. Lee hung on in the trenches at Petersburg after hope itself had died. In each man there was an indomitable quality . . . the
born fighter's refusal to give up as long as he can still remain on his
feet and lift his two fists.

Daring and resourcefulness they had, too: the ability to think 15
faster and move faster than the enemy. These were the qualities
which gave Lee the dazzling campaigns of Second Manassas and
Chancellorsville and won Vicksburg for Grant.

Lastly, and perhaps greatest of all, there was the ability, at the 16
end, to turn quickly from war to peace once the fighting was over.
Out of the way these two men behaved at Appomattox came the
possibility of a peace of reconciliation. It was a possibility not
wholly realized, in the years to come, but which did, in the end, help
the two sections to become one nation again . . . after a war whose
bitterness might have seemed to make such a reunion wholly impossible. No part of either man's life became him more than the part
he played in their brief meeting in the McLean house at
Appomattox. Their behavior there put all succeeding generations of
Americans in their debt. Two great Americans, Grant and Lee—very
different, yet under everything very much alike. Their encounter at
Appomattox was one of the great moments of American history.

MEANINGS AND VALUES

1. Clarify the assertions that through Lee "the landed nobility justified
   itself" and that "if the Lost Cause . . . had a living justification," it
   was General Lee (Par. 6). Why are these assertions pertinent to the
   central theme?

2. Does it seem reasonable that "thousands of tired, underfed, poorly
   clothed Confederate soldiers" (Par. 6) had been willing to fight for

the aristocratic system in which they would never have had even a chance to be aristocrats? Why or why not? Can you think of more likely reasons why they were willing to fight?

3.   What countries of the world have recently been so torn by internal war and bitterness that reunion has seemed, or still seems, impossible? Do you see any basic differences between the trouble in those countries and that in America at the time of the Civil War?

4.   The author calls Lee a symbol (Par. 6). Was Grant also a symbol? If so, of what? (See "Guide to Terms": *Symbol.*) How would you classify this kind of symbolism?

Expository Techniques

1.   Make an informal list of paragraph numbers from 3 to 16, and note by each number whether the paragraph is devoted primarily to Lee, to Grant, or to direct comparison or contrast of the two. This chart will show you Catton's basic pattern of development. (Notice, for instance, how the broad information of Paragraphs 4–6 and 7–9 seems almost to "funnel" down through the narrower summaries in Paragraphs 10 and 11 into Paragraph 12, where the converging elements meet and the contrast is made specific.)

2.   What new technique of development is started in Paragraph 13?

3.   What is gained, or lost, by using one sentence for Paragraph 3? For Paragraph 4?

4.   How many paragraphs does the introduction comprise? How successfully does it fulfill the three basic requirements of a good introduction? (Guide: *Introductions.*)

5.   Show how Catton has constructed the beginning of each paragraph so that there is a smooth transition from the one preceding it. (Guide: *Transition.*)

6.   What seems to be the author's attitude toward Grant and Lee? Show how his tone reflects this attitude. (Guide: *Style/Tone.*)

Diction and Vocabulary

1.   Why would a use of colloquialisms have been inconsistent with the tone of this writing?

2.   List or mark all metaphors in Paragraphs 1, 3, 5, 7–11, and 16. (Guide: *Figures of Speech.*) Comment on their general effectiveness.

3.   If you are not already familiar with the following words, study their meanings as given in the dictionary and as used in this essay: virtual, poignant (Par. 2); concept (4); sinewy, obeisance (7); implicit (8); tenacity (11); diametrically, burgeoning (12); aspiration (13); fidelity, profound, indomitable (14); succeeding (16).

READ TO WRITE

1. **Collaborating:** Catton focuses on a dramatic moment in history and explains its long-range significance. Drawing on his approach, list some dramatic moments in history. In a group, compare your lists. Does your definition of "dramatic moment" match those of other group members? Decide as a group on one moment you all agree is dramatic and, in a short essay, explain its long-range significance.

2. **Considering Audience:** Ask yourself how much you knew about the topic of "Grant and Lee" before you began reading the essay, then go through the text and highlight sections that present information that was new to you. To what extent do you think that your initial knowledge of the topic was similar to that of most readers? Why? Study the ways Catton introduces information that most readers are likely to be unfamiliar with, and identify techniques you could use to present new information in your own writing.

3. **Developing an Essay:** One special achievement of Catton's "Grant and Lee: A Study in Contrasts" is its portrait of the two generals as embodiments of contrasting societies and cultures. Consider using this strategy in an essay offering a contrast between ideas, values, or cultures by means of a contrast between people who embody the differences. The strategy can be applied to a wide variety of subjects, not simply to public or political ones. You might use it to talk about different parenting strategies, for example, or about various religious beliefs or value systems.

(NOTE: Suggestions for topics requiring development by means of COMPARISON and CONTRAST are on pp. 202–203 at the end of this chapter.)

PHILLIP LOPATE

PHILLIP LOPATE was born in 1943 in New York City. He attended
Columbia University and received a B.A. in 1964. In 1979, he re-
ceived a doctorate at Union Graduate School. He has taught cre-
ative writing in the Teachers and Writers Collaborative program in
New York City and is currently on the faculty of Hofstra University.
His publications include *The Eyes Don't Always Want to Stay Open*
(1972) and *The Daily Round* (1976) (poems); *Confessions of
Summer* (1979), *Bachelorhood: Tales of the Metropolis* (1981), and
The Rug Merchant (1987) (fiction); *Being with Children* (1975) (non-
fiction); and *Against Joie de Vivre: Personal Essays* (1989), *Portrait of
My Body* (1996), and *Totally, Tenderly, and Tragically* (1998) (col-
lections of essays). His essays have appeared in a variety of publica-
tions, including *New Age Journal, Texas Monthly,* the *New York
Times Book Review, Columbia, House and Garden, Vogue, Film
Quarterly, Cinemabook, Esquire,* and *Interview.*

A Nonsmoker with a Smoker

In this essay, which first appeared in *New Age Journal,* Lopate uses
comparison and contrast to explore his own ambiguous feelings
about smoking—and about his relationship with a smoker. In the
course of the essay, he touches on many aspects of the
smoking/nonsmoking conflict, yet he offers a personal perspective
often lost in the public controversy.

L ast Saturday night my girlfriend, Helen, and I went to a dinner   1
party in the Houston suburbs. We did not know our hosts, but
were invited on account of Helen's chum Barry, whose birthday
party it was. We had barely stepped into the house and met the
other guests, seated on a U-shaped couch under an A-framed ceiling, when Helen lit a cigarette. The hostess froze. "Uh, could you
please not smoke in here? If you have to, we'd appreciate your using
the terrace. We're both sort of allergic."

Helen smiled understandingly and moved toward the glass   2
doors leading to the backyard in a typically ladylike way, as though
merely wanting to get a better look at the garden. But I knew from
that gracious "Southern" smile of hers that she was miffed.

As soon as Helen had stepped outside, the hostess explained that   3
they had just moved into this house, and that it had taken weeks to air
out because of the previous owner's tenacious cigar smoke. A paradigmatically awkward conversation about tobacco ensued: like testifying

sinners, two people came forward with confessions about kicking the nasty weed; our scientist-host cited a recent study of indoor air pollution levels; a woman lawyer brought up the latest California legislation protecting nonsmokers; a roly-poly real estate agent admitted that, though he had given up smokes, he still sat in the smoking section of airplanes because "you meet a more interesting type of person there"—a remark his wife did not find amusing. Helen's friend Barry gallantly joined her outside. I did not, as I should have; I felt paralyzed.

For one thing, I wasn't sure which side I was on. I have never   4
been a smoker. My parents both chain-smoked, so I grew up accustomed to cloudy interiors and ever since have been tolerant of other people's nicotine urges. To be perfectly honest, I'm not crazy about inhaling smoke, particularly when I've got a cold, but that irritating inconvenience pales beside the damage that would be done to my pluralistic worldview if I did not defend smokers' rights.

On the other hand, a part of me wished Helen *would* stop   5
smoking. That part seemed to get a satisfaction out of the group's "banishing" her: they were doing the dirty work of expressing my disapproval.

As soon as I realized this, I joined her in the garden. Presently a   6
second guest strolled out to share a forbidden toke, then a third. Our hostess ultimately had to collect the mutineers with an announcement that dinner was served.

At the table, Helen appeared to be having such a good time,   7
joking with our hosts and everyone else, that I was unprepared for the change that came over her as soon as we were alone in the car afterward. "I will never go back to that house!" she declared. "Those people have no concept of manners or hospitality, humiliating me the moment I stepped in the door. And that phony line about 'sort of allergic'!"

Normally, Helen is forbearance personified. Say anything that   8
touches her about smoking, however, and you touch the rawest of nerves. I remembered the last time I foolishly suggested that she "think seriously" about stopping. I had just read one of those newspaper articles about the increased possibility of heart attacks, lung cancer, and birth deformities among women smokers, and I was worried for her. My concern must have been maladroitly expressed, because she burst into tears.

"Can't we even talk about this without your getting so sensi-   9
tive?" I had asked.

"You don't understand. Nonsmokers never understand that it   10
is a real addiction. I've tried quitting, and it was hell. Do you want

me to go around for months mean and cranky outside and angry inside? You're right, I'm sensitive, because I'm threatened with having taken away from me the thing that gives me the most pleasure in life, day in, day out," she said. I shot her a look: careful, now. "Well, practically the most pleasure. You know what I mean." I didn't. But I knew enough to drop it.

I love Helen, and if she wants to smoke, knowing the risks in-   11
volved, that remains her choice. Besides, she wouldn't quit just because I wanted her to; she's not that docile, and that's part of what I love about her. Sometimes I wonder why I even keep thinking about her quitting. What's it to me personally? Certainly I feel protective of her health, but I also have selfish motives. I don't like the way her lips taste when she's smoked a lot. I associate her smoking with nervousness, and when she lights up several cigarettes in a row, I get jittery watching her. Crazy as this may sound, I also find myself becoming jealous of her cigarettes. Occasionally, when I go to her house and we're sitting on the couch together, if I see Helen eyeing the pack I make her kiss me first, so that my lips can engage hers (still fresh) before the competition's. It's almost as though there were another lover in the room—a lover who was around long before I entered the picture, and who pleases her in mysterious ways I cannot.

A lit cigarette puts a distance between us: it's like a weapon in   12
her hand, awakening in me a primitive fear of being burnt. The memory is not so primitive, actually. My father used to smoke absentmindedly, letting the ash grow like a caterpillar eating every leaf in its path, until gravity finally toppled it. Once, when I was about nine, my father and I were standing in line at a bakery, and he accidentally dropped a lit ash down my back. Ever since, I've inwardly winced and been on guard around these little waving torches, which epitomize to me the dangers of intimacy.

I've worked hard to understand from the outside the satisfaction   13
of smoking. I've even smoked "sympathetic" cigarettes, just to see what the other person was experiencing. But it's not the same as being hooked. How can I really empathize with the frightened but stubborn look Helen gets in her eyes when, despite the fact we're a little late going somewhere, she turns to me in the car and says, "I need to buy a pack of cigarettes first"? I feel a wave of pity for her. We are both embarrassed by this forced recognition of her frailty—the "indignity," as she herself puts it, of being controlled by something outside her will.

I try to imagine myself in that position, but a certain smugness   14
keeps getting in the way (I don't have that problem and *am I glad*). We pay a price for our smugness. So often it flip-flops into envy: the

outsiders wish to be included in the sufferings and highs of others, as if to say that only by relinquishing control and surrendering to some dangerous habit, some vice or dependency, would one be able to experience "real life."

Over the years I have become a sucker for cigarette romanti-   15
cism. Few Hollywood gestures move me as much as the one in *Now Voyager,* when Paul Henreid lights two cigarettes, one for himself, the other for Bette Davis: these form a beautiful fatalistic bridge between them, a complicitous understanding like the realization that their love is based on the inevitability of separation. I am all the more admiring of this worldly cigarette gallantry because its experiential basis escapes me.

The same sort of fascination occurs when I come across a liter-   16
ary description of nicotine addiction, like this passage in Mailer's *Tough Guys Don't Dance:* "Over and over again I gave them up, a hundred times over the years, but I always went back. For in my dreams, sooner or later, I struck a match, brought flame to the tip, then took in all my hunger for existence with the first puff. I felt impaled on desire itself—those fiends trapped in my chest and screaming for one drag."

"Impaled on desire itself"! Such writing evokes a longing in me   17
for the centering of self that tobacco seems to bestow on its faithful. Clearly, there is something attractive about having this umbilical relation to the universe—this curling pillar, this spiral staircase, this prayer of smoke that mediates between the smoker's inner substance and the alien ether. Inwardness of the nicotine trance, sad wisdom ("every pleasure has its price"), beauty of ritual, squandered health—all those romantic meanings we read into the famous photographic icons of fifties saints, Albert Camus or James Agee or James Dean or Carson McCullers puffing away, in a sense they're true. Like all people who return from a brush with death, smokers have gained a certain power. They know their "coffin nails." With Helen, each cigarette is a measuring of the perishable, an enactment of her mortality, from filter to end-tip in fewer than five minutes. I could not stand to be reminded of my own death so often.

MEANINGS AND VALUES

1. Tell why you think the writer made the title say *with* rather than *and*.

2. Does the writer's portrayal of the party (Pars. 1–6) make Helen's anger (7) seem justified? Why or why not?

3. To what parts of this essay might smokers and nonsmokers react in different ways? How might their reactions differ? Be specific in answering this question.

4. What conclusion about smoking, if any, does the writer reach in the last paragraph of the essay?

EXPOSITORY TECHNIQUES

1. The focus of the essay shifts at the end of Paragraph 3. What role does the last sentence in the paragraph play, and in what way does the focus shift?

2. How would you characterize the tone and style in Paragraph 1? In Paragraph 3? (See "Guide to Terms": *Style/Tone.*) What contrast does the writer emphasize through the differences in tone and style?

3. To what extent does the focus of Paragraphs 7–11 lie on the question of smoking versus not smoking, and to what extent does it focus on the relationship between the writer and Helen? Be ready to defend your answer with specific evidence from the text.

4. What is being compared in Paragraph 11? How is this comparison related to the overall pattern of comparison in the essay?

5. In what ways do Paragraphs 13 and 14 contrast with 15 and 16?

6. State in your own words the contrast the author makes in the last two sentences of the essay. Do these sentences make an effective conclusion? (Guide: *Closings; Evaluation.*)

DICTION AND VOCABULARY

1. Identify the informal diction in Paragraph 1 and the formal diction in Paragraph 3. (Guide: *Diction.*) Why has the writer created these contrasts in diction? (Hint: see "Expository Techniques.")

2. Identify the similes in Paragraph 12, and tell what they suggest about the effect of smoking on personal relationships. (Guide: *Figures of Speech.*)

3. Explain how cigarettes act as symbols in Paragraph 15. (Guide: *Symbol.*)

4. Identify the metaphors in Paragraph 15. Discuss their meaning and their effect, both as individual metaphors and as a cluster. (Guide: *Figures of Speech.*)

5. If you do not know the meaning of some of the following words, look them up in a dictionary: tenacious, paradigmatically, ensued (Par. 3); pluralistic (4); toke (6); forbearance, maladroitly (8); epitomize (12); fatalistic, complicitious (15).

READ TO WRITE

1. **Collaborating:** In his essay, Lopate views behaviors and attitudes not so much as matters of choice but as outgrowths of our experi-

ences, personalities, and interactions with others. Follow Lopate's approach and explore in freewriting (see pp. 170–173) a pattern of behavior (perhaps one you disapprove of) by looking at the motivations of someone who engages in it and by exploring your own reactions to the behavior. Then turn your freewriting into two lists, one of motivations and one of reactions, and share your lists with a partner. Then write a short response to your partner's lists, indicating the extent to which you agree or disagree with the items on them.

2. **Considering Audience:** Compare and contrast how smokers and nonsmokers might react to this essay. Will they think Lopate is fair to both groups? Write notes for a short essay outlining the differing perspectives of two people on a similar conflict or issue such as wearing helmets while driving motorcycles or using seatbelts in cars and trucks.

3. **Developing an Essay:** Even familiar issues and controversies can be a source of new understanding for you and your readers when you take a personal approach to them and write with an expository purpose. Explore some potential subjects by asking questions like these: If smoking, wearing a fur coat, or some other activity or belief offends you, should you let the person doing the activity know about your feelings? What steps can you take to communicate your feelings without offending the other person? Should you worry about upsetting the other person?

(NOTE: Suggestions for topics requiring development by use of COMPARISON and CONTRAST are on pp. 202–203 at the end of this chapter.)

ALICE WALKER

Alice Walker was born in Georgia in 1944, the youngest in a family
of eight. Her parents were sharecroppers, and she attended rural
schools as a child, going on eventually to attend Spelman College
and Sarah Lawrence College, from which she graduated. She
worked as an editor of *Ms.* magazine and taught at several colleges. At present she teaches at the University of California,
Berkeley and lives in northern California. Her work as a poet, novelist, and essayist has been highly acclaimed, and one of her novels, *The Color Purple* (1982), received both a Pulitzer Prize and the
American Book Award for fiction. Some of her other works are
Revolutionary Petunias and Other Poems (1973) and *Her Blue Body
Everything We Know: Earthling Poems 1989–1990* (poems) (1991);
In Love and Trouble (1973) (short stories); *Meridian* (1976), *The
Temple of My Familiar* (1989), *Possessing the Secret of Joy* (1992),
and *By the Light of My Father's Smile* (1998) (novels); and *In Search
of Our Mothers' Gardens* (1983), *Living by the Word* (1988), and *The
Same River Twice: Honoring the Difficult* (1996) (essays), *The Way
Forward Is with a Broken Heart* (2000) (stories).

Am I Blue?

Humans and horses might seem at first so different that any comparison would have to take the form of an analogy—a pairing of
essentially unlike subjects whose limited similarities can be used
for explanatory purposes (see Chapter 4). Walker's strategy in this
essay from *Living by the Word* is just the opposite, however. She explains that despite their obvious differences, humans and animals
are essentially alike, at least in important matters such as the capacity to love and to communicate.

" *A* in't these tears in these eyes tellin' you?"   1

    For about three years my companion and I rented a small house   2
in the country that stood on the edge of a large meadow that appeared to run from the end of our deck straight into the mountains.
The mountains, however, were quite far away, and between us and
them there was, in fact, a town. It was one of the many pleasant aspects of the house that you never really were aware of this.

    It was a house of many windows, low, wide, nearly floor to ceil-   3
ing in the living room, which faced the meadow, and it was from one
of these that I first saw our closest neighbor, a large white horse,

cropping grass, flipping its mane, and ambling about—not over the entire meadow, which stretched well out of sight of the house, but over the five or so fenced-in acres that were next to the twenty-odd that we had rented. I soon learned that the horse, whose name was Blue, belonged to a man who lived in another town, but was boarded by our neighbors next door. Occasionally, one of the children, usually a stocky teenager, but sometimes a much younger girl or boy, could be seen riding Blue. They would appear in the meadow, climb up on his back, ride furiously for ten or fifteen minutes, then get off, slap Blue on the flanks, and not be seen again for a month or more.

There were many apple trees in our yard, and one by the fence 4 that Blue could almost reach. We were soon in the habit of feeding him apples, which he relished, especially because by the middle of summer the meadow grasses—so green and succulent since January—had dried out from lack of rain, and Blue stumbled about munching the dried stalks half-heartedly. Sometimes he would stand very still just by the apple tree, and when one of us came out he would whinny, snort loudly, or stamp the ground. This meant, of course: I want an apple.

It was quite wonderful to pick a few apples, or collect those that 5 had fallen to the ground overnight, and patiently hold them, one by one, up to his large, toothy mouth. I remained as thrilled as a child by his flexible dark lips, huge, cubelike teeth that crunched the apples, core and all, with such finality, and his high, broad-breasted *enormity;* beside which, I felt small indeed. When I was a child, I used to ride horses, and was especially friendly with one named Nan until the day I was riding and my brother deliberately spooked her and I was thrown, head first, against the trunk of a tree. When I came to, I was in bed and my mother was bending worriedly over me; we silently agreed that perhaps horseback riding was not the safest sport for me. Since then I have walked, and prefer walking to horseback riding— but I had forgotten the depth of feeling one could see in horses' eyes.

I was therefore unprepared for the expression in Blue's. Blue 6 was lonely. Blue was horribly lonely and bored. I was not shocked that this should be the case; five acres to tramp by yourself, endlessly, even in the most beautiful of meadows—and his was—cannot provide many interesting events, and once rainy season turned to dry that was about it. No, I was shocked that I had forgotten that human animals and nonhuman animals can communicate quite well; if we are brought up around animals as children we take this for granted. By the time we are adults we no longer remember. However, the animals have not changed. They are in fact *completed* creations (at least they seem to be, so much more than we) who are not likely to change; it is their nature to express themselves. What else are they going to express? And they do. And, generally speaking, they are ignored.

After giving Blue the apples, I would wander back to the house, 7 aware that he was observing me. Were more apples not forthcoming then? Was that to be his sole entertainment for the day? My partner's small son had decided he wanted to learn how to piece a quilt; we worked in silence on our respective squares as I thought. . . .

Well, about slavery: about white children, who were raised by 8 black people, who knew their first all-accepting love from black women, and then, when they were twelve or so, were told they must "forget" the deep levels of communication between themselves and "mammy" that they knew. Later they would be able to relate quite calmly, "My old mammy was sold to another good family." "My old mammy was_____ _____." Fill in the blank. Many more years later a white woman would say: "I can't understand these Negroes, these blacks. What do they want? They're so different from us."

And about the Indians, considered to be "like animals" by the 9 "settlers" (a very benign euphemism for what they actually were), who did not understand their description as a compliment.

And about the thousands of American men who marry 10 Japanese, Korean, Filipina, and other non-English-speaking women and of how happy they report they are, *"blissfully,"* until their brides learn to speak English, at which point the marriages tend to fall apart. What then did the men see, when they looked into the eyes of the women they married, before they could speak English? Apparently only their own reflections.

I thought of society's impatience with the young. "Why are they 11 playing the music so loud?" Perhaps the children have listened to much of the music of oppressed people their parents danced to before they were born, with its passionate but soft cries for acceptance and love, and they have wondered why their parents failed to hear.

I do not know how long Blue had inhabited his five beautiful, 12 boring acres before we moved into our house; a year after we had arrived—and had also traveled to other valleys, other cities, other worlds—he was still there.

But then, in our second year at the house, something happened 13 in Blue's life. One morning, looking out the window at the fog that lay like a ribbon over the meadow, I saw another horse, a brown one, at the other end of Blue's field. Blue appeared to be afraid of it, and for several days made no attempt to go near. We went away for a week. When we returned, Blue had decided to make friends and the two horses ambled or galloped along together, and Blue did not come nearly as often to the fence underneath the apple tree.

When he did, bringing his new friend with him, there was a different look in his eyes. A look of independence, of self-possession, of inalienable *horse*ness. His friend eventually became pregnant. For months and months there was, it seemed to me, a mutual feeling between me and the horses of justice, of peace. I fed apples to them both. The look in Blue's eyes was one of unabashed "this is *it*ness."   14

It did not, however, last forever. One day, after a visit to the city, I went out to give Blue some apples. He stood waiting, or so I thought, though not beneath the tree. When I shook the tree and jumped back from the shower of apples, he made no move. I carried some over to him. He managed to half-crunch one. The rest he let fall to the ground. I dreaded looking into his eyes—because I had of course noticed that Brown, his partner, had gone—but I did look. If I had been born into slavery, and my partner had been sold or killed, my eyes would have looked like that. The children next door explained that Blue's partner had been "put with him" (the same expression that old people used, I had noticed, when speaking of an ancestor during slavery who had been impregnated by her owner) so that they could mate and she conceive. Since that was accomplished, she had been taken back by her owner, who lived somewhere else.   15

Will she be back? I asked.   16

They didn't know.   17

Blue was like a crazed person. Blue *was,* to me, a crazed person. He galloped furiously, as if he were being ridden, around and around his five beautiful acres. He whinnied until he couldn't. He tore at the ground with his hooves. He butted himself against his single shade tree. He looked always and always toward the road down which his partner had gone. And then, occasionally, when he came up for apples, or I took apples to him, he looked at me. It was a look so piercing, so full of grief, a look so *human,* I almost laughed (I felt too sad to cry) to think there are people who do not know that animals suffer. People like me who have forgotten, and daily forget, all that animals try to tell us. "Everything you do to us will happen to you; we are your teachers, as you are ours. We are one lesson" is essentially it, I think. There are those who never once have even considered animals' rights: those who have been taught that animals actually want to be used and abused by us, as small children "love" to be frightened, or women "love" to be mutilated and raped. . . . They are the great-grandchildren of those who honestly thought, because   18 someone taught them this: "Women can't think," And "niggers can't faint." But most disturbing of all, in Blue's large brown eyes was a new look, more painful than the look of despair: the look of disgust with human beings, with life; the look of hatred. And it was odd what the look of hatred did. It gave him, for the first time, the look of a beast. And what that meant was that he had put up a barrier within to protect himself from further violence; all the apples in the world wouldn't change that fact.

And so Blue remained, a beautiful part of our landscape, very   19
peaceful to look at from the window, white against the grass. Once a friend came to visit and said, looking out on the soothing view: "And it *would* have to be a white horse; the very image of freedom." And I thought, yes, the animals are forced to become for us merely "images" of what they once so beautifully expressed. And we are used to drinking milk from containers showing "contented" cows, whose real lives we want to hear nothing about, eating eggs and drumsticks from "happy" hens, and munching hamburgers advertised by bulls of integrity who seem to command their fate.

As we talked of freedom and justice one day for all, we sat   20
down to steaks. I am eating misery, I thought, as I took the first bite. And spit it out.

Meanings and Values

1. In which paragraphs does Walker describe what she believes to be Blue's thoughts and feelings?

2. According to Walker, in what ways is Blue similar to a human? In what ways is he different? To what other groups does the author compare Blue and his relationships with humans in Paragraphs 8–11?

3. What thematic purposes are served by the following phrases:

   a. "human animals and nonhuman animals" (Par. 6)

   b. "who did not understand their description as a compliment" (Par. 9)

   c. "Am I Blue?" (title)

   d. "If I had been born into slavery, and my partner had been sold or killed, my eyes would have looked like that." (Par. 15)

   e. "It gave him, for the first time, the look of a beast." (Par. 18)

Expository Techniques

1. Why do you think Walker chose to wait until near the end of the essay (Par. 18) for a detailed discussion of its theme? (See "Guide to Terms": *Unity.*) To what extent does the placement of this discussion give the essay an expository rather than an argumentative purpose? (Guide: *Argument.*)

2. Discuss how the "'images'" presented in Paragraph 19 can be regarded as ironic symbols. (Guide: *Symbol; Irony.*)

3. Describe the way Walker alters the tempo of the sentences and builds to a climax in the concluding paragraph of the essay. (Guide: *Closings.*)

4. Some readers might consider the ending effective. Others might consider it overly dramatic or distasteful. Explain which reaction you consider most appropriate. (Guide: *Evaluation.*)

Diction and Vocabulary

1. Describe the ways in which Walker uses syntax and figurative language (simile) for thematic purposes in this passage: "Blue was like a crazed person. Blue *was*, to me, a crazed person" (Par. 18). (Guide: *Syntax; Figures of Speech.*)

2. In speaking of the "'settlers,'" Walker says that this term is "a very benign euphemism for what they actually were" (Par. 9). What does she mean by this comment? What other terms might be applied to them (from Walker's point of view)? Why might she have chosen not to use such terms?

3. The title of this essay is taken from a song of the same name. In terms of the content of the essay, to what ideas or themes does it refer? Can it be considered a paradox? (Guide: *Paradox.*) The quotation from the song that opens the essay points to some of the ideas discussed in the essay. What are they?

Read to Write

1. **Collaborating:** Working in groups of four, discuss different animals that you have known. What have you learned from these animals? Can you apply what you have learned to your human relationships? To your understanding of human nature? How would you contrast the behavior of animals in specific situations with typical human behavior in such situations? As a group, plan an essay comparing and contrasting likely animal and human behavior in a set of situations you have chosen.

2. **Considering Audience:** Walker repeatedly refers to expressions and feelings seemingly conveyed through Blue's eyes. How might readers who have their own pets react to Walker's descriptions of the animal's eyes? How might readers without pets react? Will readers who have

pets understand Walker's comparison of animal owners and slave owners better than non-pet owners? Will most pet owners be offended by such a comparison? Who, if anyone, might be offended by the conclusions Walker draws about Blue's and other animals' feelings and intelligence? In two to three paragraphs, offer your answers to some or all of these questions as a way of describing readers' likely reactions to Walker's essay.

3.   **Developing an Essay:** Walker's essay moves from obvious differences to surprising similarities, getting there through careful observation and comparison of horses and humans. Apply this pattern to a topic of your own choosing, using it to express hidden similarities you have already noticed or to reveal similarities as you write.

(Note: Suggestions for topics requiring development by means of comparison and contrast are on pp. 202–203 at the end of this chapter.)

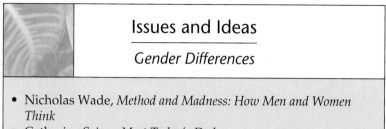

Issues and Ideas

Gender Differences

- Nicholas Wade, *Method and Madness: How Men and Women Think*
- Catherine Seipp, *Meet Today's Dad*
- Charles Hirshberg, *My Mother, the Scientist*

We understand our world by differences: wealthy, less wealthy, and a lot less wealthy; black, white, and brown; educated and uneducated; female and male. We come to understand who and what we are by learning who and what we are not.

One way we understand and deal with the world is through the difference between male and female, a distinction grounded in biological differences but extended to issues of emotion, intellectual ability, relationships, values, and social rules. These differences are maintained in various ways: through clothing styles, social organizations, sports teams, men's/women's publications, names (Kate/Carl), and kinship systems (aunt/uncle).

But how many of these differences are "real" and how many "imagined" or constructed by social custom? Just how different are men and women, and are their differences significant ones with important consequences?

As expository patterns, comparison and contrast parallel the identification of gender differences and similarities. Nicholas Wade and Charles Hirshberg make good use of the pattern to explore surprising similarities that complicate, or even call into question, differences that many readers may consider obvious and unchanging.

Nicholas Wade looks to science, specifically brain research, for hard evidence of gender contrasts. He finds evidence of real contrasts, but not simple ones. And the implications for behavior and social organization are even more complex and sometimes contradictory. Catherine Seipp looks at attempts to construct new patterns of male behavior as driven by political and social ideologies that ignore both tradition and (perhaps) biology, with unfortunate results. Charles Hirshberg, in contrast, looks at the expansion of women's roles, especially in science, as overcoming restrictive, foolish, and harmful beliefs rooted in views of women's biological inferiority.

NICHOLAS WADE

NICHOLAS WADE is a journalist who writes about science and scientific discoveries. His books include *A World Beyond Healing* (1987), *Noble Dues* (1981), and *The Ultimate Experiment* (1977). He has also edited a series of books for young people on nature and science.

Method and Madness:
How Men and Women Think

We often look to science for firm answers to hard questions but get responses that are complex and raise as many questions as they answer. Looking over current research, the author of this essay reports that although there are clearly differences between men's and women's brains, what the differences mean is not that apparent. At times the research confirms stereotypes, but just as often it challenges them. What is clear in this essay is the writer's effective use of comparison and contrast as strategies for explaining the complicated relationships among biology, behavior, and gender.

The human brain, according to an emerging new body of scientific research, comes in two different varieties, maybe as different as the accompanying physique. Men, when they are lost, instinctually fall back on their in-built navigational skills, honed from far-off days of tracking large prey miles from home. Women, by contrast, tend to find their way by the simpler methods of remembering local landmarks or even asking help from strangers. 1

Men excel on psychological tests that require the imaginary twisting in space of a three-dimensional object. The skill seems to help with higher math, where the topmost ranks are thronged with male minds like Andrew Wiles of Princeton, who proclaimed almost a year ago that he had proved Fermat's Last Theorem and will surely get around to publishing the proof almost any day now. 2

Some feminist ideologues assert that all minds are created equal and women would be just as good at math if they weren't discouraged in school. But Camilla Benbow, a psychologist at Iowa State University, has spent years assessing biases like male math teachers or parents who favor boys. She concludes that boys' superiority at math is mostly innate. 3

But women, the new studies assert, have the edge in most other ways, like perceptual speed, verbal fluency and communications 4 skills. They also have sharper hearing than men, and excel in taste, smell and touch, and in fine coordination of hand and eye. If Martians arrived and gave job interviews, it seems likely they would direct men to competitive sports and manual labor and staff most professions, diplomacy and government with women.

The measurement of intellectual differences is a field with a   5
long and mostly disgraceful past. I.Q. tests have been regularly misused, sometimes even concocted, in support of prevailing prejudices. Distinguished male anatomists used to argue that women were less intelligent because their brains weighed less, neglecting to correct for the strong influence of body weight on brain weight.

The present studies of sex differences are venturing on ground   6
where self-deception and prejudice are constant dangers. The science is difficult and the results prone to misinterpretation. Still, the budding science seems free so far of obvious error. For one thing, many of the field's leading practitioners happen to be women, perhaps because male academics in this controversial field have had their lives made miserable by militant feminists.

For another, the study of brain sex differences does not depend   7
on just one kind of subvertible measure but draws on several different disciplines, including biology and anatomy. As is described in a new book, *Eve's Rib*, by Robert Pool, and the earlier *Brain Sex*, by Anne Moir and David Jessel, the foundations of the field have been carefully laid in animal research. Experiments with rats show that exposure in the womb to testosterone indelibly imprints a male pattern of behavior; without testosterone, the rat's brain is female.

In human fetuses, too, the sex hormones seem to mold a male   8
and female version of the brain, each subtly different in organization and behavior. The best evidence comes from girls with a rare genetic anomaly who are exposed in the womb to more testosterone than normal; they grow up doing better than their unaffected sisters on the tests that boys are typically good at. There's also some evidence, not yet confirmed, that male and female brains may be somewhat differently structured, with the two cerebral hemispheres being more specialized and less well interconnected in men than in women.

If the human brain exists in male and female versions, as modu-   9
lated in the womb, that would explain what every parent knows, that boys and girls prefer different patterns of play regardless of well-meaning efforts to impose unisex toys on both.

The human mind being very versatile, however, any genetic   10
propensities are far from decisive. In math, for example, the average girl is pretty much as good as the average boy. Only among the few students at the peak of math ability do boys predominate. Within

the loose framework set by the genes, education makes an enormous difference. In Japan, boys exceed girls on the mental rotation tests, just as in America. But the Japanese girls outscore American boys. Maybe Japanese kids are just smarter or, more likely, just better taught, Japan being a country where education is taken seriously and parents and teachers consistently push children to excel.

There are some obvious cautions to draw about the social and   11
political implications that might one day flow from brain sex research. One is that differences between individuals of the same sex often far exceed the slight differences between the sexes as two population groups: "If I were going into combat, I would prefer to have Martina Navratilova at my side than Robert Reich," says Patricia Ireland, president of the National Organization for Women. Even if men in general excel in math, an individual woman could still be better than most men.

On the other hand, if the brains of men and women really are   12
organized differently, it's possible the sexes both prefer and excel at different occupations, perhaps those with more or less competition or social interaction. "In a world of scrupulous gender equality, equal numbers of girls and boys would be educated and trained for . . . all the professions. . . . [Hiring would proceed] until half of every workplace was made up of men and half, women," says Judith Lorber in *Paradoxes of Gender,* a new work of feminist theory. That premise does not hold if there are real intellectual differences between the sexes; the test of equal opportunity, when all unfair barriers to women have fallen, will not necessarily be equal outcomes.

Greek mythology tells that Tiresias, having lived both as a man   13
and a woman for some complicated reason, was asked to settle a dispute between Zeus and Hera as to which gender enjoyed sex more. He replied there was no contest—it was 10 times better for women. Whereupon Hera struck him blind for his insolence and Zeus in compensation gave him the gift of foresight. Like Tiresias, the brain sex researchers are uncovering some impolitic truths, potent enough to shake Mount Olympus some day.

Meanings and Values

1. Paragraph 6 addresses current studies of sex difference as well as Wade's belief that much of the scientific research on the subject has been misinterpreted. Wade goes on to say, "Many of the field's lead-

ing practitioners happen to be women, perhaps because male academics in this controversial field have had their lives made miserable by militant feminists." What point is Wade trying to make here? In what ways is the comment related to his statements about the misinterpretation of the data? Is his comment about feminists a conscious exaggeration? Why, or why not?

2. Why is Tiresias (Par. 13) a good choice for Wade's essay? (See "Guide to Terms": *Figures of Speech, Allusion.*)

3. Does Wade imply that one sex has a better way of thinking? Why, or why not? Is he neutral in his choice of evidence? Explain. What are the attributes people traditionally value in each of the sexes? In which paragraphs does Wade address these attributes?

EXPOSITORY TECHNIQUES

1. Wade's first five paragraphs include several comparison/contrast examples. Why might he have begun his essay this way? Is this an effective introduction for the piece? (Guide: *Introductions; Evaluation.*)

2. In Paragraph 10, the writer uses a comparison within a comparison when he addresses the differences between Japanese boys and girls as well as American boys and girls, and then continues by comparing Japanese students overall to American students overall. Why might he have chosen this technique? What point is he trying to make through this use of "dual" comparison?

DICTION AND VOCABULARY

1. How would you classify Wade's style and tone in this selection? (Guide: *Tone; Style.*) Are his word choices effective tools for communicating a message and a mood? (Guide: *Diction.*) Do you consider his use of phrases like "militant feminists" appropriate? Why, or why not?

2. This article first appeared in the *New York Times* in 1994. Was the level of difficulty of the vocabulary appropriate for the audience? Why, or why not?

3. If you do not know the meaning of some of the following words, look them up in a dictionary: ideologue (Par. 3); indelibly (7); modulated (9); propensities (10).

READ TO WRITE

1. **Collaborating:** Working in a group, make a list of what most people consider the major differences between men and women. As a group, decide how justified these generalizations are. Then choose three items from the list that all group members feel are reasonably

justified and plan a comparison/contrast paper analyzing and explaining these differences. Make sure you include supporting details and examples in your plan.

2. **Considering Audience:** Are Wade's choices of comparison/contrast examples accessible for male and female readers of a variety of ages? Why, or why not? Is his concluding story of Tiresias effective? Rewrite the conclusion of the essay (Par. 13) using a different story or example that might be more accessible for modern readers.

3. **Developing an Essay:** Wade discusses how we identify ourselves based on gender as well as how we compare ourselves to the opposite gender. He says, "The present studies of sex differences are venturing on ground where self-deception and prejudice are constant dangers" (Par. 6). What does he mean by this sentence? Prepare an essay discussing the kind of self-deception to which Wade refers. Consider how men and women typically see their gender in relation to the other gender. Think also about some clichés we often use in discussing gender differences.

(NOTE: Suggestions for topics requiring development by use of COMPARISON and CONTRAST are on pp. 202–203 at the end of this chapter.)

CATHERINE SEIPP

CATHERINE SEIPP was born in Winnipeg, Manitoba, but grew up in Los Alamitos, California. She attended UCLA, graduating with a B.A. in English and experience working on the *Daily Bruin* and writing book reviews for the *Los Angeles Times*. She has been a fashion editor and columnist, a media critic, a freelance magazine writer, and a blogger. Her writing (online and print) has appeared in *Mediaweek, TV Guide, Reason, Salon, American Journalism Review, Buzz, Wall Street Journal, Forbes, Weekly Standard,* and *New York Press,* among many other places. Her blog is *Cathy's World.*

Meet Today's Dad

In this essay, which first appeared in *National Review Online,* Seipp provides a double contrast, looking at what she calls "Today's Dad" in contrast to both mothers and "Yesterday's Dad." Her purpose is likewise twofold: to explain and to criticize the behaviors of "Today's Dad." In keeping with her satiric purpose, she employs mild exaggeration, stereotyping, and irony, but she does not allow these techniques to overwhelm her detailed examples or her explanatory purpose.

I live in the groovy Silver Lake section of Los Angeles, which is home to not only bohemians and gays but also to families who, although they voted against vouchers, still don't want their kids sitting in a classroom filled with the masses; my neighborhood has one of the few public elementary schools in L.A. where most of the kids are middle class and speak English at home. We also have around half-a-dozen preschools within just a couple of miles. Because of all this, my neighborhood is also home to an earnest creature we locals know as Silver Lake Dad.   1

Often this is a guy whose wife slaves away at an office job so dreamy artistic dad can pursue his dreamy artistic dreams. Sometimes he's divorced; by his "I [HEART] Being a Dad" bumper stickers shall ye know him. And although he and his comrades seem particularly common around here, they seem to populate hip urban centers across the country. Silver Lake Dad is just the local version of a new paternal species I think of as Today's Dad.   2

By now it's something of a cliché that men often feel they deserve a medal for what women do as a matter of course. To borrow Samuel Johnson's observation about women preachers, seeing a   3 man take care of children is sometimes like seeing a dog walk on its hind legs: It is not done well, but you are surprised to see it done at all.

Not that Today's Dad isn't helpful. On Halloween, he comes up with the best costumes, or trails along with a cooler of gin-and-tonics while bossy mom plans the trick-or-treating route. But while Today's Dad is certainly involved in his children's lives, his child-care skills aren't always quite as honed as he imagines.   4

Not long ago at Trader Joe's (a Today's Dad hotspot) I saw one of these guys in action. He was bearded (natch), wearing a faded t-shirt advertising some sort of worthy event, and making a big fuss about pork chops with his son: "OK, we'll bread them and bake them! We'll make a project out of it!" The boy looked about four and was standing up in the shopping cart the way the cart warnings always say not to do.   5

Someone came over to chat with this dad, who said he was organizing an antiwar peace vigil. "Good for you!" said the friend. At which point Today's Dad smiled and nodded, accepting the benediction with that serenely self-satisfied expression I notice these guys often assume. It's sort of like the expression men get when playing air guitar—lower lip sucked in, head bobbing up and down—only without the eyes closed shut in ecstasy.   6

Now the problem here was that even though I could see this dad was reveling in his fab daditude, like many guys he found it difficult to do two things at once—like watch a child while chatting with another adult. Men in charge of small children are like women and parallel parking: Attention must be paid or something's going to get dented. Because at this point, the son was really bouncing around in that cart, to the continued obliviousness of his father and the father's friend. The two men were too busy congratulating themselves on their moral rectitude to notice.   7

"Sir," I felt like saying, "your child and various pork products are about to spill themselves upon the ground." But I didn't. Because I know from experience that sensitive Today's Dad types are quick to dismiss women like me as Mean Ladies.   8

Now although Today's Dad is a character who is galling enough in real life, he really rankles when you see him in the concentrated modern pop-culture version. Take the popular WB drama *Everwood*, whose season finale ended with sensitive, bearded (what is with these guys and facial hair?) Dr. Brown informing his teenage son's pregnant ex-girlfriend that she was not to   9 tell the son about this unfortunate turn of events. Because that would rob the boy—who's 17—of the precious last few moments of his childhood.

There was a time when the duties of a father would have in-　10 cluded telling a son in such a situation to grow up and be a man. But then Dr. Brown (who speaks in pitch-perfect Today's Dad lingo) always describes himself as a parent, never as a father.

I once went to a press conference for a sitcom about a working　11 mom and stay-at-home dad. The show runners chuckled happily about how their own kids ran wild around the free food that's always in TV-production offices—taking bites out of cookies, then setting them back on the tray. Gee, that's cute. And it reminds me of another thing I've noticed about Today's Dad: He's fun, he's warm, and he can't be bothered to enforce proper behavior.

I know, I know; I sound cranky. Blame it on 14-plus years of　12 single Mom-dom. I'm addicted to *Everwood,* but the episode where Dr. Brown's single-mom neighbor is working herself into the ground with extra waitressing shifts, while her ex-husband just got a new $120,000 job *and no one ever says anything about child support* really got me.

O.K., so Today's Dad is a fully involved partner in all aspects of　13 the modern child-rearing process, from toting baby around in a backpack at cocktail parties to screaming at third graders on the soccer field. The thing is that, as we all know, in real life the day-in, day-out toting and chauffeuring generally falls to Mom.

My ex-husband was a great diaper-changer, but he left when　14 our daughter was just ten months old. Money became so tight that I was grateful when my own father, who like most men of his generation had never changed a diaper in his life, helped out with babysitting and eventually came to live with us. Before he changed his granddaughter's first diaper, he had to steel himself for a week by staring at dog droppings on the street. And he has no tolerance for contemporary children's lax table manners.

When my daughter had a bad day at school recently—her　15 English teacher had called her a racist for writing a paper arguing that affirmative action isn't necessary for women—Grandpa still didn't cut her any slack at dinner. "We're going to have to make a videotape of this so you can see where you're going wrong with your fork-twirling skills," he said. "We'll call it, The Racist Eating Spaghetti." Still, over the years I've come to appreciate his retro, Yesterday's Dad ways.

MEANINGS AND VALUES

1. What negative traits does Seipp identify in "Today's Dad"? What positive traits, if any, does she identify?

2. In what ways can the purpose of this essay be considered satiric? (See "Guide to Terms": *Satire.*)

3. What evidence does the essay provide of the writer's political and social outlook? How would you characterize this outlook? Explain why you think that comments reflecting her political and social values add to or detract from the effectiveness of the essay (Guide: *Evaluation.*)

EXPOSITORY TECHNIQUES

1. Where in the essay does the writer first introduce the subject of her essay? Where does she first introduce the patterns of behavior she wishes to contrast with her subject's typical behaviors?

2. Can the extended example in Paragraphs 5–8 be considered a *representative example* (see Ch. 3, "Example," p. 46) that sums up the characteristics of "Today's Dad"? Why, or why not? If so, what roles do the examples in Paragraphs 9–14 play?

3. The writer uses herself as a character in this essay—a *persona* (Guide: *Persona*). Where does she employ this technique? How does this technique aid in conveying and explaining her perspective and her values? How, if at all, does the tone of the persona's comments differ from the overall tone of the essay? (Guide: *Style/Tone*).

DICTION AND VOCABULARY

1. Identify the references to famous people, well-known places, or cultural phenomena in Paragraphs 3, 5, and 9 and explain the use the writer makes of them.

2. This essay uses *verbal irony* (consisting of both *understatement* and *sarcasm*) (Guide: *Irony*) to explain and criticize. Identify one example of each technique and discuss how the writer uses it.

3. If you do not know the meaning of some of the following words, look them up in a dictionary: bohemians (Par. 1); ye, paternal (2); honed (4); vigil, benediction (6); obliviousness, rectitude (7); lax (14).

READ TO WRITE

1. **Collaborating:** In a group, discuss the range of fathers (or mothers) that you or your friends had as children. Prepare a list of these people and the nurturing (or nonnurturing) roles they played. Extend your list by indicating which of these roles the group believes are best played by women or by men, or by either older people or

younger people. Indicate if there are any roles that can be played by only one gender or age group. Then develop at least three tentative thesis statements for essays on the many different kinds of fathers (or mothers) that people in our society need to grow up healthy and emotionally well balanced.

2. **Considering Audience:** Are most readers likely to view Seipp's views on fatherhood sympathetically? Why, or why not? Make a list of different kinds of readers who might be sympathetic and those who might be unsympathetic. Which groups does Seipp seem to address in this essay? Write out a brief plan for revising her essay to increase its appeal to groups that might be unsympathetic.

3. **Developing an Essay:** Using Seipp's essay as a starting point, prepare an essay of your own describing the range of mothers or fathers (or relatives) necessary for good social, emotional, and moral development of a child in our society. Or discuss the range of friendships you consider necessary for developing values like compassion, empathy, tolerance, and generosity.

(NOTE: Suggestions for essays requiring development by COMPARISON and CONTRAST are on pp. 202–203 at the end of this chapter.)

CHARLES HIRSHBERG

> Although he comes from a family of scientists, Charles Hirshberg
> has spent his career as a journalist. He has written for *Life* maga-
> zine, the *Washington Post Sunday Magazine, Time Digital,* and the
> *Los Angeles Times.* His work also appears in *Sports Illustrated* and
> *ESPN: The Magazine.* He is the author of three books on popular
> music, and his book *Will You Miss Me When I'm Gone* was a finalist
> for the National Book Critics Circle Award in 2002.

My Mother, the Scientist

> Hirshberg's essay, published first in *Popular Science,* looks at our
> gender expectations for careers and family roles, especially for
> people in scientific and technical fields. Though the essay contrasts
> present-day attitudes with those of an earlier generation, it also
> makes clear that the changes have not been as great as many of us
> might suppose.

In 1966, Mrs. Weddle's first-grade class at Las Lomitas Elementary   1
*School got its first homework assignment: We were to find out what our
fathers did for a living, then come back and tell the class. The next day, as
my well-scrubbed classmates boasted about their fathers, I was nervous.
For one thing, I was afraid of Mrs. Weddle: I realize now that she was probably harmless, but to a shy, elf-size, nervous little guy she looked like a
monstrous, talking baked potato. On top of that, I had a surprise in store,
and I wasn't sure how it would be received.*

"My daddy is a scientist," I said, and Mrs. Weddle turned to write   2
*this information on the blackboard. Then I dropped the bomb: "And my
mommy is a scientist!"*

Twenty-five pairs of first-grade eyes drew a bead on me, wondering   3
*what the hell I was talking about. It was then that I began to understand
how unusual my mother was.*

Today, after more than four decades of geophysical research, my   4
mother, Joan Feynman, is getting ready to retire as a senior scientist
at NASA's Jet Propulsion Laboratory. She is probably best known for
developing a statistical model to calculate the number of high-energy
particles likely to hit a spacecraft over its lifetime and for her method
of predicting sun spot cycles. Both are used by scientists worldwide.
Beyond this, however, my mother's career illustrates the enormous

change in how America regards what was, only a few decades ago, extremely rare: a scientist who's a woman and also a mother.

   To become a scientist is hard enough. But to become one while   5
running a gauntlet of lies, insults, mockeries, and disapproval—this was what my mother had to do. If such treatment is unthinkable (or, at least, unusual) today, it is largely because my mother and other female scientists of her generation proved equal to every obstacle thrown in their way.

My introduction to chemistry came in 1970, on a day when my mom was   6
*baking challah bread for the Jewish New Year. I was about ten, and though
I felt cooking was unmanly for a guy who played shortstop for Village Host
Pizza in the Menlo Park, California, Little League, she had persuaded me to
help. When the bread was in the oven, she gave me a plastic pill bottle and a
cork. She told me to sprinkle a little baking soda into the bottle, then a little
vinegar, and cork the bottle as fast as I could. There followed a violent and
completely unexpected pop as the cork flew off and walloped me in the forehead. Exploding food: I was ecstatic! "That's called a chemical reaction,"
she said, rubbing my shirt clean. "The vinegar is an acid and the soda is a
base, and that's what happens when you mix the two."*

   *After that, I never understood what other kids meant when they said   7
that science was boring.*

One of my mother's earliest memories is of standing in her crib at   8
the age of about two, yanking on her eleven-year-old brother's hair. This brother, her only sibling, was none other than Richard Feynman, destined to become one of the greatest theoretical physi- cists of his generation: enfant terrible of the Manhattan Project, pio- neer of quantum electrodynamics, father of nanotechnology, winner of the Nobel Prize, and so on. At the time, he was training his sister to solve simple math problems and rewarding each correct answer by letting her tug on his hair while he made faces. When he wasn't doing that, he was often seen wandering around Far Rockaway, New York, with a screwdriver in his pocket, repairing radios—at age eleven, mind you.

   My mother worshiped her brother, and there was never any   9
doubt about what he would become. By the time she was five, Richard had hired her for two cents a week to assist him in the elec- tronics lab he'd built in his room. "My job was to throw certain switches on command," she recalls. "I had to climb up on a box to reach them. Also, sometimes I'd stick my finger in a spark gap for the edification of his friends." At night, when she called out for a

glass of water, Riddy, as he was called, would demonstrate centrifugal force by whirling it around in the air so that the glass was upside down during part of the arc. "Until, one night," my mother recalls, "the glass slipped out of his hand and flew across the room."

Richard explained the miraculous fact that the family dog, the waffle iron, and Joan herself were all made out of atoms. He would run her hand over the corner of a picture frame, describe a right triangle, and make her repeat that the sum of the square of the sides was equal to the square of the hypotenuse. "I had no idea what it meant," she says, "but he recited it like a poem, so I loved to recite it too." One night, he roused her from her bed and led her outside, down the street, and onto a nearby golf course. He pointed out washes of magnificent light that were streaking across the sky. It was the aurora borealis. My mother had discovered her destiny. 10

That is when the trouble started. Her mother, Lucille Feynman, was a sophisticated and compassionate woman who had marched for women's suffrage in her youth. Nonetheless, when eight-year-old Joanie announced that she intended to be a scientist, Grandma explained that it was impossible. "Women can't do science," she said, "because their brains can't understand enough of it." My mother climbed into a living room chair and sobbed into the cushion. "I know she thought she was telling me the inescapable truth. But it was devastating for a little girl to be told that all of her dreams were impossible. And I've doubted my abilities ever since." 11

The fact that the greatest chemist of the age, Marie Curie, was a woman gave no comfort. "To me, Madame Curie was a mythological character," my mother says, "not a real person whom you could strive to emulate." It wasn't until her fourteenth birthday— March 31, 1942—that her notion of becoming a scientist was revived. Richard presented her with a book called *Astronomy.* "It was a college textbook. I'd start reading it, get stuck, and then start over again. This went on for months, but I kept at it. When I reached page 407, I came across a graph that changed my life." My mother shuts her eyes and recites from memory: "'Relative strengths of the Mg_+ absorption line at 4,481 angstroms . . . from *Stellar Atmospheres* by Cecilia Payne.' Cecilia Payne! It was scientific proof that a woman was capable of writing a book that, in turn, was quoted in a text. The secret was out, you see." 12

My mother taught me about resonances when I was about twelve. We were on a camping trip and needed wood for a fire. My brother and sister and I looked everywhere, without luck. Mom spotted a dead branch up in a tree. 13

She walked up to the trunk and gave it a shake. "Look closely," she told us, pointing up at the branches. "Each branch waves at a different frequency." We could see that she was right. So what? "Watch the dead branch," she went on. "If we shake the tree trunk in just the right rhythm, we can match its frequency and it'll drop off." Soon we were roasting marshmallows.

The catalogue of abuse to which my mother was subjected, begin-   14
ning in 1944 when she entered Oberlin College, is too long and relentless to fully record. At Oberlin, her lab partner was ill prepared
for the advanced-level physics course in which they were enrolled,
so my mother did all the experiments herself. The partner took copi-
ous notes and received an A. My mother got a D. "He *understands*
what he's doing," the lab instructor explained, "and you don't." In
graduate school, a professor of solid state physics advised her to do
her Ph.D. dissertation on cobwebs, because she would encounter
them while cleaning. She did not take the advice; her thesis was titled "Absorption of Infrared Radiation in Crystals of Diamond-Type
Lattice Structure." After graduation, she found that the "Situations
Wanted" section of the *New York Times* was divided between Men
and Women, and she could not place an ad among the men, the only
place anyone needing a research scientist would bother to look.

At that time, even the dean of women at Columbia University   15
argued that "sensible motherhood" was "the most useful and satisfying of the jobs that women can do." My mother tried to be a sensible mother and it damn near killed her. For three years she cooked,
cleaned, and looked after my brother and me, two stubborn and
voluble babies. One day in 1964 she found herself preparing to hurl
the dish drain through the kitchen window and decided to get professional help. "I was incredibly lucky," she remembers, "to find a
shrink who was enlightened enough to urge me to try to get a job.
I didn't think anyone would hire me, but I did what he told me
to do." She applied to Lamont-Doherty Observatory and, to her
astonishment, received three offers. She chose to work part-time,
studying the relationship between the solar wind and the magnetosphere. Soon she would be among the first to announce that the
magnetosphere—the part of space in which Earth's magnetic field
dominates and the solar wind doesn't enter—was open-ended, with
a tail on one side, rather than having a closed-teardrop shape, as had
been widely believed. She was off and running.

My mother introduced me to physics when I was about fourteen. I was   16
crazy about bluegrass music, and learned that Ralph Stanley was coming

to town with his Clinch Mountain Boys. Although Mom did not share my taste for hillbilly music, she agreed to take me. The highlight turned out to be fiddler Curly Ray Cline's version of "Orange Blossom Special," a barn burner in which the fiddle imitates the sound of an approaching and departing train. My mother stood and danced a buck-and-wing and when, to my great relief, she sat down, she said, "Great tune, huh? It's based on the Doppler effect." This is not the sort of thing one expects to hear in reference to Curly Ray Cline's repertoire. Later, over onion rings at the Rockybilt Cafe, she explained: "When the train is coming, its sound is shifting to higher frequencies. And when the train is leaving, its sound is shifting to lower frequencies. That's called the Doppler shift. You can see the same thing when you look at a star: if the light source is moving toward you, it shifts toward blue; if it's moving away, it shifts toward red. Most stars shift toward red because the universe is expanding."

I cannot pretend that, as a boy, I liked everything about having a scientist for a mother. When I saw the likes of Mrs. Brady on TV, I sometimes wished I had what I thought of as a mom with an apron. And then, abruptly, I got one.   17

It was 1971 and my mother was working for NASA at Ames Research Center in California. She had just made an important discovery concerning the solar wind, which has two states, steady and transient. The latter consists of puffs of material, also known as coronal mass ejections, which, though long known about, were notoriously hard to find. My mother showed they could be recognized by the large amount of helium in the solar wind. Her career was flourishing. But the economy was in recession and NASA's budget was slashed. My mother was a housewife again. For months, as she looked for work, the severe depression that had haunted her years before began to return.   18

Mom had been taught to turn to the synagogue in times of trouble, and it seemed to make especially good sense in this case, because our synagogue had more scientists in it than most Ivy League universities. Our rabbi, a celebrated civil rights activist, was arranging networking parties for unemployed eggheads. But when my mother asked for an invitation to one of these affairs, he accused her of being selfish. "After all—there are *men* out of work just now."   19

"But Rabbi," she said, "it's my *life*."   20

I remember her coming home that night, stuffing food into the refrigerator, then pulling out the vacuum cleaner. She switched it on, pushed it back and forth across the floor a few times, then switched it off and burst into tears. In a moment, I was crying too and my mother was comforting me. We sat there a long time.   21

"I know you want me here," she told me. "But I can either be a   22
part-time mama or a full-time madwoman."

A few months later, Mom was hired as a research scientist at the   23
National Center for Atmospheric Research, and we moved to
Boulder, Colorado. From then on, she decided to "follow research
funding around the country, like Laplanders follow the reindeer
herds." She followed it to Washington, D.C., to work for the
National Science Foundation, then to the Boston College
Department of Physics, and finally, in 1985, to JPL, where she's been
ever since. Along the way, she unlocked some of the mysteries of the
aurora. Using data from Explorer 33, she showed that auroras occur
when the magnetic field of the solar wind interacts with the magnetic field of the Earth.

In 1974, she became an officer of her professional association, the   24
American Geophysical Union, and spearheaded a committee to ensure that women in her field would be treated fairly. She was named
one of JPL's elite senior scientists in 1999 and the following year was
awarded NASA's Exceptional Scientific Achievement Medal.

Soon she'll retire, except that retirement as my mother the sci-   25
entist envisions it means embarking on a new project: comparing recent changes in Earth's climate with historic ones. "It's a pretty
important subject when you consider that even a small change in the
solar output could conceivably turn Long Island into a skating
rink—just like it was some 10,000 years ago."

The first thing I did when I came home from Mrs. Weddle's class that day   26
in 1966 was to ask my mother what my father did. She told me that he was
a scientist, and that she was a scientist too. I asked what a scientist was, and
she handed me a spoon. "Drop it on the table," she said. I let it fall to the
floor. "Why did it fall?" she asked. "Why didn't it float up to the ceiling?"
It had never occurred to me that there was a "why" involved. "Because of
gravity," she said. "A spoon will always fall, a hot-air balloon will always
rise." I dropped the spoon again and again until she made me stop. I had no
idea what gravity was, but the idea of "Why?" kept rattling around in my
head. That's when I made the decision: the next day, in school, I wouldn't
just tell them what my father did. I'd tell them about my mother too.

MEANINGS AND VALUES

1.   What is the writer's attitude toward his mother? What is the overall
     tone of the essay, and how does it contribute to conveying the au-
     thor's view of his mother and her achievements? (See "Guide to

Terms": *Style/Tone.*) How would you summarize the purpose(s) of the essay? (Guide: *Purpose.*)

2. Which sentence acts as a thesis statement for the essay (Guide: *Thesis*)? Is the thesis statement fully supported by the examples and discussion in the body of the essay? If not, what parts of the essay raise doubts about the writer's conclusions as expressed in the thesis statement?

3. What do Paragraphs 8–10 have to say about the reasons people become scientists (or choose any lifetime activity)? How are these paragraphs related to Paragraphs 6–7? What contrasts are there between the events in Paragraphs 8–10 and those in 11?

EXPOSITORY TECHNIQUES

1. What contrasts are there between the events and ideas presented in italicized Paragraphs (Pars. 1–3, 6–7, 13, 16, and 26) and those presented in nonitalicized paragraphs? In what ways does this contrast in appearance support the overall purpose and thesis of the essay? (Guide: *Thesis, Purpose.*)

2. The italicized and nonitalicized sections of the essay differ somewhat in content. How does the author make use of one or more of the following techniques in Paragraphs 4, 8, and 14 to help readers understand how they are related to the preceding paragraphs: transition words, similarity in content or idea, or echoes of phrases or words? (Guide: *Transition, Coherence, Unity*).

3. How does the writer use comparison or contrast to organize the following paragraphs: 11, 12, 15, 18, and 19? Discuss the purpose and emotional effect, if any, of each set of comparisons or contrasts.

4. What techniques does the writer use to open and close the essay? (Guide: *Introductions, Closings*). How are the opening and closing of the essay related?

DICTION AND VOCABULARY

1. What words or phrases does the writer use in Paragraphs 5, 14, and 19 to emphasize the difficulties his mother faced in becoming a scientist and achieving her professional goals? (Guide: *Diction.*)

2. What contrast does the writer present between his mother's actions and her words in Paragraph 16? (Note: You may have to look up "buck-and-wing" in a dictionary.)

3. If you do not know the meaning of the following terms, look them up in a dictionary: geophysical (Par. 4); gauntlet (5); challah (6); enfant terrible, quantum electrodynamics, nanotechnology (8); edification, centrifugal (9); aurora borealis (10); voluble (15); buck-and-wing (16).

READ TO WRITE

1. **Collaborating:** The different kinds of behaviors we notice among people are often an inheritance from the behaviors we observed in

parents and friends while growing up or from important experiences in our lives. Working in a group, consider possible topics for an essay. Think about the attitudes you encountered when you were a child. Were they consistent or contradictory? Have you accepted them or modified them? Does preserving such an inheritance help build continuity and community or is it a way of holding up necessary progress?

2.   **Considering Audience:** Insights into the ways that gender roles differ or conflict often arise in conversation. Consider opening an essay of your own with part of a conversation (recollected or invented) that touches on ideas you wish to explain and explore.

3.   **Developing an Essay:** Change (or lack of change) in gender roles, in cultural tastes, or in social outlook generally occur over time, not all-at-once. Consider opening an essay of your own with an event from your childhood or school experience that provides a contrast with current attitudes or practices. Following Hirshberg's model, draw on the earlier event or events throughout your essay as a source of contrast.

(NOTE: Suggestions for topics requiring development by use of COMPARISON and CONTRAST follow.)

Writing Suggestions for Chapter 5

COMPARISON AND CONTRAST

Base your central theme on one of the following, and develop your composition primarily by use of comparison and/or contrast. Use examples liberally for clarity and concreteness, chosen always with your purpose and reader-audience in mind.

1. Two kinds of families
2. Two Internet search engines
3. The innate qualities needed for success in two different careers
4. Dog people versus cat people
5. Two musicians
6. Two radio personalities
7. Two methods of parental handling of teenage problems
8. Two family attitudes toward the practice of religion
9. Two "moods" of the same town at different times
10. The personalities (or atmospheres) of two cities or towns of similar size
11. Two politicians with different leadership styles
12. Careers versus jobs
13. Two different attitudes toward the same thing or activity: one "practical," the other romantic or aesthetic
14. The beliefs and practices of two religions or denominations concerning one aspect of religion
15. Two courses on the same subject: one in high school and one in college
16. The differing styles of two players of some sport or game
17. The hazards of frontier life and those of life today
18. Two companies with very different styles or business philosophies
19. Two recent movies or music videos
20. Two magazines focusing on similar subjects but directed at different audiences
21. The "rewards" of two different kinds of jobs

COLLABORATIVE EXERCISES

1. Choose a partner, and using topic number 19 above, write an essay comparing and contrasting two movies or music videos. Each member of the team should be responsible for researching one of the movies or videos.

2. Working with a partner, choose a topic on which you have differing perspectives and prepare an essay, each writing a section of the essay reflecting his or her own perspective. Combine the sections into a draft, then revise each other's section so that the essay reads as a smooth, consistent, and logical whole.

6

Using *Analogy* as an Expository Device

Analogy is a special form of comparison that you can use for a specific purpose to explain something abstract or difficult to understand by showing its similarity to something concrete or easy to understand. A much less commonly used technique than comparison (and contrast), analogy is, nonetheless, a highly efficient means of explaining some difficult concepts or of giving added force to the explanations.

When you use comparison as an explanatory strategy, you need to make sure both subjects belong to the same general class of things, and you assume that readers will be more or less equally interested in both subjects. This is not the case with analogy. In analogy, you and your readers are really concerned only with one of the subjects; the second serves just to help explain the first. The two subjects, which may have little in common, also do not belong to the same class of things. The few elements they do share, however, are what give analogy the power to explain—and even to speculate about how things *might* be.

Certainly, for example, the universe is nothing like raisin bread—or so any reasonable person would think. But an analogy between the two can help explain a very difficult concept, as the following paragraph illustrates.

> If distant galaxies are really receding from the earth, and if more distant galaxies are receding faster than nearby ones, a remarkable picture of the universe emerges. Imagine that the galaxies were raisins scattered through a rising lump of bread dough. As the dough expanded, the raisins would be carried farther and farther apart from each other. If

you were standing on one of the raisins, how would things look? You wouldn't feel any motion yourself, of course, just as you don't feel the effects of the earth's motion around the sun, but you would notice that your nearest neighbor was moving away from you. This motion would be due to the fact that the dough between you and your nearest neighbor would be expanding, pushing the two of you apart.

—James Trefil, *The Dark Side of the Universe*

WHY USE ANALOGY?

In an analogy, you compare two things that are similar in some specifics but otherwise unlike. You can use this strategy to explain a complex, abstract, or unusual subject in familiar and easy-to-understand terms. Or you can use it to speculate about possible interpretations and consequences. For example, to explain how an electromagnetic field transmits radio signals from a station's transmitter to the radio in a listener's home or car, the physicist Richard Feynman asked his readers to imagine two corks floating in a pool of water. If we jiggle one cork, he pointed out, the waves in the water transmit the influence of our action and the second cork begins to jiggle, too. Like the water, an electromagnetic field transmits energy from sender to receiver in the form of waves— electromagnetic waves—conveying radio signals, a television picture, a radar image, or even plain light.

Analogy is not limited to scientific subjects, however. You can use it to explain and support your conclusions about other kinds of topics as well. For instance, a music critic, trying to explain her conclusion that jazz has influenced and will continue to influence modern music of all kinds, compares the jazz tradition to a tune that plays in the back of your mind all day, affecting your mood, the rhythm of your walk, and your tone of voice. Jazz, she explains, is a presence in the minds of composers and performers that shapes their choice of harmonies and rhythms, influences the tone of their compositions and the choice of instruments, and makes "hipness" (a mixture of sophistication, intensity, and emotional distancing) an attitude to which many of them aspire.

CHOOSING A STRATEGY

For a writer, the choice between using a brief analogy or an extended analogy is a significant one. A brief analogy, a sentence or two in length, can serve as an illustration or explanation of a difficult point or concept. To explain the need for a wide selection of college courses and the need for balance in a course of study, you might draw an analogy to a cafeteria, which serves desserts as well as meat, vegetables, and potatoes, allowing for various combinations adding up to balanced, full-course meals. If you wanted to extend this analogy to explain issues of curriculum and course choice in depth, however, you might run into problems with logic and with the adequacy of the particular analogy as an explanatory tool. Which courses, for example, should be classified as "desserts," and would all teachers and students agree on the classification? Does the concept of a well-balanced meal offer an adequate framework for understanding the specific kinds of balance appropriate for course choices?

An extended analogy, if carefully chosen for its logic and the points of comparison it offers, can serve as a framework for detailed explanation. In addition, it can offer a way to gain a fresh perspective on a problem, a controversy, or a puzzling phenomenon. For example, we often unconsciously draw on what we learn about relationships through family life in order to develop relationships within social organizations. Thus although businesses and other organizations are certainly different from families in many ways, there are still enough similarities to make an analogy worthwhile. Such an analogy asks readers to adopt a creative, "as if" perspective: let us examine the conflicts within an organization *as if* they were arguments among various members of a family to see whether the conflicts might be resolved in ways similar to those that work successfully in families. An analogy like this can be extended logically and consistently to explore a relatively broad topic, and it provides reasons for considering seriously the conclusions or interpretations the writer offers.

Analogies can take many different forms, and this flexibility is one of their appeals for both writers and readers. When you use an extended analogy to structure an essay, however, consider adopting a point-by-point arrangement to avoid confusing readers with too many comparisons at once. This is the approach taken in the following plan for an essay.

> Tentative thesis: We can better understand corporations by viewing them as if they were large, extended families.
>> Point 1: Employee ranks are similar to family roles (CEOs, board members = grandparents; VPs = parents; and so on).
>> Point 2: Different parts of the company are similar to different parts of an extended family (main office = nuclear

family; branch offices = families of uncles, aunts, cousins, and so forth).

Point 3: Conflicts over resources within a company are similar to rivalry among cousins or struggles over a will.

Point 4: Struggles over advancement within a company is similar to sibling rivalry.

Point 5: Training programs aim to help employees work together for the good of the company while family therapy tries to help maintain healthy relationships that preserve the family.

Point 6, 7, 8. . . . (if necessary)

DEVELOPING ANALOGIES

Simply stating an analogy and the specific grounds of similarity is seldom enough to make it an effective strategy, especially in the case of an extended analogy. The analogy needs to be clear to readers and developed in enough detail so that it provides convincing explanations and support for the writer's conclusions.

For an analogy to be effective, readers need to be familiar enough with the easier subject so that it really helps explain the more difficult one. Or the easier subject must be one that readers can understand with minimal discussion. An explanation of the human circulatory system, including the heart and arteries, in terms of a pump forcing water through the pipes of a plumbing system would be easily apprehended by readers. The analogy could be carried further to liken the effect of cholesterol deposits on the inner walls of the arteries to that of mineral deposits that accumulate inside water pipes and eventually close them entirely.

It is not enough for you as a writer simply to state an analogy, leaving for readers the job of understanding its significance. You need to explain both the analogy itself and its implications so that readers view it in the same way you do. To say that the world is like an overcrowded lifeboat will mean little in itself. You need also to explain that the lifeboat is in danger of sinking unless the number of passengers is reduced or the craft gains extra flotation power. And then you need to point out the implications: the world is overpopulated, and we must either limit population growth or increase our ability to sustain and feed people—without destroying the environment and, in effect, sinking the boat in which we are traveling.

Student Essay

People often use sports analogies to explain relationships and events in their lives. Kevin Nomura heard such analogies when he was growing up, especially comparisons between life and baseball. His essay draws on baseball for an extended analogy, but he uses it for a surprising purpose: to show how the analogy *fails* to explain much about life. Nonetheless, his essay makes effective use of analogy as a pattern and develops each element of the comparison in interesting, effective, and humorous detail.

Life Isn't Like Baseball
by Kevin Nomura

My father loves baseball. So does my mom. My sister was a star softball player in high school, and she is the regular shortstop on her college team. When my father tried to sign me up for Little League, however, I let him know that I would rather be playing soccer or tennis. It was about this time that he started trying to convince me that "life is like baseball." I wasn't convinced the first time he told me and I'm still not. Let me explain why.

> Introduces the analogy

> Thesis statement

Striking Out. People who think life is like baseball often talk about "striking out," "staying ahead on the count," or "taking a big swing." When you are up to bat in baseball, you get a lot of chances—not just three strikes but also four balls and any number of fouled-off pitches. I have made some serious mistakes at work, at school, and in my love life, but while I have been lucky enough to get an occasional second chance, I have never gotten any more. When I have failed at something, I have never failed as completely, as obviously, and as publicly as a baseball player does striking out. I suppose that getting booed off the stage is like striking out, but when I sang off-tune in my high school's production of *Bye, Bye Birdie*, no one yelled at me or called me back to the dugout (woops, dressing room). Instead my parents told me they were proud of me no matter what, and the director told me ways to get through my part of the song fast.

> First element of the analogy

> Why the comparison is illogical

> An inaccurate example

<u>Hitting a Home Run.</u> People seldom strike out in real life, and they do not hit home runs either. When baseball fans talk about "hitting a home run" at work or in some other activity, they mean accomplishing something dramatic whose success and importance no one can deny. Who has a job that is big enough or important enough to allow for a home run? Can the manager of a McDonald's hit a home run? Can a clerk in a department store or a steelworker do it? Who has a job that allows for dramatic and significant achievement? Can a teacher create brilliant students overnight or an artist become famous for one drawing rather than a lifetime of careful, patient effort? I don't think so, or only so seldom that such an achievement is unrealistic for us mortals.

<u>Like a Spitball.</u> People who believe that life is like baseball often ignore those parts of the game that don't fit very well with everyday experience or that are not very pleasant. Is life like a spitball? Are successful people the ones who load things up with petroleum jelly or scuff them with emery boards, then lie when confronted with evidence—and boast about their deception afterwards? And if some do, should we pretend their actions are good sport and hold them up as examples for the kids? Should we praise people for "stealing" and put the biggest thieves in the record books? Should we treat every botched move—every balk—as a serious error and a public humiliation? Would you like it if a slight slip on your part automatically allowed your competitors to advance a base and maybe even bring home the winning run?

I realize that I probably haven't convinced any real baseball fans to stop seeing life in terms of their game. I also realize that people will go on talking about "taking a good cut" or "winding up too long before the pitch." My younger brother says he agrees with me, but then he thinks life is a slap shot.

Second element of the analogy

Questions pointing out why the analogy is faulty

Third element of the analogy

Questions and examples that highlight the usefulness of the analogy

Conclusion— maintains humorous tone of the essay

JANISSE RAY

JANISSE RAY was born in 1962 in the coastal plain of southern Georgia where she grew up and now lives on her farm. She received an M.F.A. in creative writing from the University of Montana. Her essays and poetry about nature and environment have appeared in newspapers and magazines, including *Florida Wildlife, Orion, Wild Earth, Hope, Tallahassee Democrat,* and *Georgia Wildlife*. A collection of her poetry, *Naming the Unseen,* won the 1996 Merriam-Frontier Award. Her book *Ecology of a Cracker Childhood* (1999) combines memories of growing up in rural southern Georgia with an ecological portrait and lament for the longleaf pine and wiregrass range that once covered much of the southeastern United States. The book won an American Book Award in 1999. In 2003, she published a memoir *Wild Card Quilt: Taking a Chance on Home.*

Built by Fire

In "Built by Fire," an essay from *Ecology of a Cracker Childhood,* Janisse Ray uses analogy to explain how longleaf pine forests came to depend on fire for their existence and growth. Her strategy is unusual but highly effective. Instead of providing a dry, detailed scientific explanation likely to interest and enlighten few readers, she presents the biological explanation in the form of a Native American creation story. Of course, Ray is not claiming that the biological process actually involved speaking characters like "lightning" and "pine," simply that the process is easier to grasp when treated *as if* it were a story. She extends this analogy (actually a metaphor because the two unlikes are worded as if they were the same thing) throughout the essay. Despite the "poetic" effect of the writing, however, her purpose is clearly expository.

A couple of million years ago a pine fell in love with a place that   1
belonged to lightning. Flying past, a pine seed saw the open, flat land and grew covetous. The land was veined with runs of water— some bold, some fine as a reed. Seeing it unoccupied, the pine imperiously took root and started to grow there, in the coastal plains of the southern United States, and every day praised its luck. The place was broadly beautiful with clean and plentiful water sources, the sun always within reach. In the afternoons and evenings, thunderstorms lumbered across the land, lashing out rods of lightning that emptied the goatskin clouds; in those times the pine lay low.

The lightning announced itself lightly to the pine one sum- 2
mer evening, "I reign over this land," it said. "You must leave
immediately."

"There was nothing here when I came," said the pine. 3

"I was here," said lightning. "I am always here. I am here more 4
than any other place in the world." The clouds nodded, knowing
that lightning spoke true.

In that short time, however, the pine had begun to love the 5
place and called out, "Please. You live in the sky. Let me have the
earth." The clouds glowered and began to thicken.

Lightning was extremely possessive and would not agree to 6
divide.

"Then do what you will," said the pine. For years they warred. 7
The lightning would fling as many as forty million bolts a year at
the tree, striking when it could, the pine dodging and ducking. A
single thunderstorm might raise thousands of bolts. Wind helped
the tree, and although it was struck a few times, the damage was
never serious.

After the tree had reached a fair age—old enough for govern- 8
ment work, as they say—on the hottest of summer afternoons lightning crept close, hidden by towering maroon thunderheads, and
aimed for the tree, sundering its bole crown to roots. When the lightning glanced the ground, such was its ferocity that it dug a trench
wide enough to bury a horse before its force subsided. Needles from
the pine had fallen about, like a woman's long brown hairs, and they
began to smoke and then to flame, and from them fire spread out-
ward, burning easy and slow.

In its dying, the pine sprang forth a mast of cones filled with seeds. 9
The wind played with the seeds and scattered them for miles. And because the mineral soil was laid bare by fire, they could germinate.

But lightning was not worried. Kindling the whole place didn't 10
take much effort. Once lightning struck, the fire might burn slowly
through the grasses for weeks, miles at a time, arrested only by rivers,
lakes, creeks, and ponds. So if the seeds began to grow, lightning
would burn them.

Over the decades the fury and constancy of lightning knew no 11
end—every few years it would burn the place again—and the
greenhorn pines learned to lay low, sometimes for five or six years,
drilling a taproot farther and farther into the moist earth, surviving
the fast-burning, low-intensity fires of lightning's wrath by huddling,
covering their terminal buds with a tuft of long needles. Sometimes
the buds steamed and crackled inside their bonnets.

Young trees that mimicked grass survived fire. That low, they   12
didn't look like trees.

The grass-trees began to learn that if they waited until the light-   13
ning went to sleep in the rainy springs and suddenly cast themselves upward, to the height of a yard or more in one season,
drawing nutrient reserves from their long, patient roots, and if they
hurriedly thickened the bark of their trunks, a lamination, then
when the fires came again they could withstand the heat and their
terminal bud would be out of flame's reach.

Only then would the trees dare to branch.   14

Lightning was nonplussed. No matter what it did, the trees   15
flourished and multiplied. Admiring the courage of the longleaf
pine, other trees, hardwoods—sweet gum and sumac and oak—
tried to settle. Always, not knowing the secret history of longleaf's
adaptation, they burned.

And then lightning realized the pine tree was plugging its nee-   16
dles with volatile resins and oils, rendering them highly flammable.
The tree, of course, only thought to make the fires burn rapidly so
danger would pass quickly. Flammability was important in driving
wildfire through the forest, in order to leave older trees unharmed.
The longleaf grew taller, spread farther.

The lightning saw volatility as an act of remuneration.   17

Longleaf and lightning began to depend on each other and other   18
plants—the ground cover grasses and forbs, or flowering herbs—
evolved to survive and welcome fire as well. Wiregrass, for instance,
would not reproduce sexually in lightning's absence. The animals
learned to expect fire and to adapt. They scrambled off or took cover:
down into tortoise burrows, up into tree crowns. During a fire, exotic
insects never otherwise seen would scurry from the plates of bark,
scooting up the tree. Snakes and tortoises would dash for their holes.

Longleaf became known as the pine that fire built.   19

MEANINGS AND VALUES

1.   Would it be accurate to say that this essay answers a question like, "If
     fire destroys forests, how can it be necessary to the building and sur-
     vival of longleaf pine forests?" Why, or why not?

2.   What evidence is there in the essay that its purpose is expository?
     (See "Guide to Terms": *Purpose.*) Are there any additional reasons,

other than evidence directly in the essay, that readers might use to decide that the purpose is expository? If so, what are they?

3. State in your own words the meaning of the title, "Built by Fire." Where in the essay does the writer address most directly the reasons that "Longleaf became known as the pine that fire built" (Par. 18)?

EXPOSITORY TECHNIQUES

1. To what extent is personification an important part of the analogy around which this essay is built? (Guide: *Figures of Speech.*) Explain its use in the essay.

2. Which paragraphs in the essay are devoted primarily or heavily to scientific explanation? Which are devoted primarily to advancing the story and presenting its characters?

3. Why do you think the author chose not to announce the analogy (or metaphor) that structures the essay directly to readers? Is the essay more or less effective because of the absence of such an announcement? Defend your answer with evidence from the essay. (Guide: *Evaluation.*)

DICTION AND VOCABULARY

1. Which paragraphs in the essay employ scientific terms and more or less objective description? Which are more subjective in approach and tone? (Guide: *Diction; Objective/Subjective; Style/Tone.*)

2. What level of vocabulary does Ray use for this essay? Is it appropriate for the subject? Would you classify the writing as formal or informal? Explain.

3. Identify the simile in Paragraph 7 and discuss its contribution to the explanation. (Guide: *Figures of Speech.*)

4. If you do not know the meaning of some of the following words, look them up in a dictionary: covetous (Par. 1); glowered (4); sundering, bole (7); germinate (8); terminal (10); lamination (12); resins (15); volatility (16).

READ TO WRITE

1. **Collaborating:** Ray uses a myth or story to explain a complicated phenomenon. Working in groups of three, list the natural, ecological, scientific, or technical subjects that you think could be explained through a story or myth. You need not list only subjects that might take up an entire essay; you might choose a few that could be explained in several paragraphs. Discuss your list with the other groups. Are there similarities in the things or events that you have chosen? What kinds of subjects seem to lend themselves to this kind of explanation? Each group member should then write a short analy-

sis explaining the kinds of subjects that are appropriate for extended analogies (and metaphors).

2. **Considering Audience:** What emotions does this essay evoke from the reader? What attitudes toward the natural world and preservation of species and habitat does the writer want to encourage through such emotional reactions? Are all readers likely to have similar reactions? Why, or why not? Which groups or individuals might respond in different ways, and how might they respond? Rewrite Ray's essay in your own language and style, but direct it at an audience unlikely (at least initially) to share her feelings about the extraordinary and valuable nature of the longleaf pine and wiregrass environment. Make any changes you consider necessary in content, structure, emphasis, and style, but retain the scientific information Ray presents.

3. **Developing an Essay:** Love for specific natural settings and the creatures who live in them often connects people who have otherwise very little in common. Write a short essay about the roles parks, wilderness experience programs, nature and environment tours, or educational programs can play in connecting people or in altering their values.

(NOTE: Suggestions for topics requiring development by use of ANALOGY are on pp. 248–249 at the end of this chapter.)

LAN SAMANTHA CHANG

LAN SAMANTHA CHANG is a novelist and director of Writer's Workshop at the University of Iowa. She was born (in 1965) in Appleton, Wisconsin, where she lived until she left to attend college at Yale University. She also studied at Harvard, the University of Iowa, and Stanford University. She has been a creative writing instructor at Harvard University and the Bread Loaf Writer's Conference and fiction editor for the *Harvard Review*. Her short fiction has appeared in a variety of publications, including *Atlantic Monthly* and *Ploughshares*. Her books of fiction are *Hunger: A Novella and Stories* (1998) and *Inheritance* (novel) (2004).

Like Robinson Crusoe

This essay first appeared in *Prime Times: Writers on Their Favorite TV Shows* (1994). In it, Lan Samantha Chang introduces a variety of related analogies, many built around the television show *Gilligan's Island*, to explain her family's experiences as immigrants from China and to explore her feelings and her search for a "place" in which she belongs.

Desolate, my mother said. It was her first impression of the town where she would live for more than forty years. She took one step onto a pavement sheathed in ice and raised her eyes to view the narrow layer of snow-rimmed cars and houses, the edge of human evidence against the stark white sky. No people could be seen; they had stayed in against the cold. Only my father was there to welcome her. He had come weeks before, to begin his job, and now he brought my mother and sisters into the house that he had rented. It was February 1964, and my family began its life in Appleton, Wisconsin. 1

I have lived in seven states, on both coasts and in between, but in some vivid recess of my mind, I still believe I am a child in Appleton, sitting at the kitchen table with my mother. It is a quiet winter day. My sisters are at school and my mother is cleaning, sorting, and chopping vegetables to make the Chinese meals my father cannot do without. The outsized Midwestern green peppers are transformed to neat, bite-sized pieces in her hands. As she works, my mother describes the places she has lived. She was born in Shanghai, but her family moved two dozen times while seeking safety from the Japanese invasion and the civil war that followed. So 2 she speaks about Chongqing, the wartime capital, sweltering in the summer heat, and she describes the constant threat of Japanese bombers. She recalls the perfect year in Hong Kong, surrounded by palm trees and the ocean's reassuring blue. Later, she lived in Shanghai on the eve of the Nationalist collapse, a time of galloping inflation, of avenues clogged with refugees on foot and bicycle and in automobiles, terrifying days light-softened in spring sun, her last glimpse of mainland China before the Communists moved into the city, driving her and my father and thousands of others to an island in the sea.

Chongqing, Shanghai. Beijing, where my father was born. These were only names to me, but they were vivid, living cities in my parents' recollections; they were the true and real world, the world left behind. My parents fled Shanghai expecting to return, but in the months after the Communist victory, the bamboo curtain tightened. Gunboats patrolled the waters. Travel ceased. Mail halted, save a trickle of letters through Hong Kong. My mother and father heard nothing from the people they had left, and the move to Appleton detached them from all family. I was born into a house of people living in exile, a tiny island of Chinese memories and customs, surrounded by vast shimmering fields of alfalfa, corn, and soybeans, by the fertile smell of dairy cows that drifted to our neighborhood on summer nights. The faraway cities, the friends my parents had known, were sealed in ice.

What does a family in exile watch on television? We had the same programs as our neighbors, but we watched them as outsiders, stealthily, seriously, spying on the culture that the TV characters revealed so easily, took for granted. We watched each joke, each gesture, and each turn of phrase. It was from television that my grandmother learned English. It was a television sitcom that inspired my American name. My parents named me after Samantha Stephens, the domestic witch who held the power to change her circumstances in a flash. My mother hoped that I would bring our family such a rapid transformation.

After school, my sisters and I were permitted to watch television until dinner. Our time slot ensured us a steady diet of sitcom reruns. I can remember a prolonged interest in *The Flintstones* and a brief dalliance with *The Brady Bunch*, but more than anything, we watched *Gilligan's Island*. Our repeated viewings of this show went on for years, from grade school through junior high and into high school. We would switch channels to catch another episode. The

3

4

5

show ran twice and sometimes three times daily. I must have watched more than three thousand episodes of *Gilligan's Island* before leaving home for college, an average of thirty viewings per episode. For years, I found this fact embarrassing and astounding. How was it possible that we could continue to find this old sitcom, once described by the *San Francisco Chronicle* as "a new low in the networks' estimate of public intelligence," so endlessly absorbing? Why is *Gilligan* the one television show whose episodes I still remember word for word?

Now, twenty years away from Appleton, our prolonged attachment to the castaways makes better sense. The brief sea trip, the storm of change, the spinning wheel of disorientation in space and time, were elements of our own story. The seven members of my family—my maternal grandmother, my parents, my sisters, and myself—lived surrounded by "native" Americans, their speech slow, their hair blond, their customs alien. Our isolation was broken only by an occasional visit from my uncles, or a friend of the family traveling to Chicago, guest stars stopping at our way station for a home-cooked meal and an evening of reminiscence. When these visitors arrived, I saw my parents' past lives bloom before them— my father's witty Mandarin puns, the unusual snacks hand-carried from some distant Chinatown grocer—but inevitably, the visitor would leave, and we would be left alone to continue and make do.

Our cultural alienation varied according to our generation. My grandmother's homesickness was perhaps the most acute. Her age rendered her more nostalgic, less adaptive. Unlike my parents, who could look forward to a future as Americans, she had only her past in a country now closed off to her. Having reached the age when she found herself naturally turning to the past, she was obliged to reach through a geographical as well as temporal remove. The focus of her nostalgia settled on certain missing foods. Like poor Gilligan, who squandered two of his three magic wishes on ice cream, my grandmother lay awake thinking about the dishes she had once eaten and loved: the tiny seafood dumplings in Shanghai; savory chicken wrapped in lotus leaves, a specialty of Hangzhou; the flavor of a certain pepper grown only in Sichuan. These lost dishes took on the poignancy and power of her lost youth.

My parents, plunged into a new setting in midlife, spent their time and energy adapting to the change. They settled in the new country, but knew the value of the old. Each day they ventured out to work and make our family's future; at the same time, they upheld

6

7

8

the values of the past. They tried to make the foods my grandmother missed. They found a butcher willing to sell us the unpopular cuts she liked. They were able to re-create, with some effort, the paper-thin spring roll wrappers. Certain staples were acutely missed and difficult to make. My mother still recalls their struggles to make tofu. They drove out into the country and rang the doorbell of a soybean farmer, from whom they bought two bushels of beans (I remember the empty baskets in the garage). The traditional method required grinding, but my parents had no grinder, so they used an electric mixer to beat the soybeans into milk. They worked away at it for hours, burning up one mixer's motor in the process. My father, a chemist, devised a way to curdle soybean milk with salt. They wrapped the curds into cheesecloth and pressed it in the refrigerator. The final product was, my grandmother said, "good." Having nothing to compare it with, I was reluctant to agree.

Born in Appleton, I was doubly ignorant: I knew nothing of China, but I knew little of America outside our home. I grew up into the space between two ignorances. My confusion was profound. It never occurred to me that I found *Gilligan* soothing because its characters' lives were similar to my American life. After all, I was a native Appletonian. But I was first of all a resident of my family's island, a living museum, a repository for mixed-up cultural adaptations. I can remember watching an episode featuring the Professor's hand-cranked phonograph, then turning off the television and going outside to fly kites using a Chinese-style kite-flying reel that my father had constructed from an old telephone dial and the parts of fishing rods. I would watch the castaways serve pancake syrup made from tropical trees and then I'd sit down to a real dinner made of Southern-style "salt chicken" my parents had cured on the back porch. My grandmother, who often caught the episodes while watching over a pot of brewing ginseng roots, praised the Professor's efforts to treat Gilligan's eyes by concocting a keptibora berry extract. She said, "Sometimes homemade medicine can work better than those foreign doctors." 9

I was intrigued and troubled by the way that *Gilligan* preserved the shadow of my parents' war. The original series, which ran from 1964 to 1967, presented a time in which the memories of World War II's Pacific battles were not long past. In one episode, the castaways stumbled upon a hidden munitions pit. Another episode guest-starred Vito Scotti as a deranged Japanese soldier who had survived on the Pacific islands for twenty years without knowing 10 the war had ended. This particular episode left me uneasy. I felt uncomfortable with the comical portrayal of the Asian accent, his mannerisms, and his bottle-top glasses. But I felt even more disturbed by the idea of the poor, deluded man, insisting on his own version of the war, unaware that the world had gone on without him.

Of course, time does not stand still. We were caught in its flow, through the Cold War, through feminism and Watergate. My family adapted. My mother studied American customs as carefully as she had once memorized the history of the dynasties. She kept a box of file cards listing what Americans liked to eat (large cuts of meat, sweet and sour dishes) and what they did not like (rice gruel, tofu, fish with eyes and shrimp with the shells on). She earned a second degree and became a piano teacher. My father became a Packers fan. He set up a woodworking room in the basement and made our furniture. He built standing lamps bearing the characters for longevity. He built walnut end tables with the characters for "big good luck," finished and sealed under glass.   11

We grew into an accomplished, noisy family with a strong sense of identity and rich blood, squeezed into a house that was too small for us. My older sisters remember us as happy, striving. But when I think of my childhood, I remember a certain sadness in the house. It stole in on the long blue shadows of our winter evenings. It was folded into the embroidered coverlets my mother kept beneath her bed. Once, while we were cleaning, my mother showed me the basement storage bin where she and my father had stacked the dusty suitcases they had brought from overseas. There, carefully wrapped in an old sheet, my father kept the long, blue silk jacket his mother had made for him when he was a young man. His mother had been left behind; he had not heard from his parents since leaving the country in 1949. This separation lay at the heart of our sadness. We were one of many families who shape this country of transplanted people, holding the long, unspoken sorrow of those cut off from what they have known.   12

I believe we each lived on our own island. My father enveloped himself in privacy, remembering the people he had left; my mother regretted the lost dreams of her own youth. They were not entirely unhappy; it was not so simple. They were each of them a separate being, isolated, exiled by their separate losses. I was an exile as well—not a political or geographical exile, like my parents, but a child holding on to the secret, mutinous loneliness of one who is about to leave. My island was Appleton. I did not belong in town,   13 and there was not enough room for me to continue in our family's makeshift world. I knew that I was meant to leave our home. In a few years, I would pack my own suitcase and leave to see the world. I would come back to visit, never to stay.

But at the time, my stay in Appleton felt interminable. Each day,   14
I would trudge home from junior high school, where I was justifiably despised for being arrogant, a "brain," awkward, and friendless. I would be in an indignant, lonely frame of mind. The drifts of snow, which seemed to fall so thickly in those days, piled high around the house, glowed violet in the deepening dusk. Inside, when I took off my coat, I could feel the cold pressing through the windows. My sisters and I would sit in the room adjacent to the kitchen and watch television with all the lights turned on. Every day, the castaways attempted a new plan to escape. They all desired to leave, the insufferable Mr. Howell and the impossible Mary Ann. I watched carefully and seldom laughed. I found the castaways' frustration unsurprising. In every episode, they tried to leave the island, and every time, their plans were foiled. No one was getting anywhere.

And then the world changed. I remember the Chinese Ping-   15
Pong players on television. After this time of tentative outreaches, of Ping-Pong diplomacy, my oldest sister graduated and went out into the world, like a milkweed seed traveling on the wind in search of a fertile place. In September 1978, Mao died. We heard it on the evening news. My parents grew very quiet when his death was announced. I asked, "Who is Mao?" Soon afterward, my second sister left home for college. My father wrote to the mainland government for information about the whereabouts of his family. He learned their addresses and made contact with his sisters—his parents and brother had died—and in 1982 he made the long trip back through time and across the world to see them again. In 1983, I left Wisconsin to attend Thurston Howell's rival school and I stopped watching television for many years.

The world is so open now. There is an Asian grocery less than   16
two miles from my parents' house; even the supermarkets carry tofu made with local beans. In downtown Appleton, a crowded restaurant serves authentic Chinese dishes. My parents go to Lunar New Year parties with a local Chinese club. Nor need we content ourselves with China brought to us; now we can fly there ourselves. My sister and I traveled to Beijing to meet my father's sisters. We brought back for my father his own kite-flying rod and a brightly painted silk kite shaped like a butterfly with twirling eyes. He liked

the gift, although he did not use it. He has grown less sorrowful and less nostalgic, having rediscovered some old friends and reconnected with them safely, as adults. He has found a way off his island.

I have now lived away from Appleton for half my life. I moved   17
to Connecticut, then Massachusetts, Iowa, California, New Jersey. In my travels I have not found a home. It occurs to me now, once more in Massachusetts, that I have been entirely conditioned by my childhood in the Midwest, my desires shaped to a non-specified place-longing. No sooner do I settle in one town than I begin to daydream about somewhere else. But I know there is no perfect place. It is clear that I belong not to a place but to my far-flung family, my tightly knit and fractious group of former exiles.

On a recent visit to Wisconsin, while I was sitting with my   18
mother, an episode of *Gilligan's Island* came on. My mother and I were cutting up the vegetables for dinner. We sat in our old places, with the winter light at the window just as it had been when I was a child.

The castaways were still ensnared, still waiting to be saved. In   19
one episode, Mr. Howell lost $3 million to Gilligan, betting over a makeshift putting green. I discovered I could still remember the lines. But now I understood one of the jokes for the first time. "I'm having trouble adjusting to this oyster shell putter," Mr. Howell said. Lovey replied, "Why, of course, it's because there's no *r* in the month." Watching a typical exchange between Gilligan and the Skipper in their skimpy bamboo hut, I enjoyed the Skipper's exaggerated mugging, the good-natured, slapstick humor. Why hadn't I seen this, in all those years?

I asked my mother whether she thought *Gilligan* was funny.   20
Through all those years she'd caught the show from a distance, too busy, or unwilling, to sit with us for hours.

She laid down her paring knife. She was not watching the TV   21
but looking through her spectacles at some memory I couldn't see. "Yes," she said.

"Why is it funny to you?"   22

"The show is funny because the characters were in an absurd   23
situation," she replied. "They were unable to change with their environment."

"What is the difference between something funny and some-   24
thing sad?"

She did not answer. For a moment I felt that I had been trans-   25
ported to those years when my parents did not know if they would

ever be allowed to see the mainland. How many times did my parents dream that they were in China and wake up back in the Midwest, precisely where they had been? Where did they dream of being now? Finally, my mother smiled. She replied, "Some might say that problems are only sad if they don't work out. Sad times can only become funny when they're seen from far away."

MEANINGS AND VALUES

1. What roles did television play in the life of the author's family, and what effects did it have on the family as a whole or specific members of the family? (See especially Paragraphs 4 and 5.)

2. What is the "island in the sea" (Par. 2)? Why might the author have chosen to call it an "island" rather than referring to it by its (well-known) name? In what ways is the "island in the sea" linked to other islands mentioned in the essay: "a tiny island of Chinese memories and customs" (Par. 3); "each . . . our own island" (Par. 13); "Appleton" (Par. 13); and *Gilligan's Island*?

3. What answer(s) does the essay offer to this question: "Why is *Gilligan* the one television show whose episodes I still remember word for word?" (Par. 5).

4. Explain what Paragraph 23 seems to say about an important difference between the author's family and the characters in *Gilligan's Island*.

EXPOSITORY TECHNIQUES

1. What role in the organization of the essay does the rhetorical question at the end of Paragraph 5 play? (See "Guide to Terms": *Rhetorical Questions*.)

2. Where in the essay does the author first introduce and explain the main analogy she explores in the essay? Explain why you think she did not choose to introduce the analogy at the very beginning of the essay? What other analogies does the author offer in the essay (including the title)? How are they related (or unrelated) to the main analogy?

3. Identify the similarities in organization and emphasis shared by these Paragraphs: 7, 9, and 14. (Guide: *Emphasis*.) Explain what you think the author is trying to accomplish through the organization of these paragraphs.

DICTION AND VOCABULARY

1.   Identify the words the author uses in Paragraph 1 to describe the town in ways that justify her mother's use of the word *"Desolate."*

2.   To what kind of scene is the word "shimmering" often applied in a common (or clichéd) phrase? (Guide: *Clichés*.) What specific analogy does use of the word in Paragraph 3 introduce or reinforce? Do you consider this use of the word effective or ineffective? Why? (Guide: *Evaluation*.)

3.   If you do not know the meaning of some of the following words, consult a dictionary: stealthily (Par. 4); dalliance (5); disorientation, reminiscence (6); savory, poignancy (7); staples, curdle (8); cured (9); munitions (10); dynasties, characters (11); mutinous (13); interminable, indignant (14); fractious (17); mugging (19).

READ TO WRITE

1.   **Collaborating:** Break into groups of four. Discuss family relationships and experiences similar to those Chang describes that you and your classmates have had. Plan an essay using representative experiences from each member of the group. Be sure to choose the experiences carefully so that the analogy that develops from each can be connected through transitions to develop a coherent essay.

2.   **Considering Audience:** Much of this essay focuses on immigrant experience and the perspectives and history of members of a particular cultural, ethnic group. As a consequence, the writer spends some time explaining experiences and outlooks with which readers may be unfamiliar. Prepare an essay similar in style and use of analogy to Chang's that draws on sources of experiences and feelings that readers are more likely to share: youth sports, vacation travel, high school, or popular music, for example.

3.   **Developing an Essay:** As the basis for the main analogy in her essay, Chang uses episodes in a television show that come to embody ideas, values, feelings, and experiences. Use a similar source of analogies for an essay of your own that explores and explains your own experiences or ones you share with your readers.

(NOTE: Suggestions for topics requiring development by use of ANALOGY are on pp. 248–249 at the end of this chapter.)

Issues and Ideas

Humans and Animals

- Tom Wolfe, *O Rotten Gotham—Sliding Down into the Behavioral Sink*
- Barbara Kingsolver, *High Tide in Tuscon*

Like most people, you have probably spent considerable time and effort trying to understand how people behave and how they maintain (or fail to maintain) relationships with each other. One way to do this is through careful observation of social interaction. Yet the complexity of human behavior often makes it difficult to isolate the patterns that can explain our relationships or predict our actions.

For this reason, scientists and other students of human behavior often look for explanatory patterns in studies of plants, animals, or natural processes. Historians sometimes discuss a civilization in terms of its germination, growth, flowering, and decay, for example. A sociologist may use a concept like "entropy" (from physics) to explain a society's decline into chaos, and an anthropologist may turn to biology and natural history to explain our reluctance to abandon settings that once held meaning for us.

To borrow such explanatory patterns is to make use of analogy: explaining complex behaviors by those behaviors that seem simpler and easier to understand (though they may, in truth, be just as difficult and complicated). The risk in borrowing explanatory patterns is that they may oversimplify relationships (bees can represent hardworking groups, but bee societies are certainly less complex than human ones) or that they may be mostly inappropriate (we can talk of a friendship "blossoming" while we know that it has few other similarities to plants or plant life).

In reading the discussions of human behavior in Tom Wolfe's "O Rotten Gotham" and Barbara Kingsolver's "High Tide in Tucson," therefore, pay attention to how the writers use analogy as an effective expository strategy, and also to the ways they use it as a tool for understanding. Bear in mind that an explanation that is rhetorically successful may still take unfounded logical leaps or leave important questions unanswered.

TOM WOLFE

Tom Wolfe was born in 1931 and grew up in Richmond, Virginia, graduated from Washington and Lee University, and took his doctorate at Yale. After working for several years as a reporter for the *Washington Post,* he joined the staff of the *New York Herald Tribune* in 1962. He has won two Washington Newspaper Guild Awards, one for humor and the other for foreign news. Wolfe has been a regular contributor to *New York, Esquire,* and other magazines. His books include *The Kandy-Kolored Tangerine-Flake Streamline Baby* (1965), *The Electric Kool-Aid Acid Test* (1968), *The Pump House Gang* (1968), *Radical Chic and Mau-Mauing the Flak Catchers* (1970), *The New Journalism* (1973), *The Painted Word* (1975), *The Right Stuff* (1977), *In Our Time* (1980), *Underneath the I-Beams: Inside the Compound* (1981), *From Bauhaus to Our House* (1981), *The Purple Decades: A Reader* (1984), *The Bonfire of the Vanities* (1986), *A Man in Full* (1999), *Hooking Up* (2000), and *I Am Charlotte Simmons* (2004).

O Rotten Gotham—Sliding Down into the Behavioral Sink

"O Rotten Gotham—Sliding Down into the Behavioral Sink," as used here, is excerpted from a longer selection by that title in Wolfe's book *The Pump House Gang* (1968). Here, as he frequently does, the author investigates an important aspect of modern life— seriously, but in his characteristic and seemingly freewheeling style. It is a style that is sometimes ridiculed by scholars but is far more often admired. (Wolfe, as the serious student will discover, is always in complete control of his materials and methods, using them to create certain effects to reinforce his ideas.) In this piece, his analogy is particularly noteworthy for the extensive usage he is able to get from it.

I just spent two days with Edward T. Hall, an anthropologist, watching thousands of my fellow New Yorkers short-circuiting themselves into hot little twitching death balls with jolts of their own adrenalin. Dr. Hall says it is overcrowding that does it. Overcrowding gets the adrenalin going, and the adrenalin gets them hyped up. And here they are, hyped up, turning bilious, nephritic, a queer, autistic, sadistic, barren, batty, sloppy, hot-in-the-pants, chancred-on-the-flankers, leering, puling, numb—the usual in New York, in other words, and God knows what else. Dr. Hall has the theory that overcrowding has already thrown New York into a state of behavioral sink. Behavioral sink is a term from ethology, which is the study of how animals relate to their environment. Among animals, the sink winds up with a "population collapse" or "massive die-off." O Rotten Gotham.

It got to be easy to look at New Yorkers as animals, especially   2
looking down from some place like a balcony at Grand Central at the rush hour Friday afternoon. The floor was filled with the poor white humans, running around, dodging, blinking their eyes, making a sound like a pen full of starlings or rats or something.

"Listen to them skid," says Dr. Hall.   3

He was right. The poor old etiolate animals were out there skid-   4
ding on their rubber soles. You could hear it once he pointed it out. They stop short to keep from hitting somebody or because they are disoriented and they suddenly stop and look around, and they skid on their rubber-soled shoes, and a screech goes up. They pour out onto the floor down the escalators from the Pan-Am Building, from 42nd Street, from Lexington Avenue, up out of subways, down into subways, railroad trains, up into helicopters—

"You can also hear the helicopters all the way down here,"   5
says Dr. Hall. The sound of the helicopters using the roof of the Pan-Am Building nearly fifty stories up beats right through. "If it weren't for this ceiling"—he is referring to the very high ceiling in Grand Central—"this place would be unbearable with this kind of crowding. And yet they'll probably never 'waste' space like this again."

They screech! And the adrenal glands in all those poor white   6
animals enlarge, micrometer by micrometer, to the size of cantaloupes. Dr. Hall pulls a Minox camera out of a holster he has on his belt and starts shooting away at the human scurry. The Sink!

Dr. Hall has the Minox up to his eye—he is a slender man, calm,   7
52 years old, young-looking, an anthropologist who has worked with Navajos, Hopis, Spanish-Americans, Negroes, Trukese. He was the most important anthropologist in the government during the crucial years of the foreign aid program, the 1950s. He directed both the Point Four training program and the Human Relations Area Files. He wrote *The Silent Language* and *The Hidden Dimension,* two books that are picking up the kind of "underground" following his friend Marshall McLuhan started picking up about five years ago. He teaches at the Illinois Institute of Technology, lives with his wife, Mildred, in a high-ceilinged town house on one of the last great residential streets in downtown Chicago, Astor Street; he has a grown son and daughter,

loves good food, good wine, the relaxed, civilized life—but comes to New York with a Minox at his eye to record!—perfect—The Sink.

We really got down in there by walking down into the 8 Lexington Avenue line subway stop under Grand Central. We inhaled those nice big fluffy fumes of human sweat, urine, effluvia, and sebaceous secretions. One old female human was already stroked out on the upper level, on a stretcher, with two policemen standing by. The other humans barely looked at her. They rushed into line. They bellied each other, haunch to paunch, down the stairs. Human heads shone through the gratings. The species North European tried to create bubbles of space around themselves, about a foot and a half in diameter—

"See, he's reacting against the line," says Dr. Hall. 9

—but the species Mediterranean presses on in. The hell with 10 bubbles of space. The species North European resents that, this male human behind him presses forward toward the booth . . . breathing on him, he's disgusted, he pulls out of the line entirely, the species Mediterranean resents him for resenting it, and neither of them realizes what the hell they are getting irritable about exactly. And in all of them the old adrenals grow another micrometer.

Dr. Hall whips out the Minox. Too perfect! The bottom of The 11 Sink.

It is the sheer overcrowding, such as occurs in the business 12 sections of Manhattan five days a week and in Harlem, Bedford-Stuyvesant, southeast Bronx every day—sheer overcrowding is converting New Yorkers into animals in a sink pen. Dr. Hall's argument runs as follows: all animals, including birds, seem to have a built-in inherited requirement to have a certain amount of territory, space, to lead their lives in. Even if they have all the food they need, and there are no predatory animals threatening them, they cannot tolerate crowding beyond a certain point. No more than two hundred wild Norway rats can survive on a quarter acre of ground, for example, even when they are given all the food they can eat. They just die off.

But why? To find out, ethologists have run experiments on all 13 sorts of animals, from stickleback crabs to Sika deer. In one major experiment, an ethologist named John Calhoun put some domesticated white Norway rats in a pen with four sections to it, connected by ramps. Calhoun knew from previous experiments that the rats tend to split up into groups of ten to twelve and that the pen, therefore, would hold forty to forty-eight rats comfortably, assuming they formed four equal groups. He allowed them to reproduce until there were eighty rats, balanced between male and female, but did not let it get any more crowded. He kept them supplied with plenty of food, water, and nesting materials. In other words, all their more obvious needs were taken care of. A less obvious need—space— was not. To the human eye, the pen did not even look especially crowded. But to the rats, it was crowded beyond endurance.

The entire colony was soon plunged into a profound behavioral   14 sink. "The sink," said Calhoun, "is the outcome of any behavioral process that collects animals together in unusually great numbers. The unhealthy connotations of the term are not accidental: a behavioral sink does act to aggravate all forms of pathology that can be found within a group."

For a start, long before the rat population reached eighty, a sta-   15 tus hierarchy had developed in the pen. Two dominant male rats took over the two end sections, acquired harems of eight to ten females each, and forced the rest of the rats into the two middle pens. All the overcrowding took place in the middle pens. That was where the "sink" hit. The aristocrat rats at the end grew bigger, sleeker, healthier, and more secure the whole time.

In The Sink, meanwhile, nest building, courting, sex behavior,   16 reproduction, social organization, health—all of it went to pieces. Normally, Norway rats have a mating ritual in which the male chases the female, the female ducks down into a burrow and sticks her head up to watch the male. He performs a little dance outside the burrow, then she comes out, and he mounts her, usually for a few seconds. When The Sink set in, however, no more than three males—the dominant males in the middle sections—kept up the old customs. The rest tried everything from satyrism to homosexuality or else gave up on sex altogether. Some of the subordinate males spent all their time chasing females. Three or four might chase one female at the same time, and instead of stopping at the burrow entrance for the ritual, they would charge right in. Once mounted, they would hold on for minutes instead of the usual seconds.

Homosexuality rose sharply. So did bisexuality. Some males   17 would mount anything—males, females, babies, senescent rats, anything. Still other males dropped sexual activity altogether, wouldn't fight and, in fact, would hardly move except when the other rats slept. Occasionally, a female from the aristocrat rats' harems would come over the ramps and into the middle sections to sample life in The Sink. When she had had enough, she would run back up the ramp. Sink males would give chase up to the top of the ramp, which is to say, to the very edge of the aristocratic preserve. But one glance from one of the king rats would stop them cold and they would return to The Sink.

The slumming females from the harems had their adventures 18 and then returned to a placid, healthy life. Females in The Sink, however, were ravaged, physically and psychologically. Pregnant rats had trouble continuing pregnancy. The rate of miscarriages increased significantly, and females started dying from tumors and other disorders of the mammary glands, sex organs, uterus, ovaries, and Fallopian tubes. Typically, their kidneys, livers, and adrenals were also enlarged or diseased or showed other signs associated with stress.

Child-rearing became totally disorganized. The females lost the 19 interest or the stamina to build nests and did not keep them up if they did build them. In the general filth and confusion, they would not put themselves out to save offspring they were momentarily separated from. Frantic, even sadistic competition among the males was going on all around them and rendering their lives chaotic. The males began unprovoked and senseless assaults upon one another, often in the form of tail-biting. Ordinarily, rats will suppress this kind of behavior when it crops up. In The Sink, male rats gave up all policing and just looked out for themselves. The "pecking order" among males in The Sink was never stable. Normally, male rats set up a three-class structure. Under the pressure of over-crowding, however, they broke up into all sorts of unstable sub-classes, cliques, packs—and constantly pushed, probed, explored, tested one another's power. Anyone was fair game, except for the aristocrats in the end pens.

Calhoun kept the population down to eighty, so that the next 20 stage, "population collapse" or "massive die-off," did not occur. But the autopsies showed that the pattern—as in the diseases among the female rats—was already there.

The classic study of die-off was John J. Christian's study of Sika 21 deer on James Island in the Chesapeake Bay, west of Cambridge, Maryland. Four or five of the deer had been released on the island, which was 280 acres and uninhabited, in 1916. By 1955 they had bred freely into a herd of 280 to 300. The population density was only about one deer per acre at this point, but Christian knew that this was already too high for the Sikas' inborn space requirements, and something would give before long. For two years the number of deer remained 280 to 300. But suddenly, in 1958, over half the deer died; 161 carcasses were recovered. In 1959 more deer died and the population steadied at about 80.

In two years, two-thirds of the herd had died. Why? It was not starvation. In fact, all the deer collected were in excellent condition, with well-developed muscles, shining coats, and fat deposits between the muscles. In practically all the deer, however, the adrenal glands had enlarged by 50 percent. Christian concluded that the die-off was due to "shock following severe metabolic disturbance, probably as a result of prolonged adrenocortical hyperactivity. . . . There was no evidence of infection, starvation, or other obvious cause to explain the mass mortality." In other words, the constant stress of overpopulation, plus the normal stress of the cold of the winter, had kept the adrenalin flowing so constantly in the deer that their systems were depleted of blood sugar and they died of shock. 22

Well, the white humans are still skidding and darting across the floor of Grand Central. Dr. Hall listens a moment longer to the skidding and the darting noises, and then says, "You know, I've been on commuter trains here after everyone has been through one of these rushes, and I'll tell you, there is enough acid flowing in the stomachs in every car to dissolve the rails underneath." 23

Just a little invisible acid bath for the linings to round off the day. The ulcers the acids cause, of course, are the one disease people have already been taught to associate with the stress of city life. But overcrowding, as Dr. Hall sees it, raises a lot more hell with the body than just ulcers. In everyday life in New York—just the usual, getting to work, working in massively congested areas like 42nd Street between Fifth Avenue and Lexington, especially now that the Pan-Am Building is set in there, working in cubicles such as those in the editorial offices at Time-Life, Inc., which Dr. Hall cites as typical of New York's poor handling of space, working in cubicles with low ceilings and, often, no access to a window, while construction crews all over Manhattan drive everybody up the Masonite wall with air-pressure generators with noises up to the boil-a-brain decibel level, than rushing to get home, piling into subways and trains, fighting for time and for space, the usual day in New York—the whole now-normal thing keeps shooting jolts of adrenalin into the body, breaking down the body's defenses and winding up with the work-a-daddy human animal stroked out at the breakfast table with his head apoplexed like a cauliflower out of his $6.95 semi-spread Pima-cotton shirt, and nosed over into a plate of No-Kolresto egg 24 substitute, signing off with the black thrombosis, cancer, kidney, liver, or stomach failure, and the adrenals ooze to a halt, the size of eggplants in July.

One of the people whose work Dr. Hall is interested in on this   25
score is Rene Dubos at the Rockefeller Institute. Dubos's work indicates that specific organisms, such as the tuberculosis bacillus or a pneumonia virus, can seldom be considered "the cause" of a disease. The germ or virus, apparently, has to work in combination with other things that have already broken the body down in some way—such as the old adrenal hyperactivity. Dr. Hall would like to see some autopsy studies made to record the size of adrenal glands in New York, especially of people crowded into slums and people who go through the full rush-hour-work-rush-hour cycle every day. He is afraid that until there is some clinical, statistical data on how overcrowding actually ravages the human body, no one will be willing to do anything about it. Even in so obvious a thing as air pollution, the pattern is familiar. Until people can actually see the smoke or smell the sulphur or feel the sting in their eyes, politicians will not get excited about it, even though it is well known that many of the lethal substances polluting the air are invisible and odorless. For one thing, most politicians are like the aristocrat rats. They are insulated from The Sink by practically sultanic buffers—limousines, chauffeurs, secretaries, aides-de-camp, doormen, shuttered houses, high-floor apartments. They almost never ride subways, fight rush hours, much less live in the slums or work in the Pan-Am Building.

MEANINGS AND VALUES

1. Who are members of the "species Mediterranean"? The "species North European"? What could account for their differences in space requirements (Pars. 8–10)?

2. Is this writing primarily objective or subjective? (See "Guide to Terms": *Objective/Subjective*.) Why?

3. Do you get the impression that the author is being unkind, "making fun" of the harried New Yorkers? How, if at all, does he prevent such an impression?

EXPOSITORY TECHNIQUES

1. Is this analogy a success, or does the author work it too hard? Be prepared to defend your answer. (Guide: *Evaluation*.)

2. What are the benefits of the frequent return to what Dr. Hall is doing or saying (e.g., in Pars. 3, 5, 7, 9, 11, and 23)?

3. Paragraph 12 has a useful function beyond the simple information it provides—a sort of organic relation to the coming development. Explain how this is accomplished.

4. The preceding two questions highlight the ways Wolfe deals with problems of transition in this essay. (Guide: *Transition*.) How are such issues also matters of coherence? (Guide: *Coherence*.)

5. Analyze stylistic differences, with resulting effects, between the following sections of the essay (Guide: *Style/Tone*):

   a. The description of chaos at Grand Central and the information about Dr. Hall in Paragraph 7

   b. The Grand Central scene and the account of the laboratory experiment with rats in Paragraphs 8–20

   c. The Grand Central scene and the final paragraph

6. What is gained or lost by the unusual length and design of the last sentence of Paragraph 24? (We can be sure that it did not "just happen" to Wolfe—and equally sure that a sentence of such length would be disastrous in most writing.) (Guide: *Syntax*.)

Diction and Vocabulary

1. What is the significance of the word "Gotham"?

2. Why do you think the author refers to "my fellow New Yorkers" in the first sentence? What would have been the effect had he not taken such a step?

3. Why does he consistently, after Paragraph 2, refer to the people as "poor white humans," "poor human animals," etc.?

4. In Paragraph 14 he refers to the connotations of the word "sink." What are its possible connotations? (Guide: *Connotation/Denotation*.)

5. Cite examples of verbal irony to be found in Paragraphs 5, 8, and 24.

6. Consult your dictionary as needed for full understanding of the following words: autistic, puling (Par.1); etiolate (4); effluvia, sebaceous (8); pathology (14); satyrism (16); senescent (17); decibel, thrombosis (24); lethal (25).

Read to Write

1. **Collaborating:** One especially effective technique Wolfe employs in this essay is observation—specifically the overall view afforded by a balcony high above the main hall of Grand Central Station. With a team of three other people, choose a location that will provide you with a broad overview of human actions and behavior. Go to that spot with notebooks in hand and individually, without discussion,

write your observations. Return to the classroom and compare your notes. What similarities in behavior did you all observe? What different activities and images stood out in your minds? Write a short analysis of your collective observations. Be sure to include an explanation of the behaviors noticeable to all of you and reasons why other behaviors stood out to individual observers.

2. **Considering Audience:** Would this essay have a strong effect on readers raised in a rural area? What aspects of this essay might help someone from a farming environment relate to this? What other behaviors could be addressed to make this more accessible to audiences from rural areas? Choose a particular animal behavior that could be analogous to human activity in rural locations and create a plan for an essay based on the analogy.

3. **Developing an Essay:** Popular magazines can provide good summaries of contemporary research as can specialized encyclopedias and general interest books. Choose a theory or some research you think is insightful and use it to help explain common behaviors, perhaps some that you have observed in the manner described in the "collaborating" question. Prepare an essay built around two or more explanatory theories as Wolfe does in his essay.

(NOTE: Suggestions for topics requiring development by use of ANALOGY are on pp. 248–249 at the end of this chapter.)

BARBARA KINGSOLVER

BARBARA KINGSOLVER was born in 1955 in Annapolis, Maryland, and raised in eastern Kentucky. She studied biology at DePauw University (B.A., 1977) and the University of Arizona (M.S., 1981) and worked as a scientist and scientific writer before beginning her career as a writer of fiction and essays. Her highly acclaimed books include *The Bean Trees* (1988), *Animal Dreams* (1990), and *Pigs in Heaven* (1993) (novels); *Homeland and Other Stories* (1989) (stories); *Another America* (1992) (poetry); *High Tide in Tucson: Essays from Now or Never* (1996) (essays); *The Poisonwood Bible* (1998) (novel); *Prodigal Summer* (2000) (novel); and *Small Wonder* (2002) (essays).

High Tide in Tucson

This essay, from Kingsolver's book with the same title, is built around a surprising and imaginative analogy. It offers a different and more optimistic perspective on modern society and behavior than Tom Wolfe does in the preceding essay ("O Rotten Gotham"), yet, like Wolfe, the author draws heavily on scientific research for her explanations.

A hermit crab lives in my house. Here in the desert he's hiding out from local animal ordinances, at minimum, and maybe even the international laws of native-species transport. For sure, he's an outlaw against nature. So be it.

He arrived as a stowaway two Octobers ago. I had spent a week in the Bahamas, and while I was there, wishing my daughter could see those sparkling blue bays and sandy covers, I did exactly what she would have done: I collected shells. Spiky murexes, smooth purple moon shells, ancient-looking whelks sand-blasted by the tide—I tucked them in the pockets of my shirt and shorts until my lumpy, suspect hemlines gave me away, like a refugee smuggling the family fortune. When it was time to go home, I rinsed my loot in the sink and packed it carefully into a plastic carton, then nested it deep in my suitcase for the journey to Arizona.

I got home in the middle of the night, but couldn't wait till morning to show my hand. I set the carton on the coffee table for my daughter to open. In the dark living room her face glowed, in the way of antique stories about children and treasure. With perfect delicacy she laid the shells out on the table, counting, sorting, designating scientific categories like yellow-striped pinky, Barnacle Bill's pocketbook. . . . Yeek! She let loose a sudden yelp, dropped her booty, and ran to the far end of the room. The largest, knottiest whelk had begun to move around. First it extended one long red talon of a leg, tap-tap-tapping like a blind man's cane. Then came half a dozen more red legs, plus a pair of eyes on stalks, and a purple claw that snapped open and shut in a way that could not mean We come in Friendship.

Who could blame this creature? It had fallen asleep to the sound   4
of the Caribbean tide and awakened on a coffee table in Tucson, Arizona, where the nearest standing water source of any real account was the municipal sewage-treatment plant.

With red stiletto legs splayed in all directions, it lunged and   5
jerked its huge shell this way and that, reminding me of the scene I make whenever I'm moved to rearrange the living-room sofa by myself. Then, while we watched in stunned reverence, the strange beast found its bearings and began to reveal a determined, crabby grace. It felt its way to the edge of the table and eased itself over, not falling bang to the floor but hanging suspended underneath within the long grasp of its ice-tong legs, lifting any two or three at a time while many others still held in place. In this remarkable fashion it scrambled around the underside of the table's rim, swift and sure and fearless like a rock climber's dream.

If you ask me, when something extraordinary shows up in your   6
life in the middle of the night, you give it a name and make it the best home you can.

The business of naming involved a grasp of hermit-crab gender   7
that was way out of our league. But our household had a deficit of males, so my daughter and I chose Buster, for balance. We gave him a terrarium with clean gravel and a small cactus plant dug out of the yard and a big cockleshell full of tap water. All this seemed to suit him fine. To my astonishment our local pet store carried a product called Vitaminized Hermit Crab Cakes. Tempting enough (till you read the ingredients) but we passed, since our household leans more toward the recycling ethic. We give him leftovers. Buster's rapture is the day I drag the unidentifiable things in cottage cheese containers out of the back of the fridge.

We've also learned to give him a continually changing assort-   8
ment of seashells, which he tries on and casts off like Cinderella's stepsisters preening for the ball. He'll sometimes try to squeeze into ludicrous outfits too small to contain him (who can't relate?). In

other moods, he will disappear into a conch the size of my two fists and sit for a day, immobilized by the weight of upward mobility. He is in every way the perfect housemate: quiet, entertaining, and willing to eat up the trash. He went to school for first-grade show-and-tell, and was such a hit the principal called up to congratulate me (I think) for being a broad-minded mother.

It was a long time, though, before we began to understand the   9 content of Buster's character. He required more patient observation than we were in the habit of giving to a small, cold-blooded life. As months went by, we would periodically notice with great disappointment that Buster seemed to be dead. Or not entirely dead, but ill, or maybe suffering the crab equivalent of the blues. He would burrow into a gravelly corner, shrink deep into his shell, and not move, for days and days. We'd take him out to play, dunk him in water, offer him a new frock—nothing. He wanted to be still.

Life being what it is, we'd eventually quit prodding our sick   10 friend to cheer up, and would move on to the next stage of a difficult friendship: neglect. We'd ignore him wholesale, only to realize at some point later on that he'd lapsed into hyperactivity. We'd find him ceaselessly patrolling the four corners of his world, turning over rocks, rooting out and dragging around truly disgusting pork-chop bones, digging up his cactus and replanting it on its head. At night when the household fell silent I would lie in bed listening to his methodical pebbly racket from the opposite end of the house. Buster was manic-depressive.

I wondered if he might be responding to the moon. I'm partial   11 to lunar cycles, ever since I learned as a teenager that human females in their natural state—which is to say, sleeping outdoors—arrive at menses in synchrony and ovulate with the full moon. My imagination remains captive to that primordial village: the comradely grumpiness of new-moon days, when the entire world at once would go on PMS alert. And the compensation that would turn up two weeks later on a wild wind, under that great round headlamp, driving both men and women to distraction with the overt prospect of conception. The surface of the land literally rises and falls—as much as fifty centimeters!—as the moon passes over, and we clay-footed mortals fall like dominoes before the swell. It's no surprise at all if a full moon inspires lyricists to corny love songs, or inmates to slamming themselves against barred windows. A hermit crab hardly seems this impetuous, but animals are notoriously responsive to the full moon: wolves howl; roosters announce daybreak all night. Luna moths, Arctic loons, and lunatics have a sole inspiration in common. Buster's insomniac restlessness seemed likely to be a part of the worldwide full-moon fellowship.

But it wasn't, exactly. The full moon didn't shine on either end   12
of his cycle, the high or the low. We tried to keep track, but it soon became clear: Buster marched to his own drum. The cyclic force that moved him remained as mysterious to us as his true gender and the workings of his crustacean soul.

Buster's aquarium occupies a spot on our kitchen counter right   13
next to the coffeepot, and so it became my habit to begin mornings with chin in hands, pondering the oceanic mysteries while awaiting percolation. Finally, I remembered something. Years ago when I was a graduate student of animal behavior, I passed my days reading about the likes of animals' internal clocks. Temperature, photoperiod, the rise and fall of hormones—all these influences have been teased apart like so many threads from the rope that pulls every creature to its regulated destiny. But one story takes the cake. F. A. Brown, a researcher who is more or less the grandfather of the biological clock, set about in 1954 to track the cycles of intertidal oysters. He scooped his subjects from the clammy coast of Connecticut and moved them into the basement of a laboratory in landlocked Illinois. For the first fifteen days in their new aquariums, the oysters kept right up with their normal intertidal behavior: they spent time shut away in their shells, and time with their mouths wide open, siphoning their briny bath for the plankton that sustained them, as the tides ebbed and flowed on the distant Connecticut shore. In the next two weeks, they made a mystifying shift. They still carried out their cycles in unison, and were regular as the tides, but their high-tide behavior didn't coincide with high tide in Connecticut, or for that matter California, or any other tidal charts known to science. It dawned on the researchers after some calculations that the oysters were responding to high tide in Chicago. Never mind that the gentle mollusks lived in glass boxes in the basement of a steel-and-cement building. Nor that Chicago has no ocean. In the circumstances, the oysters were doing their best.

When Buster is running around for all he's worth, I can only pre-   14
sume it's high tide in Tucson. With or without evidence, I'm romantic enough to believe it. This is the lesson of Buster, the poetry that camps outside the halls of science: Jump for joy, hallelujah. Even a desert has tides.

When I was twenty-two, I donned the shell of a tiny yellow   15
Renault and drove with all I owned from Kentucky to Tucson. I was

a typical young American, striking out. I had no earthly notion that I was bringing on myself a calamity of the magnitude of the one that befell poor Buster. I am the commonest kind of North American refugee: I believe I like it here, far-flung from my original home. I've come to love the desert that bristles and breathes and sleeps outside my windows. In the course of seventeen years I've embedded myself in a family here—neighbors, colleagues, friends I can't foresee living without, and a child who is native to this ground, with loves of her own. I'm here for good, it seems.

And yet I never cease to long in my bones for what I left behind.　16 I open my eyes on every new day expecting that a creek will run through my backyard under broad-leafed maples, and that my mother will be whistling in the kitchen. Behind the howl of coyotes, I'm listening for meadowlarks, I sometimes ache to be rocked in the bosom of the blood relations and busybodies of my childhood. Particularly in my years as a mother without a mate, I have deeply missed the safety net of extended family.

In a city of half a million I still really look at every face, anticipat-　17 ing recognition, because I grew up in a town where every face meant something to me. I have trouble remembering to lock the doors. Wariness of strangers I learned the hard way. When I was new to the city, I let a man into my house one hot afternoon because he seemed in dire need of a drink of water; when I turned from the kitchen sink I found sharpened steel shoved against my belly. And so I know, I know. But I cultivate suspicion with as much difficulty as I force tomatoes to grow in the drought-stricken hardpan of my strange backyard. No creek runs here, but I'm still listening to secret tides, living as if I belonged to an earlier place: not Kentucky, necessarily, but a welcoming earth and a human family. A forest. A species.

In my life I've had frightening losses and unfathomable gifts: A　18 knife in my stomach. The death of an unborn child. Sunrise in a rain forest. A stupendous column of blue butterflies rising from a Greek monastery. A car that spontaneously caught fire while I was driving it. The end of a marriage, followed by a year in which I could barely understand how to keep living. The discovery, just weeks ago when I rose from my desk and walked into the kitchen, of three strangers industriously relieving my house of its contents.

I persuaded the strangers to put down the things they were hold-　19 ing (what a bizarre tableau of anti-Magi they made, these three unwise men, bearing a camera, an electric guitar, and a Singer sewing machine), and to leave my home, pronto. My daughter asked excitedly when she got home from school, "Mom, did you say bad words?" (I told her this was the very occasion that bad words exist for.) The police said, variously, that I was lucky, foolhardy, and "a brave lady." But it's not good luck to be invaded, and neither foolish nor brave to stand your ground. It's only the way life goes, and I did it, just as years ago I fought off the knife; mourned the lost child; bore witness to the rain forest; claimed the blue butterflies as Holy Spirit in my private pantheon; got out of the burning car; survived the divorce by putting one foot in front of the other and taking good care of my child. On most important occasions, I cannot think how to respond, I simply do. What does it mean, anyway, to be an animal in human clothing? We carry around these big brains of ours like the crown jewels, but mostly I find that millions of years of evolution have prepared me for one thing only: to follow internal rhythms. To walk upright, to protect my loved ones, to cooperate with my family group—however broadly I care to define it—to do whatever will help us thrive. Obviously, some habits that saw us through the millennia are proving hazardous in a modern context: for example, the yen to consume carbohydrates and fat whenever they cross our path, or the proclivity for unchecked reproduction. But it's surely worth forgiving ourselves these tendencies a little, in light of the fact that they are what got us here. Like Buster, we are creatures of inexplicable cravings. Thinking isn't everything. The way I stock my refrigerator would amuse a level-headed interplanetary observer, who would see I'm responding not to real necessity but to the dread of famine honed in the African savannah. I can laugh at my Rhodesian Ridgeback as she furtively sniffs the houseplants for a place to bury bones, and circles to beat down the grass before lying on my kitchen floor. But she and I are exactly the same kind of hairpin.

We humans have to grant the presence of some past adaptations, 20 even in their unforgivable extremes, if only to admit they are permanent rocks in the steam we're obliged to navigate. It's easy to speculate and hard to prove, ever, that genes control our behaviors. Yet we are persistently, excruciatingly adept at many things that seem no more useful to modern life than the tracking of tides in a desert. At recognizing insider/outsider status, for example, starting with white vs. black and grading straight into distinctions so fine as to baffle the bystander—Serb and Bosnian, Hutu and Tutsi, Crip and Blood. We hold that children learn discrimination from their parents, but they learn it fiercely and well, world without end. Recite it by rote like a multiplication table. Take it to heart, though it's neither helpful nor appropriate, anymore than it is to hire the taller of two men applying for a position as bank clerk, though statistically we're likely to do that too. Deference to the physical superlative, a preference for the scent of our own clan: a thousand anachronisms dance down the strands of our DNA from a hidebound tribal past, guiding us toward the glories of survival, and some vainglories as well. If we resent being bound by these ropes, the best hope is to seize them out like snakes, by the throat, look them in the eye and own up to their venom.

But we rarely do, silly egghead of a species that we are. We in-   21
vent the most outlandish intellectual grounds to justify discrimina-
tion. We tap our toes to chaste love songs about the silvery moon without recognizing them as hymns to copulation. We can dress up our drives, put them in three-piece suits or ballet slippers, but still they drive us. The wonder of it is that our culture attaches almost unequivocal shame to our animal nature, believing brute urges must be hurtful, violent things. But it's no less an animal instinct that leads us to marry (species that benefit from monogamy tend to prac-tice it); to organize a neighborhood cleanup campaign (rare and doomed is the creature that fouls its nest); to improvise and enforce morality (many primates socialize their young to be cooperative and ostracize adults who won't share food).

It's starting to look as if the most shameful tradition of Western   22
civilization is our need to deny we are animals. In just a few cen-turies of setting ourselves apart as landlords of the Garden of Eden, exempt from the natural order and entitled to hold dominion, we have managed to behave like so-called animals anyway, and on top of it to wreck most of what took three billion years to assemble. Air, water, earth, and fire—so much of our own element so vastly conta-minated, we endanger our own future. Apparently we never owned the place after all. Like every other animal, we're locked into our niche: the mercury in the ocean, the pesticides on the soybean fields, all comes home to our breastfed babies. In the silent spring we are learning it's easier to escape from a chain gang than a food chain. Possibly we will have the sense to begin a new century by renewing our membership in the Animal Kingdom.

Not long ago I went backpacking in the Eagle Tail Mountains.   23
This range is a trackless wilderness in western Arizona that most people would call Godforsaken, taking for granted God's preference for loamy topsoil and regular precipitation. Whoever created the Eagle Tails had dry heat on the agenda, and a thing for volcanic rock. Also cactus, twisted mesquites, and five-alarm sunsets. The hiker's program in a desert like this is dire and blunt: carry in enough water to keep you alive till you can find a water source: then fill your bottles and head for the next one, or straight back out.

Experts warn adventurers in this region, without irony, to drink their water while they're still alive, as it won't help later.

Several canyons looked promising for springs on our topo-   24
graphical map, but turned up dry. Finally, at the top of a narrow, overgrown gorge we found a blessed tinaja, a deep, shaded hollow in the rock about the size of four or five claw-foot tubs, holding water. After we drank our fill, my friends struck out again, but I opted to stay and spend the day in the hospitable place that had slaked our thirst. On either side of the natural water tank, two shallow caves in the canyon wall faced each other, only a few dozen steps apart. By crossing from one to the other at noon, a person could spend the whole day here in shady comfort—or in colder weather, follow the winter sun. Anticipating a morning of reading, I pulled *Angle of Repose* out of my pack and looked for a place to settle on the flat, dusty floor of the west-facing shelter. Instead, my eyes were startled by a smooth corn-grinding stone. It sat in the exact center of its rock bowl, as if the Hohokam woman or man who used this mortar and pestle had walked off and left them there an hour ago. The Hohokam disappeared from the earth in A.D. 1450. It was inconceivable to me that no one had been here since then, but that may have been the case—that is the point of trackless wilderness. I picked up the grinding stone. The size and weight and smooth, balanced perfection of it in my hand filled me at once with a longing to possess it. In its time, this excellent stone was the most treasured thing in a life, a family, maybe the whole neighborhood. To whom it still belonged. I replaced it in the rock depression, which also felt smooth to my touch. Because my eyes now understood how to look at it, the ground under my feet came alive with worked flint chips and pottery shards. I walked across to the other cave and found its floor just as lively with historic debris. Hidden under brittlebush and catclaw I found another grinding stone, this one some distance from the depression in the cave floor that once answered its pressure daily, for the grinding of corn or mesquite beans.

For a whole day I marveled at this place, running my fingers   25
over the knife edges of dark flint chips, trying to fit together thick red pieces of shattered clay jars, biting my lower lip like a child concentrating on a puzzle. I tried to guess the size of whole pots from the curve of the broken pieces: some seemed as small as my two cupped hands, and some maybe as big as a bucket. The sun scorched my neck, reminding me to follow the shade across to the other shelter. Bees hummed at the edge of the water hole, nosing up to the water, their abdomens pulsing like tiny hydraulic pumps; by late

afternoon they rimmed the pool completely, a collar of busy lace. Off and on, the lazy hand of a hot breeze shuffled the white leaves of the brittlebush. Once I looked up to see a screaming pair of red-tailed hawks mating in midair, and once a clatter of hooves warned me to hold still. A bighorn ram emerged through the brush, his head bent low under his hefty cornice, and ambled by me with nothing on his mind so much as a cool drink.

How long can a pestle stone lie still in the center of its mortar?   26 That long ago—that recently—people lived here. Here, exactly, and not one valley over, or two, or twelve, because this place had all a person needs: shelter, food, and permanent water. They organized their lives around a catchment basin in a granite boulder, conforming their desires to the earth's charities; they never expected the opposite. The stories I grew up with lauded Moses for striking the rock and bringing forth the bubbling stream. But the stories of the Hohokam—oh, how they must have praised that good rock.

At dusk my friends returned with wonderful tales of the   27 ground they had covered. We camped for the night, refilled our canteens, and hiked back to the land of plumbing and a fair guarantee of longevity. But I treasure my memory of the day I lingered near water and covered no ground. I can't think of a day in my life in which I've had such a clear fix on what it means to be human.

Want is a thing that unfurls unbidden like fungus, opening   28 large upon itself, stopless, filling the sky. But *needs*, from one day to the next, are few enough to fit in a bucket, with room enough left to rattle like brittlebush in a dry wind.

For each of us—furred, feathered, or skinned alive—the whole   29 earth balances on the single precarious point of our own survival. In the best of times, I hold in mind the need to care for things beyond the self: poetry, humanity, grace. In other times, when it seems difficult merely to survive and be happy about it, the condition of my thought tastes as simple as this: let me be a good animal today. I've spent months at a stretch, even years, with that taste in my mouth, and have found that it serves.

But it seems a wide gulf to cross, from the raw, green passion   30 for survival to the dispassionate, considered state of human grace. How does the animal mind construct a poetry for the modern artifice in which we now reside? Often I feel as disoriented as poor Buster, unprepared for the life that zooms headlong past my line of sight. This clutter of human paraphernalia and counterfeit necessities—what does it have to do with the genuine business of life on earth? It feels strange to me to be living in a box, hiding from the steadying influence of the moon; wearing the hide of a cow, which is supposed to be dyed to match God-knows-what, on my feet; making promises over the telephone about things I will do at a precise hour next *year*. (I always feel the urge to add, as my grandmother does, "Lord willing and the creeks don't rise!") I find it impossible to think, with a straight face, about what colors ought not to be worn after Labor Day. I can become hysterical over the fact that someone, somewhere, invented a thing called the mushroom scrubber, and that many other people undoubtedly feel they *need* to possess one. It's completely usual for me to get up in the morning, take a look around, and laugh out loud.

Strangest of all, I am carrying on with all of this in a desert, two thousand miles from my verdant childhood home. I am disembodied. No one here remembers how I was before I grew to my present height. I'm called upon to reinvent my own childhood time and again; in the process, I wonder how I can ever know the truth about who I am. If someone had told me what I was headed for in that little Renault—that I was stowing away in a shell, bound to wake up to an alien life on a persistently foreign shore—I surely would not have done it. But no one warned me. My culture, as I understand it, values independence above all things—in part to ensure a mobile labor force, grease for the machine of a capitalist economy. Our fairy tale commands: Little Pig, go out and seek your fortune! So I did. 31

Many years ago I read that the Tohono O'odham, who dwell in the deserts near here, traditionally bury the umbilicus of a newborn son or daughter somewhere close to home and plant a tree over it, to hold the child in place. In a sentimental frame of mind, I did the same when my own baby's cord fell off. I'm staring at the tree right now, as I write—a lovely thing grown huge outside my window, home to woodpeckers, its boughs overarching the house, as dissimilar from the sapling I planted seven years ago as my present life is from the tidy future I'd mapped out for us all when my baby was born. She will roam light-years from the base of that tree. I have no doubt of it. I can only hope she's growing as the tree is, absorbing strength and rhythms and a trust in the seasons, so she will always be able to listen for home. 32

I feel remorse about Buster's monumental relocation; it's a weighty responsibility to have thrown someone else's life into permanent chaos. But as for my own, I can't be sorry I made the trip. Most of what I learned in the old place seems to suffice for the new: if the seasons like Chicago tides come at ridiculous times and I have 33 to plant in September instead of May, and if I have to make up family from scratch, what matters is that I do have sisters and tomato plants, the essential things. Like Buster, I'm inclined to see the material backdrop of my life as mostly immaterial, compared with what moves inside of me. I hold on to my adopted shore, chanting private vows: wherever I am, let me never forget to distinguish *want* from *need*. Let me be a good animal today. Let me dance in the waves of my private tide, the habits of survival and love.

Every one of us is called upon, probably many times, to start a   34
new life. A frightening diagnosis, a marriage, a move, loss of a job or a limb or a loved one, a graduation, bringing a new baby home: it's impossible to think at first how this all will be possible. Eventually, what moves it all forward is the subterranean ebb and flow of being alive among the living.

In my own worst seasons I've come back from the colorless   35
world of despair by forcing myself to look hard, for a long time, at a single glorious thing: a flame of red geranium outside my bedroom window. And then another: my daughter in a yellow dress. And another: the perfect outline of a full, dark sphere behind the crescent moon. Until I learned to be in love with my life again. Like a stroke victim retraining new parts of the brain to grasp lost skills, I have taught myself joy, over and over again.

It's not such a wide gulf to cross, then, from survival to poetry.   36
We hold fast to the old passions of endurance that buckle and creak beneath us, dovetailed, tight as a good wooden boat to carry us onward. And onward full tilt we go, pitched and wrecked and absurdly resolute, driven in spite of everything to make good on a new shore. To be hopeful, to embrace one possibility after another—that is surely the basic instinct. Baser even than hate, the thing with teeth, which can be stilled with a tone of voice or stunned by beauty. If the whole world of the living has to turn on the single point of remaining alive, that pointed endurance is the poetry of hope. The thing with feathers.

What a stroke of luck. What a singular brute feat of outrageous   37
fortune: to be born to citizenship in the Animal Kingdom. We love and we lose, go back to the start and do it right over again. For every heavy forebrain solemnly cataloging the facts of a harsh landscape, there's a rush of intuition behind it crying out: High tide! Time to move out into the glorious debris. Time to take this life for what it is.

MEANINGS AND VALUES

1. In Paragraph 22, Kingsolver says, "It's starting to look as if the most shameful tradition of Western civilization is our need to deny we are animals." In what ways, according to the essay, are we like other animals?

2. What are the superficial ways Buster resembles humans (see Pars. 5, 8, 9, and 10)? What are the important (even profound) similarities (see Pars. 11, 12, 15, 19, 30, and 33)?

3. Paragraphs 15–19 of this essay are devoted to some of the disruptions and problems created by contemporary ways of living. What answers or responses to these problems does the writer offer in Paragraph 19? How do the problems and the responses help unify the essay? (See "Guide to Terms": *Unity.*)

EXPOSITORY TECHNIQUES

1. At what point in the essay does Kingsolver first make an analogy between the hermit crab and herself?

2. For what purposes does the author raise, and then dismiss, the comparison of hermit crab behaviors and those of humans and other animals in terms of their correspondence to cycles of the moon? (In answering this question, consider both the scientific reasons and those related to the purpose and design of her essay.)

3. The writer divides this essay into four parts (Pars. 1–14, 15–22, 23–28, and 29–37). Explain the content and purpose of each part, and tell why you think she chose to put them in this particular order. (Guide: *Purpose.*)

4. Discuss how the contrast between "wants" and "needs" at the end of Paragraph 28 serves as a transition to the next paragraph and those that follow. (Guide: *Transition.*)

5. Discuss how the question "What does it mean, anyway, to be an animal in human clothing?" (Par. 19) acts as a transition both within the paragraph and within the essay as a whole. (Guide: *Transition.*) Can the passage be considered a rhetorical question? Why? (Guide: *Rhetorical Questions.*)

6. Kingsolver introduces some briefer analogies in Paragraphs 32 and 36. What are they? Do they undermine or add to the effectiveness of the larger analogy around which the essay is constructed? In what ways? (Guide: *Evaluation.*)

DICTION AND VOCABULARY

1. Discuss how the repetition of the word "tide" and related words helps to unify this essay. (Guide: *Unity.*)

2. In many places, Kingsolver mixes styles and kinds of vocabulary (diction) in imaginative ways. Examine Paragraph 11 and note the instances in which she has chosen scientific terms and phrases rather than familiar, less formal wording. What seems to be the reason for her word choices? Do the same for instances of notably informal language. (Guide: *Diction; Colloquial Expressions.*) What effect does the mixed diction in the paragraph have on its overall style and tone? (Guide: *Style/Tone.*) How does the mixture serve, or fail to serve, the author's purposes?

3. If you do not know the meaning of any of the following words, look them up in a dictionary: murexes, whelks, (Par. 2); deficit, terrarium, cockleshell (7); preening, ludicrous (8); hyperactivity (10); menses, synchrony, ovulate, lyricists, impetuous (11); crustacean (12); siphoning, briny, ebbed (13); tableau, pantheon, yen, proclivity, furtively (19); deference, anachronisms, vainglories (20); copulation, ostracize (21); topographical (24); lauded (26); longevity (27); dispassionate (30); verdant (31); umbilicus (32).

READ TO WRITE

1. **Collaborating:** As mentioned in question 3 of Expository Techniques, Kingsolver divides this essay into four parts (Pars. 1–14, 15–22, 23–28, and 29–37). In a group, have each member individually focus on the analogies presented in one of these sections and critique the effectiveness of them. Compare your critiques. Do you all have similar responses to the quality of the analogies as well as the writing overall? Why or why not? Individually, write a short essay answering this question.

2. **Considering Audience:** The theme of this essay is easy to perceive for a reader who has had major life changes. Kingsolver shares her life shifts openly and relates them directly to Buster's environmental changes. Yet this piece is also effective for people who have experienced little changes in their lives. Why? Point to specific paragraphs to explain your response.

3. **Developing an Essay:** Comparing your behavior to that of a pet, as Kingsolver does, can have several advantages for you as a writer. You probably observed a pet's behavior in detail over a long period of time more carefully than you observed the activities of any other animal. You have seen the pet react to the same or similar situations that you have encountered. Follow Kingsolver's lead and prepare an essay on human and animal behavior based on your experiences with a pet.

(NOTE: Suggestions for topics requiring development by use of ANALOGY follow.)

Writing Suggestions for Chapter 6

ANALOGY

In any normal situation, the analogy is chosen to help explain a theme-idea that already exists—such as those in the first group below. But for classroom training, which is bound to be somewhat artificial, it is permissible to work from the other direction, to develop a theme that fits a preselected analogy-symbol.

1. State a central theme about one of the following general topics or a suitable one of your own, and develop it into a composition by use of an analogy of your own choosing.

   a. A well-organized school system

   b. Starting a new business or other enterprise

   c. The long-range value of programs for underprivileged children

   d. Learning a new skill

   e. The need for cooperation between management and labor

   f. Today's intense competition for success

   g. Dealing with stress

   h. The results of ignorance

2. Select an analogy-symbol from the list below and fashion a theme that it can illustrate. Develop your composition as instructed.

   a. A freeway at commuting time

   b. Building a road through a wilderness

   c. Building a bridge across a river

   d. A merry-go-round

   e. A wedding or a divorce

   f. A car wash

   g. Flood destruction of a levee

   h. The tending of a young orchard

   i. An animal predator stalking prey

   j. A baseball game

   k. A juggling act

   l. An oasis

   m. A duel

   n. An airport

COLLABORATIVE ACTIVITIES

1. Working with a partner, choose a topic from a–h in Exercise 1 on page 248, and decide on an appropriate analogy. One member of the pair should outline the points that need to be made about the theme. The other member should outline comparative (analogous) details. Combine the two outlines, and write a well-developed essay from the combined plan.

2. In groups of three or more, come up with an appropriate analogy for the theme of "adapting to college life in the freshman year." Members should brainstorm to determine the best point of analogy. Once you determine that as a group, each member should provide one point of expansion that fits the analogy, and group members should then write essays of their own drawing on material developed by the group and adding their own ideas and examples.

7

Explaining Through
Process Analysis

Process analysis focuses on *how* something happens. As an expository pattern, it appears most frequently in *instructions* that tell us how to do something or in *explanations* that explain how something is or was done. Instructions can range from the simple and everyday to the complex and challenging: from the directions for using a new appliance or piece of electronic equipment to a detailed plan showing how to make the United Nations more effective. Effective instructions do more than simply list the steps to be taken. They generally provide detailed justification for individual steps or for the plan as a whole, and they take into account readers' background knowledge and abilities.

Explanations, on the other hand, might explain the stages of a wide variety of operations or actions, of mental or evolutionary process—how stress affects judgment and health, how volcanoes cause earthquakes and mudslides, or how digital telephones work. Effective explanations take into account the things readers want or need to know about, but they can also appeal to curiosity and imagination. You can speculate how space exploration might work or how societies might be better organized.

The following process analysis by L. Rust Hills shows how process analysis can be used in imaginative ways to talk about everyday matters. It takes the form of a set of directions, and though it is short, it is a whole essay in miniature. The second example is an explanation that helps readers understand some of the reasons hurricanes can be so dangerous.

What to Do About Soap Ends

This is admittedly not a problem qualitative on the order of what to do about the proliferation of nuclear weaponry, but quantitatively it disturbs a great deal of Mankind—all those millions, in fact, who've ever used a bar of soap—except, of course, me. I've solved the problem of what to do about those troublesome, wasteful, messy little soap ends, and I'm ready now to deliver my solution to a grateful world.

The solution depends on a fact not commonly known, which I discovered in the shower. Archimedes made his great discovery about displacement ("Eureka!" and all that) in the bathtub, but I made mine in the shower. It is not commonly known that if, when you soap yourself, you hold *the same side* of the bar of soap cupped in the palm of your hand, that side will, after a few days, become curved and rounded, while the side of the bar you're soaping yourself *with* will become flat. (In between showers or baths, leave the bar curved side down so it won't stick to whatever it's resting on.) When the bar diminishes sufficiently, the flat side can be pressed onto a new bar of soap and will adhere sufficiently overnight to become, with the next day's use, a just slightly oversized new bar, ready to be treated in the same way as the one that came before it, in perpetuity, one bar after another, down through the length of your days on earth, with never a nasty soap end to trouble you ever again. Eureka, and now on to those nuclear weapons. Man is at his best, I feel, when in his problem-solving mode.

—L. Rust Hills

It's not the wind, though, that's the most dangerous part of a hurricane. It's the water, especially when something called the "storm surge" occurs. As the low-pressure eye of the hurricane sits over the ocean, the sea level literally rises into a dome of water. For every inch drop in barometric pressure, the ocean rises a foot higher. Now, out at sea, that means nothing. The rise is not even noticeable. But when that mound of water starts moving toward land, the situation becomes crucial. As the water approaches a shallow beach, the dome of water rises. It may rise ten to fifteen feet in an hour and span fifty miles. Like a marine bulldozer, the surge may rise up twenty feet high, crash onto land, and wash everything away. Then with six- to eight-foot waves riding atop this mound of water, the storm surge destroys buildings, trees, cars, and anything else in its path. It's this storm surge that accounts for 90 percent of the deaths during a hurricane.

—Ira Flatow, "Storm Surge"

WHY USE PROCESS ANALYSIS?

In almost every part of our lives, we rely on **instructions.** They help us cook a meal, repair a car, get to a vacation spot, perform an experiment, and calculate income tax. Essays offering instruction appear in newspapers, magazines, and books on topics from fashion, fitness, and sports to technology, pets, and personal relationships.

We turn to **explanations** not when we want to do things but when we want to understand how things work. Explanations can focus on mechanical or technical subjects (how computer operating systems work), on social matters (how societies create groups of insiders and outsiders), on psychological topics (how stress builds up), or on natural subjects (how cancer cells take over from normal cells).

Process analysis can have imaginative uses as well, helping us speculate about building floating cities, changing our diets for better health, or considering steps that might close the ozone hole over the South Pole. Writers sometimes explain a process in order to amuse or criticize—analyzing with a critical eye some aspects of behavior (as do Kilbourne and Mitford in this chapter) or looking at some surprising natural phenomenon. And process analysis often appears in combination with other expository patterns. You might use it to help readers understand the steps by which a cause (such as meditating) leads to an effect (reduced physical and mental stress), for example. Or you might explain differences in the processes of forming social relationships as part of an essay contrasting the behaviors of men and women.

Expository writing built around process analysis generally responds to a need for information and understanding. The need may be immediate (how to prepare for an upcoming sales meeting or an exam). It may be practical or helpful (understanding the ways our bodies respond to stress; strategies for incorporating a healthy diet and exercise into a busy schedule). Or it may be a matter of curiosity or a desire for understanding (discovering how puppeteers in Indonesia create hours-long shows that appeal to both children and adults; investigating the ways our brains process information).

CHOOSING A STRATEGY

Having encountered instructions and explanations many times before, your readers will probably expect you to employ some basic strategies. For example, they will expect the opening of a set of instructions to announce its purpose, establish the need for a step-by-step explanation of the process, and indicate any materials needed to accomplish it. The way you choose to accomplish these things should vary from situation to situation and topic to topic, however. If you are addressing a need your readers can readily recognize, such as finding effective ways to take a test, make a speech, or apply for a student loan, you might begin with a brief example of how important such knowledge is. Or you might even state the need directly: "Would you like to know how to give a speech without getting so flustered that you forget half of what you planned to say?" or "Wouldn't you like to know how to get a student loan without all the hassle and paperwork most people encounter?"

In many instances, however, you will have to convince readers that they ought to be interested in the instructions you are offering. This is the situation Heather Kaye faced when she decided to tell readers how to play the game "Bones." In response, she created an opening paragraph reminding her readers how often they get bored and telling them of the simple equipment they will need to pass the time with an amusing game.

> When boredom strikes, what can you do if you are tired of computer games, don't like chess, and don't have the money or time to go to a movie? Just collect a pad of paper, a pen, six dice, and a friend, and you are ready to play a game called "Bones." Bones provides fun and excitement, and you don't have to be Einstein to learn how to play. It is a game of chance and luck, laughter and friendship.

For an explanation, however, you may need to appeal to readers' curiosity or their desire for understanding (practical or otherwise). Emphasizing the mystery, adventure, or even oddity of a process will engage most readers' curiosity: What bodily processes allow pearl divers to stay underwater for several minutes when most of us can hold our breath for only ten or twenty seconds? How do bats produce a kind of "radar" that enables them to fly in the dark and catch minute insects? When you appeal to readers' desire for understanding, you will be most likely to succeed when you suggest a practical dimension for the knowledge. For instance, some readers interested in the natural world may be interested in the complex stages of the honey-making process. Yet to attract the majority of readers you may need to suggest that such knowledge can help them understand honey's virtues as a sweetener or choose among different kinds of honey as they shop.

Most process analyses are organized into simple, chronological units, either the *steps* involved in accomplishing the task or the *stages* of operation. In planning a set of instructions, begin by breaking it down into steps, approaching the activity as if you were doing it for the first time so that you do not leave out any necessary elements that have become so routine you might easily overlook them. Then create an organization that will help readers keep track of the many steps, perhaps dividing the task into several units, each containing smaller steps. Consider building your plan around a framework like the following.

> Introduction: Need for the information, materials, statement of purpose
> Step 1: Explanations, details
>> Substeps 1, 2, 3. . . . (if any)
> Step 2: Explanations, details
>> Substeps 1, 2, 3. . . .
> Step 3: Explanations, details
>> Substeps 1, 2, 3. . . .
> Summary (if necessary)

In planning an explanation, identify the various stages or components, including any that overlap, and create an organization that presents them in an easy-to-follow, logical order. If the process is complex, divide it into major components and subdivide each in turn, just as the following rough plan does.

> Introduction (tentative thesis identifying need for the information): Because most people do not understand the amount of energy, natural resources, and human effort needed to create paper, they use it wastefully; understanding the process and the resources it requires is an important first step for all of us concerned with preserving our environment.
> Stage 1: Bringing together natural resources
>> a. Wood—logging
>> b. Water—drawing from rivers or lakes
>> c. Fuel for heat and power (oil, gas, or electric)
> Stage 2: Turning logs into pulp
>> a. Grinding up logs (uses water and power) *or*
>> b. Breaking wood into pulp using chemicals
> Stage 3: Turning pulp into paper
>> a. Paper machine
>>> 1. Feeding pulp into machine
>>> 2. Using heated screen to congeal pulp into a mushy sheet of paper

    b. Dryer
        1. Using heat to further congeal pulp
        2. Using rollers to stretch and thin the sheet (consumes energy)
  Stage 4: Turning paper into paper products (energy and labor intensive)
    a. Creating giant rolls of paper
    b. Cutting and folding rolls of paper into tissues, newsprint, pads, paper towels, and other everyday products

Maintaining the exact order of a process is sometimes of greatest importance, as in a recipe. But occasionally the organization of an analysis may present problems. You may need to interrupt the step-by-step format to give descriptions, definitions, and other explanatory asides. Some processes may even defy a strict chronological treatment because several things occur simultaneously. In explaining the operating process of a gasoline engine, for example, you would be unable to convey at once everything that happens at the same time. Instead, you would need to present the material in *general* stages, each with subdivisions, so your readers could see each stage by itself yet also become aware of interacting relationships.

DEVELOPING A PROCESS ANALYSIS

In developing the paragraphs and sentences that make up an explanation of a process, you also need to pay attention to your readers' expectations. When you are presenting instructions, your readers will expect you to tell them of any necessary materials and will look for frequent summaries to allow them to check if they have followed the steps correctly. They will benefit from warnings of special difficulties they may encounter or any dangers the procedure entails. In addition, they will appreciate words of encouragement ("The procedure may seem strange, but it *will* work") or reminders of the goal of the process ("No pain, no gain: the only way to a flat tummy is through the hard work of repeating these exercises").

Effective explanations and instructions alike often have a visual element. Drawings can show how the parts of a mechanism fit together or help readers recognize the differences among the elements of a natural process, such as the growth of an insect or the eruption of a volcano. Pictures can help readers identify ingredients or components and show them what a finished product will look like.

To guide readers through the steps or stages of a process, to remind them of changes that will occur, or to highlight the sequence of events, consider using words that point out relationships among the various elements.

> Words identifying different stages—*step, event, element, component, phase, state, feature, occurrence*
>
> Words emphasizing relationships in time—*after, next, while, first, second, third, fourth, concurrently, the next week, later, preceding, following*
>
> Words indicating changes—*becomes, varies, transforms, causes, completes, alters, revises, uncovers, synthesizes, cures, builds*

Make sure you include enough details to allow readers to visualize the steps or stages of the process, but not so many that the details become confusing. Present major steps (or stages) in considerable detail, minor ones in less. If you choose to write in the second person (*you*), as in a set of directions ("You should then blend the ingredients"), make sure you use this point of view consistently and do not shift to the first person (*I* or *we*) or the third person (*he, she, it,* or *they*) without good reason. If you choose the first person or third person for your perspective, make sure likewise that your presentation is consistent.

Student Essay

Losing weight is not easy for most people, nor is the process a simple one, as Karin Gaffney explains in the essay that follows. As a result, she provided detailed explanations along with her dieting instructions so that readers can understand not only *how* to diet but also *why* they should follow certain steps and avoid others.

Losing Weight
by Karin Gaffney

Across the board, regardless of age, gender, race, or background, most people spend time trying to lose weight (Williamson et al.). Some people want to lose only five or ten pounds while others worry about getting rid of seventy-five pounds or more. As a result, weight loss is both a universal concern and a highly individualized matter.

Losing weight must mean a lot to Americans. After all, they spend over three billion dollars on weight-loss programs each year ("Rating" 353). If you think you need to diet, think again. Many people think they are overweight because they compare themselves to impossibly thin models or imagine themselves in the slimmest of new fashions. So if you think you need to diet, consult a doctor and other reliable sources of health information. Then go to a good weight-loss program—if you really need one.

Why should you be careful about going on a diet? A study in 1988 by the Centers for Disease Control concluded that any change of weight either up or down led to a higher rate of heart disease in the people studied ("Losing" 350). This does not necessarily mean that you should forget about dieting, however, because weight loss can also help you avoid other health problems ("Losing" 348, 350).

To lose weight, some people turn to commercial diets and hospital programs, yet the majority rely on self-help. For those people who are trying to lose weight on their own, I can offer some general advice along with a simple weight-loss program. The simple advice is no different from what most of us have already heard, but it probably still needs to be repeated: 1) cut down on high-fat foods, 2) eat moderate portions of healthy foods, and 3) get regular exercise. Above all, consult your doctor not only to determine whether you should diet but to make sure your dietary and exercise programs are appropriate for you (and not for the models and athletes who appear on exercise tapes or talk about their health and muscle-power diets in magazines).

A person who is overweight probably has a diet heavy in fat (Beitz 281). A calorie of fat in food becomes part of body fat much more easily than does a calorie of carbohydrate, which is easily burned as energy (Delaney 46). In other words, the body often keeps the fat it takes in, but the carbohydrates it uses up. Moreover, a gram of fat has about 2.25 times as many calories as one gram of carbohydrate or protein does (Beitz 281).

The first step in a healthy weight-loss plan is to reduce the fat in your diet. If you eliminate high-fat foods such as ice creams, cheese, hamburgers, and butter from your diet, your body will respond immediately to the change. Low-fat substitutes, such as low-fat milk, can also have a positive effect, as can steps like cutting the fat off meat or taking the skin off poultry ("Losing" 352).

The second step is to eat more foods that are low in fat but high in fiber and carbohydrates. Here are several choices:

1. Potatoes (baked, not fried, and without butter or sour cream)
2. Beans (pinto, kidney, lentil, and so on)
3. Whole grains (cereals, pastas, breads)
4. Fresh fruits
5. Skim milk (and skim milk products)

When you eat foods like these, your blood sugar levels stabilize and you get "filled up," yet you take in only about one-half the number of calories that fatty alternatives provide (Delaney 44–45).

The third step is to snack wisely. Limit your snacks, of course, and choose from foods like the following: string cheese, corn-on-the-cob (without butter), vegetables, angel food cake, pita bread, soft pretzels, fruits, bagels, nonfat yogurt, juice, animal crackers, or fig bars ("30 Low Fat" 3). Food companies have also been adding fat-free items to grocery shelves in recent years, so when you shop, look for low-fat frozen desserts, low-fat cookies, and the like.

The fourth step is to exercise regularly. Exercise can burn up to 200–300 calories per day (Delaney 46). You may also be surprised to learn that exercise can decrease your weight even if you do not radically change your eating habits. Regular exercise increases basal metabolism, the energy needed just to stay alive. One-half of the calories in a person's diet, for example, can go to basal metabolism. Exercise can increase the basal metabolism rate so that a person can lose more calories by just living and breathing. The amount of muscle a person has also affects basal metabolism. A person with more muscle has a higher basal metabolism and burns up more of the calories in food through this means ("Losing" 357).

Your exercise routine does not have to be strenuous or exhausting like that of an Olympic trainee. Moderate exercise, such as one half-hour to an hour of good-paced walking, is beneficial. If you need an incentive to start your exercise program, remember that a person who goes from a nonexerciser to a moderate exerciser will notice the results more than someone going from moderate to advanced. There are other side benefits to exercise as well. For example, people who exercise regularly develop adult diabetes 40 percent less frequently than nonexercisers do ("Losing" 351).

The fifth step is to set reasonable goals for weight loss. Concentrate on losing a pound or two at a time, and try to maintain this small weight loss before continuing ("Losing" 350). This approach will help make you confident of your ability to lose weight and help you avoid the yo-yo effect of losing a lot of weight, then gaining it right back.

The final step is to keep several key points in mind.

1. Make eating right and exercising (not dieting) the focus of your attention and effort.

2. Concentrate on maintaining your healthy lifestyle so that you can make your weight loss permanent and benefit over the long term from good eating and exercise habits.

3. Remember that you are an individual and that the advice offered here may or may not apply to you. Always consult a doctor who knows you and your medical history.

Works Cited

Beitz, Donald C. "Nutrition." <u>McGraw-Hill Yearbook of Science and Technology.</u> New York: McGraw-Hill, 1993.

Delaney, Lisa. "The 'No-Hunger' Weight-Loss Plan." <u>Prevention</u> Sept. 1993: 43–46.

"Losing Weight: What Works, What Doesn't."
    Consumer Reports June 1993: 347–52.
"Rating the Diets." Consumer Reports June 1993:
    353–57.
"30 Low Fat Foods to Grab." Thinline Sept./Oct. 1993: 3.
Williamson, David F., Mary K. Serdula, Robert F.
    Auclay, Alan Levy, and Tim Byers. "Weight Loss
    Attempts in Adults: Goals, Duration, and Rate of
    Weight Loss." American Journal of Public Health
    Sept. 1992: 82–89.

JOE BUHLER AND RON GRAHAM

JOE BUHLER, a professor of mathematics at Reed College, has published many scholarly articles as well as essays for more general audiences. Among the latter are essays on science, juggling, and the game Go.

RON GRAHAM is associated with Bell Labs in Murray Hill, New Jersey, and has had a distinguished career as a mathematician. He has published many articles in his field of research and his work has been honored with membership in the National Academy of Sciences. He is a past president of the International Jugglers' Association.

Give Juggling a Hand!

This instructional essay, a particularly compact explanation of an intriguing activity, was first published in *The Sciences.* It reflects the authors' enjoyment of juggling as well as their expertise. By providing some historical background, clear directions, and interesting explanations, the writers make the activity seem as enjoyable to readers as it is to them.

Nothing could be simpler than a game of catch. But just add an- 1
other ball or two and the game turns magical—the juggled balls take on a life of their own. Suddenly, simple motions and common objects blur into one stunning display after another.

In recent years, juggling has experienced a renaissance. Street 2
performers and skilled amateurs are practicing the ancient art in parks, back yards, and on campuses around the globe. Membership in the largely amateur International Jugglers' Association (IJA) has more than doubled since 1979.

Juggling is actually 4000 years young. In Egypt, Asia, and the 3
Americas, it was once associated with religious ritual. In medieval Europe, wandering minstrels often juggled; the term derives from these *jongleurs.*

Amazing jugglers imported from the Orient—in particular the 4
"East Indian" Ramo Samee, who was said to string beads in his mouth while turning rings with his fingers and toes, and the Japanese artist Takashima, who manipulated a cotton ball with a stick held in his teeth—convinced 19th-century Europeans that juggling could be extraordinary show business.

Perhaps the greatest juggler of all time was variety-show virtu-   5
oso Enrico Rastelli. By his death in 1931, he had taught himself to
juggle eight clubs, eight plates or ten balls; he could even bounce
three balls continuously on his head.

Most people assume that a skilled juggler can manage up to   6
20 objects. In fact, even five-ball juggling is very difficult and requires about a year to master. Only a few jugglers worldwide
have perfected seven-ball routines. At the 1986 IJA competition,
one entrant separately juggled nine rings, eight balls, and seven
clubs.

Jugglers use a bewildering variety of objects, including bowl-   7
ing balls, whips, plastic swimming pools, cube puzzles, fruit,
flaming torches, and playing cards. Performers trying for the
largest number of objects usually choose rings, which allow a
tighter traffic pattern and are stable when thrown to great heights.
Several jugglers can manage ten or 11 rings, and some are trying
for 12 or 13.

Clubs are the most visually pleasing objects to juggle. They're   8
especially suited for passing back and forth between performers.
Because they take up a lot of space when they rotate and must be
caught at one end, juggling even five is tricky. Almost nobody can
manage seven, even for a few seconds.

Throughout history, all jugglers—from South Sea Islanders to   9
Aztec Indians—have used the same fundamental patterns:

The Cascade. Here, each ball travels from one hand to the other   10
and back again, following a looping path that looks like a figure
eight lying on its side. The juggler starts with two balls in his right
hand, using a scooping motion and releasing a ball when his throwing hand is level with his navel. As the first ball reaches its highest
point, the other hand scoops and releases a second ball, and as that
one reaches *its* apogee, he throws the third. Skilled jugglers can keep
three, five, or even seven balls going in a cascade, but never four or
six. With an even number, balls collide at the intersection of the figure eight.

The Shower. In this more difficult pattern, the balls follow a cir-   11
cular path as they are thrown upward by the right hand, caught by
the left and quickly passed back to the right. Since the right does all
the long-distance throwing, the shower is inherently asymmetrical
and, therefore, inefficient; it is difficult with more than three objects.

The Fountain. This figure allows for a large number of balls. In a   12
four-ball fountain, each hand juggles two balls independently in a
circular motion. For symmetry, the number of balls is usually even.

If the hands throw alternately and the two patterns interlock, it is surprisingly hard to discern that the fountain is made of two separate components and not one.

Because gravity causes objects to accelerate as they fall, a juggler has only a short time to catch and throw one ball before another drops into his hand—even if he throws high. A juggler who throws a ball eight feet in the air, for example, must catch it 1.4 seconds later, but throwing it four times that high only doubles the flight time.   13

The best way to understand juggling is to learn to do it yourself. Some people get the hang of the three-ball cascade in minutes, although most need at least a few days. Limit your sessions to ten minutes rather than frustrate yourself with a two-hour binge.   14

Step 1: One Ball. Practice throwing a ball from your right hand to your left and back, letting the ball rise to just above your head. Make the ball follow the path of a figure eight lying on its side, by "scooping" the ball and releasing it near the navel. Catch the ball at the side of your body, then repeat the sequence.   15

Step 2: Two Balls. Put one in each hand. Throw the ball in the left hand as in Step 1, and then, just as the ball passes its high point, throw the right-hand ball. Avoid releasing the second throw too early or tossing the balls to unequal heights.   16

At first it may be difficult to catch the balls. Don't worry. Focus instead on the accuracy and height of the throws. Catching will come naturally as soon as the throws are on target. If things seem hectic, try higher throws.   17

Step 3: Two Balls Reversed. Reverse the order of throws so that the sequence is right, then left.   18

Step 4: Three Balls. Now put two balls in your right hand and one in your left. Try to complete Step 2 while simply holding the extra ball. Pause, then do Step 3.   19

The third ball can make it difficult to catch the second throw. To solve this, throw the third ball just after the second reaches its high point. The sequence is thus right, left, right. At first it may be tough to persuade your right hand to make its second throw. Remember: catches are irrelevant in the beginning. Throw high, accurately and slowly. Don't rush the tempo, and don't forget the figure-eight pattern.   20

Once you've mastered the three-ball cascade you'll want to try other patterns. A juggler is never finished: there is always one more ball.   21

MEANINGS AND VALUES

1. Are readers in general likely to find the topic of this essay interesting? Why or why not? How do the authors encourage readers to consider juggling an amusing or worthwhile activity? Are these reasons presented directly or indirectly?

2. People often think juggling is difficult because it *looks* difficult. What do the writers say about the process to convince readers that they can master it?

3. What purposes are served by the historical background in Paragraphs 3, 4, and 5? (See "Guide to Terms": *Purpose.*)

EXPOSITORY TECHNIQUES

1. What technique do Buhler and Graham use to begin the essay? To conclude it? What makes these techniques successful (or unsuccessful) in this particular essay? (Guide: *Introductions; Closings.*)

2. Why do the authors describe different juggling patterns before they provide specific advice on beginning to juggle? Would the selection be more effective or less effective if the order were reversed? (Guide: *Evaluation.*)

3. Which expository patterns, other than PROCESS ANALYSIS, do the authors use to make juggling readily understandable and to help readers believe that they can master it?

DICTION AND VOCABULARY

1. Tell how the diction and vocabulary choices in Paragraphs 10–12 help make juggling seem simple. (Guide: *Diction.*)

2. How does the diction in Paragraphs 14–20 contribute to the message that getting started with juggling is not as difficult as most readers might think?

3. If you do not know the meaning of some of the following terms, look them up in a dictionary: renaissance (Par 2); virtuoso (5); cascade (10).

READ TO WRITE

1. **Collaborating:** Physical activities can be difficult or challenging, but so can mental, social, or artistic activities. Working in a group, discuss activities you undertake with some success that others might find difficult, and list as many as you can. From the list, choose several that you and other group members are interested in writing or reading about. Note which ones you might be able to explain in ways

that will intrigue readers and teach them something useful. Choose one as the topic for an essay and, as a group, prepare a plan for the essay.

2.   **Considering Audience:** In the first seven paragraphs of their essay, Buhler and Graham offer a variety of information about juggling. Looking at each paragraph, describe the kinds of readers who might find the information it presents particularly interesting. Explain why you think these paragraphs are successful or unsuccessful in appealing to a wide range of readers.

3.   **Developing an Essay:** Many sports and hobbies can seem difficult or mystifying. Drawing on Buhler and Graham's essay as a model, create a set of instructions to simplify a seemingly challenging, dangerous, or mysterious sport or activity. Make the activity interesting and encourage readers to try it.

(NOTE: Suggestions for topics requiring developing by use of PROCESS ANALYSIS are on pp. 313–314 at the end of this chapter.)

DAVID FONTANA

DAVID FONTANA teaches at the University of Wales, Cardiff, and the University of Minho in Portugal. He is a psychologist and a fellow of the British Psychological Society. He has written many books on subjects such as dreaming, meditation, and psychotherapy. These include *Dreamlife: Understanding and Using Your Dreams* (1990), *The Secret Language of Symbols* (1994), and *The Secret Language of Dreams: A Visual Key to Dreams and Their Meanings* (1994).

Working with Dreams

This chapter from *The Secret Language of Dreams* provides concrete advice for remembering, analyzing, and interpreting dreams, supported with explanations of the dreaming process. Though the primary expository pattern David Fontana employs is analysis of a process, he also makes frequent use of examples, some in narrative form and some in visual form.

The first stage of working with dreams is the art of remembering them. Many people claim never to recall their dreams, and some deny having dreams at all. However, with practice, and the right technique, it is not unusual to remember five or more dreams each morning.

Start with a positive attitude. Remembering dreams is a habit, and can be cultivated. The best way is to tell yourself during the day that you will remember your dreams, and upon awakening lie still for a while, focusing your conscious mind on whatever ideas or emotions have emerged from your sleep, and allowing them through association to prompt dream recall.

Keeping a dream diary makes it possible to build up a detailed, sustained picture of your dream life. Write down (or sketch) everything you can remember—small details as well as main themes—and make a note of any emotions or associations that emerge from the dream's contents. During the day, think back to the dream of the night before, even if its details have faded, and try to re-live the emotions associated with it. Re-read your notes and be patient: it may take weeks or months before you regularly remember your dreams, but success will come if you persevere. To speed things up, occasionally set an alarm clock for about two hours after you usually fall asleep: you will stand a good chance of awakening immediately after the first, dream-laden period of REM sleep.

Some dream researchers advise subjects to collect at least a hundred dreams before starting analysis, as it may take this length of time before the common themes emerge coherently. It is always worth searching for connections with the events of the day, but remember—the dream has a reason for choosing these events, and may be using them to symbolize deeper material. Note anything significant about these events and any memories that they spark off. Such memories may lead back to long-forgotten experiences to which the dream is trying to draw your attention. 4

Keeping a Dream Record

A dream sketchbook can often capture the mood of a dream better than a written record. Moreover, making notes immediately after waking requires a mental adjustment that will often interpose itself between the dreamer and the dream, whereas a sketch can often be made without losing touch with the remembered experience. The example on these pages is a dream by a 15-year-old girl; her spoken account is given on this page, with a note on the symbolism; the sketch is in her visual notebook. 5

> First I saw a hairy caterpillar eating a leaf, which then gradually changed into the keyboard of one of those old upright typewriters. The keys were moving by themselves and the paper coming out of the machine was all crumpled and had glistening raindrops on it—but there was no rain. The paper then appeared on a table and someone had spilt a cup of coffee over it. The caterpillar turned into a butterfly and flew off. Suddenly, I was in a rain storm trying to bring in the laundry, and the caterpillar was there also crawling along the washing line. 6

Dream Analysis

The best way to analyze dreams is through the recurring themes that emerge from a dream diary. Whether analysis concentrates on these themes or on powerful individual dreams, a good way to start is to separate the dream material into discrete categories: for example, scenery, objects, characters, events, colours, emotions. One should not strive for detailed accuracy: these categories may well overlap, and the memories themselves may be vague or confused. But try not to ignore apparently unimportant details, because these may be the very aspects that carry the most meaning. 7

Start by selecting something from whichever of the categories appears most relevant, and subject it to the process of Jungian direct 8 association. . . . Write down the object (or whatever) in the centre of a piece of paper, hold it in the mind, and note down all associated images and ideas that come to you. Keep returning to the original stimulus. Try to ensure that each association is specific: if the dream contained a red car, it may be its colour, rather than the fact that it is a car, that is of most symbolic significance. When no more associations come to mind, put the paper aside and go on to the next dream symbol with which you want to deal, and so on, until all the desired categories have been covered.

[Carl] Jung, [a psychologist] suggested that direct association 　9 becomes easier if the dreamer imagines that he or she is describing each element to someone who has never encountered such a thing before. He also advocated elaborating upon direct associations, linking them to any personal reactions or responses that arise for the dreamer in response to the original dream image.

If few associations arise from a dream's main elements, the 　10 dream may be operating at Level 1, carrying little representational or symbolic meaning, and simply serving as a reminder of the significance owed to certain events in the dreamer's life. It may be hinting, for example, that particular emotions may need more acknowledgment, or may be providing clues about the solution to problems that have been worrying the dreamer at a conscious level.

If the dream appears to carry a further level of meaning that re- 　11 mains undetectable by direct association, Freudian[1] free association may be helpful, allowing the mind freely to follow a whole chain of thoughts and images set off by the individual dream element, with one idea emerging spontaneously from another. Jung complained that such free and unspecific associations lead the dreamer too far away from the original dream, but Freud's method can reveal significant repressed memories, urges or emotions that direct association may fail to reach.

If the memories and ideas that emerge from dreams are purely 　12 personal associations, the chances are that they emerge from a Level 2 dream, but if they seem to be working as archetypal symbols[2]. . . they are probably operating at Level 3.

Jung stressed that no dream interpretation should be imposed 　13 upon the dreamer: the meaning is uncovered only if it provides the

[1]From the psychologist Sigmund Freud. [ed.]

[2]"Archetypes are the common themes . . . that emerge from the collective unconscious and reappear in symbolic form again and again in myths, symbol systems and dreams. . . . archetypes appear as symbols, or take personified form as the particular gods and goddesses, heroes and heroines, fabulous beasts and powers of good and evil."

dreamer with a self-insight, whether welcome or unwelcome, that rings true. Interpretations should "act" for the dreamer, setting his or her "life in motion again". To be truly effective, a dream interpretation should be confirmed not only by subsequent dreams, but also by subsequent life-events.

Dream Control

Once interpretation has led us into the scenery of our dreams, and once we have recognized their landscapes as the symbols and archetypes of our unconscious mind, we can often begin directly to influence our dream life by trying by various techniques to carry aspects of our waking consciousness into sleep.   14

The ability regularly to become more conscious in our dreams is known as lucid dreaming . . . and is often found in people who have a high degree of concentration and awareness in waking life. It is also associated with spiritual and occult powers. Tibetan Buddhism teaches that to gain control in the land of our dreams gives us control in the realms after death, where conscious awareness can free the initiate from the illusory cycle of birth and death.   15

There are several techniques for establishing awareness in dreams, and thus for experiencing them with the conscious mind. Hindu, Buddhist and Western esoteric orders link these methods with more general exercises, such as meditation and self-observation, designed to develop enhanced psychological and spiritual awareness. For example, some Western occultists advocate building up during prolonged and intensive meditation a clear visualization of oneself sitting opposite the physical body, and then transferring consciousness to this. Later, during sleep, this body can be used as the conscious dream body. It is also suggested that by co-hypnosis (which involves two practitioners simultaneously hypnotizing each other) it is even possible consciously to share and control experiences in the dream world.   16

Shamans attempt to fix a power object of some kind so firmly in the waking mind that it can even be visualized in sleep, reminding them that they are dreaming. The anthropologist Carlos Castaneda was advised by Don Juan, his Yaqui shaman guide to other worlds, to control his dreams and other altered states of consciousness by visualizing his own hands before sleeping, so that if they appeared in his dreams he would become aware that he was dreaming. Shamans also teach that if we vividly re-create the dream worlds in the imagination while we are consciously remembering our dreams, it be-   17 comes progressively easier to re-enter them in a conscious state while dreaming. Falling asleep determined to find a particular object, or hear a particular song, may also help to develop conscious control over dreaming.

The *reflection technique* involves asking oneself as often as possible during the day, "How do I know that I am not dreaming now?", and being as specific as possible with the answers. It then becomes easier to recognize an actual dream for what it is, and so assert control over it. A variation on this is the *intention technique,* in which the dreamer is encouraged constantly to tell himself or herself during the day that particular events in the dream world will be recognized as such by the aware, dreaming mind. If, for example, we frequently dream of horses, or trains, or schools, we should impress upon our waking mind that the appearance of such objects in dreams will alert us to the fact of dreaming. 18

A similar technique is to imagine ourselves dreaming of certain common objects or actions, like climbing stairs or running across a field, and attempt to visualize them as frequently as possible in waking life. Again, when the chosen image occurs in a dream, we become conscious of dreaming. 19

Autosuggestion, repeating to oneself again and again on the verge of our sleep that conscious awareness *will* emerge in our dreams, can also help. 20

Recent research on dream control has experimented with laboratory techniques. By recording eye movements or changes in pulse or in breathing, experimenters can detect the moment when REM dreaming commences. Alerting the dreamer with a mild electric shock from a device strapped to the wrist may induce a conscious understanding that a dream is in progress, thus bringing the dream within the dreamer's control. 21

A somewhat different approach, used by various Eastern traditions and by Jung in his technique of *active imagination,* is to imagine that one is dreaming while awake. Thus we enter a "virtual" waking dream world: everything is seen as an illusion which has been created by the mind, and can be changed at will. By reminding ourselves constantly that we are exercising this will when carrying out every waking action, we can potentially build a bridge between waking and dream consciousness, thus creating a single level of awareness that extends throughout waking, dreaming and dreamless sleep. 22

A similar technique of mind control is to develop the habit of asking ourselves when remembering dreams why it is that a particularly 23 unusual dream event did not prompt us into realizing that we were dreaming. This technique trains the mind by reminding it of its past failures to alert us to the fact of dreaming, and encouraging it not to repeat such failures.

Many of the above techniques can be used in conjunction with each other as aids to lucid dreaming, as can more conventional methods such as keeping a dream diary or meditation. However, a key requirement for all techniques is patience: do not be too discouraged if the desired results are some time in coming.   24

It is also vital not to try too hard. Lucid dreaming is achieved by an act of will, but not by an act of teeth-gritting determination. Like any creative activity, it is most readily achieved by a mind that is concentrated, motivated and persistent, but at the same time light and playful.   25

Solving Problems

The prescription that we should sleep upon problems is well known. Although the conscious ego is inactive while we sleep, some part of the mind continues working on the problems that beset it during the day, so that when we awake the solutions may be already in place.   26

Sometimes answers are actually given in dreams. A famous example is that of the German chemist Friedrich Kekulé who claimed that his ground-breaking discovery of the molecular structure of benzene, in 1961, came to him in a dream. Working hard on the problem, he fell asleep and dreamed of molecules dancing before his eyes, forming into patterns, then joining like a snake catching its tail in a dream representation of the so-called "benzene ring."   27

We can sometimes obtain a demonstration of the problem-solving power of the dreaming mind if we visualize an unsolved anagram or mathematical puzzle while drifting to sleep. Instructing the mind to work on the puzzle, just before sleep descends, can often stimulate a dream solution.   28

The answer may come literally, unfiltered by symbol. The Russian chemist Dmitri Mendeleev, after many fruitless attempts to tabulate the elements according to their atomic weight, dreamed their respective values and subsequently found all but one to be correct, a discovery that led to the publication of his periodic law in 1869.   29

When dreams offer symbolic rather than literal solutions, interpretation can be more difficult. The scientist Neils Bohr identified the model of a hydrogen atom in 1913 after a dream in which   30 he stood on the sun and saw the planets attached to its surface by thin filaments as they circled overhead. Numerical solutions, in particular, may be conveyed in symbolic form, perhaps using associations lodged deep in the personal unconscious. For example, the number 3 might be indicated by an old three-legged stool from the dreamer's childhood.

One of the most astonishing of all dream discoveries, involving visitation by a dream ghost, is that of H.V. Hilprecht, Professor of Assyrian at the University of Pennsylvania. In 1893, Hilprecht was trying to decipher inscriptions on drawings of two agate fragments believed to come from finger rings, dating from c. 1300 BC and excavated from the ruins of a temple at Nippur in modern Iraq. Discouraged by lack of success, Hilprecht retired to bed and dreamed that an ancient Babylonian priest appeared before him to inform him with a wealth of background detail that the fragments were not separate rings at all but part of a cylinder that the priests had cut up to make earrings for a statue. If they were put together, the priest told him, the original inscription could be read with ease. Hilprecht awoke and confirmed the truth of his dream, receiving final proof when he examined the fragments in the museum at Istanbul.

31

MEANINGS AND VALUES

1. In Paragraphs 1, 7, 14, and 26 the writer introduces elements of the larger process of "working with dreams." What are each of these elements? Identify the smaller steps or techniques the writer presents within each one.

2. What overall logical pattern does the writer follow in organizing the essay? How does it help unify the essay, if at all? (See "Guide to Terms": *Unity*.)

3. To what extent do the examples that Fontana presents in Paragraphs 27 and 29–31 help make the explanation in Paragraphs 26–31 convincing? What qualities do these examples have in common?

EXPOSITORY TECHNIQUES

1. The writer uses a number of subheadings to introduce the sections of the essay. How accurately do they describe and introduce the contents of each section? If you think they are not as accurate as they need to be, suggest alternatives.

2.   Why do you think the writer provides alternative techniques for con-
     trolling and analyzing dreams or for solving problems through
     dreams? Does he offer readers any explanation of why there are mul-
     tiple techniques or advice for choosing among them? If not, suggest
     some ways the author might give readers more guidance, and rewrite
     two paragraphs from the essay providing such advice for readers.

3.   What is the tone of this essay? (Guide: *Tone.*) How does the author
     feel about the subject that he is discussing? What evidence is there of
     his feelings in the essay? What does he appear to assume about his
     reader's attitudes toward the subject?

DICTION AND VOCABULARY

1.   Paragraphs 2–4, 7–11, and 18–25 offer specific directions to readers.
     Analyze the words (especially verbs) that the writer uses to present
     these directions. What pattern does he follow in his word choice?
     Does he make different kinds of choices in each of the sections? If so,
     what are the differences? Do his specific word choices help him
     avoid seeming "bossy"? Why, or why not? (Guide: *Diction.*)

2.   What does the diction in the sections listed above (in Question 1) con-
     tribute to the overall tone of the essay? (Guide: *Tone.*)

3.   Use a dictionary to define the following words and use each appropri-
     ately in a sentence you create: REM (Par. 3); illusory (15); esoteric (16);
     shamans (17); tabulate (29).

READ TO WRITE

1.   **Collaborating:** In a group, share some dreams and compose an
     analysis of one of them following Fontana's advice.

2.   **Considering Audience:** Some people dismiss dream interpretation
     on the grounds that it is unscientific or that it is uncertain and
     flawed. Create a list of the varied objections readers might have to
     dream interpretation. For each objection, search Fontana's essay for
     information, ideas, or statements that might provide an answer. For
     those he does not address, compose for the essay a paragraph or two
     that might convince readers of the seriousness and importance of
     what Fontana has to say.

3.   **Developing an Essay:** Do some research of your own on dream in-
     terpretation and develop an essay offering advice on the subject that
     differs in significant ways from Fontana's advice. If possible, make
     direct reference to his work and indicate why your advice provides a
     worthwhile alternative.

(NOTE: Suggestions for essays requiring development by PROCESS ANALYSIS are on
pp. 313–314 at the end of this chapter.)

SRIDHAR PAPPU

SRIDHAR PAPPU currently is a correspondent for *The Atlantic Monthly,* based out of New York. At the time of this article's publication, he was a staff writer for T*he Chicago Reader.* In addition to stints as a reporter and staff writer at *Money* and *Sports Illustrated,* Pappu served as a media columnist for *The New York Observer* from June 2001 to February 2004. Pappu holds a B.S. and M.S. from Northwestern University's Medill School of Journalism and resides in the Park slope section of Brooklyn, New York.

Deranged Marriage

This essay was published in *Life as We Know It: A Collection of Personal Essays from Salon.com.* In it, Sridhar Pappu describes a process of "courtship" and marriage likely to be unfamiliar to many readers. What makes this analysis of a process even more interesting is that in the particular events Pappu presents, the process doesn't work—though it is clear that it has worked for other people for many years.

In the days before last Christmas, a girl I had never met or spoken   1
to called me to see if I wanted to marry her. It wasn't the girl, really, but her family. And they didn't call me, exactly. They called my mother.

Thus began a series of events that concluded on a Saturday   2
night in January with me sitting in the dark, sobbing into a pillowcase, drinking a bottle of He'brew beer that I'd saved from a friend's Hanukkah party, and listening to Merle Haggard. I had taken on the antiquated custom of arranged marriage, in its modern incarnation, and it had beaten me into a state of previously unfathomable self-pity that happened to include very bad beer.

This was new terrain for me. I am Indian by birth, but I grew up   3
as a white kid in southwest Ohio. I drank beer in open fields in high school and still consider my greatest adolescent achievement the night I walked into the homecoming dance with the prettiest girl in my senior class. I worship Johnny Bench. And until last December, the prospect of an arranged marriage was an abstract idea to me, the appropriate narrative vein for someone else's story; my grandparents', my parents', even my sister's, but never my own.

Of course, I had distaste for all of it: a feeling, which informed   4
every John Hughes movie I ever saw, that any kind of outside involvement in finding that "someone" was, well, wrong. I can say truthfully

now that I felt the right girl would just come to me on, say, the Wilson Avenue Bridge in Chicago, or within the basement-level environs of the old Knitting Factory in New York. Tabula rasa. I'm here.

I believed my future would be spent in apartments on the   5
Upper East Side or in Greenwich Village, where, my hands shoved into the pockets of a tweed sports coat, I would find myself asking a waiflike brunet why she was leaving me or coming back to me, or if she had ever loved me at all. I saw my brows furrowed and my eyes drawn close. "Jenny," I'd say, "what's this all about?"

The fact of the matter is that I have passed through nearly half   6
of my twenties without experiencing anything close to that exchange, and I realize that, on some level, the idea of an arranged marriage has always been with me. It has served as both an emboldening force against loneliness, and the precise cause of that loneliness, since it has hovered in the background as Plan B while I have searched for nothing less than the perfect girl.

Which brings us to the events of the past few months.   7

It all began with my hesitant approval of my mother's decision   8
to start "the process." I did this without knowing precisely where or to whom that process might lead. Arranged marriage has changed a great deal since it was shipped to this country in the late 1960s, having been forced to embrace the exterior trappings of a world that it is designed to circumvent. There are (or can be) phone calls, dates, and months of courtship, supposedly meant to give the participants access to traits, qualities, and annoying habits not obvious at first glance. More important, these new aspects of the ritual seek to first simulate, then stimulate the intermittent passion, the plain pining, experienced in unmatched love.

My own faux dating started with a match to a girl from   9
Louisiana that never got past the picture-viewing stage, then moved to a match with a soon-to-be-graduating medical school student from Florida. Nearly giddy in the days before Christmas, my mother and father called to say that, yes, "this one" was pretty, and soon, in a hotel room in Boston, they showed me her picture—with résumé.

The photograph showed her standing in profile, her face turned   10
just slightly. She was wearing a sari with her hands placed over one another in an attempt to display a kind of grace. Her vita said her career goals include a "fellowship in gastroenterology" and listed her interests as "Languages, Literature" as well as travel and running. It went on to say that she enjoyed "people, social and fun loving." My father said she'd be coming to Chicago on the residency-interview trail in January, and that was when I could meet her.

"For now," said my father as I sat on the edge of the bed, pre-   11
tending to only half-listen while watching *The Sopranos,* "we're going to just concentrate on doctors."

I met her two weeks later on a cold, sunless day. She had on a   12
long, dark coat and a blue shawl, and a smile—bright and assured
and unironic—that made her seem irreducibly pretty. We were, I
felt, what a young couple should look like: well dressed and un-
wrinkled, what Eudora Welty once described as a "matched team—
like professional, Spanish dancers wearing masks."

We spent seven hours together—beginning with a tense el ride   13
and a tenser, chitchatty lunch at the Berghoff meant to create casual-
ness where there was none. Of course, the easiest way for characters
in any story to address the large, overarching dilemmas and issues
(Why am I with you? What is going on between the two of us? How
can I make things better?) is to talk about them, which, initiated by
her, is what we did.

"Are your parents traditional?" she asked as we walked around   14
the Art Institute.

"I guess they have traditional ideas," I said. "My dad likes to   15
play the liberal, but my mom's the real heavy. They're pretty great,
though. I dunno. I mean, what do you mean by 'traditional'?"

"I guess," she said, "I mean, what do they expect out of this?"   16
"I'm not sure," I said, and I wasn't.   17
"What do you expect out of this?"   18
"I don't know," I said, taken by her matter-of-factness. "How   19
about you?"

She went on to tell me that her parents first brought up the idea   20
a year ago, saying that as long as she was going to visit these cities,
she "might as well" begin to meet "these" boys.

Listening to this, I felt my limbs entirely weaken and my head   21
grow light. I thought about the Cincinnati Bengals' inability to
keep their lead against the San Francisco 49ers in the 1989 Super
Bowl, about the need for the Cincinnati Reds to pick up another
quality starting pitcher. I saw my picture pasted on a bulletin
board along with those of other earnest, nearsighted young Indian
men. How did my looks rate next to theirs? My clothes? My hair?
How did she feel when I told her that I felt unnerved around large
groups of Indian people, that most of my close friends were
Jewish?

I wanted to go home, but of course I didn't. Instead, I finished   22
the museum tour with her and walked north up Michigan Avenue,
talking to her about city politics in Chicago and Miami. She told me

that she loved Cuban coffee, and I said that my father had raised my sister and me to drink Maxwell House black. She said there was nothing so pretty as a Florida sunset, but that she wanted to live in a place with hip, young professionals. I didn't ask but was pretty certain that she really, really liked *Friends.*

"So, Sridhar," she said before we entered a Starbucks, "what else?"   23

"About me," I replied, "or about this?"   24

"About this," she said. "What are your concerns?"   25

That night in my notebook, I would write that I was "gripped   26
by an acute sensation to hold her and only let go 30 or 40 years later." I know, yeech. But I suppose that a good deal of me had thought this was a moment of real definition, where she could see something that set me apart from the rest of the Sanjays and Ajays, the would-be radiologists and software engineers. The future had in fact unfolded. Now it just needed ironing out.

Inside, over a tall mocha and a tall house coffee, we spoke about   27
our problems with the process and what we expected from a potential spouse. She said she didn't want to get married for two more years, and that she wanted to move to Houston. Proximity, she said, was a definite issue. I expressed the sentiment that part of me didn't feel Indian enough, that I wanted someone not entirely freaked out by my intention to eventually write a novel.

Smitten is the word for what I felt. In the course of the day I had   28
premonitions of attending her medical school graduation in May, of buying a fixer-upper in Houston's Rice Village with a large sunporch and a home office in the attic. Premature feelings perhaps, but not entirely out of line with the heightened sense that comes with these things, where every word choice, every pause, every action takes on 400 to 500 additional pounds in emotional weight.

I told her that I'd like to see her before she left town, and she   29
said that she felt the same. When I called her two days later, however, she said seeing me again wasn't possible, that she had gone ahead and made plans with other people. "I guess," she said, "it's just not going to happen."

A pretty good piece of dialogue for someone who is not a   30
writer, good enough to plunge me into a rueful weekend of darkness and "Mama Tried."

Since then, however, in talks with my parents and my sister, I   31
have come to see this experience for what it was: the first match, the initial act in a process that seeks to remove the randomness from life, that deals with affection directly and is meant to eliminate the ambi-

guities and missed signals that plague us once we enter the love life of adults.

I'm not sure if it will ever "happen" for me, not in this way. But for now I'm willing to try. 32

MEANINGS AND VALUES

1. What is the process Sridhar Pappu describes in this essay?

2. What do the imagined events described in Paragraph 5 reveal about the writer's cultural and social values?

3. How does the process Pappu presents differ from more traditional versions of the process? Can these differences account for the reactions he describes in Paragraph 2? Why, or why not?

EXPOSITORY TECHNIQUES

1. Describe the strategy Pappu uses to open the essay. (See "Guide to Terms": *Introductions.*)

2. Is the opening to the essay likely to be effective in getting the attention of most readers? Why, or why not? (Guide: *Evaluation.*)

3. Why does the writer describe the failure of the process in Paragraph 2?

4. Where in the essay does the presentation of the process begin? Why do you think the writer waits so long to begin the presentation?

DICTION AND VOCABULARY

1. Why does the writer use the phrase "faux dating"? Is the meaning of this phrase likely to be apparent to most readers? Why, or why not?

2. At several points in the essay, the writer includes quotations from himself and from other people. For what purposes does he include these quotations?

READ TO WRITE

1. **Collaborating:** Working with a group of writers, make a list of activities that your parents and other people from earlier generations accomplish in ways different from those that are common or fashionable today. Make a list of the differences among present and

past (or "traditional") processes. Then choose one process, and summarize the differences between present and past versions in a paragraph or two.

2. **Considering Audience:** Choose one of the processes from activity 1, above, and explore in writing what people from different age groups need to know about the values and ideas that shape each different version of the process.

3. **Developing an Essay:** Write an essay about the topic you explored in activity 2, presenting different versions of the process, and explain it to both contemporary and "traditional" audiences.

(NOTE: Suggestions for topics requiring development by analysis of PROCESS ANALYSIS are on pp. 313–314 at the end of this chapter.)

JIM HARRISON

> JIM HARRISON has written poems, novels, and screenplays. His books
> include *Legends of the Fall* (1980), *Wolf: A False Memoir* (1989), *Just
> Before Dark: Collected Nonfiction* (1991), *The Woman Lit by Fireflies*
> (1991), *The Theory and Practice of Rivers and New Poems* (1989),
> *After Ikkyu and Other Poems* (1996), *The Shape of the Journey:*
> *Collected Poems* (1998), and *Sundog: The Story of an American*
> *Foreman, Robert Corvus Strang* (1999).

Going Places

"Going Places" first appeared in *Outside* magazine. In this essay,
Harrison presents an unusual set of directions, for drivers "obsessed with going places, pure and simple, for the sake of movement, anywhere and practically anytime." Since the people he
claims to be addressing are not the kind likely to follow instructions step-by-step, he adopts a slightly different approach, offering instead a set of suggestions and precepts. At the same time,
however, he speaks to those readers who are less adventurous or
independent in their ways, providing a blueprint for adventure
and (self-)discovery that he encourages them to follow if only in
parts, on short journeys as well as long ones. By the end of the essay, most writers are likely to agree that Harrison's larger purpose
is to suggest ways for readers to live richer, freer, and more imaginative lives.

Everyone remembers those kindergarten or first-grade jigsaw   1
puzzles of the forty-eight states, not including Hawaii and
Alaska, which weren't states when I was a child and perhaps for
that reason are permanently beyond my sphere of interest. I'm not at
all sure at what age a child begins to comprehend the abstraction of
maps—Arthur Rimbaud's line about the "child crazed with maps"
strikes home. Contiguous states in the puzzle were of different colors, establishing the notion that states are more different from one
another than they really are. The world grows larger with the child's
mind, but each new step doesn't abolish the previous steps, so it's
not much more than a big child who finally gets a driver's license,
certainly equivalent to losing your virginity in the list of life's prime
events.

It is at this point that pathology enters: Out of a hundred dri-   2
vers the great majority find cars pleasant enough, and some will be

obsessed with them in mechanical terms, but two or three out of the hundred will be obsessed with going places, pure and simple, for the sake of movement, anywhere and practically anytime.

"You haven't been anywhere until you've taken Route 2   3 through the Sand Hills of Nebraska," they're liable to say, late at night.

"Or Route 191 in Montana, 35 in Wisconsin, 90 in West Texas,   4 28 in the Upper Peninsula of Michigan, 120 in Wyoming, 62 in Arkansas, 83 in Kansas, 14 in Louisiana," I reply, after agreeing that 2 in Nebraska is one of my favorites. To handle Route 2 properly, you should first give a few hours to the Stuhr Museum in Grand Island to check on the human and natural history of the Great Plains. If you don't care all that much about what you're seeing, you should stay home, or, if you're just trying to get someplace, take a plane.

There is, of course, a hesitation to make any rules for the road;   5 the main reason you're out there is to escape any confinement other than that of change and motion. But certain precepts and theories should be kept in mind:

- Don't compute time and distance. Computing time and distance vitiates the benefits to be gotten from aimlessness. Leave that sort of thing to civilians with their specious categories of birthdays, average wage, height and weight, the number of steps to second floors. If you get into this acquisitive mood, make two ninety-degree turns and backtrack for a while. Or stop the car and run around in a big circle in a field. Climbing a tree or going swimming also helps. Remember that habit is a form of gravity that strangulates.
- Leave your reason, your logic, at home. A few years ago I flew all the way from northern Michigan to Palm Beach, Florida, in order to drive to Livingston, Montana, with a friend. Earlier in life I hitchhiked 4,000 miles round-trip to see the Pacific Ocean. Last year I needed to do some research in Nebraska. Good sense and the fact that it was January told me to drive south, then west by way of Chicago, spend a few days, and drive home. Instead I headed due north into a blizzard and made a three-day backroad circle to La Crosse, Wisconsin, one of my favorite hideouts. When I finished in Nebraska, I went to Wyoming, pulled a left for Colorado and New Mexico, a right for Arizona, headed east across Texas and Louisiana to Alabama, then north toward home. My

spirit was lightened by the thirty-five days and 8,000 or so miles. The car was a loaner, and on deserted back roads I could drive on cruise control, standing on the seat with shoulders and head through the sunroof.

- Spend as little time as possible thinking about the equipment. Assuming you are not a mechanic, and even if you are, it's better not to think too much about the car over and above minimum service details. I've had a succession of three four-wheel-drive Subaru station wagons, each equipped with a power winch, although recently I've had doubts about this auto. I like to take the car as far as I can go up a two-track, then get out and walk until the road disappears. This is the only solution to the neurotic pang that you might be missing something. High-performance cars don't have the clearance for back roads, and orthodox four-wheel drives are too jouncy for long trips. An ideal car might be a Saab turbo four-wheel-drive station wagon, but it has not as yet been built by that dour land without sunshine and garlic. A Range Rover is a pleasant, albeit expensive, idea, but you could very well find yourself a thousand miles from a spare part.

- A little research during downtime helps. This is the place for the lost art of reading. The sort of driving I'm talking about is a religious impulse, a craving for the unknown. You can, however, add to any trip immeasurably by knowing something about the history of the area or location. For instance, if you're driving through Chadron, Nebraska, on Route 20, it doesn't hurt to know that Crazy Horse, He Dog, American Horse, Little Big Man, and Sitting Bull took the same route when it was still a buffalo path.

- Be careful about who you are with. Whiners aren't appropriate. There can be tremendous inconveniences and long stretches of boredom. It takes a specific amount of optimism to be on the road, and anything less means misery. A nominal Buddhist who knows that "the goal is the path" is at an advantage. The essential silence of the highway can allow couples to turn the road into a domestic mud bath by letting their petty grievances preoccupy them. Marriages survive by garden-variety etiquette, and when my wife and I travel together we forget the often suffocating flotsam and jetsam of marriage.

If you're driving solo, another enemy can be the radio or tape   6
deck. This is an eccentric observation, but anyone under fifty in

America has likely dissipated a goodly share of his life listening to music. Music frequently draws you out of where you belong. It is hard work to be attentive, but it's the only game in town. D. H. Lawrence said that "the only true aristocracy is consciousness," which doesn't mean you can't listen to music; just don't do it all the time. Make your own road tapes: Start with cuts of Del Shannon, Merle Haggard, Stravinsky, Aretha Franklin, Bob Seger, Mozart, Buffett, Monteverdi, Woody Guthrie, Jim Reeves, B. B. King, George Jones, Esther Lammandier, Ray Charles, Bob Wills, and Nicholas Thorne. That sort of thing.

If you're lucky, you can find a perfect companion. During a   7
time of mutual stress I drove around Arizona with the grizzly bear expert Douglas Peacock, who knows every piece of flora, fauna, and Native American history in that state. In such company, the most unassertive mesa becomes verdant with possibility.

- Pretend you don't care about good food. This is intensely difficult if you are a professional pig, gourmand, and trencherman like I am. If you're going to drive around America you have to adopt the bliss-ninny notion that less is more. Pack a cooler full of disgusting health snacks. I am assuming you know enough to stay off the interstates with their sneeze shields and rainbow Jell-Os, the dinner specials that include the legendary "fried, fried," a substantial meal spun out of hot fat by the deep-fry cook. It could be anything from a shoe box full of oxygen to a cow plot to a dime-store wig. In honor of my own precepts I have given up routing designed to hit my favorite restaurants in Escanaba, Duluth, St. Cloud (Ivan's in the Park), Mandan, Miles City, and so on. The quasi–food revolution hasn't hit the countryside; I've had good luck calling disc jockeys for advice. You generally do much better in the South, particularly at barbecue places with hand-painted road signs. Along with food you might also consider amusements: If you stop at local bars or American Legion country dances don't offer underage girls hard drugs and that sort of thing. But unless you're a total asshole, *Easy Rider* paranoia is unwarranted. You are technically safer on the road than you are in your own bathroom or eating a dinner of unrecognizable leftovers with your mother.
- Avoid irony, cynicism, and self-judgment. If you were really smart, you probably wouldn't be doing this. You would be

in an office or club acting nifty, but you're in a car and no one knows you, and no one calls you because they don't know where you are. Moving targets are hard to hit. You are doing what you want, rather than what someone else wants. This is not the time to examine your shortcomings, which will certainly surface when you get home. Your spiritual fathers range from Marco Polo to Arthur Rimbaud, from Richard Halliburton to Jack Kerouac. Kerouac was the first actual novelist I ever met, back in 1957 or 1958 at the Five Spot, a jazz club in New York City. I saw him several times, and this great soul did not dwell on self-criticism, though, of course, there is an obvious downside to this behavior.

- Do not scorn day trips. You can use them to avoid nervous collapse. They are akin to the ardent sailor and his small sailboat. You needn't travel very far unless you live in one of our major urban centers, strewn across the land like immense canker sores. Outside this sort of urban concentration, county maps are available at any courthouse. One summer in Michigan's Upper Peninsula, after a tour in Hollywood had driven me ditzy, I logged more than 5,000 miles in four counties on gravel roads and two-tracks, lifting my sodden spirits and looking for good grouse and woodcock cover (game birds literally prefer to live in their restaurants, their prime feeding areas). This also served to keep me out of bars and away from drinking, because I don't drink while driving.

- Plan a real big one—perhaps hemispheric, or least national. Atrophy is the problem. If you're not expanding, you're growing smaller. As a poet and novelist I have to get out of the study and collect some brand-new memories, and many of our more memorable events are that of the childish, the daffy and irrational. "How do you know but that every bird that cuts the airy wavy is an immense world of delight closed to your senses five?" asked Blake. If you're currently trapped, your best move is to imagine the next road voyage.

I'm planning a trip when I finish my current novel, for which I 8 had to make an intense study of the years 1865 to 1900 in our history, also the history of Native Americans. I intend to check out locations where I sensed a particular magic in the past: certain culverts in western Minnesota, nondescript gullies in Kansas, invisible graveyards in New Mexico, moonbeam targets in Nebraska, buffalo jumps in Montana, melted ice palaces in the Dakotas, deserted but well-stocked wine warehouses in California. Maybe I'll discover a new bird or animal. Maybe I'll drive up a gravel road that winnows into a two-track that stops at an immense swale, in the center of which is a dense woodlot. I'll wade through the bog into the woods, where I'll find an old, gray farmhouse. In this farmhouse I'll find all my beloved dead dogs and cats in perfect health, tended by the heroines in my novels. I'll make a map of this trip on thin buckskin that I'll gradually cut up and add to stews. Everyone must find his own places.

MEANINGS AND VALUES

1. Why does Harrison begin this essay with a reflection on experiences of learning geography as a child? Is this an appropriate introduction for the remainder of the essay? Explain your response. (See "Guide to Terms": *Introductions; Evaluation.*)

2. Why does Harrison provide readers with statistics (though somewhat unscientific ones) in Paragraph 2? Describe the types of people to whom Harrison refers.

3. Why (in Paragraph 11) does Harrison refer to the tape deck and radio as potential enemies? What point might he be trying to make? How successful do you think his alternative is in avoiding the negative aspects of such equipment?

EXPOSITORY TECHNIQUES

1. Harrison's "list" (Paragraphs 6–10) is not the same kind of step-by-step list that Buhler and Graham present in "Give Juggling a Hand!" (pp. 262–264). What type of organization does he use to present the process? How effective is this approach? (Guide: *Evaluation.*)

2. What predominant tone does Harrison use throughout this essay? (Guide: *Tone.*) Where does the essay vary in tone, and why?

3. What type of reality is Harrison attempting to shape or present in his essay? Why does he use quotations in Paragraphs 3 and 4? What is the effect of these quotations in shaping reality?

DICTION AND VOCABULARY

1. For what level of reader is Harrison's work written? Make a list of the characteristics you think Harrison assumes his readers will have. What parts of the essay support your conclusions?

2. Highlight any words in the essay that are unfamiliar to you. Look up each of the words in a dictionary and use each one appropriately in a sentence.

READ TO WRITE

1. **Collaborating:** From your own perspective, write a list of key elements for a good automobile "travel" experience. Then, working in a group, compare lists. Look for common threads and write out a plan for an essay similar to Harrison's that expresses your collective thoughts on travel.

2. **Considering Audience:** People who travel frequently by automobile might respond positively to Harrison's essay. Even if they disagree with some of his points, they will likely understand his emphasis on the importance of the process of traveling by car. In writing, describe briefly how you might compose a similar kind of essay for people who generally travel by train, bus, or plane.

3. **Developing an Essay:** The term "rugged individualism" is often applied in a positive way to the character of Americans, particularly those who explored the Western frontier. The trait still shapes the behavior of some Americans today, including people who set out on cross-country drives with no particular destination. Write an essay comparing the concept of "going places" during the exploration and settlement of the Western frontier to travel and exploration today. You may need to do some research on the exploration and settlement in nineteenth-century America for your essay.

(NOTE: Suggestions for essays requiring development by PROCESS ANALYSIS are on pp. 313–314 at the end of this chapter.)

Issues and Ideas

Advertising and Appearances

- James B. Twitchell, *We Build Excitement*
- Jean E. Kilbourne, *Beauty . . . And the Beast of Advertising*
- Jessica Mitford, *To Dispel Fears of Live Burial*

Do appearances count? When they come to us on television, in movies, or through advertisements, they do—at least, that is what the authors of the essays that follow suggest.

James Twitchell explains how the images and strategies of advertising create and maintain a culture of which we are a part: a culture based on ever-present images and texts encouraging us to buy brand-name products, which he refers to as "adcult." Adcult makes one product appear better or more desirable than others and helps shape our tastes, choices, environment, and values, a process Twitchell analyzes in detail.

Jean E. Kilbourne offers a sharply critical analysis of the images of physical appearance and of behavior that dominate various media and have influenced our attitudes toward our bodies, our values, and our behaviors in harmful ways. She focuses especially on the ways women participate in and are affected by this process, but her conclusions also apply to society at large.

Jessica Mitford's treatment of our fascination with appearances has an even harder edge. She offers a bitingly satiric and humorous view of our concern with the appearance of the dead, a form of manipulation that amounts almost to a denial of the reality of death. Though she puts primary blame on the funeral industry for creating and maintaining this obsession with false appearances, she includes in her indictment all of us who willingly tolerate the sham process.

Taken together, these essays demonstrate the importance of media images in contemporary life and suggest ways of interpreting and analyzing these images that can lead to further writing.

JAMES B. TWITCHELL

JAMES B. TWITCHELL was born in Burlington, Vermont, in 1943. He received his B.A. (1962), M.A. (1966), and Ph.D. (1969) from the University of North Carolina at Chapel Hill. He has taught at Duke University, California State University Bakersfield, and the University of Florida, where he is currently Alumni Professor of English. Though much of Twitchell's writing has appeared in scholarly journals and in books issued by university presses, his work is nonetheless interesting and accessible to a wide audience of readers. Among his books are *Forbidden Partners: The Incest Taboo in Modern Culture* (1986); *Dreadful Pleasures: An Anatomy of Modern Horror* (1987); *Preposterous Violence: Fables of Aggression in Modern Culture* (1989); *Carnival Culture: The Trashing of Taste in America* (1992) (nominated for a National Book Award and a National Book Critics Circle Award); and *Adcult USA: The Triumph of Advertising in American Culture* (1996).

We Build Excitement

In this selection from *Adcult USA* (1996), James Twitchell talks about the process by which advertising became part of our culture and now serves as a primary force in shaping our culture, our perceptions, and our values. The selection is primarily informational and makes use of numerous examples in its analysis of the process. Twitchell is critical, at times, of the work of advertisers, but his criticism is much less harsh than that of many other writers, for, as he admits in the preface to *Adcult USA*, "I have always loved advertising."

The Hatter in the Strand of London, instead of making better felt-hats than another, mounts a huge lath-and-plaster Hat, seven feet high, upon wheels; sends a man to drive it through the streets; hoping to be saved *thereby*. He has not attempted to *make* better hats, as he was appointed by the Universe to do, and as with this ingenuity of his he could very probably have done, but his whole industry is turned to *persuade* us that he has made such! He too knows that the Quack has become God.

—Thomas Carlyle,
"Past and Present," 1843

Thomas Carlyle just didn't get it. The Hatter in the Strand of   1
London was not in the business of making hats to make better
hats. He made hats to make money. The Victorians may have

commanded the manufacturer to make the best of what he set out to do, but the culture of capitalism does not care so much about what he makes as about what he can sell. Hence the "best" hat becomes the most profitable hat. Ironically, perhaps he cannot make hats profitably unless he can market what he makes efficiently. The selling determines the making. And once he makes those best hats, especially if he has a machine to help him, heaven help him if he makes too many. If he has to spend some of his productive time acting like a nut in order to sell those hats, so be it.

The ingredients necessary to concoct an Adcult [culture of advertising] are not complex. The Hatter in the Strand of London is crucial. Because the Hatter probably has enough hats for his own use, he makes something that has exchange value. Assuming that he can control the retail price, the more he manufactures, the more he takes advantage of the economies of mass production and the greater the profit. To control that retail price however, he needs some method to differentiate his hat or he will produce more than he can sell. After all, because the product is partially machine made, it is essentially interchangeable with a competitor's product made with the same machinery.

The process of differentiation, called branding, is the key ingredient in all advertising. Make all the machine-made felt hats, biscuits, shoes, cigarettes, automobiles, or computer chips you want, but you cannot sell effectively until you can call it a Fedora, a Ritz, a Nike, a Marlboro, a Chevrolet, or an Intel 386. If everybody's biscuits are in the same barrel, and if they look pretty much the same, urging people to buy biscuits probably won't do the trick. Chances are, they won't buy your biscuit. As Thomas J. Barratt said at almost the same time that Carlyle was having at the Hatter, "Any fool can make soap. It takes a clever man to sell it."[3] Barratt was a clever man. He made a fortune by the end of the century by calling his soap Pears' Soap and making sure everyone knew about it by defacing miles of Anglo-American wall and newsprint space with "Have you had your Pears' today?" In many ways modern culture has been a battle between Carlyle and Barratt. If you aren't sure who won, look around you.

Adcult also requires purchasers with sufficient disposable income to buy your product. And it doesn't hurt if your audience members have enough curiosity to listen to you tell them your

2

3

4

[3]E. S. Tuner, *The Shocking History of Advertising* (New York: Dutton, 1953).

biscuits are different when they know all biscuits are the same. But watch out: this process is not without risk. When money is tight, brands take flight. For reasons no one can understand, from time to time markets fall apart, advertising loses its grip, and the charade has to be reenacted. Procter & Gamble spent billions building its soap brands, Philip Morris did the same with premium cigarettes, as did IBM with the personal computer, only to have the demand for their brands suddenly plummet. Generics appear to eat up what advertising created. Brands can suddenly become just commodities again. The Hatter in the Strand soon responds by dropping his prices and by making a still larger lath-and-plaster hat.

With those ingredients in the pot all an Adcult still needs is a 5 plasma, or conduit, between producer and consumer within which producers can, in the jargon of modern criticism, *inscribe* their message. The ever bigger lath-and-plaster hat is soon subject to diminishing returns. The brand may appear *on* his hat, but its name recognition is created *in* a medium. So along with his sign the Hatter may even decide to hire someone to advertise his product by voice. In the nineteenth century consumers still heard the cries of the costermonger (the coster is a kind of English apple) or other traders announcing their wares:

> *One-a-penny, two-a-penny, hot cross buns!*
> *One-a-penny, two for tup'ence, hot cross buns!*
>
> *Dust, O! Dust O! Bring it out today.*
> *Bring it out today! I shan't be here tomorrow!*
>
> *I sweep your Chimnies clean, O!*
> *I sweep your Chimney clean, O!*
>
> *Buy my Diddle Dumplings, hot! hot!*
> *Diddle, Diddle, Diddle, Dumplings, hot!*
>
> *Maids, I mend old Pans or Kettles,*
> *Mend old Pans or Kettles, O!*
>
> *Muffins, O! Crumpets! Muffins to-day!*
> *Crumpets, O! Muffins, O! Fresh to-day!*

Street cries and moving hats "set upon wheels" are no longer 6 major conduits in modern Adcult. True, the urban bus has become a billboard. And the billboard plastered on a truck is making a comeback in cluttered cities (the sides of such rolling billboards are lit fluorescently and can change panels every ten minutes), and the human voice can still be heard on street corners.[4] But they are no match for ink and electrons.

With the advent of print and paste, signs moved to walls.   7 From the late seventeenth century to the middle of the nineteenth the great cities of western Europe were nightly plastered over—sometimes twice a night—with what became known as posters. Seventeenth-century London streets were so thick with signs that Charles II proclaimed that "no sign shall be hung across the streets shutting out the air and light of the heavens." Although it was against the law, even Fleet Street Prison was posted. As the "post no bills" regulations took hold, posters became free-standing bill-boards. The "boards" grew so thick in America that people could barely see Niagara Falls through the forest of Coca-Cola and Mennen's Toilet powder signs. N. W. Ayer Company executives bragged that if all the boards they had erected for Nabisco were painted on a fence, the fence would enclose the Panama Canal on either side, from sea to shining sea.

What distinguishes modern advertising is that it has jumped   8 from the human voice and printed posters to anything that can carry it. Almost every physical object now carries advertising, almost every human environment is suffused with advertising, almost every moment of time is calibrated by advertising.

Start the day with breakfast. What's on the cereal box but the Ninja   9 Turtles, Batman, or the Addams Family? Characters real or imagined once sold cereal; now they *are* the cereal. Once Wild Bill Hickock, Bob Mathias, Huckleberry Hound, and Yogi Bear touted Sugar Pops or Wheaties. Now the sugar gobs reappear every six months, renamed to cross-promote some event. When the most recent Robin Hood movie was released, a Prince of Thieves Cereal appeared on grocery shelves. Alas, the movie did not show Mr. Hood starting the day with his own brand. But Kellogg has tried for this brass ring of promotion anyway. It has marketed cereals with Jerry Seinfeld and Jay Leno on the boxes and then gone on to buy commercial time on their network, NBC. It is of some comfort that while cereals sporting

---

[4]In a sense, of course, advertising in various media is ancient. Commercial speech starts with the snake's spiel in the Garden of Eden, is heard in the cries of vendors in ancient Persia, is seen on walls of Pompeii as the marks listing prices of various prostitutes, is carried in our surnames (as with Smith, Weaver, Miller, Taylor, Baker. . . .), and remains in the coats of arms over European hostelries with names like the Red Crown, the Gold Fox, and the Three Stars as well as in the symbolic images of the barber's pole or the golden balls of a pawn shop.

Barbie and Donkey Kong have gone stale on the shelves, the re-doubtable Fred Flintstone and his Flintstones cereal survive.

Go to school. The classroom is the Valhalla of place-based media.   10
Better than the doctor's office, the shopping mall, the health club, the hospital, and the airport, here you have the ideal—a captive audience with more disposable income than discretion. Advertising material is all over the place. For home economics classes Chef Boyardee supplies worksheets on how to use pasta; Prego counters with the Prego Science Challenge complete with an "instructional kit" to test the thickness of various spaghetti sauces. General Mills sends out samples of its candy along with a pamphlet, "Gushers: Wonders of the Earth," which encourages the kids to learn about geysers by biting the "fruit snack." Monsanto donates a video sug-gesting that the world cannot be fed without using pesticides; Union Carbide does the same, saying chemicals "add comfort to your lives." Exxon has an energy awareness game in which nonrenew-able natural resources are not losers. K-Swiss sneakers provides shoes for participants in a video creation of an ad for . . . you guessed it. And Kodak, McDonald's, and Coca-Cola plaster a na-tional essay contest about why kids should stay in school with cor-porate logos and concern. Clearly, one reason to stay in school is to consume more advertising.

Go shopping. The war, as they say, is in the store. Food shoppers   11
make almost two-thirds of their buying decisions when they set foot in the aisle. Capitalizing on these last-minute decisions is why gro-cers don't alphabetize soup sections, why all the raisin bran cereals are not bunched together, and why high-profit toothbrushes are both nestled with toothpastes and stacked almost at random throughout the store. With more than fifteen hundred new items in-troduced to supermarkets each month, the need to inform and con-vince the querulous shopper of the new product is intense. The experience of food buying has become an advertising adventure.

A company called Ad-Tiles puts its ads on the floors in   12
Pathmark stores, charging what amounts to 50 cents per thousand impressions. Flashing coupon dispensers are omnipresent, except near the upright freezers and open dairy case, because shoppers do not like to open doors to compare prices—too cold. They won't even open the door for coupons. The latest hot places for advertising are the checkout line and the shopping cart. The shopping cart, which revolutionized food shopping as much as self-service, because it de-termined the amount of food a shopper could buy, has come alive.

VideOcart is here, almost. This shopping cart has a six-by-nine-inch screen affixed to what used to be the kiddie rumble seat, and infrared censors on the ceiling cause it to flash ads, messages, and recipes as you pass various products. The same technology that scans the Universal Product Code on your can of beans now scans the shopper. You are the can.

Go to a sporting event. It's football season. Let's go to a bowl   13 game. Which one? Or which product? The Orange Bowl has become the Federal Express Orange Bowl, the Cotton Bowl has become the Mobil Cotton Bowl, the Sugar Bowl has become the USF&G Sugar Bowl, and the Sun Bowl has become the John Hancock Bowl. Not to mention the Sunkist Fiesta Bowl (now the IBM OS/2 Fiesta Bowl), the Mazda Gator Bowl (now the Outback Steakhouse Gator Bowl), the Sea World Holiday Bowl, the Domino's Pizza Copper Bowl, the California Raisin Bowl, and everyone's favorite, the Poulan/Weed Eater Independence Bowl. For a while even the Heisman Memorial Trophy was up for grabs. Merrill Lynch paid $1.5 million for promotional rights but not for a name change. Not yet. No matter: Merrill Lynch already has a golf tournament.

Take a trip. Get away from Adcult. Weren't we told in the fa-   14 mous Cunard advertisement that getting there is half the fun? Hop in a taxi. Some urban cabs have alphanumeric signs that scroll ten ads per minute across a panel on the back of the front seat. Gannett, the billboard-and-newspaper conglomerate, has been experimenting with installing these "electronic gutters" in subway cars and has contracted with the Transit Authority of New York to put them in six thousand cars. Nothing revolutionary here, just the electrifying of the advertising card, which has been a staple of public transportation since the first trolley. The company has also introduced what it calls the brand train and the brand bus in which a sponsor can buy all the ad space on a particular vehicle that runs a specific route. So Donna Karan's DKNY line has taken over an entire ten-car train that runs under Lexington Avenue on Manhattan's East Side, endlessly running beneath DKNY's superstore at Bloomingdale's. Gannett also installed radio equipment in bus shelters around midtown Manhattan for a news and business station. The New York City Department of Transportation ordered Gannett to pull the plug—too much noise.

No destination is safe. The Russian government has even sold   15 space inside Red Square. For something less than $1 million your message can be part of the May Day celebration. Coca-Cola and

Pepsi are already in Pushkin Square. For $100,000 the side of GUM, the largest department store in the world, is yours. Lenin's tomb is off-limits, but above Lenin's tomb is OK. For about $30,000 you can float a blimp. Who's itching to get onto Russian space? The usual suspects: AT&T, Reebok, Sara Lee, and of course the ever-present tobacco companies.[5]

Finally, no matter where you go in this world or beyond, when   16 you get home, your credit card bill for the trip will eventually appear. When it does, it may have that tear-off tag on the envelope upon which is printed yet another ad.

Almost as interesting as where advertising is, is where it might   17 be. Here are some of the more interesting venues contributed by advertising men and women who make hundreds of thousands of dollars thinking up and trying out some of these locations:

- Subway tokens.
- The backs of chairs in commuter trains.
- The Gateway Arch in St. Louis.
- Postage stamps and paper currency.
- In place of the telephone dial tone.
- Polo ponies.
- The bottom of golf holes, to be observed while putting and then while removing the ball.
- Self-serve gasoline pumps. Messages scroll along with the amount of gas pumped.
- Rural mailboxes. Although the Postal Service prohibits advertising on boxes, John Deere has produced a green and yellow version that retails for about $50.
- Astronauts' uniforms.
- Postcards. Laden with advertising, they are given to patrons by restaurants.
- School buses.
- Slot machines. Why should they come up cherries and oranges? Why not boxes of Tide?

[5]Nor would you be ad free in outer space. For $500,000 NASA agreed that Columbia Pictures could cover a rocket with an ad for Arnold Schwarzenegger's *Last Action Hero* (the movie bombed before the missile flew). And Joel Babbit, an Atlanta advertising executive, almost succeeded in launching a billboard high in the heavens. The space billboard was to be an unfolding screen set in geosynchronous orbit 250 miles above the equator; in the evening it would appear to be about the size of the moon— just right for a logo. The usual suspects were interested, but the U.S. Department of Transportation nixed the idea.

- Catalogs. This has been done, most notably by *The Sharper Image,* but the reverse is almost as interesting—a recent *Lands' End* catalog included a story by David Mamet.
- Video games. "Cool Spot" is a game like "Pac Man," except it stars "Spot," the 7-Up mascot. "Yo! Noid" is a game centered around the Domino's Pizza character. "Mick and Mack: Global Gladiators" has a black hero who battles pollution. To get from level to level the player has to collect golden arches passed out by a gate-tending Ronald McDonald.

It may be of some comfort to critics of this use of the human 18 imagination that a new advertising medium has begun appearing *inside* advertising agencies. Called Media News, it appears on a never ending fifty-four-by-eight-inch alphanumeric display similar to the Dow Jones market ticker. Running across the board is information interspersed with thirty seconds of commercials. Advertisers pay $5,000 for thirteen weeks of ads in a medium described by its creators as "invasive without being aggravating." Poetic justice?

The rise of place-based (as it is known in the trade), in your face 19 (as it is experienced), or new media (as it is presented to the public) follows the principle that where blank space exists, there shall advertising be. The triumph of Adcult is attributable not so much to new products as to new media reaching new audiences. Each new invasion by commercialism is greeted with an outcry, followed by tentative acceptance, assumption, and expectation. And finally, of course, neglect.

MEANINGS AND VALUES

1. What, according to the writer, did Thomas Carlyle fail to understand (see Par. 1)? What key point about business and advertising does the writer make in rejecting Carlyle's point of view?

2. What are the ingredients of an Adcult, and where does the writer discuss them? Is this definition satisfactory? In what ways, if any, might it be improved?

3. How does modern advertising differ from that of previous centuries? Be specific.

Expository Techniques

1. In what way are the italicized sentences beginning Paragraphs 10, 11, 12, 14, and 15 linked to the second sentence in Paragraph 9? Discuss how this linking provides coherence within the second half of the selection. (See "Guide to Terms": *Coherence.*) In what ways does Paragraph 9, as a whole, help unify the selection? (Guide: *Unity.*)

2. In which paragraphs does the writer employ extended examples? In which does he use clusters of brief examples? Which paragraphs containing brief examples are especially effective? Why? Are any markedly less effective? Explain why.

3. How would you describe the overall tone of this selection? In what ways, if at all, does the tone add to or detract from the informational goals of the piece? Can the tone in Paragraphs 10, 11, and 16 be considered either ironic or sarcastic? (Guide: *Irony.*) If so, does this tone undermine the writer's claim that "I have always loved advertising"? Explain. If not, what do you believe is the tone of these paragraphs?

Diction and Vocabulary

1. Would you characterize the diction in Paragraphs 11–13 as *specific* or *general?* As *abstract* or *concrete?* (Guide: *Specific/General; Concrete/Abstract.*) Cite examples to support your conclusions. How does the diction contribute to the purpose and effect of these paragraphs? (Guide: *Purpose.*)

2. Compare the diction in Paragraphs 5–6 and 15–16. Which makes greater use of formal diction, and why? Which makes greater use of colloquial language, and why? (Guide: *Colloquial Expressions.*) To what extent does the writer use the connotations of terms as well as their denotations to criticize advertisers? (Guide: *Connotation/Denotation.*) Is this criticism harsh or mild, direct or indirect? Explain.

3. If you do not know the meaning of some of the following terms, look them up in a dictionary: lath, quack (Par 1); differentiate (3); charade, plummet (5); conduit, inscribe, costermonger (6); suffused, calibrated (9); redoubtable (10); Valhalla (11); omnipresent (13); invasive (18); attributable, tentative, assumption (19).

Read to Write

1. **Collaborating:** Advertising is a good subject for expository writing. Working with a group, make up a set of questions about advertising and then list details, ideas, and possible topics under each. When you are finished, look through the list to see if you can discover possible focuses for essays. Choose the two you find most promising, and develop an essay plan for each. Here are several questions to get you started: Other than manufacturers, who sponsors advertising? What different kinds of advertising do we encounter in a typical day? Do

different kinds of advertising achieve their effects through different processes?

2.   **Considering Audience:** Twitchell uses many examples in his essay, and in so doing he represents the tastes, values, and interests of many groups of readers. But he does not include all possible readers. What significant groups (ethnic, occupational religious, or otherwise) are not represented in the examples? Do any of these omissions seriously weaken the essay? If so, which ones? Suggest several examples that might be added to the essay to broaden its appeal or make it more effective in some other way.

3.   **Developing an Essay:** Drawing on "We Build Excitement" as a model, create an essay of your own showing how the contemporary form of some activity or process (fishing, basketball, or clothing design and manufacture, for example) differs from earlier forms. Also explain the special features of the contemporary process in detail.

(NOTE: Suggestions for topics requiring development by PROCESS ANALYSIS are on pp. 313–314 at the end of this chapter.)

JEAN E. KILBOURNE

JEAN E. KILBOURNE is a media critic whose award-winning films *Still Killing Us Softly* and *Calling the Shots* explore the relationships between media and advertising images and our values and behaviors. She lectures regularly on alcohol and cigarette advertising, images of women in advertising, and related issues.

Beauty . . . And the Beast of Advertising

In this essay, first published in *Media & Values* in 1989, Kilbourne analyzes the ways media images shape perceptions and values, particularly those of women. This essay blends a number of patterns, including definition, process analysis, and cause-and-effect analysis.

"You're a Halston woman from the very beginning," the adver-   1
tisement proclaims. The model stares provocatively at the viewer, her long blonde hair waving around her face, her bare chest partially covered by two curved bottles that give the illusion of breasts and a cleavage.

The average American is accustomed to blue-eyed blondes se-   2
ductively touting a variety of products. In this case, however, the blonde is about five years old.

Advertising is an over $100 billion a year industry and affects   3
all of us throughout our lives. We are each exposed to over 2,000 ads a day, constituting perhaps the most powerful educational force in society. The average adult will spend one and one-half years of his/her life watching television commercials. But the ads sell a great deal more than products. They sell values, images and concepts of success and worth, love and sexuality, popularity and normalcy. They tell us who we are and who we should be. Sometimes they sell addictions.

Advertising's foundation and economic lifeblood is the mass   4
media, and the primary purpose of the mass media is to deliver an audience to advertisers, just as the primary purpose of television programs is to deliver an audience for commercials.

Adolescents are particularly vulnerable, however, because they   5
are new and inexperienced consumers and are the prime targets of many advertisements. They are in the process of learning their

values and roles and developing their self-concepts. Most teenagers are sensitive to peer pressure and find it difficult to resist or even question the dominant cultural messages perpetuated and reinforced by the media. Mass communication has made possible a kind of nationally distributed peer pressure that erodes private and individual values and standards.

But what does society, and especially teenagers, learn from the   6
advertising messages that proliferate in the mass media? On the most obvious level they learn the stereotypes. Advertising creates a mythical, WASP-oriented world in which no one is ever ugly, overweight, poor, struggling or disabled either physically or mentally (unless you count the housewives who talk to little men in toilet bowls, animated germs in drains or muscle-bound giants clad in white clothing). And it is a world in which people talk only about products.

Housewives or Sex Objects

The aspect of advertising most in need of analysis and change is the   7
portrayal of women. Scientific studies and the most casual viewing yield the same conclusion: Women are shown almost exclusively as housewives or sex objects.

The housewife, pathologically obsessed by cleanliness and lemon-   8
fresh scents, debates cleaning products with herself and worries about her husband's "ring around the collar."

The sex object is a mannequin, a shell. Conventional beauty is   9
her only attribute. She has no lines or wrinkles (which would indicate she had the bad taste and poor judgment to grow older), no scars or blemishes—indeed, she has no pores. She is thin, generally tall and long-legged, and, above all, she is young. All "beautiful" women in advertisements (including minority women), regardless of product or audience, conform to this norm. Women are constantly exhorted to emulate this ideal, to feel ashamed and guilty if they fail, and to feel that their desirability and lovability are contingent upon physical perfection.

Creating Artificiality

The image is artificial and can only be achieved artificially (even the   10
"natural look" requires much preparation and expense). Beauty is something that comes from without; more than one million dollars is

spent every hour on cosmetics. Desperate to conform to an ideal and impossible standard, many women go to great lengths to manipulate and change their faces and bodies. A woman is conditioned to view her face as a mask and her body as an object, as *things* separate from and more important than her real self, constantly in need of alteration, improvement, and disguise. She is made to feel dissatisfied with and ashamed of herself, whether she tries to achieve "the look" or not. Objectified constantly by others, she learns to objectify herself. (It is interesting to note that one in five college-age women have an eating disorder.)

"When *Glamour* magazine surveyed its readers in 1984, 75 per-   11
cent felt too heavy and only 15 percent felt just right. Nearly half of those who were actually underweight reported feeling too fat and wanting to diet. Among a sample of college women, 40 percent felt overweight when only 12 percent actually were too heavy," according to Rita Freedman in her book *Beauty Bound.*

There is evidence that this preoccupation with weight begins   12
at ever-earlier ages for women. According to a recent article in *New Age Journal*, "Even grade-school girls are succumbing to sticklike standards of beauty enforced by a relentless parade of wasp-waisted fashion models, movie stars, and pop idols." A study by a University of California professor showed that nearly 80 percent of fourth-grade girls in the Bay Area are watching their weight.

A recent *Wall Street Journal* survey of students in four Chicago-   13
area schools found that more than half the fourth-grade girls were dieting and three-quarters felt they were overweight. One student said, "We don't expect boys to be that handsome. We take them as they are." Another added, "But boys expect girls to be perfect and beautiful. And skinny."

Dr. Steven Levenkron, author of *The Best Little Girl in the World*,   14
the story of an anorexic, says his blood pressure soars every time he opens a magazine and finds an ad for women's fashions. "If I had my way," he said, "every one of them would have to carry a line saying, 'Caution: This model may be hazardous to your health.'"

Women are also dismembered in commercials, their bodies sepa-   15
rated into parts in need of change or improvement. If a woman has "acceptable" breasts, then she must also be sure that her legs are worth watching, her hips slim, her feet sexy, and that her buttocks look nude under her clothes ("like I'm not wearin' nothin'"). This image is difficult and costly to achieve and impossible to maintain (unless you buy the product)—no one is flawless and everyone ages.

Growing older is the great taboo. Women are encouraged to remain little girls ("because innocence is sexier than you think"), to be passive and dependent, never too mature. The contradictory message— "sensual, but not too far from innocence"—places women in a double bind; somehow we are supposed to be both sexy and virginal, experienced and naïve, seductive and chaste. The disparagement of maturity is, of course, insulting and frustrating to adult women, and the implication that little girls are seductive is dangerous to real children.

Influencing Sexual Attitudes

Young people also learn a great deal about sexual attitudes from   16
the media and from advertising in particular. Advertising's approach to sex is pornographic; it reduces people to objects and de-emphasizes human contact and individuality. This reduction of sexuality to a dirty joke and of people to objects is the real obscenity of the culture. Although the sexual sell, overt and subliminal, is at a fevered pitch in most commercials, there is at the same time a notable absence of sex as an important and profound human activity.

There have been some changes in the images of women. Indeed,   17
a "new woman" has emerged in commercials in recent years. She is generally presented as superwoman, who manages to do all the work at home and on the job (with the help of a product, of course, not of her husband or children or friends), or as the liberated woman, who owes her independence and self-esteem to the products she uses. These new images do not represent any real progress but rather create a myth of progress, an illusion that reduces complex sociopolitical problems to mundane personal ones.

Advertising images do not cause these problems, but they   18
contribute to them by creating a climate in which the marketing of women's bodies—the sexual sell and dismemberment, distorted body image ideal and children as sex objects—is seen as acceptable.

This is the real tragedy, that many women internalize these   19
stereotypes and learn their "limitations," thus establishing a self-fulfilling prophecy. If one accepts these mythical and degrading images, to some extent one actualizes them. By remaining unaware of the profound seriousness of the ubiquitous influence, the redundant message and the subliminal impact of advertisements, we ignore one of the most powerful "educational" forces in the culture—one that greatly affects our self-images, our ability to relate to each other,

and effectively destroys any awareness and action that might help to change that climate.

MEANINGS AND VALUES

1. According to the writer, what does advertising tell women they should be, and by what process does it convey this message? Does the beginning of Paragraph 18 accurately summarize the process the writer has been analyzing? If not, what is missing from the summary? Would the essay be stronger if the missing information were included? Why or why not? (See "Guide to Terms": *Evaluation.*)

2. Who or what is the "new woman" (Par. 7)? Why does the writer believe that this image does "not represent any real progress"? Why would the absence of any discussion of the "new woman" weaken the expository purpose of the selection? (Guide: *Purpose.*)

3. At several places in the essay, Kilbourne discusses the consequences of advertising on teenagers while in much of the rest of the essay she focuses on women. Does the focus on teenagers undermine the unity of the essay? Why, or why not? (Guide: *Unity.*)

EXPOSITORY TECHNIQUES

1. What strategy does Kilbourne use to begin her essay (Pars. 1–2)? (Guide: *Introductions.*) Can the opening of this essay be considered ironic? Why, or why not? (Guide: *Irony.*) What strategy does she use to conclude the essay? (Guide: *Closings.*)

2. What kinds of evidence does the author provide to support her conclusions about the process of advertising and its consequences? Which kind of evidence do you consider most effective, and which seems least effective? Why? (Guide: *Evaluation.*)

3. Discuss how Kilbourne varies sentence length (and structure) to achieve emphasis in Paragraphs 3, 9, and 15. (Guide: *Emphasis; Syntax.*)

DICTION AND VOCABULARY

1. Where in the essay does the writer use numbers to present information? Be specific. Why can these numbers be considered a form of concrete diction? (Guide: *Concrete/Abstract; Diction.*) What do they contribute to the effects of the various passages in which they appear?

2. If you do not know the meaning of some of the following words, look them up in a dictionary: provocatively, cleavage (Par. 1); touting (2);

stereotypes, WASP (6); pathologically (8); mannequin, attribute, exhorted, contingent (9); anorexic (14); sensual, disparagement (15); overt, subliminal (16); mundane (17); ubiquitous, redundant (19).

READ TO WRITE

1. **Collaborating:** Working with a group of classmates, spend some time observing advertisements on television or analyzing them in magazines. Take notes on the process by which they achieve their effects as well as the effects themselves. Discuss the notes and arrive at a focus and a thesis for a possible essay.

2. **Considering Audience:** Read (or reread) Brent Staples's essay, "Just Walk on By" (pp. 5–9), for another example of an essay that begins with a reversal of readers' expectations. Create an opening for an essay of your own with a reversal of readers' expectations similar to the ones created by Kilbourne and Staples.

3. **Developing an Essay:** Using Kilbourne's essay as a model, discuss the process of advertising as it affects a group or groups other than women in general. Feel free to take a positive view of advertising in contrast to Kilbourne's generally negative perspective.

(NOTE: Suggestions for topics requiring development by means of PROCESS ANALYSIS are on pp. 313–314 at the end of this chapter.)

JESSICA MITFORD

JESSICA MITFORD was born in 1917, the daughter of an English peer. Her brother was sent to Eton, but she and her six sisters were educated at home by their mother. At the age of nineteen Mitford left home, eventually making her way to the United States in 1939. She made her home in San Francisco and became an American citizen in 1944. She did not begin her writing career until she was thirty-eight. Her books are *Lifeitselfmanship* (1956); her autobiography, *Daughters and Rebels* (1960); the bestseller *The American Way of Death* (1963); *The Trial of Dr. Spock* (1969); *Kind and Usual Punishment* (1973), a devastating study of the American penal system; *A Fine Old Conflict* (1977); and *Poison Penmanship* (1979). Mitford's articles have appeared in the *Atlantic, Harper's,* and *McCall's.*

To Dispel Fears of Live Burial

"To Dispel Fears of Live Burial" (editor's title) is a portion of *The American Way of Death,* a book described in the *New York Times* as a "savagely witty and well-documented exposé." The "savagely witty" style, evident in this selection, does not obscure the fact of its being a tightly organized, step-by-step process analysis.

Embalming is indeed a most extraordinary procedure, and one must wonder at the docility of Americans who each year pay hundreds of millions of dollars for its perpetuation, blissfully ignorant of what it is all about, what is done, how it is done. Not one in ten thousand has any idea of what actually takes place. Books on the subject are extremely hard to come by. They are not to be found in most libraries or bookshops. 1

In an era when huge television audiences watch surgical operations in the comfort of their living rooms, when, thanks to the animated cartoon, the geography of the digestive system has become familiar territory even to the nursery school set, in a land where the satisfaction of curiosity about almost all matters is a national pastime, the secrecy surrounding embalming can, surely, hardly be attributed to the inherent gruesomeness of the subject. Custom in this regard has within this century suffered a complete reversal. In the early days of American embalming, when it was performed in the home of the deceased, it was almost mandatory for some relative to stay by the embalmer's side and witness the procedure. Today, family members 2 who might wish to be in attendance would certainly be dissuaded by the funeral director. All others, except apprentices, are excluded by law from the preparation room.

A close look at what does actually take place may explain in   3
large measure the undertaker's intractable reticence concerning a procedure that has become his major *raison d'être*. Is it possible he fears that public information about embalming might lead patrons to wonder if they really want this service? If the funeral men are loath to discuss the subject outside the trade, the reader may, understandably, be equally loath to go on reading at this point. For those who have the stomach for it, let us part the formaldehyde curtain. . . .

The body is first laid out in the undertaker's morgue—or rather,   4
Mr. Jones is reposing in the preparation room—to be readied to bid the world farewell.

The preparation room in any of the better funeral establish-   5
ments has the tiled and sterile look of a surgery, and indeed the embalmer-restorative artist who does his chores there is beginning to adopt the term "dermasurgeon" (appropriately corrupted by some mortician-writers as "demisurgeon") to describe his calling. His equipment, consisting of scalpels, scissors, augers, forceps, clamps, needles, pumps, tubes, bowls and basins, is crudely imitative of the surgeon's as is his technique, acquired in a nine- or twelve-month post-high-school course in an embalming school. He is supplied by an advanced chemical industry with a bewildering array of fluids, sprays, pastes, oils, powders, creams, to fix or soften tissue, shrink or distend it as needed, dry it here, restore the moisture there. There are cosmetics, waxes and paints, to fill and cover features, even plaster of Paris to replace entire limbs. There are ingenious aids to prop and stabilize the cadaver: A Vari-Pose Head Rest, the Edwards Arm and Hand Positioner, the Repose Block (to support the shoulders during the embalming), and the Throop Foot Positioner, which resembles an old-fashioned stocks.

Mr. John H. Eckels, president of the Eckels College of Mortuary   6
Science, thus describes the first part of the embalming procedure: "In the hands of a skilled practitioner, this work may be done in a comparatively short time and without mutilating the body other than by slight incision—so slight that it scarcely would cause serious inconvenience if made upon a living person. It is necessary to remove the blood, and doing this not only helps in the disinfecting, but removes the principal cause of disfigurements due to discoloration."

Another textbook discusses the all-important time element: "The earlier this is done, the better, for every hour that elapses between death and embalming will add to the problems and complications encountered. . . ." Just how soon should one get going on the embalming? The author tells us, "On the basis of such scanty information made available to this profession through its rudimentary and haphazard system of technical research, we must conclude that the best results are to be obtained if the subject is embalmed before life is completely extinct—that is, before cellular death has occurred. In the average case, this would mean within an hour after somatic death." For those who feel that there is something a little rudimentary, not to say haphazard, about this advice, a comforting thought is offered by another writer. Speaking of fears entertained in early days of premature burial, he points out, "One of the effects of embalming by chemical injection, however, has been to dispel fears of live burial." How true; once the blood is removed, chances of live burial are indeed remote.

To return to Mr. Jones, the blood is drained out through the veins and replaced by embalming fluid pumped in through the arteries. As noted in *The Principles and Practices of Embalming,* "Every operator has a favorite injection and drainage point—a fact which becomes a handicap only if he fails or refuses to forsake his favorites when conditions demand it." Typical favorites are the carotid artery, femoral artery, jugular vein, subclavian vein. There are various choices of embalming fluid. If Flextone is used, it will produce a "mild, flexible rigidity. The skin retains a velvety softness, the tissues are rubbery and pliable. Ideal for women and children." It may be blended with B. and G. Products Company's Lyf-Lyk tint, which is guaranteed to reproduce "nature's own skin texture . . . the velvety appearance of living tissue." Suntone comes in three separate tints: Suntan; Special Cosmetic Tint, a pink shade "especially indicated for young female subjects"; and Regular Cosmetic Tint, moderately pink.

About three to six gallons of dyed and perfumed solution of formaldehyde, glycerin, borax, phenol, alcohol, and water are soon circulating through Mr. Jones, whose mouth has been sewn together with a "needle directed upward between the upper lip and gum and brought out through the left nostril," with the corners raised slightly "for a more pleasant expression." If he should be bucktoothed, his teeth are cleaned with Bon Ami and coated with colorless nail polish. His eyes, meanwhile, are closed with flesh-tinted eye caps and eye cement.

The next step is to have at Mr. Jones with a thing called a trocar.   10
This is a long, hollow needle attached to a tube. It is jabbed into the
abdomen, poked around the entrails and chest cavity, the contents
of which are pumped out and replaced with "cavity fluid." This
done, and the hole in the abdomen sewn up, Mr. Jones's face is heavily creamed (to protect the skin from burns which may be caused by
leakage of the chemicals), and he is covered with a sheet and left un-
molested for a while. But not for long—there is more, much more, in
store for him. He has been embalmed, but not yet restored, and the
best time to start the restorative work is eight to ten hours after embalming, when the tissues have become firm and dry.

The object of all this attention to the corpse, it must be remem-   11
bered, is to make it presentable for viewing in an attitude of healthy
repose. "Our customs require the presentation of our dead in the
semblance of normality . . . unmarred by the ravages of illness, disease or mutilation," says Mr. J. Sheridan Mayer in his *Restorative Art.*
This is rather a large order since few people die in the full bloom of
health, unravaged by illness and unmarked by some disfigurement.
The funeral industry is equal to the challenge: "In some cases the
gruesome appearance of a mutilated or disease-ridden subject may
be quite discouraging. The task of restoration may seem impossible
and shake the confidence of the embalmer. This is the time for intestinal fortitude and determination. Once the formative work is begun and affected tissues are cleaned or removed, all doubts of
success vanish. It is surprising and gratifying to discover the results
which may be obtained."

The embalmer, having allowed an appropriate interval to   12
elapse, returns to the attack, but now he brings into play the skill and
equipment of sculptor and cosmetician. Is a hand missing? Casting
one in plaster of Paris is a simple matter. "For replacement purposes,
only a cast of the back of the hand is necessary; this is within the ability of the average operator and is quite adequate." If a lip or two, a
nose or an ear should be missing, the embalmer has at hand a variety
of restorative waxes with which to model replacements. Pores and
skin texture are simulated by stippling with a little brush, and over
this cosmetics are laid on. Head off? Decapitation cases are rather
routinely handled. Ragged edges are trimmed, and head joined to
torso with a series of splints, wires and sutures. It is a good idea to
have a little something at the neck—a scarf or high collar—when
time for viewing comes. Swollen mouth? Cut out tissue as needed
from inside the lips. If too much is removed, the surface contour can

easily be restored by padding with cotton. Swollen necks and cheeks are reduced by removing tissue through vertical incisions made down each side of the neck. "When the deceased is casketed, the pillow will hide the suture incisions . . . as an extra precaution against leakage, the suture may be painted with liquid sealer."

The opposite condition is more likely to present itself—that of   13
emaciation. His hypodermic syringe now loaded with massage cream, the embalmer seeks out and fills the hollowed and sunken areas by injection. In this procedure the backs of the hands and fingers and the under-chin area should not be neglected.

Positioning the lips is a problem that recurrently challenges   14
the ingenuity of the embalmer. Closed too tightly, they tend to give a stern, even disapproving expression. Ideally, embalmers feel, the lips should give the impression of being ever so slightly parted, the upper lip protruding slightly for a more youthful appearance. This takes some engineering, however, as the lips tend to drift apart. Lip drift can sometimes be remedied by pushing one or two straight pins through the inner margin of the lower lip and then inserting them between the two front upper teeth. If Mr. Jones happens to have no teeth, the pins can just as easily be anchored in his Armstrong Face Former and Denture Replacer. Another method to maintain lip closure is to dislocate the lower jaw, which is then held in its new position by a wire run through holes which have been drilled through the upper and lower jaws at the midline. As the French are fond of saying, *il faut souffrir pour être belle.*[6]

If Mr. Jones has died of jaundice, the embalming fluid will   15
very likely turn him green. Does this deter the embalmer? Not if he has intestinal fortitude. Masking pastes and cosmetics are heavily laid on, burial garments and casket interiors are color-correlated with particular care, and Jones is displayed beneath rose-colored lights. Friends will say, "How *well* he looks." Death by carbon monoxide, on the other hand, can be rather a good thing from the embalmer's viewpoint: "One advantage is the fact that this type of discoloration is an exaggerated form of a natural pink coloration." This is nice because the healthy glow is already present and needs but little attention.

The patching and filling completed, Mr. Jones is now shaved,   16
washed and dressed. Cream-based cosmetic, available in pink, flesh,

[6]"You have to suffer if you want to be beautiful" (editor's note).

suntan, brunette and blond, is applied to his hands and face, his hair is shampooed and combed (and, in the case of Mrs. Jones, set), his hands manicured. For the horny-handed son of toil special care must be taken; cream should be applied to remove ingrained grime, and the nails cleaned. "If he were not in the habit of having them manicured in life, trimming and shaping is advised for better appearance—never questioned by kin."

Jones is now ready for casketing (this is the present participle of the verb "to casket"). In this operation, his right shoulder should be depressed slightly "to turn the body a bit to the right and soften the appearance of lying flat on the back." Positioning the hands is a matter of importance, and special rubber positioning blocks may be used. The hands should be cupped slightly for a more lifelike, relaxed appearance. Proper placement of the body requires a delicate sense of balance. It should lie as high as possible in the casket, yet not so high that the lid, when lowered, will hit the nose. On the other hand, we are cautioned, placing the body too low "creates the impression that the body is in a box."   17

Jones is next wheeled into the appointed slumber room where a few last touches may be added—his favorite pipe placed in his hand or, if he was a great reader, a book propped into position. (In the case of little Master Jones a Teddy bear may be clutched.) Here he will hold open house for a few days, visiting hours 10 A.M. to 9 P.M.   18

Meanings and Values

1. What is the author's tone? (See "Guide to Terms": *Style/Tone.*) What does the tone reveal about the writer's attitude toward the intense concern with the appearance of the dead exhibited by embalmers (and other people)?

2. Why was it formerly "almost mandatory" for some relative to witness the embalming procedure (Par. 2)?

3. Do you believe that public information about this procedure would cost mortuaries much embalming business (Par. 3)? Why, or why not? Why *do* people subject their dead to such a process?

4. Use the three-part system of evaluation found under *Evaluation* in the "Guide to Terms" to judge the success of this process analysis.

EXPOSITORY TECHNIQUES

1. What is the central theme? (Guide: *Unity*.) Which parts of the writing, if any, do not contribute to the theme, thus damaging unity? Which contribute to unity?

2. Beginning with Paragraph 4, list or mark the transitional devices that help to bridge paragraphs. (Guide: *Transition*.) Briefly explain how coherence is aided by such interparagraph transitions.

3. In this selection, far more than in most, emphasis can best be studied in connection with style. In fact, the two are almost indistinguishable here, and few, if any, of the other methods of achieving emphasis are used at all. (Guide: *Emphasis; Style/Tone*.) Consider each of the following stylistic qualities (some may overlap; others are included in diction) and illustrate, by examples, how each creates emphasis.

   a. Number and selection of details—for example, the equipment and "aids" (Par. 5)

   b. Understatement—for example, the "chances of live burial" (Par. 7)

   c. Special use of quotations—for example, "that the body is in a box" (Par. 17)

   d. Sarcasm and/or other forms of irony—for example, "How *well* he looks" (Par. 15) (Guide: *Irony*.)

DICTION AND VOCABULARY

1. Much of the essay's unique style (with resulting emphasis) comes from qualities of diction. Use examples to illustrate the following. (Some may be identical to those of the preceding answer, but they need not be.)

   a. Choice of common, low-key words to achieve sarcasm through understatement—for example, "This is nice. . . ." (Par. 15)

   b. Terms of violence—for example, "returns to the attack" (Par. 12)

   c. Terms of the living—for example, "will hold open house" (Par. 18)

   d. The continuing use of "Mr. Jones"

2. Illustrate the meaning of "connotation" with examples of the quotations from morticians. (Guide: *Connotation/Denotation*.) Are these also examples of "euphemism"?

3. Use the dictionary as needed to understand the meanings of the following words: docility, perpetuation (Par. 1); inherent, mandatory (2); intractable, reticence, *raison d'être* (3); ingenious (5); rudimentary, cellular, somatic (7); carotid artery, femoral artery, subclavian vein (8); semblance (11); simulated, stippling, sutures (12); emaciation (13); dispel (7, title).

READ TO WRITE

1. **Collaborating:** Working in a group, think of any other common practices in which we alter appearances to hide reality or create a new reality. Choose one practice and analyze it in detail as the potential subject for an essay.

2. **Considering Audience:** Many of the processes Mitford describes would be likely to upset or offend many readers, yet she presents them in a way that does not do so except to help readers regard them critically. Choose one such passage and discuss in writing the techniques Mitford employs to present the subject critically but without making it seem distasteful to most readers.

3. **Developing an Essay:** Mitford presents an unpleasant subject—dead bodies—in such detail that it becomes intriguing (her humor helps here, too). Use a similar strategy in your own writing about a subject that readers might at first consider distasteful or boring.

(NOTE: Suggestions for topics requiring development by PROCESS ANALYSIS follow.)

Writing Suggestions for Chapter 7

ANALOGY

From one of the following topics, develop a central theme into an informational process analysis, showing:

1. How you selected a college
2. How you selected your future career or major field of study
3. How your family selected a home
4. How an unusual sport is played
5. How religious faith is achieved
6. How gasoline is made
7. How the air (or water) in _____ becomes polluted
8. How lightning kills
9. How foreign policy is made
10. How political campaigns are financed
11. How _____ was rebuilt
12. How fruit blossoms are pollinated
13. How a computer chip is designed or made

COLLABORATIVE EXERCISES

1. As a group, write an informative paper on the process of completing a collaborative project. Consider how you plan team meetings, team tasks, team evaluations, and so on.

2. For topics 2a–h, have each member of a group write the directional process for a different audience-reader. Predefine each person's audience profile using an audience profile sheet.

    a. How to do any of the processes suggested by topics 1a–e (This treatment will require a different viewpoint, one that is completely objective, and it may require a different organization.)

    b. How to overcome shyness

    c. How to overcome stage fright

    d. How to make the best use of study time

    e. How to write a college composition

    f. How to sell an ugly house

    g. How to prepare livestock or any other entry for a fair

    h. How to start a club (or some other kind of recurring activity)

8

Analyzing *Cause-and-Effect* Relationships

Writing built around cause-effect analysis addresses questions like "Why did that happen?" and "What is likely to happen next?" It can grow from simple curiosity about the *why* of events or from a practical desire to avoid unpleasant or unforeseen consequences. Above all, cause-effect analysis focuses on relationships, the links between one phenomenon and another. When you employ the pattern in expository writing, you need to do more than identify possible causes or consequences. You need to establish a reasonable relationship among them by showing how both logic and the available evidence point to the relationship. After all, two things that often occur together, such as storms and tornadoes, are not *necessarily* related. Since many storms occur without the accompaniment of tornadoes, a cause-effect analysis would focus first on identifying those kinds of storms frequently associated with the appearance of tornadoes, then isolate specific causal features that can be demonstrably linked to funnel clouds and destructive winds.

A search for cause and effect can be rigorously scientific ("Researchers debate possible links between caffeine consumption and heart disease") or it can be personal ("Why do I always end up arguing with my parents over things we all know are unimportant?"). It can take the form of causal analysis, trying to identify all the links in a causal chain: remote causes, necessary conditions, and direct causes to immediate effects and more distant consequences. Or it can identify the many conditions and forces that work together in no particular pattern to shape a person's life, create a particular situation, or help bring about events.

Most expository uses of the pattern do not require scientific rigor, however. For social or cultural events, like the growth of a political movement or the rise of a new form of art, we can seldom hope to pinpoint exact causes and effects. Instead, we can identify the roots of contemporary phenomena and develop an awareness of the kinds of changes that may be going on today. This is the kind of explanation provided by the following paragraph, which looks at the early development of a popular kind of music.

> Rap started in the discos, not the midtown glitter palaces like Studio 54 or New York, New York, but at Mel Quinn's on 42nd Street and Club 371 in the Bronx, where a young Harlemite who called himself D.J. Hollywood spun on the weekends. It wasn't unusual for black club jocks to talk to their audiences in the jive style of the old personality deejays. Two of the top black club spinners of the day, Pete (D.J.) Jones and Maboya, did so. Hollywood, just an adolescent when he started, created a more complicated, faster style, with more rhymes than his older mentors and call-and-response passages to encourage reaction from the dancers. At local bars, discos, and many illegal after-hours spots frequented by street people, Hollywood developed a huge word-of-mouth reputation. Tapes of his parties began appearing around the city on the then new and incredibly loud Japanese portable cassette players flooding into America. In Harlem, Kurtis Blow, Eddie Cheeba, and D.J. Lovebug Star-ski; in the Bronx, Junebug Star-ski, Grandmaster Flash, and Melle Mel; in Brooklyn, two kids from the projects called Whodini; and in Queens, Russell and Joey, the two youngest sons from the middle-class Simmons household—all shared a fascination with Hollywood's use of the rhythmic breaks in his club mixes and his verbal dexterity. These kids would all grow up to play a role in the local clubs and, later, a few would appear on the national scene to spread Hollywood's style. Back in the 1970s, while disco reigned in the media, the Black Main Streets of New York were listening to D.J. Hollywood, and learning.

> —Nelson George, *The Death of Rhythm and Blues*

WHY USE CAUSE-EFFECT ANALYSIS?

Some causes and effects are not very complicated; at least their explanation requires only a simple statement. New parking facilities are not built because a college (or town) lacks the money in its budget. But frequently a much more thorough analysis is required. New parking facilities are not built partly because of expense and partly because they simply seem to encourage more traffic and rapidly become jammed. The college (or town) delays the project until it can study *why* parking facilities quickly become overloaded. In writing, cause-effect as an expository pattern helps address these kinds of complicated relationships.

Writers often respond to puzzling or intriguing phenomena with causal explanations. In its simplest form, the strategy consists of a description of a puzzling phenomenon (the persistence of alcoholism in families, for example) followed by an explanation or an examination of possible causes. The simplicity of this pattern gives it considerable power and flexibility. Writers speculating about social patterns and individual behavior often use the strategy or vary it to consider possible consequences. In dealing with effects, the strategy consists of discussion of a new or previously unnoticed phenomenon whose consequences are unfamiliar followed by consideration of its likely effects, or it begins with discussion of desired effects followed by examination of actions or arrangements most likely to produce these consequences.

Causal explanations appear frequently in academic and research writing. Scholars often look for a particularly puzzling element in a subject or for a point over which there has been much disagreement and then build an essay in an attempt to explain the phenomena: "Perhaps the most interesting feature of early jazz is . . . ."; "Over the last decade researchers have argued about the role of aggressive behavior in corporate organizations. . . ."

CHOOSING A STRATEGY

To explain fully the causes of a phenomenon, writers must seek not only *immediate* causes (the ones encountered first) but also *ultimate* causes (the basic, underlying factors that help to explain the more apparent ones). Business or professional people, as well as students, often have a pressing need for this type of analysis. How else could they fully understand or report on a failing sales campaign, diminishing church membership, a local increase in traffic accidents, or a decline in crime and the use of drugs? The immediate cause of a disastrous warehouse fire could be faulty electrical wiring, but this might be attributed in turn to the company's unwise economic measures, which might be traced even further to undue pressures on the management to show large profits. The written analysis might logically stop at any point of course, with the actual strategy a writer employs depending on the purpose of the writing and the audience for which it is intended.

Similarly, both the immediate and ultimate *effects* of an action or situation may, or may not, need to be fully explored. If a 5 percent pay raise is granted, what will be the immediate effect on the cost of production, leading to what ultimate effects on prices and, in some cases, on the economy of a business, a town, or perhaps the entire region?

Whatever the extent of the reasoning your writing task demands, you need to make certain strategic choices. Will you focus on causes, effects, or both? Will you focus on a single clear chain of causes and effects or provide a more general discussion, highlighting many contributing factors? How will you use the opening of your writing to convince readers of the importance of understanding the causes or effects of a phenomenon or situation and interest them in reading about the topic?

Because causes and effects often form intricate, potentially confusing relationships, you should develop a straightforward plan for your writing—an organization that will help readers understand the order you have discovered within the complexity. This is particularly important when a phenomenon has multiple causes, as in the following example.

> Introduction: Example of a diverse audience at a horror movie responding with fear and pleasure to the film
>> Tentative thesis: People choose to watch horror films for many different reasons, each depending on the individual's taste and psychological makeup.
> Cause 1: The "thrill" of being shocked and scared
>> Support: Some people are psychologically disposed to get pleasure from danger, especially when it is imaginary.
>> Support: Certain people's brain chemistry may mean that they (like people who engage in extreme sports) get a feeling of well-being after feeling that they have placed themselves in danger.
> Cause 2: The twists and turns of the plot
>> Support: Many people enjoy the kinds of complicated, surprising plots they find in horror movies (similar in some ways to the kinds of plots people enjoy in adventure stories).
> Cause 3: The pleasure of "escape"
>> Support: The dangers faced by characters in the films allow viewers to escape for a short time from their somewhat less serious but more real everyday problems.

Cause 4: Fashion
> Support: Horror movies are popular. Going to them with friends and talking about them afterwards is a pleasant social experience.

Summary

Your writing will need to do more than identify causes and effects. It will need to provide readers with evidence that you have correctly identified the relationships. As a result, much writing that employs this pattern relies on detailed research. Printed sources, television documentaries, and interviews can provide you with useful information. You should keep such research focused, however, so you don't stray too far into areas that are interesting but not really related to the causes or consequences you will be discussing.

DEVELOPING CAUSE-EFFECT ANALYSIS

Discussions of causes and effects can easily become complex and confusing, so consider using the following strategies for alerting readers to the relationships among causes and effects. A concise statement near the beginning of an essay can point out relationships you plan to examine. Statements in the body of an essay can remind readers of the points you are making and the supporting details and reasoning you are providing. Likewise, terms that identify causes and effects or that indicate their relationships can help guide readers' attention:

result	effect	accomplishment	development
outcome	antecedent	source	first
cause	instrument	as a result	second
means	thus	motive	third
consequence	reason	agent	next

When you analyze causes and effects, your readers must always have confidence in the thoroughness and logic of your reasoning. Here are some ways to avoid the most common faults in causal reasoning:

1. Never mistake the fact that something happens with or after another occurrence as evidence of a causal relationship—for example, that a black cat crossing the road caused the flat tire a few minutes later, or that a course in English composition caused a student's nervous breakdown that same semester.

2. Consider all possible relevant factors before attributing causes. Perhaps studying English did result in a nervous breakdown, but the cause may also have been ill health, trouble at home, the stress of working while attending college, or the anguish of a love affair. (The composition course, by providing an "emotional" outlet, may even have helped postpone the breakdown!)

3. Support the analysis by more than mere assertions: offer evidence. It would not often be enough to *tell* why Shakespeare's wise Othello believed the villainous Iago—the dramatist's lines should be used as evidence, possibly supported by the opinions of at least one literary scholar. If you are explaining that capital punishment deters crime, do not expect the reader to take your word for it—give before-and-after statistics or the testimony of reliable authorities.

4. Be careful not to omit any links in the chain of causes or effects unless you are certain that the readers for whom the writing is intended will automatically make the right connections themselves—and this is frequently a dangerous assumption. To unwisely omit one or more of the links might leave the reader with only a vague, or even erroneous, impression of the causal connection, possibly invalidating all that follows and thus making the entire writing ineffective.

5. Be honest and objective. Writers (or thinkers) who bring their old prejudices to the task of casual analysis, or who fail to see the probability of *multiple* causes or effects, are almost certain to distort their analyses or to make them so superficial, so thin, as to be almost worthless.

Student Essay

As an expository pattern, cause-effect can explore personal matters as well as those of broader public interest. Aware of her difficulties in coming to terms with her mother's death, Sarah Egri used the pattern to explore one possible reason for her feelings.

How a Public Document Affected My Life

Public documents are a part of everyday life. The presence of these documents can affect a person's life in many different ways. However, the <u>absence</u> of such documents may also affect a person's life, such as my

Gives topic an
interesting
twist: an
absence

own. I believe the absence of my mother's death certificate has affected my life.

When I was around 12 years old, my mother became
very ill with cancer. She was diagnosed with lymphoma,
which is cancer within the lymph nodes. She sought several types of medical treatment, but nothing seemed to
help her. During this time, the doctor told my family
that my mom did not have much longer to live. The
doctor also told my mom this, but she did not believe
him, nor did she want to. At this point, I did not know
what was happening. Since I was so young, I did not understand. I listened to my mom and believed her because I did not want her to die. She and I were quite
close. I was able to talk to her about anything and
everything. There was still so much I had to learn from
her, still so many more memories to be made.

When I was 14 years old my mother passed away. I
will never forget that night, for it seemed like a dream;
it seemed as though it were not really happening. I
awoke to a phone call at one-thirty in the morning saying that my mom had passed away. No more would I be
able to talk with her, or learn from her, or make precious memories. She was gone, yet it felt like it was not
real. I could not grasp the concept that she would no
longer be a part of my life. The years passed by and I
only got <u>used</u> to my mom not being there; I never faced
the fact that she had died. The day that my mother
died, I never saw her death certificate. Perhaps if I had
seen it, her death would have seemed more realistic.

Now as I think back, I <u>never</u> saw my mother's death
certificate. A death certificate is a document that is signed
by a doctor, giving information about the time, place, and
cause of a person's death. This document finalizes everything. It may be that since I never saw this document, I
never came to the realization that she had passed. Since I
did not believe she <u>would</u> die, I cannot bring myself to
believe that she <u>did</u> die. If I had seen the death certificate,
I would have come to terms with her death.

*rather than a
presence is
the cause.*

**Thesis
statement**

**Background
to help
readers
understand
the cause and
the effects**

*One of the
effects*

The cause

**Examines and
explains the
cause**

*Generalizes
about the
effects*

How can such a <u>small</u> document make such a <u>big</u> difference in my life? All a death certificate is, is a small piece of paper with a person's name on it. I think it might have made a difference because it's an <u>official</u> notification of my mom's death. It's a <u>real</u>, physical thing; it is more real than just <u>thinking</u> someone has died.

My mother's death certificate has affected my life, even though I never did see it. The absence of this document affects my life, because if I had seen it, I would have come to the realization that she is really gone. If I had seen that document, her death would have been finalized in my mind and I would not just be <u>used to</u> her not being around; I would <u>know</u> that she has passed and is no longer with us. The death certificate finalizes a person's death, and if I had seen my mom's it would have finalized her death for me. Since I did not see this document, I have not brought my mom's death to a close. Perhaps the <u>absence</u> of some documents, such as my mother's death certificate, can affect a person's life more than the presence of other documents.

Explains the force and importance of public documents

Explores effects

Ends with a contrast between absence and presence

SUSAN PERRY AND JIM DAWSON

> SUSAN PERRY is a former staff writer for Time-Life, Inc., and now works full-time as a freelance writer specializing in health, business, and women's issues. Her articles have appeared in such publications as *Ms.,* the *Washington Post,* and the *Minneapolis Star-Tribune.* She is the author of *Nightmare* (1985) and *Natural Menopause* (1992).
>
> JAMES DAWSON is a science reporter who writes regularly for the *Minneapolis Star-Tribune.* Perry and Dawson coauthored *The Secrets Our Body Clocks Reveal* (1988).

What's Your Best Time of Day?

> This essay, published as a magazine article, is drawn from *The Secrets Our Body Clocks Reveal.* The piece opens with examples of some puzzling behaviors, looks at their causes in the rhythms of our bodies, then examines some further effects of these rhythms. The authors make use of examples, classification, and process to support the cause-effect pattern and provide practical advice for taking advantage of the biological patterns that help govern our lives.

Every fall, Jane, a young mother and part-time librarian, begins to eat more and often feels sleepy. Her mood is also darker, especially when she awakens in the morning; it takes all her energy just to drag herself out of bed. These symptoms persist until April, when warmer weather and longer days seems to lighten her mood and alleviate her cravings for food and sleep. 1

Joseph, a 48-year-old engineer for a Midwestern computer company, feels cranky early in the morning. But as the day progresses, he becomes friendlier and more accommodating. 2

All living organisms, from mollusks to men and women, exhibit biological rhythms. Some are short and can be measured in minutes or hours. Others last days or months. The peaking of body temperature, which occurs in most people every evening, is a daily rhythm. The menstrual cycle is a monthly rhythm. The increase in sexual drive in the autumn—not in the spring, as poets would have us believe—is a seasonal, or yearly, rhythm. 3

The idea that our bodies are in constant flux is fairly new—and goes against traditional medical training. In the past, many doctors were taught to believe the body has a relatively stable, or homeostatic, 4 internal environment. Any fluctuations were considered random and not meaningful enough to be studied.

As early as the 1940s, however, some scientists questioned the homeostatic view of the body. Franz Halberg, a young European scientist working in the United States, noticed that the number of white blood cells in laboratory mice was dramatically higher and lower at different times of day. Gradually, such research spread to the study of other rhythms in other life forms, and the findings were sometimes startling. For example, the time of day when a person receives X-ray or drug treatment for cancer can affect treatment benefits and ultimately mean the difference between life and death.

This new science is called chronobiology, and the evidence supporting it has become increasingly persuasive. Along the way, the scientific and medical communities are beginning to rethink their ideas about how the human body works, and gradually what had been considered a minor science just a few years ago is being studied in major universities and medical centers around the world. There are even chronobiologists working for the National Aeronautics and Space Administration, as well as for the National Institutes of Health and other government laboratories.

With their new findings, they are teaching us things that can literally change our lives—by helping us organize ourselves so we can work *with* our natural rhythms rather than against them. This can enhance our outlook on life as well as our performance at work and play.

Because they are easy to detect and measure, more is known of daily—or circadian (Latin for "about a day")—rhythms than other types. The most obvious daily rhythm is the sleep/wake cycle. But there are other daily cycles as well: temperature, blood pressure, hormone levels. Amid these and the body's other changing rhythms, you are simply a different person at 9 A.M. than you are at 3 P.M. How you feel, how well you work, your level of alertness, your sensitivity to taste and smell, the degree with which you enjoy food or take pleasure in music—all are changing throughout the day.

Most of us seem to reach our peak of alertness around noon. Soon after that, alertness declines, and sleepiness may set in by midafternoon.

Your short-term memory is best during the morning—in fact, about 15 percent more efficient than at any other time of day. So, students, take heed: when faced with a morning exam, it really does pay to review your notes right before the test is given.

Long-term memory is different. Afternoon is the best time for learning material that you want to recall days, weeks or months later. Politicians, business executives or others who must learn speeches would be smart to do their memorizing during that time of day. If you are a student, you would be wise to schedule your more difficult classes in the afternoon, rather than in the morning. You should also try to do most of your studying in the afternoon, rather than late at night. Many students believe they memorize better while burning the midnight oil because their short-term recall is better during the wee hours of the morning than in the afternoon. But short-term memory won't help them much several days later, when they face the exam.

By contrast, we tend to do best on cognitive tasks—things that 12 require the juggling of words and figures in one's head—during the morning hours. This might be a good time, say, to balance a checkbook.

Your manual dexterity—the speed and coordination with which 13 you perform complicated tasks with your hands—peaks during the afternoon hours. Such work as carpentry, typing or sewing will be a little easier at this time of day.

What about sports? During afternoon and early evening, your 14 coordination is at its peak, and you're able to react the quickest to an outside stimulus—like a baseball speeding toward you at home plate. Studies have also shown that late in the day, when your body temperature is peaking, you will *perceive* a physical workout to be easier and less fatiguing—whether it actually is or not. That means you are more likely to work harder during a late-afternoon or early-evening workout, and therefore benefit more from it. Studies involving swimmers, runners, shot-putters and rowing crews have shown consistently that performance is better in the evening than in the morning.

In fact, all of your senses—taste, sight, hearing, touch and 15 smell—may be at their keenest during late afternoon and early evening. That could be why dinner usually tastes better to us than breakfast and why bright lights irritate us at night.

Even our perception of time changes from hour to hour. Not 16 only does time seem to fly when you're having fun, but it also seems to fly even faster if you are having that fun in the late afternoon or early evening, when your body temperature is also peaking.

While all of us follow the same general pattern of ups and 17 downs, the exact timing varies from person to person. It all depends on how your "biological" day is structured—how much of a morning or night person you are. The earlier your biological day gets going, the earlier you are likely to enter—and exit—the peak times for performing various tasks. An extreme morning person and an extreme night person may have circadian cycles that are a few hours apart.

Each of us can increase our knowledge about our individual   18
rhythms. Learn how to listen to the inner beats of your body; let them set the pace of your day. You will live a healthier—and happier—life. As no less an authority than the Bible tells us, "To every thing there is a season, and a time to every purpose under heaven."

MEANINGS AND VALUES

1. What cause(s) and effect(s) do the writers discuss in this selection?

2. According to the explanations in this essay, what are the best times to undertake the following activities, and why?

    a. Play a sport

    b. Balance a checkbook

    c. Learn a speech

    d. Prepare for an exam

EXPOSITORY TECHNIQUES

1. What functions do the examples that open the essay perform for readers? (See "Guide to Terms": *Introductions.*)

2. Where in the essay do the authors use classification? Why? Where do the authors use process analysis? Why?

3. Would this essay be more effective if discussions of the causes and the effects were more clearly separated? Why, or why not? (Guide: *Evaluation.*)

4. Discuss the arrangement of Paragraphs 9–12, paying special attention to parallel structures and transitions within and between paragraphs. (Guide: *Unity; Parallel Structure.*)

DICTION AND VOCABULARY

1. In what ways does the diction in Paragraphs 1 and 2 emphasize the contrasts being illustrated? (Guide: *Diction.*)

2. Discuss how the authors provide explanations of the following scientific or otherwise unfamiliar terms in the text so that readers will not have to pause to look them up: homeostatic (Par. 4); circadian (8); cognitive tasks (12); manual dexterity (13).

3. Does the allusion that concludes the essay seem appropriate? Why, or why not? Try looking up the passage in the Bible (Ecclesiastes 3:1) to see if its original meaning is similar to the one it has in the context of this essay.

READ TO WRITE

1. **Collaborating:** Assume for a moment that Perry and Dawson's view of the cause-effect relationship of body cycles and behavior is accurate. In a group, discuss how typical academic or work schedules might need to be altered to take into account the patterns described by the authors. What common practices seem particularly in need of change given the information provided here? As a group, plan an essay with such practical consequences as its topic.

2. **Considering Audience:** In a magazine like *Discover* or *Scientific American,* read an article that offers a physical explanation of human behavior. Or in a magazine like *Psychology Today,* read an article that offers a psychological or social explanation of behavior. Then prepare a brief analysis of the different kinds of audiences to which this article and Perry and Dawson's essay are directed.

3. **Developing an Essay:** Perry and Dawson use numerous examples to explain and confirm the effects of body cycles. Do your experiences agree with what the authors say about the cycles that guide our behavior? In an essay of your own, provide examples that either support or contradict their conclusions, or that do the same for some other well-known explanation of behavior.

(NOTE: Suggestions for topics requiring development by analysis of CAUSE AND EFFECT are on pp. 351–352 at the end of this chapter.)

CULLEN MURPHY

Cullen Murphy grew up in Greenwich, Connecticut, and attended
school in both Greenwich and Dublin, Ireland. He received a B.A.
from Amherst College in 1974 and soon after began working in
the production department of *Change* magazine. In 1977 he was
named editor of the *Wilson Quarterly,* and he has been managing
editor of the *Atlantic Monthly* since 1985. In his parallel career, he
has written the comic strip *Prince Valiant* since the middle 1970s
(a comic strip that his father draws). Murphy is an essayist and
nonfiction writer as well. His essays on many different topics have
appeared in the *Atlantic Monthly* and other magazines, including
Harper's. His first book, *Rubbish!* (with William Rathje), appeared
in 1992, and a collection of his essays, *Just Curious,* was published
in 1995.

Hello, Darkness

"Hello, Darkness" was first published in the *Atlantic Monthly* in
1996. With touches of humor, Murphy looks at a subject that trou-
bles many people: lack of sleep. His explanations of a phenomenon
that most of us view as a matter of personal behavior may at first
seem surprising; nonetheless, they point convincingly to technology and social change as the culprits who have stolen sleep.

Americans today have plenty of reasons to be thankful that they   1
were not Americans a hundred years ago, but they also have
more than a few reasons to wish they had been. On the one hand, a
hundred years ago there was no Voting Rights Act, no penicillin,
and no zipper, and the first daily comic strip was still more than a
decade away. On the other hand there was no income tax, no nuclear
bomb, and no Maury Povich. Also on the plus side, the average
American a hundred years ago was able to sleep 20 percent longer
than the average American today.

That last figure, supported by various historical studies over   2
the years, comes from a report released by the Better Sleep Council.
Americans in the late 1800s are believed to have slept an average of
about nine and a half hours a night. The average today is about
seven and a half hours. A survey by the Better Sleep Council reveals
that on a typical weeknight almost 60 percent of Americans get *less*
than seven hours of sleep. Other evidence seems to indicate that the
rate of sleep loss is in fact accelerating.

Some may argue that the Better Sleep Council's news should be discounted, on the grounds that the council has an interest in the story—it is supported (comfortably?) by the mattress industry.

I would counter that the data simply confirm what anecdotal evidence already suggests is true. Independent experts at universities and hospitals speak as one on the subject, observing that as a nation we are laboring under a large and increasingly burdensome "sleep deficit," defined as the difference between how much sleep we need and how much we get.

Would that we could pass this particular deficit on to our children! But the only way we can pay it back, the experts say, is by getting more sleep ourselves. Apparently, we're trying. A recent article in *The Wall Street Journal* took note of the growing phenomenon of employees napping at work, but I suspect that this barely covers the interest payments, which go right to Japan. (As you may have noticed, the Japanese are asleep most of the time that we're awake.)

Why, by degrees, are we banishing sleep? In a handful of instances, arguably, the cause has been government over-regulation. I am thinking of the recent case of Sari Zayed, of Davis, California. Ms. Zayed, after being overheard by a neighbor, was awakened at 1:30 A.M. by a municipal "noise-abatement officer" who gave her a $50 citation for snoring too loudly. The amount of money that Ms. Zayed subsequently received in damages from the city of Davis would allow her to pay for nightly snoring citations from now to the end of the year.

America's sleep deficit, though, is surely a systemic phenomenon. Many commentators would blame it on what might be called the AWOL factor—that is, the American Way of Life. We are by nature a busy and ambitious people whom tectonic social forces—declining average wage, high rate of divorce, two-paycheck families, instant telecommunications, jet travel across time zones, growing popularity of soccer for everyone older than four—have turned into a race of laboratory rats on a treadmill going nowhere ever faster. And there is obviously something to this explanation. It is noteworthy that television shows like *Seinfeld* and *Cheers*, on which nobody seems to have any real responsibilities (circumstances that accord more fully with most viewers' fantasies than with their actual lives), have come to constitute a distinct broadcast genre known as "time porn."

It is hard not to credit the importance of the AWOL factor, but I wonder if the driving force behind the sleep deficit is in fact more pervasive, and indeed global in nature: the triumph of light. I am by no means a romantic or a Luddite when it comes to electricity (any-one who is should read Robert Caro's *The Years of Lyndon Johnson* for its haunting description of life in west Texas in the days before rural electrification), and I also don't subscribe to the fashionable opinion that electronic labor-saving devices (personal computers possibly excepted) end up consuming more labor than they save. Yet electric-ity's ubiquitous and seemingly most innocuous use—to power the common light bulb—could not help exacting a price in sleep. Electricity made it possible for the first time in history for masses of humanity to vanquish darkness.

I had never given much thought to the role of darkness in ordi-nary human affairs until I read a monograph prepared by John Staudenmaier, a historian of technology and a Jesuit priest, for a re-cent conference at MIT. (The essay appears in a book called *Progress: Fact or Illusion,* edited by Leo Marx and Bruce Mazlish.) Staudenmaier makes the point—obvious when brought up, though we've mostly lost sight of it—that from the time of the hominid Lucy, in Hadar, Ethiopia, to the time of Thomas Edison, in West Orange, New Jersey, the onset of darkness sharply curtailed most kinds of activity for most of our ancestors. He writes,

> Living with electric lights makes it difficult to retrieve the experience of a non-electrified society. For all but the very wealthy, who could af-ford exorbitant arrays of expensive artificial lights, nightfall brought the works of daytime to a definitive end. Activities that need good light—where sharp tools are wielded or sharply defined boundaries maintained; purposeful activities designed to achieve specific goals; in short, that which we call work—all this subsided in the dim light of evening. Absent the press of work, people typically took themselves safely to home and were left with time in the evening for less urgent and more sensual matters: storytelling, sex, prayer, sleep, dreaming.

Staudenmaier's comments on electric light occupy only a few passages. His larger subject is Western intellectual history, and how metaphors of "enlightenment" came to be associated with orderli-ness, objectivity, and progress, even as metaphors of darkness came to signify the chaotic, the nonrational, the terrifying. He argues that we have lost, to our detriment, the medieval view that some aspects of life and understanding are not necessarily helped by clarity or harmed by ambiguity. Observing that Enlightenment ideals have "taken a fair beating" in the course of this century, Staudenmaier wonders if it is time to rediscover the metaphysical dark, that place "where visions are born and human purpose renewed."

I'll leave that thought where it is. But the implication of electric-　11
ity in the sleep deficit seems hard to argue with. Whatever it is that
we wish or are made to do—pursue leisure, earn a living—there are
simply far more usable hours now in which to do it. Darkness was
once an ocean into which our capacity to venture was greatly limited; now we are wresting vast areas of permanent lightness from
the darkness, much the way the Dutch have wrested polders of dry
land from the sea. So vast are these areas that in composite satellite
photographs of the world at night the contours of civilization are
clearly illuminated—the boundaries of continents, the metastases of
cities. Even Wrigley Field, once a reliable pool of nocturnal darkness, would now show up seventeen nights during the baseball season. In the United States at midnight more than five million people
are at work at full-time jobs. Supermarkets, gas stations, copy
shops—many of these never close. I know of a dentist in Ohio who
decided to open an all-night clinic, and has had the last laugh on
friends who believed that he would never get patients. The supply-
side theory may not have worked in economics, but it has certainly
worked with regard to light: the more we get, the more we find
ways to put it to use. And, of course, the more we get, the more we
distance ourselves from the basic diurnal rhythm in which our evolution occurred.

Thomas Edison, famous for subsisting on catnaps, would have　12
wanted it this way. In contrast, Calvin Coolidge, a younger man
with an older temperament, slept at least ten and often as much as
eleven hours a day. Two world views collide here, and somewhere
between them is a balance waiting to be struck. Where and how?
The only useful contribution I can make is to recall life in Ireland in
the mid-1960s. One of the elements that made it so congenial was a
shared expertise among engineers at the Electricity Supply Board
which resulted in regular but unpredictably occurring blackouts.
The relentless march of time would suddenly be punctuated by a
limbo of uncertain duration. Lights were extinguished. Clocks
stopped. Television screens went black. Drivers became hesitant and
generous at traffic signals. Society and all its components took a
blessed time out.

There was also something in Ireland called "holy hour," a pe-　13
riod in the afternoon when all the pubs would close. Perhaps what
Americans need is a holy hour in the form of a blackout—a brief
caesura in our way of life that might come every day at perhaps
nine-thirty or ten at night. Not the least of the holy hour's benefits, I
might add, would be an appealing new time slot for Maury Povich.

MEANINGS AND VALUES

1. The writer mentions "anecdotal evidence" of a "'sleep deficit'" (Par. 4) but does not present it directly. Why do you think he chose not to offer it in detail? Is the essay weakened—or perhaps strengthened— by this omission? Explain. (See "Guide to Terms": *Evaluation*.)

2. Are we to take the example in Paragraph 6 seriously? If not, what is its role in the essay? Is it an indication that we should not take other examples in the essay seriously? Why or why not?

3. Explain why the author might be justified in referring to certain television shows as "time porn." Do you think most readers will agree or disagree with his conclusion? Why?

4. According to this essay, what was lost when electricity made it possible to "vanquish darkness" (8)?

EXPOSITORY TECHNIQUES

1. Where does Murphy first announce the phenomenon he wishes to explain? Should this announcement be considered a thesis? Why or why not? (Guide: *Thesis*.)

2. What is the role of the rhetorical question that opens Paragraph 6? (Guide: *Rhetorical Questions*.)

3. Which causes of the sleep deficit does the author consider most important, and how does he signal their importance to readers? Which of the strategies for creating emphasis does he use with frequency in this essay? (Guide: *Emphasis*.)

4. Where in the essay does the author begin discussing the effects of electricity?

5. What is the role of the extended discussion of Staudenmaier's work in Paragraphs 10 and 11? To what extent do these paragraphs contradict or complement Murphy's tone and approach in the rest of the essay? (Guide: *Style/Tone*.)

6. What strategy does the writer use to conclude the essay? (Guide: *Closings*.) How effective is the conclusion?

DICTION AND VOCABULARY

1. To what does the title allude? (Guide: *Figures of Speech*.) How is the allusion related to the rest of the essay? Discuss how repetition of the word "darkness," beginning with the title, serves to create unity and coherence in the essay. (Guide: *Unity; Coherence*.) Is the title effective even for readers who do not recognize the allusion? Why or why not?

2. What choices of words and phrases does the writer make in Paragraph 8 to indicate the importance of electricity as one of the causes of the sleep deficit and the disappearance of "darkness" in our daily lives? (Guide: *Diction.*) Do you think the diction in this paragraph is appropriate to its purposes, or is it excessive? Explain. (Guide: *Evaluation.*)

3. If you do not know the meaning of some of the following terms, look them up in a dictionary: anecdotal (Par. 4); systemic, tectonic (7); Luddite, innocuous, vanquish (8); hominid, curtailed (9); metastases, diurnal (11); subsisting, limbo, duration (12); caesura (13).

READ TO WRITE

1. **Collaborating:** In a group, think of other modern inventions (airplanes, television, the Internet, credit cards) and the ways they have changed our society and shaped our lives. The inventions can be seemingly insignificant (cup holders in automobiles, telephone calling cards, zippers, or Velcro) and still be topics worth exploring because of their consequences, both good and bad. Then plan an essay exploring the consequences of one or more of the inventions.

2. **Considering Audience:** This essay is partly humorous, partly serious. Prepare an essay analyzing the role of each element and discussing how readers are likely to respond to the combination.

3. **Developing an Essay:** This essay makes effective use of the concept of a "deficit," that is, the difference between what we have and what we ought to have. Use a similar strategy to begin an essay of your own by introducing some other kind of "deficit" whose causes and consequences are worth exploring.

(NOTE: Suggestions for topics requiring development by analysis of CAUSE AND EFFECT are on pp. 351–352 at the end of this chapter.)

MARY ROACH

> MARY ROACH is a freelance writer whose work has appeared in a
> number of magazines. She lives in San Francisco.

My Father the Geezer

> In "My Father the Geezer," Susan Roach begins with the assump-
> tion that most readers hold negative views about the likely effects
> of having older parents, then goes on to undermine them by pre-
> senting in often humorous detail the consequences in her own life
> of having a "geezer" for a parent. This essay first appeared in the
> *New York Times Magazine.*

My father was 65 when I was born. Even to myself, the statement   1
sits funny, like one of those how-so brain teasers with the hidden loophole—the boy's mother is the doctor. But there is no loophole. He was my biological father, 20 years older than my mother. He
had children late because he married late. I came in under the wire.

People invariably want to know what it was like growing up   2
with an old father. Some want to know because they're coming to
parenthood relatively late themselves and wonder how it will affect
their children. Most are just rubbernecking. There's a "Good God!"
in their tone, as though I'd been suckled by wolves. Who fed whom,
they're wondering. Did I dress him or did he dress me? To which I
reply that he was a young 65, white-haired but red-blooded.

Granted, my upbringing seemed a little odd. I could recite the   3
names of all the members of the Lawrence Welk musical family. I
practiced phonemes by reading aloud from *Modern Maturity.* My
first paying job, at age 7, was to sit on my father's lap with a pair of
tweezers and cull overgrown ear hairs for 2 cents a pluck.

One thing I didn't do was engage in those "When I'm age X,   4
he'll be X" calculations. Children live in the moment. If he was
around next Saturday to drive me to the riding ring, that was good
enough. We'd deal with the strangeness when we got to it. How will
an 82-year-old cope with a 16-year-old? As best he could, and with
frequent naps.

Fortunately for all involved, I wasn't a particularly difficult   5
teen-ager. I remember one summer afternoon, walking out of the
A&P with a roll of "Ripe for Tonight" avocado stickers I'd swiped
from a stockboy's cart. My father, who'd been waiting in the car,

said, "What's under your sweatshirt?" "Nothing," I lied. He just shook his head and went back to his newspaper. For whatever reason, I never moved on to the big stuff: jewelry, clothing, actual avocados. I like to think my father's indifference took the thrill out of shoplifting. More likely, he was just lucky.

In the end, what most people fixate on is that my father was too 6 old to—as they often put it—play ball with me. This is true. I can't recall ever seeing him run. He didn't swim or ride a bicycle or roller-skate. The extent of my father's physical activity was an evening constitutional to the end of Dogford Road, in his Irish tweed hat, whistling a tune and swinging a Hanover Hardware yardstick as if it were a brass-tipped cane. Perhaps that's why I didn't learn to swim as a child, why I was chosen last for gym teams. Perhaps, and who cares. Show me the support group for children of sedentary parents.

What stands out about my father are not the things he couldn't 7 do but the things he did. That most of them were done from a sitting position hardly seems to matter. My father was an artist, a story-teller, a character. When I was 11, he painted a life-size elephant on the basement floor because elephants were my favorite animal. He taught me to draw, making a squiggle on a sheet of paper and challenging me to finish the picture. He framed my finger paintings and hung them on the living room wall, and when guests commented, he'd make up the name of "a noted abstract artist" and wink at me. My father, in short, was a very cool dad. So he mixed Metamucil in his orange juice. So he turned the TV up loud. So his hands shook on the steering wheel. Of all the undesirable things fathers can be (absent, cruel, cold, immature), old is pretty weak poison.

Parenthood over 60 has its advantages. My father spent a good 8 deal more time with me than the average 30-year-old father can afford to. Retirement is like endless paternity leave. Pop was my day care, my baby sitter, my play date. We didn't break a sweat together, but we had a lot of fun.

To be sure, it could easily have been otherwise. Old fathers are 9 more likely to be invalid fathers, senile fathers, dead fathers. (I like to think I kept mine young at heart.) Sixty-five is not the ideal age to have a baby. You can be too old to be a parent. You can also be too young. Neither has all that much to do with years.

Would my father have been a better parent had he been 30 at the 10 time I was born? Probably not. My father spent his 30's on the road with a theater troupe. He would have resented my arrival, the shelved aspirations, the loss of freedom I represented. As it was, I was a gift (or so I like to think), an unexpected coda on a long, full life.

MEANINGS AND VALUES

1. Why does Roach point out that people "fixated" on the fact that her father was "too old to play ball" (Par. 1)? What is the traditional value placed on children playing ball with their fathers? What activities "replaced" this for Roach?

2. Why is the phrase "retirement is endless paternity leave" (Par. 8) significant for readers today who often come from homes with two working parents?

3. What is the significance of the last line of the essay? Why is the musical reference appropriate for an essay on Roach's father?

EXPOSITORY TECHNIQUES

1. Roach tells us that her father married late and consequently was an older parent (Par. 1). Only at the end of the essay does the reader learn what career Roach's father had and the potential reason that he may have settled into marriage later in life. Is it important for the reader to know why Roach's father had children later in life early on in the essay? Would it have been more effective? Why might Roach have waited to share that information with her readers?

2. What positive and negative effects of having an older father does Roach list in this essay? Do they support her response to people that she shares with her readers at the end of Paragraph 2 ("to which I reply that he was a young 65, white-haired but red-blooded")?

DICTION AND VOCABULARY

1. What is the tone of Roach's essay? Does she make light of a serious topic, or is her use of humor very deliberate? Explain. (See "Guide to Terms": *Tone*.)

2. At what point does she take on a serious voice? Why might she have chosen this spot?

3. What kinds of readers might enjoy this piece? Explain.

READ TO WRITE

1. **Collaborating:** Roach shares particular memories of episodes and events with her father. Individually, write a list of the times that you remember the most with one of your parents. Compare your list with a partner and look for any common threads or activities that you might have. Then look at what you did differently. Write an individual comparison and contrast essay of the memories that you and

your partner have with your respective parents. Be sure to include a cause-effect analysis explaining the differences.

2. **Considering Audience:** How would readers who have grown up without a father in the household respond to this essay? Would it have the same impact? Rewrite this essay for a reader who might better identify with a mother or some other woman who was a strong role model. Use a woman in your life as the basis for the essay.

3. **Developing an Essay:** Choose a role model in your life who may have been somewhat different from role models in your friends' lives (i.e., Roach's father was different because of his age). Write an essay similar in style sharing with your reader the experiences that you remember. Be sure that the experiences reflect the different quality that the person you choose possesses.

(NOTE: Suggestions for topics requiring development by analysis of CAUSE AND EFFECT are on pp. 351–352 at the end of this chapter.)

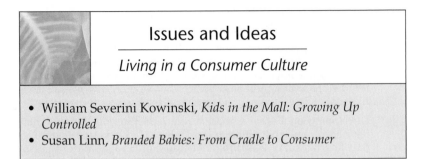

Issues and Ideas

Living in a Consumer Culture

- William Severini Kowinski, *Kids in the Mall: Growing Up Controlled*
- Susan Linn, *Branded Babies: From Cradle to Consumer*

Malls, trademarks, and logos: these three phenomena are essential features of a consumer culture. Their consequences for our behavior and values are significant, at least according to writers like Susan Linn and William Severini Kowinski. Consumer culture shapes our values and habits (Kowinski) and it shapes our perceptions, sometimes from infancy (Linn).

Many people are inclined to consider the elements of a consumer culture as separate from the values that "really" define us. Or they consider the consumer culture so much a part of everyday life that we have already learned to deal effectively with it. Yet if consumer culture is a part of everyday life, then it must be important because it is an element in almost everything we do, say, or believe.

William Severini Kowinski regards consumer culture in the form of malls as one of the causes of "passivity" and a lack of emphasis on risk-taking and imagination in contemporary life. Kowinski's outlook is relatively pessimistic. He takes a detailed look at the social forces ranged against people growing up in today's complex but controlled environment—forces that leave them with few alternatives.

Susan Linn tries to surprise readers with the extent to which consumer culture pervades our lives, even on noncommercial television and in the cradles of newborns in our hospitals. To the extent that Linn sees her job as alerting her readers to surprising developments, we might be tempted to see her outlook as more optimistic than Kowinski's. Nonetheless, the social developments she explains are both powerful and hard to notice, and they are likely to have significant effects.

WILLIAM SEVERINI KOWINSKI

WILLIAM SEVERINI KOWINSKI grew up in Greensburg, Pennsylvania. In 1964, the year before the first mall was built in Greensburg, he left to attend Knox College in Illinois. While attending Knox he spent a semester studying in the fiction and poetry workshops at the University of Iowa. Kowinski was a writer and editor for the Boston *Phoenix* and the Washington *Newsworks* and has written articles for a number of national newspapers and magazines including *Esquire, New Times,* and the *New York Times Magazine.* His book *The Malling of America: An Inside Look at the Great Consumer Paradise* (1985) is based on his travels to malls throughout the United States and Canada.

Kids in the Mall: Growing Up Controlled

Over the past 30 years, the number, size, and variety of suburban shopping malls have grown at astonishing rates, replacing, in many cases, both plazas and urban shopping districts. They are now important economic and cultural forces in American and Canadian society. In this chapter from *The Malling of America,* Kowinski looks at some of the ways malls have affected the teenagers who spend much of their time shopping, working, or just hanging around at the mall.

Butch heaved himself up and loomed over the group. "Like it was different for me," he piped. "My folks used to drop me off at the shopping mall every morning and leave me all day. It was like a big free baby-sitter, you know? One night they never came back for me. Maybe they moved away. Maybe there's some kind of a Bureau of Missing Parents I could check with."

—Richard Peck, *Secrets of the Shopping Mall,* a novel for teenagers

From his sister at Swarthmore, I'd heard about a kid in Florida   1
whose mother picked him up after school every day, drove him straight to the mall, and left him there until it closed—all at his insistence. I'd heard about a boy in Washington who, when his family moved from one suburb to another, pedaled his bicycle five miles every day to get back to his old mall, where he once belonged.

Their stories aren't unusual. The mall is a common experience   2
for the majority of American youth; they have probably been going there all their lives. Some ran within their first large open space, saw their first fountain, bought their first toy, and read their first book in

a mall. They may have smoked their first cigarette or first joint or turned them down, had their first kiss or lost their virginity in the mall parking lot. Teenagers in America now spend more time in the mall than anywhere else but home and school. Mostly it is their choice, but some of that mall time is put in as the result of two-paycheck and single-parent households, and the lack of other viable alternatives. But are these kids being harmed by the mall?

I wondered first of all what difference it makes for adolescents to experience so many important moments in the mall. They are, after all, at play in the fields of its little world and they learn its ways; they adapt to it and make it adapt to them. It's here that these kids get their street sense, only it's mall sense. They are learning the ways of a large-scale artificial environment: its subtleties and flexibilities, its particular pleasures and resonances, and the attitudes it fosters. 3

The presence of so many teenagers for so much time was not something mall developers planned on. In fact, it came as a big surprise. But kids became a fact of mall life very early, and the International Council of Shopping Centers found it necessary to commission a study, which they published along with a guide to mall managers on how to handle the teenage incursion. 4

The study found that "teenagers in suburban centers are bored and come to the shopping centers mainly as a place to go. Teenagers in suburban centers spent more time fighting, drinking, littering and walking than did their urban counterparts, but presented fewer overall problems." The report observed that "adolescents congregated in groups of two to four and predominantly at locations selected by them rather than management." This probably had something to do with the decision to install game arcades, which allow management to channel these restless adolescents into naturally contained areas away from major traffic points of adult shoppers. 5

The guide concluded that mall management should tolerate and even encourage the teenage presence because, in the words of the report, "The vast majority support the same set of values as does shopping center management." *The same set of values* means simply that mall kids are already preprogrammed to be consumers and that the mall can put the finishing touches to them as hard-core, lifelong shoppers just like everybody else. That, after all, is what the mall is about. So it shouldn't be surprising that in spending a lot of time there, adolescents find little that challenges the assumption that the goal of life is to make money and buy products, or that just about everything else in life is to be used to serve those ends. 6

Growing up in a high-consumption society already adds ines-   7
timable pressure to kids' lives. Clothes consciousness has invaded
the grade schools, and popularity is linked with having the best,
newest clothes in the currently acceptable styles. Even what they
read has been affected. "Miss [Nancy] Drew wasn't obsessed with
her wardrobe," noted *Wall Street Journal.* "But today the mystery in
teen fiction for girls is what outfit the heroine will wear next."
Shopping has become a survival skill and there is certainly no better
place to learn it than the mall, where its importance is powerfully reinforced and certainly never questioned.

The mall as a university of suburban materialism, where Valley   8
Girls and Boys from coast to coast are educated in consumption, has
its other lessons in this era of change in family life and sexual mores
and their economic and social ramifications. The plethora of products in the mall, plus the pressure on teens to buy them, may contribute to the phenomenon that psychologist David Elkind calls "the
hurried child": kids who are exposed to too much of the adult world
too quickly, and must respond with a sophistication that belies their
still-tender emotional development. Certainly the adult products
marketed for children—form-fitting designer jeans, sexy tops for
preteen girls—add to the social pressure to look like an adult, along
with the home-grown need to understand adult finances (why
mothers must work) and adult emotions (when parents divorce).

Kids spend so much time at the mall partly because their par-   9
ents allow it and even encourage it. The mall is safe, it doesn't seem
to harbor any unsavory activities, and there is adult supervision; it
is, after all, a controlled environment. So the temptation, especially
for working parents, is to let the mall be their babysitter. At least the
kids aren't watching TV. But the mall's role as a surrogate mother
may be more extensive and more profound.

Karen Lansky, a writer living in Los Angeles, has looked into   10
the subject and she told me some of her conclusions about the effects
on its teenaged denizens of the mall's controlled and controlling environment. "Structure is the dominant idea, since true 'mall rats'
lack just that in their homelives," she said, "and adolescents about to
make the big leap into growing up crave more structure than our
modern society cares to acknowledge." Karen pointed out some of
the elements malls supply that kids used to get from their families,
like warmth (Strawberry Shortcake dolls and similar cute and cuddly merchandise), old-fashioned mothering ("We do it all for you,"
the fast-food slogan), and even home cooking (the "homemade"
treats at the food court).

The problem in all this, as Karen Lansky sees it, is that while   11
families nurture children by encouraging growth through the assumption of responsibility and then by letting them rest in the bosom of the family from the rigors of growing up, the mall as a
structural mother encourages passivity and consumption, as long as
the kid doesn't make trouble. Therefore all they learn about becoming adults is how to act and how to consume.

Kids are in the mall not only in the passive role of shoppers—   12
they also work there, especially as fast-food outlets infiltrate the
mall's enclosure. There they learn how to hold a job and take responsibility, but still within the same value context. When *CBS
Reports* went to Oak Park Mall in suburban Kansas City, Kansas, to
tape part of their hour-long consideration of malls, "After the Dream
Comes True," they interviewed a teenaged girl who worked in a
fast-food outlet there. In a sequence that didn't make the final program, she described the major goal of her present life, which was to
perfect the curl on top of the ice-cream cones that were her store's
specialty. If she could do that, she would be moved from the lowly
soft-drink dispenser to the more prestigious ice-cream division, the
curl on top of the status ladder at her restaurant. These are the
achievements that are important at the mall.

Other benefits of such jobs may also be overrated, according to   13
Laurence D. Steinberg of the University of California at Irvine's social ecology department, who did a study on teenage employment.
Their jobs, he found, are generally simple, mindlessly repetitive and
boring. They don't really learn anything, and the jobs don't lead
anywhere. Teenagers also work primarily with other teenagers;
even their supervisors are often just a little older than they are.
"Kids need to spend time with adults," Steinberg told me.
"Although they get benefits from peer relationships, without parents and other adults it's one-sided socialization. They hang out
with each other, have age-segregated jobs, and watch TV."

Perhaps much of this is not so terrible or even so terribly differ-   14
ent. Now that they have so much more to contend with in their lives,
adolescents probably need more time to spend with other adolescents without adult impositions, just to sort things out. Though it is
more concentrated in the mall (and therefore perhaps a clearer target), the value system there is really the dominant one of the whole
society. Attitudes about curiosity, initiative, self-expression, empathy, and disinterested learning aren't necessarily made in the mall;
they are mirrored there, perhaps a bit more intensely—as through a
glass brightly.

Besides, the mall is not without its educational opportunities.   15
There are bookstores, where there is at least a short shelf of classics
at great prices, and other books from which it is possible to learn
more than how to do sit-ups. There are tools, from hammers to
VCRs, and products, from clothes to records, that can help the
young find and express themselves. There are older people with stories, and places to be alone or to talk one-on-one with a kindred
spirit. And there is always the passing show.

The mall itself may very well be an education about the future.   16
I was struck with the realization, as early as my first forays into
Greengate,[1] that the mall is only one of a number of enclosed and
controlled environments that are part of the lives of today's young.
The mall is just an extension, say, of those large suburban schools—
only there's Karmelkorn instead of chem lab, the ice rink instead of
the gym: It's high school without the impertinence of classes.

Growing up, moving from home to school to the mall—from   17
enclosure to enclosure, transported in cars—is a curiously continu-
ous process, without much in the way of contrast or contract with
unenclosed reality. Places must tend to blur into one another. But
whatever differences and dangers there are in this, the skills these
adolescents are learning may turn out to be useful in their later
lives. For we seem to be moving inexorably into an age of pre-
planned and regulated environments, and this is the world they will
inherit.

Still, it might be better if they had more of a choice. One   18
teenaged girl confessed to *CBS Reports* that she sometimes felt she
was missing something by hanging out at the mall so much. "But
I'm here," she said, "and this is what I have."

Meanings and Values

1. Do teenagers who spend their time in malls display any obviously
   unusual behavior? If so, in what ways do they behave? If not, how
   might one describe their behavior?

2. What question does this essay attempt to answer? Where in the essay
   is the question asked? Other than providing an answer to the question, what purpose or purposes does this selection have? (See "Guide
   to Terms": *Purpose.*)

[1]Greengate Mall in Greensburg, Pennsylvania, where Kowinski began his research on
malls (Editors' note).

3. What does Kowinski see as the major effects of malls on teenagers? What other, less important effects (if any) does he identify? Discuss whether or not the author presents enough evidence to convince most readers that he has correctly identified the effects.

4. Where in the essay does Kowinski consider causes other than the mall environment for the attitudes and behaviors of teenagers? Explain how the alternative explanation either undermines or adds to his view of the malls.

EXPOSITORY TECHNIQUES

1. What strategies does the author employ in the introduction (Pars. 1–3) to help convince readers of the importance of reading and thinking about what happens to teenagers as a result of the time they spend at malls? (Guide: *Introductions.*)

2. Discuss how the author uses examples, quotations from authorities, and various strategies of emphasis in Paragraphs 8, 9, 11, 13, and 14 to indicate whether or not the effects of malls can be considered harmful. (Guide: *Emphasis.*)

3. Which chapters of the essay are devoted *primarily* to exploring the effects of the mall environment? Which are devoted *primarily* to discussing whether or not the effects are harmful?

4. What use does the author make of qualification in presenting his conclusions in Paragraphs 15 and 17–19? (Guide: *Qualification.*) Explain why this strategy adds to or weakens your confidence in his conclusions.

5. Explain how parallelism in Paragraphs 17 and 18 helps emphasize similarities in the environments. (Guide: *Parallel Structure.*)

DICTION AND VOCABULARY

1. Who is the Nancy Drew alluded to in Paragraph 8? (Guide: *Figures of Speech.*) What is the purpose of this allusion?

2. What transitional devices are used to tie together Paragraphs 7–9? (Guide: *Transition.*) Which are used to link Paragraphs 10–13?

3. If you do not know the meaning of some of the following words, look them up in the dictionary: loomed, piped (Par. 1); viable (3); resonances, fosters (4); incursion (5); inestimable (8); mores, ramifications, plethora (9); surrogate (10); denizens (11); nurture (12); socialization (14); impositions, empathy, disinterested (15); kindred (16); forays, impertinence (17); inexorably (18).

READ TO WRITE

1. **Collaborating:** Working in a group, use these questions to help develop a topic and plan for an essay: Were malls as important to you as they were to the people Kowinski describes in his essay? Based on

your experience and observations, does Kowinski appear to be overstating the effects of malls on teenagers? What other influences on the lives of teenagers are as important or more important than malls (or than shopping in general)? Are malls important in people's lives because of the special experiences they offer, or simply because they bring together large numbers of people and offer work to many individuals?

2. **Considering Audience:** Kowinski takes a partly negative view of malls and the work they provide. Are readers in general likely to agree or disagree with him? What do you think? Prepare a brief essay analyzing readers' likely reactions to the essay.

3. **Developing an Essay:** What experiences and activities condition us for success or failure? Which ones give us important goals for work, personal relationships, and civic responsibility? Taking an approach similar to the one Kowinski employs in "Kids in the Mall," criticize the influence of the activities that characterize contemporary teenage life. Or, reverse Kowinski's approach and praise the effects of particular activities and experiences.

(NOTE: Suggestions for topics requiring development by analysis of CAUSE AND EFFECT are on pp. 351–352 at the end of this chapter.)

SUSAN LINN

Susan Linn is Associate Director of the Media Center for Children at Harvard University-affiliated Judge Baker Children's Center. She is also an Instructor in Psychiatry at Harvard Medical School. She has published articles in the *Boston Globe,* the *Los Angeles Times,* the *Christian Science Monitor,* the *Washington Post,* and *Newsweek.* Her book, *Consuming Kids: The Hostile Takeover of Childhood* was published in 2004. She has also created video programs for children, including *Different and the Same: Helping Children Identify and Prevent Prejudice* (1966).

Branded Babies: From Cradle to Consumer

In this selection from *Consuming Kids,* Susan Linn discusses the possible effects of a surprising advertising strategy: introducing infants and toddlers to product and corporate logos. As Linn points out, the strategy can include gift packages for newborns, and many readers might wonder how such a tactic could possibly have any consequences for consumer habits in later years.

On September 1, 1998, in maternity wards all around the country, 1 newborns got a jump-start on their lives as media consumers and marketing targets. PBS Kids, along with Ragdoll Productions, Itsy Bitsy Entertainment, and Warner Home Video, celebrated the release of a series of *Teletubbies* videos by making "Teletubby Gift Packs" available to babies born on that day. Hospitals distributed the packs—including copies of two videos, *Here Come the Teletubbies* and *Dance With the Teletubbies,* and a mini-Teletubby plush toy from Hasbro—free of charge.

Teletubbies, in case you don't know, are small humanoid crea- 2 tures with television sets embedded in their tummies. Their heads are topped by antennae, which in their incarnation as stuffed toys are conveniently sized to fit in a baby's grasp, like a plush rattle. On their television program, the Teletubbies babble unintelligibly in a language sounding a lot like toddler talk as they frolic in a lush, fairy-tale landscape. Under the watchful eyes of a blue-eyed, giggling baby ensconced in a glowing sun, they interact with things of great interest to young children—a butterfly, a giant ball, a toaster. One of the program's main characters is a vacuum cleaner. The Teletubbies' TV tummies show films of real toddlers and caring adults engaged in such activities as playing games or fixing bicycles.

Periodically a speaker set on a tall pole calls the Teletubbies to assemble at an appointed place: "Teletubbies, come here!"

As a television series, *Teletubbies* first appeared on BBC (British   3
Broadcasting Corporation). It debuted in the United States on the Public Broadcasting Service in 1998, accompanied by a slew of toys and accessories. It is the first television series ever marketed as educational for children as young as one.

Whenever I think about the recent explosion of marketing to   4
"under twos," I find myself face to face with *Teletubbies.* The program may seem like old news—it exists only in reruns today—but the success of this particular series and its spin-offs raises several important and very current issues all at once. These include the efforts of marketers to promote brand recognition even before a baby can talk. . . .

By the 1990s, it was inevitable that babies and toddlers would   5
be included in the deluge of child-targeted marketing. As an article published in *KidScreen* explains, "When it comes to building kids [*sic*] brands, executives speak in terms of growing with a child from cradle to university. Yet when it comes to building a kid property's product offering, often the only way to grow is 'backward'"—that is, to cultivate an ever younger demographic.

As they mature, children often discard playthings or clothing or   6
other items that they associate with their younger selves—"But that's for babies," a new kindergartner might announce about a toy he played with the previous summer. Therefore, from the sole perspective of profit, it makes perfect sense to try to reach one step further back and market that product to the babies themselves.

When it comes to products specifically designed for children,   7
"cradle to university" may be the most one can hope for, but many manufacturers are looking for brand loyalty to last from cradle to the grave. James McNeal, a psychologist who has written extensively about how and why companies should market to children, estimates that a lifetime customer could be worth $100,000 to an individual retailer. Babies are a once and future gold mine for marketers, which helps explain why companies such as Ralph Lauren and Harley Davidson are now targeting infants and toddlers by putting out items like tiny T-shirts and sweatshirts with their logos on them.

But wait a minute. Aren't such infant and toddler products   8
really marketed to parents? Well, yes—and no. Infants certainly can't ask for brands. Remember, however, that according to industry research, toddlers are requesting brands as soon as they can speak.

This would suggest that children may develop positive feelings about logos or licensed characters *before* they have words to ask for the products associated with them. As any parent can attest, even before a child has language, a tiny pointing finger accompanied by excited noises is enough to indicate "I want that." By marketing nursery linens, mobiles, and crib toys decorated with brand logos or images of licensed characters, marketers are doing what they can to ensure that babies will recognize and request similarly adorned products ranging from cereal to stuffed toys as their verbal skills evolve.

Whenever I see crib sheets emblazoned with Looney Tunes   9
characters, or the Sesame Street "First Years Elmo" two-in-one bathtub, which positions a large portrait of the famed Muppet character to face the bathing baby, I can't help thinking of what I learned in undergraduate psychology classes about what the Nobel Prize-winning behavioral scientist Konrad Lorenz called imprinting. In a well-known series of papers published on the eve of World War II, Lorenz documented a phenomenon he had first observed when he himself was a boy—that baby geese who are exposed to a human being rather than to their mother at a certain time just after hatching will (presumably for the rest of their goslinghood) follow that human being around as if he or she were their parent. The human image becomes "imprinted" in their brains as "Mother."

It's always risky to extrapolate from animals to humans with-   10
out research to prove specific parallels, but for what other reason would companies *make* baby paraphernalia adorned with media characters and corporate logos? They might be marketing to parents and grandparents attracted to a particular familiar brand, but they also believe it provides a jump-start on brand loyalty that could last through preschool and early elementary school, if not, for companies like Ralph Lauren, for life.

I suppose the kind of positive link between an image and a   11
product that marketers hope to foster is based on building an association through what social scientists call "conditioning" rather than on imprinting. If the baby who snuggles in Sesame Street sheets and drinks from a Bugs Bunny bottle is also regularly plopped in front of a television to watch programs featuring the same characters she sees on her crib, clothes, mobile, and toys, her familiarity with those characters means (perhaps even before she's fully verbal) that trips to the grocery store will be characterized by squeals of joy every time she sees them on cereal boxes and cries of disappointment if the cereal doesn't land in the grocery cart.

The *Teletubbies* gift package for newborns looks a lot like the 12
kind of preemptive strike that corporations have often used to establish brand loyalty among purchasers of products for infants and
toddlers—and eventually among the children themselves.

MEANINGS AND VALUES

1. According to Paragraph 8, why does it make sense for companies to
    direct marketing campaigns at infants?

2. What specific causes and effects does the writer explain in
    Paragraph 8?

3. According to the writer, what psychological or social explanations
    might account for the effectiveness of marketing to infants?

4. How would you describe the tone of this essay, especially the sec-
    tions where the writer describes specific marketing strategies, actual
    or possible? (See "Guide to Terms": *Tone.*)

EXPOSITORY TECHNIQUES

1. Where in the essay does the writer introduce the advertising strategy
    whose causes and effects she plans to explore?

2. What elements of the advertising strategy does she emphasize in or-
    der to convince readers that its causes and effects are worth analyz-
    ing? (Guide: *Emphasis.*)

3. Why do you think the writer provides so much background informa-
    tion on Teletubbies? Is this information likely to be necessary for
    most readers, including yourself? Why, or why not?

4. Why is the writer's explanation of cause and effect based on the work
    of Konrad Lorenz (Pars. 9–10) convincing or unconvincing to you?
    How do you think most readers are likely to evaluate its effective-
    ness? (Guide: *Evaluation.*)

DICTION AND VOCABULARY

1. What view of the motivations and values of advertisers and toy man-
    ufacturers is conveyed through phrases like "preemptive strike"
    (Par. 12), "got a jump-start on their lives as media consumers and
    marketing targets" (1), and "a once and future gold mine" (7)?

2. If you do not know the meaning of some of the following words,
    look them up in a dictionary: humanoid, incarnation, unintelligibly,
    frolic (Par. 2); slew (3); mobiles, verbal (8); paraphernalia (10);
    preemptive (12).

READ TO WRITE

1. **Collaborating:** It is easy to identify advertising and marketing strategies that seem absurd or amusing yet are likely to be successful. Working in a group, make a list of such strategies. As part of the list, indicate briefly what makes each strategy amusing or absurd and indicate why group members feel that it is nonetheless likely to succeed.

2. **Considering Audience:** Talk to several people about their reactions to specific advertising or marketing campaigns and prepare a brief report of similarities and differences among their responses.

3. **Developing an Essay:** Using Linn's essay as a model, take a critical look at the causes and effects of a particular marketing or advertising campaign. Draw your evidence from the ads and products themselves and from talking to people who are familiar with the products and the advertising.

(NOTE: Suggestions for topics requiring development by analysis of CAUSE AND EFFECT follow.)

Writing Suggestions for Chapter 8

CAUSE AND EFFECT

Analyze the immediate and ultimate causes and/or effects of one of the following subjects or another suggested by them. (Be careful that your analysis does not develop into a mere listing of superficial "reasons.")

1. The ethnic makeup of a neighborhood
2. Some *minor* discovery or invention
3. The popularity of some modern singer or other celebrity
4. The popularity of some fad of clothing or hairstyle
5. The widespread fascination for antique cars (or guns, furniture, dishes, motorcycles, old bottles, etc.)
6. The widespread enjoyment of fishing or hunting
7. Student cheating
8. Too much pressure (on you or an acquaintance) for good school grades
9. Your being a member of some minority, ethnic, or religious group
10. Your association, as an outsider, with members of such a group
11. The decision of some close acquaintance to enter the religious life
12. Some unreasonable fear or anxiety that afflicts you or someone you know well
13. The reluctance of many women today to enter what used to be primarily women's professions such as nursing
14. Your tendency toward individualism
15. The popularity of computer games
16. The mainstreaming of handicapped children
17. The appeal of careers that promise considerable financial rewards
18. The appeal of a recent movie or current television series
19. The willingness of some people to sacrifice personal relationships for professional success
20. The disintegration of a marriage or family
21. A family's move (or reluctance to move) to a new home
22. A candidate's success in a local or national election
23. A recent war or international conflict

24. A trend in the national economy
25. The concern with diet and physical fitness
26. Worry about crime
27. Attention to gender roles
28. Personal stress or depression
29. Desire for success
30. Willingness to take risks, even extreme ones

COLLABORATIVE EXERCISES

1. As a group, research the causes of a war or other armed conflict. Decide collectively which causes were most central, and together write an essay showing how the combination of such causes led to the conflict. Look at immediate (direct) causes as well as indirect causes.

2. Split into teams of four. Divide each team into two halves, one that will analyze the causes and one that will analyze the effects of number 20 (p. 351). Create a thesis based on your analyses that would work as a claim for an essay on the topic.

3. Perform the same task for the above question for the topic of "the high percentage of women in the workforce."

9

Using *Definition* to Help Explain

$\mathbf{F}$ew barriers to communication are as great as those created by key terms or concepts that have various meanings or shades of meaning. For this reason, expository writing often provides definitions of words and ideas whose precise meaning is important to the writer's purpose. Sometimes **definitions** merely clarify meanings of concrete or noncontroversial terms. This simple process is similar to that often used in dictionaries:

1. providing a synonym, for example

   cinema: a motion picture

   or

2. placing the word in a class and then showing how it differs from others of the same class, for example

Term	Class	Details

   metheglin: an alcoholic liquor made of fermented honey

Often, however, definitions specify the meanings of abstract, unusual, or newly minted terms. Definitions of this sort are particularly useful when the experiences or knowledge of readers does little to help them with the meaning of a term or idea that is nonetheless a key element of an overall explanation.

Sometimes a term or concept (or perhaps a process, a natural phenomenon, a group of people, or a relationship) is itself the subject of an explanation, leading to an *extended definition,* as in the following example.

353

This is *orienteering,* a mixture of marathon, hike, and scavenger hunt, a cross-country race in which participants must locate a series of markers set in unfamiliar terrain by means of map and compass. The course, which may range from an acre of city park to twenty square miles of wilderness, is dotted with anywhere from four to fifteen "controls," red-and-white flags whose general locations are marked on the map by small circles. At each control there is a paper punch that produces a distinctive pattern on a card the racer carries. In most events the order in which the card must be punched is fixed; the route taken to reach each control, however, is up to the participant.

—Linton Robinson, "Marathoning with Maps"

Extended definitions may take a paragraph or two or may be the primary pattern for all or most of an essay, depending on the complexity of the subject being defined, the amount of controversy or confusion it has generated, the likely interest of readers in the discussion, and the writer's purpose.

WHY USE DEFINITION?

When your subject requires you to write about terms, ideas, or phenomena likely to be unfamiliar to your audience, or when the concepts and words you are using have conflicting or controversial meanings, then you probably need to prepare an extended definition for your readers. For years, discussions of how much people work each week excluded housework and other time spent on activities important to home and family. The definition of *work* included only labor outside the home for a specific wage. Women were rightly angered by this definition, which excluded the hours many of them labored creating homes and maintaining families. If you were to write today about how much work people do in an average week, you would need to provide an extended definition of work including such activities. Few people would argue your definition, but they would expect you to be aware of the different (and conflicting) meanings of the term and to make your choice among them clear. If some readers are likely to disagree with your choice, however, you will need to present reasons for it. You might even need to stipulate (or dictate) the meaning of the term as you use it in the essay so that your audience will not misread your essay by substituting their preferred meaning for your own.

When your writing focuses on a fashion, artistic trend, social phenomenon, political movement, or set of ideas or behaviors whose impact is widespread enough to interest most readers but new enough to require definition, you might consider creating an essay that presents an *informative definition,* one that explores and explains the various aspects of your subject. In contrast, when your readers already have some ideas about your subject, but you think these ideas (or perspectives) need to be changed, you could create a *redefinition* essay. A redefinition begins with the ideas readers hold and tries to substitute new and different ones. For example, people often try to make pets of wild animals because they consider the creatures cute, cuddly, or amusing. You might attempt to redefine the favorable images people hold of animals like koala bears, monkeys, boa constrictors, ocelots, or raccoons to show that these and similar creatures are likely to make troublesome, unpleasant, or even dangerous pets.

CHOOSING A STRATEGY

Extended definitions, unlike the simple dictionary type, follow no set pattern. Often when extended definitions are part of an essay, readers are not specifically aware of the process of definition. This lack of specific awareness arises because the definitions are frequently part of the overall subject, are written in the same tone as the rest of the exposition, and are closely tied to the writer's thesis and purpose.

When an extended definition is the primary pattern for an essay, however, the essay itself may follow one of several broad strategies. An informative definition often begins by explaining the reason for the subject's current importance as well as the need to define it. It may then move to a brief, sometimes formal definition; continue with a discussion of the historical background and present instances; and conclude with a review of the subject's features. The following informal plan for an essay includes these strategies in an order appropriate to the subject.

    Introduction
        Tentative thesis: If you look carefully at your calendar
            for the month of December, you are likely to come
            across the holiday Kwanzaa, which may be unfa-
            miliar to you but which is celebrated each year by
            an increasing number of your friends, coworkers,
            and neighbors.
        Current importance: Examples
    Definition
        Brief formal definition
        Historical background

Features: Seven principles, various activities, clothing, participants, meaning of celebration, food, stories, and materials and resources
Present instances: Current and growing popularity
Conclusion: Summary and sources for further information

A redefinition essay grows from the assumption that readers already have some ideas about the subject but these ideas should be modified or discarded altogether. Redefinitions often begin in the same matter as informative definitions—by creating interest in the topic. Then they generally proceed to mention the ways the subject is normally interpreted, following each with an alternate interpretation, or redefinition. Or they review various aspects of the subject and suggest fresh ways of looking at each.

DEVELOPING DEFINITIONS

A definition helps writers and readers agree on the meaning of a term, concept, or phenomenon by providing answers to some important questions. As you develop a definition, try keeping in mind the questions you will need to address in order to help readers understand your subject. These sample questions can provide a start.

For subjects that can be observed, measured, and known:

What are its features?

What is its history?

What does it do?

What doesn't it do?

For concepts, values, or terms whose meaning depends on the ways people use them:

How do people use it?

What has its meaning been historically, and how has the meaning changed?

How is this set of values or concepts different from others? Similar?

Definitions use many familiar techniques of expository writing, including examples, comparisons, and classifications. There are, however, some techniques peculiar to definition. You can give the *background* of a word, answering the question "What is the history of the term or concept?" (that is, its *etymology*) and providing valuable hints to its meanings. For example, *catholic* originally, in ancient times, meant pertaining to the universal Christian church. Its present meaning—of or concerning the Roman Catholic Church—retains some of the original force because the Roman Catholic Church views itself as the direct descendant of the ancient, undivided Christian church.

You can also enumerate the *characteristics* of the term or subject, sometimes isolating an essential one for special treatment. In defining a social group, such as triathletes, for example, you might list the physical qualities they share (endurance, strength, versatility, and exceptional fitness), their mental qualities (high endurance for pain, desire to exceed normal levels of achievement, and pleasure in physical exertion), and their social preferences (tolerance for solitary training routines, desire to excel, and preference for individual achievement rather than group membership). In so doing, you would be explaining the common elements that define the group and distinguish it from other groups.

You might define by *negation,* sometimes called "exclusion" or "differentiation," by showing what is *not* the meaning of the term, concept, or phenomenon. (This is an important technique for a redefinition essay.) To do this, you answer the question, "What is it *not?*": "*Intelligence* is neither a puzzle-solving activity that enables people to do well on a standardized example like the SAT or ACT, nor the ability to remember columns of facts and figures that may have no real use." If you employ this technique, however, remember that readers will expect you also to provide a positive definition, indicating what the definition *is* as well as what it *is not.*

But perhaps the most dependable techniques for defining are basic expository patterns. You can illustrate the meaning of a term or define a phenomenon by drawing *examples* from your own experience, from newspaper or online reports, from books and magazines, or from interviews and surveys. For instance, you might help explain the range of behaviors included in the term *deviant behavior* by offering examples not only of thieves, drug dealers, and pornographers, but also of people who live alone in the wilderness for spiritual enlightenment or who participate in dangerous sports. You might even include yourself in the category by telling how you climbed the side of a glacier or parachuted from a bridge into a river gorge. Or you might define by *classifying,* sorting kinds of deviant behavior into those that are socially acceptable, even honorable (the search for spiritual enlightenment); those that are harmful only to the individual (dangerous sports); and those that harm other people (thievery and other activities generally considered criminal).

Comparisons are useful, too, both those that identify *synonyms* (*naïve* means innocent, unsophisticated, natural, unaffected, and artless) or that distinguish among concepts with similar, though not identical, meanings, such as *consensus* (general agreement among a group of people on their attitude toward an issue or problem) and *dissensus* (general agreement among a group of people on the ways their attitudes toward an issue or problem differ). Comparisons respond to the question "What is the subject like or unlike?" So, too, do *similes* and *metaphors,* two techniques that are especially useful in defining concepts and attitudes that are difficult to grasp directly ("an *epiphany* is a moment of sudden clarity and insight, like the moment your eyes become accustomed to the dark and you can suddenly see your surroundings," "a *transition* in writing is a bridge between ideas").

A narrative or an account of a process can also help you define. An explanation of *courage,* for example, might include the story of a 10-year-old saving a friend from drowning in an icy pond. A discussion of *open-heart surgery* might include a description of the process.

Few extended definitions would use all these methods, but the extent to which you use them should depend on three factors: (1) the term or concept itself, since some are more elusive and subject to misunderstanding than others; (2) the function the term serves in your writing, since it is foolish to develop several pages defining a term that serves only a casual or unimportant purpose; and (3) your prospective audience, since the extent of your readers' knowledge and their likely responses to your definition of a disputed or controversial concept or phenomenon should lead you to choose the most convincing or persuasive strategies for the particular audience.

Finally, remember that reference works can be valuable sources for definition. The *Oxford English Dictionary*, for example, traces the meanings of a word during various historical periods; the *Dictionary of Slang and Unconventional English* or the *Encyclopedia of Pop, Rock, and Soul* can provide you with surprising and useful information. A reference librarian or an Internet search engine can provide you with many more sources.

Student Essay

In the following essay, Lori L'Heureux uses a variety of definition techniques to define and redefine *stars.*

Stars

by Lori L'Heureux

How many of us as children longed to be famous when we grew up? Many of us admired a certain celebrity and wanted to be just like him or her when we got older. We wanted to be a star.

**Importance of
term**

**Word/concept
to be defined**

The word "star," used to describe a celebrity, first came into use around 1830. Before this, there was no special term to label performers who, on their own, could draw large numbers of spectators to a performance or an athletic contest. The lack of a term for such a celebrity probably reflected a greater emphasis on the performance or athletic event than on the individual performer or athlete. But as the role of talented individuals became more important, a word for it was needed. Many words, old or newly fashioned, might have served, but the noun borrowed from gazing at the night sky somehow captured the emerging role (Braudy 9).

**Background
and history**

Stars, indeed, have an enormous impact on our lives. They are recognized throughout society, observed closely onstage and off, thought about, talked about, emulated, even dreamed about. Stardom is a vital force in our culture.

**Effects and
importance**

Because so many people perceive the work stars do as a form of upgraded play, they understand only imperfectly the work life of celebrity entertainers. According to Jib Fowles, many stars resent the stereotypes that have been created for them over the last century. Many people, thinking that the majority of stars spend the hours of the day at leisure, imagine them living a lavish lifestyle characterized by money and glamour. Stars are thought to be greedy and to associate only with people whose social status matches their own. Stars are frequently imagined as leading relaxed lives: this one reclining in a chaise lounge, reading a script; that one stretched out on a massage table, getting worked on by a team's trainer; several others poolside and prone. But in reality, the life of most stars is quite the opposite (Fowles 59).

**Define by
negation**

I conducted a survey of my own to see if most people hold these misconceptions of celebrities' lives. I asked 15 people to tell me what type of lives they felt celebrities lead. Twelve people said that stars were rich and had easy careers. Only three said celebrities led hard lives in the public eye and had difficult jobs. Two people added that they were never tempted to become stars (L'Heureux).

But what exactly is a star? Is there a downside to being constantly in the public eye? Is being a star really a lot of work? What is the cost of being famous?

It must be understood that being a star is a social role that an individual adopts. Every day of our lives, we, too, take on social roles; we accept the obligations and behaviors of being an employee, a parent, a spouse, and so forth. Celebrity performers are similar; they wake up in the morning and step into the star role.

A star's talent delights audiences of all ages. A star acts or sings or cracks jokes or even just poses, and does these things with such style that we are fascinated and refreshed. We pay attention to stars because their performances are so successful at entertaining us. Because the audience for television shows, films, and recordings has become so large and so appreciative, the acclamation a star receives has become greater and more ferocious in recent decades. Through ticket sales, high ratings, and fan mail, an audience makes known its jubilant or waning response to a star's performance. When the response is good, the flow of good tidings certifies a star in public regard and elevates him or her to a special glory. At some moments for certain stars and their captivated fans, the reaction can be manic, as when the Beatles first toured the U.S. in 1964.

Becoming a star is sometimes a difficult task. Trying to become known in the industry, to be liked by directors, and to get parts, hopefuls embark on endless rounds of auditions. Most will spend more time at auditions than they ever will before the camera. Athletes struggling to become star players generally spend many years in the minor leagues (or the equivalent) waiting for a call to "the show."

What readers believe

Rhetorical questions provide structure

Examples

Redefining star

Examples

Meanwhile, between roles, struggling actors have to sustain themselves. Usually this means menial jobs of one sort or another. For example, Marilyn Monroe labored in a wartime defense plant where she packed parachutes. For aspiring athletes, a job in the off-season is generally a necessity.

Example

Fame may require much in the way of disappointment, strain, and heartache. Since so many people are striving to become stars, and since so few will make it, the typical aspirant's work life is a ceaseless round of rejection and exclusion. He or she may attempt to maintain motivation with visions of ultimate stardom, but the daily experience of trudging from audition to audition can prove devastating. Celebrity George C. Scott commented about acting, "I think it is a psychologically damaging profession, just too much rejection to cope with every day of your life."

Redefining

Example and quote

Aspirants may initially set themselves on the path to stardom because, in their rosy view, fame promises freedom beyond compare. But in fact the job of the celebrity performer is subject to suffocating impositions and strangling constraints. Asked what it means to become a star, Cary Grant replied, "Does it mean happiness? Yeah, for a couple of days. And then what happens? You find out that your life is not your own anymore, and that you're on show every time you step out on the street."

Example and quote

According to Yoti Lane, such a reaction is altogether typical, for "one of the most characteristic symptoms of having actually become a celebrity is a certain disillusionment, which sets in—after the first thrill of seeing one's name in headlines—upon discovering the obligations and inconveniences of being known by everyone everywhere" (130).

Underestimated by the public, a star's work is one of the most strenuous occupations that a person can have. Fred Astaire commented, "People will come up to me and say, 'Boy, it must have been fun making those old MGM musicals.' Fun? I suppose you could have considered them that—if you like beating your brains and feet out."

Redefinition continues

Knocking oneself out to deliver first-rate performances to the public, time after time, is the fate of those ensconced in the star role. The occupation calls for extraordinary effort and ceaseless toil.

For most stars, the preparation for performing begins with a general readiness. Professional athletes work out for countless hours to maintain their physical condition. Singers exercise their voices daily, practicing their delivery and keeping their vocal cords in shape. Actors take classes to strengthen their performance or spend time carefully observing others.

From a base of readiness, the star prepares for the performance. The rock band practices its songs for a concert, the comedian works on new material, and the actor concentrates on a new character to become familiar with it. Actors must go over their lines again and again, working to get them right. Before going on, the star has to be costumed and made up, a process that can be very time-consuming.

The hard work for a star truly begins when he or she must concentrate on the task at hand. What a performer must do is create wonderfully and completely, on cue. The star has been engaged to deliver, within the framework of the performance, the right act at the right moment. The audience expects the comedian to have the perfect punchline, the center fielder to catch the ball in the sun, and the actress to cry when required.

Being a star can also be dangerous. Actor Sylvester Stallone calculates that in making some of his action films he has broken his nose three times, his hand twice, and has suffered a concussion and a ruptured stomach. Also a danger to stars is their public. Fan letters pour in by the thousands each day, and the letter writers often want to enter into some sort of transaction with their idols. This can be dangerous when fans strive to encounter a star in person, pushing and shoving for contact, or when outraged fans try to injure a star.

For the privilege of staring at a star, fans will follow an entertainer into parties, restaurants, and even bathrooms.

Process

Effects of stardom

Sometimes stars have to live with the unremitting presence of fans camped at their front doors. The romance and obsession that are in a fan's mind can lead them to stalk an idol. Brooke Shields was the object of the affections of one Mark Bailey, who attempted to break into her New Jersey home; the judge put him on five years' probation. While David Letterman was on the West Coast, a mentally ill woman who claimed to be his wife installed herself in his East Coast home (Fowles 310).

The media can also invade the privacy of a star. Interviews may seem endless and prove to be very draining. The press tends to emphasize personal questions that make the subject of an interview understandably uncomfortable. Magazines such as <u>The National Enquirer</u> strive to create rumors about different stars, often relying on questionable sources and rumors that later prove to be unfounded. A personal problem that any of us could easily encounter and that most of us would like to face in privacy frequently ends up on the front pages of newspapers, creating stress and embarrassment for the celebrity and threatening his or her career.

Even if their lives do not fit within stereotypes, stars are not people who lead normal lives. Celebrities are widely admired and often receive considerable money for their work, yet they must face situations that the general public does not fully understand. Stars face danger; give up their privacy; and work long, hard hours. Referring to celebrities as "stars" is quite appropriate because their lives are as far from ours as the stars are distant from the ground we stand on.

Summary

Works Cited

Braudy, Leo. <u>Frenzy of Renown: Fame and Its History</u>. New York: Oxford UP, 1986.

Fowles, Jib. <u>Starstruck</u>. Chicago: Smithsonian, 1992.

Lane, Yoti. <u>The Psychology of the Actor</u>. Westport, CT: Greenwood, 1959.

L'Heureux, Lori. Survey. 7–10 Nov. 1995.

JOHN BERENDT

> JOHN BERENDT was born in Syracuse, New York, in 1939. He was a
> student at Harvard and received his B.A. in 1961. A journalist, es-
> sayist, and writer of nonfiction, he has also worked as an editor and
> columnist at *Esquire,* an editor at *Holiday* and *New York* magazines,
> and as an associate producer of the *David Frost Show* and the
> *Dick Cavett Show.* His essays and articles have appeared in nu-
> merous magazines, including *Forbes, Publisher's Weekly, Esquire,*
> *Architectural Digest,* and the *New Yorker.* His best-selling book,
> *Midnight in the Garden of Good and Evil* (1994) is a nonfiction account
> of unusual characters and scandalous goings-on in Savannah,
> Georgia.

The Hoax

In this essay, first published in *Esquire,* Berendt takes a relatively
straightforward approach to definition, yet through skillful writing and wit, he manages to offer a fresh and insightful understanding of a familiar term and the behavior it designates.

When the humorist Robert Benchley was an undergraduate at   1
Harvard eighty years ago, he and a couple of friends showed
up one morning at the door of an elegant Beacon Hill mansion,
dressed as furniture repairmen. They told the housekeeper they had
come to pick up the sofa. Five minutes later they carried the sofa out
the door, put it on a truck, and drove it three blocks away to another
house, where, posing as deliverymen, they plunked it down in the parlor. That evening, as Benchley well knew, the couple living in house A
were due to attend a party in house B. Whatever the outcome—and
I'll get to that shortly—it was guaranteed to be a defining example of
how proper Bostonians handle social crises. The wit inherent in
Benchley's practical joke elevated it from the level of prank to the
more respectable realm of hoax.

To qualify as a hoax, a prank must have magic in it—the word   2
is derived from *hocus-pocus,* after all. Daring and irony are useful ingredients, too. A good example of a hoax is the ruse perpetrated by
David Hampton, the young black man whose pretense of being
Sidney Poitier's son inspired John Guare's *Six Degrees of Separation.*
Hampton managed to insinuate himself into two of New York's
most sophisticated households—one headed by the president of

the public-television station *WNET,* the other by the dean of the Columbia School of Journalism. Hampton's hoax touched a number of sensitive themes: snobbery, class, race, and sex, all of which playwright Guare deftly exploited.

Hampton is a member of an elite band of famous impostors that   3 includes a half-mad woman who for fifty years claimed to be Anastasia, the lost daughter of the assassinated czar Nicholas II; and a man named Harry Gerguson, who became a Hollywood restaurateur and darling of society in the 1930s and 1940s as the ersatz Russian prince Mike Romanoff.

Forgeries have been among the better hoaxes. Fake Vermeers   4 painted by an obscure Dutch artist, Hans van Meegeren, were so convincing that they fooled art dealers, collectors, and museums. The hoax came to light when van Meegeren was arrested as a Nazi collaborator after the war. To prove he was not a Nazi, he admitted he had sold a fake Vermeer to Hermann Göring for $256,000. Then he owned up to having created other "Vermeers," and to prove he could do it, he painted *Jesus in the Temple* in the style of Vermeer while under guard in jail.

In a bizarre twist, a story much like van Meegeren's became the   5 subject of the book *Fake!,* by Clifford Irving, who in 1972 attempted to pull off a spectacular hoax of his own: a wholly fraudulent "authorized" biography of Howard Hughes. Irving claimed to have conducted secret interviews with the reclusive Hughes, and McGraw-Hill gave him a big advance. Shortly before publication, Hughes surfaced by telephone and denied that he had ever spoken with Irving. Irving had already spent $100,000 of the advance; he was convicted of fraud and sent to jail.

As it happens, we are used to hoaxes where I come from. I grew   6 up just a few miles down the road from Cardiff, New York—a town made famous by the Cardiff Giant. As we learned in school, a farmer named Newell complained, back in 1889, that his well was running dry, and while he and his neighbors were digging a new one, they came upon what appeared to be the fossilized remains of a man twelve feet tall. Before the day was out, Newell had erected a tent and posted a sign charging a dollar for a glimpse of the "giant"— three dollars for a longer look. Throngs descended on Cardiff. It wasn't long before scientists determined that the giant had been carved from a block of gypsum. The hoax came undone fairly quickly after that, but even so—as often happens with hoaxes—the giant became an even bigger attraction *because* it was a hoax.

P. T. Barnum offered Newell a fortune for the giant, but Newell refused, and it was then that he got his comeuppance. Barnum simply
made a replica and put it on display as the genuine Cardiff Giant.
Newell's gig was ruined.

The consequences of hoaxes are what give them spice. Orson   7
Welles's lifelike 1938 radio broadcast of H. G. Well's *War of the
Worlds* panicked millions of Americans, who were convinced that
martians had landed in New Jersey. The forged diary of Adolf Hitler
embarrassed historian Hugh Trevor-Roper, who had vouched for its
authenticity, and *Newsweek* and the *Sunday Times* of London, both of
which published excerpts in 1983 shortly before forensic tests
proved that there were nylon fibers in the paper it was written on,
which wouldn't have been possible had it originated before 1950.
The five-hundred-thousand-year-old remains of Piltdown man,
found in 1912, had anthropologists confused about human evolution until 1953, when fluoride tests exposed the bones as an elaborate modern hoax. And as for Robert Benchley's game on Beacon
Hill, no one said a word about the sofa all evening, although there it
sat in plain sight. One week later, however, couple A sent an anonymous package to couple B. It contained the sofa's slipcovers.

MEANINGS AND VALUES

1. State Berendt's definition of a hoax in your own words, and indicate
   the difference between a hoax and a practical joke or prank. Look up
   hoax in a dictionary, and tell how Berendt's definition differs, if at all,
   from the one you encounter there.

2. Restate the meaning of this sentence, "The consequences of hoaxes
   are what give them spice" (Par. 7), and discuss whether the examples
   that follow it provide satisfactory support for the writer's conclusion.
   (See "Guide to Terms": *Evaluation*.)

3. Other than defining the term *hoax*, what purposes do you think the
   writer had in mind for this essay? (Guide: *Purpose*.)

EXPOSITORY TECHNIQUES

1. Discuss how the way Berendt presents the examples in Paragraphs 2,
   3, and 6 makes them seem imaginative (and somewhat harmless) escapades rather than criminal frauds or deceptions.

2. Determine what definition strategies Berendt uses in this essay.
   Which seem most effective, and why? (Guide: *Evaluation*.)

3.   Evaluate the strategy Berendt uses to open and close the essay. What makes it successful or unsuccessful?

DICTION AND VOCABULARY

1.   To what extent does Berendt's presentation of the hoaxes described in Paragraphs 2, 3, and 6 as escapades rather than crimes depend on the terms he uses to present them? (See Expository Techniques, Question 1.) (Guide: *Diction*.)

2.   If you do not know the meaning of some of the following terms, look them up in a dictionary: perpetrated (Par. 2); ersatz (3); reclusive (5); gypsum, gig (6); vouched, forensic (7).

READ TO WRITE

1.   **Collaborating:** Pranks, jokes, humorous events, adventures, and absurd occurrences make enjoyable examples in essays, and they often reveal a good deal about human beings and their relationships. Working in a group, make a list of possible examples of this sort. Then freewrite individually about the examples as a way of discovering a possible topic and thesis for an essay of your own.

2.   **Considering Audience:** Make a list of words that most readers are likely to believe imply some sort of trickery and deception. Then prepare an essay in which you *redefine* one of the words and attempt to alter readers' views of its meaning.

3.   **Developing an Essay:** Using Berendt's essay as a general pattern, create a definition of your own about a very different subject—such as the greatest loss, the most difficult task, or the biggest disappointment.

(NOTE: Suggestions for topics requiring development by DEFINITION are on pp. 404–405 at the end of this chapter.)

DAGOBERTO GILB

> Dagoberto Gilb was born in Los Angeles in 1950 and has lived for
> many years in Texas, first in El Paso, now in Austin. He spent six-
> teen years in construction, twelve years as a highrise carpenter
> with the United Brotherhood of Carpenters. His collection of sto-
> ries, *The Magic of Blood* (1994) won the PEN/Hemingway Award.
> He has also published a novel, *The Last Known Residence of Mickey
> Acuna* (1995) and another collection of stories, *Woodcuts of Women*
> (2000). His collection of essays, *Gritos,* appeared in 2003.

Pride

> In medieval times, pride was considered one of the seven deadly
> sins. (The others were gluttony, envy, sloth, lechery, wrath, and
> greed.) In this essay, from his collection *Gritos,* Dagoberto Gilb
> treats pride as a positive trait—a virtue. He also focuses on the ac-
> tions of ordinary people in everyday circumstances, treating them
> as sources of pride.

It's almost time to close at the northwest corner of Altura and   1
Copia in El Paso. That means it is so dark that it is as restful as the
deepest unremembering sleep, dark as the empty space around this
spinning planet, as a black star. Headlights that beam a little cross-
eyed from a fatso American car are feeling around the asphalt road
up the hill toward the Good Time Store, its yellow plastic smiley
face bright like a sugary suck candy. The loose muffler holds only
half the misfires, and, dry springs squeaking, the automobile curves
slowly into the establishment's lot, swerving to avoid the new self-
serve gas pump island. Behind it, across the street, a Texas flag—out
too late this and all the nights—pops and slaps in a summer wind
that finally is cool.

A good man, gray on the edges, an assistant manager in a   2
brown starched and ironed uniform, is washing the glass windows
of the store, lit up by as many watts as Venus, with a roll of paper
towels and the blue liquid from a spray bottle. Good night, m'ijo! he
tells a young boy coming out after playing the video game, a Grande
Guzzler the size of a wastebasket balanced in one hand, an open bag
of Flaming Hot Cheetos, its red dye already smearing his mouth and
the hand not carrying the weight of the soda, his white T-shirt, its

short sleeves reaching halfway down his wrists, the whole XXL of it billowing and puffing in the outdoor gust.

A plump young woman steps out of that car. She's wearing a 3 party dress, wide scoops out of the top, front, and back, its hemline way above the knees.

Did you get a water pump? the assistant manager asks her. Are 4 you going to make it to Horizon City? He's still washing the glass of the storefront, his hand sweeping in small hard circles.

The young woman is patient and calm like a loving mother. I 5 don't know yet, she tells him as she stops close to him, thinking. I guess I should make a call, she says, and her thick-soled shoes, the latest fashion, slap against her heels to one of the pay phones at the front of the store.

Pride is working a job like it's as important as art or war, is the 6 happiness of a new high score on a video arcade game, of a pretty new black dress and shoes. Pride is the deaf and blind confidence of the good people who are too poor but don't notice.

A son is a long time sitting on the front porch where he 7 played all those years with the squirmy dog who still licks his face, both puppies then, even before he played on the winning teams of Little League baseball and City League basketball. They sprint down the sidewalk and across streets, side by side, until they stop to rest on the park grass, where a red ant, or a spider, bites the son's calf. It swells, but he no longer thinks to complain to his mom about it—he's too old now—when he comes home. He gets ready, putting on the shirt and pants his mom would have ironed but he wanted to iron himself. He takes the ride with his best friend since first grade. The hundreds of moms and dads, abuelos y abuelitas, the tios and primos, baby brothers and older married sisters, all are at the Special Events Center for the son's high school graduation. His dad is a man bigger than most, and when he walks in his dress eel-skin boots down the cement stairs to get as close to the hardwood basketball-court floor and cere- mony to see—m'ijo!—he feels an embarrassing sob bursting from his eyes and mouth. He holds it back, and with his hands, hides the tears that do escape, wipes them with his fingers, because the chavalitos in his aisle are playing and laughing and they are so small and he is so big next to them. And when his son walks to the stage to get his high school diploma and his dad wants to scream his name, he hears how many others, from the floor in caps and gowns and from around the arena, are already screaming it—could be any name, it could be any son's or daughter's: Alex! Vanessa! Carlos! Veronica! Ricky! Tony! Estella! Isa!—and sees his boy waving back to all of them.

Pride hears gritty dirt blowing against an agave whose stiff fertile stalk, so tall, will not bend—the love of land, rugged like the people who live on it. Pride sees the sunlight on the Franklin Mountains in the first light of morning and listens to a neighbor's gallo—the love of culture and history. Pride smells a sweet, musky drizzle of rain and eats huevos con chile in corn tortillas heated on a cast-iron pan—the love of heritage.   8

Pride is the fearless reaction to disrespect and disregard. It is knowing the future will prove that wrong.   9

Seeing the beauty: look out there from a height of the mountain and on the north and south of the Rio Grande, to the far away and close, the so many miles more of fuzz on the wide horizon, knowing how many years the people have passed and have stayed, the ancestors, the ones who have medaled, limped back on crutches or died or were heroes from wars in the Pacific or Europe or Korea or Vietnam or the Persian Gulf, the ones who have raised the fist and dared to defy, the ones who wash the clothes and cook and serve the meals, who stitch the factory shoes and the factory slacks, who assemble and sort, the ones who laugh and the ones who weep, the ones who care, the ones who want more, the ones who try, the ones who love, those ones with shameless courage and hardened wisdom, and the old ones still so alive, holding their grandchildren, and the young ones in their glowing prime, strong and gorgeous, holding each other, the ones who will be born from them. The desert land is rock-dry and ungreen. It is brown. Brown like the skin is brown. Beautiful brown.   10

MEANINGS AND VALUES

1. What purposes do you think the writer is trying to achieve in this essay? (See "Guide to Terms": *Purpose*.)

2. Explain the extent to which you believe most readers are likely to feel Gilb succesfully achieves his purposes in this essay. (Guide: *Evaluation*.)

3. Does Gilb focus on a particular ethnic group in this essay? If so, which one? Do his ideas apply to other groups as well or to people in general? Why, or why not?

4. In your own words, state the definition of *pride* this essay offers. (Hint: Be ready to take more than one sentence to present your definition.)

EXPOSITORY TECHNIQUES

1. Which paragraphs in the essay provide definition in the form of extended examples?

2. Which paragraphs in the essay provide definition in the form of brief statements or examples?

3. What advantages (if any) does the writer's stratagy of providing multiple (though related) definitions of *pride* have over the more familiar strategy of providing a single, detailed definition followed by supporting examples. What disadvantages does it have? (Guide: *Evaluation*.)

4. Identify the parallel structures in Paragraphs 6, 8, and 9, and discuss the role they play in conveying the central theme of the essay. (Guide: *Unity*.)

DICTION AND VOCABULARY

1. Point out the concrete words in Paragraphs 2 and 7. Discuss what these words contribute to the examples presented in the paragraph. (Guide: *Concrete/Abstract*.)

2. If you do not know the meaning of some of the following words, look them up in a dictionary, either English or English/Spanish, as appropriate: m'ijo (par. 2); abuelos y abuelitas, tios, primos, chavalitos (7); gallo, huevos con chile (8).

READ TO WRITE

1. **Collaborating:** Working in a group, create a list of examples of behavior that illustrate and define a virtue (such as kindness or loyalty) or that help readers understand the positive sides of more questionable behaviors such as stubbornness or anger. Choose two examples and write three brief paragraphs (total) defining and explaining the behavior.

2. **Considering Audience:** Rewrite parts of Gilb's essays by substituting examples from your own experience or from a social, cultural, or ethnic group to which you belong. Or use the essay as a model for a discussion of other kinds of behavior.

3. **Developing an Essay:** Gilb finds positive traits and values in everyday behavior. Take a similar approach in an essay of your own by looking at everyday behaviors and ordinary people and emphasizing qualities within them deserving praise and admiration.

(NOTE: Suggestions for topics requiring development by use of DEFINITION are on pp. 404–405 at the end of this chapter.)

CARINA CHOCANO

> CARINA CHOCANO lives in Los Angeles and is the television critic for
> the *Los Angeles Times*. She also writes film reviews for the online
> magazine *Salon.com*. Her book, *Do You Love Me, or Am I Just
> Paranoid: The Serial Monogamist's Guide to Love* (2003), takes a
> satirical look at contemporary relationships. She has directed the
> film *Samuel Becket Orders Out* (1997).

Pilgrim

> "Pilgrim" was first published in *Border-Line Personalities* (2004), a
> collection of essays by contemporary Latina writers. In the essay,
> Chocano defines and describes a kind of "global" identity that is
> becoming increasingly common in an era when international trade
> and travel are rapidly altering familiar cultures and identities.

When I was a little kid, I used to fantasize about having a pilgrim friend. I think I got the idea from the episode of *Bewitched* in which Aunt Clara sends the Stephenses back to Plymouth Rock, and Darrin gets accused of being a witch for using a pencil. In my fantasy, my pilgrim friend would show up at my house, lonely, scared, and disoriented, and I would take her under my wing. I'd be very careful to introduce her to her new environment— the modern world, with all its crazy high-tech wonders—slowly and carefully. I'd do it in small doses and make sure not to overwhelm her.

I would begin with little things, easy things, like pencils (perhaps she would have already seen Darrin's) and breakfast cereal. I would make sure she was ready, that she had her bearings, before moving on to mind-blowing things like lamps and toasters. I would try to imagine what it might be like to be unable to fathom a toaster. I would break it down for her, teach her not to fear the toaster, assure her that the toaster was not, in fact, an instrument of the devil but an instrument of General Electric, which was a very large company that had offices and manufacturing plants and employees all over the world.

I would wait a reasonable amount of time before letting my pilgrim friend see a car, or a television, or anything else that might startle her into the kind of culture shock from which she might never recover. I didn't want my Pilgrim friend going into some state of catatonic stupor before I could show her off to my modern-day friends, who would be very impressed and forget for a moment that I was new.

By the time I was nine, about the age I was when I thought up my pilgrim friend, I had moved a total of five times. I had lived in four countries, three continents, and two states. I had learned three languages and forgotten one of them. I would have forgotten another if my parents had let me, but it was theirs, so they wouldn't. (There you have the difference between an immigrant and an expatriate.) I learned English, in what now seems like a few hours, with a New Jersey accent, which I promptly dropped within minutes of arriving in Illinois two years later. I identified, in a way that was totally incommensurate to the duration and timing of my previous sojourn there, with Chicago, the accidental city of my birth.

By the time I was nine, I was a world-weary jet traveler, the kind of kid who knew how to get on the good side of a stewardess, because getting on the good side of the stewardess means getting into the cockpit, a pair of plastic wings, and an extra dessert. I had spent a cumulative total of about one year living in hotels. (Room service held no mystery for me, though it never lost its charm.) On the day I turned nine, halfway through the third grade, I started at a new school. I was greeted at the door of the classroom with a rendition of "Happy Birthday." Most kids drew a blank after the word "dear."

If you grew up as a corporate nomad, particularly a non-American one, and your camel was the plodding conglomerate known as a "multinational corporation," then you understand what I'm talking about, and the geo-biographical rundown that follows won't strike you as romantic, exotic, exciting, or terribly interesting. If you didn't, and odds are you didn't, then you will likely find it to be all of those things. You will lament your own boring childhood in Shaker Heights, New Brunswick, or Fremont—the one you are constantly apologizing for—and I will envy you with a runny, inchoate, E.T.-like longing that no amount of phoning could curb.

I have told this story, in more or less detail, so many times I no longer know if it's even true. It's my story, but I have the distinct feeling that the most important parts happened without me. My parents were born and raised in Lima, Peru. Shortly after they got married, my father got accepted to graduate school in Chicago and the two of them went together. A year and a half later, I was born. We moved back to Lima six months later, and after that, thanks to a series of promotions and job changes timed almost exactly two years apart, we went from Brazil to New Jersey to Chicago to Spain. Beyond whatever house my family was living in at the time, which my mother was always careful to decorate almost exactly like the previous place to preserve a sense of continuity, like they do in the movies, any notion of home was completely abstract to me.

My family's first stay in Madrid lasted for six years. We went to   8
the American School, which might as well have been a stray mother ship that had briefly alighted on a stretch of arid land just to try and get its bearings. Some of the American kids I went to school with were spending their first and only years away from home, but others seemed never to have actually lived in the United States, or had left when they were so young, they had no firsthand recollection of it. They might have had American passports, and they might have spent the bulk of their childhoods in Spain, Saudi Arabia, or Mexico, but they were really Firestonian, Exxonese, Merckan.

These were the kids that seemed frozen in a kind of cultural am-   9
ber, still dressing, cutting their hair, and listening to the music that perhaps their older siblings or the cool neighbor kids had listened to "back home" when they still lived "back home." They referred to whatever town qualified, as if they'd gotten together on this, as "back home," a phrase that, for all its imperialist shucksiness, always struck a chord of deep longing in me. Even though these kids, with their ten-years-too-late southern rock records and their feathered hair, had a way of making their hometowns sound like a compound in Guyana; even though I knew deep down that "back home" was bound to disappoint one day, bound to fail to live up to its twangy, bucolic promise; as much as I just knew that their reentry "back home" would be turbulent and alienating after all those years abroad, at least they were talking about places you could actually locate on a map.

After I'd lived in Madrid long enough to adopt the accent, I   10
more or less adopted it as my home. Between my freshman year in high school and my junior year in college, my family moved back to Chicago, then back to Madrid, then back to New Jersey, then back to Madrid. I went away to college (back to Chicago) as they were moving back to New Jersey. I spent the year in Paris the year they moved back to Madrid. Then I returned to school, graduated, moved to California, and somehow, without really intending to, I never really went back home again.

When I go to Madrid now, which is infrequently, I am re-   11
minded of a movie I saw once when I was a kid, in which a city was

hit by a bomb that killed all the life-forms but left all the buildings intact. I held on to the idea of Madrid as my home for as long as I could sustain it. When I was 25, my parents and siblings still lived there. About a year later, my parents had separated, my mom had moved back to Lima, my brother took a job in London, and my sister went to school in Texas. When my dad died about five years after that, all the buildings were officially empty.

12 I have lived in California for thirteen years, the longest I have ever lived anywhere. Even though it is, technically, my home, and I have all the documentation, it can't be home because I don't long for it. It can't be home because it's all around me. When you move a lot, you travel through space at the same rate you travel through time. Everything becomes relative. You pick things up along the way. You leave things behind and you miss them later. Some things you carry with you, even if they were never yours. You cling to things that weren't important in the first place. You hedge your bets. You are not one thing and you are not another. You are everything to all people. You are, as the American kids at school used to say when asked about their religion, "nothing." You find you can't listen to a national anthem sung with sloppy sentimentality without blushing or cringing or both. You are literally neither here nor there.

13 As a kid, on the last night of our annual Christmas visits to Lima, I would stand in the doorway of my grandfather's den, clutching a small bottle of salt water (my grandfather was fanatical about the Pacific Ocean and lamented most of all that we were being raised nearer to the subpar Atlantic), and will myself to commit everything in it to memory—his poker table, his coin collection, the low midcentury sofas upholstered in burnt orange tweed, the mirrored shelves that held his collection of amoeba-shaped crystal ashtrays and colored genie bottles, his ridiculous framed *Playboy* cartoons, in which stacked nurses in straining uniforms were humorously sexually harassed by doctors and patients alike, his extensive collection of *Playboy* magazines, which he had leather-bound by year. I would stand in this late '50s James Bond fantasy of a room, my favorite, naturally, in his old-fashioned house of the future, and think: Remember this. Remember this. This is where I am from. This is mine. This is me.

14 It was and it wasn't. Home is not a place I can find on a map. It's still undiscovered. It has mystical powers. It's the place I'm trying to get to when I set out, every day, to journey in a foreign land. I am my own pilgrim friend. I'm showing myself around.

MEANINGS AND VALUES

1. What does the passage "... I could show her off to my modern-day friends, who would be very impressed and forget for a moment that I was new" (Par. 3) reveal about the psychological motivation for the writer's fantasy about a pilgrim friend? What description of the imaginary pilgrim friend's feelings seems to apply equally well to the writer's state of mind as a child?

2. What does the writer mean when she refers to some of the kids she met as "Firestonian, Exxonese, Merckan"?

3. In what ways would the imaginary pilgrim described in the opening paragraphs of the essay fit the common definitions of *pilgrim:* "somebody who goes on a journey to a holy place for religious reasons" and "somebody who is making a journey of any kind"? In what ways do modern pilgrims like the writer fit these definitions?

EXPOSITORY TECHNIQUES

1. From Paragraph 4 on, the writer describes herself in ways that fit the definition of *pilgrim.* Not until the last paragraph, however, does she state directly, "I am my own pilgrim friend" (Par. 14). Why do you think she waits until the end of the essay to announce the theme of the essay directly? (See "Guide to Terms": *Unity.*)

2. Where in the essay does the writer indicate that her purpose is to extend the traditional definition of *pilgrim* to include contemporary experiences? Do you think this purpose is made clear enough for most readers? (Guide: *Purpose/Evaluation.*) Why, or why not? If not, how might the writer have made it clearer?

3. Where in the essay does the writer include examples of people other than herself to explain her understanding of contemporary pilgrims? What do these examples add to the meaning and effectiveness of the essay?

DICTION AND VOCABULARY

1. The events presented in Paragraph 5 are likely to lead most readers to feel a sense of pity for the child's isolation and loneliness. How does the writer prevent this response from becoming excessively emotional, or sentimental? (Guide: *Sentimentality.*) Pay particular attention to the writer's objective style of presentation and choice of words. (Guide: *Objective/Subjective, Diction.*)

2. Identify the metaphor and the allusion in Paragraph 6 and discuss their contribution to the main point of the paragraph. (Guide: *Figures of Speech.*)

3.　If you do not know the meaning of some of the following words, look them up in a dictionary: disoriented (Par. 1); catatonic, stupor (3); expatriate, incommensurate, duration, sojourn (4); rendition (5); conglomerate, inchoate (6); continuity (7); arid, bearings (8); amber, imperialist, bucolic (9); infrequently (11).

READ TO WRITE

1.　**Collaborating:** Working with classmates, try to think of any other personal or cultural phenomena that our contemporary experience of frequent travel, emigration, and global business has had on people's lives has altered in ways that require new definitions or revisions of traditional definitions. List as many phenomena as you can along with ideas for definitions. Then create an informal plan for presenting a definition of one phenomenon in an essay.

2.　**Considering Audience:** Chocano introduces an imaginary character at the beginning of her essay that represents (in part) more traditional definitions of a concept. Create the opening for an essay of your own using a similar strategy.

3.　**Developing an Essay:** Do Activity 2, then, using "Pilgrim" as a model, prepare an entire essay of your own.

(NOTE: Suggestions for topics requiring development by use of DEFINITION are on pp. 404–405 at the end of this chapter.)

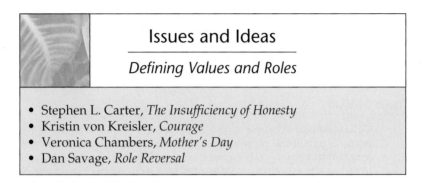

Issues and Ideas

Defining Values and Roles

- Stephen L. Carter, *The Insufficiency of Honesty*
- Kristin von Kreisler, *Courage*
- Veronica Chambers, *Mother's Day*
- Dan Savage, *Role Reversal*

Leave It to Beaver represents for many people a time and a culture whose values, relationships, and roles were simple, clear, and unchanging. Things were probably never that simple, though the television program certainly made them appear that way. Nonetheless, values, identities, and relationships are certainly undergoing more changes and redefinition now than they were five decades ago. The changes involve not only the development of new identities but also the recognition that all our identities are constructed from multiple—and sometimes seemingly incompatible—elements.

Though we are always the children of our parents, sometimes we end up playing parental roles toward them, offering advice or counsel, just as Veronica Chambers explains in her essay, "Mother's Day." Though we might like to think of ourselves as typically middle class, Midwestern, or business/labor minded in our values and outlooks, few, if any, of us are so easily defined. As Dan Savage points out in his essay, "Role Reversal," we may end up redefining ourselves and our values as we encounter new situations and challenges, whatever our primary ethnic, social, economic, religious, or gender identification might be. Even such seemingly clear roles as "mother" and "father" can be filled by many different people and by more than one person, especially in this age of blended families. Kristin von Kreisler takes these issues one step further by pointing out that we might have to extend our definitions of important human qualities like courage and bravery to include animals whose behavior seems to display these virtues.

Each of these essays reminds us that the need to understand our values, identities, and roles in relation to other people makes definition an important pattern of thought and analysis. Each essay also demonstrates many other expository patterns.

STEPHEN L. CARTER

Stephen L. Carter is professor of law at Yale Law School and the author of several controversial but highly respected and tightly reasoned books that explore issues in contemporary ethics, politics, and social relationships. After graduating from Yale Law School, he had a variety of professional experiences, including clerking for U.S. Supreme Court Justice Thurgood Marshall and working in a prestigious law firm. Carter's books are *Reflections of an Affirmative Action Baby* (1992), *The Culture of Disbelief: How American Law and Politics Trivialize Religious Devotion* (1994), *The Confirmation Mess: Cleaning Up the Federal Appointments Mess,* (1995), *Integrity* (1997), and *Civility* (1999) (nonfiction); and *The Emperor of Ocean Park* (2002) (a novel).

The Insufficiency of Honesty

Integrity is not simply a term or idea. It refers to a way of acting and of discerning the qualities of our actions. Integrity may be something we all claim to admire and wish to have ourselves, but as Stephen L. Carter points out in this essay first published in the *Atlantic Monthly*, it can be very difficult to achieve.

A couple of years ago I began a university commencement ad- 1
dress by telling the audience that I was going to talk about integrity. The crowd broke into applause. Applause! Just because they had heard the word "integrity": that's how starved for it they were. They had no idea how I was using the word, or what I was going to say about integrity, or, indeed, whether I was for it or against it. But they knew they liked the idea of talking about it.

Very well, let us consider this word "integrity." Integrity is like 2
the weather: everybody talks about it but nobody knows what to do about it. Integrity is that stuff that we always want more of. Some say that we need to return to the good old days when we had a lot more of it. Others say that we as a nation have never really had enough of it. Hardly anybody stops to explain exactly what we mean by it, or how we know it is a good thing, or why everybody needs to have the same amount of it. Indeed, the only trouble with integrity is that everybody who uses the word seems to mean something slightly different.

For instance, when I refer to integrity, do I mean simply "hon- 3
esty"? The answer is no; although honesty is a virtue of importance,

it is a different virtue from integrity. Let us, for simplicity, think of honesty as not lying; and let us further accept Sissela Bok's definition of a lie: "any intentionally deceptive message which is *stated*." Plainly, one cannot have integrity without being honest (although, as we shall see, the matter gets complicated), but one can certainly be honest and yet have little integrity.

When I refer to integrity, I have something very specific in   4
mind. Integrity, as I will use the term, requires three steps: discerning what is right and what is wrong; acting on what you have discerned, even at personal cost; and saying openly that you are acting on your understanding of right and wrong. The first criterion captures the idea that integrity requires a degree of moral reflectiveness. The second brings in the ideal of a person of integrity as steadfast, a quality that includes keeping one's commitments. The third reminds us that a person of integrity can be trusted.

The first point to understand about the difference between honesty and integrity is that a person may be entirely honest without   5
ever engaging in the hard work of discernment that integrity requires: she may tell us quite truthfully what she believes without ever taking the time to figure out whether what she believes is good and right and true. The problem may be as simple as someone's foolishly saying something that hurts a friend's feelings; a few moments of thought would have revealed the likelihood of the hurt and the lack of necessity for the comment. Or the problem may be more complex, as when a man who was raised from birth in a society that preaches racism states his belief in one race's inferiority as a fact, without ever really considering that perhaps this deeply held view is wrong. Certainly the racist is being honest—he is telling us what he actually thinks—but his honesty does not add up to integrity.

Telling Everything You Know

A wonderful epigram sometimes attributed to the filmmaker Sam   6
Goldwyn goes like this: "The most important thing in acting is honesty; once you learn to fake that, you're in." The point is that honesty can be something one *seems* to have. Without integrity, what passes for honesty often is nothing of the kind; it is fake honesty—or it is honest but irrelevant and perhaps even immoral.

Consider an example. A man who has been married for fifty   7
years confesses to his wife on his deathbed that he was unfaithful thirty-five years earlier. The dishonesty was killing his spirit, he says. Now he has cleared his conscience and is able to die in peace.

The husband has been honest—sort of. He has certainly unbur-   8
dened himself. And he has probably made his wife (soon to be his
widow) quite miserable in the process, because even if she forgives
him, she will not be able to remember him with quite the vivid image of love and loyalty that she had hoped for. Arranging his own
emotional affairs to ease his transition to death, he has shifted to his
wife the burden of confusion and pain, perhaps for the rest of her
life. Moreover, he has attempted his honesty at the one time in his
life when it carries no risk; acting in accordance with what you think
is right and risking no loss in the process is a rather thin and unad-
mirable form of honesty.

Besides, even though the husband has been honest in a sense,   9
he has now twice been unfaithful to his wife: once thirty-five years
ago, when he had his affair, and again when, nearing death, he decided that his own peace of mind was more important than hers. In
trying to be honest he has violated his marriage vow by acting toward his wife not with love but with naked and perhaps even cruel
self-interest.

As my mother used to say, you don't have to tell people   10
everything you know. Lying and nondisclosure, as the law often
recognizes, are not the same thing. Sometimes it is actually illegal
to tell what you know, as, for example, in the disclosure of certain
financial information by market insiders. Or it may be unethical,
as when a lawyer reveals a confidence entrusted to her by a
client. It may be simple bad manners, as in the case of a gratuitous comment to a colleague on his or her attire. And it may be
subject to religious punishment, as when a Roman Catholic priest
breaks the seal of the confessional—an offense that carries automatic excommunication.

In all the cases just mentioned, the problem with telling every-   11
thing you know is that somebody else is harmed. Harm may not be
the intention, but it is certainly the effect. Honesty is most laudable
when we risk harm to ourselves; it becomes a good deal less so if we
instead risk harm to others when there is no gain to anyone other
than ourselves. Integrity may counsel keeping our secrets in order to
spare the feelings of others. Sometimes, as in the example of the
wayward husband, the reason we want to tell what we know is precisely to shift our pain onto somebody else—a course of action dic-
tated less by integrity than by self-interest. Fortunately, integrity
and self-interest often coincide, as when a politician of integrity is
rewarded with our votes. But often they do not, and it is at those
moments that our integrity is truly tested.

Error

Another reason that honesty alone is no substitute for integrity is   12
that if forthrightness is not preceded by discernment, it may result in
the expression of an incorrect moral judgment. In other words, I
may be honest about what I believe, but if I have never tested my beliefs, I may be wrong. And here I mean "wrong" in a particular
sense: the proposition in question is wrong if I would change my
mind about it after hard moral reflection.

Consider this example. Having been taught all his life that   13
women are not as smart as men, a manager gives the women on his
staff less-challenging assignments than he gives the men. He does
this, he believes, for their own benefit: he does not want them to fail,
and he believes that they will if he gives them tougher assignments.
Moreover, when one of the women on his staff does poor work, he
does not berate her as harshly as he would a man, because he expects nothing more. And he claims to be acting with integrity because he is acting according to his own deepest beliefs.

The manager fails the most basic test of integrity. The question   14
is not whether his actions are consistent with what he most deeply
believes but whether he has done the hard work of discerning
whether what he most deeply believes is right. The manager has not
taken this harder step.

Moreover, even within the universe that the manager has con-   15
structed for himself, he is not acting with integrity. Although he is
obviously wrong to think that the women on his staff are not as
good as the men, even were he right, that would not justify applying
different standards to their work. By so doing he betrays both his
obligation to the institution that employs him and his duty as a manager to evaluate his employees.

The problem that the manager faces is an enormous one in our   16
practical politics, where having the dialogue that makes democracy
work can seem impossible because of our tendency to cling to our
views even when we have not examined them. As Jean Bethke
Elshtain has said, borrowing from John Courtney Murray, our politics are so fractured and contentious that we often cannot even reach
disagreement. Our refusal to look closely at our own most cherished
principles is surely a large part of the reason. Socrates thought the
unexamined life not worth living. But the unhappy truth is that few
of us actually have the time for constant reflection on our views—on
public or private morality. Examine them we must, however, or we
will never know whether we might be wrong.

None of this should be taken to mean that integrity as I have 17
described it presupposes a single correct truth. If, for example, your
integrity-guided search tells you that affirmative action is wrong, and
my integrity-guided search tells me that affirmative action is right, we
need not conclude that one of us lacks integrity. As it happens, I
believe—both as a Christian and as a secular citizen who struggles
toward moral understanding—that we *can* find true and sound answers to our moral questions. But I do not pretend to have found
very many of them, nor is an exposition of them my purpose here.

It is the case not that there aren't any right answers but that, 18
given human fallibility, we need to be careful in assuming that we
have found them. However, today's political talk about how it is
wrong for the government to impose one person's morality on
somebody else is just mindless chatter. *Every* law imposes one person's morality on somebody else, because law has only two functions: to tell people to do what they would rather not or to forbid
them to do what they would.

And if the surveys can be believed, there is far more moral agree- 19
ment in America than we sometimes allow ourselves to think. One of
the reasons that character education for young people makes so much
sense to so many people is precisely that there seems to be a core set of
moral understandings—we might call them the American Core—that
most of us accept. Some of the virtues in this American Core are, one
hopes, relatively noncontroversial. About 500 American communities
have signed on to Michael Josephson's program to emphasize the
"six pillars" of good character: trustworthiness, respect, responsibility, caring, fairness, and citizenship. These virtues might lead to a
similarly noncontroversial set of political values: having an honest
regard for ourselves and others, protecting freedom of thought and
religious belief, and refusing to steal or murder.

Honesty and Competing Responsibilities

A further problem with too great an exaltation of honesty is that it 20
may allow us to escape responsibilities that morality bids us bear. If
honesty is substituted for integrity, one might think that if I say I am
not planning to fulfill a duty, I need not fulfill it. But it would be a
peculiar morality indeed that granted us the right to avoid our
moral responsibilities simply by stating our intention to ignore
them. Integrity does not permit such an easy escape.

Consider an example. Before engaging in sex with a woman, 21
her lover tells her that if she gets pregnant, it is her problem, not his.

She says that she understands. In due course she does wind up pregnant. If we believe, as I hope we do, that the man would ordinarily have a moral responsibility toward both the child he will have helped to bring into the world and the child's mother, then his honest statement of what he intends does not spare him that responsibility.

This vision of responsibility assumes that not all moral obliga- 22 tions stem from consent or from a stated intention. The linking of obligations to promises is a rather modern and perhaps uniquely Western way of looking at life, and perhaps a luxury that only the well-to-do can afford. As Fred and Shulamit Korn (a philosopher and an anthropologist) have pointed out, "If one looks at ethnographic accounts of other societies, one finds that, while obligations everywhere play a crucial role in social life, promising is not preeminent among the sources of obligation and is not even mentioned by most anthropologists." The Korns have made a study of Tonga, where promises are virtually unknown but the social order is remarkably stable. If life without any promises seems extreme, we Americans sometimes go too far the other way, parsing not only our contracts but even our marriage vows in order to discover the absolute minimum obligation that we have to others as a result of our promises.

That some societies in the world have worked out evidently 23 functional structures of obligation without the need for promise or consent does not tell us what *we* should do. But it serves as a reminder of the basic proposition that our existence in civil society creates a set of mutual responsibilities that philosophers used to capture in the fiction of the social contract. Nowadays, here in America, people seem to spend their time thinking of even cleverer ways to avoid their obligations, instead of doing what integrity commands and fulfilling them. And all too often honesty is their excuse.

Meanings and Values

1.   Most readers are likely to consider honesty a good trait. Why, therefore, do you think Carter created a definition that points out its shortcomings? What do you think was his overall purpose in writing the essay? Do you believe the essay has more than one purpose? If so, what are they? (See "Guide to Terms": *Purpose*.)

2. List the reasons the author gives for considering honesty insufficient. State in your own words why the author believes that the men in Paragraphs 7–9 and 21 have honesty but lack integrity.

3. Does this essay have a thesis statement? If so, where is it? Does it adequately sum up the main idea of the entire essay? Why, or why not? If the essay does not have a thesis statement, is it nonetheless organized around a main idea or theme? What is it? (Guide: *Thesis.*) Explain why you consider the essay unified or not unified. (Guide: *Unity.*)

EXPOSITORY TECHNIQUES

1. If one of the main purposes of this essay is to define *integrity,* why does the writer spend so much time discussing the meaning of *honesty?* In formulating your answer, take into account various definition strategies and the likely responses of readers to concepts like honesty.

2. What is the main definition strategy Carter employs in this essay? How is the organization of the essay related to this strategy? Be specific in answering this question. What other definition patterns does the writer employ, and where in the essay does he use them?

3. Which paragraphs in the essay are devoted wholly, or mostly, to qualification? (Guide: *Qualification.*) What role(s) do they play in helping develop the definitions? Why would the essay be weaker without them?

4. Where in the essay does the writer use transitions at the beginnings of paragraphs to highlight the essay's organization and indicate the definition strategy he is employing? (Guide: *Transition.*)

DICTION AND VOCABULARY

1. Throughout the essay, Carter uses contrasting words and concepts to explain the difference between honesty and integrity. Sometimes the contrasts involve the denotation of words and sometimes the connotations. (Guide: *Connotation/Denotation.*) Discuss the contrasts as they appear in Paragraphs 6, 8, and 9, and explain the use Carter makes of them. (Guide: *Diction.*) Explain the extent to which Carter reinforces the contrasts through sentence structure. (Guide: *Syntax.*)

2. In the course of the essay, Carter repeats a small number of words quite frequently, often varying their form. What are the words? How are they related to the essay's thesis (or theme)? How do they contribute to the essay's coherence? (Guide: *Coherence.*)

3. If you do not know the meanings of some of the following terms, look them up in a dictionary: discerning, criterion, steadfast (Par. 4); epigram (6); gratuitous, excommunication (10); laudable, counsel (11); forthrightness (12); contentious (16); presupposes (17); fallibility, impose (18); parsing (22).

READ AND WRITE

1. **Collaborating:** Working in a group, create a list of terms naming qualities that most people would agree are virtues (like *honesty* and *integrity*). Choose two and write three brief examples for each word that help define it. Choose examples that indicate what the term means and also some that indicate what it does not or should not mean. Include examples focusing on women as well as men.

2. **Considering Audience:** Rewrite Carter's essay by substituting examples from women's experiences, or use the essay as a model for a discussion of moral concepts as they apply to both men and women.

3. **Developing an essay:** Carter's title, "The Insufficiency of Honesty," suggests both a focus for the essay and an interesting approach to explaining why a particular quality is inadequate. Borrow this approach for an essay. Explain why your subject is inadequate, insufficient, or incomplete.

(NOTE: Suggestions for topics requiring development by use of DEFINITION are on pp. 404–405 at the end of this chapter.)

KRISTIN VON KREISLER

KRISTIN VON KREISLER has taught English at the University of Hawaii and journalism at San Jose State University. She is also a writer whose work has appeared in magazines and newspapers, including *Glamour, Animal People, Ladies' Home Journal, Family Circle, Parade, Reader's Digest, Washington Post, Los Angeles Times,* and *Christian Science Monitor.* She has also published a book, *I Do, I Don't* (1988), but is best known for two other books focusing on the emotional and moral life of animals, *The Compassion of Animals* (1997) and *Beauty in the Beasts* (2002).

Courage

Courage is a quality usually applied to humans. In this selection from *Beauty in the Beasts,* Kristin von Kreisler defines courage and a related quality, bravery, in ways that apply to the actions of animals. She is aware, of course, that many people might argue that animals act simply from instinct or lack the kind of awareness necessary for acts of courage and bravery. As a result, she uses a variety of definition strategies to show that the concepts clearly apply to at least some animal behavior.

Two days after Beauty, a chestnut mare, gave birth to her foal, 1 Sultan, the winter weather turned bitter cold. And the Jan du Toit's River, which flowed through the South African farm where Beauty lived, turned into a torrent of rushing, foaming water.

In freezing rain, Hank Gorter went to find Beauty and Sultan in 2 the afternoon to bring them to their stable. But, apparently, horses whinnying on the other side of the river were more compelling than a warm barn; Beauty and Sultan leapt into the dangerous water and swam across to join them. In the strong current, Beauty nudged Sultan along and kept him steady. Just as the foal climbed out, however, the muddy riverbank collapsed and he fell back, neighing with terror, into the water.

With all her strength, Beauty paddled through the raging cur- 3 rent and tried to reach Sultan before he was carried downstream to his death. Gorter ran down the bank and also tried to grab the foal as the water took him away, but Gorter slipped and was swept into the torrent, too. Sputtering for air, he bobbed to the surface next to Beauty, whose eyes, he remembers, were bulging in fear. In spite of her panic, Beauty stopped trying to get to Sultan just long enough to shove Gorter with her nose toward the safety of the riverbank. As Gorter clung to tree roots, Beauty finally reached her foal and guided him to an island in the middle of the river.

When Beauty behaved so valiantly in such terrifying circum-   4 stances, it's impossible for us to know with certainty what was on her mind. Perhaps she was acting impulsively, like a human mother who doesn't think of herself for an instant when her child is in trouble; she does whatever she has to do, including dying herself, to save her child. On the other hand, Beauty also stopped her efforts on behalf of her foal to rescue Gorter, whom she barely knew, in spite of Sultan's desperate situation and her own danger. That seems to me to be a deliberate—and even moral—choice. When Beauty acted as she did, she clearly showed great courage.

If people risk their lives to help someone, we don't seem to care   5 if they're acting on impulse or choice. The outcome is the same: These heroes are congratulated for their bravery and showered with accolades. But bravery is bravery, whether shown by a person or a horse, and I believe that animals should be recognized in this way, too. So often, though, animals' courage goes unacknowledged. Or it's dismissed, negated, or explained away as something else.

That isn't fair. In circumstances that might leave many of us im-   6 mobilized with fear, animals can choose to act in amazing ways, especially when they help their human guardians. But researchers often dismiss animal courage, by saying, simply, that animals don't feel fear. Since winning a victory over fear is usually the basis of courage, then animals can't be called brave, or so the argument goes.

"Fear is an inference. We don't know anything about animals'   7 direct experience, if anything," explains Peter Lang, a research professor of clinical and health psychology at the University of Florida. When I asked him if animals' pounding hearts and trembling bodies weren't physical signals of fear (as they are with us), he said that "physiological signs don't tell us what animals are experiencing." In other words, when an animal displays those signs, it may be showing only an automatic biological response, not an emotional one. Fear is out of the picture.

But from laboratory experiments, other experts have concluded   8 that animals *can* be fearful.

For one thing, certain drugs seem to bring fear out in some   9 species. In several studies, researchers rewarded rats for pressing a bar in threatening situations but did not reward them for pressing it in nonthreatening ones. After the researchers then gave the rats a drug called pentaline tetrazol (PTZ), the rats pressed the bar just as they did when threatened. When the rats have taken PTZ, "they feel scared. In other words, there is a consistent, subjective experience associated with fear," explains Caroline Blanchard, a research professor at the University of Hawaii's Pacific Biomedical Research Center. "On the basis of these subjective effects, the rats can determine that the situation [with the drug] is more similar to when they're scared than to when they're not scared."

Certain situations also seem to draw fear out of experimental 10 animals. If lab rats are allowed to live happily for generations with nothing to fear, and then researchers set even a gentle, well-behaved cat near them for fifteen minutes, says Blanchard, "you change those rats' lives for a long, long time. Before, they never realized that anything was scary. But now they know. For at least the next several days, those guys are really nervous." The rats stick their heads out of their burrowing tunnels and cautiously sniff and look around for the cat before venturing out. They eat less, drink less, and have less sex. "Now they're worried," Blanchard adds. "The fear is built in them, only requiring certain types of stimuli to release it."

If chickens are faced with something unfamiliar, they can show 11 fear, too. In a study at the Victorian Institute of Animal Science in Australia, researcher John Barnett studied the position and posture of hens when someone stood close to their cages. The person's sex, height, or eyeglasses seemed not to phase the hens at all. But they crouched down or tried to escape when the person wore overalls instead of their usual clothes. Barnett concluded that the birds were not accustomed to seeing overalls; that novelty, which they sensed as danger, apparently, set off a fearful reaction.

Outside of labs, other experts have observed animals' behavior 12 and determined that they can be afraid of many things. Bob Andrysco, a pet behaviorist in Columbus, Ohio, has worked with dogs who cowered at firecrackers, thunder, people wearing hats, and a window that a burglar had once come through. One dog whined and ran to hide from lights reflected on walls. Another dog would tremble at the sight of blimps. A cat, threatened by unfamiliar people in his home, sank his claws into a visitor's anklebone and refused to let loose for twenty agonizing minutes. By recognizing danger in this way, Andrysco says, the cat was "like a person getting so afraid during a scary TV movie that he grabs and holds a pillow."

What better way is there for animals to tell us of their fear than 13 by their behavior? And what could make the fear more obvious than their trembling, crouching, or trying to run? The signs of animal fear are too apparent to ignore, as are stories of animals who have overcome fear and, in so doing, demonstrated its opposite: courage. Yet several experts, including those who give animals credit for being afraid, winced when I suggested that animals could be brave. That concept seemed out of the question.

Once again we have to decide for ourselves if we should go along with widely accepted expert opinion—or, specifically, if we might conclude that animals can override their fears and be courageous. In many of the stories I've collected, I see no other way of interpreting the action of the animals except to see it in these terms.   14

One such animal was Ole, a chocolate Lab, known for being so timid and fearful that he'd take cover, like a prairie dog, every time that hawks flew overhead. When chased by a moose once, he ran and hid his head between the legs of his guardian, Stan Anderson. With ears like flaps on a hunter's cap and fur glossy as a seal, Ole seemed to have the courage of toast—until one hike he and Anderson took near Rex Ford, Montana.   15

As man and dog walked along a grassy logging road, a black bear cub trundled out of the woods. Anderson's stomach squeezed into a knot of apprehension. Sure that the cub's mother would undoubtedly show up in a minute, Anderson whispered to Ole, "Let's get out of here." But before they could turn and run, the mother bear rose out of a ditch a hundred feet away.   16

Rearing up on her hind legs to a menacing six feet, the bear charged and swept her paw across Anderson's face. Blood poured down his cheek, and he was sure he'd lost an eye. He was also sure he'd soon be dead; Ole, always so fearful, couldn't possibly be brave enough to come to his aid. But Ole snarled and barked and snapped at the bear. He clamped his teeth into her leg with such ferocity, in fact, that she paused for an instant, perhaps wondering if killing Anderson with this fierce dog around was more trouble than it was worth. She turned and loped back to her cub.   17

About to go into shock, Anderson staggered, bleeding, toward his car. It was parked a mile away, and he wasn't sure he could make it that far and then drive the five miles home. Things got even worse when he heard scratching in the earth behind him, then felt breath on the back of his neck. Dread flashing through his mind, he braced himself.   18

The mother bear rammed her head against Anderson and bit his shoulder, then grabbed his elbow in her teeth and, with a terrible grinding sound, champed clear to his bone. Ole went crazy. Barking, yowling, and snapping, he hurled himself at the bear and bit any part of her that he could reach.   19

Anderson, as terrified for Ole as for himself, shoved the bear   20
with his free arm in a last desperate attempt to turn her away.
Thrown off balance, she momentarily unclamped her jaw, and Ole
sank his teeth into her hindquarters. She whirled around and again
lumbered back to her cub as Ole kept barking. All his life Ole had
been a fierce closet gladiator. Anderson realized, and not a trembling butterfly.

When they finally reached the car, Ole set aside his new   21
bravery and ferocity and again became his usual gentle, sensitive
self. He plastered his body against Anderson and supported him,
then licked his face to keep him from passing out on the drive
home. Anderson, who required hundreds of stitches for his
wounds, says. "Ole was determined to save me. He knew what
he was doing." Thrown into a crisis, he went against his basic,
fearful nature and mustered the courage to do what he knew
needed to be done.

Researchers' arguments to the contrary, plenty of animals, like   22
Ole, find themselves in dangerous situations, feel fear, and choose
to override it. And when they do, it seems to me that we owe them
an honest appraisal of their action. They deserve to be called
"brave."

MEANINGS AND VALUES

1.   a. What definition of courage (and bravery) does the writer offer in
Paragraphs 4–6? State it in your own words.

b. Why do you think the author does not offer a fuller, more formal
definition of these concepts? Is her main purpose in this selection
to define the concepts, or does she have some other purpose? If so,
what is it? (See "Guide to Terms": *Purpose.*)

2.   What main point does the author make in Paragraphs 6–12? Does
she state it directly anywhere in the paragraphs? If so, where does
the statement appear?

3.   Paragraph 14 offers a definition of courage that can be applied to
animal behavior. What is it?

EXPOSITORY TECHNIQUES

1.   a. In your own words, state the main point of this essay.

b. Tell how each of the following sections contributes to or supports
the main point (thesis): Paragraphs 1–4, 5–6, 7–11, 12–14, and
15–22? (Guide: *Unity.*)

2. The selection does not open with a definition, although the writer does indicate its subject in the title. What strategy does the writer use to begin the selection? (Guide: *Openings.*) Is this an appropriate choice, given the purpose and subject matter? (Guide: *Evaluation.*)

3. Apart from definition, what expository techniques does the writer use to organize this essay as a whole? What do they contribute to the process of definition?

4. This essay makes use of a variety of expository patterns. Explain why it is accurate or inaccurate to refer to the overall pattern as one of definition. Defend your answer with evidence from the text. (Guide: *Unity; Purpose.*)

DICTION AND VOCABULARY

1. a. Tell how the choice of words in each of these selections emphasizes the emotional impact of the events: Pars. 1–3 and 15–21. (Guide: *Diction.*)

   b. How, if at all, does the writer avoid sentimentality in presenting each of these extended examples? (Guide: *Sentimentality.*)

   c. Many of the words the writer uses to describe the animal's actions in each example emphasize the self-conscious nature of the acts. Identify these words and tell why they do, or do not, help the writer achieve her apparent purpose. (Guide: *Evaluation.*)

   d. What role does the simile in Paragraph 4 play in achieving this purpose? (Guide: *Figures of Speech.*)

2. If you do not know the meanings of some of the following terms, look them up in a dictionary: foal (Par. 1); accolades (5); inference, physiological, automatic (7).

READ TO WRITE

1. **Collaborating:** Working in a group, make a list of questions relating to the concepts *courage, bravery, self-sacrifice,* and similar moral traits that might lead to topics for an essay. Here are some to get you started: To what extent is physical bravery no longer possible in our society? Does taking risks for recreation (mountain climbing, sky-diving, and so on) involve bravery and courage or not? What contemporary films endorse self-sacrifice or other moral traits and which do not?

2. **Considering Audience:** People with different moral or religious beliefs might react in different ways to essays defining and endorsing what the authors consider virtues: self-sacrifice, charity, and abstinence from drugs or premarital sex, for example. Analyze Kristin von Kreisler's essay and prepare a written response explaining what kind of moral system it assumes will be guiding readers' responses and what kind of readers might not react the way she hopes.

3.   **Developing an Essay:** Following Kristin von Kreisler's example, build an essay of your own around a series of examples displaying a particular virtue (or vice) in the behavior of animals or people. Consider choosing a group of people or animals that readers may not usually consider capable of such behavior: birds, for example, or very young children.

(NOTE: Suggestions for topics requiring development by DEFINITION are on pp. 404–405 at the end of this chapter.)

VERONICA CHAMBERS

> VERONICA CHAMBERS is a writer living in New York City. She was a
> contributing editor for *Glamour* and *Esquire* and has published a
> memoir, *Mama's Girl* (1996).

Mother's Day

In this selection from her book *Mama's Girl,* also published as an
essay in *Glamour* magazine, Chambers uses a variety of expository patterns (comparison, example, narrative, cause and effect)
to help understand why her Mother's Day gift received such a
cool reception. As she considers the differences between her perspective as an African American professional woman and college-
educated writer with that of her mother, who struggled to raise
her child on a secretary's salary in the days when educational
and occupational opportunities for African Americans were strictly
limited, Chambers comes to a deeper appreciation of her mother's
achievements.

A couple of years ago, I earned a good salary for the first time and   1
I wanted to do something special for my mother. So I sent her a
gift certificate for a day at Elizabeth Arden. Included were a massage, facial, sauna and makeover—the works, plus tips. My mother
wouldn't have to spend a dime, only the subway token it would
take to get her there. I called her up on Mother's Day, all excited
about the gift. She was excited, too, and described how it had come
gift-wrapped with a big red bow. Then she asked me a question that
broke my heart in two. "Vee?" she whispered. "Do they allow black
people in those places?"

It was 1992 and my mother was asking whether Elizabeth Arden   2
would slam the red door in her black face. "Of course they allow black
people!" I said, using an angry voice to conceal how hurt I felt. "I've
paid for everything, including a tip for everyone who touches your
body. So if anybody so much as looks at you funny, you tell me!"

Months went by and my mother did not use the gift certificate.   3
"*You* use it," she would tell me. "You work so hard. Burning the can-
dle at both ends. . . ." Finally, I got furious with her and made some
empty threat about refusing to talk to her until she went to Elizabeth
Arden. She wouldn't budge.

In my frustration I reimagined the situation as a Daliesque fan-   4
tasy in which I was an avenging angel pushing my mother through

the Red Door. When a friend suggested that perhaps my mother did not want to go to Elizabeth Arden alone, I sent her neighbor a gift certificate too, but it didn't help: She turned out to be just as afraid to go as my mother.

Finally, almost a year later, my mother called and said, "Guess where I've just been? Elizabeth Arden." 5

My heart almost stopped. "How was it?" I asked. 6

"Nice . . . but everyone there was just like you," she said coyly. 7

"Just like *me?*" I repeated disbelievingly, picturing the Fifth Avenue crowd of older white women laid out on massage tables. 8

"Professionals. Upper-class women. You know," she replied. 9

While I was thrilled that she'd gone, that exchange made me wonder what my mother saw when she looked at me. I wondered if everything about me that she chose to see as being white—my education, my career, my social activities—obscured everything about me that was black—my family, my community, my mother herself. I always knew she saw me as different from her, but not until she went to Elizabeth Arden did I realize how different. 10

I never stop feeling that I want to make things up to my mother—make up for her difficulties with my father, from whom she was eventually divorced, for my brother's failure to do well in school or in a job, for the ways in which we all left her. So I buy her things. If I'm shopping and I buy myself a suit, I'll get my mother a blouse. I send her vases and candles and antique dolls. One of the first questions I ask when I enter a store is: "Can you ship this somewhere for me?" I'd be a liar if I said my generosity was only about bestowing kindnesses on my mother. It is also about easing my own guilt. 11

I am more aware now of how my schooling and experiences separate us, but I cannot get used to the distance. She is so much a part of me that I half felt I graduated college for both of us. To me, the newfound abundance of the money I can earn has meaning for both of us. But my mother sees things differently. We are separated by education and economics. 12

When I was in college, my mother once called me an Oreo— black on the outside, white on the inside. The word, so cruel when it comes from a black person's peers, was like a punch in the face coming from my mother—as if I were a total stranger and not her own child. Later, when I told her how much it had hurt me, she said, "But I was just joking!" 13

Now that I am working, she is fond of calling me a Buppie. I hate it, I tell her, and ask her to stop. But if I talk about wanting to 14 see a certain play or deliberate over whether to buy a painting, she can't help but let it slip: "You're such a Buppie." There is a texture of affection and pride in her voice that suggests she's glad I'm not as poor as she was when she was my age, but it is a pride I have trouble absorbing. Her voice says, "I am proud of you—but you are now an entirely different being than I am."

Going from poor to middle class was both the longest and the shortest transition I have ever made. Long, because every day that I went without was just one of an unending stretch of days in which I'd always done without. Once I'd craved things so deeply that I kept myself away from malls and shops, so as not to preoccupy myself with what I could not have. In college I collected mail-order catalogs, marking them up with stars and circling the outfits I liked in the colors and sizes I wanted. Desire became a game and playing the game was satisfying in its own way. At the end of freshman year, a friend asked, "Why do you always mark up those catalogs when you never order anything?" I hadn't realized that anyone noticed what had become a mindless habit, and I didn't know what to say. Was he being cruel?   15

"I don't know," I said, feigning dumbness and vowing to keep the catalogs out of sight.   16

But the jump from poverty to solvency seemed short and sudden because it was one I made alone. It was just me in an apartment, staring at a paycheck that was bigger than any I'd ever seen. Who could I call, without it sounding like I was bragging? Who wouldn't immediately ask for a loan? Who would understand how a thousand dollars could feel so much like a million? I wanted my mother there on the other end of the phone.   17

But I also felt guilty, because I felt she was much more deserving of that check than I was. I watched my mother work all her life with no reward greater than a cost-of-living raise; she was always just getting by. I knew that hard work was no guarantee of success. Success was only a dream—the big payoff that never came from my father's get-rich-quick schemes, or a winning lottery number that came to you in a vision. My life had been different. And even after going to college, even after years of hard work, I still felt deep inside that I was more lucky than successful. As if I had dreamed of a number and that number had come in.   18

My mother was neither lucky nor successful. She believed in the promise of the civil rights movement, but never really thought what those rights would mean to her. She taught her children the importance of equality and pride, but never expected to live in equality herself.   19

I can see now that although she was affected by the benefits of integration—no more sitting in the back of the bus, no more separate water fountains—most of the triumphs of the movement remained for my mother events that happened on TV. In 1970, my mother gave birth to me and worked as a secretary. In the 1990s, my mother is still a secretary. She's worked hard all her life, mostly for white people, and the civil rights movement did not change that. What it changed was me, and I wasn't some bright, young black woman that my mother saw on TV. I was her daughter. My success brought the benefits of integration through her front door, and that scared her. She could call me an Oreo and a Buppie and try to keep what I represented at a safe distance, but the things I bought her, the restaurants I took her to, forced her to consider life differently. Maybe it wouldn't take a winning lottery ticket for her to be able to lead a better life. 20

I called my mother recently and had a long talk about money. My mother is only 45. She has so much life ahead of her. I was hoping that I could use some of what I've learned about saving and investing to make her life more comfortable, so I began to ask her questions: What do your retirement savings look like? What are your financial goals? She had to stop and think. 21

"You mean goals besides paying the rent and putting dinner on the table?" She laughed nervously. 22

"Yes," I said. "What do you want to own? What trips do you want to take?" 23

There wasn't much she wanted to own. What she really wanted to do was travel. She wanted to go to Jamaica, Ghana, and Brazil. The tentativeness in her voice was so clear, as if just by speaking her wishes aloud, she might cause the genie to dive back into its bottle. My mother had never been able to see further ahead than the next day or next month. I knew then why it had scared her when, as a ten-year-old, I started talking about college. She didn't know what we were going to eat for the next seven days, much less where she would find tuition in seven years. 24

Now as we discussed *her* money for the first time, I told my mother that if she didn't dream, if she didn't think about what she wanted to have, then she was going to wake up and another 20 years would be gone. "There's nothing to save," she said, I asked if I could see her weekly budget. I told her I knew it was personal, but I needed to know exactly how much she and my stepfather made and where it was going. "What budget?" she said. 25

I wrote down all my mother's figures—how much she owed, what little she had saved, how much she and my stepfather made. I 26 did a budget and a savings plan and outlined a retirement plan that would give her some sort of nest egg.

"It's not a lot," I told her. "You'd probably still need to work. 27 But maybe you could save enough to open a business." I wrote out the plan and mailed it to her. When she called me back, I could tell she was impressed. She told me that she and my stepfather had gone over my plan and they thought they could stick to it.

My mother told me she had tried to save money when we were 28 little, but often she was too embarrassed to take a five dollar bill up to the teller's window and deposit it, so she would keep it in an envelope. By the next week, it would be gone.

"I feel like I can really be hopeful now," she said. "Like I have 29 something to look forward to besides bills." Then she paused and added, "I'm still going to play the lottery, and if I hit it, then to hell with your savings plan." I laughed and said that would be fine.

For the first time in my life, I hear in my mother's voice that she 30 is more than just coping, more than just figuring out how to get by. When I hear my mother talk, I can hear her dreaming and it's the sweetest sound in the world to me.

MEANINGS AND VALUES

1. In what ways does the author's mother define her daughter? In what ways does the author define her mother? In what ways does the author define herself?

2. What social movements and changes in values and attitudes make necessary the redefinition of identity and roles the author undertakes in this essay? How many of these social movements are mentioned in the essay, and where are they mentioned?

3. How are readers likely to react to the question at the end of Paragraph 1? What might determine the ways different readers react? What proportion of readers do you think are likely to react as the writer does? Why?

EXPOSITORY TECHNIQUES

1. In what ways does the question at the end of Paragraph 1 act as a justification for the redefining of roles that Chambers undertakes in this essay? Does it provide justification for most readers as well as for the writer? If not, how else does the writer justify the need for new definitions?

2. Can the sentence at the end of Paragraph 1 be considered a thesis statement? Why, or why not? If not, where else in the essay does the author make plain the purpose or thesis (main theme) of the piece? (See "Guide to Terms": *Thesis; Purpose.*)

3. Which paragraphs in the essay use comparison as an expository pattern? What do they contribute to the process of definition?

DICTION AND VOCABULARY

1. Many of the paragraphs in this essay discuss conflicting definitions and misunderstandings. Discuss how the writer uses transitions in Paragraphs 12–14 and 17–20 to emphasize such conflicts and contrasting perspectives. (Guide: *Transition; Emphasis.*)

2. To what does the word "Daliesque" in Paragraph 4 allude? (Guide: *Figures of Speech.*) What does this reveal about the speaker's attitudes and perspective? What is a "Buppie"? Why would the writer be offended by the term?

3. If you do not know the meaning of some of the following words, look them up in a dictionary: sauna (Par. 1); disbelievingly (8); bestowing (11); tentativeness (24).

READ TO WRITE

1. **Collaborating:** Working with a partner, discuss some aspect of your individual upbringings that distinguishes you from each other. Discuss the differences, and plan an essay comparing the definition of your childhood lifestyle with that of your partner.

2. **Considering Audience:** Throughout her essay, Chambers employs definitions of race, education, socioeconomic class, and even gender to explain the differences between her thinking and that of her mother. Choose one of these categories or another, similar one to help you better understand some of the differences between you and a member of your immediate family from a previous generation. Write an essay on parent-child relationships that addresses the feelings and values of readers who are in your age group.

3. **Developing an Essay:** In what ways are college-educated children likely to view the world differently from parents who have not attended college? Are there likely differences in the perspective between children who have attended graduate school and parents who attended college? Do differences in careers and kinds of work also lead to different perspectives? Consider exploring these and other contrasting outlooks (or definitions of values and identities) in an expository essay.

(NOTE: Suggestions for topics requiring development by DEFINITION are on pp. 404–405 at the end of the chapter.)

DAN SAVAGE

> DAN SAVAGE is a syndicated columnist, editor of an online magazine,
> and frequent contributor to radio and television news and infor-
> mation programs. For several years he wrote an advice column for
> ABCNews.com. (His mother is also an online columnist for
> WebMD.com.) Savage is the author of several books. Among them
> are *Skipping Towards Gomorrah: The Seven Deadly Sins and the
> Pursuit of Happiness in America* (2002); *The Kid: What Happened
> After My Boyfriend and I Decided to Go Get Pregnant: An Adoption
> Story* (2000); and *Savage Love: Straight Answers from America's
> Most Popular Sex Columnist* (1992).

Role Reversal

> In this essay, first published in the *New York Times Magazine*, Dan
> Savage redefines notions of gender, parenthood, and responsibil-
> ity while at the same time affirming a number of traditional values
> and concepts. This dual movement of redefinition and affirmation
> within the essay makes it interesting to read and at the same time
> makes it difficult to pigeonhole Savage's views. In addition, the
> changes Savage reports in his own attitudes and values may re-
> mind readers that their outlooks, too, are likely to be subject to re-
> definition as they encounter new situations and challenges.

She was homeless by choice and seven months pregnant by acci- 1
dent when she selected my boyfriend and me from our adoption
agency's pool of prescreened parent wannabes. Six weeks later, the
three of us sat in a recovery room at the hospital taking turns holding our son, DJ. Some adoptive parents abuse pronouns (*"our* son,"
"my child") to establish possession; it's as if they're saying, "Our
child now, not her child anymore." But doing an open adoption
means embracing the "most plural" definition of every plural pronoun, at least where your child is concerned. When I say "our" son,
his mother is included. We may be DJ's full-time parents, but she is
his parent, too, and stealth-hostile pronouns can't change that.

But one parent was missing that day in the hospital. 2

When DJ's mom was a 19-year-old street kid, she had hooked up 3
with Bacchus, our son's biological father, for a few weeks one summer. By the time she realized she was pregnant, the god of wine was
gone. When we adopted DJ, Bacchus didn't know he was a father—or
that his son had been adopted by a gay couple. We were tense when

Bacchus surfaced in New Orleans, appropriately enough, shortly before DJ's first birthday, but in the end Bacchus wanted only what we had agreed to give his mother: pictures a few times a year and the occasional visit. DJ met his biological father, whose real name is Jacob, in a hotel off Bourbon Street a few weeks later. When Jacob's own dad, a truck driver living in Texas, called to thank us for taking "good care of my grandson," we started sending him pictures too. The gay thing didn't appear to be an issue with Jacob or his father. It never came up.

Since the day we brought DJ home from the hospital, people have 4 been asking us if we're going to bring DJ up gay. The idea that two gay men, of all people, would even think it possible for a parent to select their child's sexual orientation is absurd. Didn't our own parents try that on us? Didn't it fail? Yet the question is put to us by the most unlikely people; relatives present at our long-ago coming-out dramas; friends we assumed to be more sophisticated. And as a result of hearing it so many times, my boyfriend and I have come to feel . . . scrutinized.

So watching my son tear into an unexpected late bonus round of 5 Christmas gifts, I couldn't help wondering if the gay thing was coming up. Last month, Jacob's father and his father's new wife sent an enormous package filled with a toy workbench, a battery-powered toy drill, a battery-powered toy saw, a hammer and two screwdrivers. It looked to my slightly paranoid eyes like a grow-up-straight care package from some concerned grandparents. (Of course, as my boyfriend points out, there's a good chance DJ's biograndparents bought him tools because DJ's a boy.)

Most hip, modern, urban parents have a sense of humor about 6 sex roles. Not us. I had given the sons of straight friends little pink dresses as baby gifts for years. "Don't assume anything," I wanted each pink dress to say. Almost all of my friends put their sons in their pink dresses once and took a picture before exchanging them. A few payback pink dresses arrived in the first weeks we had DJ, but we didn't have a single pink-dress photo-op. If we put him in a dress, my God, people might think we were trying to make him gay.

Walking home with DJ the day his preschool teacher painted 7 DJ's fingernails red, I wanted to scream, "I didn't do it!" Then there was the neighbor who started calling our sons, who play together, "cute little boyfriends," much to her husband's consternation—and mine. A friend threatened to give DJ a "Future Hooters Girl" T-shirt on his birthday until I told him it would wind up at Goodwill faster than a crate of eight-track tapes.

So if DJ's Texan grandparents sent tools because they worry his 8 gay dads are buying him nothing but Barbie dolls, well, their fears are misplaced. All we buy DJ are trucks and planes and cars and trains and blocks—which, as it turns out, is all DJ wants. He's a standard-issue boy, not a sissy like I was. Of course, I would love him just as much if he were into dolls, even if I have to admit it's a relief that he isn't.

But if he wanted dolls, I would give him dolls; if he wanted to   9 paint his nails red and wear a "Future Hooters Girl" T-shirt to school, I would let him. But I would still worry that people might think that my boyfriend and I were, as a relative put it, "pushing DJ in *that* direction." So I guess we're lucky DJ loves—adores—his new tools. He could still grow up gay; I know plenty of adult gay men who played with toolboxes when they were boys. I never did, but I'm playing with them now. Being DJ's dad has forced me to take a be-lated interest in all the boy stuff I wouldn't touch when I was a kid. I spend an awful lot of time on the floor with my son these days play-ing with cars and trucks, blocks and Legos, hammers and saws. DJ is the kind of boy I never was, and now, thanks to my son, so am I.

MEANINGS AND VALUES

1. What unexpected behaviors or attitudes are readers likely to en-counter in the first paragraph?

2. According to the essay, in what ways does the writer's definition of adoption (at least as he practices it) differ from most people's defin-ition of the practice? To what extent can his definition be seen as a redefinition?

3. What new definitions of family, parenthood, gender roles, and re-sponsibility toward children is Savage offering in this essay? Try stat-ing these definitions in your own words. Why do you think that Savage does not offer his own concise definitions of these concepts in the essay? Is the essay more—or less—effective without them? (See "Guide to Terms": *Evaluation.*)

4. Does the writer appear to believe that gender roles and sexual prefer-ence are determined by parenting practices or that they are the result of the nature of each individual? Be ready to provide evidence from the essay to support your conclusion. If you think the essay does not take an explicit stand on the issue, explain why you think so and why you think the writer might have avoided clearly announcing his perspective.

EXPOSITORY TECHNIQUES

1. What strategy does Savage use to open the essay? (Guide: *Introductions.*) In what ways is it appropriate for the purposes of the essay? (Guide: *Purpose.*)

2. What strategy does Savage use to conclude the essay? (Guide: *Closings.*) In what ways does it reinforce the essay's main point and echo the emphasis on redefinition? (Guide: *Unity.*)

3. Part of the effectiveness of this essay lies in its use of the toys and gifts that both symbolize gender roles or sexual preference and, some people think, even create them. Discuss the use of these examples to present and redefine roles and preferences in Paragraphs 5–9. Which of the examples can be regarded as symbols, and why? Are they natural, personal, or conventional symbols? (Guide: *Symbol.*)

DICTION AND VOCABULARY

1. Examine the language used to present details in Paragraphs 5, 6, and 7 and indicate where most of it seems to fall on a sliding scale from abstract to concrete. (Guide: *Concrete/Abstract.*) Indicate how the relative concreteness or abstractness of the language aids in the effective presentation of the details and the ideas (values, attitudes, or definitions) they represent. (Guide: *Evaluation.*)

2. What qualities are suggested by the two names: DJ and Bacchus? (Guide: *Connotation/Denotation.*)

3. What is meant by the phrases "stealth-hostile pronouns" (Par. 1) and "coming-out dramas"?

READ TO WRITE

1. **Collaborating:** Think of situations that rob children of parents, for example AIDS, drugs, and the like, or that result in family structures other than traditional ones. Working in a group, consider who might act as role models for these children. Choose one of these topics and plan an essay that redefines that role model as "parent" for victims of biological parental loss. Your group may need to do some outside research to plan your essay.

2. **Considering Audience:** Think of the parenting roles various people have played in your life and in the lives of people you know. Think of how people who are not blood relatives have acted like siblings, aunts, uncles, or grandparents. Freewrite about different ways of viewing families and family relationships until you decide on a topic and direction for an essay. Then share your essay ideas with classmates to discover how many of your definitions they (and your potential readers) are likely to share.

3. **Developing an Essay:** Develop a definition essay of your own in which you give new meaning to a term or concept. Consider waiting until the end of the essay to fully explain the new term or concept and its consequences, just as Savage does.

(NOTE: Suggestions for topics requiring development by use of DEFINITION follow.)

Writing Suggestions for Chapter 9

DEFINITION

Develop a composition for a specified purpose and audience, using whatever methods and expository patterns will help convey a clear understanding of your meaning of one of the following terms:

1. Country music
2. Conscience
3. Religion
4. Bigotry
5. Success
6. Empathy
7. Family
8. Hypocrisy
9. Humor
10. Sophistication
11. Naïveté
12. Cowardice
13. Wisdom
14. Integrity
15. Morality
16. Greed
17. Social poise
18. Intellectual (the person)
19. Pornography
20. Courage
21. Patriotism
22. Equality (or equal opportunity)
23. Loyalty
24. Stylishness (in clothing or behavior)
25. Fame
26. Obesity

27. Cheating

28. Hero

29. Feminine

30. Masculine

COLLABORATIVE EXERCISE

Working in a group, choose a term from the list below. Have each member of your group define the term for a reader/audience of a particular age group. As a group, compare your choices of definition strategies based on each intended audience.

a. Success

b. Family

c. Cowardice

d. Loyalty

e. Hero

f. Integrity

10

Explaining with the Help of *Description*

You can make your expository writing more vivid, and hence more understandable, with the support of **description,** sometimes even using the pattern as the basic plan for an exposition. In writing, you can use sensory details—sight, sound, touch, taste, and smell—to re-create *places:* a portrait of the steamy closeness of the Brazilian jungle; the gray stone, narrow streets, tall houses, and church spires of an Eastern European city. You can create portraits of *people, qualities, emotions,* or *moods:* a beloved aunt whose cheerfulness was part of a long fight against pain and illness, the physical and spatial on-court "intelligence" of a star basketball player, the despair of a child crying for her puppy just killed by a car, or the contrasting moods of a city where excited theatergoers pass a drunk slumped against a building.

Descriptive writing depends on detail, and your first and most important job as a writer employing description is to select the details to be included. There are usually many from which to choose, and it is easy to become so involved in a subject—especially one that is visually or emotionally intriguing—that you lose sight of the expository purpose of your writing. As you draft and revise, therefore, you need to keep in mind the kind of picture you want to paint with words, one that accomplishes *your* purpose for *your* intended audience. Such a word picture need not be entirely visual, for the dimensions of sound, smell, and even touch can create a vivid and effective image in your readers' minds.

When used as a pattern for much or all of an expository essay, description does more than set a mood, add a vivid touch to an explanation, or provide an occasional supporting detail. It becomes the primary strategy for explaining a subject or supporting a thesis, as in the following example.

> It's not winter without an icestorm. When Robert Frost gazed at bowed birch trees and tried to think that boys had bent them playing, he knew better: "Icestorms do that." They do that and a lot more, trimming disease and weakness out of the tree—the old tree's friend, as pneumonia used to be the old man's. Some of us provide life-support systems for our precious shrubs, boarding them over against the ice, for the icestorm takes the young or unlucky branch or birch as well as the rotten or feeble. One February morning we look out our windows over yards and fields littered with kindling, small twigs and great branches. We look out at a world turned into one diamond, ten thousand carats in the line of sight, twice as many facets. What a dazzle of spinning refracted light, spider webs of cold brilliance attacking our eyeballs! All winter we wear sunglasses to drive, more than we do in summer, and never so much as after an icestorm, with its painful glaze reflecting from maple and birch, granite boulder and stone wall, turning electric wires into bright silver filaments. The snow itself takes on a crust of ice, like the finish of a clay pot, that carries our weight and sends us swooping and sliding. It's worth your life to go for the mail. Until sand and salt redeem the highway, Route 4 is quiet. We cancel the appointment with the dentist, stay home, and marvel at the altered universe, knowing that midday sun will strip ice from tree and roof and restore our ordinary white winter world.
>
> —Donald Hall, *Seasons at Eagle Pond*

WHY USE DESCRIPTION?

Descriptions help readers create mental images of a subject or scene. To do this, the writer uses concrete, specific detail ("The floodwater turned the carpet into a slippery mess that smelled like dead fish and covered the electronic insides of the TV with a thin coat of black mud") rather than abstract, general impressions ("The flood soaked everything in the living room"). You can put descriptive detail to work for a variety of purposes, however.

You might choose to focus on a particular place or scene, using description to convey and support your thoughts and conclusions about it. Writing of this sort often appears in brief essays focusing on a limited scene: a beach in winter, a small corner of the Sonoran Desert, or a mall parking lot just before Christmas, for example. On the other hand, a description of a typical family apartment in Cairo might provide important conclusions and support for a study of family structure in Egypt, or descriptions of the Arctic landscape might contribute to an understanding of the habits of polar bears. When used for such expository purposes, descriptive writing goes beyond simply recording details to offering conclusions and explanations of the effects of a setting on those who live in it.

You might also use descriptive writing to create a portrait of a person. To do this, you combine descriptive detail with narration (see Chapter 11), usually in the form of brief but representative incidents. Your aim is to highlight the characteristics of your subject: details of appearance, speech, action, and feeling. In such a context, descriptive detail serves to support and convey your understanding of an individual's outlook and motivation, a sense of his or her personality, and your insight into the individual's influence on others.

Technical descriptions, common in scientific and professional writing, are another use for descriptive writing. In this form of writing, you provide a precise understanding of the elements of a subject and their relationship, and in so doing you convey necessary information or evidence to support your conclusions. Biologists, for example, might describe features of a frog that are marks of evolution or function; art historians might focus on color, line, shape, and brush stroke as a way of supporting a thesis about an artist or a particular painting.

CHOOSING A STRATEGY

Descriptive writing generally follows one of two strategies— *objective* description or *subjective* description—though some overlapping is also common. In objective description you aim at conveying the details of a subject thoroughly and accurately without suggesting your feelings or biases and without trying to evoke an emotional response from readers. Scientific papers, business reports, and academic writing often take this stance. In choosing details, writers of objective descriptions aim at precision and try to avoid emotional overtones. In arranging the details for presentation, writers either pay attention to the need to support a conclusion or to the function of the object or process being presented, as in the following example.

Cathode Ray Tube

The most familiar example is a television picture tube, and the simplest kind is the black and white. The inside of the tube is coated with a *phosphor*, a substance that glows when struck by electrons. At the rear of the tube (the neck) is an electron gun that shoots a beam of electrons toward the front. Electromagnetic coils or electrically charged metal plates direct this stream from side to side and top to bottom, forming a glow-picture of the "message" being received by the cathode ray tube. Color tubes are similar except that the face is coated with thousands of groups of dots. Each group, called a *pixel* (picture element), consists of three dots, one for each of the three primary colors—red, green, and blue.

—Herman Schneider and Leo Schneider, *The Harper Dictionary of Science in Everyday Language*

In subjective description, however, you make your values and feelings clear and often encourage readers to respond emotionally. Often, instead of describing how something *is* objectively, you describe how it *seems* subjectively. To do this, you may make occasional use of direct statement, but you are likely to find it more effective to rely on a choice of vivid, concrete, or emotionally laden detail or on the connotations of words. *Connotations* are the feelings or associations that accompany a word, not its dictionary or literal meaning. Subjective descriptions express your conclusions about a subject or your attitudes toward it. Thus, in arranging details for presentation, you should pay attention to the dominant impression or interpretation you wish to convey as well as to the arrangement of details in the setting (right to left, top to bottom, for example).

In creating a subjective description, pay attention to the dominant impression you create, making sure it conveys and supports your overall purpose or interpretation. In the following passage, for example, the dominant impression clearly conveys the writer's insights into the effects of atmosphere—in this case, fog—on human perceptions, even though she does not directly state this conclusion.

It begins in late afternoon, a wall of gray blocking the entrance to the harbor, moving imperceptibly, closing in. The sun becomes a bright thing in the sky for a moment before a thick grayness takes over. Trails of vapor drift by. Roads taper off into mist. Pine trees, encircled by the fog, take on different shapes. Inside vacation houses, people make tea, read books, play cards with old decks. Outside, the air smells of soaked wharves. Down by the rocks the surf crashes, but it is a muffled sound, heard while asleep. Bay bushes hunch together, woolly and wet. Walking through fields of Queen Anne's lace, lupine, and goldenrod, their colors muted, is like moving through dreamland. A foghorn blows. Other people are out—a figure appears near the raspberry bushes, spectral, with a basket. A dog runs by, and from the leaves drops fall.

—Susan Minot, "Lost in the Light of Gray"

DEVELOPING DESCRIPTION

The first and most important job in descriptive writing is to select the details. The questions you ask about a subject can help you identify significant details and suggest ways of interpreting it.

For scenes or objects:

- What does it look like (colors, shapes, height, depth)?
- What does it sound like (loud, soft, rasping, soothing, musical, like a lawn mower)?
- What does it smell like (smoky, acrid, like gasoline, like soap, like a wood fire)?
- What does it feel like (smooth, sticky, like a cat's fur, like a spider's web, like grease)?
- What does it taste like (bitter, salty, like grass, like feathers)?

For emotions or ideas:

- What effect does it have on behavior (anger: red face, abrupt gestures)?
- What is it like (freedom: like taking a deep breath of air after leaving a smoky room)?

For people:

- What does the person look like (hair neatly combed, rumpled blouse, muddy boots)?
- What are some characteristic behaviors (rubs hands on skirt, picks ear)?
- What has the person done or said (cheated on a chemistry test, said cruel things to friends)?
- How do others respond to the person (turn to her for advice, call him a "slob")?

Successful subjective descriptions generally focus on a single *dominant impression,* which can act in place of a conclusion or thesis. To create a dominant impression, you select those details that will help create a mood or atmosphere or emphasize a feature or quality. But more than the materials themselves are involved in creating a dominant impression. The words you choose, and both their literal and suggestive meanings (denotations and connotations), convey an impression. So, too, do the arrangements of words in sentences, as in the use of short, hurried sentences to help convey a sense of urgency or excitement.

The actual arrangement of the material is perhaps less troublesome in description than in most other expository patterns. Nonetheless, you need to follow a sequence that is clear to your reader and that helps you achieve your purpose or support your thesis. A clear spatial organization, for example, will help readers understand a visually complex subject. You can move from left to right, top to bottom, or near to far. You can describe a person from head to toe, or vice versa, or begin with the most noticeable feature and work from there. Or you could start with an overall view of a scene and then move to a focal point.

A chronological arrangement enables you to look at a scene from several perspectives: early morning, midday, and night, for example, or in different weather conditions. Such a strategy allows you to make a point by contrasting the scenes, and it provides variety and interest. A thematic organization emphasizes the dominant impression or thesis through focus and repetition. You might emphasize by repeating clusters of key words (grim, grasping, hard, short-tempered) or images (pink ribbons, the scent of violets). You might also arrange segments of the description by increasing order of importance or in another manner that best supports a thesis.

You can also choose a point of view, either first person ("I looked . . .") or third person ("He sighed . . . ," "It moved . . . ."). You might also choose a perspective, including the location of the observer and any limitation on the observer's ability to see and understand, perhaps observing a familiar family scene from a child's perspective to provide a new understanding of relationships.

Whatever techniques you choose, however, try to avoid excessive description, which creates confusion and boredom, or description without a clear purpose, which offers your readers no goal or reward for their effort.

Student Essay

In preparing the following essay, Carey Braun tried to combine technical descriptions of the effects of light with her subjective responses and perceptions. In linking the two, she makes some interesting observations about the way we humans are linked to the natural world.

Bright Light

by Carey Braun

The sun woke me by sneaking its way through the narrow cracks of the vertical blinds. I squinted at the bright sun, then kept my eyes closed and enjoyed its warmth on my face and shoulders. After a time, I slid across the bed to the window and peeked through the blinds to look out on a day that reminded me of my version of Andrew Lloyd Webber's song, "Light" changes everything"—or at least the sun does.

What better place to see light, feel light, and become one with the sun, I thought, than at the beach? I rushed out of bed, got dressed, had a bite of breakfast, grabbed my bathing suit and suntan lotion, and headed for the beach.

As I stepped out of the car in the parking lot, I felt a sunwarmed breeze across my face. It blew my hair across my cheek and made me wonder what it would be like to be a bird, about to skim across the waves of wind with the sun on my back. I hurried down the walkway. On each side of the path, dilapidated summer cottages managed to look fresh and new in the early morning rays. Crossing the hot sand, I stepped gingerly on it, a recognition that even this early in the day we need to shape our actions to the sun's heat and power.

I sat on the blanket and rubbed the suntan lotion over my body. My skin shined, reflecting the sun's rays and making me seem for a moment like a second source of light. But soon I began to feel like a frying pan that would sizzle if a drop of water hit me. In the background I could hear the sound of many boom boxes blending together forming a lighthearted hymn that took away thoughts of everything else but this time and place. People were splashing the water, sending luminous drops into the air and breaking the surface of the water into a million mirroring pieces. During brief breaks in the music and the sounds of splashing, I could hear the sound of birds singing.

Initial setting

Time: morning

Thesis-stated somewhat indirectly

Observer moves from place to place— observations show the effect of light at different times of day

Observer is also participant

Detailed, specific observations

Time: Midday

The sun's heat relaxed me so that I fell asleep. When I woke, there was sweat covering my face and my arms and refracting the sun's rays. If I looked just right, I could see rainbow dots on the surface of my skin. I woke up slowly and decided to head for the cool, refreshing water in front of me. I could feel my body temperature dropping as it moved into the water. As I dove into a wave, chills went through my body like shock waves. I was ready to move back to the beach and the sun.

Appeals to a variety of senses

I couldn't taste the sun, but as I walked back to my blanket, I licked the salt off my lips, which had dried quickly in the heat. Salt, I decided, must be the taste of light, at least this morning. The salt on my skin made it feel like stretched leather, tight across my cheekbones and shoulders and stiffening at my joints. I walked across the glinting sand, through midday air heated to luminous, shimmering waves, to the outdoor shower.

More senses

As I let the water wash away the salt, I looked at the sky and realized that the sun was beginning to descend. The subtle change in light made me feel cooler even though the sand was just as hot as I returned to my blanket. As the light turned to afternoon, people began looking at each other, perhaps noticing the growing shadows and the loss of brilliance. Light now turned to haze, luminous and bright, but still haze. People began straggling up the sand, looking as if their energy, too, had begun to wane. The music left and the song that remained was the crash of waves, glinting here and there as the growing fog broke to let through a stray ray.

Transition to late afternoon

Change in mood and effects of light

I gathered my belongings and shook all the sand off. As I drove away, I took one last look in the mirror to mourn the passing of the sun's power and light; startled by the electrifying colors of reds, yellows, and oranges spreading from the horizon through the sky, I realized once again the power of light to change everything.

Restates thesis

GARY SOTO

GARY SOTO was born in 1952 in Fresno, California, and currently teaches at the University of California, Berkeley. He has won numerous awards for his poetry and novels as well as for his essays and other nonfiction writing. These include ten volumes of poetry and two novels. *Nickel and Dime* (2000) and *Poetry Lover* (2001). His essays have been collected in *Small Faces* (1982), *Lesser Evils* (1988), *A Summer Life* (1995), and *The Effects of Knut Hamsun on a Fresno Boy* (2000) as well as in periodicals such as the *Iowa Review, El Andar,* and *American Literary History.* His memoir, *Living up the Street* (1985), received an American Book Award.

The Jacket

"The Jacket" was first published in *Small Faces.* It illustrates the subjective form of description that is generally known as impressionistic description. At the same time, the writer seems to stand outside the scenes and brief incidents, making the reader aware of what the jacket reveals about the psychological and social dimensions of growing up. In this way, the description serves an expository purpose.

My clothes have failed me. I remember the green coat that I wore   1
in fifth and sixth grades when you either danced like a champ or pressed yourself against a greasy wall, bitter as a penny toward the happy couples.

When I needed a new jacket and my mother asked what kind I   2
wanted, I described something like bikers wear: black leather and silver studs with enough belts to hold down a small town. We were in the kitchen, steam on the windows from her cooking. She listened so long while stirring dinner that I thought she understood for sure the kind I wanted. The next day when I got home from school, I discovered draped on my bedpost a jacket the color of day-old-guacamole. I threw my books on the bed and approached the jacket slowly, as if it were a stranger whose hand I had to shake. I touched the vinyl sleeve, the collar, and peeked at the mustard-colored lining.

From the kitchen mother yelled that my jacket was in the closet.   3
I closed the door to her voice and pulled at the rack of clothes in the closet, hoping the jacket on the bedpost wasn't for me but my mean brother. No luck. I gave up. From my bed, I stared at the jacket. I wanted to cry because it was so ugly and so big that I knew I'd have

to wear it a long time. I was a small kid, thin as a young tree, and it would be years before I'd have a new one. I stared at the jacket, like an enemy, thinking bad things before I took off my old jacket whose sleeves climbed halfway to my elbow.

I put the big jacket on. I zipped it up and down several times, and rolled the cuffs up so they didn't cover my hands. I put my hands in the pockets and flapped the jacket like a bird's wings. I stood in front of the mirror, full face, then profile, and then looked over my shoulder as if someone had called me. I sat on the bed, stood against the bed, and combed my hair to see what I would look like doing something natural. I looked ugly. I threw it on my brother's bed and looked at it for a long time before I slipped it on and went out to the backyard, smiling a "thank you" to my mom as I passed her in the kitchen. With my hands in my pockets I kicked a ball against the fence, and then climbed it to sit looking into the alley. I hurled orange peels at the mouth of an open garbage can and when the peels were gone I watched the white puffs of my breath thin to nothing. 4

I jumped down, hands in my pockets, and in the backyard on my knees I teased my dog, Brownie, by swooping my arms while making bird calls. He jumped at me and missed. He jumped again and again, until a tooth sunk deep, ripping an L-shaped tear on my left sleeve. I pushed Brownie away to study the tear as I would a cut on my arm. There was no blood, only a few loose pieces of fuzz. Damn dog, I thought, and pushed him away hard when he tried to bite again. I got up from my knees and went to my bedroom to sit with my jacket on my lap, with the lights out. 5

That was the first afternoon with my new jacket. The next day I wore it to sixth grade and got a D on a math quiz. During the morning recess Frankie T., the playground terrorist, pushed me to the ground and told me to stay there until recess was over. My best friend, Steve Negrete, ate an apple while looking at me, and the girls turned away to whisper on the monkey bars. The teachers were no help: they looked my way and talked about how foolish I looked in my new jacket. I saw their heads bob with laughter, their hands half-covering their mouths. 6

Even though it was cold, I took off the jacket during lunch and played kickball in a thin shirt, my arm feeling like braille from the goose bumps. But when I returned to class I slipped the jacket on and shivered until I was warm. I sat on my hands, heating them up, while my teeth chattered like a cup of crooked dice. Finally warm, I slid out of the jacket but a few minutes later put it back on when the fire bell rang. We paraded out into the yard where we, the sixth 7 graders, walked past all the other grades to stand against the back fence. Everybody saw me. Although they didn't say out loud, "Man, that's ugly," I heard the buzz-buzz of gossip and even laughter that I knew was meant for me.

And so I went, in my guacamole-colored jacket. So embar- 8 rassed, so hurt, I couldn't even do my homework. I received Cs on quizzes, and forgot the state capitals and rivers of South America, our friendly neighbor. Even the girls who had been friendly blew away like loose flowers to follow the boys in neat jackets.

I wore that thing for three years until the sleeves grew short and 9 my forearms stuck out like the necks of turtles. All during that time no love came to me—no little dark girl in a Sunday dress she wore on Monday. At lunchtime I stayed with the ugly boys who leaned against the chainlink fence and looked around with propellers of grass spinning in our mouths. We saw girls walk by alone, saw couples, hand in hand, their heads like bookends pressing air together. We saw them and spun our propellers so fast our faces were blurs.

I blame that jacket for those bad years. I blame my mother for 10 her bad taste and her cheap ways. It was a sad time for the heart. With a friend I spent my sixth-grade year in a tree in the alley, waiting for something good to happen to me in that jacket, which had become the ugly brother who tagged along wherever I went. And it was about that time that I began to grow. My chest puffed up with muscle and, strangely, a few more ribs. Even my hands, those fleshy hammers, showed bravely through the cuffs, the fingers already hardening for the coming fights. But that L-shaped rip on the left sleeve got bigger, bits of stuffing coughed out from its wound after a hard day of play. I finally Scotch-taped it closed, but in rain or cold weather the tape peeled off like a scab and more stuffing fell out until that sleeve shriveled into a palsied arm. That winter the elbows began to crack and whole chunks of green began to fall off. I showed the cracks to my mother, who always seemed to be at the stove with steamed-up glasses, and she said that there were children in Mexico who would love that jacket. I told her that this was America and yelled that Debbie, my sister, didn't have a jacket like mine. I ran outside, ready to cry, and climbed the tree by the alley to think bad thoughts and watch my breath puff white and disappear.

But whole pieces still casually flew off my jacket when I played 11 hard, read quietly, or took vicious spelling tests at school. When it became so spotted that my brother began to call me "camouflage," I flung it over the fence into the alley. Later, however, I swiped the jacket off the ground and went inside to drape it across my lap and mope.

I was called to dinner; steam silvered my mother's glasses as   12
she said grace; my brother and sister with their heads bowed made
ugly faces at their glasses of powdered milk. I gagged too, but eagerly ate big rips of buttered tortilla that held scooped-up beans.
Finished, I went outside with my jacket across my arm. It was a cold
sky. The faces of clouds were piled up, burting. I climbed the fence,
jumping down with a grunt. I started up the alley and soon slipped
into my jacket, that green ugly brother who breathed over my shoulder that day and ever since.

MEANINGS AND VALUES

1. What is the general tone of this writing? (See "Guide to Terms": *Style/ Tone.*)

2. At what points in the essay are readers likely to notice a difference between the feelings and perceptions of the boy and those of the writer as an adult? In what ways does this contrast contribute to what the writer has to say about the process of growing up?

3. Discuss the possible meanings of the last sentence. "I started up the alley and soon slipped into my jacket, that green ugly brother who breathed over my shoulder that day and ever since."

4. Has this author avoided the excesses of sentimentality? Try to dis- cover how. (Guide: *Sentimentality.*) If not, where does he fail?

EXPOSITORY TECHNIQUES

1. Can the jacket be considered a symbol as well as a concrete object? Is it a natural, conventional, or personal symbol? (Guide: *Symbol.*)

2. Should this writing be classed as primarily impressionistic, rather than objective? If so, what is the dominant impression? Or should it be classed as having a double perspective, impressionistic and objec- tive? Why, or why not? Does the jacket function as object or as sym- bol depending on whether the emphasis is on impressionistic or objective description? Explain your answer.

3. a. Analyze the role that selection of details plays in creating the dom- inant impression in Paragraphs 2, 7, 9, 10, and 12. Provide exam- ples of the type of details that could have been included but were not. Are such omissions justifiable?

   b. Discuss the extent to which the details in these paragraphs reflect the social and economic circumstances in which the writer grew up.

4. Identify the paragraphs in this essay that can be viewed as examples (see Chapter 3, "Example"). Explain how this pattern of exposition supports the purpose of the essay. (Guide: *Purpose.*)

Diction and Vocabulary

1. Discuss the ways in which the simple (often one-syllable) words and short sentences convey the perceptions and feelings of the writer as a young boy. (Guide: *Diction.*)

2. Discuss how the choice of words and the relatively complicated sentence structures in Paragraphs 10 and 12 reflect the writer's perceptions as an older boy and his perspective as an adult. (Guide: *Diction; Syntax.*) Pay particular attention to the use of parallel structures in Paragraph 10. (Guide: *Parallel Structure.*)

Read to Write

1. **Collaborating:** Working with a group to identify and explore topics for writing, think about some common childhood experiences (schooling, loss of a parent or friend, sibling relationships, choice of clothing or toys, sports, and the like) that reflect important stages in social and psychological development. The stages and the quality of the experiences may vary greatly according to individual experience and social or cultural background, of course. Put the group's thoughts in the form of questions you could attempt to answer in an essay. Here are three questions to get you started: What kinds of clothing or other objects are likely to play important roles in childhood and adolescent development or to reflect different stages of development? What kinds of behavior, appearance, or background are likely to play a role in the social groupings common in schools or neighborhoods? What kinds of childhood memories are likely to remain vivid and laden with emotion into adulthood?

2. **Considering Audience:** Soto's essay begins with some forceful, slightly puzzling statements whose meaning becomes clearer in the course of the selection. Use a similar reader-centered strategy to begin an essay of your own. Start with statements or conclusions about the objects, incidents, people, relationships, or things you plan to explain and describe, and go on to discuss and explore them in the body of your essay.

3. **Developing an Essay:** A description is not a form of exposition unless it is used for expository purposes, as in "The Jacket." Follow Soto's lead by using detailed description in an essay to explain a relationship, problem, or phenomenon. Consider focusing on a subject whose importance and possible consequences may not be immediately apparent to readers, or consider using description to encourage readers to critically view actions and attitudes they take for granted.

(NOTE: Suggestions for topics requiring development by use of DESCRIPTION are on pp. 464–465 at the end of this chapter.)

DONNA TARTT

> DONNA TARTT was born in 1963 in Greenwood, Mississippi. She at-
> tended the University of Mississippi and Bennington College. Her
> first novel, *The Secret History,* was published in 1992 and her sec-
> ond, *The Little Friend,* in 2003, winning the WHSmith Literary
> Award and making the list of finalists for the Orange Prize for fic-
> tion. She has also published nonfiction essays and short stories.

A Garden Party

> The power of childhood experiences over your values and per-
> spectives as well as the briefness of life (and beauty) are some of
> the ideas explored through description in this essay, originally
> published in the *Guardian* (U.K.) newspaper and in *When We Were
> Young: An Anthology of Childhood.* Instead of describing a single
> scene in this essay, the Tartt presents several detailed examples,
> each related to the central theme.

Not long ago, my little godson came to stay with me for the first   1
time: his first summer vacation, and also his first trip to the
countryside. Though still an infant, not yet able to speak, his eyes
were round and ringing with astonishment all weekend long.
Everything at my house was shocking and utterly new: velvet sofa
cushions, purple flowers, elderly pug (bigger than he was, a frightening but friendly lion). In the photographs from that weekend (swimming pool; absurd yellow kiddie float) his face is alight with violent
wonder—an expression very similar to the dazed, incredulous joy
that I remember on the faces of some sombre little hill-children in
India at the watermelon sparklers I gave them. These were a racy treat
of my American childhood—clear candies of a biting, gorgeous pink,
deliciously sour, smooth and sparkling like jewels when you took
them out of your mouth and held them up to the light after you'd
sucked on them for a while. But though they are pretty enough to
look at, their taste is the real stunner—an overpowering electric tang
to make a grown-up's eyes water, but that children adore. As a child I
craved these candies, was driven mad by them, saved my nickels and
dimes for them—all the children on my school bus did—but there, in
the high Himalayas, they were unheard of, pure magic: I might as
well have been handing out rubies.

Of course, it's not at all remarkable that children are captivated   2
by new things, because to children everything is new. But what is re-

markable is how fleeting impressions of childhood delight can linger and change and vanish and re-appear unexpectedly over the years, winking like fireflies throughout the arduous and complicated darks of a lifetime. It has been remarked that a poet's most powerful, passionate metaphors—the ones that recur again and again, the ones that carry the deepest personal meaning—are fixed irrevocably in the mind before the age of 12. So, too, I think, for the rest of us. Someday, long after I am dead, my little godson may be an old man of 80 or 90 sitting in a deck chair in Miami Beach, inexplicably transfixed with a wordless pang of joy at a striped beach ball, at dazzling turquoise pool water—just as someday (I hope) a particular impossible shade of watermelon pink, glimpsed in passing, may perhaps strike an old lady in a Himalayan hill village as the very sweetness of youth.

Quite often there's a pattern to these haphazard and apparently random flashes of childhood memory—a pattern that doesn't emerge or make itself known until later in life. One particularly vivid memory that has stayed with me throughout my life, and will be with me until I die, is of the first time I saw a hummingbird. The incident was inconsequential enough; I was about four years old, and had accompanied my beloved great-grandmother (then in her late 70s) to a garden party given for a distant relative: a young bride-to-be. It was springtime; the azaleas were in spectacular bloom; the astonishing little ruby-throated creature flew right in front of me—down at my eye level, practically in front of my face—and hovered there for some moments before it buzzed forward, then backward, then flew away across the green lawn for ever.

That was all. It can have lasted no more than 10 seconds, yet this tiny incident has left a much more intense and lasting impression on me than many of the great landmark events of my childhood. For many years, I wondered exactly why I remembered this specific incident so vividly and not some thing else, something more powerful. Why the hummingbird? What was it trying to tell me? Why had this memory, and not some other, struck me so forcefully in the first place; why does it come back to me so persistently, in memory and in dream?

Only now—at mid-life, in my 40th year—am I starting to realise what the hummingbird means, and why, at unexpected moments, it returns to me still. It is a premonition of heaven, and of death. My great-grandmother (who was leaning beside me, holding my hand, as the hummingbird paused in mid-air before me) did not have long to live. Nor did the bride herself—lovely laughing Ginger, who died young, of cancer. I couldn't have understood it then, and scarcely understand it now, but my entire subsequent impressions of death, and beauty, and mutability, and the brevity of life itself are somehow crystallised perfectly in those few moments, when the tiny iridescent hummingbird darted before my face, hovered briefly, then flew away. All I know of the sublime is somehow encapsulated and encoded in that instant: flowers everywhere, white-gloved ladies in pastel dresses. Then beautiful Ginger, in an apple-green dress, kneeling to say hello.

MEANINGS AND VALUES

1. Where in the essay does the writer announce the central theme (thesis)? (See "Guide to Terms": *Thesis.*) State the central theme in your own words.

2. Why should this essay be regarded as expository in purpose rather than simply a vivid recreation of experiences? (Guide: *Purpose.*)

3. If you have read E.B. White's essay, "Once More to the Lake" (beginning on p. 455), compare Tartt's views on death, beauty, and life's briefness with White's.

EXPOSITORY TECHNIQUES

1. What "fleeting impressions of childhood delight" does the writer present as examples in this essay?

2. Where does the writer locate the statement of the essay's central theme (thesis) in relationship to the two main examples? Why do you think she chose this location?

3. Can the watermelon candy and the hummingbird be considered symbols? (Guide: *Symbol.*) If so, what does each symbolize?

DICTION AND VOCABULARY

1. Identify the words and phrases the writer uses in paragraph 1 to help readers imagine the taste and appearance of the watermelon candy. How effective are her choices in conveying the candy's qualities? (Guide: *Diction.*)

2. What words does the writer use in paragraph 5 to emphasize the briefness and fragility of life and beauty? (Guide: *Diction.*)

3. If you do not know the meaning of some of the following words, look them up in the dictionary: pug, incredulous, somber (par. 1); captivated, arduous, irrevocably, inexplicably, transfixed (2); haphazard, inconsequential (3); premonition, subsequent, mutability, brevity, iridescent, sublime, encapsulated (5).

READ TO WRITE

1. **Collaborating:** Working in a group, use the following questions and make up others like them in order to examine the relationship among places, childhood experiences, and values, and develop a list of possible topics for writing. Do many people today have a chance to return to the homes or neighborhoods in which they grew up, which helped shape their values and personalities? Are experiences with food, weather, natural settings, animals, or social events likely to be central to people's values? How are the childhood memories of people who grew up in settings unlike those described by Tartt likely to differ? Are their values likely to differ also?

2. **Considering Audience:** Consider how readers who grew up in settings very different from those describe by Tartt likely to respond to her essay. Write an essay describing the likely reactions of such readers, focusing especially on passages they might not fully appreciate or to which they might respond negatively.

3. **Developing an Audience:** Preparing an essay describing one or more experiences you had as a child, paying particular attention to the physical and sensory details. Follow Tartt's lead and deal with questions of change, loss, growth, continuity, death, and beauty, offering your insights, of course, and not Tartt's.

(NOTE: Suggestions for topics requiring development by use of DESCRIPTION are on pp. 464–465 at the end of this chapter.)

GEORGE SIMPSON

GEORGE SIMPSON, born in Virginia in 1950, received his B.A. in journalism from the University of North Carolina at Chapel Hill. He went to work for *Newsweek* in 1972, and in 1978 he became public affairs director for that magazine. Before joining *Newsweek,* Simpson worked for two years as a writer and editor for the *Carolina Financial Times* in Chapel Hill, North Carolina, and as a reporter for the *News-Gazette* in Lexington, Virginia. He received the Best Feature Writing award from Sigma Delta Chi in 1972 for a five-part investigative series on the University of North Carolina football program. He has written stories for the *New York Times, Sport, Glamour,* the *Winston-Salem* (North Carolina) *Journal,* and *New York.*

The War Room at Bellevue

"The War Room at Bellevue" was first published in *New York* magazine. The author chose, for good reason, to stay strictly within a time sequence as he described the emergency ward. This essay is also noteworthy for its cumulative descriptive effect, which was accomplished almost entirely with objective details.

Bellevue. The name conjures up images of an indoor war zone: the wounded and bleeding lining the halls, screaming for help while harried doctors in blood-stained smocks rush from stretcher to stretcher, fighting a losing battle against exhaustion and the crushing number of injured. "What's worse," says a longtime Bellevue nurse, "is that we have this image of being a hospital only for . . ." she pauses, then lowers her voice, "for crazy people."

Though neither battlefield nor Bedlam is a valid image, there is something extraordinary about the monstrous complex that spreads for five blocks along First Avenue in Manhattan. It is said best by the head nurse in Adult Emergency Service: "If you have any chance for survival, you have it here." Survival—that is why they come. Why do injured cops drive by a half-dozen other hospitals to be treated at Bellevue? They've seen the Bellevue emergency team in action.

9:00 P.M. It is a Friday night in the Bellevue emergency room. The after-work crush is over (those who've suffered through the day, only to come for help after the five-o'clock whistle has blown) and it is nearly silent except for the mutter of voices at the admitting desk, where administrative personnel discuss who will go for coffee.

Across the spotless white-walled lobby, ten people sit quietly, passively, in pastel plastic chairs, waiting for word of relatives or to see doctors. In the past 24 hours, 300 people have come to the Bellevue Adult Emergency Service. Fewer than 10 percent were true emergencies. One man sleeps fitfully in the emergency ward while his heartbeat, respiration, and blood pressure are monitored by control consoles mounted over his bed. Each heartbeat trips a tiny bleep in the monitor, which attending nurses can hear across the ward. A half hour ago, doctors in the trauma room withdrew a six-inch stiletto blade from his back. When he is stabilized, the patient will be moved upstairs to the twelve-bed Surgical Intensive Care Unit.

9:05 P.M. An ambulance backs into the receiving bay, its red and   4
yellow lights flashing in and out of the lobby. A split second later, the glass doors burst open as a nurse and an attendant roll a mobile stretcher into the lobby. When the nurse screams, "Emergency!" the lobby explodes with activity as the way is cleared to the trauma room. Doctors appear from nowhere and transfer the bloodied body of a black man to the treatment table. Within seconds his clothes are stripped away, revealing a tiny stab wound in his left side. Three doctors and three nurses rush around the victim, each performing a task necessary to begin treatment. Intravenous needles are inserted into his arms and groin. A doctor draws blood for the lab, in case surgery is necessary. A nurse begins inserting a catheter into the victim's penis and continues to feed in tubing until the catheter reaches the bladder. Urine flows through the tube into a plastic bag. Doctors are glad not to see blood in the urine. Another nurse records pulse and blood pressure.

The victim is in good shape. He shivers slightly, although the   5
trauma room is exceedingly warm. His face is bloodied, but shows no major lacerations. A third nurse, her elbow propped on the treatment table, asks the man a series of questions, trying to quickly outline his medical history. He answers abruptly. He is drunk. His left side is swabbed with yellow disinfectant and a doctor injects a local anesthetic. After a few seconds another doctor inserts his finger into the wound. It sinks in all the way to the knuckle. He begins to rotate his finger like a child trying to get a marble out of a milk bottle. The patient screams bloody murder and tries to struggle free.

Meanwhile in the lobby, a security guard is ejecting a derelict   6
who has begun to drink from a bottle hidden in his coat pocket. "He's a regular, was in here just two days ago," says a nurse. "We checked him pretty good then, so he's probably okay now. Can you

believe those were clean clothes we gave him?" The old man, blackened by filth, leaves quietly.

9:15 P.M. A young Hispanic man interrupts, saying his pregnant 7 girl friend, sitting outside in his car, is bleeding heavily from her vagina. She is rushed into an examination room, treated behind closed doors, and rolled into the observation ward, where, much later in the night, a gynecologist will treat her in a special room—the same one used to examine rape victims. Nearby, behind curtains, the neurologist examines an old white woman to determine if her headaches are due to head injury. They are not.

9:45 P.M. The trauma room has been cleared and cleaned merci- 8 lessly. The examination rooms are three-quarters full—another overdose, two asthmatics, a young woman with abdominal pains. In the hallway, a derelict who has been sleeping it off urinates all over the stretcher. He sleeps on while attendants change his clothes. An ambulance—one of four that patrol Manhattan for Bellevue from 42nd Street to Houston, river to river—delivers a middle-aged white woman and two cops, the three of them soaking wet. The woman has escaped from the psychiatric floor of a nearby hospital and tried to drown herself in the East River. The cops fished her out. She lies on a stretcher shivering beneath white blankets. Her eyes stare at the ceiling. She speaks clearly when an administrative worker begins routine questioning. The cops are given hospital gowns and wait to receive tetanus shots and gamma globulin—a hedge against infection from the befouled river water. They will hang around the E.R. for another two hours, telling their story to as many as six other policemen who show up to hear it. The woman is rolled into an examination room, where a male nurse speaks gently: "They tell me you fell into the river." "No," says the woman, "I jumped. I have to commit suicide." "Why?" asks the nurse. "Because I'm insane and I can't help [it]. I have to die." The nurse gradually discovers the woman has a history of psychological problems. She is given dry bedclothes and placed under guard in the hallway. She lies on her side, staring at the wall.

The pace continues to increase. Several more overdose victims 9 arrive by ambulance. One, a young black woman, had done a striptease on the street just before passing out. A second black woman is semiconscious and spends the better part of her time at Bellevue alternately cursing at and pleading with the doctors. Attendants find a plastic bottle coated with methadone in the pocket of a Hispanic O.D. The treatment is routinely the same, and sooner or later involves vomiting. Just after doctors begin to treat the O.D., he vomits great quantities of wine and methadone in all directions. "Lovely business, huh?" laments one of the doctors. A young nurse confides that if there were other true emergencies, the overdose victims would be given lower priority. "You can't help thinking they did it to themselves," she says, "while the others are accident victims."

10:30 P.M. A policeman who twisted his knee struggling with an 10
"alleged perpetrator" is examined and released. By 10:30, the lobby is jammed with friends and relatives of patients in various stages of treatment and recovery. The attendant who also functions as a translator for Hispanic patients adds chairs to accommodate the overflow. The medical walk-in rate stays steady—between eight and ten patients waiting. A pair of derelicts, each with battered eyes, appear at the admitting desk. One has a dramatically swollen face laced with black stitches.

11:30 P.M. The husband of the attempted suicide arrives. He 11
thanks the police for saving his wife's life, then talks at length with doctors about her condition. She continues to stare into the void and does not react when her husband approaches her stretcher.

Meanwhile, patients arrive in the lobby at a steady pace. A 12
young G.I. on leave has lower-back pains; a Hispanic man complains of pains in his side; occasionally parents hurry through the adult E.R. carrying children to the pediatric E.R. A white woman of about 50 marches into the lobby from the walk-in entrance. Dried blood covers her right eyebrow and upper lip. She begins to perform. "I was assaulted on 28th and Lexington, I was," she says grandly, "and I don't have to take it *anymore*. I was a bride 21 years ago and, God, I was beautiful then." She has captured the attention of all present. "I was there when the boys came home—on Memorial Day—and I don't have to take this kind of treatment."

As midnight approaches, the nurses prepare for the shift 13
change. They must brief the incoming staff and make sure all reports are up-to-date. One young brunet says, "Christ, I'm gonna go home and take a shower—I smell like vomit."

11:50 P.M. The triage nurse is questioning an old black man 14
about chest pains, and a Hispanic woman is having an asthma attack, when an ambulance, its sirens screaming full tilt, roars into the receiving bay. There is a split-second pause as everyone drops what he or she is doing and looks up. Then all hell breaks loose. Doctors and nurses are suddenly sprinting full-out toward the trauma room. The glass doors burst open and the occupied stretcher is literally run past me. Cops follow. It is as if a comet has whooshed by. In the

trauma room it all becomes clear. A half-dozen doctors and nurses surround the lifeless form of a Hispanic man with a shotgun hole in his neck the size of your fist. Blood pours from a second gaping wound in his chest. A respirator is slammed over his face, making his chest rise and fall as if he were breathing. "No pulse," reports one doctor. A nurse jumps on a stool and, leaning over the man, begins to pump his chest with her palms. "No blood pressure," screams another nurse. The ambulance driver appears shaken, "I never thought I'd get here in time," he stutters. More doctors from the trauma team upstairs arrive. Wrappings from syringes and gauze pads fly through the air. The victim's eyes are open yet devoid of life. His body takes on a yellow tinge. A male nurse winces at the gunshot wound. "This guy really pissed off somebody," he says. This is no ordinary shooting. It is an execution. IV's are jammed into the body in the groin and arms. One doctor has been plugging in an electrocardiograph and asks everyone to stop for a second so he can get a reading. "Forget it," shouts the doctor in charge. "No time." "Take it easy, Jimmy," someone yells at the head physician. It is apparent by now that the man is dead, but the doctors keep trying injections and finally they slit open the chest and reach inside almost up to their elbows. They feel the extent of the damage and suddenly it is all over. "I told 'em he was dead," says one nurse, withdrawing. "They didn't listen." The room is very still. The doctors are momentarily disgusted, then go on about their business. The room clears quickly. Finally there is only a male nurse and the still-warm body, now waxy-yellow, with huge ribs exposed on both sides of the chest and giant holes in both sides of the neck. The nurse speculates that this is yet another murder in a Hispanic political struggle that has brought many such victims to Bellevue. He marvels at the extent of the wounds and repeats, "This guy was really blown away."

Midnight. A hysterical woman is hustled through the lobby 15 into an examination room. It is the dead man's wife, and she is nearly delirious. "I know he's dead, I know he's dead," she screams over and over. Within moments the lobby is filled with anxious relatives of the victim, waiting for word on his condition. The police are everywhere asking questions, but most people say they saw nothing. One young woman says she heard six shots, two louder than the other four. At some point, word is passed that the man is, in fact, dead. Another woman breaks down in hysterics; everywhere young Hispanics are crying and comforting each other. Plainclothes detectives make a quick examination of the body, check on the time of pronouncement of death, and begin to ask questions, but the bereaved are too stunned to talk. The rest of the uninvolved people in the lobby stare dumbly, their injuries suddenly paling in light of a death.

12:30 A.M. A black man appears at the admissions desk and says   16
he drank poison by mistake. He is told to have a seat. The ambulance brings in a young white woman, her head wrapped in white gauze. She is wailing terribly. A girl friend stands over her, crying, and a boyfriend clutches the injured woman's hands, saying, "I'm here, don't worry, I'm here." The victim has fallen downstairs at a friend's house. Attendants park her stretcher against the wall to wait for an examination room to clear. There are eight examination rooms and only three doctors. Unless you are truly an emergency, you will wait. One doctor is stitching up the eyebrow of a drunk who's been punched out. The friends of the woman who fell down the stairs glance up at the doctors anxiously, wondering why their friend isn't being treated faster.

1:10 A.M. A car pulls into the bay and a young Hispanic asks if a   17
shooting victim has been brought here. The security guard blurts out, "He's dead." The young man is stunned. He peels his tires leaving the bay.

1:20 A.M. The young woman of the stairs is getting stitches in a   18
small gash over her left eye when the same ambulance driver who brought in the gunshot victim delivers a man who has been stabbed in the back on East 3rd Street. Once again the trauma room goes from 0 to 60 in five seconds. The patient is drunk, which helps him endure the pain of having the catheter inserted through his penis into his bladder. Still he yells, "That hurts like a bastard," then adds sheepishly, "Excuse me, ladies." But he is not prepared for what comes next. An X-ray reveals a collapsed right lung. After just a shot of local anesthetic, the doctor slices open his side and inserts a long plastic tube. Internal bleeding had kept the lung pressed down and prevented it from reinflating. The tube releases the pressure. The ambulance driver says the cops grabbed the guy who ran the eight-inch blade into the victim's back. "That's not the one," says the man. "They got the wrong guy." A nurse reports that there is not much of the victim's type blood available at the hospital. One of the doctors says that's okay, he won't need surgery. Meanwhile blood pours from the man's knife wound and the tube in his side. As the nurses work, they chat about personal matters, yet they respond immediately to orders from either doctor. "How ya doin'?" the doctor asks the patient. "Okay," he says. His blood spatters on the floor.

So it goes into the morning hours. A Valium overdose, a woman   19
who fainted, a man who went through the windshield of his car.
More overdoses. More drunks with split eyebrows and chins. The
doctors and nurses work without complaint. "This is nothing, about
normal, I'd say," concludes the head nurse. "No big deal."

MEANINGS AND VALUES

1. What is the author's point of view? (See "Guide to Terms": *Point of View.*) How is this reflected by the tone? (Guide: *Style/Tone.*)

2. Does Simpson ever slip into sentimentality—a common failing when describing the scenes of death and tragedy? (Guide: *Sentimentality.*) If so, where? If not, how does he avoid it?

3. Cite at least six facts learned from reading this piece that are told, not in general terms but by specific, concrete details—for example, that a high degree of cleanliness is maintained at Bellevue, illustrated by "the spotless white-walled lobby" (Par. 3) and "the trauma room has been cleared and cleaned mercilessly" (Par. 8). What are the advantages of having facts presented in this way?

EXPOSITORY TECHNIQUES

1. Do you consider the writing to be primarily objective or impressionistic? What is the dominant impression, if any?

2. What is the value of using a timed sequence in such a description?

3. Does it seem to you that any of this description is excessive—that is, unnecessary to the task at hand? If so, how might the piece be revised?

4. List, in skeletal form, the facts learned about the subject from reading the two-paragraph introduction. How well does it perform the three basic purposes of an introduction? (Guide: *Introductions.*)

5. What is the significance of the rhetorical question in Paragraph 2? (Guide: *Rhetorical Questions.*) Why is it rhetorical?

6. Is the short closing effective? (Guide: *Closings.*) Why, or why not?

DICTION AND VOCABULARY

1. Cite the clichés in Paragraphs 4, 5, 8, and 14. (Guide: *Clichés.*) What justification, if any, can you offer for their use?

2. Cite the allusion in Paragraph 2, and explain its meaning and source. (Guide: *Figures of Speech.*)

3. Simpson uses some slang and other colloquialisms. Cite as many of these as you can. (Guide: *Colloquial Expressions*.) Is their use justified? Why, or why not?

READ TO WRITE

1. **Collaborating:** Working in a group, discuss a job or an activity (sport, organization) that to an outsider might seem hectic or hazardous. Consider describing it in an essay so that readers can come to understand it more clearly.

2. **Considering Audience:** Descriptive writing can create events for readers who have not experienced it. Much of the power of Simpson's writing comes from the sensational nature of the subjects he describes and his careful selection of detail. If you have witnessed or participated in some other kind of "extreme" experience, help your readers understand it by describing and explaining it with the same mix of detail and commentary that Simpson offers.

3. **Developing an Essay:** Consider arranging an expository essay of your own by using a time frame as Simpson does. Your purposes for using this device need not be the same, however, and you can use this strategy for expository patterns other than description.

(NOTE: Suggestions for topics requiring development by use of DESCRIPTION are on pp. 464–465 at the end of this chapter.)

EDWIDGE DANTICAT

> EDWIDGE DANTICAT has written novels, short stories, nonfiction, and
> essays drawing frequently on the scenes and traditions of Haiti,
> where she spent much of her childhood before emigrating to New
> York at age 12. She received a degree in French literature from
> Barnard College and an M.F.A. from Brown University. Her award-
> winning first novel, *Breath, Eyes, Memory* (1994), was followed by a
> collection of stories, *Krik? Krak!* (1995) (nominated for a National
> Book Award), and a second novel, *The Farming of Bones* (1998). In
> addition, she has edited several collections of stories. Her essays
> and stories have appeared in a variety of periodicals. Her most re-
> cent book is the nonfiction *After the Dance: A Walk Through
> Carnival in Jacmel, Haiti* (2002).

Carnival of the Dead

> "Carnival of the Dead," from *After the Dance*, takes readers to a
> cemetery in Haiti. Danticat uses the elements of the scene to ex-
> plain a perspective on the closeness of life and death that may be
> unfamiliar to many readers. She also draws on the details to ex-
> plain the complex religious traditions embodied in the place she
> calls "a carnival of stone."

I have always enjoyed cemeteries. Altars for the living as well as   1
resting places for the dead, they are entryways, I think, to any
town or city, the best places to become acquainted with the tastes of
the inhabitants, both present and gone.

The cemetery in Jacmel is no different. In fact, it is downright   2
colorful in its vibrant and disorganized mix of old and new architec-
ture, a carnival of stone.

After I ask the poet Rodney Saint-Eloi, who is traveling with me,   3
to accompany me to the Jacmel cemetery. Rodney works for the cultural affairs section of Haiti's oldest daily newspaper, *Le Nouvelliste*,
and is the codirector of one of the few publishing houses in Port-au-
Prince. Since he has written a long poem that includes a verse about
cemeteries, I figure he won't mind coming along. Besides, we have
traveled together before and he has always shown a singular reverence for the dead, going as far as dipping his hands in rivers and
streams and raising his fingers to his forehead to connect himself to
those who have crossed the waters, literally and figuratively, before
him. In that way he is a kindred spirit, so I know he will not think it

strange if I say hello to the graves, which is something I do now and then when I am in a cemetery.

We head out in midafternoon, when the heat will least interfere   4
with our walk along Avenue Baranquilla, the central road leading out of town. Once we pass the Rue Vaivres and the corner where the carnival's official viewing stand is being built for Sunday, the sidewalk abruptly ends and the large white-and-blue public transportation buses, which are repainted school buses from the United States, double their speed.

The necropolis of Jacmel is off the main road, down a hill with a   5
row of houses on either side. Crossing a wide unpaved road, we reach one of its side walls. A few sections of the wall are decorated with advertisements, one for a cine club where you can sit in a small room and watch a kung fu movie or a Hollywood feature a year or two out of the theaters, the other for a construction-materials store called Kay Dodo. While the cine club's announcement is written in chalk, the Kay Dodo message is painted in red and blue to recall the colors of the Haitian flag. On the walls are also fading campaign posters from the last presidential election, which took place the previous November, images of the recently inaugurated president Jean-Bertrand Aristide, his bespectacled glare fixed on the hills surrounding the cemetery as he appears to be whispering his campaign slogan, "*Lapè nan tèt, lapè nan vant*"—Peace in the head, peace in the belly. The other writing is plain old graffiti, scribbled in chalk rather than spray paint. I find one unerringly appropriate. It is a simple word over a hole in the wall large enough to stick one's head through: BYE.

We enter the cemetery through the back because the wall is   6
missing a stretch there, forming an impromptu rear entrance. Rodney points out that this is a good way to enter a cemetery, for it alerts the dead that we are only on a visit, as they must have learned by now that if one doesn't come through the front gates accompanied by a large entourage, one is probably not there to stay.

There is a saying here: Houses don't have owners, only cemeter-   7
ies do. In that spirit, this cemetery seems to belong to everyone. Through it runs a well-beaten path, which the neighborhood people use as a shortcut. Teenagers on the way home from school. Young men en route to a soccer game. Scrolling lovers. Two girls carrying a *sèvis* of food to a sick relative, rushing because the food is getting cold.

Aside from the area residents, the cemetery has also drawn its   8
share of foreign visitors. The Lonely Planet's guide to the Dominican Republic and Haiti makes a brief mention of it, as does the British writer Ian Thomson in his travelogue *Bonjour Blanc*. Thomson is not

at all impressed, noting that the cemetery has "fallen into a ragged state of desuetude. Hibiscus has rooted in the shattered tombs, the lead lettering on monuments bored out of marauding weeds."

As Rodney and I follow the public trail toward the middle of the   9
cemetery, it is hard to avoid these old marble tombs. Many of them are cracked, and rendered anonymous by the dissolution of their markers, some are nearly covered with moss, wild grasses, and weeds, others are reburied under mounds of brown dirt in places where the ground suddenly slopes upward above them.

In 1951, in a public lecture at one of the social clubs of Jacmel, a   10
local resident, the journalist Louis Pélissier Baptiste, bemoaned the disintegration and, in some cases, the disappearance of many of the cemetery's tombstones. "It is regrettable," he is reported to have said, "that the rise of the orange trees and the vandalism of thieves have removed the marble tombstones which would tell us so much about the old city."

To better see the cemetery requires that we zigzag through it,   11
crisscrossing the pebbled soil between the graves. Rodney asks an old woman passing by what the bright green vines with crimson berrylike buds at the foot of the tombs are called. The old woman's knee-length black dress, mourning garb, suggests that she has recently buried a loved one here, or elsewhere. Gently tugging at the short salt-and-pepper plaits framing her wizened face, she looks into the distance, over the uneven rows of old graves and new mausoleums, and speaks in a soft, almost whispery voice.

"*Se fiè kouwòn lavyèj*," she says. These are the flowers of the   12
crown of the Virgin Mary.

The Virgin Mary, who does not have the heart to leave her chil-   13
dren by themselves in death, gardens their graves to keep them company, she adds. After Jesus was entombed, the Virgin Mary went to the site and wept so much that her tears rained on the ground and created these vines, the green leaves representing her uncontrollable sorrow and the red buds symbolizing Christ's shed blood, the cause of her pain.

And the reason you see the vines sometimes standing at the foot   14
of the graves, she says, sometimes crawling around and over them, sometimes somewhere in between as if kneeling, is because they represent all the physical stages of the Virgin Mary's grief. "And now these same vines grow in all the places where Christ's children, the Virgin Mary's children, are buried."

We walk from the older graves to the newer mausoleums.   15
Painted in bright yellows, pinks, and blues, they are as elaborate or as simple as the tastes of the owners and their families. Some are built in

the shape of houses, with rain drains protruding from the rooftops, steps leading up to the front galleries, an anterior room, as if to receive visitors, and metal grillwork gates and windows with heart- and diamond-shaped designs. The "flowers of the crown of the Virgin Mary" are so high and so symmetrical around some of them that it appears as though the mausoleums have their own gardens. Unlike the older tombs, which were meant for one person, the contemporary mausoleums are family affairs. Rodney points out one that's labeled FAMILIE EDNER TOUTEBON, with only the name of the apparent patriarch painted in red block letters at the pinnacle. The others entombed with Monsieur Toutebon would remain as overshadowed by their progenitor in death as perhaps they had been in life.

Other mausoleums look like small churches, with pitched roofs   16
and steeples topped by a cross. The crosses can be interpreted in many ways: as symbols of Christianity, Christ's crucifixion and death, as with the Virgin Mary vines, but also as representations of the guardian of the cemetery, the *Vodou* divinity Baron Samedi. Baron Samedi, the patron god, or *lwa,* of the cemetery, is honored with Day of the Dead services, held in cemeteries in early November.

During my early childhood in Haiti, the dictator François "Papa   17
Doc" Duvalier would dress like Baron Samedi. Donning a black hat, dark suit, and coattails, he was reminding all Haitians that he literally held the key to the cemeteries and could decide at will who the next inhabitants would be. (A 1963 *Life* magazine article quotes Duvalier as saying, "When they [Haitians] ask me, 'Who is our Mother?' I tell them, 'The Virgin.' But when they ask, 'Who is our Father?' then I must answer, 'No one—you have only me.' ")

Along with its religious connections, the Haitian cemetery cross   18
can also be artistic space, representing, as art historian Robert Farris Thompson writes in *Flash of the Spirit,* "the circular motion of human souls."

As we weave our way through the maze of the cemetery, I am   19
reminded of the story of Georges Liautaud, who is the originator of a now very popular form of Haitian flat metal sculpture. Born in Croix-des-Bouquets, a small town fifteen miles or so north of the capital, Liautaud was a blacksmith who carved distinctive wrought-iron wreathlike crosses embellished with heart- and diamond-shaped silhouettes for his local cemetery. Liautaud did not consider himself an artist until his crosses in the cemetery were noticed and admired and he was encouraged to create more of them as objets d'art.

Pauleus Vital, an artist who paints biblical tales such as the   20
judgment of Christ by Pontius Pilate and the beheading of John the Baptist, only staged in the Victorian manors of Jacmel, has set one of

his better-known paintings, *Judgement Day,* in what appears to be this cemetery. In the painting, a dark-skinned, long-haired Christ, surrounded by mermaids serving as angels, is floating over Jacmel. Beneath the Christ's feet are the tombs and mausoleums with skeletons leaping out of them.

One of Jacmel's best-known artists, Vital's half brother Préfète   21 Duffaut, has repeatedly painted Jacmel as a city of mountains spiraling toward the sky. In a painting called *Earth, Paradise and Hell,* the dead must pass through an arched doorway with a Liautaud-like cross on top to reach the sky. Once they have crossed this threshold, they turn either right or left, one side leading to Lucifer and a flaming hell in the clouds, the other leading to a paradise guarded by angels with features like those of the Arawak Indians, who were the first inhabitants of the island. The paradise, with its cathedral and narrow streets of ascending steps and cemetery, looks an awful lot like Jacmel. The seventy-eight-year-old Duffaut recently created what some have called his best work: his own coffin, brightly decorated with the real and imagined mountains of Jacmel.

Meaning and Values

1. a. The first two paragraphs of the essay contain statements that seem to indicate the central theme and purpose of the essay. What are the statements?

   b. Does the rest of the essay follow the theme and purpose outlined in these paragraphs? Why, or why not? (See "Guide to Terms": *Unity; Thesis.*)

2. What does the writer mean when she refers to Rodney Saint-Eloi as a "kindred spirit" who "will not think it strange if I say hello to the graves" (Par. 3).

3. What do Paragraphs 6 and 7 have to say about the relationships of the living and the dead in Haitian society? According to this essay, in what ways can the dead be said to be "alive"?

4. What do the people who criticize the run-down condition of the cemetery (Pars. 8, 10) fail to understand about it, at least according to the perspective the writer offers in Paragraphs 11–14?

Expository Techniques

1. Which paragraphs make up what might be called the "introduction"? Which comprise the body of the essay? The conclusion?

2. What strategy does the writer employ in concluding the selection? (Guide: *Closings.*)

3. How is the description arranged? What point of view does the writer employ? (See this chapter's introduction.)

4. In which paragraphs does Danticat discuss the religious significance of the monuments? In which does she discuss its significance and meaning as an artistic expression? Is her essay impressionistic or objective? Explain.

5. What symbols does the author present in Paragraph 21? Are they personal or conventional? (Guide: *Symbol.*) Explain their meaning.

DICTION AND VOCABULARY

1. In what ways can the phrase "carnival of stone" (Par. 2) be considered paradoxical? (Guide: *Paradox.*)

2. Identify the concrete diction in Paragraphs 9 and 11. How does this contribute to the effectiveness of the paragraphs and of the essay?

3. Look up the following words in the dictionary and write definitions for any that are unfamiliar to you: necropolis, cine, unerringly (Par. 5); entourage (6); desuetude (8); dissolution (9); plaits, wizened, mausoleums (11); anterior, symmetrical, progenitor (15); objets d'art (19).

READ TO WRITE

1. **Collaborating:** Working in a group, list aspects of public places (buildings, monuments, parks, streets, malls, cemeteries, and the like) that are highly detailed. Choose two examples from your group, then list and collectively write descriptive paragraphs for each. Be sure to use concrete language to "paint" a picture.

2. **Considering Audience:** Would a reader who had never seen a cemetery like the one in "Carnival of the Dead" be able to visualize the phenomenon based on Danticat's description? Choose an example that might better suit such an audience and write a descriptive essay using a style and arrangement similar to Danticat's.

3. **Developing an Essay:** Danticat's essay brings together two contrasting states (life and death) in a single scene. Think of some other contrasts (happy/sad, optimistic/fearful, old/young, for example) and a scene that brings them together. Write an essay similar to Danticat's using elements of the scene to explain the relationship, both contrasts and similarities.

(NOTE: Suggestions for topics regarding development by two of DESCRIPTION are on pp. 464–465 at the end of this chapter.)

Issues and Ideas

Place and Person

- Barry Lopez, *A Passage of Hands*
- Maya Angelou, *Champion of the World*
- E. B. White, *Once More to the Lake*

Our environments shape us, but we in turn shape them, in large ways and small. This probably seems so obvious to you that you seldom stop to notice the many relationships between place and person. This, however, is exactly what the next essays ask you to do. Barry Lopez's "A Passage of Hands" and E. B. White's "Once More to the Lake" offer two rather different perspectives on the relationship of people and their surroundings.

Though a feeling of nostalgia—a sense of fond memories and loss—might seem most appropriate for journeys back to childhood settings, the tone Barry Lopez creates is far more complex. E. B. White also asks readers to move beyond sentimental responses in his descriptions of places from the past. Indeed, when description is used as an expository strategy, it goes beyond simple re-creation of a setting to analysis and explanation.

An effective analysis of place and its relationship to character needs to focus not only on the details of the setting but also on the extent to which they embody and enact social, cultural, and psychological influences. But although it can be insightful, this use of description is seldom objective, especially when the writer is describing scenes and events from his or her own experience, as does Maya Angelou in "Champion of the World." As a writer, therefore, you should try to remain aware of the extent to which your perspective shapes and reshapes the scenes you are presenting. As a reader, you also need to stay alert to this further dimension of the relationship between person and place.

BARRY LOPEZ

BARRY LOPEZ was born in 1945 in Port Chester, New York. He attended the University of Notre Dame and the University of Oregon and works as a writer and photographer specializing in natural subjects. His writing and photography have been published in *Audubon, National Wildlife, Harper's, National Geographic,* and many other magazines. Among his books are *Desert Notes: Reflections in the Eye of the Raven* (1976), *Of Wolves and Men* (1978), *River Notes: The Dance of the Herons* (1979), *Winter Count* (1982), *Arctic Dreams* (1986) (winner of the National Book Award), *The Rediscovery of North America* (1990), and *About This Life* (1998).

A Passage of Hands

In this essay, first published in the collection *About This Life,* Barry Lopez links a number of descriptions as a way of recording and exploring changes in his life as well as the development of his values and a growing sense of self. Though the hands remain physical objects throughout, engaged in all sorts of activities, they simultaneously act as symbols summing up the meaning Lopez discovers in the various activities in which the hands are engaged.

My hands were born breech in the winter of 1945, two hours before sunrise. Sitting with them today, two thousand miles and more from that spot, turning each one slowly in bright sunshine, watching the incisive light raise short, pale lines from old cuts, and seeing the odd cant of the left ring finger, I know they have a history, though I cannot remember where it starts. As they began, they gripped whatever might hold me upright, surely caressed and kneaded my mother's breasts, yanked at the restrictions of pajamas. And then they learned to work buttons, to tie shoelaces and lift the milk glass, to work together.

The pressure and friction of a pencil as I labored down the spelling of words right-handed raised the oldest permanent mark, a callus on the third joint of the middle finger. I remember no trying accident to either hand in these early years, though there must have been glass cuts, thorn punctures, spider bites, nails torn to the cuticle, scrapes from bicycle falls, pin blisters from kitchen grease, splinters, nails blackened from door pinches, pain lingering from having all four fingers forced backward at once, and the first true weariness, coming from work with lumber and stones, with tools made for larger hands.

It is from these first years, five and six and seven, that I am able   3
to remember so well, or perhaps the hands themselves remember, a great range of texture—the subtle corrugation of cardboard boxes, the slickness of the oilcloth on the kitchen table, the shuddering bend of a horse's short-haired belly, the even give in warm wax, the raised oak grain in my school-desk top, the fuzziness of dead bumblebees, the coarseness of sheaves immediate to the polished silk of unhusked corn, the burnish of rake handles and bucket bails, the rigidness of the bony crest rising beneath the skin of a dog's head, the tackiness of flypaper, the sharpness of saws and ice picks.

It is impossible to determine where in any such specific mem-   4
ory, of course, texture gives way to heft, to shape, to temperature. The coolness of a camellia petal seems inseparable from that texture, warmth from the velvet rub of a horse's nose, heft from a brick's dry burr. And what can be said, as the hand recalls the earliest touch and exploration, or how texture changes with depth? Not alone the press of the palm on a dog's head or fingers boring to the roots of wool on a sheep's flank, but of, say, what happens with an orange: the hands work in concert to disassemble the fruit, running a thumb over the beaded surface of the skin, plying the soft white flay of the interior, the string net of fiber clinging to the translucent skin cases, dividing the yielding grain of the flesh beneath, with its hard, wrinkled seeds. And, further, how is one to separate these textures from a memory of the burst of fragrance as the skin is torn, or from the sound of the sections being parted—to say nothing of the taste, juice dripping from the chin, or the urge to devour, then, even the astringent skin, all initiated by the curiosity of the hands?

Looking back, it's easy to see that the education of the hands   5
(and so the person) begins like a language: a gathering of simple words, the assembly of simple sentences, all this leading eventually to the forging of instructive metaphors. Afterward nothing can truly be separated, to stand alone in the hands' tactile memory. Taking the lay of the dog's fur, the slow petting of the loved dog is the increasingly complicated heart speaking with the hand.

Still, because of an occasional, surprising flair of the hands, the   6
insistence of their scarred surfaces, it is possible for me to sustain the illusion that they have a history independent of the mind's perception, the heart's passion; a history of gathering what appeals, of expressing exasperation with their own stupidity, of faith in the

accrual of brute work. If my hands began to explore complex knowledge by seeking and sorting texture—I am compelled to believe this—then the first names my memory truly embraced came from the hands' differentiating among fruits and woven fabrics.

Growing on farms and in orchards and truck gardens around 　7
our home in rural California was a chaos of fruit: navel and Valencia oranges, tangerines, red and yellow grapefruit, pomegranates, lemons, pomelos, greengage and damson plums, freestone and cling peaches, apricots, figs, tangelos, Concord and muscadine grapes. Nectarines, Crenshaw, casaba, and honeydew melons, watermelons, and cantaloupes. My boyish hands knew the planting, the pruning, and picking, and the packing of some of these fruits, the force and the touch required. I sought them all out for the resilience of their ripeness and knew the different sensation of each—pips, radius, cleavage. I ate even tart pomegranates with ardor, from melons I dug gobs of succulent meat with mouth and fingers. Slicing open a cantaloupe or a melon with a knife, I would hesitate always at the sight of the cleft fistula of seeds. It unsettled me, as if it were the fruit's knowing brain.

The fabrics were my mother's. They were stacked in bolts 　8
catawampus on open shelves and in a closet in a room in our small house where she both slept and sewed, where she laid out skirts, suits, and dresses for her customers. Lawn, organdy, batiste, and other fine cottons; cambric and gingham; silks—moiré, crepe de chine, taffeta; handkerchief and other weights of linen; light wools like gabardine; silk and cotton damasks; silk and rayon satins; cotton and wool twills; velvet; netted cloths like tulle. These fabrics differed not only in their texture and weave, in the fineness of their threads, but in the way they passed or reflected light, in their drape, and, most obviously from a distance, in their color and pattern.

I handled these fabrics as though they were animal skins, open- 　9
ing out bolts on the couch when Mother was working, holding them against the window light, raking them with my nails, crumpling them in my fist, then furling them as neatly as I could. Decades later, reading "samite of Ethnise" and "uncut rolls of brocade of Tabronit" in a paperback translation of Wolfram von Eschenbach's *Parzival,* I watched my free hand rise up to welcome the touch of these cloths.

It embarrassed and confounded me that other boys knew so lit- 　10
tle of cloth, and mocked the knowledge; but growing up with orchards and groves and vine fields, we shared a conventional, peculiar intimacy with fruit. We pelted one another with rotten

plums and the green husks of walnuts. We flipped gourds and rolled melons into the paths of oncoming, unsuspecting cars. The prank of the hand—throwing, rolling, flipping—meant nothing without the close companionship of the eye. The eye measured the distance, the crossing or closing speed of the object, and then the hand—the wrist snapping, the fingers' tips guiding to the last— decided upon a single trajectory, measured force, and then a rotten plum hit someone square in the back or sailed wide, or the melon ex- ploded beneath a tire or rolled cleanly to the far side of the road. And we clapped in glee and wiped our hands on our pants.

In these early years—eight and nine and ten—the hands be- came attuned to each other. They began to slide the hafts of pitch- forks and pry bars smoothly, to be more aware of each other's placement for leverage and of the light difference in strength. It would be three or four more years before, playing the infield in baseball, I would sense the spatial and temporal depth of awareness my hands had of each other, would feel, short-hopping a sharp grounder blind in front of third base, flicking the ball from gloved- left to bare-right hand, making the cross-body throw, that balletic poise of the still fingers after the release, would sense how mindless the beauty of it was.   11

I do not remember the ascendancy of the right hand. It was the one I was forced to write with, though by that time the right hand could already have asserted itself, reaching always first for a ham- mer or a peach. As I began to be judged according to the perfor- mance of my right hand alone—how well it imitated the Palmer cursive, how legibly it totaled mathematical figures—perhaps here is where the hands first realized how complicated their relationship would become. I remember a furious nun grabbing my six-year-old hands in prayer and wrenching the right thumb from under the left. Right over left, she insisted. *Right over left.* Right over left in praying to God.   12

In these early years my hands were frequently folded in prayer. They, too, collected chickens' eggs, contended with the neat assembly of plastic fighter planes, picked knots from bale twine, clapped chalkboard erasers, took trout off baited hooks, and trenched flower beds. They harbored and applauded homing pi- geons. When I was eleven, my mother married again and we moved east to New York. The same hands took on new city tasks, struggled more often with coins and with tying the full Windsor knot. Also, now, they pursued a more diligent and precise combing of my hair. And were in anxious anticipation of touching a girl.   13

And that caress having been given, one hand confirmed the memory later with the other in exuberant disbelief. They overhauled and pulled at each other like puppies.

I remember from these years—fourteen and fifteen and sixteen— 14 marveling at the dexterity of my hands. In games of catch, one hand tipped the falling ball to the other, to be seized firmly in the same instant the body crashed to the ground. Or the hands changed effortlessly on the dribble at the start of a fast break in basketball. I remember disassembling, cleaning, and reassembling a two-barrel carburetor, knowing the memory of where all the parts fit was within my hands. I can recall the baton reversal of a pencil as I wrote then erased, wrote then erased, composing sentences on a sheet of paper. And I remember how the hands, so clever with a ball, so deft with a pair of needle-nose pliers, fumbled attaching a cymbidium orchid so close to a girl's body, so near the mysterious breast.

By now, sixteen or so, my hands were as accustomed to books, 15 to magazines, newspapers, and typing paper, as they were to mechanic's tools and baseballs. A blade in my pocketknife was a shape my fingers had experienced years earlier as an oleander leaf. The shape of my fountain pen I knew first as a eucalyptus twig, drawing make-believe roads in wet ground. As my hands had once strained to bring small bluegills to shore, now they reeled striped bass from the Atlantic's surf. As they had once entwined horses' manes, now they twirled girls' ponytails. I had stripped them in those years of manure, paint, axle grease, animal gore, plaster, soap suds, and machine oil; I had cleaned them of sap and tar and putty, of pond scum and potting soil, of fish scales and grass stains. The gashes and cuts had healed smoothly. They were lithe, strenuous. The unimpeded reach of the fingers away from one another in three planes, their extreme effective span, was a subtle source of confidence and wonder. They showed succinctly the physical intelligence of the body. They expressed so unmistakably the vulnerability in sexual desire. They drew so deliberately the curtains of my privacy.

One July afternoon I stood at an ocean breakwater with a friend, 16 firing stones one after another in long, beautiful arcs a hundred feet to the edge of the water. We threw for accuracy, aiming to hit small breaking waves with cutting *thwips*. My friend tired of the game and lay down on his towel. A few moments later I turned and threw in a single motion just as he leaped to his feet. The stone caught him full in the side of the head. He was in the hospital a month with a fractured skull, unable to speak clearly until he was operated on. The following summer we were playing baseball together again, but I could not throw hard or accurately for months after the accident, and I shied away completely from a growing desire to be a pitcher.

My hands lost innocence or gained humanity that day, as they   17
had another day when I was pulled off my first dog, screaming, my hands grasping feebly in the air, after he'd been run over and killed in the road. Lying awake at night I sometimes remember throwing the near deadly stone, or punching a neighbor's horse with my adolescent fist, or heedlessly swinging a 16-gauge shotgun, leading quail—if I hadn't forgotten to switch off the trigger safety, I would have shot an uncle in the head. My hands lay silent at my sides those nights. No memory of their grace or benediction could change their melancholy stillness.

While I was in college I worked two summers at a ranch in   18
Wyoming. My hands got the feel of new tools—foot nips, frog pick, fence pliers, skiving knife. I began to see that the invention, dexterity, and quickness of the hands could take many directions in a man's life; and that a man should be attentive to what his hands loved to do, and so learn not only what he might be good at for a long time but what would make him happy. It pleased me to smooth every wrinkle from a saddle blanket before I settled a saddle squarely on a horse's back. And I liked, too, to turn the thin pages of a Latin edition of the *Aeneid* as I slowly accomplished them that first summer, feeling the impression of the type. It was strengthening to work with my hands, with ropes and bridles and hay bales, with double-bitted axes and bow saws, currying horses, scooping grain, adding my hands' oil to wooden door latches in the barn, calming horses at the foot of a loading ramp, adjusting my hat against the sun, buckling my chaps on a frosty morning. I'd watch the same hand lay a book lovingly on a night table and reach for the lamp's pull cord.

I had never learned to type, but by that second summer, at nine-   19
teen, I was writing out the first few stories longhand in pencil. I liked the sound and the sight of the writing going on, the back pressure through my hand. When I had erased and crossed out and rewritten a story all the way through, I would type it out slowly with two or sometimes four fingers, my right thumb on the space bar, as I do to this day. Certain keys and a spot on the space bar are worn through to metal on my typewriters from the oblique angles at which my fingernails strike them.

Had I been able to grasp it during those summers in Wyoming,   20
I might have seen that I couldn't get far from writing stories and

physical work, either activity, and remain happy. It proved true that in these two movements my hands found their chief joy, aside from the touching of other human beings. But I could not see it then. My hands only sought out and gave in to the pleasures.

I began to travel extensively while I was in college. Eventually I   21
visited many places, staying with different sorts of people. Most worked some substantial part of the day with their hands. I gravitated toward the company of cowboys and farmers both, to the work of loggers and orchardists, but mostly toward the company of field biologists, college-educated men and women who worked long days open to the weather, studying the lives of wild animals. In their presence, sometimes for weeks at a time, occasionally in stupefying cold or under significant physical strain, I helped wherever I could and wrote in my journal what had happened and, sometimes, what I thought of what had happened. In this way my hands came to know the prick and compression of syringes, and the soldering of radio collars, the arming of anesthetizing guns, the setting of traps and snares, the deployment of otter trawls and plankton tows, the operation of calipers and tripod scales, and the manipulation of various kinds of sieves and packages used to sort and store parts of dead animals, parts created with the use of skinning and butchering knives, with bone saws, teasing needles, tweezers, poultry shears, and hemostatic clamps. My hands were in a dozen kinds of blood, including my own.

Everywhere I journeyed I marveled at the hands of other crea-   22
tures, at how their palms and digits revealed history, at how well they performed tasks, at the elegant and incontrovertible beauty of their design. I cradled the paws of wolves and polar bears, the hooves of caribou, the forefeet of marine iguanas, the foreflippers of ringed seals and sperm whales, the hands of wallabies, of deer mice. Palpating the tendons, muscles, and bones beneath the skin or fur, I gained a rough understanding of the range of ability, of expression. I could feel where a broken bone had healed and see from superficial scars something of what a life must have been like. Deeper down, with mammals during necropsy, I could see how blood vessels and layers of fat in a paw or in a flipper were arranged to either rid the creature of its metabolic heat or hoard it. I could see the evidence of arthritis in its phalanges, how that could come to me.

I have never touched a dead human, nor do I wish to. The living   23
hands of another person, however, draw me, as strongly as the eyes. What is their history? What are their emotions? What longing is

there? I can follow a cabinetmaker's hands for hours as they verify and detect, shave, fit, and rub; or a chef's hands adroitly dicing vegetables or shaping pastry. And who has not known faintness at the sight of a lover's hand? What man has not wished to take up the hands of the woman he loves and pore over them with reverence and curiosity? Who has not in reverie wished to love the lover's hands?

Years after my mother died I visited her oldest living friend. We were doing dishes together and she said, "You have your mother's hands." Was that likeness a shade of love? And is now I say out of respect for my hands I would buy only the finest tools, is that, too, not love? 24

The hands evolve, of course. The creases deepen and the fingers begin to move two or three together at a time. If the hands of a man are put to hard use, the fingers grow blunt. They lose dexterity and the skin calluses over like hide. Hardly a pair of man's hands known to me comes to mind without a broken or dislocated finger, a lost fingertip, a permanently crushed nail. Most women my age carry scars from kitchen and housework, drawer pinches, scalds, knife and glass cuts. We hardly notice them. Sunlight, wind, and weather obscure many of these scars, but I believe the memory of their occurrence never leaves the hands. When I awaken in the night and sense my hands cupped together under the pillow, or when I sit somewhere on a porch, idly watching wind crossing a ripening field, and look down to see my hands nested in my lap as if asleep like two old dogs, it is not hard for me to believe they know. They remember all they have done, all that has happened to them, the ways in which they have been surprised or worked themselves free of desperate trouble, or lost their grip and so caused harm. It's not hard to believe they remember the heads patted, the hands shaken, the apples peeled, the hair braided, the wood split, the gears shifted, the flesh gripped and stroked, and that they convey their feelings to each other. 25

In recent years my hands have sometimes been very cold for long stretches. It takes little cold now to entirely numb thumbs and forefingers. They cease to speak what they know. When I was thirty-one, I accidentally cut the base of my left thumb, severing nerves, leaving the thumb confused about what was cold, what was hot, and whether or not it was touching something or only thought so. When I was thirty-six, I was helping a friend butcher a whale. We'd been up for many hours under twenty-four-hour arctic daylight and 26 were tired. He glanced away and without thinking drove the knife into my wrist. It was a clean wound, easy to close, but with it I lost the nerves to the right thumb. Over the years each thumb has regained some sensitivity, and I believe the hands are more sympathetic to each other because of their similar wounds. The only obvious difference lies with the left hand. A broken metacarpal forced a rerouting of tendons to the middle and ring fingers as it healed and raised a boss of carpal bone tissue on the back of the hand.

At the base of the right thumb is a scar from a climbing accident. On the other thumb, a scar the same length from the jagged edges of a fuel-barrel pump. In strong sunlight, when there is a certain tension in the skin, as I have said, I can stare at my hands for a while, turning them slowly, and remember with them the days, the weather, the people present when some things happened that left scars behind. It brings forth affection for my hands. I recall how, long ago, they learned to differentiate between cotton and raw silk, between husks of the casaba and the honeydew melon, and how they thrilled to the wire bristle of a hog's back, how they clipped the water's surface in swimming-pool fights, how they painstakingly arranged bouquets, how they swung and lifted children. I have begun to wish they would speak to me, tell me stories I have forgotten. 27

I sit in a chair and look at the scars, the uneven cut of the nails, and reminisce. With them before me I grin as though we held something secret, remembering bad times that left no trace. I cut firewood for my parents once, winter in Alabama, swamping out dry, leafless vines to do so. Not until the next day did I realize the vines were poison ivy. The blisters grew so close and tight my hands straightened like paddles. I had to have them lanced to continue a cross-country trip, to dress and feed myself. And there have been days when my hands stiffened with cold so that I had to quit the work being done, sit it out and whimper with pain as they came slowly back to life. But these moments are inconsequential. I have looked at the pale, wrinkled hands of a drowned boy, and I have seen handless wrists. 28

If there were a way to speak directly to our hands, to allow them a language of their own, what I would most wish to hear is what they recall of human touch, of the first exploration of the body of another, the caresses, the cradling of breast, of head, of buttock. Does it seem to them as to me that we keep learning, even when the caressed body has been known for years? How do daydreams of an idealized body, one's own or another's affect the hands' first tentative inquiry? Is the 29

hand purely empirical? Does it apply an imagination? Does it retain
a man's shyness, a boy's clumsiness? Do the hands anguish if there is
no one to touch?

Tomorrow I shall pull blackberry vines and load a trailer with   30
rotten timber. I will call on my hands to help me dress, to turn the
spigot for coffee, to pull the newspaper from its tube. I will put my
hands in the river and lift water where the sunlight is brightest, a
playing with fractured light I never tire of. I will turn the pages of a
book about the history of fire in Australia. I will sit at the typewriter,
working through a story about a trip to Matagorda Island in Texas. I
will ask my hands to undress me. Before I turn out the light, I will
fold and set my reading glasses aside. Then I will cup my hands, the
left in the right, and slide them under the pillow beneath my head,
where they will speculate, as will I, about what we shall handle the
next day, and dream, a spooling of their time we might later remember together and I, so slightly separated from them, might recognize.

Meanings and Values

1.   Lopez uses his hands as the thread for an autobiographical essay.
     Why might he have chosen hands to represent the changes in his life?
     (See "Guide to Terms": *Symbol*.)

2.   Lopez says, "Looking back, it's easy to see that the education of the
     hands (and so the person) begins like a language: a gathering of sim-
     ple words, the assembly of simple sentences, all this leading eventu-
     ally to the forging of instructive metaphors" (Par. 5). Why might he
     have chosen such a simile? What is the connection between hands
     and language as Lopez explains it?

3.   Find all of Lopez's references to writing in the essay. What theme
     emerges from the repetitive use of the physical act of writing?

Expository Techniques

1.   Identify where Lopez uses transition to represent the passage of
     time. How does he use the subject of hands to link stages in his life?
     (Guide: *Transitions*.)

2.   Does Lopez primarily use concrete or abstract images in this essay?
     Point to examples of each and analyze their success. (Guide:
     Evaluation.)

3.   Compare the references to dogs in Paragraph 5 ("Taking the lay of
     the dog's fur, the slow petting of the loved dog is the increasingly
     complicated heart speaking with the hand") to that in Paragraph 17

("My hands lost innocence or gained humanity that day, as they had another day when I was pulled off my first dog, screaming, my hands grasping feebly in the air, after he'd been run over and killed in the road"). How do these acts of placing hands on a dog differ? How has the author grown as a result of these experiences?

DICTION AND VOCABULARY

1. Compare the tasks of the hands in Paragraphs 1 and 30. What words and actions are repeated? Explain the significance of Lopez's linked introduction and conclusion in this essay. (Guide: *Introductions; Conclusions.*)

2. Why does Lopez emphasize his right hand throughout the essay? What connotation does the left hand evoke in many readers? (Guide: *Denotation/Connotation.*)

3. Look up any of the following words with which you are unfamiliar: heft (Par. 4); casaba (7); cambric (8); hafts (11); necropsy (22).

READ TO WRITE

1. **Collaborating:** Lopez "grows up" in this essay. Consider the various stages in your own lives. List those stages in an outline. Working in a group, identify the specific passages that indicate a new phase of Lopez's life and outline them. Compare Lopez's stages with your own and with those of other group members. Write a paragraph analyzing the similarities and differences among your choices.

2. **Considering Audience:** Lopez shares many experiences with his audience. With how many of these experiences might a majority of his readers be familiar? Can you think of any personal experiences with your hands that could be added and that readers would readily understand? Choose one and write a paragraph that could fit into Lopez's essay.

3. **Developing an Essay:** "A Passage of Hands" relies on clear description of touch. Choose one of your other senses and write an autobiographical essay similar to Lopez's.

(NOTE: Suggestions for topics regarding development by use of DESCRIPTION are on pp. 464–465 at the end of this chapter.)

MAYA ANGELOU

> MAYA ANGELOU was born in 1928 in St. Louis and raised in rural
> Arkansas in a segregated society. Angelou has had a wide-ranging
> career as a writer, actress, producer, director, and civil rights ac-
> tivist. She is currently Reynolds Professor of American Studies at
> Wake Forest University. Angelou has published numerous books
> and articles, winning her both Pulitzer Prize and National Book
> Award nominations.

Champion of the World

In this selection from the first volume of her autobiography, *I Know
Why the Caged Bird Sings,* published in 1969, the writer uses descriptive detail to recreate a scene from the 1930s during the era of
segregation. There are three sets of descriptive details in the selection: those recreating the immediate scene in the Store; those pointing toward the social setting for the events; and those describing
the fight that come through the words of the radio announcer.
These details help Angelou explain why Joe Louis was so much
more than just another boxer.

The last inch of space was filled, yet people continued to wedge   1
themselves along the walls of the Store. Uncle Willie had turned
the radio up to its last notch so that youngsters on the porch
wouldn't miss a word. Women sat on kitchen chairs, dining-room
chairs, stools, and upturned wooden boxes. Small children and babies perched on every lap available and men leaned on the shelves
or on each other.

The apprehensive mood was shot through with shafts of gaiety,   2
as a black sky is streaked with lightning.

"I ain't worried 'bout this fight. Joe's gonna whip that cracker   3
like it's open season."

"He gone whip him till that white boy call him Momma."   4

At last the talking finished and the string-along songs about ra-   5
zor blades were over and the fight began.

"A quick jab to the head." In the Store the crowd grunted. "A   6
left to the head and a right and another left." One of the listeners
cackled like a hen and was quieted.

"They're in a clinch, Louis is trying to fight his way out."   7

Some bitter comedian on the porch said, "That white man don't   8
mind hugging that niggah now, I betcha."

"The referee is moving in to break them up, but Louis finally   9
pushed the contender away and it's an uppercut to the chin. The
contender is hanging on, now he's backing away. Louis catches him
with a short left to the jaw."

A tide of murmuring assent poured out the door and into the   10
yard.

"Another left and another left. Louis is saving that mighty   11
right . . ." The mutter in the Store had grown into a baby roar and it
was pierced by the clang of a bell and the announcer's "That's the
bell for round three, ladies and gentlemen."

As I pushed my way into the Store I wondered if the announcer   12
gave any thought to the fact that he was addressing as "ladies and
gentlemen" all the Negroes around the world who sat sweating and
praying, glued to their "Master's voice."

There were only a few calls for RC Colas, Dr. Peppers, and   13
Hires root beer. The real festivities would begin after the fight. Then
even the old Christian ladies who taught their children and tried
themselves to practice turning the other cheek would buy soft
drinks, and if the Brown Bomber's victory was a particularly bloody
one they would order peanut patties and Baby Ruths, also.

Bailey and I laid coins on top of the cash register. Uncle Willie   14
didn't allow us to ring up sales during a fight. It was too noisy and
might shake up the atmosphere. When the gong rang for the next
round we pushed through the near-sacred quiet to the herd of children outside.

"He's got Louis against the ropes and now it's a left to the body   15
and a right to the ribs. Another right to the body, it looks like it was
low . . . Yes, ladies and gentlemen, the referee is signaling but the
contender keeps raining the blow on Louis. It's another to the body,
and it looks like Louis is going down."

My race groaned. It was our people falling. It was another lynch-   16
ing, yet another Black man hanging on a tree. One more woman am-
bushed and raped. A Black boy whipped and maimed. It was hounds
on the trail of a man running through slimy swamps. It was a white
woman slapping her maid for being forgetful.

The men in the Store stood away from the walls and at atten-   17
tion. Women greedily clutched the babes on their laps while on the
porch the shufflings and smiles, flirtings and pinching of a few minutes before were gone. This might be the end of the world. If Joe lost
we were back in slavery and beyond help. It would all be true, the
accusations that we were lower types of human beings. Only a little

higher than apes. True that we were stupid and ugly and lazy and dirty and, unlucky and worst of all, that God Himself hated us and ordained us to be hewers of wood and drawers of water, forever and ever, world without end.

We didn't breathe. We didn't hope. We waited.   18

"He's off the ropes, ladies and gentlemen. He's moving towards   19
the center of the ring." There was no time to be relieved. The worst might still happen.

"And now it looks like Joe is mad. He's caught Carnera with a   20
left hook to the head and a right to the head. It's a left jab to the body and another left to the head. There's a left cross and a right to the head. The contender's right eye is bleeding and he can't seem to keep his block up. Louis is penetrating every block. The referee is moving in, but Louis sends a left to the body and it's an uppercut to the chin and the contender is dropping. He's on the canvas, ladies and gentlemen."

Babies slid to the floor as women stood up and men leaned to-   21
ward the radio.

"Here's the referee. He's counting. One, two, three, four, five,   22
six, seven . . . Is the contender trying to get up again?"

All the men in the store shouted, "NO."   23

"—eight, nine, ten." There were a few sounds from the audi-   24
ence, but they seemed to be holding themselves in against tremendous pressure.

"The fight is all over, ladies and gentlemen. Let's get the micro-   25
phone over there to the referee . . . Here he is. He's got the Brown Bomber's hand, he's holding it up . . . Here he is . . ."

Then a voice, husky and familiar, came to wash over us—"The   26
winnah, and still heavyweight champeen of the world . . . Joe Louis."

Champion of the world. A black boy. Some Black mother's son.   27

He was the strongest man in the world. People drank Coca-   28
Colas like ambrosia and ate candy bars like Christmas. Some of the men went behind the Store and poured white lightning in their soft-drink bottles, and a few of the bigger boys followed them. Those who were not chased away came back blowing their breath in front of themselves like proud smokers.

It would take an hour or more before people would leave the   29
Store and head home. Those who lived too far had made arrange-ments to stay in town. It wouldn't do for a Black man and his family to be caught on a lonely country road on a night when Joe Louis had proved that we were the strongest people in the world.

MEANINGS AND VALUES

1. What details does Angelou present to indicate the people's reaction when Louis appears to be losing the fight? What details does she present to indicate the reaction when Louis appears to be winning?

2. To what extent is Angelou's purpose to re-create an event, and to what extent is her purpose to explain the social attitudes, feelings and values of a particular place and time? (See "Guide to Terms": *Purpose.*) Explain your answer by referring to the details mentioned in question #1.

3. Where in the selection does Angelou mention more or less directly the racial tensions and conflicts of the period? What evidence is there that her purpose is to explain the outlook of one side in the conflict and to make it understandable even to people living in different times and places?

EXPOSITORY TECHNIQUES

1. In what specific ways do the radio announcer's descriptions of the fight differ from the descriptions of the crowd and its reactions?

2. In several sections, the selection alternates between descriptions of the fight and descriptions of the crowd. What is the purpose of these alternations? (Guide: *Purpose.*)

3. In which paragraphs of the selection does the writer comment on the significance of the events? In what ways are these comments important for the expository purpose of the selection? (Guide: *Purpose.*)

4. When does Angelou make comments in her role as writer? When does she make comments in her role as participant in the events? What significant differences are there, if any, between the comments she makes in each role?

DICTION AND VOCABULARY

1. Where in the selection does Angelou quote passages in rural African-American dialect? What does the language of the dialect add to her explanation of the social relationships of the time and place she is portraying?

2. Identify the simile in paragraph 2 and discuss its meaning and effect. (Guide: *Figures of Speech.*)

3. In what ways, if at all, might the "lightning" of paragraph 2 be said to symbolize both Louis and his effect on the community in the selection? (Guide: *Symbol.*)

READ TO WRITE

1. **Collaborating:** Working in a group, identify a performance, a film, a television show, or some other event that has an audience. Choose

one in which the event reveals something about cultural or social relationships and in which the audience's reactions are similarly revealing. You might search for an event in which the crowd is diverse and offers diverse or even conflicting reactions. List some of the elements in the setting and in the audience's reaction that might be of particular use in an expository essay developed through description.

2. **Considering Audience:** Angelou focuses on an event in which she is both a participant and, as a writer, the observer. Can you think of an event or situation in which you were a participant but might also act as an observer? Does this event contain a third perspective, too, like the perspective of the radio announcer in Angelou's selection? Write a paragraph describing part of this situation or event, and play the roles of both participant and observer.

3. **Developing an Essay:** "Champion of the World" relies on multiple perspectives: the writer as participant and observer, and another event described by a third voice. Write an autobiographical essay similar to Angelou's in which you use at least two similar perspectives to explain social and cultural relationships you have experienced.

(NOTE: Suggestions for topics regarding development by use of DESCRIPTION are on pp. 464–465 at the end of this chapter.)

E. B. WHITE

E. B. WHITE, distinguished essayist, was born in Mount Vernon, New York, in 1899 and died in 1985 in North Brooklin, Maine. A graduate of Cornell University, White worked as a reporter and advertising copywriter, and in 1926 he joined the staff of the *New Yorker* magazine. After 1937 he did most of his writing at his farm in Maine, for many years contributing a regular column, "One Man's Meat," to *Harper's* magazine and freelance editorials for the "Notes and Comments" column of the *New Yorker.* White also wrote children's books, two volumes of verse, and, with James Thurber, *Is Sex Necessary?* (1929). With his wife, Katherine White, he compiled *A Subtreasury of American Humor* (1941). Collections of his own essays include *One Man's Meat* (1942), *The Second Tree from the Corner* (1953), *The Points of My Compass* (1962), and *Essays of E. B. White* (1977). In 1959 he revised and enlarged William Strunk's *The Elements of Style,* a textbook still widely used in college classrooms. White received many honors and writing awards for his crisp, highly individual style and his sturdy independence of thought.

Once More to the Lake

In this essay White relies primarily on description to convey his sense of the passage of time and the power of memory. The vivid scenes and the clear yet expressive prose in this essay are characteristic of his writing.

August 1941

One summer, along about 1904, my father rented a camp on a lake in Maine and took us all there for the month of August. We all got ringworm from some kittens and had to rub Pond's Extract on our arms and legs night and morning, and my father rolled over in a canoe with all his clothes on; but outside of that the vacation was a success and from then on none of us ever thought there was any place in the world like that lake in Maine. We returned summer after summer—always on August 1 for one month. I have since become a salt-water man, but sometimes in summer there are days when the restlessness of the tides and the fearful cold of the sea water and the incessant wind that blows across the afternoon and into the evening make me wish for the placidity of a lake in the woods. A few weeks ago this feeling got so strong I bought myself a couple of bass hooks and a spinner and returned to the lake where we used to go, for a week's fishing and to revisit old haunts.

I took along my son, who had never had any fresh water up his nose and who had seen lily pads only from train windows. On the journey over to the lake I began to wonder what it would be like. I wondered how time would have marred this unique, this holy spot—the coves and streams, the hills that the sun set behind, the camps and the paths behind the camps. I was sure that the tarred road would have found it out, and I wondered in what other ways it would be desolated. It is strange how much you can remember about places like that once you allow your mind to return into the grooves that lead back. You remember one thing, and that suddenly reminds you of another thing. I guess I remembered clearest of all the early mornings, when the lake was cool and motionless, remembered how the bedroom smelled of the lumber it was made of and of the wet woods whose scent entered through the screen. The partitions in the camp were thin and did not extend clear to the top of the rooms, and as I was always the first up I would dress softly so as not to wake the others, and sneak out into the sweet outdoors and start out in the canoe, keeping close along the shore in the long shadows of the pines. I remembered being very careful never to rub my paddle against the gunwale for fear of disturbing the stillness of the cathedral.

The lake had never been what you would call a wild lake. There were cottages sprinkled around the shores, and it was in farming country although the shores of the lake were quite heavily wooded. Some of the cottages were owned by nearby farmers, and you would live at the shore and eat your meals at the farmhouse. That's what our family did. But although it wasn't wild, it was a fairly large and undisturbed lake and there were places in it that, to a child at least, seemed infinitely remote and primeval.

I was right about the tar: it led to within half a mile of the shore. But when I got back there, with my boy, and we settled into a camp near a farmhouse and into the kind of summertime I had known, I could tell that it was going to be pretty much the same as it had been before—I knew it, lying in bed the first morning, smelling the bedroom and hearing the boy sneak quietly out and go off along the shore in a boat. I began to sustain the illusion that he was I, and therefore, by simple transposition, that I was my father. This sensation persisted, kept cropping up all the time we were there. It was not an entirely new feeling, but in this setting it grew much stronger. I seemed to be living a dual existence. I would be in the middle of some simple act, I would be picking up a bait box or laying down a table fork, or I would be saying something, and suddenly it would be not I but my father who was saying the words or making the gesture. It gave me a creepy sensation.

We went fishing the first morning. I felt the same damp moss covering the worms in the bait can, and saw the dragonfly alight on the tip of my rod as it hovered a few inches from the surface of the water. It was the arrival of this fly that convinced me beyond any doubt that everything was as it always had been, that the years were a mirage and that there had been no years. The small waves were the same, chucking the rowboat under the chin as we fished at anchor, and the boat was the same boat, the same color green and the ribs broken in the same places, and under the floorboards the same fresh-water leavings and débris—the dead helgramite, the wisps of moss, the rusty discarded fishhook, the dried blood from yesterday's catch. We stared silently at the tips of our rods, at the dragonflies that came and went. I lowered the tip of mine into the water, tentatively, pensively dislodging the fly, which darted two feet away, poised, darted two feet back, and came to rest again a little farther up the rod. There had been no years between the ducking of this dragonfly and the other one—the one that was part of memory. I looked at the boy, who was silently watching his fly, and it was my hands that held his rod, my eyes watching. I felt dizzy and didn't know which rod I was at the end of.

We caught two bass, hauling them in briskly as though they were mackerel, pulling them over the side of the boat in a businesslike manner without any landing net, and stunning them with a blow on the back of the head. When we got back for a swim before lunch, the lake was exactly where we had left it, the same number of inches from the dock, and there was only the merest suggestion of a breeze. This seemed an utterly enchanted sea, this lake you could leave to its own devices for a few hours and come-back to, and find that it had not stirred, this constant and trustworthy body of water. In the shallows, the dark, water-soaked sticks and twigs, smooth and old, were undulating in clusters on the bottom against the clean ribbed sand, and the track of the mussel was plain. A school of minnows swam by, each minnow with its small individual shadow, doubling the attendance, so clear and sharp in the sunlight. Some of the other campers were in swimming, along the shore, one of them with a cake of soap, and the water felt thin and clear and unsubstantial. Over the years there had been this person with the cake of soap, this cultist, and here he was. There had been no years.

Up to the farmhouse to dinner through the teeming, dusty field,   7
the road under our sneakers was only a two-track road. The middle
track was missing, the one with the marks of the hooves and the
splotches of dried, flaky manure. There had always been three
tracks to choose from in choosing which track to walk in; now the
choice was narrowed down to two. For a moment I missed terribly
the middle alternative. But the way led past the tennis court, and
something about the way it lay there in the sun reassured me; the
tape had loosened along the backline, the alleys were green with
plantains and other weeds, and the net (installed in June and removed in September) sagged in the dry noon, and the whole place
steamed with midday heat and hunger and emptiness. There was a
choice of pie for dessert, and one was blueberry and one was apple,
and the waitresses were the same country girls, there having been
no passage of time, only the illusion of it as in a dropped curtain—
the waitresses were still fifteen; their hair had been washed, that was
the only difference—they had been to the movies and seen the
pretty girls with the clean hair.

Summertime, oh, summertime, pattern of life indelible, the   8
fade-proof lake, the woods unshatterable, the pasture with the
sweetfern and the juniper forever and ever, summer without end;
this was the background, and the life along the shore was the design, their tiny docks with the flagpole and the American flag floating against the white clouds in the blue sky, the little paths over the
roots of the trees leading from camp to camp and the paths leading
back to the outhouses and the can of lime for sprinkling, and at the
souvenir counters at the store the miniature birch-bark canoes and
the postcards that showed things looking a little better than they
looked. This was the American family at play, escaping the city heat,
wondering whether the newcomers in the camp at the head of the
cove were "common" or "nice," wondering whether it was true that
the people who drove up for Sunday dinner at the farmhouse were
turned away because there wasn't enough chicken.

It seemed to me, as I kept remembering all this, that those times   9
and those summers had been infinitely precious and worth saving.
There had been jollity and peace and goodness. The arriving (at the
beginning of August) had been so big a business in itself, at the rail-
way station the farm wagon drawn up, the first smell of the pine-
laden air, the first glimpse of the smiling farmer, and the great
importance of the trunks and your father's enormous authority in
such matters, and the feel of the wagon under you for the long ten-
mile haul, and at the top of the last long hill catching the first view of

the lake after eleven months of not seeing this cherished body of water. The shouts and cries of the other campers when they saw you, and the trunks to be unpacked, to give up their rich burden. (Arriving was less exciting nowadays, when you sneaked up in your car and parked it under a tree near the camp and took out the bags and in five minutes it was all over, no fuss, no loud wonderful fuss about trunks.)

Peace and goodness and jollity. The only thing that was wrong   10
now, really, was the sound of the place, an unfamiliar nervous sound of the outboard motors. This was the note that jarred, the one thing that would sometimes break the illusion and set the years moving. In those other summertimes all motors were inboard; and when they were at a little distance, the noise they made was a sedative, an ingredient of summer sleep. They were one-cylinder and two-cylinder engines, and some were make-and-break and some were jump-spark, but they all made a sleepy sound across the lake. The one-lungers throbbed and fluttered, and the twin-cylinder ones purred and purred, and that was a quiet sound, too. But now the campers all had outboards. In the daytime, in the hot mornings, these motors made a petulant, irritable sound; at night, in the still evening when the afterglow lit the water, they whined about one's ears like mosquitoes. My boy loved our rented outboard, and his great desire was to achieve single-handed mastery over it, and authority, and he soon learned the trick of choking it a little (but not too much), and the adjustment of the needle valve. Watching him I would remember the things you could do with the old one-cylinder engine with the heavy flywheel, how you could have it eating out of your hand if you got really close to it spiritually. Motorboats in those days didn't have clutches, and you would make a landing by shutting off the motor at the proper time and coasting in with a dead rudder. But there was a way of reversing them, if you learned the trick, by cutting the switch and putting it on again exactly on the final dying revolution of the flywheel, so that it would kick back against compression and begin reversing. Approaching a dock in a strong following breeze, it was difficult to slow up sufficiently by the ordinary coasting method, and if a boy felt he had complete mastery over his motor, he was tempted to keep it running beyond its time and then reverse it a few feet from the dock. It took a cool nerve, because if you threw the switch a twentieth of a second too soon you would catch the flywheel when it still had speed enough to go up past center, and the boat would leap ahead, charging bull-fashion at the dock.

We had a good week at the camp. The bass were biting well   11
and the sun shone endlessly, day after day. We would be tired at
night and lie down in the accumulated heat of the little bedrooms
after the long hot day and the breeze would stir almost imperceptibly outside and the smell of the swamp drift in through the rusty
screens. Sleep would come easily and in the morning the red squir-
rel would be on the roof, tapping out his gay routine. I kept remembering everything, lying in bed in the mornings—the small
steamboat that had a long rounded stern like the lip of a Ubangi,
and how quietly she ran on the moonlight sails, when the older
boys played their mandolins and the girls sang and we ate dough-
nuts dipped in sugar, and how sweet the music was on the water in
the shining night, and what it had felt like to think about girls then.
After breakfast we would go up to the store and the things were in
the same place—the minnows in a bottle, the plugs and spinners
disarranged and pawed over by the youngsters from the boys'
camp, the Fig Newtons and the Bee-man's gum. Outside, the road
was tarred and cars stood in front of the store. Inside, all was just as
it had always been, except there was more Coca-Cola and not so
much Moxie and root beer and birch beer and sarsaparilla. We
would walk out with the bottle of pop apiece and sometimes the
pop would backfire up our noses and hurt. We explored the
streams, quietly, where the turtles slid off the sunny logs and dug
their way into the soft bottom; and we lay on the town wharf and
fed worms to the tame bass. Everywhere we went I had trouble
making out which was I, the one walking at my side, the one walking in my pants.

One afternoon while we were there at that lake a thunder-   12
storm came up. It was like the revival of an old melodrama that I
had seen long ago with childish awe. The second-act climax of
the drama of the electrical disturbance over a lake in America had
not changed in any important respect. This was the big scene, still
the big scene. The whole thing was so familiar, the first feeling of
oppression and heat and a general air around camp of not wanting to go very far away. In mid-afternoon (it was all the same) a
curious darkening of the sky, and a lull in everything that had
made life tick; and then the way the boats suddenly swung the
other way at their moorings with the coming of a breeze out of
the new quarter, and the premonitory rumble. Then the kettle
drum, then the snare, then the bass drum and cymbals, then
crackling light against the dark, and the gods grinning and lick-
ing their chops in the hills. Afterward the calm, the rain steadily

rustling in the calm lake, the return of light and hope and spirits, and the campers running out in joy and relief to go swimming in the rain, their bright cries perpetuating the deathless joke about how they were getting simply drenched, and the children screaming with delight at the new sensation of bathing in the rain, and the joke about getting drenched linking the generations in a strong indestructible chain. And the comedian who waded in carrying an umbrella.

When the others went swimming, my son said he was going in, too. He pulled his dripping trunks from the line where they had hung all through the shower and wrung them out. Languidly, and with no thought of going in, I watched him, his hard little body, skinny and bare, saw him wince slightly as he pulled up around his vitals the small, soggy, icy garment. As he buckled the swollen belt, suddenly my groin felt the chill of death.

13

Meanings and Values

1. In what ways have the lake and its surroundings remained the same since White's boyhood? In what ways have they changed? Be specific.

2. Can the lake be considered a personal symbol for White? (See "Guide to Terms": *Symbol.*) If so, what does it symbolize?

3. At one point in the essay, White says, "I seemed to be living a dual existence" (Par. 4). What is the meaning of this statement? How does this "dual existence" affect his point of view in the essay? (Guide: *Point of View.*) Is the dual existence emphasized more in the first half of the essay or the second half? Why?

4. Where in the essay does White link differences between the lake now and in his youth with a difference between his son's outlooks and his own? Is this distance between father and son caused by changes in the world around them or merely the passage of time? Explain.

5. After spending a day on the lake, White remarks, "There had been no years" (Par. 6). What other direct or indirect comments does he make about time and change? Be specific.

6. What is the tone of the essay? (Guide: *Style/Tone.*) Does the tone change or remain the same throughout the essay?

7. What is meant by the closing phrase of the essay, "suddenly my groin felt the chill of death" (Par. 13)? Is this an appropriate way to end the essay? Why, or why not?

EXPOSITORY TECHNIQUES

1. In the first part of the essay, White focuses on the unchanged aspects of the lake; in the second part, he begins acknowledging the passage of time. Where does this shift in attitude take place? What strategies, including transitional devices, does White use to signal to the reader the shift in attitude? Be specific.

2. How does White use the discussion of outboard motors and inboard motors (Par. 10) to summarize the differences between life at the lake in his youth and at the time of his return with his son?

3. Many of the descriptive passages in this essay convey a dominant impression, usually an emotion or mood. Discuss how the author's choice of details and the author's comments suggest that the impressions are more a reflection of the observer's perspective than an objective description of the lake. (Guide: *Syntax; Diction.*)

4. In many places the author combines description and comparison. Select a passage from the essay and discuss in detail how he combines the patterns. In what ways is the combination of description and comparison appropriate to the theme and the point of view of the essay?

DICTION AND VOCABULARY

1. How much do the connotations of the words used in Paragraph 8 contribute to the dominant impression the author is trying to create? (Guide: *Connotation/Denotation.*) In Paragraph 10? What do these connotations suggest about the relation of person to place? Of observer to subject of observation?

2. Is the diction in this passage sentimental: "Summertime, oh, summertime, pattern of life indelible, the fade-proof lake, the woods unshatterable, the pasture with the sweetfern and the juniper forever and ever, summer without end. . . ." (Par. 8)? (Guide: *Sentimentality.*) If so, why would the author choose to use this style in the passage? Does the passage contain an allusion? If so, what is alluded to and why? (Guide: *Figures of Speech.*)

3. In what sense can a tennis court steam "with midday heat and hunger and emptiness" (Par. 7)?

4. What kind of paradox is presented in this passage: "the waitresses were the same country girls, there having been no passage of time, only the illusion of it as in a dropped curtain—the waitresses were still fifteen; their hair had been washed, that was the only difference—they had been to the movies and seen the pretty girls with the clean hair" (Par. 7)? (Guide: *Paradox.*)

5. Study the author's uses of the following words, consulting the dictionary as needed: incessant, placidity (Par. 1); gunwale (2); primeval (3); transposition (4); helgramite, pensively (5); petulant (10); premonitory (12); languidly (13).

READ TO WRITE

1. **Collaborating:** Working with a group, make a list of your memorable vacations and holidays, then choose three and develop for each a tentative thesis statement that sums up the meaning of the event.

2. **Considering Audience:** In his descriptions, White creates symbols to convey his ideas about the passing of time. How else might readers respond to the incidents White describes? To what extent might responses be shaped by differing religious, social, economic, or cultural backgrounds? Prepare a short essay considering the possible range of reactions.

3. **Developing an Essay:** Drawing on the strategies White employs in "Once More to the Lake," choose some place you remember from your childhood and have seen recently, and write a description of it comparing its present appearance with your memories of it. As you write, take into account the relationships of place and person, permanence and change, and the effect of experience on perception.

(NOTE: Suggestions for topics requiring development by use of DESCRIPTION follow.)

Writing Suggestions for Chapter 10

DESCRIPTION

1. Primarily by way of impressionistic description that focuses on a single dominant impression, show and explain the mood or atmosphere of one of the following:

   a. A country fair

   b. A ball game

   c. A rodeo

   d. A wedding

   e. A funeral

   f. A busy store

   g. A ghost town

   h. A cave

   i. A beach in summer (or winter)

   j. An antique shop

   k. A party

   l. A family dinner

   m. A traffic jam

   n. Reveille

   o. An airport (or a bus depot)

   p. An automobile race (or a horse race)

   q. A home during one of its rush hours

   r. The last night of holiday shopping

   s. A natural scene at a certain time of day

   t. The campus at examination time

   u. A certain person at a time of great emotion—for example, joy, anger, or grief

2. Using objective description as your basic pattern, explain the functional qualities or the significance of one of the following:

   a. A house for sale

   b. A public building

   c. A dairy barn

   d. An ideal workshop (or hobby room)

   e. An ideal garage

    f. A fast-food restaurant

    g. The layout of a town (or airport)

    h. The layout of a farm

    i. A certain type of boat

    j. A sports complex

COLLABORATIVE EXERCISES

1. Have each member of your team brainstorm a list of words that describe the mood or atmosphere he or she feels when attending any one of the events listed in 1 a–c. From your individual lists, look for similar experiences and moods. Collaboratively write an essay based on one of those events and the team similarities.

2. Have each member of the group describe a designated building on campus. Compare and contrast your descriptions.

3. Consider an ideal gymnasium or dormitory. Have each student in the group research this building by talking to other students on campus. Share your results and write a collaborative essay incorporating each member's research.

11

Using *Narration* as an Expository Technique

When is narration a pattern of exposition rather than a story told for its own purposes? The answer: when it serves to explain a subject, present conclusions, or support an interpretation or a thesis. For example, a writer who wishes to explain the role of risk-taking individuals (rather than corporations) in developing new ideas and products might tell the story of an entrepreneur who perfected the frozen French fry in the early 1950s only to discover that there was little demand for his product. The story would emphasize his perseverance in struggling to develop a market for the product—a perseverance that paid off for all concerned a decade later when the rapidly growing fast-food industry discovered the usefulness of frozen fries for ready-in-a-minute menus.

Whether you use narration as the pattern for an entire essay or for support and explanation within an essay, your readers will expect you to do certain things. They will expect your narrative to help them understand *what happened*, including the *who, where, what,* and *to whom* of events. They will expect the narrative to *re-create* events, showing (through concrete detail or the actual words of participants) rather than merely telling what happened (through summary). Finally, your readers will expect your narrative to help them understand the *significance* of the events. They will look for the point you are making, for what you have to say about the events, or for the way the events support your thesis.

In a book explaining the extraordinary character and physical courage of early Antarctic explorers, the writer Edwin Mickleburgh offers the following narrative to support his thesis about the explorer

Ernest Shackleton's abilities as a leader and about the courage of his crew.

> For anyone who has looked up from the sullen South Georgia shore [an island near Antarctica] towards the soaring, razor-edged peaks and the terrible chaos of glaciers topped by swirling clouds and scoured by mighty winds, the knowledge of the crossing made by these three men adds a wider dimension to an already awe inspiring sight. How they did it, God only knows, but they crossed the island in thirty-six hours. They were fortunate that the weather held, although many times great banks of fog rolled in from the open sea, creeping toward them over the snow and threatening to obscure their way. Confronted by precipices of ice and walls of rock they had often to retrace their steps adding many miles to the journey. They walked almost without rest. At one point they sat down in an icy gully, the wind blowing the drift around them, and so tired were they that Worseley and Crean fell asleep immediately. Shackleton, barely able to keep himself awake, realized that to fall asleep under such conditions would prove fatal. After five minutes he woke the other two, saying that they had slept for half an hour.

Introduces narrative and its relation to writer's main point

Narrative

—Edwin Mickleburgh,
Beyond the Frozen Sea: Visions of Antarctica

WHY USE NARRATION?

Perhaps the most familiar form of expository narrative is the personal narrative, based on personal experience or observation, that offers insights into events or conclusions about relationships and the importance of certain kinds of experience. These include memoirs focusing on the author's personal and intellectual development, on an unusual and significant childhood event, or on other experiences. They include autobiographies of media stars, politicians, and other well-known people, especially those that shed light on the fields in which they have worked or on the important events they have witnessed. And they include personal narratives embedded in other kinds of works in order to give the works a sense of authenticity.

Another use of narrative is to present a profile on an unfamiliar or unusual activity or the people involved in it. Typically, such a narrative begins by presenting an interesting person in action (a day in the life of a computer game creator, for example) or by focusing on an activity (workers changing light bulbs on the spire of the Empire State Building; divers searching in deep water for wreckage from an airplane crash). As a way of creating drama and interest, such narratives frequently reveal surprising tensions or contradictions, such as the quiet home life and personal kindness of an off-shore boat racer also known for his fearlessness, abrasiveness, spectacular crashes, and narrow escapes from death.

A narrative can also provide a framework for commentary and analysis, with passages of narrative interspersed with discussions of the significance and implications of the events. Or narratives can add convincing detail or emotional force to explanations built around some other expository pattern, such as comparison (Chapter 5), cause-and-effect (Chapter 8), or definition (Chapter 9).

CHOOSING A STRATEGY

A narrative is a chronological account of events. You do not always have to present the events in chronological order or give them all equal emphasis. When you are creating an event for expository purposes, begin your planning process with questions like these:

- What events are most important to my purpose for writing?
- What ideas and emotions surrounding the events are worth sharing with my readers?
- What point do I want to make with this narrative?

Your answers to questions like these should help you limit the time frame of your narrative and focus on the most important events of the story. Many writers are gripped by a compulsion to get all the details of a story down—important and unimportant. Radical surgery often helps. Instead of covering a whole week or day, consider focusing on the single most important incident—the four or five minutes when all the forces came together—and summarizing the rest.

Remember that you can arrange the events to suit your purpose(s). In basic form, a narrative sets the scene; introduces characters; presents, in chronological order, episodes that introduce a conflict or prepare for the central event; then, finally, explores in detail the most important incident in which the conflict is resolved or the writer's outlook is made clear. Yet the chronological approach can make it hard to emphasize the most important element. You may instead want to start in the middle of things, perhaps at the climactic episode, and fill in prior events through flashbacks. Or you might stop in the middle of events to provide important background information or comment on the characters and their actions.

And you need to choose whether to provide an explicit thesis statement to organize your narrative and direct commentary on the events, or to let the events speak for themselves, assuming that their relationship to your main point will be sufficiently clear to readers.

DEVELOPING A NARRATIVE

As you draft and revise a narrative, pay attention to the following concerns that can contribute to the success (or failure) of your efforts.

- **Selection of Details.** You will probably have many more details you might include in a narrative than you need. Keep in mind that too many details can overwhelm readers, making them lose sight about the point the narrative is making or the explanation it is offering. Focused, unified writing makes use only of those details that are most relevant to the writer's purpose and desired effect. Whenever possible, try to include concrete, specific details that make the narrative vivid and believable and that will be likely to hold your readers' interest.
- **Time Order.** You can employ straight chronology, relating events as they happened, or the flashback method, leaving the sequence temporarily in order to go back and relate some now-significant happening of a time prior to the main action. If you use flashback, do so deliberately, not merely because you neglected to mention the episode earlier.
- **Transitions.** Watch out for overly simple and repetitive transitions between events in the narrative: "And then we. . . . And then she. . . . And then we . . . ." As you revise, make a conscious effort to create variety in transitions: "next," "following," "subsequently," "as a consequence," "reacting to," "later," "meanwhile," "at the same time," "concurrently," and the like.
- **Point of View.** Decide whether you want to tell the story from the point of view of a participant, such as yourself or a character, or from the overall perspective of a spectator. The vividness and immediacy possible from a participant's point of view can make

the narrative more dramatic, but the spectator's point of view can allow for an easier transition from narrative to commentary and may be especially useful in expository writing. Whichever point of view you choose, keep it consistent throughout the narrative.

- **Dialogue.** Remember that quoting the words of participants can help make narrative more convincing and dialogue, which can reveal conflicting perspectives among the participants, can also be a springboard to your commentary on the meaning of the events.

Student Essay

One important use of narrative in expository writing is to explore values and the ways they change. In the following essay, Hrishikesh Unni uses flashback and a dream sequence to explain a set of personal values—love of ivory and of ivory carvings—that may be unfamiliar to many of his readers. He then returns to the main narrative of his encounter with a herd of elephants in Zambia and uses it to explain his change in attitude toward ivory collecting.

Elephants, Ivory, and an Indelible Experience

by Hrishikesh Unni

The roar of the engine increased to a crescendo as the driver revved the engine of the open van. This sound broke the monotonous atmosphere of the dry and deserted African grassland of the Luangwa Valley in Zambia and made me shift in my rear seat. I had been sitting there for at least three hours since noon and had not seen any game, apart from the impala and zebra that intermittently spotted the grasslands. These creatures are a common sight in all national parks in Zambia, including the Luangwa. The drought had taken its toll. What was once a land filled with green vegetation was turned into a brown and heavily scorched area by the menacing October sun that was callously beating down on my back. I clutched my Canon camera even more firmly and could feel the heat radiating from the surface of its black case.

> *Opening incident— starts in the middle of events*
>
> *Unusual, exotic—gets readers' attention*
>
> *Appeals to senses*

"You sure are unlucky, aren't you, Hrishi? No elephants yet!" said Musa, the guide, who was the only other person in the spacious van besides Banda.

> *Uses quotation*

Banda was a local driver who could only speak the local language, Nyanga. I merely nodded to this statement, admitting my disappointment. I had come all the way from Ndola (another town in Zambia) to see the well-known elephants of the Luangwa National Park. I had given up hope because it was the third and final day of my visit, and I had not seen any so far. What irritated me was the fact that I had lost a long-awaited opportunity to see these beasts. To overcome my disappointment, I looked at the metallic body of the van that was painted white. It blazed in the sun and blinded my eyes. It reminded me of something I had once loved and treasured: ivory.

Fills in background of events

I had an affinity for ivory. I loved its color, texture, and appearance. My positive feelings for this substance had begun after I received my first ivory carving for my ninth birthday from a Zambian friend. It was a superb carving of a baby elephant, and I instantly liked it. I would gaze at it, admiring its dominant white color and its smooth texture. Also, its different shades of light brown never seemed to bore me. Since receiving that gift, I had bought every ivory item I could get my hands on and had a magnificent collection that I kept in my room.

Uses key word to set off flashbacks

Introduces his values

Flashbacks— source of values

My eyes could no longer take the glare and in an attempt to reduce the strain, I allowed my eyelids to drop over them. I realized how tired I was when I closed my eyes. Every muscle in my body seemed to be screaming in desperation, ordering my brain to sleep. I felt sleep gradually overtake me like an ivy conquering an old dilapidated castle. Soon I was fast asleep and dreaming of the time. . . .

Back to main narrative

Dream event

I entered my room and switched on my titanium-white tube light. I stared in awe as the light fell on my ivory collection, enhancing its already immaculate white coating. The furniture in my room consisted of a bed, a table, a chair, and a couple of shelves that were attached to the wall. It was decorated with my extravagant ivory collection. I stood at the doorway and began surveying the room, casting my eyes on each and every piece of ivory. I admired and absorbed every detail of the carvings and was aware of the hours of work involved in creating a single delicate carving from a long curved elephant tusk. The dexterity and skill the African craftsmen possessed amazed me, and I never got tired of looking at my collection. I saw a variety of things: old traditional men, dogs, a range of birds, daggers, kudu, impala, elephants, rhino, leopards, cheetahs—all in ivory. My eyes finally came to rest on the carving I admired the most—an elephant bull, which I had named Tusker Bull. It was the largest piece I had. Its place on the highest shelf and its majestic posture gave it an authority over the other animals in my collection. Its ominous, evil eyes and its cocked ears portrayed tyranny. I had a sudden urge to look into its lifeless eye. I daringly did this and saw a look I had never seen before. It was one of anger and rage. This look sent a chill down my spine as I wondered if my imagination was mocking me. The look in its eye seemed to be saying. . . .

Explains values; love of ivory helps readers understand appeal of art that may be unfamiliar to them

"Wake up, Hrishi, elephants!" shouted the guide.

I awoke with a jump, expecting to see my room, but the heat waves of the national park that enveloped me made me aware that I was a long way away from there. The painful process of adjusting to the amber sunlight took quite a while. The sky was an orange-yellow, and the ground seemed to have darkened to a beige color. It was nearly dusk, and I realized I had been sleeping for at least two hours. Musa repeated the word "elephant," the word I longed to hear. I knew he had spotted a couple of them.

Brief transition paragraph

Back to main narrative

"Where?" I asked anxiously.

He pointed in between two brown-colored thickets and said, "By that dry waterhole."

He was right, and I could see the posterior of two African elephants. I could not see the entire waterhole because the dry trees and scrub that had adapted to drought conditions partially obliterated our view. I was filled with excitement as images of elephants and my ivory collection flashed in my mind. I quickly set my camera to "operate" as the driver steered the van toward the elephants. We took an unorthodox and meandering path toward the elephants. As the van cut through the dry scrub, I could hear the twigs being crushed by its enormous tires and the dry grass, grazing and caressing the sides of the van. We finally reached the brown-colored thicket, and the driver deftly steered around it enabling us to see the entire expanse of the waterhole that merely had shallow puddles of water.

What we saw shocked us. There were not two elephants; there were two thousand of them! From where we were before, we could only get a glimpse of this enormous herd.

"What a sight! Ten years in this business, and I have not seen this many at once!" exclaimed Musa.

"Hitut, hitut!" said Banda, in awe.

Everywhere I looked, I only saw elephants. They completely superimposed the entire landscape, which now looked like a dark gray Persian carpet. The faint sunlight that reflected off the elephants transformed the color of their bodies to a stone-gray. It was an absolutely fantastic and awesome sight! I began surveying them in the manner I surveyed my ivory collection in my dream, slowly and meticulously, but this time I wasn't looking at elephant ivory carvings but at real elephants. My eyes swept across the herd, and I was amazed at the unique behavior of each individual elephant I saw. There were numerous bulls with gigantic tusks. Their white tusks contrasted with their black bodies and made me think of ivory. From our position the tusks looked like curved toothpicks. The females were nurturing and tending to their playful calves. The elephants were of different sizes, but all the bulls were above eleven feet. Their postures conveyed a strong sense of magnanimity as they marched slowly in unison, every step serving a purpose. I admired the ease with which they moved, taking all the time in the world. They deliberately swung their trunks from side to side, like pendulums, and their tails moved naturally to their

Experience of seeing elephants more dramatic and moving than their representations in ivory

rhythmic walk. The mild deep grunts of the bulls were amplified by the wind that blew toward us. This natural sound enabled them to coax the members of the herd that were extremely slow. The pitch of this sound was lower than the sound the baby elephants made, which was like notes played on a trumpet that was not in tune. The calves pranced around playfully and used their trunks to mock and tease each other, not aware of their vulnerability to predators. A huge bull raised its head and arched its trunk in a form of imperious salute. He was definitely the largest and seemed to be leading the herd, ready to admonish the herd of any potential danger. I wanted a photo of this elephant.

Concrete details appeal to senses throughout narrative

"Let's get closer, I want a photo of that bull," I said, pointing to the conspicuous animal.

Dialogue

"I think we'll be asking for trouble if we get any closer. This herd is definitely overprotective because there are so many young," replied Musa.

"Oh, come on, this is the only opportunity we've had of seeing so many elephants. I mean, this is a rare sight, and we haven't seen any all day. I want that bull. We must get closer," I persisted.

Musa and Banda conversed in the local language about my idea. I could tell Banda was not pleased, but finally he reluctantly nodded his head in apparent consent.

"Okay, but Banda says only a couple of meters," he said firmly.

I gave them both a "thumbs up" sign showing my appreciation. Banda furtively drove the van toward the herd that had not noticed us yet, and he stopped near it. As a precaution he left the engine on and did not remove his foot from the accelerator, establishing a ready position to take off if something went terribly wrong. From the expressions on Banda's and Musa's faces, I could tell that they were not pleased. I was told that the elephants were used to the sound of the van, and if you maintained a safe distance, you would be fine even if they were aware of you. I knew the elephants had seen us because some turned their heads in our direction.

Now we were a dangerous fifteen meters from the herd, and I was now in a position to take a photo of the largest elephant that was closer to us than the rest of the herd. I set the flash on my camera and peered at the bull through the eyepiece. It was out of focus, and I had the lateral view of the elephant. I quickly brought it into focus and waited, hoping it would turn toward me. I had to wait for approximately forty seconds until the moment I longed for arrived, but it was a moment I have never forgotten to this day. The bull turned its head towards me, and I stared into its eye the way I stared into the eye of the elephant carving in my dream. I saw the same look of rage and anger in its eye. The menacing look seemed to be accusing me of an unforgivable crime I seemed to have committed. I avoided its eyes and pressed the button on my camera. This was a big mistake because the flash disturbed the elephant, and it let out an ear-shattering sound that I had never heard before. This sound seemed to be the warning alarm because it caused the whole herd to simultaneously bellow in this fashion. It sounded like a loud never-ending echo, which punished our ears. The ground reverberated beneath us as they moved impetuously and tried to form a cordon around their young. There were so many of them, causing them to nearly trample on each other. Some began running away from us, while others advanced toward us, their ears flapping rapidly and fervently in a form of defense. What had once been a calm and benign atmosphere turned into a calamitous one at the push of a camera button.

Link to dream sequence— effect on his values

I was speechless and could hear Musa shouting, "Tieni, tieni fast!" to the driver. Instinctively, Banda slammed the foot on the accelerator causing the engine to roar strongly, but this sound was barely audible due to the louder angry grunts of the elephants. He then turned the van away from the herd in an attempt to reach safety.

"Abuil abuil ei tiuti hamba isa tieni tieni fast!" shouted Musa frantically to Banda as he ducked below a seat. I did not know what this had meant, but I soon

Dramatic climax of narrative

found out. The massive bull, which I had tried to photo-graph, began charging at us from the rear, flapping its ears vigorously and grunting vehemently. Its tusks were raised, like a tank with two white-colored barrels, ready for battle. I had a clear view of its tusks and they made me think of ivory—yet not as a smooth and attractive substance, as I once did, but as something dangerous to be in possession of. Now the thought of ivory did not amaze me but frightened me. I have never seen ivory the same way since that day. At that moment, the im-age of Tusker Bull, my biggest piece in the ivory collec-tion, flashed into my mind. It seemed as if it had come alive and was after me. I was surprised at the pace the bull was running because I didn't expect such a large animal to run at such a fast speed. I honestly thought I was going to die and was terrified because it was merely ten feet away from the van and was gaining on us. I held on to the side of the van and shut my eyes, not looking behind me. Yet, I could see the elephant in my mind, charging angrily at us. Banda was doing his best to escape from this animal, but his efforts seemed to be futile.

> Reference to dream sequence and to underlying discussion of values

It seemed hours had passed when suddenly Musa yelled in relief, "It's stopped! It's stopped!" pointing at the elephant that had become stationary.

It gave an indignant salute that meant to say, "Don't ever come near my herd again. We are much more powerful than you."

> Warning symbolic of writer's changed perspectives

"Hiny in hyi it fl,ungo," replied Banda in a tone of relief.

"Are you all right?" Musa asked me.

Since I was in a state of shock, I did not say a word and merely nodded.

"We'll be at the lodge soon so don't worry. It's over, and everything will be all right," said Musa.

I responded to him with a slight smile and then closed my eyes, while thinking of my close brush with death. The roar of the engine increased to a crescendo as the driver revved the engine of the open van and

followed the dusty route to Mfuwe Lodge of the
Luangwa National Park of Zambia.

The ten-minute encounter with the elephants and the
charging bull changed my perspective of elephants and
gave me second thoughts about collecting ivory. This
frightening experience made me aware of how protective an elephant community is and of the similarities in
its character to that of a human society. It was during
this time that I realized the natural power these animals
possess and that a human is only able to overpower
them with the use of guns and other weapons. My respect for these animals and nature in general has increased. I felt that the elephants were trying to make
me aware of the cruelty of people and how they have
killed elephants to get ivory. Just the fact that I collected ivory betrayed my insensitivity toward these creatures. I burned my collection when I got home, and now
I am no longer interested in collecting ivory. Now I
don't value my collection in terms of money but in terms
of the amount of life that was wasted in obtaining every
piece that was present in my collection. I was taught a
lesson by the victims that I feel is the best way to be
punished. I will never collect ivory again, and I am planning to become part of the organization that plans to
ban ivory and abolish poaching. Yes, the actual substance of ivory I will continue to admire, but differently,
because I now think that ivory looks best on an elephant
and not as carvings placed on a shelf in my room.

*Discussion of
changed
values—
summarizes
main ideas of
essay*

MARTIN GANSBERG

> Martin Gansberg was born in Brooklyn, New York, in 1920 and re-
> ceived a Bachelor of Social Sciences degree from St. John's
> University. He has been an editor and reporter for the *New York
> Times,* including a three-year period as editor of its international
> edition in Paris. He also served on the faculty of Fairleigh Dickinson
> University. Gansberg has written for many magazines, including
> *Diplomat, Catholic Digest, Facts,* and *U.S. Lady.*

38 Who Saw Murder Didn't Call the Police

> "38 Who Saw Murder . . ." was written for the *New York Times* in
> 1964, and for obvious reasons it has been anthologized frequently
> since then. Cast in a deceptively simple news style, it still provides
> material for serious thought, as well as a means of studying the use
> and technique of narration.

For more than half an hour 38 respectable, law-abiding citizens in   1
Queens watched a killer stalk and stab a woman in three separate attacks in Kew Gardens.

Twice their chatter and the sudden glow of their bedroom lights   2
interrupted him and frightened him off. Each time he returned,
sought her out, and stabbed her again. Not one person telephoned
the police during the assault; one witness called after the woman
was dead.

That was two weeks ago today.   3

Still shocked is Assistant Chief Inspector Frederick M. Lussen,   4
in charge of the borough's detectives and a veteran of 25 years of
homicide investigations. He can give a matter-of-fact recitation on
many murders. But the Kew Gardens slaying baffles him—not because it is a murder, but because the "good people" failed to call
the police.

"As we have reconstructed the crime," he said, "the assailant   5
had three chances to kill this woman during a 35-minute period. He
returned twice to complete the job. If we had been called when he
first attacked, the woman might not be dead now."

This is what the police say happened beginning at 3:20 A.M. in   6
the staid, middle-class, tree-lined Austin Street area:

Twenty-eight-year-old Catherine Genovese, who was called Kitty   7
by almost everyone in the neighborhood, was returning home from

her job as manager of a bar in Hollis. She parked her red Fiat in a lot adjacent to the Kew Gardens Long Island Rail Road Station, facing Mowbray Place. Like many residents of the neighborhood, she had parked there day after day since her arrival from Connecticut a year ago, although the railroad frowns on the practice.

She turned off the lights of her car, locked the door, and started to walk the 100 feet to the entrance of her apartment at 82–70 Austin Street, which is in a Tudor building, with stores in the first floor and apartments on the second.   8

The entrance to the apartment is in the rear of the building because the front is rented to retail stores. At night the quiet neighborhood is shrouded in the slumbering darkness that marks most residential areas.   9

Miss Genovese noticed a man at the far end of the lot, near a seven-story apartment house at 82–40 Austin Street. She halted. Then, nervously, she headed up Austin Street toward Lefferts Boulevard, where there is a call box to the 102nd Police Precinct in nearby Richmond Hill.   10

She got as far as a street light in front of a bookstore before the man grabbed her. She screamed. Lights went on in the 10-story apartment house at 82–67 Austin Street, which faces the bookstore. Windows slid open and voices punctuated the early-morning stillness.   11

Miss Genovese screamed: "Oh, my God, he stabbed me! Please help me! Please help me!"   12

From one of the upper windows in the apartment house, a man called down: "Let that girl alone!"   13

The assailant looked up at him, shrugged and walked down Austin Street toward a white sedan parked a short distance away. Miss Genovese struggled to her feet.   14

Lights went out. The killer returned to Miss Genovese, now trying to make her way around the side of the building by the parking lot to get to her apartment. The assailant stabbed her again.   15

"I'm dying!" she shrieked, "I'm dying!"   16

Windows were opened again, and lights went on in many apartments. The assailant got into his car and drove away. Miss Genovese staggered to her feet. A city bus, Q-10, the Lefferts Boulevard line to Kennedy International Airport, passed. It was 3:35 A.M.   17

The assailant returned. By then, Miss Genovese had crawled to the back of the building, where the freshly painted brown doors to the apartment house held out hope for safety. The killer tried the first door; she wasn't there. At the second door, 82–62 Austin Street,   18 he saw her slumped on the floor at the foot of the stairs. He stabbed her a third time—fatally.

It was 3:50 by the time the police received their first call, from a   19
man who was a neighbor of Miss Genovese. In two minutes they were at the scene. The neighbor, a 70-year-old woman, and another woman were the only persons on the street. Nobody else came forward.

The man explained that he had called the police after much de-   20
liberation. He had phoned a friend in Nassau County for advice and then he had crossed the roof of the building to the apartment of the elderly woman to get her to make the call.

"I didn't want to get involved," he sheepishly told the police.   21

Six days later, the police arrested Winston Moseley, a 29-year-   22
old business-machine operator, and charged him with homicide. Moseley had no previous record. He is married, has two children and owns a home at 133–19 Sutter Avenue, South Ozone Park, Queens. On Wednesday, a court committed him to Kings County Hospital for psychiatric observation.

When questioned by the police, Moseley also said that he had   23
slain Mrs. Annie May Johnson, 24, of 146–12 133rd Avenue, Jamaica, on Feb. 29 and Barbara Kralik, 15, of 174–17 140th Avenue, Springfield Gardens, last July. In the Kralik case, the police are holding Alvin L. Mitchell, who is said to have confessed to that slaying.

The police stressed how simple it would have been to have got-   24
ten in touch with them. "A phone call," said one of the detectives, "would have done it." The police may be reached by dialing "O" for operator or SPring 7–3100.

Today witnesses from the neighborhood, which is made up of   25
one-family homes in the $35,000 to $60,000 range with the exception of the two apartment houses near the railroad station, find it diffi-cult to explain why they didn't call the police.

A housewife, knowingly if quite casually, said, "We thought it   26
was a lover's quarrel." A husband and wife both said, "Frankly, we were afraid." They seemed aware of the fact that events might have been different. A distraught woman, wiping her hands on her apron, said, "I didn't want my husband to get involved."

One couple, now willing to talk about that night, said they   27
heard the first screams. The husband looked thoughtfully at the bookstore where the killer first grabbed Miss Genovese.

"We went to the window to see what was happening," he said,   28
"but the light from our bedroom made it difficult to see the street." The wife, still apprehensive, added: "I put out the light and we were able to see better."

Asked why they hadn't called the police, she shrugged and   29
replied: "I don't know."

A man peeked out from the slight opening in the doorway to   30
his apartment and rattled off an account of the killer's second attack.
Why hadn't he called the police at the time? "I was tired," he said
without emotion. "I went back to bed."

It was 4:25 A.M. when the ambulance arrived to take the body of   31
Miss Genovese. It drove off. "Then," a solemn police detective said,
"the people came out."

MEANINGS AND VALUES

1. What is Gansberg's central (expository) theme? How might he have
   developed this theme without using narration at all? Specify what
   patterns of exposition he could have used instead. Would any of them
   have been as effective as narration *for the purpose?* Why, or why not?

2. Why has this narrative account of old news (the murder made its
   only headlines in 1964) retained its significance to this day? Are you
   able to see in this event a paradigm of any larger condition or situation? If so, explain, using examples as needed to illustrate your ideas.

EXPOSITORY TECHNIQUES

1. What standard introductory technique is exemplified in the first
   paragraph? ("Guide to Terms": *Introductions.*) How effective do you
   consider it? If you see anything ironic in the fact stated there, explain
   the irony. (Guide: *Irony.*)

2. Where does the main narration begin? What, then, is the function of
   the preceding paragraphs?

3. Study several of the paragraph transitions within the narration itself
   to determine Gansberg's method of advancing the time sequence (to
   avoid overuse of "and then") What is the technique? Is another
   needed? Why, or why not?

4. What possible reasons do you see for the predominant use of short
   paragraphs in this piece? Does this selection lose any effectiveness
   because of the short paragraphs?

5. Undoubtedly, the author selected with care the few quotations from
   witnesses that he uses. What principle or principles do you think applied to his selection?

6. Explain why you think the quotation from the "solemn police detective" was, or was not, deliberately and carefully chosen to conclude
   the piece. (Guide: *Closings.*)

7.   Briefly identify the point of view of the writing. (Guide: *Point of View.*) Is it consistent throughout? Show the relation, as you see it, between this point of view and the author's apparent attitude toward his subject matter.

DICTION AND VOCABULARY

1.   Why do you think the author used no difficult words in this narration? Do you find the writing at all belittling to college people because of this fact? Why, or why not?

READ TO WRITE

1.   **Collaborating:** Gansberg's narration is written as a news account except that it clearly editorializes about the apathetic attitude of citizens. Working in a group, identify the places in the essay that Gansberg injects his bias. With your group, rewrite those sections where Gansberg expresses his perspective, taking the opposite point of view—supporting people who do not get involved in a situation like the one presented in the essay.

2.   **Considering Audience:** The general plot of this story is as believable for audiences of the twenty-first century as it was for audiences of the 1960s—perhaps even more so because levels of violence in society have increased in the intervening decades. However, how might the behaviors of the people involved have been different if the incident had occurred today? Write out your answer and a brief explanation of it.

3.   **Developing an Essay:** Though he certainly has his own view of the events he reports, Gansberg allows readers to question the motivations of the observers and to make their own judgments about the lack of involvement. Prepare an account of some incident you witnessed and use a similar approach. Call attention to the various motivations expressed by the participants, to any inconsistencies in their behavior, and to any other elements you wish readers to analyze and question. The event itself need not be of more than local significance (an account of a meeting or a sports event can offer interesting insights, for example), but your exposition should offer readers insights worth considering.

(NOTE: Suggestions for topics requiring development by NARRATION are on pp. 513–514 at the end of this chapter.)

GEOFFREY CANADA

GEOFFREY CANADA is the President/CEO of the Harlem Children's
Zone in New York City.

Pain

"Pain," an excerpt from the book *Reaching Up for Manhood,* draws on
the writer's training and experience as a psychologist. He uses the
narrative to explain the power of memory in our lives, especially
memory of painful experiences. His particular focus is on boys and
on the ways they are taught to repress the wounds caused by
painful experiences. Nonetheless, it should be easy for readers to
apply his insights to the experiences of girls.

Boys are taught to suffer their wounds in silence. To pretend that 1
it doesn't hurt, outside or inside. So many of them carry the
scars of childhood into adulthood, never having come to grips
with the pain, the anger, the fear. And that pain can change boys
and bring doubts into their lives, though more often than not they
have no idea where those doubts come from. Pain can make you
afraid to love or cause you to doubt the safety of the ground you
walk on. I know from my own experience that some pain changes
us forever.

It all started because there was no grass. Actually, there was 2
grass, you just couldn't walk on it.

In the late fifties and early sixties, the projects were places peo- 3
ple moved to get away from tenement buildings like mine. We
couldn't move into the projects because my mother was a single parent. Today most projects are crammed full of single parents, but
when I was a child your application for the projects was automatically rejected if that was your situation. The projects were places for
people on the way up. They had elevators, they were well maintained, and they had grass surrounding them. Grass like we had
never seen before. The kind of grass that was like walking on carpet.
Grass that yelled out to little girls and boys to run and tumble and
do cartwheels and roll around on it. There was just one problem, it
was off limits to people. All the projects had signs that said "Keep
Off the Grass." And there were men keeping their eyes open for children who dared even think of crossing the single-link chain that en-

closed it. The projects didn't literally have the only grass we could find in the Bronx. Crotona Park, Pelham Bay Park, and Van Cortland Park were available to us. But the grass in those parks was a sparse covering for dirt, rocks, and twigs. You would never think about rolling around in that grass, because if you did you'd likely be rolling in dog excrement or over a hard rock.

There was one other place where we found grass in our neigh-   4
borhood. Real grass. Lawn-like grass. It was in the side yard of a small church that was on the corner of Union Avenue and Home Street. The church was small and only open on Sundays. The yard and its precious grass were enclosed by a four-foot-high fence. We were not allowed in the yard by the pastor of the church.

Occasionally we would sneak in to retrieve a small pink   5
Spaulding ball that had gone off course during a game of stickball or punch ball, but if we were seen climbing the fence there would be a scene, with screams, yells, and threats to tell our parents. So although we often looked at that soft grass with longing, the church-yard was off limits.

It would have stayed off limits if it had not been for football.   6
Football came into my life one fall when I was nine years old, and I played it every fall for the rest of my childhood and adolescence. But football in the inner city looked very different than football played other places. The sewer manhole covers were the end zones. Anywhere in the street was legal playing territory, but not the side-walk. There could be no tackling on pavement, so the game was called two-hand touch. If you touched an opponent with both hands, play had to stop. The quarterback called colorful plays: "Okay now. David, you go right in front of the blue Chevy. I'm gonna fake it to you. Geoff, see the black Ford on the right? No, don't look, stupid—they're gonna know our play. You go there, stop, then cross over toward William's stoop. I'll look for you short. Richard, go to the first sewer and turn around and stop. I'll pump it to you, go long, Geoff, you hike on three. Ready! Break!"

All we needed was grass. All our eyes were drawn to the   7
churchyard. A decision had to be made. Rory was the first to bring it up. "We should sneak into the churchyard and play tackle."

We all walked over to Home Street and, out of sight of front   8
windows, climbed over the fence and walked onto the grass. A thick carpet of grass that felt like falling on a mattress. We were in heaven.

Football in the churchyard was everything we had imagined.   9
We could finally block and tackle and not worry about falling on the

hard concrete or asphalt streets. We didn't have to worry about cars coming down the block the way we did when we played two-hand touch. And because we were able to tackle, we could have running plays. We loved it. We played for hours on end.

There was one problem with our football field, which was   10
about thirty yards long and fifteen yards wide: at the far end there was a built-in barbecue pit, right in the middle of the end zone. If we were running with the football, or going out for a pass, we had to avoid the barbecue pit with its metal rods along the top, set into its concrete sides. We knew that no matter what you were doing when in that area of the yard, you had to keep one eye on the barbecue pit. To run into its concrete sides—or, even worse, the metal bars— would be very painful and dangerous.

I was fast and crafty. I loved to play split end on the offense. I   11
could fake out the other kids and get free to catch the ball. I had one problem, though—I hadn't mastered catching a football thrown over my head. To do this you have to lean your head back and watch as the football descends into your hands. Keep your eye on the ball, that's the trick to catching one over the shoulder. We all wanted to go deep for "the bomb"—a ball thrown as far as possible, where a receiver's job is to run full speed and catch it with out-stretched hands. It took me forever to learn to concentrate on the football, with my head back as far as it would go, while running full speed. But finally I mastered it. I was now a truly dangerous receiver. If you played too far away from me I could catch the ball short, and if you came too close I could run right by the slower boys and catch the bomb.

The move I did on Ned was picture perfect. I ran ten yards,   12
turned around, and faced Walter. He pumped the ball to me. I felt Ned take a step forward, going for the fake as I turned and ran right by him. Walter launched the bomb. As the football left his hand I stopped looking over my shoulder at him and started my sprint to the end zone. After running ten yards I tilted my head back and looked up at the bright blue fall sky. Nothing. I looked forward again and ran harder, then looked up again. There it was, the brown leather football falling in a perfect arc toward the earth, toward where I would be in three seconds, toward the winning touchdown.

And then pain. The bar of the barbecue pit caught me in mid-   13
stride in the middle of my shin. I went down in a flurry of ashes, legs and arms flying every which way. The pain was all-enveloping. I grabbed my leg above and below where it had hit; I couldn't bear to

touch the place where it had slammed into the bar. The pain was too much. I lay flat on the ground, trying to cry out. I could only make a humming sound deep in the back of my throat. My friends gathered around and I tried to act like a big boy, the way I had been taught. I tried not to cry. Then the pain consumed me and I couldn't see any of my friends anymore. I howled and then cried and then howled some more. The boys saw the blood seeping through my dungarees and my brother John said, "Let me see. Be still. Let me see." He rolled my pants leg up to my knee to look at the damage. All the other boys who had been playing or watching were in a circle around me. They all grimaced and turned away. I knew it was bad then, and I howled louder.

Catching the metal bar in full stride with my shin had crushed a   14
quarter-sized hole in my leg. The skin was missing and even to this day I can feel the indentation in my shinbone where the bar gouged out a small piece of bone. I was off my feet for a few days and it took about two weeks for my shin to heal completely. Still, I was at the age where sports and friends meant everything to me. I couldn't wait to play football in the churchyard again, but I was a much more cautious receiver than before.

Several years later, when I finished the ninth grade at a junior   15
high school in the South Bronx and was preparing to go to high school, I knew that my life had reached a critical juncture. My high school prospects were grim. I didn't pass the test to get into the Bronx High School of Science (I was more interested in girls than prep work), so my choices were either Morris High School or Clinton High School. Both of these were poor academically and suffered from a high incidence of violence. I asked my mother if I could stay with my grandparents in the house they had just built in Wyandanch, a quiet, mostly African-American town on Long Island. She agreed and they agreed, so I went there for my three years of high school.

That first year I went out for the junior varsity football team at   16
Wyandanch High and played football as a receiver. I was a good receiver. The years of faking out kids on the narrow streets of the Bronx made me so deceptive that I couldn't be covered in the wide-open area of a real football field. But I had one problem—I couldn't catch the bomb. My coach would scream at me after the ball had slipped through my fingers or bounced off my hands. "Geoff! What's the matter with you? Concentrate, goddamn it! Concentrate!" I couldn't. No matter how I tried to focus on the ball coming down out of the sky, at the last minute I would have

to look down. To make sure the ground wasn't playing tricks on me. No hidden booby traps. What happened in the churchyard would flash into my mind and even though I knew I was in a wide-open field, I'd have to glance down at the ground. I never made it as a receiver in high school. I finished my career as quarterback. Better to be looking at your opponent, knowing he wanted to tackle you, sometimes even getting hit without seeing it coming, but at least being aware of that possibility. Never again falling into the trap of thinking you were safe, running free, only you and the sky and a brown leather ball dropping from it.

Boys are conditioned not to let on that it hurts, never to say, 17 "I'm still scared." I've written here only about physical trauma, but every day in my work I deal with boys undergoing almost unthinkable mental trauma from violence or drug abuse in the home, or carrying emotional scars from physical abuse or unloving parents. I have come to see that in teaching boys to deny their own pain we inadvertently teach them to deny the pain of others. I believe this is one of the reasons so many men become physically abusive to those they supposedly love. Pain suffered early in life often becomes the wellspring from which rage and anger flow, emotions that can come flooding over the banks of restraint and reason, often drowning those unlucky enough to get caught in their way. We have done our boys an injustice by not helping them to acknowledge their pain. We must remember to tell them "I know it hurts. Come let me hold you. I'll hold you until it stops. And if you find out that the hurt comes back, I'll hold you again. I'll hold you until you're healed."

Boys are taught by coaches to play with pain. They are told by 18 parents that they shouldn't cry. They watch their heroes on the big screen getting punched and kicked and shot, and while these heroes might groan and yell, they never cry. And even some of us who should know better don't go out of our way to make sure our boys know about our pain and tears, and how we have healed ourselves. By sharing this we can give boys models for their own healing and recovery.

Even after I was grown I believed that ignoring pain was part of 19 learning to be a man, that I could get over hurt by simply willing it away. I had forgotten that when I was young I couldn't run in an open field without looking down, that with no one to talk to me about healing, I spent too many years unable to trust the ground beneath my feet.

MEANINGS AND VALUES

1. What is the main expository point (thesis) of the essay, and where does the writer state it? (See "Guide to Terms": *Unity*.)

2. What desires or aspirations did grass represent for the writer as a young man?

3. a. What, according to the writer, are the consequences of painful experiences (physical or emotional) suffered in youth?

    b. Why might the writer have chosen to focus on the consequences of pain for boys? How might the essay's conclusions be applied to or adapted for understanding the experiences of girls?

EXPOSITORY TECHNIQUES

1. Which paragraphs in the essay are devoted primarily to retelling events? Which focus on analyzing the events and generalizing about behavior?

2. Why do you think the writer waited until the end of the essay to offer an extended discussion of the psychological consequences of painful events? Where else in the essay might he have undertaken such an explanation?

3. Discuss the strategies the writer employs to create transitions between the paragraphs in the following pairs: 1 and 2, 5 and 6, 6 and 7, 12 and 13, and 17 and 18.

DICTION AND VOCABULARY

1. Discuss the use of the repetition of the word *pain* and its synonyms in Paragraph 17 to provide emphasis for the writer's main ideas. (Guide: *Emphasis*.)

2. For what purposes does the writer employ repetition and parallel structures in Paragraph 3? (Guide: *Parallel Structures*.)

3. Look up in a dictionary any of the following words with which you are unfamiliar: excrement (Par. 3); grimaced (13); trauma, wellspring (17).

READ TO WRITE

1. **Collaborating:** Working in a group, list and describe briefly the earliest recollections that each group member has of a painful event, either physical or emotional. From the list, choose several that your group finds particularly intriguing and plan a narrative essay around each one.

2.   **Considering Audience:** How might girls' (and womens') experiences of pain differ from the experience described in Canada's essay? Write a brief essay exploring the similarities and differences between boys' and girls' experiences of pain.

3.   **Developing an Essay:** Think of some central event from your youth that continues to affect your behavior today, positively or negatively. Write a narrative similar to Canada's, emphasizing that distinguishing part of your experience and commenting on the way such experiences are likely to affect many other people. To expand your perspective on the events, include your point of view, then and now, and describe the reactions of others to the events.

(NOTE: Suggestions for topics requiring development by NARRATION are on pp. 513–514 at the end of this chapter.)

KUMIKO MAKIHARA

> KUMIKO MAKIHARA has been a correspondent for the Tokyo bureau of *Time* magazine. She continues to write and to live in Tokyo.

Making the Grade

> In some societies, including Japan, the pressures for social confor-
> mity are strong. Outsiders often assume that only two responses
> are possible: conformity or rebellion. As Kumiko Makihara's essay
> explains, however, the reality is more complex. Makihara looks at
> the pressure for conformity from the inside of a society—from the
> point of view of someone struggling to balance unconventional be-
> havior and individual principles against conventional behavior
> and values. Her narrative explores the many complexities and ne-
> gotiations involved in such a struggle, including both compro-
> mises and victories.

When I started inquiring about cram schools for my 5-year-old   1
son's primary-school entrance exams, I knew I would be chastised for starting late. It was May, and most children in Tokyo had
already been studying a year or two for the tests in November. "You
haven't done any preparation yet?" one woman from a major chain
of cram schools asked me. I confessed that I was a single parent
working full time. "Oh, you are on your own," she replied. "A private
school might be difficult."

Single working mothers are increasingly common in Japan but   2
remain a rarity in the exclusive world of primary-school entrance
examinations, where the two-parent family with a stay-at-home
mom is the norm. Most schools consider a single mother too harried
to raise a well-adjusted child and too poor to afford the tuition. For
eight years, my ex-husband and I lived in Berlin, Beijing and
Moscow, where we had adopted our son from Kazakhstan. After
our divorce three years ago, my ex, who is American, stayed abroad
and I came home with Yataro.

Since our return, I still hadn't grown accustomed to being un-   3
derestimated. I kept hoping for the best for Yataro with or without a
father. I was not alone. One aspiring mother put it plainly on an
exam-information Web site fittingly called Espoir: "Can one not enter a private elementary school without a father?" The reply from the
site wasn't encouraging: "The highly competitive schools or schools

for boys and girls of good upbringing would be difficult," adding
that for lower-ranked schools "we don't rule out the possibility."

Of course, Seikei Elementary, the school I was interested in, had   4
five stars. My father is an alumnus, but that wasn't guaranteed to
help. As luck would have it, Seikei is known for denying entrance to
many children of graduates in the name of fairness.

During the next months, several afternoons a week, Yataro at-   5
tended one cram school for his written exam and craft making and
another for sports and more crafts. I relied on my mother and baby
sitters to take him to the schools and often rushed in at the end when
the teachers summarized the lesson and offered pointers to parents.
"Don't take such a big bag to the test," one teacher told me, gestur-
ing toward my briefcase. A handbag and tote were preferred. We
were also instructed to wear dark suits to the schools even if we
were just picking up an application.

These were easy compromises; my divorce was going to be   6
more of a stumbling block. At a lecture on parental interviews, a former private-school teacher advised, "Just explain, before you take
your seat, that you are divorced and therefore had to come to the interview alone." Translation: admit your guilt before being charged.
Two of Yataro's cram-school teachers recommended toning down
our application essay. There was no need to spell out that I was divorced and had adopted Yataro (another quirk considered suspect).
I didn't want to hide facts I felt had shaped Yataro. But was I sacrificing my son's opportunities for some lofty principles? I caved in
and took out the word "divorced" and just said that Yataro and I
lived alone.

In the frenzied run-up to exams, a cram-school teacher asked stu-   7
dents to name what they had eaten for breakfast. Yataro answered:
yogurt, a kiwi and a prune, bread and cheese. "That is an excellent
breakfast, everyone," the teacher exalted. "The school will think,
There is a wonderful mother." Praised as a good mother before a
room of full-time moms, I was beaming.

But later when I was coaching Yataro with another question—   8
"When does your mother praise you?"—he replied, "When I give
the correct response about breakfast." I started to laugh then caught
myself. Here I was twisting truths to come across as the best parent,
and Yataro had called my bluff.

On interview day at Seikei, two days after Yataro took his writ-   9
ten exam, mothers and fathers in nearly identical dark blue or black
suits and children in navy shorts or skirts and white shirts filled the
waiting room. I ran into a business acquaintance and her attractive

husband. I wondered if Yataro had noticed that we were the only pair among threesomes.

First, the children were sent to classrooms where teachers ob-   10
served them in group activities—Seikei's alternative to individual child interviews. Once I was called, I entered a room with three young male teachers. I skipped the suggested apologetic divorce confession and sat down. One teacher asked, "What considerations do you have in raising Yataro?"

"He needs to be strong to survive societal prejudices," I said.   11
"But I hope he can also, because of his background, understand the pain of others and be that much kinder."

Two days later, Yataro's registration number was on the accep-   12
tance list posted at the school. I'll never know what got him in, but standing there next to other parents, all in the requisite dark suits, I had become part of the group.

Meanings and Values

1. List the ways that the writer and her son are "different" from the normal or conventional.

2. List the different ways people urge or pressure the writer to conform to expected behaviors.

3. When does she choose to conform? When does she stick to her individuality or "difference"?

4. What does the last sentence reveal about the essay's theme: "I'll never know what got him in, but standing there next to other parents, all in the requisite dark suits, I had become part of the group"?

5. Sum up the theme of this essay in a thesis statement of your own. (See "Guide to Terms": *Thesis Statement.*)

Expository Techniques

1. How has the writer designed the opening sentence to alert readers that she will be talking about a culture unfamiliar to most of them?

2. What strategies does the writer employ to begin the essay? (Guide: *Openings/Introductions.*)

3. Does the introduction provide necessary background information? What more information might the writer provide, if any, to make the essay more effective?

4. Where in the essay does the writer present the situation or problem she plans to explore?

5.   In addition to a narrative organization, this essay is arranged according to the various elements of the situation being discussed. Into what segments can the essay be divided?

Diction and Vocabulary

1.   Why do you think the writer chose the word "chastised" in Paragraph 1 rather than more familiar words like "criticized" or "punished"? (Look up some of these words if you are not familiar with their meanings or connotations. (Guide: *Connotation/Denotation*.)

2.   Where do the vocabulary and sentence structure in the quoted passages in the essay fit on a scale from informal to formal? (Guide: *Colloquial Expressions, Syntax*.) What does the level of formality indicate about the society and the pressures it produces on individuals?

3.   If you do not know the meaning of some of the following words, look them up in a dictionary: chastised (Par. 1); harried (2); exalted (7); requisite (12).

Read to Write

1.   **Collaborating:** This essay consists of a series of conflicts in which the writer either compromises or refuses to compromise. Working in a group, identify each of these conflicts and identify the tone and language the writer uses to describe her response (compromise or refusal to compromise). Then compare the descriptions, answering these questions: Is there a consistent pattern in the way she narrates each kind of response? If so, what is it? If not, does she narrate each response differently, or does she take some other approach in which various kinds of responses are distinguished but not according to a clear plan?

2.   **Considering Audience:** People who have not grown up in a culture that places a high value on conformity or who have not experienced pressures similar to those described in this essay may not respond to the essay in the same way as people who have. Create a brief essay describing the possible reactions of three different groups of readers, each differing from the other (and from the writer of the essay) in cultural background and experience. Include analysis of any strategies used in the essay to help readers with differing backgrounds and experiences understand the events being presented.

3.   **Developing an Essay:** List several situations in which you have felt pressure to conform to social or cultural expectations that were contrary to your personal outlook, habits, or values. Create a narrative exploring the conflicts and your responses to them.

(Note: Suggestions for topics requiring development by NARRATION are on pp. 513–514 at the end of this chapter.)

Issues and Ideas

Stories and Values

- George Orwell, *A Hanging*
- Wayne Worcester, *Arms and the Man*
- Chang-rae Lee, *Uncle Chul Gets Rich*

Sometimes speaking directly about our values or perspectives does not clarify or convey them effectively. The situation that gives rise to a particular moral judgment or that leads to an ethical perspective can give someone else a better understanding than a detailed definition or even a careful comparison of differing perspectives. The more complex the idea or outlook, the more we may need to know about the events surrounding it. A detailed narrative can perhaps give readers a better understanding of causes and effects than an explanation that attempts to isolate them from the surrounding details.

The three essays that follow demonstrate the effectiveness of narration as an expository pattern for dealing with questions of value. Capital punishment has been the subject of many argumentative and expository essays, but few have offered the kind of insight into the minds of the prisoner and of those responsible for carrying out the sentence that George Orwell provides in "A Hanging." And few essays explore the moral ambiguities surrounding the practice as well as Orwell does.

Wayne Worcester's "Arms and the Man" provides an insider's view of some of the values associated with gun ownership and use. Although his perspective is in one way linked to his (and his friend's) experience, it nonetheless gains power and depth for others from the same experience. Finally Chang-rae Lee, in "Uncle Chul Gets Rich," uses narrative to explore interesting sets of values: personal, family, and cultural. He also uses the immigrant experience to explore American values from the perspective of outsiders struggling to become insiders.

GEORGE ORWELL

Gᴇᴏʀɢᴇ Oʀᴡᴇʟʟ (1903–1950), whose real name was Eric Blair, was a British novelist and essayist well known for his satire. He was born in India and educated at Eton in England; he was wounded while fighting in the Spanish Civil War. Later he wrote the books *Animal Farm* (1945), a satire on Soviet history; and *1984* (1949), a vivid picture of life in a projected totalitarian society. He was, however, also sharply aware of injustices in democratic societies and was consistently socialistic in his views. Many of Orwell's essays are collected in *Critical Essays* (1946), *Shooting an Elephant and Other Essays* (1950), and *Such, Such Were the Joys* (1953).

A Hanging

"A Hanging" is typical of Orwell's essays in its setting—Burma—and in its subtle but biting commentary on colonialism, on capital punishment, and even on one aspect of human nature itself. Although he is ostensibly giving a straightforward account of an execution, the author masterfully uses descriptive details and dialogue to create atmosphere and sharply drawn characterizations. The essay gives concrete form to a social message that is often delivered much less effectively in abstract generalities.

It was in Burma, a sodden morning of the rains. A sickly light, like yellow tinfoil, was slanting over the high walls into the jail yard. We were waiting outside the condemned cells, a row of sheds fronted with double bars, like small animal cages. Each cell measured about ten feet by ten and was quite bare within except for a plank bed and a pot for drinking water. In some of them brown, silent men were squatting at the inner bars, with their blankets draped round them. These were the condemned men, due to be hanged within the next week or two.   1

One prisoner had been brought out of his cell. He was a Hindu, a puny wisp of a man, with a shaven head and vague liquid eyes. He had a thick, sprouting mustache, absurdly too big for his body, rather like the mustache of a comic man on the films. Six tall Indian warders were guarding him and getting him ready for the gallows. Two of them stood by with rifles and fixed bayonets, while the others handcuffed him, passed a chain through his handcuffs and fixed it to their belts, and lashed his arms tight to his sides. They crowded very close about him, with their hands always on him in a careful,   2 caressing grip, as though all the while feeling him to make sure he was there. It was like men handling a fish which is still alive and may jump back into the water. But he stood quite unresisting, yielding his arms limply to the ropes, as though he hardly noticed what was happening.

Eight o'clock struck and a bugle call, desolately thin in the wet air, floated from the distant barracks. The superintendent of the jail, who was standing apart from the rest of us, moodily prodding the gravel with his stick, raised his head at the sound. He was an army doctor, with a grey toothbrush mustache and a gruff voice. "For God's sake, hurry up, Francis," he said irritably. "The man ought to have been dead by this time. Aren't you ready yet?"   3

Francis, the head jailer, a fat Dravidian in a white drill suit and gold spectacles, waved his black hand. "Yes sir, yes sir," he bubbled. "All iss satisfactorily prepared. The hangman iss waiting. We shall proceed."   4

"Well, quick march, then. The prisoners can't get their breakfast till this job's over."   5

We set out for the gallows. Two warders marched on either side of the prisoner, with their rifles at the slope; two others marched close against him, gripping him by arm and shoulder, as though at once pushing and supporting him. The rest of us, magistrates and the like, followed behind. Suddenly, when we had gone ten yards, the procession stopped short without any order or warning. A dreadful thing had happened—a dog, come goodness knows whence, had appeared in the yard. It came bounding among us with a loud volley of barks and leapt round us wagging its whole body, wild with glee at finding so many human beings together. It was a large woolly dog, half Airedale, half pariah. For a moment it pranced around us, and then, before anyone could stop it, it had made a dash for the prisoner, and jumping up tried to lick his face. Everybody stood aghast, too taken aback even to grab the dog.   6

"Who let that bloody brute in here?" said the superintendent angrily. "Catch it, someone!"   7

A warder detached from the escort, charged clumsily after the dog, but it danced and gambolled just out of his reach, taking everything as part of the game. A young Eurasian jailer picked up a handful of gravel and tried to stone the dog away, but it dodged the stones and came after us again. Its yaps echoed from the jail walls. The prisoner, in the grasp of the two warders, looked on incuriously, as though this was another formality of the hanging. It was several minutes before someone managed to catch the dog. Then we put my   8 handkerchief through its collar and moved off once more, with the dog still straining and whimpering.

It was about forty yards to the gallows. I watched the bare   9 brown back of the prisoner marching in front of me. He walked clumsily with his bound arms, but quite steadily, with that bobbing gait of the Indian who never straightens his knees. At each step his muscles slid neatly into place, the lock of hair on his scalp danced up and down, his feet printed themselves on the wet gravel. And once, in spite of the men who gripped him by each shoulder, he stepped lightly aside to avoid a puddle on the path.

It is curious; but till that moment I had never realized what it   10 means to destroy a healthy, conscious man. When I saw the prisoner step aside to avoid the puddle, I saw the mystery, the unspeakable wrongness, of cutting a life short when it is in full tide. This man was not dying, he was alive just as we are alive. All the organs of his body were working—bowels digesting food, skin renewing itself, nails growing, tissues forming—all toiling away in solemn foolery. His nails would still be growing when he stood on the drop, when he was falling through the air with a tenth-of-a-second to live. His eyes saw the yellow gravel and the grey walls, and his brain still re-membered, foresaw, reasoned—even about puddles. He and we were a party of men walking together, seeing, hearing, feeling, un-derstanding the same world; and in two minutes, with a sudden snap, one of us would be gone—one mind less, one world less.

The gallows stood in a small yard, separate from the main   11 grounds of the prison, and overgrown with tall prickly weeds. It was a brick erection like three sides of a shed, with planking on top, and above that two beams and a crossbar with the rope dangling. The hangman, a greyhaired convict in the white uniform of the prison, was waiting beside his machine. He greeted us with a servile crouch as we entered. At a word from Francis the two warders, grip-ping the prisoner more closely than ever, half led, half pushed him to the gallows and helped him clumsily up the ladder. Then the hangman climbed up and fixed the rope round the prisoner's neck.

We stood waiting, five yards away. The warders had formed in   12 a rough circle round the gallows. And then, when the noose was fixed, the prisoner began crying out to his god. It was a high, reiter-ated cry of "Ram! Ram! Ram! Ram!" not urgent and fearful like a prayer or cry for help, but steady, rhythmical, almost like the tolling of a bell. The dog answered the sound with a whine. The hangman, still standing on the gallows, produced a small cotton bag like a flour bag and drew it down over the prisoner's face. But the sound, muffled by the cloth, still persisted, over and over again: "Ram! Ram! Ram! Ram! Ram!"

The hangman climbed down and stood ready, holding the   13
lever. Minutes seemed to pass. The steady, muffled crying from the prisoner went on and on, "Ram! Ram! Ram!" never faltering for an instant. The superintendent, his head on his chest, was slowly poking the ground with his stick; perhaps he was counting the cries, allowing the prisoner a fixed number—fifty, perhaps, or a hundred. Everyone had changed colour. The Indians had gone grey like bad coffee, and one or two of the bayonets were wavering. We looked at the lashed, hooded man on the drop, and listened to his cries—each cry another second of life; the same thought was in all our minds; oh, kill him quickly, get it over, stop that abominable noise!

Suddenly the superintendent made up his mind. Throwing up   14
his head he made a swift motion with his stick. "Chalo!" he shouted almost fiercely.

There was a clanking noise, and then dead silence. The prisoner   15
had vanished, and the rope was twisting on itself. I let go of the dog, and it galloped immediately to the back of the gallows; but when it got there it stopped short, barked, and then retreated into a corner of the yard, where it stood among the weeds, looking timorously out at us. We went round the gallows to inspect the prisoners's body. He was dangling with his toes pointed straight downwards, very slowly revolving, as dead as a stone.

The superintendent reached out with his stick and poked the   16
bare brown body; it oscillated slightly. "*He's* all right," said the superintendent. He backed out from under the gallows, and blew out a deep breath. The moody look had gone out of his face quite suddenly. He glanced at his wrist-watch. "Eight minutes past eight. Well, that's all for this morning, thank God."

The warders unfixed bayonets and marched away. The dog,   17
sobered and conscious of having misbehaved itself, slipped after them. We walked out of the gallows yard, past the condemned cells with their waiting prisoners, into the big central yard of the prison. The convicts, under the command of warders armed with lathis, were already receiving their breakfast. They squatted in long rows, each man holding a tin pannikin, while two warders with buckets marched around ladling out rice; it seemed quite a homely, jolly scene, after the hanging. An enormous relief had come upon us now that the job was done. One felt an impulse to sing, to break into a run, to snigger. All at once everyone began chattering gaily.

The Eurasian boy walking beside me nodded towards the way 18
we had come, with a knowing smile. "Do you know, sir, our friend
(he meant the dead man) when he heard his appeal had been dismissed, he pissed on the floor of his cell. From fright. Kindly take one
of my cigarettes, sir. Do you not admire my new silver case, sir? From
the boxwallah, two rupees eight annas. Classy European style."

Several people laughed—at what, nobody seemed certain. 19

Francis was walking by the superintendent, talking garru- 20
lously: "Well, sir, all has passed off with the utmost satisfactori-
ness. It was all finished—flick! Like that. It iss not always so—oah,
no! I have known cases where the doctor was obliged to go beneath the gallows and pull the prissoner's legs to ensure decease.
Most disagreeable!"

"Wriggling about, eh? That's bad," said the superintendent. 21

"Ach, sir, it iss worse when they become refractory! One man, I 22
recall, clung to the bars of hiss cage when we went to take him out.
You will scarcely credit, sir, that it took six warders to dislodge him,
three pulling at each leg. We reasoned with him, 'My dear fellow,'
we said, 'think of all the pain and trouble you are causing to us!' But
no, he would not listen! Ach, he wass very troublesome!"

I found that I was laughing quite loudly. Everyone was laugh- 23
ing. Even the superintendent grinned in a tolerant way. "You'd better all come out and have a drink," he said quite genially. "I've got a
bottle of whisky in the car. We could do with it."

We went through the big double gates of the prison into the 24
road. "Pulling at his legs!" exclaimed a Burmese magistrate suddenly, and burst into a loud chuckling. We all began laughing again.
At that moment Francis' anecdote seemed extraordinarily funny.
We all had a drink together, native and European alike, quite amica-
bly. The dead man was a hundred yards away.

Meanings and Values

1. What was the real reason for the superintendent's impatience?

2. On first impression it may have seemed that the author gave undue at-
    tention to the dog's role in this narrative. Why was the episode such a
    "dreadful thing" (Par. 6)? Why did the author think it worth noting
    that the dog was excited at "finding so many human beings together"?
    Of what significance was the dog's trying to lick the prisoner's face?

3. Explain how the prisoner's stepping around a puddle could have given
    the author a new insight into what was about to happen (Par. 10).

4. Why was there so much talking and laughing after the hanging was finished?

5. What is the broadest meaning of Orwell's last sentence?

EXPOSITORY TECHNIQUES

1. Cite examples of both objective and impressionistic description in the first paragraph.

2. What is the primary time order used in this narrative? If there are any exceptions, state where.

3. Considering the relatively few words devoted to them, several of the characterizations in this essay are remarkably vivid—a result, obviously, of highly discriminating selection of details from the multitude of those that must have been available to the author. For each of the following people, list the character traits that we can observe, and state whether these impressions come to us through details of description, action, and/or dialogue.

   a. The prisoner

   b. The superintendent

   c. Francis

   d. The Eurasian boy

4. Why do you think the author included so many details of the preparation of the prisoner (Par. 2)? Why did he include so many details about the dog and his actions? What is gained by the assortment of details in Paragraph 10?

5. How would your characterize the tone of this selection? (Guide: *Style/Tone.*)

DICTION AND VOCABULARY

1. A noteworthy element of Orwell's style is his occasional use of figurative language. Cite six metaphors and similes, and comment on the author's choice of them and on their effectiveness. (Guide: *Figures of Speech.*)

2. Orwell was always concerned with the precise effects that words could give to meaning and style. Cite at least six nonfigurative words that seem to you particularly well chosen for their purpose. Show what their careful selection contributes to the description of atmosphere or to the subtle meanings of the author. (Guide: *Style/Tone.*)

READ TO WRITE

1. **Collaborating:** Discuss in a group people who have jobs that place their "duty" in conflict with their "conscience." Choose one such

person or profession and write a collaborative essay similar in style to Orwell's. You may choose to make group members responsible for one or two concrete examples each, to be combined into a unified paper.

2. **Considering Audience:** Orwell's approach in his essay makes his discussion of capital punishment approachable even to readers who may be in disagreement with his views. Identify places in the essay where Orwell deals with opposing views, and prepare an analysis of his success in dealing with them.

3. **Developing an Essay:** Draw on Orwell's expository technique in an essay of your own by recounting a minor incident (like the actions of the dog in "A Hanging") that led to much deeper insight. Or use a minor incident to reveal and emphasize insights that readers probably have not considered before.

(Note: Suggestions for topics requiring development by NARRATION are on pp. 513–514 at the end of this chapter.)

WAYNE WORCESTER

WAYNE WORCESTER is a former newspaper reporter and editor. He now teaches journalism at the University of Connecticut.

Arms and the Man

In "Arms and the Man," first published as a newspaper essay, Wayne Worcester narrates a brief incident, largely through dialogue, that explores a variety of values and issues associated with guns and their personal use.

In an especially rural part of southern New Hampshire, where the hills in early spring roll to mottled green and the roads turn to deep mud-brown, I have two old friends who live as they please. 1

He drives a truck. She works in a dentist's office. They have three children, and on most days the kids' toys sprawl in abandon across the living-room floor, directly in front of the gun cabinet, which has no lock. 2

"Doesn't it bother you?" I asked on a recent visit. "The kids' playing around the gun cabinet?" 3

"Nope. We brought 'em up to not touch it." 4

He handed me his newest gun. It was flat and small, only slightly larger than my hand, and the room's bright light died on its coal-black barrel. No reflection. Not a hint. 5

"Isn't that a sweetheart?" 6

"Very small." 7

"It's hers, but it's got real stoppin' power. Great protection." 8

I popped the magazine out, and saw the stack of bullets. 9

"You always keep it loaded?" I asked. 10

"Course." 11

"She carry it?" 12

"No point havin' it, she gonna leave it to home." 13

"She works for a dentist, for Chrissake! He use this instead of Novocain? What's she need a gun for?" 14

His lips went tight, as though I'd insulted him, which I had. 15

"You never know." 16

"How did she get a permit?" 17

"A what? C'mon." 18

"Well, why's she carrying?" 19

"I told you. Protection." 20

"Right. What else have you got in there?" 21

"Couple rifles. Shotgun. My AR 15. God, that's fun. Last year, 22
me and a couple guys from work, we just went out and set up a target on a red oak out back, and we hit it with the AR so many times
the damned tree just broke in half like we'd sawed it off. Thing just
toppled right over."

"Your neighbor must love you." 23

"Yeah, he called the cops up, but they didn't do nothing—just 24
checked to see we was on our own property."

"'Live free or die,' right? What'd the neighbor do?" 25

"Bout three days later, he comes over. His wife's bein' a pain in 26
the ass. He says, 'We're moving in two months, but if you keep the
shootin' down till then, you can have this.'"

From the top shelf of the cabinet, my friend took down a long- 27
barreled, chrome-plated .357-magnum, the kind of handgun that'll
stop a speeding car, or most anything else.

"But this one here's my pride 'n' joy," he said. It was a .22-caliber 28
handgun, jet black with a long, heavy barrel.

"Real accurate. Wanna try her out?" 29

We walked to the edge of the woods, and he set a bright-blue 30
Maxwell House can swinging from a tree limb.

For a small-caliber weapon, the gun was bone-heavy, and in 31
the palm of my hand it felt oddly substantial, as though it were
even more than its true weight. I walked slowly back toward the
house, flipped off the safety, turned—quickly, for some reason—
and squeezed the trigger the instant the barrel fell in line with the target. The shot was loud. It was sharp and clear and flat, as though it
had hard, cutting edges, and before the sound had died the can had
jumped and the chamber slide had recoiled and kicked out a casing
with that matchlessly pleasing sound that metal on metal can make
only when the parts have been properly and ever-so-precisely ma-
chined. I was pleased, and I fired again, and then, quickly in the echo,
twice again, and I could smell the shots and feel the recoil of the
bone-weight as though it were an extension of me, and I squeezed
the trigger again, and then again in affirmation, counting silently in
the loud and hard flat noise and clink-sliding of the chamber—seven
shots now—and the can danced some more and in a far shadow I
thought I could see old man Bergevin, whom I'd worked for as a
teenager and hated and do to this day, though he is long dead and
not thought of in years. I considered him in his grave, all scraps and
maggoty bone, and was glad. Eight shots, and the can finally fell to

the ground, and I lowered the gun toward the fallen target and squeezed the trigger for the ninth time and sent the can skittering.

We were quiet on the way back. I was still listening to the gun,   32
feeling its weight, thinking about a quip I'd overheard: "You know what N.R.A. stands for? Not a Rational Adult." I chuckled aloud.

"What?" my friend asked.   33

"Just thinking. You ever wonder who you really need protect-   34
ing from?"

He just smiled.   35

Meanings and Values

1.   Why, in Paragraph 2, does Worcester discuss the parents' careers, present a description of the toys, and mention the gun cabinet? What is the significance of these three topics mentioned in conjunction with each other?

2.   Worcester says, "His lips went tight as though I'd insulted him, which I had" (Par. 14). What did he say that was potentially offensive? Was his friend justified in being insulted? Why, or why not?

3.   What is the overall meaning of the last four paragraphs of the essay (31–34)? Who needs protecting, and from whom?

Expository Techniques

1.   Worcester uses dialogue to present much of his narrative. How does this dialogue provide a context for the only substantially nonconversational section (Par. 30)? Is this heavy use of dialogue an effective technique? Please explain.

2.   Identify the descriptive details in Paragraph 30. What ideas or qualities do they emphasize? (See "Guide to Terms": *Emphasis*.) How does this paragraph serve to unify the essay? (Guide: *Unity*.)

Diction and Vocabulary

1.   Why does Worcester use few difficult words in this essay? Who is his target audience? Is it fair to say that he is belittling the characters in this essay by using such relatively simple language? Why, or why not?

Read to Write

1.   **Collaborating:** "Arms and the Man" could serve as an introduction to a larger research essay on gun control. Working in a group, choose

another controversial issue and write an anecdote similar in style to Worcester's (either fiction or nonfiction) that could be an introduction to an essay on that issue.

2. **Considering Audience:** What does Worcester assume about the attitude most of his readers will have toward gun use? Identify those places in the essay where he makes his assumptions about his audience clear. Then prepare an essay analyzing the way Worcester addresses, identifies, and interacts with his audience's attitudes.

3. **Developing an Essay:** Think of a time you disagreed with the course of behavior or values of a friend because of the implications of the action or behavior. Write an essay about that relationship, similar to Worcester's essay, and incorporate dialogue and detailed description in your narration.

(NOTE: Suggestions for topics requiring development by NARRATION are on pp. 513–514 at the end of this chapter.)

CHANG-RAE LEE

> CHANG-RAE LEE was born in South Korea in 1967. When he was 3 years
> old, he and his family emigrated to the United States. He is a gradu-
> ate of Phillips Exeter Academy and Yale University. He earned his
> M.F.A. degree from the University of Oregon where he taught cre-
> ative writing. Lee's novel, *Native Speaker* (1996), was awarded the
> Ernest Hemingway Foundation/PEN Award for First Fiction. His sec-
> ond novel is entitled *A Gesture of Life* (1999).

Uncle Chul Gets Rich

In "Uncle Chul Gets Rich," first published in 1996, Lee offers a familiar narrative form—a story of success in business—set amid
contrasting values and cultures typical of immigrant experiences.
The issues Lee explores, however, will be familiar and important
for most readers.

My father's youngest brother, Uncle Chul, shared the Lees' fa- 1
mously bad reaction to liquor, which was to turn beet-red in
the face, grow dizzy and finally get sick. In spite of this, he was always happy to stay up late at family gatherings. After a few Scotches
he would really loosen up, and, with the notable exception of my
mother, we all appreciated his rough language and racy stories.
Only when Mother came in from the kitchen would his talk soften,
for he knew he had always fallen short in her eyes. If they were ever
alone together, say in the kitchen, after dinner, he would use the
most decorous voice in asking for a glass or a fresh bucket of ice,
and even offer to help load the dishwasher or run an errand to the
store.

On one of those nights we sped off, both happy for a break in 2
the long evening. He asked me about school, what sports I was playing, but the conversation inevitably turned toward my parents, and
particularly my mother—how much she had invested in me, that I
was her great hope. I thought it was odd that he was speaking this
way, like my other relatives, and I answered with some criticism of
her—that she was too anxious and overbearing. He stared at me
and, with a hard solemnity I had not heard from him before, said
that my mother was one of the finest people one could ever know.
He kept a grip on the wheel and in the ensuing quiet of the drive I
could sense how he must have both admired and despised her. In

many respects, my mother was an unrelenting woman. She tended to measure people by the mark of a few principles of conduct: ask no help from anyone, always plan for the long run and practice (her own variation of) the golden rule, which was to treat others much better than oneself.

In her mind, Uncle Chul sorely lacked on all these accounts. In the weeks following our drive, my father would be deciding whether to lend him $10,000 to start a business. As always after dinner, my parents sat in the kitchen (the scent of sesame oil and pickled vegetables still in the air) and spoke in Korean, under the light of a fluorescent ring. My mother, in many ways the director of the family, questioned my uncle's character and will. Hadn't he performed poorly in school, failed to finish college? Hadn't he spent most of his youth perfecting his skills as a black belt in taekwondo and his billiards game? Wasn't he a gambler in spirit?   3

My father could defend him only weakly. Uncle Chul had a history of working hard only when reward was well within sight, like cash piled high on the end of a pool table. His older brothers were all respected professionals and academics. My father was a doctor, a psychiatrist who had taught himself English in order to practice in America. Uncle Chul had left Korea after a series of failed ventures and odd jobs, and found himself broke with a wife and new baby. How valuable were his taekwondo trophies now? What could he possibly do in this country?   4

My parents argued fiercely and my father left the kitchen. But as was my mother's way, she kept on pushing her side of the issue, thinking aloud. My father was throwing away his hard-earned money on the naïve wish that his little brother had magically changed. Uncle Chul was a poor risk and even now was complaining about his present job, hauling and cleaning produce for a greengrocer in Flushing. He would get to the store at 4 A.M. to prepare vegetables for the day's selling. While he shared a sofa bed with his nephew in his older brother's tiny apartment, his wife and infant daughter were still in Seoul, waiting for him to make enough money to send for them.   5

But his wages were only $250 a week for 70 hours of work and he loathed the job, the brutal effort that went into clearing a few cents a carrot, a quarter a soda, the niggling, daily accrual. The owners themselves would toil like slaves to see a till full of tattered ones and fives at day's end.   6

I knew Uncle Chul craved the big score, the quick hit, a rain of cash. For the very reasons my mother had so little faith in him—his   7 brashness, his flagrant ambitions—I admired him. Over Scotch and rice crackers, he would tell my father about the millions he was going to make by moving merchandise wholesale, in bigger-ticket items with decent margins. He would never touch another orange again. I remember my father absently nodding his head at each vague and grandiose idea, probably hearing my mothers' harangues.

The other men in my father's family were thick-lensed scribblers who worked through their days from A to Z, assiduously removing uncertainty by paying close attention to the thousand details of each passing hour. My father worked long days at the hospital, and spent weekends pouring over volumes of Freud and Rank and Erickson in his second language, to "catch up" with the American doctors. When my father decided to lend Uncle Chul the $10,000, making it clear that no further discussion was needed, my mother transferred her worrying energy squarely onto me. It seemed no accident that her latest criticism was that I was "always looking for the easy way." I had, in fact, been feeling moody and rebellious, weary of being a good student and good boy. I was in the eighth grade, and my friends were beginning to drink beer and smoke pot. I secretly resolved to join them.   8

I was also taking solo train trips from Pleasantville, N.Y., down to the city to visit my older cousins on the weekends, prompting questions from my mother about what kind of fun we were having. I didn't tell her that what thrilled me most was riding the elevated trains between Flushing and Grand Central, shuttling back and forth with the multitude. My new comer's heart was fearful and enthralled, and I naïvely thought Uncle Chul felt the same way. He had quit working for the greengrocer after getting the money, and brought over his wife and child. He was busy scouting out stores for his first business in America.   9

But Uncle Chul found that the leases for even the smallest stores were $4,000 a month, and he seemed tense and even a little scared. I felt a strange pang of guilt because of the extra pressure on him— the $10,000 and the tenuous faith behind it. The only thing worse than losing the money was what my mother would never have to mention again: that he started working a little too late.   10

But he did find a store, in the Bronx, and we drove down one Sunday to see it in all its new glory. It seemed as if half the tenement buildings on the block were burned out or deserted, and the sidewalks were littered with garbage, broken glass and the rubble of bricks and mortar. My father pulled up behind Uncle Chul's car and we peered out to see if we had the right address. The shop couldn't   11 have been more than eight feet wide. A single foot-wide corridor running its length was lined with accessories, odd-lot handbags and tie clips and lighters; the stuff hung on plastic grids on the walls and overhead. In the back, there was a hot plate on the floor, two stools and a carton of instant ramen noodles.

Uncle Chul proudly showed us the merchandise and, from a glass display box, gave me a watch; my sister got a faux-pearl necklace. A customer peered in but waved her hand and scurried away. My mother said that we were disturbing the business, and after a rush of bows and goodbyes we were in the car, heading back to Westchester.   12

Uncle Chul had no choice but to be in that neighborhood, in that quarter-size store, with the risk of crime and no insurance. The trade-off was the low rent, and it soon became clear that he had made an excellent choice. With little competition on the block, the money started coming in, and soon he moved to a larger store nearby, and then moved again. His volume and cash flow surged, and after sell-ing each successive business, he staked his profit on the next store.   13

We didn't see him much during this time, but when we did he made sure to show off his success to my parents. My aunt wore de-signer clothes, and Uncle Chul sported a fat gold Rolex. If we were out somewhere, he would casually pull out a rolled wad of $100's when a check arrived, proclaiming affably to his brothers that it was his turn to pay.   14

But I noticed, too, that he and my aunt looked haggard and pressed. They spoke hurriedly and ate as quickly as they could. My mother would say something like, "You've developed such expen-sive tastes," and tell him that he was still frittering away his money on useless luxuries.   15

When Uncle Chul amassed the war chest he needed to open the wholesale business he had hoped for, he moved away from New York. He had heard of opportunities in Texas, where goods could be im-ported across the border and sold at big profits. Within a few years he had more than 50 people working for him, selling, by containers and truckloads, the same purses and belts he started with years before.   16

He bought a sprawling ranch house, brand-new and fitted with jet-action bathtubs and wide-screen televisions. He hired a team of Mexican maids to keep the place running. He traded in his Cadillacs for BMW's and sent his daughters to private school. One summer he paid my sister outrageous wages to sit in his air-conditioned office and practice her Spanish with the retailers. The business was on automatic pilot—effortless. Uncle Chul was now a millionaire sev-eral times over, richer than all his brothers combined.   17

I spent time with him again years later, when my mother be-   18
came terminally ill. He visited regularly, always bearing gifts for the
family. To me, he simply gave money. He knew I had quit my first
job to become a writer, which meant little to him, except that I would
be poor forever. Maybe, someday, my name would be famous, and
he invested in that possibility, slipping me a couple of $100's when
my mother wasn't looking. He did this naturally, with an ease and
power in his grip full of cash. His money was like a weight outside
his body, which he could press upon others, like me. But in my
mother's presence, his swagger vanished, and he was just Uncle
Chul again, prodigal and bereft.

He was especially solemn on the day of her funeral. Of the many   19
people who made their way to the cemetery and later to the house, I
suspect Uncle Chul knew he was among those she would be most
closely watching. My mother's friends had brought food and electric
rice cookers and the men were in the living room, drinking companionably, speaking in low voices. My mother had been dying for
nearly two years, and now that it was over waves of exhaustion and
relief were washing over everyone in the house.

I remember Uncle Chul padding softly about the house, wary of   20
disturbing even the layer of dust on her furniture. He was speaking
in a soft register, his voice faltering, like a nervous young minister
on his first encounter with the bereaved. He was nodding and bow-
ing, even helping the ladies gather cups and plates, exercising until
the last visitor left a younger brother's respect and obedience to the
family and the dead.

In the Korean tradition, mourners brought offerings of money, all   21
token amounts, except for Uncle Chul's fat envelope, which held
thousands of dollars. He would have given more, he said, but his
wholesale business wasn't doing so well anymore. I knew that wasn't
the real reason. He must have known what my mother would have
said, perhaps was telling him now—that he couldn't help but be the
flashy one again.

MEANINGS AND VALUES

1. How would you define an "all-American success story"? In what ways
    is Uncle Chul's story like an all-American success story? Be specific.

2. How do the values embodied by Uncle Chul and the narrative of his
    success differ from those embodied and expressed by the writer's
    mother?

3. Does the writer endorse either his mother's values or Uncle Chul's? If so, why and how? If not, why do you think he refrains from making his own opinion known?

EXPOSITORY TECHNIQUES

1. What strategy does the writer use to begin this selection? To conclude it? (See "Guide to Terms"; *Introductions; Closings.*) Are both strategies effective? Why, or why not? (Guide: *Evaluation.*)

2. What ideas does the writer highlight or emphasize by his choice of opening and closing strategies? Where else in the essay do these ideas receive emphasis, and through what means? (Guide: *Emphasis.*)

3. Where and for what purposes does this essay employ comparison and contrast as an expository pattern? (See Chapter 5.) Why should we consider narration, not comparison and contrast, as the dominant expository pattern in the selection?

DICTION AND VOCABULARY

1. Choose a paragraph describing one of the characters and explain how the terms the writer has chosen reflect the values of the character. (Guide: *Diction.*)

2. If you do not know the meaning of some of the following terms, look them up in a dictionary: decorous (Par. 1); taekwondo (3); niggling, accrual (6); tenuous (10).

READ TO WRITE

1. **Collaborating:** Uncle Chul seems to believe he can get wealthy quickly. Working in a group, discuss what you consider to be the American dream. Did Uncle Chul leave Korea for an American dream? Did the dream exist in the form that he perceived? Draw on your notes of the group's discussion to write an essay about a person you know or a particular experience that helps define that American dream.

2. **Considering Audience:** Many of the situations in Lee's essay cross cultural boundaries. "Get rich quick" schemes and disagreements between family members are widespread. Identify situations that Lee presents that are relevant for most readers. Choose one that resonates as part of your life and narrate it in a short essay.

3. **Developing an Essay:** Create a narrative essay using selected scenes from over a considerable period of time. Choose the scenes so that they reflect differing outlooks or perspectives, and arrange them as Lee does for an expository purpose.

(NOTE: Suggestions for topics requiring development by NARRATION follow.)

Writing Suggestions for Chapter 11

NARRATION

Use narration as a primary or partial pattern (e.g., in developed examples or in comparison) for one of the following expository themes or another suggested by them. Avoid the isolated personal account that has little broader significance. Remember, too, that development of the essay should itself make your point, without excessive moralizing.

1. People can still succeed without a college education.
2. The frontiers are not all gone.
3. When people succeed in communicating, they can learn to get along with each other.
4. Even with "careful" use of capital punishment, innocent people can be executed.
5. Sports don't always build character.
6. Physical danger can make us more aware of ourselves and our values.
7. Conditioning to the realities of the job is as important for police officers as it is in professional training.
8. It is possible for employees themselves to determine when they have reached their highest level of competence.
9. Wartime massacres are not a new development.
10. "Date rape" and sexual harassment on the job are devastating and generally unexpected.
11. Both heredity and environment shape personality.
12. Physical and mental handicaps can be overcome in some ways, but they are still a burden.
13. Toxic wastes pose a problem for many communities.
14. Hunting is a worthwhile and challenging sport.
15. Lack of money places considerable stress on a family or a marriage.
16. Exercise can become an obsession.
17. People who grow up in affluent surroundings don't understand what it is like to worry about money, to be hungry, or to live in a dangerous neighborhood.
18. Some jobs are simply degrading, either because of the work or because of the fellow workers.

COLLABORATIVE EXERCISES

1. Consider item 6 from the list of writing suggestions. Have each member of a group relate a story of physical danger and self-awareness that affected the group member or a friend. Each group member can then combine the examples into a unified paper narrating the effects that physical dangers may have upon people. When the papers are completed, group members can compare them and discuss the different choices the writers made.

2. Item 9 from the list of writing suggestions addresses analyzing wartime massacres. Have each member of your group choose some wartime atrocity (e.g., from the Gulf War, the Holocaust, or the like). Group members can then choose from these examples to create unified narratives.

12

Reasoning by Use of *Induction* and *Deduction*

Sometimes you can best explain a subject by asking readers to fol-low the line of reasoning you use to *understand it:* either *inductive reasoning* or *deductive reasoning. Induction* is the process by which we accumulate evidence until, at some point, we can make the "induc-tive leap" and thus reach a useful *generalization.* The science labora-tory employs this technique: hundreds of tests and experiments and analyses may be required before the scientist will generalize, for in-stance, that a disease is caused by a certain virus. It is also one of the primary techniques of the prosecuting attorney who presents pieces of inductive evidence, asking the jury to make the inductive leap and conclude that the accused did indeed kill the victim.

Whereas induction is the method of reaching a potentially use-ful generalization (for example, people attending meetings after lunch are invariably less attentive than those at morning meetings), *deduction* is the method of *using* such a generality, now accepted as a fact (for example, because we need an attentive audience, we had better schedule this meeting at 10:30 A.M. rather than 1:00 P.M.). Working from a generalization already formulated—by ourselves, by someone else, or by tradition—we may deduce that a specific thing or circumstance that fits into the generality will act the same. Hence, if we are convinced that orange-colored food tastes bad, we will be reluctant to try pumpkin pie.

A personnel manager may have discovered over the years that electrical engineering majors from Central College are invariably well trained in their field. His induction may have been based on the evidence of observations, records, and opinions of people at his

515

company; and, perhaps without realizing it, he has made the usable generalization about the training of Central College electrical engineering majors. Later, when he has an application from Nancy Ortega, a graduate of Central College, his deductive process will probably work as follows: Central College turns out well-trained electrical engineering majors; Ortega was trained at Central; therefore, Ortega must be well trained. Here he has used a generalization for a specific case.

In written form, you can use inductive reasoning to help readers explore the details of a subject and arrive at the same conclusion or interpretation you do, as in the following paragraph.

> Roaming the site, I can't help noticing that when men start cooking, the hardware gets complicated. Custom-built cookers—massive contraptions of cast iron and stainless steel—may cost $15,000 or more; they incorporate the team's barbecue philosophy. "We burn straight hickory under a baffle," Jim Garts, coleader of the Hogaholics, points out as he gingerly opens a scorching firebox that vents smoke across a water tray beneath a 4-by-8-foot grill. It's built on a trailer the size of a mobile home. Other cookers have been fashioned from a marine diesel engine; from a '76 [Nissan], with grilling racks instead of front seats, a chimney above the dash, and coals under the hood; and as a 15-foot version of Elvis Presley's guitar (by the Graceland Love Me Tenderloins). It's awesome ironmongery.

Preliminary observation states topic

Inductive evidence/ details

Inductive generalization

—Daniel Cohen,
"Cooking-Off for Fame and Fortune"

You can use deductive reasoning to help readers use a generalization as a way of understanding a complex situation or complicated evidence and details, as in this paragraph.

> It is an everyday fact of life that competitors producing similar products claim that their own goods or services are better than those of their rivals. Every product advertised—from pain relievers to fried chicken—is claimed to be better than its competitor's. If all these companies sued for libel, the courts would be so overloaded with cases that they would grind to a halt. For years courts dismissed criticisms of businesses, products, and performances as expressions of

Background for generalization

Deductive generalizations

opinion. When a restaurant owner sued a guidebook to New York restaurants for giving his establishment a bad review, he won a $20,000 verdict in compensatory damages and $5 in punitive damages. But this was overturned by the court of appeals. The court held that, with the exception of one item, the allegedly libelous statements were expressions of opinion, not fact. Among these statements were that the "dumplings, on our visit, resembled bad ravioli . . . chicken with chili was rubbery and the rice . . . totally insipid. . . ." Obviously, it would be impossible to prove the nature of the food served at that particular meal. What is tender to one palate may be rubbery to another. The one misstatement of fact, that the Peking duck was served in one dish instead of three, was in my opinion, a minor and insignificant part of the entire review. Had the review of the restaurant been considered as a whole . . . , this small misstatement of fact would have been treated as *de minimis.* That is a well established doctrine requiring that minor matters not be considered by the courts. In this case, the court held that the restaurant was a public figure and had failed to prove actual malice.

Specific instance to be explained using the generalizations

—Lois G. Forer,
*A Chilling Effect: The Mounting
Threat of Libel and Invasion of Privacy Actions
to the First Amendment*

WHY USE INDUCTION AND DEDUCTION?

One useful way to think of induction and deduction is as a way of arriving at a generalization (induction) and of applying a generalization as an explanatory strategy (deduction). Once you start thinking of the patterns this way, you can develop questions to help you decide when to employ them in your writing. You might ask, for example, "Why should I lead readers through the process of arriving at a generalization when I could simply announce it at the beginning of an essay and then provide examples, comparisons, and other kinds of evidence to explain the generalization and show how reasonable it is?" One answer is that you employ deduction whenever the process of arriving at a generalization is as important as the conclusion itself. For example, in explaining a particular kind of childhood behavior, you may also wish to model for readers a way of drawing conclusions about such behavior.

Another occasion when induction is an appropriate pattern of explanation is when the evidence leading to your conclusion is quite complicated or your conclusion is unusual or surprising. In such cases, readers may be more likely to understand and agree with your conclusion if you lead them through the process of reasoning. Inductive reasoning is also appropriate when you want to create tension or drama by building toward your conclusion or when you want to arrive at it by considering and rejecting other explanations until you arrive at a satisfactory one.

Before employing deduction as an explanatory strategy, you might ask, "How will my readers benefit if I use deductive reasoning to guide my explanation?" The importance of deductive reasoning as an explanatory pattern lies in the careful logic (and hence reliability) it can lend to conclusions. Put in simplified form (which, in writing, it seldom is), the deductive process is also called a "syllogism"—with the beginning generality known as the "major premise" and the specific that fits into the generality known as the "minor premise." For example:

Major premise—Orange-colored food is not fit to eat.
Minor premise—Pumpkin pie is orange-colored.
Conclusion—Pumpkin pie is not fit to eat.

As this example makes clear, however, deductive reasoning can be only as reliable as the original generalizations that were used as deductive premises. If the generalizations themselves were based on flimsy or insufficient evidence, any future deduction using them is likely to be erroneous.

Working together, induction and deduction can be good strategies for exploring an unfamiliar or complicated topic. Inductive reasoning can suggest a generalization about the topic; deductive reasoning can use the generalization to explore and explain whatever details, applications, and consequences call for understanding.

CHOOSING A STRATEGY

The organization of writing employing induction, deduction, or both generally parallels the process of reasoning. The following example may make this clear. Suppose that after a careful process of reasoning, you concluded that your family's dog treats you and other family members as if they were part of her own dog pack. This would be a somewhat startling conclusion for many readers, so to help make your explanation convincing, you might wish to follow an inductive-deductive pattern.

> *Tentative Thesis* (to be presented in full at the end of the essay): My family's dog treats my parents and my siblings as if we were all members of the same pack of dogs.
>
> *Inductive Explanation:* Dogs behave in ways that surprise humans.
> 1. They often try to sleep with their owners or members of the family. Dogs in packs like to sleep together.
> 2. Dogs often like to carry around bits of smelly clothing (ugh!) from their owners or family members. Dogs in packs recognize and relate to each other through scent.
> 3. Dogs choose one family member as most important and others as less so. Dog packs are strictly hierarchical; a dog is content when he or she can recognize the "Alpha" dog and his or her own place in the pack.
>
>   4, 5, 6. . . .
>
> *Inductive Generalization:* Dogs relate to humans in ways similar to the ways they relate to other dogs in a pack.
>
> *Deductive Explanation:* Much of my dog's behavior can be explained by considering my family as her pack.
> 1. Every time one of the family sits down, our female beagle comes over and falls asleep on one of our feet. She's "cuddling" with us and feeling comfortable when she is literally "in touch" with her pack.
> 2. I have lots of single socks; the dog has the other ones, which she chews, then "lovingly" drapes over her head or muzzle when she falls asleep in her bed. My dog isn't trying to be a pest or to cause me trouble. She's "complimenting" me by letting me know that my scent is an important element in her life.
> 3. My mother says that even though she feeds and walks the dog, our beagle still thinks my father and my brothers are the most important people in the house. Beagles aren't politically correct; the lead dog is still generally a male, even if the "dog" walks on two legs.
>
>   4, 5, 6. . . .

One particularly effective and familiar pattern of induction in writing is the "process of elimination." If it can be shown, for instance, that "A" does not have the strength to swing the murder weapon, that "B" was in a drunken sleep at the time of the crime, and that "C" had recently become blind and could not have found her way to the boathouse, then we may be ready for the inductive leap—that the foul deed must have been committed by "X," the only other person on the island. This organization can help you explain to readers why a particular explanation or interpretation of a subject is the only reasonable one.

> Details of the subject to be explained
> Explanation 1
> > Strengths and weaknesses
> Explanation 2
> > Strengths and weaknesses
> Explanation 3
> > Strengths and weaknesses
> 4, 5. . . .
> Deductive Generalization
> > This explanation is the only one with significant strengths and few significant weaknesses. It is probably the most accurate one.

DEVELOPING INDUCTION AND DEDUCTION

To develop an explanation using induction and deduction, you need to pay attention to the logic of your reasoning. These two faults are common in induction: (1) the use of *flimsy* evidence— mere opinion, hearsay, or analogy, none of which can support a valid generalization—instead of verified facts or opinions of reliable authorities; and (2) the use of *too little* evidence, leading to a premature inductive leap. The amount of evidence needed in any situation depends, of course, on purpose and audience. The success of two Central College graduates might be enough to convince some careless personnel director that all Central College electronics graduates would be good employees, but two laboratory tests would not convince medical researchers that they had learned anything worthwhile about a disease-causing virus.

Deductive reasoning can fall victim to questionable premises or any of a number of flaws in logic (see Chapter 13, p. 568). Induction and deduction are highly logical processes, and any trace of weakness can seriously undermine an exposition that depends on their reasonableness. Although no induction or deduction ever reaches absolute, 100 percent certainty, we should try to get from these methods as high a degree of *probability* as possible.

Student Essay

In the following essay, Sheilagh Brady shows how an essay can use induction and deduction to organize a complicated explanation in a way readers will consider clear and easy to understand. She takes readers through the history of MADD, leading up to some of its key positions, then explores the positions in detail.

Mad About MADD

Sheilagh Brady

On May 3, 1980, Cari Lightner was walking through a suburban neighborhood on her way to a church carnival in Fair Oaks, California, when she was killed by a hit-and-run drunk driver. The driver was Clarence Busch, 46 years old with four prior arrests for drunk driving. Busch had just been released on bail for a hit-and-run drunk-driving charge a week before.

Background

Cari's mother, Candy Lightner, was 33 at the time, a divorced mother of two other children working as a real estate agent. She was told by two police officers investigating the accident that Busch would probably receive little jail time, if any, because "'That's the way the system works'" (Lightner and Hathaway 224).

Faced with these circumstances, many of us might have concluded that the only possible responses were despair and frustrated rage. Candy Lightner reached another conclusion. Mulling over the police officers' words during dinner the same night, Lightner conceived of the organization that eventually became MADD, Mothers Against Drunk Driving. She felt the need to do something to take away her pain. MADD became a way for her to use her anger and to come to terms with the death of her daughter. For the next five years, Lightner devoted her time and effort to the creation of MADD.

Events in the history of MADD and its efforts lead up to the inductive conclusion

Lightner moved to Dallas, Texas, the eventual headquarters of MADD, to begin working on organizing the
new group. In March 1983, NBC aired a documentary,
"Mothers Against Drunk Driving: The Candy Lightner
Story." According to James B. Jacobs, MADD chapters
doubled across the United States by 1985, and in the
same year *Time* magazine reported that there were
320 chapters nationwide, and 600,000 volunteers and
donors (Otto 41).

MADD's response to drunk driving has been to emphasize jail sentences and legislation. MADD members
get angry when people feel "that a killer drunk driver
deserves a lesser penalty than other homicidal offenders" (Jacobs). MADD has been successful in focusing
public attention on the problems associated with drinking and driving and mobilizing legal changes to create
stiffer penalties for drunk driving. MADD aims to have
these stiffer penalties made mandatory and plea bar-
gaining abolished (Voas and Lacey 126–27).

Not only has MADD focused public attention but
it has also had considerable effect on local, state,
and federal governments. In 1988, S. Ungerleider and
S. A. Bloch did an evaluation of MADD that has been
summarized as concluding that MADD was "more successful in state legislatures where a large number of
laws were enacted in an effort to produce more severe
sanctions for the drunk driving offense" (qtd. in Voas
and Lacey 137).

Yet according to Dave Russel, a member of the
Rhode Island Chapter of MADD, the past few years
have been difficult. During the 1980s legislation was
passed quickly because of the sudden public support
through pressure groups concerned about drinking and
driving. Since then, the progress of drunk-driving legislation has slowed considerably. Russel says that the
number of deaths per year has steadily decreased since
1980 but that alcohol related accidents still take close to
19,000 lives each year. As a response to this situation,
MADD chapters nationally have concluded that there is

still a need for more drunk-driving legislation, even if legislators do not see it.

Having reached this conclusion, MADD chapters nationwide have decided to submit three different bills annually to their state legislatures. Some states have turned these bills into laws, but many have not. Just what are these MADD chapters proposing? Are the laws they want enacted reasonable or unreasonable?

Inductive generalization

One bill aims to reduce the BAC (blood alcohol content) level from .10 to .08 as the legal limit of intoxication. In 1988 in a report focusing on BAC levels, researchers Moskowitz and Robinson found that although theoretically impairment begins with the first drink, significant impairment occurs in most people at .05 BAC or lower. At the Surgeon General's Workshop, December 14–16, 1988, C. Everett Koop called for lowering the BAC limit in all states to .08, as did the National Highway Transportation Safety Administration in reports sent to the United States Congress. According to MADD's national office, lowering the BAC level to .09 will reduce drunk driving by making it more likely that drunk drivers will be caught, and also by acting to discourage driving under the influence. If research evidence and reliable authorities suggest reducing the BAC level from .10 to .08 will save lives, then most of us are likely to conclude that the legislative proposal seems reasonable.

First deductive explanation

Another bill is the ALR Bill or the Administrative License Revocation Bill. This law would eliminate the period between the arrest of a drunk driver and the hearing suspending the license. Right now, in many states, that period is supposed to be around 30 days but inevitably becomes much longer, a delay that allows the drunk driver to continue driving for that much longer legally under a valid license. The ALR would be a process that would allow the police officer to take the drunk driver's license if there is a refusal to take the breathalyzer test. In return, the driver would be given a temporary permit, good for ten to 15 days, following an

Second deductive explanation

appearance at a hearing. If the driver does not appear
for the hearing or cannot provide reasonable evidence
for refusing the test, the license is suspended. In the
case of a "no show," the driver must appear later to answer to the charge against him or her, but what is important is that the license will have already been
suspended.

The Administrative License Revocation was recommended by the Presidential Commission on Drunk
Driving, which developed the National Commission
Against Drunk Driving. According to several researchers,
"Administrative revocation has widespread support
among researchers, highway safety experts, and the
public in general because it has been shown to be an
effective administrative action that protects innocent
drivers" in an experiment conducted in California,
Washington, and Minnesota (Peck, Sadler, and Perrine).
Most of us would probably conclude that ALR is a reasonable procedure, yet 17 states have not yet turned
the ALR bill into a law.

Last, MADD chapters propose annually an Open
Container Law requiring that open containers of alcohol
not be allowed in the passenger compartments of vehicles. According to MADD's national chapter, it is fundamental to separate drinking and driving because this
separation is essential to the public interest and to the
public's understanding of the crisis created by drunk
driving. MADD argues that banning open containers of
alcoholic beverages in a vehicle is one way to make sure
drivers do not start drinking while driving or to become
even more intoxicated while driving. Moskowitz and
Robinson, in <u>Effects of Low Doses of Alcohol on Driving
Skills</u>, report that drinking while driving is dangerous because ingesting even a small amount of alcohol begins
the impairment process. For most of us, the Open
Container Law probably also seems quite reasonable.

Even though the bills proposed by MADD chapters
are likely to seem reasonable to most people, many
states have not turned them into laws. At the same

*Third
deductive
explanation*

time, the combination of alcohol and driving remains a problem. Nineteen thousand deaths per year may be lower than in previous years, but this is still too many avoidable tragedies. One appropriate response is for each of us to become involved in working for a solution. If MADD's three proposals seem reasonable to you, if they are not yet law in your state, and if you want these policies in place to protect you, your family, and your friends, call your local MADD chapter and ask what you can do to help.

Works Cited

Jacobs, James B. Drunk Driving: An American Dilemma. Chicago: U of Chicago P, 1989.

Lightner, Candy, and Nancy Hathaway. "The Other Side of Sorrow." Ladies' Home Journal Sept. 1990: 158–224.

Moskowitz, H., and C. D. Robinson. Effects of Low Doses of Alcohol on Driving Skills. Washington: National Highway Traffic Safety Administration, 1988.

Otto, Friedrich. "Seven Who Succeeded." *Time* 7 Jan. 1985: 40.

Peck, Raymond C., D. D. Sadler, and M. W. Perrine. "The Comparative Effectiveness of Alcohol Rehabilitation and Licensing Control Actions for Drunk Driving Offenders: A Review of the Literature." Alcohol, Drugs and Driving: Abstracts and Reviews 1 (1985): 15–39.

Russel, Dave. Personal interview. 19 Nov. 1993.

Voas, Robert B., and John H. Lacey. "Drunk Driving Enforcement Adjudication, and Sanctions in the United States." Drinking and Driving: Advances in Research and Prevention. Ed. Robert E. Mann and R. Jean Wilson. New York: Guilford, 1990. 130–45.

NANCY FRIDAY

NANCY FRIDAY is the author of numerous books, including *My Mother, My Self: The Daughter's Search for Identity* (1977); *My Secret Garden: Women's Sexual Fantasies* (1988); *Jealousy* (1997); and *Our Looks, Our Lives: Sex, Beauty, Power, and the Need to Be Seen* (1999).

The Age of Beauty

In "The Age of Beauty," first published in the *New York Times Magazine,* Friday uses induction and deduction to explain a parallel process of personal discovery and change. Her effective use of the pattern illustrates its versatility.

I had stood, all eagerness and impatience, while my sister's old 1
evening dress was pinned on me before that fateful dance at the yacht club. I didn't even know enough to look critically at the mirror and see that the strapless gown didn't suit me, especially after the dark brown velvet straps had been added to keep the dress up on my flat chest. I placed no value on looks. Having not had this rite of passage explained to me, I hadn't a clue that beauty was *the* prerequisite to adolescent stardom. Certainly, this new longing for boys had made me awkward in their presence; but I had noticed that they were awkward, too. Accustomed to being chosen first for any team of girls, I didn't question success that night, couldn't remember failure, so carefully had I buried nursery angers under trophies of recent accomplishments. I'm sure I was prepared to solve any hesitancy the boys might have in approaching us girls by taking the initiative myself. Assuming responsibility was who I was. In recent years my life had been a great adventure, in which there had been no comparisons made to my mother and sister. In my mind, they were boring in their tedious arguing over my sister's looks and her evenings with boys.

That night at the yacht club marked the end of childhood, the 2
finish of that adventure story with me as heroine. In one momentous night I took it all in and made my concession speech to myself. I watched my friends, whose leader I had been for years, watched them happy in the arms of desirable boys, and I recognized what they had that I lacked; saw it so clearly that I can recreate the film today, frame by frame: they had a look I lacked that went beyond beauty. It wasn't curls, breasts, prettiness, but a quality of acquies-

cence: the agreeable offer to be led instead of to lead. My own face was too eager, too open, too sure of itself. I needed a mask. I needed a new face that belied the intelligent leader inside and portrayed the little girl, no, the tiny, helpless baby who hadn't been held enough in the first years of life and had been waiting all these years for boys now to care for her.

3   I stood in my horrible dress, shoulder blades pressing into the wall, watching my dear friends dance by in the arms of handsome boys, with a frozen, ghastly smile on my face, denying I needed to be rescued. Why, even the girl who couldn't hit a ball danced by. Though they all whispered for me to hide in the ladies' room, I stood my ground.

4   Miserable as I was, I recognized the work ahead: the girl I had invented, so full of words waiting to be spoken and skills to be mastered, she had to be pushed down like an ugly jack-in-the-box. No boy was going to take a package like me.

5   A part of me was filled with rage at having to abandon what I thought to be a fine person. But I had no voice for rage. I belonged to a family of women who wept, and by not weeping I had made myself different from my mother and sister. But that night I became a woman; I wept and wept after someone's father drove me home while the rest of my group went off to a late party with boys. I showed my grief but not my rage. I did what most women still do: I swallowed anger, choked on it. I bowed my head, in part to be shorter, but also, like a cornered cow, to signal I had given up.

6   By morning I had buried and mourned my 11-year-old self, the leader, the actress, the tree climber, and had become an ardent beauty student. From now on I would ape my beautiful friends, smile the group smile, walk the group walk and, what with hanging my head and bending my knees, approximate as best I could the group look.

7   I have a photograph of myself taken in our yard on what looks like The First Day of Adolescence. I am sitting in a white wicker chair, hunched forward, staring at the ground, hands tightly clasped in my lap, swathed in the loser's agony of defeat. I remember the box camera aimed at me and that awful skirt and sweater, which had been my sister's—as had the awful dress at the yacht club, fine for a beauty but oh, so wrong for the tomboy I had been.

8   Twenty years later, I would go through countless hours of physical therapy to realign my spine, which has never recovered from the bent-leg posture I mastered in learning the art of being less. Neither professional success, great friendships nor the love of men

could recapture the self-confidence, the inner vision and, yes, the kindness of generosity I owned before I lost myself in the external mirrors of adolescence.

MEANINGS AND VALUES

1.   In Paragraph 2, Friday says, "That night at the yacht club marked the end of childhood, the finish of that adventure story with me as the heroine." Explain the significance of that one evening. What did it symbolize for Friday? (See "Guide to Terms": *Symbol.*)

2.   What does Friday mean when she says, "It wasn't curls, breast, prettiness, but a quality of acquiescence: the agreeable offer to be led instead of to lead" (Par. 2)? How is Friday defining the "role" of a successful woman from her adolescent perspective?

3.   Why did Friday have to undergo physical therapy for her spine (Par. 8)? What is the significance of this reference as the conclusion of her essay?

EXPOSITORY TECHNIQUES

1.   What inductive generalizations does the adolescent Friday make? Does the author still regard that generalization as valid? Why, or why not?

2.   Throughout the essay, the author uses masculine imagery to describe her youthful self, for example "adventure story" (Par. 2), "the girl who couldn't hit a ball" (3), and "the loser's agony of defeat" (7). Why might she have used such masculine and athletic references?

3.   What is the tone of Friday's essay? (Guide: *Tone.*) Is it successful in supporting the inductive pattern that she presents?

DICTION AND VOCABULARY

1.   Look up any of the following words with which you may be unfamiliar: tedious (Par. 1); acquiescence (2); ardent (6); swathed (7).

READ TO WRITE

1.   **Collaborating:** In a group, share stories from your adolescence that had a particular impact on the way that you defined yourself. Do group members share any similar experiences? Write a collaborative essay using one of those similar experiences as a basis for an inductive essay.

2. **Considering Audience:** Most women who read this essay would have some understanding of Friday's experiences. The image of the dress, the moving from "tomboy" to adolescent "girl," and the effort to "fit" are somewhat universal examples for young women. What images might be universal for men? Think of experiences that young boys have that mark their adolescence. Write an essay similar to Friday's looking at some adult male behaviors that may be outcomes of adolescent experiences. You may have to do some research in the form of interviews.

3. **Developing an Essay:** Think of something physical or emotional that is part of your adult character and that developed as a result of adolescent experiences. Write an essay incorporating an inductive generalization like Friday's to help your reader understand the impact of adolescence on your life.

(NOTE: Essays requiring development by means of INDUCTION and DEDUCTION are on p. 545 at the end of this chapter.)

Issues and Ideas

Digital Realities

- Maia Szalavitz, *A Virtual Life*
- J. C. Herz, *Superhero Sushi*

To some people, computers may be simply one more appliance whose effects on daily life seem to b°e minimal. However, the number of people who can avoid working on computers seems to be shrinking, just as computer influence seems to be growing. Computers, the software they run, and their many networked connections change the way we run our lives. They alter the time we need to spend at a task, the kind of tasks we can undertake, and our creative abilities. They alter our schedules, our places of work and play, and maybe even our friendships and personal relationships.

We can say that computers create new realities for us, digital realities. The essays that follow use inductive and deductive reasoning to explore these digital realities. Maia Szalavitz, in "A Virtual Life," considers her experiences as a computer user, sums them up, and then reviews her experiences to see if her perceptions and values have indeed changed as much as she suspects. J. C. Herz, in "Superhero Sushi," shows how cultures blend in remarkable ways once they are drawn into cyberspace. Both authors are a bit tentative in their conclusions because new digital realities may emerge in just a few years.

MAIA SZALAVITZ

Maia Szalavitz, formerly a television producer, now spends her time as a writer and is co-author of *Recovery Options: The Complete Guide, How You and Your Loved Ones Can Understand and Treat Alcohol and Other Drug Problems.* She lives in New York City. She has also written numerous articles for magazines, newspapers, and online publications.

A Virtual Life

In this essay from the *New York Times Magazine,* Szalavitz uses induction and deduction to explore digital reality and its consequences. Along the way, she compares the digital world to the "real" world, acknowledging the attractions of the electronic dimension.

After too long on the Net, even a phone call can be a shock. My boyfriend's Liverpudlian accent suddenly becomes indecipherable after the clarity of his words on screen; a secretary's clipped tonality seems more rejecting than I'd imagined it would be. Time itself becomes fluid—hours become minutes, and alternately seconds stretch into days. Weekends, once a highlight of my week, are now just two ordinary days. 1

For the last three years, since I stopped working as a producer for Charlie Rose, I have done much of my work as a telecommuter. I submit articles and edit them via E-mail and communicate with colleagues on Internet mailing lists. My boyfriend lives in England, so much of our relationship is also computer-mediated. 2

If I desired, I could stay inside for weeks without wanting anything. I can order food, and manage my money, love and work. In fact, at times I have spent as long as three weeks alone at home, going out only to get mail and buy newspapers and groceries. I watched most of the blizzard of '96 on TV. 3

But after a while, life itself begins to feel unreal. I start to feel as though I've merged with my machines, taking data in, spitting them back out, just another node on the Net. Others on line report the same symptoms. We start to feel an aversion to outside forms of socializing. It's like attending an A.A. meeting in a bar with everyone holding a half-sipped drink. We have become the Net naysayers' worst nightmare. 4

What first seemed like a luxury, crawling from bed to com-   5
puter, not worrying about hair, and clothes and face, has become an
evasion, a lack of discipline. And once you start replacing real human contact with cyber-interaction, coming back out of the cave can
be quite difficult.

I find myself shyer, more circumspect, more anxious. Or, con-   6
versely, when suddenly confronted with real live humans, I get
manic, speak too much, interrupt. I constantly worry if I'm dressed
appropriately, that perhaps I've actually forgotten to put on leggings and walked outside in the T-shirt and underwear I sleep and
live in.

At times, I turn on the television and just leave it to chatter in   7
the background, something that I'd never done previously. The
voices of the programs soothe me, but then I'm jarred by the commercials. I find myself sucked in by soap operas, or compulsively
needing to keep up with the latest news and the weather. *Dateline,*
Frontline, Nightline, CNN, New York 1, every possible angle of every
story over and over and over, even when they are of no possible use
to me. Work moves from foreground to background. I decide to
check my E-mail.

On line, I find myself attacking everyone in sight. I am irritable,   8
and easily angered. I find everyone on my mailing list insensitive,
believing that they've forgotten that there are people actually reading their invective. I don't realize that I'm projecting until after I've
been embarrassed by someone who politely points out that I've
flamed her for agreeing with me.

When I'm in this state, I fight with my boyfriend as well, misin-   9
terpreting his intentions because of the lack of emotional cues given
by our typed dialogue. The fight takes hours, because the system
keeps crashing. I say a line, then he does, then crash! And yet we
keep on, doggedly.

I'd never realized how important daily routine is: dressing for   10
work, sleeping normal hours. I'd never thought I relied so much on
co-workers for company. I began to understand why long-term unemployment can be so insidious, why life without an externally supported daily plan can lead to higher rates of substance abuse, crime,
suicide.

To counteract my life, I forced myself back into the real world.   11
I call people, set up social engagements with the few remaining
friends who haven't fled New York City. I try to at least get to the
gym, so as to differentiate the weekend from the rest of my week.

I arrange interviews for stories, doctor's appointments—anything to get me out of the house and connected with others.

But sometimes, just one engagement is too much. I meet a friend   12
and her ripple of laughter is intolerable—the hum of conversation in the restaurant, overwhelming. I make my excuses and flee. I re-enter my apartment and run to the computer as though it were a sanctuary.

I click on the modem, the once-grating sound of the connection   13
now as pleasant as my favorite tune. I enter my password. The real world disappears.

MEANINGS AND VALUES

1.   What is the inductive generalization the author arrives at after spending "too long on the Net" (Par. 1)? Where does she state it?

2.   In which paragraphs does she apply this generalization in a deductive manner?

3.   Explain the meaning of the following phrases: "just another node on the Net" (Par. 4); "I've flamed her for agreeing with me" (8); and "The fight takes hours, because the system keeps crashing" (9).

EXPOSITORY TECHNIQUES

1.   How does the essay's conclusion reinforce the inductive generalization arrived at earlier in the essay? What strategy does the writer employ to conclude the essay? (See "Guide to Terms": *Closings*.)

2.   What do the beginning sentences of Paragraphs 6–13 have in common in terms of wording or structure? (Guide: *Syntax*.) In what ways are these similarities related to the inductive generalization? Discuss how they help create coherence in the essay. (Guide: *Coherence*.)

3.   Discuss the use of parallelism to provide emphasis in the sentences in Paragraphs 3 and 11. (Guide: *Parallel Structure*.)

DICTION AND VOCABULARY

1.   Discuss the essay's use of computer terminology and slang used by people familiar with computers. Does this add to or detract from most readers' understanding of the essay? How would the essay be different if the terminology and slang were not used? (Guide: *Colloquial Expressions*.)

2. If you do not know the meaning of some of the following words, look them up in a dictionary: mediated (Par. 2); aversion (4); evasion, cyber (5); circumspect, manic (6); invective (8); doggedly (9); insidious (10); counteract (11).

READ TO WRITE

1. **Collaborating:** Freewrite about your computer experiences or about typical behaviors of computer users that you have observed. Compare your freewrite with other members of a group. As a team, focus on one or two particularly interesting areas, examples, or topics that you have in common. Develop these areas into passages that might be collected for a collaborative essay.

2. **Considering Audience:** Most readers have probably experienced the online environment to which Szalavitz refers in her essay. Most, therefore, would understand her references to the "virtual life." List other mechanical/technical devices that have removed people from human contact in past generations. Choose one with which you are familiar and write an essay similar to Szalavitz's, making an inductive generalization about the consequences of this other device.

3. **Developing an Essay:** Draw on Szalavitz's comparisons of the digital and the physical world in order to develop further comparisons in an essay of your own.

(NOTE: Suggestions for essays requiring development by INDUCTION and DEDUCTION are on p. 545 at the end of this chapter.)

J. C. HERZ

J. C. HERZ was a graduate student at Harvard University when she set out to explore the world of video games. Her reports on this virtual world have appeared in numerous magazines and in two books, *Surfing on the Internet* (1995) and *Joystick Nation: How Videogames Ate Our Quarters, Won Our Hearts, and Rewired Our Minds* (1997).

Superhero Sushi

For J. C. Herz, induction and deduction serve to explain the complicated mixture of American and Japanese characteristics and cultures that appear in the figures of video game heroes. The essay is a detailed and sometimes disturbing (though entertaining) exploration of the worlds of virtual reality and their complex relationships to everyday life. This essay first appeared in *Joystick Nation.*

After walloping her opponent, *Tekken* 2's heroine, Michelle Chang, swivels within the videogame arena and turns to face the camera, the viewer, the players. And it's a disconcerting moment, because she looks at you intelligently, and there are so many polygons in her face that she almost seems real, and because she is such a confusing mix of signals. She's a slender girl who beats up rippling hypermasculine bruisers. She's computer generated, yet more true-to-life than most of the silicon-enhanced, digitally retouched dreamgirls staring vacantly out from real world magazine racks. She's got an Asian name but ambiguous features—a Western nose, almond-shaped eyes. If you saw her on the street, you'd peg her as Amerasian.

In a way, she is a perfect metaphor for videogames themselves. She's a hybrid, of mixed Asian and American heritage, a creature made possible by the technological innovation of two hemispheres. Videogame characters are a bicontinental crossbreed of American and Japanese pop culture, with elements of Japanese comic books (manga) and animation as well as Western comics and science fiction.

On the Pacific side, videogames' family resemblance to manga and Japanimation are undeniable. In some cases, the games themselves are playable translations of popular Japanese comic books and animated films. In the last decade, hundreds of manga titles have been made into videogames in Japan, crossing over into the United States as manga shifts from cult status to mass acceptance, mostly via MTV. *Dragonball* alone has spawned six arcade games, a dozen titles for the Super Famicon (the Japanese equivalent of the Super NES), and a *Dragonball* Game Boy cartridge.

The salient feature of manga heroes—and the game characters   4
based on them—is a preternatural cuteness and almost freakish babylike quality, which takes the form of oversized heads, tiny noses, and saucerlike, impossibly liquid eyes. This way of drawing characters translated easily into early videogames, which didn't have the graphic resolution to represent characters with adult proportions. Small, cute characters had fewer pixels per inch and were easier to use, and so videogames borrowed, for reasons of expediency, what manga had developed as a matter of convention. Even a character like Mario the Plumber, who's supposed to be an adult, with facial hair no less, is rendered with the roly-poly proportions of a child, like a manga character. You would expect characters to take on mature dimensions as technology enables videogame manufacturers to animate large, complex, realistic forms. But instead, companies like Sega hew even closer to the babyland aesthetic. To paraphrase Gordon Gekko in *Wall Street,* cuteness is good. Cuteness works.

The reason cuteness works, as Scott McCloud notes in *Under-*   5
standing Comics,[1] is that abstraction fosters identification. It is only because an animated character is abstract and cartoony that we can project our own expressions onto him. We can't really map ourselves onto truly realistic characters—we see them as objects, separated from us by their details. To use an annoying but useful postmodern term, they read as the Other. The most realistically rendered characters in videogames are usually enemies. The good guys are rounded, simplified, and childlike, a puttylike visual glove into which our own hands and faces fit. If anything, early videogames were especially powerful in this sense. The more photorealistic characters become, the less we relate to them. Seeing a cast of TV actors in a full-motion video makes you into more of a spectator or an editor than a part of the story, whereas the polygon people in *Tekken 2* are easy to slide into, and a character like Mario or Sonic is even easier to identify with. A primitive, completely minimal figure like Pac-Man takes this link between pixel and personality to the nth degree.

---

[1]Scott McCloud, *Understanding Comics: The Invisible Art* (New York: HarperCollins, 1993).

Characters in *Mortal Kombat* have fingers and stubble. You watch them. Pac-Man has one black dot for an eye, and you *become* him.

Videogame companies are well aware of this, which is why   6
their figureheads are all round and minimal and cute, just like, well, jeepers, just like Mickey Mouse. Sega is even working on a version of *Virtua Fighter 2* called *Virtua Fighter Kizu* ("kizu" is Japlish for "kids") where all the adult martial arts characters are rendered with gigantic toddler heads. From a distance, it looks like ferocious dueling lollipops. If you count the height of their hair, the giant toddlers' heads are as tall as the rest of their bodies. The eyes are bigger than their flying fists.

Americans usually read these saucer eyes as Western, as a sign   7
of whiteness. After all, the reasoning goes, Western eyes are bigger and rounder than Asian eyes. This must be the way that they see us. And for some strange reason, they're drawing us all over their comic books. But actually, that's not the case, says Matt Thorn, a doctoral candidate at Columbia University who is writing his dissertation on teen-girl comic books in Japan. "Japanese readers don't think of the characters as white," he says. "Of course, they have these huge eyes. And so to us, the characters do look white, because Westerners expect that the Japanese will represent themselves the way that Westerners represent them. That is, we have these certain standardized ways of indicating to a viewer this character is Asian or this character is black or this character is anything but white, including the slanty eyes and the black hair. And of course, the Japanese don't draw themselves that way. Those characters aren't white, and the readers don't think of them as being white, despite those features. There's a concept in linguistics called the unmarked category. And in the West, which is white-dominated, white is the unmarked category. Everything else is marked and has to be indicated, but white is taken for granted. But in Japan, Japanese is the unmarked category, the one that's taken for granted. They've developed that style with the huge eyes—that's the way that they've developed for drawing people, which means Japanese people. And when they want to indicate that a character is not Japanese, they have different ways of doing it. Like, for white people and black people they use exaggerated features. Like for white people, they'll have big noses or really big bodies or really sharply defined eyelashes."

So within a typical martial arts videogame, the racial contin-   8
uum is deceptive. It's not a simple matter of ethnic blur. It's a matter of reading the signs in completely different ways. All the indeterminate characters that to Western eyes would read as white look

Japanese to kids playing the games in Tokyo. Figuratively speaking, we read these faces left to right. The Japanese read them up and down. This isn't their way of drawing us. It's their way of drawing themselves. Meanwhile, both sets of videogame players look at the screen and think the characters look native. It's counterintuitive. But when you think about it, really, *no one* has eyes that big.

There are characters in videogames that are visibly Asian, the   9
way Westerners would draw Asians. But these characters are never supposed to be from Japan. They are supposed to be from China or Korea or Mongolia or some other part of Asia. "The irony," says Thorn, "is that the techniques that Westerners use to draw Asians are the same techniques the Japanese use when they're drawing Asians other than themselves. So you'll have a manga in which there are Japanese characters, which to us read as white. And then you'll have a Chinese character, and the Chinese character is drawn in such a way as to indicate to players that this character is not Japanese but Chinese. And they'll use the same kinds of techniques that we use: the straight black hair, the slanty eyes, etc."

And Americans? Usually, when a videogame character hails   10
from the United States, he's blond. He's broad. He's buff. And he's larger than life, or at least larger than the other videogame characters. He looks more like an American comic book character than a manga hero. And he's not nearly as unassuming and cute. In fact, the more videogames borrow from American comic books, the less cute they get. Whereas Japanese manga characters are generally childlike and unassuming, American cartoon heroes in the Marvel/DC vein are, if anything, hyperadult. "In America," writes comic book historian Fred Schodt, "almost every comic book hero is a 'superhero' with bulging biceps (or breasts, as the case may be), a face and physique that rigidly adhere to the classical traditions, invincibly accompanied by superpowers, and a cloying, moralistic personality."[2] Like the drawings in a Western superhero comic, American characters in Japanese fighting games have wildly distorted, hyperrealistic, hypersexual bodies. And in American software houses, where Superman takes native precedence over Speed Racer and Astro Boy, the videogames themselves are absolutely devoid of blinking sweetness, offering instead the beloved stateside menagerie of larger-than-life comic book mutants. Capcom's *Marvel*

[2]Frederik Schodt, *Manga Manga: The World of Japanese Comics* (Tokyo: Kodansha, 1983), 77, 78.

Superheroes arcade cabinet, which is seven feet tall and physically towers over its Japanese counterparts, pumps out sound effects at blockbuster volume and stars veiny, spandex-clad standbys like the Incredible Hulk, Spiderman, and Captain America. The arcade game is, essentially, a moving comic book that replaces Pow! Boom! Zap! bubbles with gut-rattling audio effects. In this way, a Marvel Comics videogame is a more intense comic book experience than the paper it's based on. Comic book characters have always been drawn swooping and swinging and flying through the air. Now they can do it in real time. Comic book videogames are comic books squared. And with this added dimension the blurry line between comic books and videogames finally dissolves.

This blur between media is epitomized by *Comix Zone,* a   11 videogame for the Sega Saturn. The premise, whose only precedent is Swedish pop group A-Ha's *Take on Me* video, is that your character, Sketch, is trapped in a Marvelesque comic book universe and forced to battle through it, panel by panel, combating enemies drawn by Mortus, an evil comic book artist. Along the way, helper characters yell out from the corner of the screen ("Watch out, Sketch!") in comic book dialogue boxes. The object, ultimately, is to defeat the evil illustrator and rip yourself out of his two-dimensional paper universe. It's like an Escher drawing, where you break out of one trompe l'oeil tableau only to find yourself in another impossible illusion. Beyond the simulated comic book page is a simulated TV cartoon, when, really, there aren't any pages, or any television, for that matter. There are only the conventions of paper and television, twined around each other, to float the action of a videogame.

Of course, to kids playing *Comix Zone* or *Marvel Superheroes* or   12 *Tekken 2,* the distinction between comic book and videogame or Asian and Western is completely irrelevant. The only categories they recognize are "fun" and "not fun." If you walk into an arcade, you don't see white kids choosing white characters and black kids choosing black characters. Kids routinely choose any and all of these options and don't think twice about it, because the only factor in their decision is a given character's repertoire of kick-ass fighting moves. Ironically, all considerations of race, sex, and nationality are shunted aside in the videogame arena, where the only goal is to clobber everyone indiscriminately.

But on a deeper level, the kids playing these games intuitively   13 understand that they're operating in a disembodied environment where your virtual skin doesn't have to match your physical one, and that you can be an Okinawan karate expert, a female Thai kick-boxer, a black street fighter from the Bronx, or a six-armed alien from outer space, all within the span of a single game. Members of the previous generation might have a problem with the idea of playing a Japanese schoolgirl in a combat game. At the very least, they would be aware of their decision to choose this character, and maybe even a little smug about being enlightened enough to do so. For kids of the eighties and nineties, shuffling videogame bodies and faces is like playing with a remote control. The game starts, cycles through a bunch of avatars, and you punch the fire button when you see one you like. It's channel surfing.

In this milieu, the classic distinctions between heroes and villains break down. In older videogames, and in all previous media, the good guys look one way and the bad guys look another. It may be as simple as black hats and white hats or as fraught as cowboys and Indians. In movies and TV shows, we know what the hero and the villain are supposed to look like, and those images are very loaded. Heroes talk like midwestern news anchors and own dogs. Bad guys speak with foreign accents and stroke cats. Heroines are slender and blond and adorably helpless. Bad girls have dark hair and red nails and hips and guns they're ready to use. And because of the way these people look, and the way they're lit, it's clear for whom you're supposed to root.   14

But in an arcade fighting game like *Virtua Fighter 2*, you can't do that, because those categories don't exist at all. You can play any character, and it's every gladiator for himself. This type of videogame doesn't label opposing forces as evil or good, because that would imply a scripted outcome, that the designated "hero" is supposed to win, when really no one is supposed to win. Everyone is supposed to play. It's the skill of the competitors that determines who wins and who loses. In a videogame, unlike in novels or movies or other fictions like history, no one—not even the game designer—knows the outcome of a given contest. And so it's impossible to cast a moral hair light on one character versus another.[3] There are no heroes and villains in a round-robin martial arts game. There are only combatants, each with his or her own special weapons, attributes,   15

[3]This becomes patently obvious when you play a game like *Tekken 2,* where even the more wholesome characters are monstrously broad-shouldered, earnest, square-jawed, and monumental in the style of socialist realism. This is when you realize that monstrosity is in the eye of the beholder. This is also when you realize that most of the superheroes we hold up for children to admire are freaks.

and fighting style. In the post–Cold War world, this seems an even-handed approach. Everyone's a hero. Everyone is also a monster.

Or, to paraphrase the Red Dog beer motto, you are your own   16
monster. Now that the videogame hero is freed from the cosmetic constraints of gallant poster boyhood, you can play a whole menagerie of creatures, from werewolves to ice creatures to dinosaurs. Superhuman strength and/or demonic powers seem to be the only prerequisites for inclusion in the videogame bestiary, which draws from martial arts movies, Arthurian legend, the Greek pantheon, science fiction, Norse mythology, and Jurassic Park. And that's just *Primal Rage,* one of the hotter fighting games of 1996.

Primal Rage is mythic stuff. It's a fight-to-the-death among an-   17
gry, violent demigods who are also dinosaurs. According to the epic back story, "Before there were humans, gods walked the earth. They embodied the essence of Hunger, Survival, Life, Death, Insanity, Decay, Good, and Evil. They fought countless battles up through the Mesozoic Wars." When these conflicts threatened to destroy the planet, a wiser, more mature deity in another dimension decided to launch a kind of mythological NATO peacekeeping mission to shut them up. "He was not powerful enough to kill the gods," the story goes, "so instead he banished one to a rocky tomb within the moon. This disrupted the fragile balance between the gods; pandemonium ensued, and a great explosion threw clouds of volcanic dust into the atmosphere. The dinosaurs died out, and the surviving gods went into suspended animation. Now, the impact of a huge meteor strikes the Earth. Its destructive force wipes out civilization, rearranges the continents, and frees the imprisoned gods. Get ready to rumble . . . ."

The game ensues, throwing you into a kind of fossil fantasy   18
Ragnarok scenario where you choose one of these reptilian gods to fight against all the others. Each of them has its own repertoire of decay-related weapons, most of which involve bodily functions. The God of Survival is a crafty velociraptor lacking in brute strength but incredibly agile and slippery.

In addition to its personal eccentricities, each character also has   19
a coordinated epic backdrop. The fire-breathing Tyrannosaurus rex dukes it out in the Inferno, an active volcanic island oozing lava. The serpentine Goddess of Insanity fights on a Stonehengian knoll under a full moon with petrified enemies planted like lawn sculptures in the background. And, if you make it through all these themed battlegrounds, the final scene of *Primal Rage* is set in a dinosaur graveyard littered with the bones of fallen reptiles. Red cracks split the

ground, and a huge vortex swirls in the sky as you leap, bite, and strike as best you can against a very scary-looking, dragonish God of Death. It's a perfect frappé of paleontology and the supernatural, prehistory and the apocalypse. Like the science fiction universe, videogames are where technology melts into the occult. This is a place where missile launchers and mojo are both legitimate weapons. All the old monsters, harpies, dragons, and divinities are excavated from their mythological sediment, sampled, looped, remixed, cross-faded, and digitally recycled. Videogames do to dusty legends what deejays do to vintage vinyl. They weave the old grooves into something accessible to teenagers.

And increasingly, it doesn't matter where those teenagers are. 20 The same way a transcendent house mix leaps from a mixing board in London to sound systems in Tokyo, Los Angeles, and Helsinki, good videogames have a way of becoming popular everywhere. It's all digital. And a certain echelon of global youth all have access to the technology. So if it's fun, it quickly goes transnational. And in the process, it ceases to connote nationality. A successful dance track or videogame doesn't read Japanese or American, German, or British. It's all just pop. And it's yours for fifty cents.

The finest digital architects on the planet have built these play- 21 grounds out of comic books, Hong Kong cinema, scroll paintings and music videos, ancient monsters and digital technology. They pour in their myths and suck out quarters.

And this is what it's about, finally, as the cultural streams of 22 East and West swirl into the Tastee-Freez of global entertainment. Mythic figures resonate, all the more if they're engaged in some kind of combat or action adventure, real or simulated, the most popular forms being basketball and video games. They resonate for the same reasons mythic figures have always resonated. Only now, the audience numbers in the millions, and the object is not to celebrate ancestors or teach lessons or curry favor with the spirits. It's commerce. And the people transmitting their stories to the next generation aren't priests or poets or medicine women. They're multinational corporations. And they are not trying to appease the gods. They are trying to appease the shareholders. It's not just videogames. It's everything, with the possible exception of the Internet. All the mythic pop stars in Hollywood, the NBA, and MTV are purchasable commodities. Videogames are just the logical extreme, because all the superheroes in them are computer gener- ated for maximum resonance and marketing kick. Unlike sports stars or actors, they don't get addicted, arrested, or petulant. They perform. They may look and act superhuman. They may throw lightning or breathe fire. And when you're in the game, they may really inspire or scare you. But unlike the mythic monsters that preceded them, videogame demons are caged in their arcade cabinets, firmly under the control of their corporate wardens. Demigods used to make people docile. Now it's the other way around. It is Sega and Namco and Capcom and Williams Entertainment, finally, that have tamed the dragons.

MEANINGS AND VALUES

1. Explain the significance of the title of the essay. How does it connect to Herz's message?

2. Why does Herz open with a description of a female, Japanese video character? What is significant about this character as opposed to other characters that Herz might have chosen to use in an introduction?

3. What is the significance of Paragraph 4? Does technology control other images that we see? Can it define or create stereotypes? Please explain.

4. In the first section of this essay (Par. 1–11), Herz explains the different images of heroes from different nations. But in Paragraph 12, she makes a clear shift into limiting the importance of gender, race, and nationality. What is the significance of this shift?

EXPOSITORY TECHNIQUES

1. Herz repeatedly uses comparison and contrast in this essay. Identify the different things that she compares. How successful is this technique for a reader who may have limited knowledge of video games?

2. What is the thesis of this essay? (See "Guide to Terms": *Thesis.*) What type of reasoning (inductive, deductive, or a combination of both) does Herz employ to clarify and support the thesis?

3. Herz uses the second person (*you*) at various points in the essay. How effective is this? Why might she have chosen that technique in the places that she did?

DICTION AND VOCABULARY

1. Identify slang and jargon in "Superhero Sushi." (Guide: *Slang.*) Is the use of such language excessive? Could a person unfamiliar with

video games and the language associated with them understand the essay? Please explain.

2.   To what age group(s) is this essay targeted? Explain how Herz's language helps to define the age of her intended audience.

READ TO WRITE

1.   **Collaborating:** List as many video game characters as you can think of and identify their race, gender, nationality, or species (if appropriate). Working with a group, compare your lists. Write a plan for an essay analyzing the various trends in video game characters.

2.   **Considering Audience:** This essay clearly will be more easily understood by readers who have played video games or at least observed others play them. Using Herz's thesis as the basis for an essay, write a similar piece for an audience that might be less familiar with such technology.

3.   **Developing an Essay:** Choose two or three virtual characters with which you are familiar, then go to a local arcade and study the newest games. Write an essay similar to Herz's that uses these characters collectively as a basis for an inductive generalization about the latest trends in video game characters.

(NOTE: Suggestions for essays requiring development by INDUCTION and DEDUCTION follow.)

Writing Suggestions for Chapter 12

INDUCTION AND DEDUCTION

Choose one of the following unformed topics and shape your central theme from it. This could express the view you prefer or an opposing view. Develop your composition primarily by use of induction, alone or in combination with deduction. Unless otherwise directed by your instructor, be completely objective and limit yourself to exposition, rather than engaging in argumentation.

1. Little League baseball (or the activities of 4-H clubs, Boy Scouts, Girl Scouts, etc.) as a molder of character
2. Conformity as an expression of insecurity
3. Pop music as a mirror of contemporary values
4. The status symbol as a motivator to success
5. The liberal arts curriculum and its relevance to success in a career
6. Student opinion as the guide to better educational institutions
7. The role of public figures (including politicians, movie stars, and business people) in shaping attitudes and fashions
8. The values of education, beyond dollars and cents
9. Knowledge and its relation to wisdom
10. The right of individuals to select the laws they obey
11. Television commercials as a molder of morals
12. The "other" side of one ecological problem
13. The value of complete freedom from worry
14. Homosexuality as inborn or as voluntary behavior
15. Raising mentally challenged children at home
16. Fashionable clothing as an expression of power (or as a means of attaining status)

COLLABORATIVE EXERCISE

Using number 3, 5, or 10 from the Writing Suggestions list above, have each member of your group write an inductive generalization for the topic. Then as a group, create a plan for a unified essay that presents one of the inductive generalizations.

13

Using Patterns for *Argument*

Argument and exposition have many things in common. They both use the basic patterns of exposition; they share a concern for the audience; and they often deal with similar subjects, including social trends (changing social relationships, the growth of the animal rights movement), recent developments (the creation of new strains of plants through genetic manipulation, developments in health care), and issues of widespread concern (the quality of education, the effects of pollution). As a result, the study of argument is a logical companion to the study of exposition. Yet the two kinds of writing have very different purposes.

Expository writing shares information and ideas; it explores issues and explains problems. Argumentative writing has a different motivation. It asks readers to choose one side of an issue or take a particular action, whether it is to choose a career, vote for a candidate, or build a new highway. In exposition we select facts and ideas to give a clear, interesting, and thorough picture of a subject. In argument we select facts and ideas that provide strong support for our point of view and arrange this evidence in the most logical and persuasive order, taking care to provide appropriate background information and to acknowledge and refute opposing points of view.

The evidence we choose for an argument is determined to a great extent by the attitudes and needs of the people we are trying to persuade. For example, suppose you want to argue successfully for a new approach to secondary education in your community—an approach that enrolls students in "mini-schools" according to their interests. Your essay would need to provide enough examples, facts, and reasons to convince parents and community leaders that the approach would be best for *their* children, not just for children in general. You would need to show that the community could afford the approach and that the benefits would justify the added expense. To be effective, moreover, your essay would also need to answer possible objections to the proposal and demonstrate that it is preferable to other approaches a reasonable school board and community might consider.

Your argumentative writing needs to focus on your thesis: the opinion you wish readers to share, the action you want them to undertake, or the assertion you wish them to endorse. The twin poles of argumentative writing—your thesis and the needs and values of your readers—need to be linked by evidence and reasoning. Evidence and reasoning extend your thesis to readers, and they bring readers closer to it.

WHY USE ARGUMENT?

Argumentative writing responds to situations in which there are two or more conflicting points of view. An argument attempts to resolve or at least modify disagreements by encouraging people to agree upon an action or a point of view. You can recognize an argumentative thesis and an argumentative essay by the writer's evident awareness of opposing perspectives. When readers are likely to require good reasons before they will agree with your thesis or when they are likely to resist your point of view, your situation is one that calls for argumentative writing.

In addition, a simple argumentative essay can serve one of three purposes. Some essays ask readers to agree with a *value judgment* ("The present day care system is inadequate and inefficient"). Others propose a *specific action* ("Money from the student activity fee at this college should be used to establish and staff a fitness program available to all students"). And still others advance an *opinion* quite different from that held by most people ("The supposed 'revolution' of Internet shopping is no more than the logical next step in catalog retailing").

In situations calling for more complex arguments, however, you should feel free to combine these purposes as long as the relationship among them is made clear to the reader. In a complex argument, for instance, you might *first* show that the city government is inefficient and corrupt and *then* argue that it is better to change the city charter to eliminate the opportunities for the abuse of power than it is to try to vote a new party into office or to support a reform faction within the existing political machine.

Some people draw a distinction between situations calling for *logical argument* (usually called, simply, *argument*) and *persuasive argument* (usually termed *persuasion*). Whereas logical argument appeals to reason, persuasive argument appeals to the emotions. The aim of both, however, is to convince, and they are nearly always blended into whatever mixture seems most likely to do the convincing. After all, reason and emotion are both important human elements. The two often work together, with reason helping to change minds and emotion helping to prompt action.

CHOOSING A STRATEGY

Argument begins with an issue, moves to a thesis (or assertion) addressing the issue, and concludes with evidence and reasoning to convince readers and deal with opposing perspectives. This is an admittedly oversimplified view of the components of an argument (and the process of composing), yet it serves to point out that choosing strategies for an argumentative essay calls for a number of different activities.

First, you need to *identify an issue* that you can effectively address through argument. Without an issue—a difference in point of view—you have nothing to argue about. Some issues will take a clear shape before you begin writing: matters of social justice, environmental regulation, civil and criminal law, education, community relationships, and the like are filled with familiar and significant matters of disagreement and difference. In preparing to address such an issue, you need to make sure that you understand them well enough to present them in clearly defined form to readers and to provide appropriate background. You should be ready to stress the significance of an issue and the need to make a judgment or take an action.

Some familiar issues have been argued so often that readers are not likely to be receptive to further argument; others are matters of taste that are beyond argument. For instance, no amount of reasoning is likely to convince people who dislike action movies to begin enjoying them. And some issues involve matters of deeply held religious or ethical beliefs that are difficult, if not impossible, to address through logical argument.

Many issues will take a clear shape only when you think and write about them, however. Perhaps you have been irritated for some time by the concert arrangements at a local civic center, and you believe other people share your irritation. Your irritation is not itself an issue, but it can point to one. If you propose changing the arrangements, and you realize that your proposals are not the only ones that ought to be considered, then you have begun to shape an issue. As you write, you need to be ready to explain the issue to your readers, perhaps drawing on their own irritation with the arrangements to stress the importance of considering changes. Of course, when an issue takes shape in your writing, the opposing points of view are probably not well developed, if at all. For instance, you may not be aware of any alternate concert arrangements that other people have proposed, but you can probably think of some plausible alternatives to your own. In exploring them for readers, however, you identify the opposing points of view that create the issue.

Next, you need to *articulate your stance.* At the heart of an argumentative essay is the opinion you want readers to share or the action you are proposing they undertake. Being able to state this *thesis* (or *proposition*) concisely and clearly to yourself is essential to developing your strategy for an argumentative essay. Conveying your thesis in convincing form is, after all, the main purpose of the essay. Expressing your stance concisely and clearly in a *thesis statement* is perhaps the best way to alert readers to the point of your argument.

Some writers like to arrive at a sharply focused thesis statement early in the process of composing and use it to guide the selection and arrangement of evidence, for example,

> The inconvenience and discontent that accompanies concerts at the Civic Center can be greatly reduced by moving the box office further away from the main entrance doors, doubling the number of rest rooms, improving the lighting, and removing the temporary seating that partially obstructs the central aisles.

Other writers settle on a tentative ("working") thesis, which they revise as an essay takes shape. In either case, checking frequently to see that factual evidence and supporting ideas or arguments are clearly linked to the thesis is a good way for writers to make sure their finished essays are coherent, unified arguments.

Finally, you need to develop evidence and reasoning that supports your thesis and arrange it in ways that readers will consider clear and convincing. Variety in evidence gives writers a chance to present an argument fully and persuasively. Examples, facts and figures, statements from authorities, personal experience, or the experience of other people—all these can be valuable sources of support. The basic patterns of exposition, too, can be supporting strategies.

For example, to persuade people to take driving lessons at an automobile racing school, you might tell the story of someone whose life was saved through the evasive maneuver she learned in her first day at such a school. Or you might follow this narrative example with a classification of the most common kinds of accidents, comparing them, in turn, with the parallel kinds of safety lessons the schools provide.

The expository patterns can also be easily adapted to argumentative purposes. Writers frequently turn to example, comparison and contrast, cause and effect, definition, and induction or deduction to organize arguments. A series of *examples* can be an effective way of showing that a government social policy does not work and in fact hurts the people it is supposed to serve. *Comparison and contrast* can guide choices among competing products, among ways of disposing toxic waste, or among ways of revising student loan policies. *Cause and effect* can organize an argument over who is to blame for a problem or over the possible consequences of a new program. *Definition* is helpful when a controversy hinges on the interpretation of a key term or when the meaning of an important word is itself the subject of disagreement. *Induction* and *deduction* are useful in argument because they provide the kind of careful, logical reasoning necessary to convince many readers, especially those who may at first have little sympathy for the writer's opinion.

An argument need not be restricted to a single pattern. The choice of a pattern or a combination of patterns depends on the subject, the specific purpose, and the kinds of evidence needed to convince the audience to which the essay is directed. Some arguments about complicated, significant issues use so many patterns that they can be called *complex arguments.*

In arranging your evidence and reasoning, you should also consider the potential impact on readers. Three common and effective arrangements from which you can choose are ascending order, refutation-proof, and pro-con. In an *ascending order* arrangement, the strongest, most complex, or most emotionally moving evidence comes last, where it can build on the rest of the evidence in the essay and is likely to have the greatest impact on readers, as in the following example.

> Introduction: The issue—some people are trying to have genetically altered farm products banned while others are arguing for an increase in the number of such products.
> Tentative thesis: Despite a few drawbacks, genetically altered farm products are a great benefit to us all.

Support 1: The regulations governing genetic alteration and extensive testing means the products are generally quite safe; problems have been minor and worries have not been warranted by experience.

Support 2: Genetic alteration can create crops that are less resistant to disease and that are easier to cook and digest.

Support 3: Genetic alteration can make farms more productive and in so doing lower food costs, make more food available, and help fight undernourishment throughout the world [strongest, most moving support; even if there are some problems, these benefits may outweigh them].

Conclusion: Sums up, restates, and reinforces the thesis and the evidence.

In a *refutation-proof* arrangement, the writer acknowledges opposing points of view early in the essay and then goes on to show why the author's outlook is superior.

Tentative thesis: Genetically altered farm products benefit farmers and consumers.

Opposing points of view: Genetically engineered products are often less tasty and less nutritious; they can have unintended health consequences for farmers and consumers.

Refutation: The products can be engineered to be both tasty and nutritious—the choice is up to the producers and consumers; all natural products can have unintended consequences, and we forget this when dealing with "scientific products"; more extensive testing can help us deal with any unfortunate consequences.

Support 1: Genetically altered products can be more disease and pest-resistant, reducing the dangers of exposure to pesticides and other chemicals.

Support 2: Genetically altered products provide greater variety for consumers and choices for farmers looking for products appropriate for their soil and climate.

Support 3, 4, 5. . . .

Conclusion

A *pro-con* arrangement allows the writer to present an opposing point of view and then refute it, continuing until all opposition has been dealt with and all positive arguments voiced. This strategy is particularly useful when there is a strong opposition to the writer's thesis.

Tentative thesis: The benefits of genetically altered farm products far outweigh the liabilities.

Con 1: The engineered products may end up replacing "natural" ones.

Pro 1: Some "natural" products may be less common, but the success of organic and other specialty products indicates that there will be a demand for both "new" and "natural" foods.

Con 2: Genetically altered products are often designed for the needs of large corporate farms and will contribute to the demise of smaller, family farms.

Pro 2: The shift to larger farms and agribusinesses has been occurring for many reasons other than genetic engineering of crops; the new crops will have only a small effect, if any.

Con 3, 4, 5. . . .

Pro 3, 4, 5. . . .

Conclusion

DEVELOPING ARGUMENTS

In developing an argument, you need to pay attention to your choice of evidence and to make sure your reasoning is clear and logical. It is never possible to arrive at absolute proof—argument, after all, assumes that there are at least two sides to the matter under discussion—yet a carefully constructed case will convince many readers.

One way to construct arguments is to follow the pattern of *data-warrant-claim reasoning* as outlined by the philosopher Stephen Toulmin. *Data* correspond to your evidence and *claim* to your thesis or assertion. *Warrant* refers to the mental process by which a reader connects the data to the claim. To argue effectively, you need to show your readers how the warrant connects the data to your claim, as in the following sequence.

Data: Children's books are relatively expensive, generally costing between ten and 30 dollars.

Warrant: Buying children a variety of books can be very expensive.

Warrant: Children learn to love books by reading; playing with books on a regular basis is something that helps them become good readers.

Warrant: Children get easily bored with a book, so they need a variety of books to keep them occupied—though the book

that bores them today will interest them tomorrow and the day after.
Claim: The high cost of children's books keeps many children from learning to love books and becoming better readers.

At the same time, a flaw in logic can undermine an otherwise reasonable argument and destroy a reader's confidence in its conclusions. The introduction to Chapter 12, "Reasoning by Use of *Induction* and *Deduction*," discusses some important errors to avoid in reasoning or in choosing evidence. Here are some others:

Post hoc ergo propter hoc ("After this therefore because of this")— Just because one thing happened *after* another does not mean that the first event caused the second. In arguing without detailed supporting evidence that a recent drop in the crime rate is the result of a newly instituted anticrime policy, a writer might be committing this error, because there are other equally plausible explanations: a drop in the unemployment rate, for example, or a reduction in the number of people in the 15–25 age bracket, the segment of the population that is responsible for a high proportion of all crimes.

Begging the question—A writer "begs the question" when he or she assumes the truth of something that is still to be proven. An argument that begins this way, "The recent, unjustified rise in utility rates should be reversed by the state legislature," assumes that the rise is "unjustified," though this important point needs to be proven.

Ignoring the question—A writer may "ignore the question" by shifting attention away from the issue at hand to some loosely related or even irrelevant matter: for example, "Senator Jones's plan for encouraging new industries cannot be any good because in the past he has opposed tax cuts for corporations" (this approach shifts attention away from the merits of Senator Jones's proposal). A related problem is the *ad hominem* (toward the person) argument, which substitutes personal attack for a discussion of the issue in question.

Student Essay

In recent years, many new foods have been developed, including some that are substitutes for "natural foods." The development of these products has gone hand-in-hand with growing controversies over their safety, with most people willing to at least listen to the criticisms on the grounds that food safety is one of the most important public health issues all of us face. In the face of such controversy, Julie Richardson sets out to defend an "artificial" food, olestra, in her essay, "The Fight on Fat Controversy."

The Fight on Fat Controversy
by Julie Richardson

Today, Americans are realizing the importance of a healthy lifestyle, which includes exercising and following a balanced diet. Reducing fat in the diet decreases the risk of health problems such as heart disease and obesity and is a vital step in achieving an improved lifestyle. Food manufacturers are responding to the consumer's needs by adding more reduced-fat foods to product lines. A trip down the grocery aisle is evidence of the increased "better-for-you" products, tempting the consumer with less salt, less sugar, and sugarless, lower fat, and nonfat items.

Background

Importance of topic for readers

After nine years of research, the U.S. Food & Drug Administration (FDA) approved a fat-free cooking oil known as olestra to be used in frying savory snacks. Olestra has been hailed as a breakthrough solution for millions of Americans who are looking to reduce fat and calories from the foods they want to eat without sacrificing the quality of taste. Excitement, curiosity, and confusion have followed the new lineup of products made with olestra. This new discovery is slowly, yet dramatically changing food processing, and consumers need to educate themselves on the facts surrounding this innovative alternative to fat.

Information about specific issue/ disagreement

"Confusion" suggests potential disagreements

Olestra, marketed by Procter & Gamble as Olean, is made from vegetable oil and sugar, then used in place of regular cooking oils or fats. This revolutionary fat substitute does not break down like other fats; instead, it passes through the stomach and intestines without being digested or absorbed by the body. As a result, olestra provides all the taste of vegetable oil but none of the calories or harmful saturated fats of regular vegetable oils. The results are snacks that taste great with no fat and half of the calories.

Heralded as a waistline-whittling savior by millions of consumers, olestra has been condemned by others as a nutritional saboteur with distressing gastrointestinal side effects. The Center for Science in the Public Interest (CSPI) believes there are serious health risks when products made with olestra are consumed. This nonprofit health group believes the FDA should ban olestra or, at the very least, require a prominent warning label on the front of packages stating that olestra can cause severe side effects. Currently there is only a small warning on the back of packaging, warning consumers that they could experience soft stools when consuming olestra.

Concise statement of issue

Arguments against the product

Challengers of olestra also advocate that the body is robbed of vitamins or carotenoids (found in fresh fruits and vegetables) that have already been digested. Michael Jacobson, executive director of CSPI, reveals that carotenoids protect against chronic diseases. Jacobson also states that long-term use of olestra in snack foods is likely to cause thousands of cases of cancer and heart disease each year. Opponents of olestra believe additional research should be completed to ensure the protection of consumers' health.

More arguments against

Proponents of olestra, including Procter & Gamble and the FDA, are quick to point out the fallacy of olestra "robbing" the body of vitamins and carotenoids that have already been digested, as Jacobson implies. Olestra can only interact with vitamins or carotenoids that are in the digestive system at the exact same time as the olestra; and even then, the level of interaction has not been outside the acceptable range. Results from the FDA Advisory Committee review in June 1998 determined there is no direct evidence that carotenoids are responsible for lower risk of disease, which disproves Jacobson's theory that carotenoids protect against chronic diseases. These results also show the absurdity of Jacobson's claim that long-term use of olestra causes cancer.

Arguments and evidence for the product— refuting opponents of olestra

Frito-Lay has been allowed to fortify their WOW! Chips with extra vitamins to insure there is no net loss or reduction in vitamin levels due to normal absorption. However, the FDA is preventing Frito-Lay from adding extra carotenoids to their WOW! Chips because the jury in the scientific community is still out as to whether or not carotenoids are actually good or bad. In a study conducted in Sweden, a compelling argument raises the possibility of carotenoids actually causing cancer.

Admits to some validity in worries about the product

Michael Jacobson's research is anecdotal and unscientific. Most of his research is obtained through questionnaires completed on the CSPI website, not in a laboratory by scientists. In contrast, P&G has spent 25 years and $200 million researching olestra, in one of the most comprehensive reviews of any food additive in history. The FDA received 150,000 pages of data from studies of 8,000 adults and children. Results from a follow-up study were reviewed in June 1998 by a FDA panel of leading health, medical, and nutrition experts who overwhelmingly reaffirmed the safety of Olean. The committee also discussed the possibility of removing or rewording the warning label on Frito-Lay's WOW! Chips.

Direct refutation of major objections supported by statistics and authoritative testimony

Another issue of concern with olestra rivals is the labeling of "fat-free" on snacks made with olestra. Opponents feel the packaging is misleading to consumers since olestra is an indigestible fat. I do understand the dispute over labeling, even though olestra technically is a fat substitute and does not have the same effect as regular fat in the body.

Agrees with objections to packaging of product

Side effects from olestra in some people have given way for public scrutiny. Olestra's larger and tighter molecules pass through the body undigested. Since the olestra is mixed in with other food products in the digestive system, it may physically soften the stool, similar to adding oil or water to bread dough. The symptoms experienced may depend on consumption, other eaten foods, and the individual body reaction.

Another objection

Followed by two paragraphs of refutation

Prior to olestra's approval, it was determined that digestive symptoms were common among the general population. As recorded in the FDA's report on olestra in 1996, 40 precent of adults noted that they experienced some digestive effect within the past month. Also, a study published in the Journal of the American Medical Association (January 1998) said that potato chips made with Olean are no more likely to cause digestive changes than potato chips made with regular vegetable oil.

Common digestive symptoms are caused by a range of other foods, such as beans, some milk products, and fruit, especially in those who eat too much. Usually when people determine that certain foods do not agree with them, they avoid them. To ban olestra since it may cause diarrhea in some instances is like banning milk because it causes illness for those that are lactose intolerant.

Opponents of olestra, namely the CSPI group, have fought loud and hard at attacking the new fat substitute by relying on the media to circulate their allegations. They have become the nation's most familiar nutrition watchdog group; however, some people may view CSPI's intentions as being more interested in publicity rather than protecting the public's interest. Let's face it, the media loves drama brought on by interest groups representing "victims," and CSPI is good at digging out victims from their website. According to a Reader's Digest article titled, "Attack of the Food Police," Jacobson has not only thrashed olestra, but has also attempted bans on movie theater popcorn and Chinese food.

Questions motivation of opponents

CSPI has also petitioned the Federal Trade Commission to stop deceptive multimillion-dollar advertising campaigns for Olean and products made with it. As a result, Michael Jacobson persuaded The New England Journal of Medicine to pull Olean advertisements on the basis that NEJM was biased and had received funds from manufacturer, Procter & Gamble, for its support.

The truth of the matter is that <u>NEJM</u> elected to discontinue the Olean ad because it did not want to compromise its position while receiving advertising money from P&G. It is common for prestigious magazines to make decisions such as this to protect their interests; however, it was even more critical with Olean. The backlash and rhetoric the magazine would receive from Jacobson if it were to publish a positive report on olestra while still accepting ad funds from P&G would be damaging to its credibility. This is a good example of the effectiveness of Jacobson's scare tactics and persuasiveness.

Refutes the reasoning of criticisms of the product

Since Olean's approval, tens of millions of people have eaten over half-a-billion servings of new snacks made with this ingredient. These consumers have avoided more than 10 million pounds of fat and 40 billion calories, fat and calories they would have eaten in full-fat snacks. That's particularly noteworthy, considering the country's struggle with obesity and concern for cardiovascular diseases.

Pro-evidence of safety (facts)

Proctor & Gamble is continuing to study olestra, including possible nutrient depletion, and will report its findings to the FDA. The company has signed agreements with 12 other firms interested in making olestra snacks. P&G has tested olestra in several other foods, such as ice cream and mayonnaise, and states it will submit another application to the FDA for olestra's use within a year.

Evidence of trustworthiness of the manufacturer

I believe the protests made by opponents of olestra to be exaggerated, unfounded, and sensationalized. The Center for Science in the Public Interest is leading the crusade against olestra in its typical melodramatic fashion by twisting and eliminating the true facts. Consumers owe it to themselves to be aware of the organizations supporting olestra, such as The Food & Drug Administration, The American Medical Association, The American Dietetics Association, The American Academy of Pediatrics, and The National Consumer League.

Argumentative proposition implied throughout— now stated directly

The evidence from years of research has proven that olestra can be worked into a healthy diet, just like any other food. Olestra has confirmed its safety and effectiveness to the medical and scientific community as well as gained momentum in the consumer's "fight on fat" battle. Olestra alone is not the answer to trim the fat off America's belly; however, it is a safe and effective way to enjoy favorite foods without sacrificing the taste. Olestra has opened the doors; now it's up to the American people to open their eyes to the truth. As Abraham Lincoln said "Truth is generally the best vindication against slander," and the truth of olestra's safety will prevail over Michael Jacobson and the CSPI group.

Summarizes evidence for and ends with a quotation summing up the writer's opinion of critics

Issues and Ideas

Current Controversies

An issue is a subject on which there is more than one point of view. Since arguments address differences and disagreements, they necessarily begin with an issue. When an issue disappears, however, so does the usefulness and relevance of an argument—unless, of course, the argument is expressed in language so moving and effective or with reasoning so precise and convincing that it remains admirable even though the immediate concerns of the author and the audience may pass away.

The essays in this chapter address contemporary questions, though the issues themselves have been around in some form for quite a while and are likely to remain with us in coming years. Christopher B. Daly's "How the Lawyers Stole Winter" focuses not only on concerns about children's safety and legal liability, but also on the much larger issue of personal responsibility. Mike Rose's "Extol Brains as Well as Brawn of the Blue Collar," focuses on the stereotypes we impose on blue collar workers that cause us to fail to notice their real abilities. Stephanie Mills's "Could You Live with Less?" and David Quammen's "Who Swims with the Tuna" both focus on issues resulting from our current ways of living and interacting with nature and our environments. Gregg Easterbrooks's "All This Progress Is Killing Us, Bite by Bite," calls into question an important definition that many of us take for granted, and in so doing argues that the effects of progress may be less beneficial than we think. Anna Quindlen's "The Drug That Pretends It Isn't" redefines a behavior that many resist labeling as extreme because it is something they enjoy. Barbara Lawrence's essay, "Four-Letter Words Can Hurt You," was first published a little more than 20 years ago. Nonetheless, although the particular words we use may have changed somewhat, the issues are still alive. Sarah Min, in "Language Lessons," takes a personal and refreshing approach to the issue of bilingualism.

ARGUMENT THROUGH COMPARISON AND CONTRAST

CHRISTOPHER B. DALY

CHRISTOPHER B. DALY grew up in Medford, Massachusetts. He now lives with his family in Newton, Massachusetts, and is a freelance writer and contributor to magazines.

How the Lawyers Stole Winter

In this essay, which appeared first in *Atlantic Monthly,* Daly uses comparison to make the case that in our attempts to prevent dangerous accidents, we (and, in particular, the lawyers among us) have not only stolen some enjoyment from our lives but also lessened responsibility for our own actions. He suggests that the result may be more danger, not less.

When I was a boy, my friends and I would come home from school each day, change our clothes (because we were not allowed to wear "play clothes" to school), and go outside until dinnertime. In the early 1960s in Medford, a city on the outskirts of Boston, that was pretty much what everybody did. Sometimes there might be flute lessons, or an organized Little League game, but usually not. Usually we kids went out and played.

In winter, on our way home from the Gleason School, we would go past Brooks Pond to check the ice. By throwing heavy stones onto it, hammering it with downed branches, and, finally, jumping on it, we could figure out if the ice was ready for skating. If it was, we would hurry home to grab our skates, our sticks, and whatever other gear we had, and then return to play hockey for the rest of the day. When the streetlights came on, we knew it was time to jam our cold, stiff feet back into our green rubber snow boots and get home for dinner.

I had these memories in mind recently when I moved, with my wife and two young boys, into a house near a lake even closer to Boston, in the city of Newton. As soon as Crystal Lake froze over, I grabbed my skates and headed out. I was not the first one there, though: the lawyers had beaten me to the lake. They had warned the town recreation department to put it off limits. So I found a sign that said DANGER. THIN ICE. NO SKATING.

Knowing a thing or two about words myself, I put my own gloss on the sign. I took it to mean *When the ice is thin, there is danger and there should be no skating.* Fair enough, I thought, but I knew that the obverse was also true: *When the ice is thick, it is safe and there should be skating.* Finding the ice plenty thick, I laced up my skates and glided out onto the miraculous glassy surface of the frozen lake. My wife, a native of Manhattan, would not let me take our two boys with me. But for as long as I could, I enjoyed the free, open-air delight of skating as it should be. After a few days others joined me, and we became an outlaw band of skaters.

What we were doing was once the heart of winter in New England—and a lot of other places, too. It was clean, free exercise that needed no StairMasters, no health clubs, no appointments, and hardly any gear. Sadly, it is in danger of passing away. Nowadays it seems that every city and town and almost all property holders are so worried about liability and lawsuits that they simply throw up a sign or a fence and declare that henceforth there shall be no skating, and that's the end of it.

As a result, kids today live in a world of leagues, rinks, rules, uniforms, adults, and rides—rides here, rides there, rides everywhere. It is not clear that they are better off; in some ways they are clearly *not* better off.

When I was a boy skating on Brooks Pond, there were no grown-ups around. Once or twice a year, on a weekend day or a holiday, some parents might come by with a thermos of hot cocoa. Maybe they would build a fire (which we were forbidden to do), and we would gather round.

But for the most part the pond was the domain of children. In the absence of adults, we made and enforced our own rules. We had hardly any gear—just some borrowed hockey gloves, some hand-me-down skates, maybe an elbow pad or two—so we played a clean form of hockey, with no high-sticking, no punching, and almost no checking. A single fight could ruin the whole afternoon. Indeed, as I remember it, thirty years later, it was the purest form of hockey I ever saw—until I got to see the Russian national team play the game.

But before we could play, we had to check the ice. We became serious junior meteorologists, true connoisseurs of cold. We learned that the best weather for pond skating is plain, clear cold, with starry nights and no snow. (Snow not only mucks up the skating surface but also insulates the ice from the colder air above.) And we learned that moving water, even the gently flowing Mystic River, is a lot less likely to freeze than standing water. So we skated only on the pond. We learned all the weird whooping and cracking sounds that ice makes as it expands and contracts, and thus when to leave the ice.

Do kids learn these things today? I don't know. How would 10 they? We don't let them. Instead we post signs. Ruled by lawyers, cities and towns everywhere try to eliminate their legal liability. But try as they might, they cannot eliminate the underlying risk. Liability is a social construct; risk is a natural fact. When it is cold enough, ponds freeze. No sign or fence or ordinance can change that.

In fact, by focusing on liability and not teaching our kids how to 11 take risks, we are making their world more dangerous. When we were children, we had to learn to evaluate risks and handle them on our own. We had to learn, quite literally, to test the waters. As a result, we grew up to be savvier about ice and ponds than any kid could be who has skated only under adult supervision on a rink.

When I was a boy, despite the risks we took on the ice no one I 12 knew ever drowned. The only people I heard about who drowned were graduate students at Harvard or MIT who came from the tropics and were living through their first winters. Not knowing (after all, how could they?) about ice on moving water, they would innocently venture out onto the half-frozen Charles River, fall through, and die. They were literally out of their element.

Are we raising a generation of children who will be out of their 13 element? And if so, what can we do about it? We cannot just roll back the calendar. I cannot tell my six-year-old to head down to the lake by himself to play all afternoon—if for no other reason than that he would not find twenty or thirty other kids there, full of the collective wisdom about cold and ice that they had inherited, along with hockey equipment, from their older brothers and sisters. Somewhere along the line that link got broken.

The whole setting of childhood has changed. We cannot change 14 it again overnight. I cannot send my children out by themselves yet, but at least some of the time I can go out there with them. Maybe that is a start.

As for us, last winter was a very unusual one. We had ferocious 15 cold (near-zero temperatures on many nights) and tremendous snows (about a hundred inches in all). Eventually a strange thing happened. The town gave in—sort of. Sometime in January the recreation department "opened" a section of the lake, and even dispatched a snowplow truck to clear a good-sized patch of ice. The boys and I skated during the rest of winter. Ever vigilant, the town officials kept the THIN ICE signs up, even though their own truck could safely drive on the frozen surface. And they brought in "lifeguards" and all sorts of rules about the hours during which we could skate and where we had to stay.

But at least we were able to skate in the open air, on real ice.   16
And it was still free.

Meanings and Values

1. Summarize in your own words the issue the author is addressing in
    this essay. In what ways is this issue representative of similar issues
    in other settings and climates? Explain. Does this "representative-
    ness" make the argument significant and interesting for people who
    are not worried about thin ice and have no interest in skating? Why,
    or why not? (See "Guide to Terms": *Evaluation.*)

2. Daly presents his examples of growing up in the early 1960s as illus-
    trations of a good way to teach children responsibility and to allow
    them to have healthy fun. Does he succeed in doing so? If so, what
    details in the examples or statements of interpretation are most con-
    vincing? If not, what keeps the examples from being successful?

3. What opposing points of view, if any, does Daly acknowledge?
    Would the essay be more (or less) effective if he spent more time
    dealing with possible objections to his argument? Make a list of pos-
    sible objections to his argument and evidence that could be used to
    support them.

4. Does the writer offer possible answers to the problem he identifies? If
    so, what are they? Does the essay make a clear case that lawyers are
    to blame for the problem? If not, does this weaken the essay? Why, or
    why not?

Argumentative Techniques

1. Why does the writer wait until Paragraph 6 to offer an argumenta-
    tive proposition (thesis)? What role(s) do the opening paragraphs
    play? Do they explain an issue or problem? Do they provide evi-
    dence that can be used to support the thesis? Be specific in your an-
    swer, and point to specific evidence to support your conclusions.
    (Guide: *Introductions.*)

2. Which sentence or sentences state the argumentative proposition
    (thesis)? (Guide: *Thesis.*) Restate it in your own words. Are all parts of
    the essay clearly related to this thesis? If not, what are the functions
    of any parts not clearly related to the thesis? (Guide: *Unity.*) How is
    the comparison-contrast pattern related to the thesis? Explain.
    Would another arrangement of ideas and evidence be likely to pro-
    vide more convincing development and support for the thesis? What
    arrangement, and why?

3. In what ways does the concluding sentence "echo" the beginning of
    the essay? Which paragraphs should be considered the conclusion of
    the essay? What functions do they perform? (Guide: *Closings.*)

DICTION AND VOCABULARY

1. The effectiveness of this essay depends to a considerable extent on the writer's ability to make the account of his childhood experiences seem like a realistic ideal and not merely a sentimental, nostalgic excursion. How does the diction in Paragraphs 1–2 and 7–9 aid him in staying away from too much sentimentality while at the same time making the experience seem attractive and worth reclaiming? If you think the examples are overly sentimental, explain why. (Guide: *Sentimentality.*)

2. What words with positive connotations does Daly associate with skating and playing hockey (see Pars. 4 and 8)? (Guide: *Connotation/ Denotation.*) How do the connotations of these words help support his thesis?

3. If you do not know the meaning of some of the following words, look them up in a dictionary: gloss, obverse (Par. 4); high-sticking, checking (8); meteorologists, connoisseurs (9); liability, construct (10); vigilant (15).

READ TO WRITE

1. **Collaborating:** Working in a group, make a list of other valuable childhood activities that have been curtailed, limited, or threatened by legal concerns. Should we ignore these concerns, find a way to accommodate them, or come up with different and less dangerous activities? Consider making an issue from this general subject area the focus of an argumentative essay.

2. **Considering Audience:** Using Daly's essay as a model, argue that in an attempt to deal with a problem, threat, or danger, we have taken steps that create more problems and dangers by taking away the need to be responsible for our actions. In developing the essay, acknowledge that many readers have legitimate fears, and avoid being too critical of such readers.

3. **Developing an Essay:** Begin an argumentative essay of your own with examples of how things should be, then develop your argument by contrasting how they are with how they ought to be.

(NOTE: Suggestions for topics requiring development by ARGUMENT are on pp. 601–602 at the end of this chapter.)

ARGUMENT THROUGH COMPARISON

MIKE ROSE

> Mike Rose teaches in the Graduate School of Education and Information Studies at UCLA. For most of his career, he has been concerned with how students learn to read and write and how these skills can transform their lives. His books include *Lives on the Boundary: The Struggles and Achievements of American's Underprepared* (1989), *Possible Lives* (1999), and *The Mind at Work: Valuing the Intelligence of the American Worker* (2004).

Extol Brains as Well as Brawn
of the Blue Collar

> In this essay, Rose introduces the contrast between white collar work and blue collar work that is typical in our society—and attempts to undo it, at least partly. One key point in his argument is suggested in the title: blue collar work takes considerable intelligence and ought to be given credit for it. In undoing the contrast, he suggests that the two kinds of work are comparable in many ways.

I am watching a carpenter install a set of sliding French doors in a   1
tight wall space. He stands back, surveying the frame, imagining the pieces as he will assemble them.

What angle is required to create a threshold that will shed   2
water? Where might the sliding panels catch or snag? How must the casings be remade to match the woodwork in the rest of the room? And how can he put it all together fast enough and smart enough to make his labor pay?

This isn't the usual stuff of a Labor Day tribute. Our typical trib-   3
utes spotlight the economic contribution that the labor force has made to the country, the value of the work ethic. But what about the intelligence of the laborer—the thought, the creativity, the craft it takes to do work, any work, well?

Over the last six years, I've been studying the thinking involved   4
in what is often dismissed as manual labor, exploring the way knowledge is gained and used strategically on job sites, in trade schools and in businesses such as beauty salons and restaurants, auto factories and welding shops. And I've been struck by the intellectual demands of what I saw.

Consider what a good waitress or waiter has to do in a busy   5
restaurant. Remember orders and monitor them, attend to an ever-
changing environment, juggle the flow of work, make decisions on
the fly. Or the carpenter: To build a cabinet, a staircase or a pitched
roof requires complex mathematical calculations, a high level of precision. The hairstylist's practice is a mix of scissors technique, knowledge of biology, aesthetic judgment and communication skills. The
mechanic, electrician and plumber are troubleshooters and problem-
solvers. Even the routinized factory floor calls for working smart.
Yet we persist in dividing labor into the work of the hand and the
work of the mind.

Distinctions between blue collar and white collar do exist.   6
White-collar work, for example, often requires a large investment of
money and time in formal schooling. And, on average, white-collar
work leads to higher occupational status and income, more autonomy and less physical risk. But these distinctions carry with them
unfair assumptions about the intelligence of the people who do
physical work. Those assumptions have a long history, from portrayals of 18th century mechanics as illiterate and incapable of par-
ticipating in government to the autoworkers I heard labeled by one
supervisor as "a bunch of dummies."

Such beliefs are intensified in our high-tech era. Listen to the   7
language we use: Work involving electronic media and symbolic
analysis is "neck up" while old-style manufacturing or service work
is "neck down."

If society labels whole categories of people, identified by their   8
occupations, as less intelligent, then social separations are reinforced
and divisions constrict the kind of civic life we can create or imagine. And if society ignores the intelligence behind the craft, it mistakes prejudice for fact.

Many Labor Day tributes will render the muscled arm, sleeve   9
rolled tight. How many also will celebrate the link between hand
and brain? It would be fitting, on this day especially, to have a truer,
richer sense of all that is involved in the wide range of work that surrounds and sustains us. We need to honor the brains as well as the
brawn of American labor.

MEANINGS AND VALUES

1.   What kinds of work does the author present as examples of blue
collar work?

2. According to the author, what do most people consider the differences between blue collar and white collar work?

3. In your own words, state the argumentative thesis presented and supported in this essay.

4. State the reasons you think the author is successful or unsuccessful in presenting and supporting this thesis. (See "Guide to Terms": *Thesis.*)

ARGUMENTATIVE STRATEGIES

1. What is the purpose of the rhetorical questions in paragraph 2? ("Guide": *Rhetorical Questions.*)

2. Does the rhetorical question at the end of paragraph 3 state the thesis of the essay? If not, where is the thesis stated? ("Guide": *Thesis.*)

3. What strategy does the author use to begin the essay? (Guide: *Introductions.*)

4. What strategy does he use to conclude the essay? (Guide: *Closings.*)

DICTION AND VOCABULARY

1. Identify the terms the writer uses in paragraphs 3 and 5 to emphasize the intelligence involved in blue-collar work. (Guide: *Diction.*) Which terms rely on denotation alone, and which involve connotation as well. (Guide: *Denotation and Connotation*).

2. If you do not know the meaning of some of the following terms, look them up in a dictionary: pitched, aesthetic (par. 5); autonomy (6); symbolic (7).

READ TO WRITE

1. **Collaborating:** Working with fellow students, make a list of as many blue collar occupations as you can, and for each, list two special skills or forms of intelligence involved in the occupation.

2. **Considering an Audience:** One assumption Rose seems to make about his readers is that they will consider blue collar work as more a matter of physical effort than mental effort. Prepare a paragraph in which you discuss and define what you believe to be typical views of blue collar work and blue collar workers.

3. **Developing an Essay:** We often underestimate (and sometimes overestimate) the intelligence, imagination, and skill involved in different occupations—blue collar, white collar, or professional. Prepare an essay in which you argue that a particular occupation or profession takes more (or less) skill and ability than most people think.

(NOTE: Suggestions for topics requiring development by ARGUMENT are on pp. 601–602 at the end of this chapter.)

ARGUMENT THROUGH EXAMPLE

STEPHANIE MILLS

> STEPHANIE MILLS is an activist and writer. She has written and edited
> a number of books on environmental and social issues, including *In
> Praise of Nature* (ed.) (1991); *In Service of the Wild: Restoring and
> Reinhabiting Damaged Land* (1995); *Turning Away from Technology:
> A New Vision for the 21st Century* (ed.) (1997); and *Epicurean
> Simplicity* (2002).

Could You Live with Less?

The examples in this essay, first published in *Glamour* magazine,
are drawn from Mills's experience and, she suggests, are arguments intended primarily to justify her frugal, natural lifestyle. It
should be clear to most readers, however, that she intends them to
encourage readers to take seriously the choices she has made and
perhaps even make similar choices themselves. What helps make
this essay more than a statement of personal belief is the time Mills
spends dealing with potential objections to her reasoning. In appearing to deal with objections, she is actually arguing in favor of
her outlook—and addressing these arguments to readers, hoping
to persuade them to agree with her.

Compared to the lifestyle of the average person on Earth, my   1
days are lush with comfort and convenience: I have a warm
home, enough to eat, my own car. But compared to most of my urban American contemporaries, I live a monastically simple life.

Since 1984 I've made my home outside a small city in lower   2
Michigan, where the winters are snowy but not severely cold. My
snug 720-square-foot house is solar- and wood-heated. No thermostat, just a cast-iron stove. There's electric lighting, indoor plumbing,
a tankless water heater, a secondhand refrigerator and range—but
no microwave oven, no dishwasher, no blow-dryer, no cordless
phone. My gas-sipping compact station wagon has 140,000 miles on
it and spreading patches of rust. I've never owned a television set.
My home entertainment center consists of a thousand books, a CD-
less stereo system, a picture window and two cats.

Part of the reason I live the way I do is that as a freelance writer,   3
my income is unpredictable and at best fairly unspectacular. Thus it
behooves me to keep in mind the difference between wants and

needs. Like all human beings, I have some needs that are absolute: about 2,500 calories a day, a half a gallon of water to drink, a sanitary means of disposing of my bodily wastes, water to bathe in, something muscular to do for part of the day and a warm, dry place to sleep. To stay sane I need contact with people and with nature, meaningful work and the opportunity to love and be loved.

I don't need, nor do I want, to complicate my life with gadgets.   4
I want to keep technology at the periphery rather than at the center of my life, to treat it like meat in Chinese cuisine—as a condiment rather than as a staple food. Technology should abet my life, not dominate or redefine it. A really good tool—like a sharp kitchen knife, a wheelbarrow or a baby carrier, all of which have been with us in some form for thousands of years—makes a useful difference but doesn't displace human intelligence, character or contact the way higher technologies sometimes do. Working people need the tools of their trade, and as a writer, I do have a fax, but I've resisted the pressure to buy a personal computer. A manual typewriter has worked well for me so far. Noticing that the most computer-savvy people I know are always pining for more megabytes and better software, I've decided not to climb on the purchasing treadmill of planned obsolescence.

Doing with less is easier when I remember that emotional needs   5
often get expressed as material wants, but can never, finally, be satisfied that way. If I feel disconnected from others, a cellular phone won't cure that. If I feel like I'm getting a little dowdy, hours on a tanning bed can't eradicate self-doubt.

Why live in a snowy region when I don't use central heat? I   6
moved here for love several years ago, and while that love was brief, my affection for this place has grown and grown. I like the roots I've put down; living like Goldilocks, moving from chair to chair, seems like not much of a life to me.

Being willfully backward about technology suits my taste—I like   7
living this way. Wood heat feels good, better than the other kinds. (Central heating would make my home feel like it was just anywhere.) Fetching firewood gets me outdoors and breathing (sometimes gasping) fresh air in the wintertime when it's easy to go stale. It's hard, achy work to split and stack the eight or 12 cords of stove wood I burn annually. I've been known to seek help to get it done. But the more of it I do myself, the more I can brag to my city friends.

My strongest motivation for living the way I do is my knowl-   8
edge, deep and abiding, that technology comes at a serious cost to the planet and most of its people. Burning fossil fuels has changed the

Earth's climate. Plastics and pesticides have left endocrine-disrupting chemicals everywhere—in us and in wildlife, affecting reproductive systems. According to Northwest Environment Watch in Seattle, the "clean" computer industry typically generates 139 pounds of waste, 49 of them toxic, in the manufacture of each 55-pound computer.

I refuse to live as if that weren't so. In this, I'm not unique.   9
There are many thousands of Americans living simply, questioning technology, fighting to preserve what remains of nature. We're bucking the tide, acting consciously and succeeding only a little. Yet living this way helps me feel decent within myself—and that, I find, is one luxury worth having.

MEANINGS AND VALUES

1. To what extent does the title of this essay act as a statement of the argumentative thesis (admittedly an *indirect* statement)? Is the thesis stated anywhere else in the essay? If not, does it need to be? (See "Guide to Terms": *Unity.*)

2. Summarize in your own words the issue the author is addressing in this essay. What evidence is there in the essay that the writer's purpose is to take a stand on the issue rather than simply to make a statement of personal belief? (Guide: *Purpose.*)

3. What opposing points of view does Mills acknowledge? Identify each and tell how effective you think she is at rebutting it. (Guide: *Evaluation.*) Do you think other readers are likely to agree with your estimate of Mills's success or failure? Why? What kinds of readers would be likely to disagree with you, if any?

ARGUMENTATIVE TECHNIQUES

1. Why does the writer not announce her argumentative proposition (thesis) clearly in the opening paragraphs of the essay? What role(s) do the opening paragraphs play? Do they explain an issue or problem? Do they provide evidence that can be used to support the thesis? Be specific in your answer, and point to specific evidence to support your conclusions. (Guide: *Introductions.*)

2. Examine the opening sentences of Paragraphs 3–8. How are they related to the argumentative thesis? Which parts of the essay, if any, do not support or explain the thesis? Could the essay be revised in any way to make it more unified? (Guide: *Thesis; Unity.*)

3. In what ways does the concluding paragraph sentence "echo" or refer to the beginning of the essay? What appeal to readers to agree with her does Mills offer in the conclusion? (Guide: *Closings.*)

DICTION AND VOCABULARY

1.   The effectiveness of this essay depends to a considerable extent on the writer's ability to make her way of living seem like a realistic ideal and not merely an impractical, foolish, or sentimental exercise. How do the diction and the details in Paragraphs 3–4 and 7–8 emphasize the realistic and practical side of her way of living and help her stay away from too much sentimentality or nostalgia in portraying a lifestyle many will see as pointing back to the "good old times"? If you think the examples are overly sentimental, explain why. (Guide: *Sentimentality.*)

2.   What words with positive connotations does Mills associate with her lifestyle (see Pars. 3, 4, 6, 7, and 8)? (Guide: *Connotation/Denotation.*) How do the connotations of these words help support her thesis?

READ TO WRITE

1.   **Collaborating:** Working in a group, list other ways of living that most people might not endorse immediately. Decide with your group which patterns of development might be used for an essay defending one of these ways of living.

2.   **Considering Audience:** Envision yourself as a modern suburban or urban dweller reading Mills's essay (this will not be much of a stretch for many people). Write a letter to the editor of the magazine in which it appeared (*Glamour*), responding to the issue from your perspective.

3.   **Developing an Essay:** Mills clearly lets her readers know how she feels without excessive moralizing. Choose a controversial issue and write an essay similar to Mills's in which you share your belief without judging harshly or openly criticizing those in opposition.

(NOTE: Suggestions for essays requiring development by ARGUMENT are on pp. 601–602 at the end of this chapter).

ARGUMENT THROUGH CAUSE AND EFFECT

GREGG EASTERBROOK

GREGG EASTERBROOK recevied a bachelor's degree from Colorado College and a master's degree from Northwestern University. He is a senior editor of *The New Republic* and has also written on sports for *Slate,* ESPN.com, and NFL.com. He is the author of a book *The Progress Paradox: How Life Gets Better While People Feel Worse* (2003).

All This Progress Is Killing Us, Bite by Bite

Most people assume that progress is always (or almost always) good; the term *progress* itself is seldom associated with negative ideas or feelings. But any cause can have unintended as well as intended effects. Easterbrook looks at the unintended (and negative) effects of progress to encourage readers to change their outlooks.

Your great-great grandparents would find it hard to believe the   1
Boeing 747, but perhaps they'd have a harder time believing last week's news that obesity has become the second-leading cause of death in the United States. Too much food a menace instead of too little! A study released by the federal Centers for Disease Control ranked "poor diet and physical inactivity" as the cause of 400,000 United States deaths in 2000, trailing only fatalities from tobacco. Obesity, the C.D.C. said, now kills five times as many Americans as "microbial agents," that is, infectious disease.

Moon landings might seem less shocking to your great-great   2
grandparents than abundance of food causing five times as many deaths as germs; OutKast might seem less bizarre to them than the House passing legislation last week to exempt restaurants from being sued for serving portions that are too large.

Your recent ancestors would further be stunned by the notion   3
of plump poverty. A century ago, the poor were as lean as fence posts; worry about where to get the next meal was a constant companion for millions. Today, America's least well-off are so surrounded by double cheeseburgers, chicken buckets, extra-large pizzas and supersized fries that they are more likely to be overweight than the population as a whole.

But the expanding waistline is not only a problem of lower-   4
income Americans who dine too often on fast food. Today, the typical

American is overweight, according to the C.D.C., which estimates that 64 percent of American citizens are carrying too many pounds for their height. Obesity and sedentary living are rising so fast that their health consequences may soon supplant tobacco as the No. 1 preventable cause of death, the C.D.C. predicts. Rates of heart disease, stroke and many cancers are in decline, while life expectancy is increasing—but ever-rising readings on the bathroom scale may be canceling out what would otherwise be dramatic gains in public health.

O.K., it's hard to be opposed to food. But the epidemic of obe- 5 sity epitomizes the unsettled character of progress in affluent Western society. Our lives are characterized by too much of a good thing—too much to eat, to buy, to watch and to do, excess at every turn. Sometimes achievement itself engenders the excess: today's agriculture creates so much food at such low cost that who can resist that extra helping?

Consider other examples in which society's success seems to be 6 backfiring on our health or well-being.

PRODUCTIVITY   Higher productivity is essential to rising 7 living standards and to the declining prices of goods and services. But higher productivity may lead to fewer jobs.

Early in the postwar era, analysts fretted that automation 8 would take over manufacturing, throwing everyone out of work. That fear went unrealized for a generation, in part because robots and computers weren't good at much. Today, near-automated manufacturing is becoming a reality. Newly built factories often require only a fraction of the work force of the plants they replace. Office technology, meanwhile, now allows a few to do what once required a whole hive of worker bees.

There may come a point when the gains from higher productiv- 9 ity pale before the job losses. But even if that point does not come, rapid technological change is instilling anxiety about future employment: anxiety that makes it hard to appreciate and enjoy what productivity creates.

TRAFFIC   Cars are much better than they were a few decades 10 ago—more comfortable, powerful and reliable. They are equipped with safety features like air bags and stuffed with CD players, satellite radios and talking navigation gizmos. Adjusted for consumers' rising buying power, the typical powerful new car costs less than one a generation ago.

But in part because cars are so desirable and affordable, roads 11 are increasingly clogged with traffic. Today in the United States, there are 230 million cars and trucks in operation, and only 193 million licensed drivers—more vehicles than drivers! Studies by the Federal Highway Administration show that in the 30 largest cities, total time lost to traffic jams has almost quintupled since 1980.

Worse, prosperity has made possible the popularity of S.U.V.'s   12
and the misnamed "light" pickup trucks, which now account for half of all new-car sales. Exempt from the fuel-economy standards that apply to regular cars, sport utility vehicles and pickup trucks sustain American dependence on Persian Gulf oil. A new study in the Journal of Risk and Uncertainty showed that the rise in S.U.V.'s and pickup trucks "leads to substantially more fatalities" on the road.

So just as longevity might be improving at a faster clip were it   13
not for expanding waistlines, death rates in traffic accidents might show a more positive trend were it not for the S.U.V. explosion.

The proliferation of cars also encourages us to drive rather than   14
walk. A century ago, the typical American walked three miles a day; now the average is less than a quarter mile a day. Some research suggests that the sedentary lifestyle, rather than weight itself, is the real threat; a chubby person who is physically active will be O.K. Studies also show that it is not necessary to do aerobics to get the benefits of exercise; a half-hour a day of brisk walking is sufficient. But more cars, driven more miles, mean less walking.

STRESS   It's not just in your mind: Researchers believe stress   15
levels really are rising. People who are overweight or inactive experience more stress than others, and that now applies to the majority. Insufficient sleep increases stress, and Americans now sleep on average only seven hours a night, versus eight hours for our parents' generation and 10 hours for our great-grandparents'.

Research by Bruce McEwen, a neuroendocrinologist at Rocke-   16
feller University in New York, suggests that modern stress, in addition to making life unpleasant, can impair immune function—again, canceling out health gains that might otherwise occur.

Prosperity brings many other mixed blessings. Living stan-   17
dards keep rising, but so does incidence of clinical depression. Cellphones are convenient, but make it impossible to escape from office calls. E-mail is cheap and fast, if you don't mind deleting hundreds of spam messages. The Internet and cable television improve communication, but deluge us with the junkiest aspects of culture.

Americans live in ever-nicer, ever-larger houses, but new homes   18
and the businesses that serve them have to go somewhere. Sprawl

continues at a maddening pace, while once-rustic areas may now be gridlocked with S.U.V.'s and power boats.

Agricultural yields continue rising, yet that means fewer family   19
farms are needed. Biotechnology may allow us to live longer, but may leave us dependent on costly synthetic drugs. There are many similar examples.

Increasingly, Western life is afflicted by the paradoxes of   20
progress. Material circumstances keep improving, yet our quality of life may be no better as a result—especially in those cases, like food, where enough becomes too much.

"The maximum is not the optimum," the ecologist Garrett   21
Hardin, who died last year, liked to say. Americans are choosing the maximum, and it does not necessarily make us healthier or happier.

MEANINGS AND VALUES

1. What different kinds of progress does the writer offer as evidence to support his opinion? Which do you find particularly effective, and why? (See "Guide to Terms": *Evaluation.*)

2. Is it possible that some readers will consider the positive effects of some of the developments cited in the essay as far more important than the negative effects? If so, which ones are most likely to get such a response. Is such a reaction likely to undermine the author's argument? Why, or why not? Or is it simply necessary for the author to undermine readers' beliefs in the positive nature of progress in order to succeed in convincing readers to share his outlook? Please explain your answer.

3. In your own words, state the argumentative thesis of this essay.

ARGUMENTATIVE STRATEGIES

1. In which paragraph does the author first state clearly his argumentative thesis? Why does he wait so long to do so?

2. The author offers a wide range of examples to support his opinion. What are the different kinds of examples he uses?

3. In what ways does the variety of examples make the essay more effective or less effective? (Guide: *Evaluation.*)

4. Discuss the way the surprising twist (or reversal) the writer adds to many otherwise positive examples is a major strategy for persuading readers, and identify paragraphs that employ this strategy.

DICTION AND VOCABULARY

1. Describe how the writer uses the connotation of words to encourage readers to view the effects of progress negatively. Choose three paragraphs from the essay for examples to use in your answer. (Guide: *Denotation and Connotation.*)

2. If you do not know the meaning of some of the following words, look them up in a dictionary: sedentary (par. 3); affluent (4); productivity (6); longevity (12).

READ TO WRITE

1. **Collaborating:** Working with a group of classmates, identify ten recent developments you (or most people) are likely to consider examples of "progress." Then list several reasons why each might also be viewed as having negative as well as positive effects.

2. **Considering an Audience:** What is progress for some people might be an unpleasant or objectional new development for others. Prepare a brief essay in which you look at two different ways of viewing a recent social, cultural, or political development from two contrasting viewpoints, one positive, one negative.

3. **Developing an Essay:** Take a recent social, cultural, or political development that most people are likely to view in a similar light (positive or negative) and develop an essay in which you argue that readers ought to take the opposite view.

(NOTE: Suggestions for essays requiring development by ARGUMENT are on pp. 601–602 at the end of this chapter).

ARGUMENT THROUGH DEFINITION

ANNA QUINDLEN

> ANNA QUINDLEN has been a reporter and columnist for the *New York Times* and a columnist for *Newsweek*. She has written four novels: *Blessings* (2002), *Black and Blue* (1998), *One True Thing* (1994), and *Object Lessons* (1991). Her books of nonfiction essays include *Living Out Loud* (1988), *Thinking Out Loud* (1993), *How Reading Changed My Life* (1998), and *Loud and Clear* (2004).

The Drug That Pretends It Isn't

> In this essay, Quindlen employs a particularly useful (and flexible) argument strategy: choose a definition about which most people agree, and then show that a controversial subject or issue fits within the definition. Quindlen begins by pointing out that most people see illegal drug use as a big problem, and then argues that we need to view alcohol as a drug and its misuse as a significant problem. She builds on this framework, too, paying attention to arguments and evidence likely to be most persuasive to her readers.

Spring break in Jamaica, and the patios of the waterfront bars are   1
so packed that it seems the crowds of students must go tumbling into the aquamarine sea, still clutching their glasses. Even at the airport one drunken young man with a peeling nose argues with a flight attendant about whether he can bring his Red Stripe, kept cold in an insulated sleeve, aboard the plane heading home.

The giggle about Jamaica for American visitors has always been   2
the availability of ganja; half the T-shirts in the souvenir shops have slogans about smoking grass. But the students thronging the streets of Montego Bay seem more comfortable with their habitual drug of choice: alcohol.

Whoops! Sorry! Not supposed to call alcohol a drug. Some of   3
the people who lead antidrug organizations don't like it because they fear it dilutes the message about the "real" drugs, heroin, cocaine, and marijuana. Parents are offended by it: as they try to figure out which vodka bottle came from their party and which from their teenager's, they sigh and say, "Well, at least it's not drugs." And naturally the lobbyists for the industry hate it. They're power guys, these guys: The wine guy is George W.'s brother-in-law, the beer guy meets regularly with House majority whip Tom DeLay. When you lump a cocktail in with a joint, it makes them crazy.

And it's true: Booze and beer are not the same as illegal drugs. 4
They're worse. A policy research group called Drug Strategies has
produced a report that calls alcohol "America's most pervasive drug
problem" and then goes on to document the claim. Alcohol-related
deaths outnumber deaths related to drugs four to one. Alcohol is a
factor in more than half of all domestic violence and sexual assault
cases. Between accidents, health problems, crime, and lost productivity, researchers estimate alcohol abuse costs the economy $167 bil-
lion a year. In 1995 four out of every ten people on probation said
they were drinking when they committed a violent crime, while only
one in ten admitted using illicit drugs. Close your eyes and substitute
the word blah-blah for alcohol in any of those sentences, and you'd
have to conclude that an all-out war on blah-blah would result.

Yet when members of Congress tried to pass legislation that 5
would make alcohol part of the purview of the nation's drug czar,
the measure failed. Mothers Against Drunk Driving faces opposition to both its education programs and its public service ads from
principals and parents who think illicit drugs should be given
greater priority. The argument is this: Heroin, cocaine, and marijuana are harmful and against the law, but alcohol is used in moderation with no ill effects by many people.

Here's the counterargument: There are an enormous number of 6
people who cannot and will never be able to drink in moderation.
And what they leave in their wake is often more difficult to quantify
than DWIs or date rapes. In his memoir *A Drinking Life,* Pete Hamill
describes simply and eloquently the binges, the blackouts, the routine: "If I wrote a good column for the newspaper. I'd go to the bar
and celebrate; if I wrote a poor column, I would drink away my re-
gret. Then I'd go home, another dinner missed, another chance to
play with the children gone, and in the morning, hung over, thick-
tongued, and thick-fingered, I'd attempt through my disgust to
make amends." Hamill and I used to drink, when we were younger,
at a dark place down a short flight of stairs in the Village called the
Lion's Head. There were book jackets covering the walls that I used
to look at covertly with envy. But then I got older, and when I
passed the Head I sometimes thought of how many books had never
been written at all because of the drinking.

Everyone has a friend/an uncle/a coworker/a spouse/a neigh- 7
bor who drinks too much. A recent poll of seven thousand adults
found that 82 percent said they'd even be willing to pay more for a
drink if the money was used to combat alcohol abuse. New Mexico
and Montana already use excise taxes on alcohol to pay for treatment programs. It's probably just coincidence that, as Drug

Strategies reports, the average excise tax on beer is nineteen cents a gallon, while in Missouri and Wisconsin, homes to Anheuser-Busch and Miller, respectively, the tax is only six cents.

A wholesale uprising in Washington against Philip Morris,   8 which owns Miller Brewing and was the largest donor of soft money to the Republicans in 1998, or against Seagram's, which did the same for the Democrats in 1996, doesn't seem likely. Homeschooling is in order, a harder sell than even to elected officials, since many parents prefer lessons that do not require self-examination. Talking about underage drinking and peer pressure lets them off the hook by suggesting that it's all about sixteen-year-olds with six-packs. But the peer group is everywhere, from the frogs that croak "Bud" on commercials to those tiresome folks who behave as if wine were as important as books (it's not) to parents who drink to excess and teach an indelible life lesson.

Prohibition was cooked up to try to ameliorate the damage that   9 drinking does to daily life. It didn't work. But there is always self-prohibition. It's not easy, since all the world's a speakeasy. "Not even wine?" Hamill recalls he was asked at dinner parties after he stopped. Of course, children should not drink, and people who sell them alcohol should be prosecuted. Of course, people should not drink and drive, and those who do should be punished. But twenty-one is not a magic number, and the living room is not necessarily a safe place. There is a larger story that needs to be told, loud and clear, in homes and schools and on commercials given as much prominence and paid for in the same way as those that talk about the dangers of smack or crack: that alcohol is a mind-altering, mood-altering drug, and that lots of people should never start to drink at all. "I have no talent for it," Hamill told friends. Just like that.

Meanings and Values

1. Summarize the reasons why, as this essay claims, people resist viewing alcohol as a drug.

2. Summarize the arguments and evidence the essay offers in favor of viewing alcohol as a drug.

3. Where in this essay does the writer offer readers a definition of illegal drugs, and in what ways does she provide this definition? Will the definition be precise enough so that most readers will be able to follow the argument? Why, or why not? (See "Guide to Terms": *Evaluation*.)

ARGUMENTATIVE TECHNIQUES

1. Identify the thesis statement in this essay. Tell why you find it either clear, focused, and appropriately limited in scope or unclear, vague, and too broad (or too narrow). (Guide: *Thesis.*)

2. What strategy does the writer employ to introduce opposing points of view? What strategies does she employ to introduce her refutation of the opposing points of view?

3. Identify the elements of this essay that are consistent with a refutation proof organization (see p. 566). Does the essay, in general, follow a refutation-proof pattern? Why, or why not?

4. Can this essay be said to combine strategies of definition and refutation-proof? If so, why? If not, why not?

DICTION AND VOCABULARY

1. Discuss how the author's choice of words in Paragraphs 3 and 8 is a strategy for criticizing people and groups unwilling to take strong measures against alcohol use and abuse. (Guide: *Diction.*)

2. Analyze the use of the words "blah-blah" in Paragraph 4 as a strategy consistent with the author's use of definition for purposes of argument.

3. What words or phrases in Paragraph 7 are used ironically? (Guide: *Irony.*)

4. If you do not know the meaning of some of the following words, look them up in a dictionary: aquamarine (Par. 1); lobbyists (2); purview (5); eloquently, amends, covertly (6); excise (7).

READ TO WRITE

1. **Collaborating:** Working in a group, focus on drinking or some other activity some people may regard as "recreational" and others as "dangerous." List as many reasons as you can for each judgment. Summarize these *pro* and *con* perspectives in a brief informative essay.

2. **Considering Audience:** The range of responses to Quindlen's essay is likely to be broad, depending on a reader's experiences, values, and background. Identify four kinds of people likely to have differing responses, and summarize briefly the likely responses from each kind of reader as well as reasons for the responses.

3. **Developing an Essay:** Using Quindlen's essay as a model, develop an argumentative essay of your own about how a particular activity generally regarded in either a positive or negative light should be redefined as the opposite.

(NOTE: Suggestions for topics requiring development by ARGUMENT are on page 601–602, at the end of this chapter.)

ARGUMENT THROUGH DEFINITION

DAVID QUAMMEN

DAVID QUAMMEN has won several National Magazine Awards for his writing on scientific and natural subjects. He has written regularly for *Outside* magazine and is the author of three novels and other books, including the award-winning *The Song of the Dodo* (1996). His essays have been collected in *The Flight of the Iguana* (1988), *Wild Thoughts from Wild Places* (1988), *Natural Acts* (1991), and *The Boilerplate Rhino* (2000).

Who Swims with the Tuna

This essay was first published in 1990 in *Outside* magazine, yet its subject and Quammen's approach remain fresh and relevant today. Quammen makes use of several patterns of argument, including, most obviously, comparison and contrast. Yet the heart of his argument lies in his attempt to redefine tuna so that they elicit our sympathy and action in their behalf just as dolphins do.

The yellowfin tuna is not celebrated for its intelligence. It's cele- 1
brated for its flavor. The spotted dolphin, on the other hand, is famously brainy and no one will tell us how it tastes. The killing of dolphins is a national outrage; the killing of tuna is a given. I keep asking myself why. There are some good reasons and some bad reasons, I think, which haven't been closely examined, or even sorted apart.

One of these animals breathes air. The other doesn't. One is a 2
mammal, one isn't. And so on: Among the possible ways of describing dolphins and tuna, though not the only way, is to recite a litany of such invidious comparisons. One is homoiothermic and one isn't. One seems to have an elaborate system of social behavior, and one doesn't. One has performed altruistic and astonishing rescues of human swimmers; the other is prized for sushi. One shrieks with terror and squeals with pain. The other maintains a stoic piscine silence. Furthermore, on our grocery shelves nowadays we find cans of a product called dolphin-safe tuna. But no tuna-safe dolphin.

There are other differences. Entangled in a net, unable to swim 3
backward, panicked, hampered from raising its blowhole clear of the water, a dolphin will drown. The sight is pathetic and gruesome—as I can attest, having once watched a certain videotape of dolphin

misfortunes at the hands of tuna fishermen during a purse-seining operation. To be more precise, I did not watch this videotape *once*—I watched it over and over in the course of a week, immersing myself in ugly visions of drowning dolphins, crushed dolphins, bleeding dolphins. I froze frames, rewound, and jabbed the play button again to see large dolphin bodies, mashed and twisted beyond hope of recovery, being tossed back into the ocean like so much offal. It's an important document, this particular tape, potently distressing yet eloquent on the subject of humankind's wasteful, abusive treatment of other creatures. It was shot by a young man named Sam LaBudde, at serious personal risk, while he worked for some months on a tuna boat in the Eastern Tropical Pacific, that zone of ocean encompassing the warm waters along the west coast of Latin America.

During the past thirty years, dolphins of several different   4
species have died in great number because commercial tuna fishermen found it convenient and cost-effective, at least in the Eastern Tropical Pacific, to catch one kind of animal by setting their nets around another. By a conservative estimate, purse-seining for tuna has caused more than six million dolphin deaths. Although U.S. tuna fishermen claim that they are more careful than their foreign competitors, that they safely release almost all the dolphins they net, those same U.S. fishermen have fought stubbornly for a legal provision that lets them continue killing up to 20,050 dolphins each year.

The dolphins are netted because they serve as a marker: encircle   5
them and chances are good that you've also got tuna. Despite all their differences, the fish and mammal tend to associate closely. Maybe that connection is symbiotic, or maybe it's just coincidence. We humans don't know. We aren't privy. Trapped in a huge corral of floating net, along with their tuna associates, the dolphins can in some cases be released unharmed. In other cases they turn hysterical, or the boat captain simply ignores them; the net is hauled, the dolphins tangle themselves and flail desperately, like antelope caught in the web of a gigantic spider; a few are lifted high, to be crushed in the power block (the huge spool) that gobbles up the net; more than a few, still trapped in the water beneath doubled-over netting, drown. Drowning is ugly; drowning makes four minutes seem like eternity. A tuna will not drown, though it will suffocate inconspicuously while it flops around on a deck.

For all the value of the LaBudde tape, something is missing. At   6
least it's missing from the edited version, supplied to me by Earth

Island Institute, the organization with which LaBudde is affiliated. There's no footage, not so much as a glimpse, of dead or dying tuna.

Tuna are not the point, I know. Canned tunafish is the given; dolphin-safe or dolphin-unsafe is the point. But it still seems to me odd that tuna, as living and dying creatures, have so completely disappeared. Not just from the videotape. From our minds.   7

Are we concerned with humanity's relationship with nature, or are we merely concerned about Man's Special Friend at Sea, the dolphin? These are two different things.   8

A few years ago, Kenneth Brower published in *The Atlantic* a long, excellent article about the destruction of dolphins by tuna fishermen in the Eastern Tropical Pacific, and about the daring gambit of Sam LaBudde. The article is full of facts, full of fair-minded argument, but its most subtle effect is achieved by another method—point of view. It begins: 9

> Of the thirty-odd species of oceanic dolphins, none makes a more striking entrance than *Stenella attenuata,* the spotted dolphin. Under water spotted dolphins first appear as white dots against the blue. The beaks of the adults are white-tipped, and that distinctive blaze, viewed head-on, makes a perfect circle. When the vanguard of the school is "echolocating" on you—examining you sonically—the beaks all swing your way, and each circular blaze reflects light before any of the rest of the animal does.

Brower describes the habitat of these dolphins—clear, deep, tropical ocean—and the sensation of floating within it. A blue void, he calls it, seemingly sterile as a desert. Then:

> Five or six quick strokes of the flukes and they are upon you, sleek, fast, graceful legions. They come a little larger than life, for water magnifies. They animate the void. With barrages of clicks and choruses of high-pitched whistling, with speed and hydrodynamic perfection, with curiosity, mission, agenda, and something like humor, they fill up the empty blue.

You are surrounded by dolphins, caressed by their clicking voices. And then: "The last dolphin of the last wave pumps by, glances at you in passing, hurries to catch up." Kenneth Brower has been in the water with these animals, obviously, and before even mentioning tuna boats or purse seines, he deftly pulls the reader in there with him. He offers a vicarious opportunity to look dolphins in the face and share the sensation of being explored, known, by their sonar and their big liquidy eyes. Why? Because he wants us—you and me and whoever else might pick up *The Atlantic*—to feel especially bonded with dolphins, and he evidently believes that direct physical acquaintance (or even a literary rendition of it) is the best way to generate such a bond.

Later in the article, he makes that premise explicit. Alluding to   10 the doom awaiting a certain newborn dolphin calf that LaBudde saw pitched back into the water, where without its mother it faced starvation and sharks, Brower declares: "Anyone who has swum with wild dolphins can imagine how it went."

Ani H. Moss, a former fashion model living in Los Angeles and   11 latterly a conservation activist, broke into public view about the same time as Brower's article, representing a physical embodiment of the anyone-who-has-swum-with-them premise. Like Brower, she harbors a warm and specific affinity for dolphins. One newspaper photograph shows her, afloat, in a life jacket, kissing a pleased-looking dolphin on the side of its beak. According to the *San Francisco Chronicle*, Ani Moss has swum with dolphins in Bermuda, Florida, and Hawaii. This fact merits newsprint because she is one of the cluster of people—including Sam LaBudde, David Phillips of Earth Island Institute, Anthony J. F. O'Reilly of the H. J. Heinz Company, and Ani's husband, a music-industry executive named Jerry Moss— most responsible for a great triumph won in the crusade to protect dolphins. On April 12, 1990, Heinz announced that its StarKist subsidiary, the world's largest tuna-canning business, would no longer purchase any tuna caught by methods that were harmful to dolphins.

Behind that decision lay a domino chain of persuasion that went   12 roughly like this: Ani Moss saw LaBudde's videotape and talked with her husband; Mr. and Mrs. Moss talked with Phillips about dolphin conservation and Earth Island's consumer boycott against Heinz; Jerry Moss then talked honcho-to-honcho with Anthony J. F. O'Reilly; the Heinz people eventually talked with Phillips and even, it seems, with Sam LaBudde. Behind the boardroom doors at H. J. Heinz, there was "an epic debate, almost theological in tone," as O'Reilly himself later told the *New York Times*. At last, with a suddenness that startled everyone on the outside and probably more than a few people on the inside, Heinz decided to leap acrobatically from one side of the issue to the other. Seldom in the history of conservation politics has jawboning proven so concretely effective.

The announcement caused an abrupt revolution in the interna-   13
tional tuna trade. That same afternoon, StarKist's two main competitors, Chicken of the Sea and Bumble Bee, vowed that they also
would cease their complicity in the death of dolphins; StarKist had
seized what appeared to be the moral high ground, and in this case
the moral high ground was so good for public relations, perhaps
also for business, that Chicken of the Sea and Bumble Bee were compelled to scramble up-slope in the same direction. Before long, tuna
canners in Thailand, France, and Italy made similar announcements.
Some of the U.S. tuna boats in the Eastern Tropical Pacific immediately applied for clearance to move westward, into waters where
tuna and dolphins don't associate. Heinz began printing "dolphin-
safe" labels, while Earth Island Institute declared victory and offered peace with honor.

Anthony J. F. O'Reilly, the man who effected (or at least accepted)   14
this sea change, is a hardheaded Irish millionaire and a fancier of race-
horses. If he has ever jumped into a tank or an ocean and swum with
dolphins, the newspaper accounts don't mention it. But the calculus of
the businessman has its own heartfelt power.

Back when the Earth Island boycott was in force, before the   15
Heinz capitulation, Sam LaBudde said: "The reason this issue remains an issue, and the reason that it's not going to go away, is that
human beings have a very special kinship with dolphins." It's an
honest and accurate statement, so far as it goes, and one with which
Anthony J. F. O'Reilly came to agree.

The LaBudde videotape does not diminish in grisliness with repeated   16
viewing. While the information content becomes familiar, while the
words and the numbers blur away, the moving images come forward
more vividly. Like the photographer played by David Hemmings
in the movie *Blowup,* you start noticing nasty details that you had
missed. You see the flying bits of flesh from some anatomical
breakage—a fin ripped away, maybe, or a beak—when a tangled dolphin suddenly falls from the hoisted net. You see an animal pass
through the power block, like wet laundry through a wringer, and
you recognize that its thrashing has turned into twitching. On the
fourth replay, as you stare at the sleek dark shapes in a pocket of
tightened seine, big animals bunched like sprawling salmon, you realize that they are all floating limp with their blowholes submerged.
Watching the crewmen work, you begin to distinguish between when
they're releasing live dolphins and when they're disposing of carcasses. Mostly it's the latter. Then there's the scene with the knife.

The captain of LaBudde's ship, a burly man wearing only a pair   17
of soaked shorts, is stooping over the body of a dolphin, filleting it
deftly. With quick slashes, he strips off a long panel of muscle. He
glances up into the camera—once, then back to his work, then up
again. The tape ends.

This scene with the knife is hard to watch and tricky to contem-   18
plate. It's a crux at which the emotional import of the LaBudde
videotape diverges (for some of us, anyway) from the philosophical
import. The captain's knife cuts through more than flesh; it also divides attitudes. It divided my own, clarifyingly, into two successive
but contradictory reactions. First reaction: My God, he's slicing that
dolphin into meat. My God, they're going to *eat* it. Witnessing the
butchery, you feel a surge of horrified outrage to which you may not
be entitled. I know I felt one to which I'm probably not entitled.
Butchery, not as a metaphor but the literal fact, is just what brings
animal parts—including, occasionally, a bit of mammal—to my
kitchen counter. Sam LaBudde, when he made the tape, was a vegetarian; so arguably he was entitled. Maybe he also felt some outrage
at the notion of eating tuna. Or maybe not. Second reaction: Who am
I, a confirmed carnivore, to say that they *shouldn't* eat dolphin flesh?
If the creature is dead, better to eat it than to discard it. Both these
reactions have merit, I think, and the dichotomy between them
helps untangle that confusion of good logic and bad logic, earned
emotion and specious emotion, surrounding the subject of dolphin-
unsafe tuna.

A person might object to the killing on grounds that dolphins are   19
big-brained mammals. If that were my position, I'd want also to know
more than I know about the size of the brain of a Hereford, and I'd be
uncomfortable with reports of high intelligence among octopuses and
pigs. A person might object on the grounds that dolphins are charming
and communicative creatures capable of forming exceptional bonds
with our species. That position is admirably loyal. But if it were mine I'd
feel forced to admit that my view of nature was rigidly anthropocentric,
and that I was therefore prevented from arguing that a hectare of beetle-
infested rainforest might be more valuable than a hectare of slash-and-
burn rice. A person might object on grounds that the death of six million
dolphins in thirty years—as a by-product of purse-seining, merely to
bring us cheap tuna, with most of those six million carcasses dumped
back into the ocean—has been unconscionably wasteful; and that just
such contemptuous, self-indulgent wastefulness is the greatest sin that
our species commits against nature. This *is* my position. But probably
it's no more consistent than the others.

Or a person might object, as some have, that the drownings of   20
dolphins are slow and cruel, much worse than the quick death of a
cow or a chicken in a slaughterhouse. If that were my position, I'd
deserve to be haunted by a nightmare of suffocating tuna, big fish
flopping paroxysmally on a deck, their sticky-dry gills unable to
extract oxygen from the air. And I'd need to swear off live-boiled
lobster.

Mix all these positions together and what you don't get is a sin-   21
gle, unassailable ethical stance. What you do get is a successful consumer boycott against one kind of canned fish. The fight to protect
dolphins from tuna fishermen brought a great victory for mammalian
empathy, but not for clear thinking about humanity's responsibility
within the wider diversity of life.

There's no question that *Stenella attenuata* and the other dol-   22
phins have an unmatched appeal to us humans. From our point of
view, as Sam LaBudde said, it's a special kinship. They are bright,
sophisticated, cheery, generous, perceptive, affectionate, and yet
mysterious—all the things that we value in our friends. They seem to
possess important secrets. They seem to reciprocate our infatuation.
Plus they consent to let us swim with them.

On the other hand, who swims with the yellowfin tuna? The   23
answer is that dolphins do.

Meanings and Values

1. Where in the essay does the writer describe the issue he is address-
    ing? Summarize it in your own words.

2. What is Quammen's argumentative thesis, and where does he pre-
    sent it to readers? (See "Guide to Terms": *Thesis*.)

3. What criticisms does the writer offer of those who have campaigned
    in favor of saving dolphins? Is his purpose to undermine their ef-
    forts? If not, what is his purpose? (Guide: *Purpose*.)

4. What strategies of definition does Quammen employ in arguing for a
    new definition of tuna and a new attitude toward the species? (See
    Chapter 6, "Definition.")

Argumentative Techniques

1. How does Quammen manage to encourage readers to develop sym-
    pathy for tuna and to urge readers to take action without arguing
    against sympathy for dolphins and action on their behalf?

2. Quammen employs several patterns of development in advancing his argument. What are they? Which are particularly effective? (Guide: *Evaluation*.) Is it accurate to say that definition (or redefinition) is the dominant pattern? Why, or why not?

3. How does Quammen shift readers' attention from dolphins to tuna (Pars. 6–7)?

4. What role does the rhetorical question in Paragraph 8 play in the overall organization of the essay and in the logic of Quammen's argument? (Guide: *Rhetorical Question*.)

DICTION AND VOCABULARY

1. How do the connotations and denotations of the words Quammen uses to describe dolphins caught in nets (Pars. 3, 5, 16) and tuna caught in nets (20) help develop sympathy for them? (Guide: *Denotation/Connotation*.)

2. If you do not know the meaning of some of the following words, look them up in a dictionary: litany, invidious, homoiothermic, altruistic, piscine (Par. 2); purse-seining, offal (3); symbiotic (5); gambit (9); grisliness (16); dichotomy (18); Hereford, anthropocentric, hectare, contemptuous (19); paroxysmally (20).

READ TO WRITE

1. **Collaborating:** Working in a group, list as many environmental or wildlife policies you can think of that harm one group of animals or people or one ecological setting at the expense of another. Write an argumentative essay of your own on one or more of the issues suggested by the group's list.

2. **Considering Audience:** Are most readers likely to agree with Quammen that tuna have been treated unfairly? Or are they likely to think that Quammen has treated dolphin advocates unfairly? Write a brief essay analyzing the essay and answering these questions.

3. **Developing an Essay:** Is Quammen justified in his criticism of LaBudde and others campaigning for saving dolphins? Do some research on the subject and develop a thesis of your own regarding the current and future efforts to save dolphins and tuna from needless destruction. Then write an essay defending this thesis.

(NOTE: Suggestions for topics to be developed by means of ARGUMENT are on page 601–602, at the end of this chapter.)

ARGUMENT THROUGH DEFINITION

BARBARA LAWRENCE

BARBARA LAWRENCE was born in Hanover, New Hampshire. After receiving a B.A. in French literature from Connecticut College, she worked as an editor on *McCall's, Redbook, Harper's Bazaar,* and the *New Yorker.* During this period she also took an M.A. in philosophy from New York University. Currently a professor of humanities at the State University of New York's College at Old Westbury, Lawrence has published criticism, poetry, and fiction in *Choice, Commonweal, Columbia Poetry,* the *New York Times,* and the *New Yorker.*

Four-Letter Words Can Hurt You

"Four-Letter Words Can Hurt You" first appeared in the *New York Times* and was later published in *Redbook.* In arguing against the "earthy, gut-honest" language often preferred by her students, Lawrence also provides a thoughtful, even scholarly, extended definition of *obscenity* itself. To accomplish her purpose, the author makes use of several other patterns as well.

W hy should any words be called obscene? Don't they all describe natural human functions? Am I trying to tell them, my students demand, that the "strong, earthy, gut-honest"—or, if they are fans of Norman Mailer, the "rich, liberating, existential"—language they use to describe sexual activity isn't preferable to "phony-sounding, middle-class words like 'intercourse' and 'copulate'"? "Cop You Late!" they say with fancy inflections and gagging grimaces. "Now, what is *that* supposed to mean?" 1

Well, what is it supposed to mean? And why indeed should one group of words describing human functions and human organs be acceptable in ordinary conversation and another, describing presumably the same organs and functions, be tabooed—so much so, in fact, that some of these words still cannot appear in print in many parts of the English-speaking world? 2

The argument that these taboos exist only because of "sexual hangups" (middle-class, middle-age, feminist), or even that they are a result of class oppression (the contempt of the Norman conquerors for the language of their Anglo-Saxon serfs), ignores a much more likely explanation, it seems to me, and that is the sources and functions of the words themselves. 3

The best known of the tabooed sexual words, for example,   4
comes from the German *ficken,* meaning "to strike"; combined, according to Partridge's etymological dictionary *Origins,* with the
Latin sexual verb *futuere:* associated in turn with the Latin *fustis,* "a
staff or cudgel"; the Celtic *buc,* "a point, hence to pierce"; the Irish
bot, "the male member"; the Latin *battuere,* "to beat"; the Gaelic
batair, "a cudgeller"; the Early Irish *bualaim,* "I strike"; and so forth.
It is one of what etymologists sometimes called "the sadistic group
of words for the man's part in copulation."

The brutality of this word, then, and its equivalents ("screw,"   5
"bang," etc.) is not an illusion of the middle class or a crotchet of
Women's Liberation. In their origins and imagery these words carry
undeniably painful, if not sadistic, implications, the object of which
is almost always female. Consider, for example, what a "screw" actually does to the wood it penetrates; what a painful, even mutilating, activity this kind of analogy suggests. "Screw" is particularly
interesting in this context, since the noun, according to Partridge,
comes from words meaning "groove," "nut," "ditch," "breeding
sow," "scrofula" and "swelling," while the verb, besides its explicit
imagery, has antecedent associations to "write on," "scratch," "scarify," and so forth—a revealing fusion of a mechanical or painful action with an obviously denigrated object.

Not all obscene words, of course, are as implicitly sadistic or   6
denigrating to women as these, but all that I know seem to serve a
similar purpose: to reduce the human organism (especially the female organism) and human functions (especially sexual and procreative) to their least organic, most mechanical dimension; to substitute
a trivializing or deforming resemblance for the complex human reality of what is being described.

Tabooed male descriptives, when they are not openly denigrat-   7
ing to women, often serve to divorce a male organ or function from
any significant interaction with the female. Take the word *"testes,"* for
example, suggesting "witnesses" (from the Latin *testis*) to the sexual
and procreative strengths of the male organ; and the obscene counter-
part of this word, which suggests little more than a mechanical shape.
Or compare almost any of the "rich," "liberating" sexual verbs, so
fashionable today among male writers, with that much-derived Latin
word "copulate" ("to bind or join together") or even that Anglo-
Saxon phrase (which seems to have had no trouble surviving the
Norman Conquest) "make love."

How arrogantly self-involved the tabooed words seem in com-   8
parison to either of the other terms, and how contemptuous of the

female partner. Understandably so, of course, if she is only a "skirt," a "broad," a "chick," a "pussycat" or a "piece." If she is, in other words no more than her skirt, or what her skirt conceals; no more than a breeder, or the broadest part of her; no more than a piece of a human being or a "piece of tail."

The most severely tabooed of all the female descriptives, inci-   9
dentally, are those like a "piece of tail," which suggests (either explicitly or through antecedents) that there is no significant difference between the female channel through which we are all conceived and born and the anal outlet common to both sexes—a distinction that pornographers have always enjoyed obscuring.

This effort to deny women their biological identity, their indi-   10
viduality, their humanness, is such an important aspect of obscene language that one can only marvel at how seldom, in an era preoccupied with definitions of obscenity, this fact is brought to our attention. One problem, of course, is that many of the people in the best position to do this (critics, teachers, writers) are so reluctant today to admit that they are angered or shocked by obscenity. Bored, maybe, unimpressed, aesthetically displeased, but—no matter how brutal or denigrating the material—never angered, never shocked.

And yet how eloquently angered, how piously shocked many   11
of these same people become if denigrating language is used about any minority group other than women; if the obscenities are racial or ethnic, that is, rather than sexual. Words like "coon," "kike," "spic," "wop," after all, deform identity, deny individuality and humanness in almost exactly the same way that sexual vulgarisms and obscenities do.

No one that I know, least of all my students, would fail to ques-   12
tion the values of a society whose literature and entertainment rested heavily on racial or ethnic pejoratives. Are the values of a society whose literature and entertainment rest as heavily as ours on sexual pejoratives any less questionable?

MEANINGS AND VALUES

1. Explain the meaning of *irony* by use of at least one illustration from the latter part of this essay. (See "Guide to Terms": *Irony.*)

2. Inasmuch as the selection itself includes many of the so-called "strong, earthy, gut-honest" words, could anyone logically call it obscene?

Why, or why not? To what extent, if at all, does the author's point of view help determine your answer? (Guide: *Point of View.*)

3. Compose, in your own words, a compact statement of Lawrence's thesis. (Guide: *Thesis.*) Are all parts of the essay completely relevant to this thesis? Justify your answer.

4. Evaluate this composition by use of our three-question system. (Guide: *Evaluation.*)

ARGUMENTATIVE TECHNIQUES

1. What is the purpose of this essay? (Guide: *Purpose.*)

2. What objection to her opinion does the author refute in Paragraph 3, and how does she refute it? (Guide: *Refutation.*) Where else in the essay does she refute opposing arguments?

3. Are the evidence and supporting arguments in this essay arranged in a refutation-proof pattern? If not, describe the arrangement of the essay.

4. Which of the methods "peculiar to definition alone" (see the introduction to Chapter 9) does the author employ in developing this essay? What other patterns of exposition does she also use?

5. Which of the standard techniques of introduction are used? (Guide: *Introductions.*) Which methods are used to close the essay? (Guide: *Closing.*)

DICTION AND VOCABULARY

1. How, if at all, is this discussion of words related to *connotation?* (Guide: *Connotation/Denotation.*) To what extent would connotations in this matter depend on the setting and circumstances in which the words are used? Cite illustrations to clarify your answer.

2. In view of the fact that the author uses frankly many of the "gut-honest" words, why do you suppose she plainly avoids others, such as in Paragraphs 4 and 7?

3. The author says that a "kind of analogy" is suggested by some of the words discussed (Par. 5). If you have studied Chapter 6 of this book, does her use of the term *analogy* seem in conflict with what you believed it to mean? Explain.

4. Study the author's uses of the following words, consulting the dictionary as needed: existential, grimaces (Par. 1); etymological, cudgel (4); sadistic (4–6); crotchet, scrofula, explicit, antecedent, scarify (5); denigrated (5–7, 10–11); aesthetically (10); pejoratives (12).

READ TO WRITE

1. **Collaborating:** Why do people use obscene language? Are these reasons satisfactory enough to keep from stigmatizing it or considering it impolite? Have our views of obscene language undergone any

recent changes? Should we discourage the use of obscene language in more social situations than we currently do? Working in a group, continue this list of questions until you have identified several possible topics for an essay. Words characterizing ethnic groups are likely to get strong responses from readers.

2.   **Considering Audience:** Does the author make a justifiable comparison between obscene words and ethnic pejoratives? Using illustrations for specificity, carry the comparison further to show why it is sound, or explain why you consider it a weak comparison.

3.   **Developing an Essay:** Following Lawrence's lead, discuss some other closely related group of terms and its significance, and suggest ways we should alter the way we use these terms.

(NOTE: Suggestions for topics requiring development by ARGUMENT are on pp. 601–602 at the end of this chapter.)

ARGUMENT THROUGH NARRATIVE

SARAH MIN

SARAH MIN works at *Glamour* magazine.

Language Lessons

Issues of bilingualism and bilingual education along with proposals for "English Only" in government and schools have drawn
much interest over the past decade. Sarah Min takes a somewhat
different, and personal, approach to bilingualism, arguing for its
importance through her own story.

Even though I could understand only snippets of their conversa-   1
tion, I comprehended enough to know that the manicurists at the
nail salon were talking about me.

What a shame! Another Korean who cannot speak the language, the   2
woman filing my fingernails said to her colleague, both of them
shaking their heads in disapproval. Her remark hit me, and I stumbled for the right words to defend myself.

The fact is, I traded my own Korean voice to give my parents   3
their English ones: My mom and dad came to this country 27 years
ago with an English vocabulary dominated by brand names like
Tropicana and Samsonite. But they were determined to master the
language of their new home. When I was in grade school, my dad
read my English textbooks and asked me to give him the same
lessons I had learned that day. On long car trips, my parents spent
the confined hours in our Impala station wagon practicing their pro-
nunciation aloud. My brother and I, captive tutors, led them in oral
exercises, repeating the difficult distinction between *ear* and *year*,
war and *wore*.

As my parents' fluency increased, their use of Korean dwindled.   4
Though they spoke to each other in their native tongue, with my
brother and me they used only one language: English. They didn't
want us to speak Korean, they said, because they didn't want even a
trace of an accent to infect our American-style speech.

Still, I absorbed bits and pieces of Korean, important phrases   5
like "Oh-mo-mo" and "Whey-goo-deh?"—the equivalent of "Oh
no!" and "What's your problem?"—subtleties that can't be precisely

translated but are understood as readily as "oy vey" or "cool." In private, I'd practice the sound effects—the gasps and clucks that are a part of the Korean language.

In public, though, I was reluctant to speak. My words sounded clunky, choppy, unlike the rhythmic cadences of my mother's voice. Once when I attempted conversation with a Korean-speaking woman in my neighborhood, my efforts were clearly unimpressive: She snickered at my accent and answered me in English. By the time I was in college, I had stopped trying to speak Korean, a decision only I noticed. No one expected me to speak the language anyway.   6

Yet I always felt that a part of me had been silenced. As I got older and moved to a city where I met more Koreans, I began to feel as the women in the nail salon did: That those of us who didn't speak Korean had something to be ashamed of, that we were distancing ourselves from our cultural heritage. Language, after all, involves much more than the ability to communicate. It conveys a desire to understand and participate in a culture, to make it one's own. Could I ever fully understand and appreciate my heritage if I couldn't speak the language of my ancestors?   7

So I registered for a course in Korean at an adult education school. I expected my classmates to be Americans who were going abroad, but I discovered most of the students had come for the same reason that I had: to find their Korean voices.   8

To my surprise, I picked up the language quickly. Even though my vocabulary was limited and my grammar was rough, I realized I knew quite a bit, as if the Korean words had been lurking somewhere in a quiet corner of my brain. The teacher taught phrases that sounded familiar and came to me effortlessly; I practiced the new tongue placements and inflections to hide my American accent. The first time I called my parents and said, in flawless Korean, "Hello, we haven't spoken in such a long time," I was 24 years old, but they reacted as proudly as if I were a toddler who had just uttered her first words. And when I walked into a Korean restaurant and casually greeted the waiter, who responded in Korean that I could sit anywhere I liked, I knew he took me for the genuine article.   9

Now whenever I visit my parents, I ask them to speak Korean with me at least some of the time. Although I'm still struggling, still studying so I can become more fluent, I know enough now that my parents can tell me stories, jokes and proverbs that would otherwise have gotten garbled in the static of translation. Eagerly, I listen, laugh and nod in full understanding.   10

Being able to speak Korean has some surprising bonuses: In   11
American restaurants, my dad and I figure the tip right in front of
the waiter. And among Koreans, knowing the language forges an almost instant camaraderie.

That day at the nail salon, when I finally worked up the courage   12
to respond to the manicurist, I spoke slowly, but confidently: *I understand you and yes, it is shameful that I can only speak a little.*

The young woman polishing my fingernails paused. She   13
looked up at me and smiled, as if she were seeing me for the first
time. And, for the first time, I too was seeing a new part of myself: a proud Korean American who could finally hear her own
voice.

MEANINGS AND VALUES

1. Min devotes much of Paragraphs 3 and 4 in her essay to a discussion
   of her parents' efforts to learn English and to encourage their children to speak English. Explain why her parents may have felt they
   needed to do this. As a young girl, how does Min react to her parents' effort?

2. What feelings inspired Min to take adult education courses in Korean
   (Par. 8)? Is she justified in her concerns about heritage? How important are these cultural issues in the contemporary America?

ARGUMENTATIVE TECHNIQUES

1. The anecdote in Min's introduction (Pars. 1 and 2) is readdressed in
   her conclusion. What element of surprise does she incorporate into
   this story? Does she convince her reader of the importance of her
   conversation with the manicurists?

2. Much of Min's argument is in the form of narrative. How effective is
   this technique? Why do you think she chose a first-person narrative
   for this topic?

DICTION AND VOCABULARY

1. Are there any words in this essay with which you are unfamiliar?
   Why might Min have used a basic vocabulary for this piece? Who
   might her target audience include?

2. Min writes this as an autobiographical narrative. Point to specific
   uses of transitions, dialogue, and other techniques that help the narrative have a storylike quality.

READ TO WRITE

1. **Collaborating:** Working in a group, list the native languages of your ancestors. How many of you still speak that language? Discuss with your teammates the reasons why you feel that your family no longer speaks in the native tongue, or if your family still does, why the members have chosen to continue. Compare your reasons and look for underlying cultural connections regarding the maintenance of native tongues. Keeping in mind your group discussions, write an individual paper in a style similar to Min's discussing your use or lack of use of your family's native tongue. If your ancestry is of English-speaking people, write about a friend or someone you know who has had this issue arise in his or her family.

2. **Considering Audience:** Min says, "And among Koreans, knowing the language forges an almost instant camaraderie" (Par. 11). Would non-Korean readers identify with this statement? Does her point apply to others besides Koreans? Write a short analysis explaining your response.

3. **Developing an Essay:** Min's essay clearly encourages the maintaining of a native tongue, but not at the sacrifice of learning English when living in the United States. This is one facet of a debate on language. Research the question of whether or not the United States should have a unified language and the impact of maintaining a native tongue in some capacity. Consider the unifying qualities of language both inside and outside of the cultural boundaries. Write an argumentative essay employing multiple patterns of development in which you address the issue of either the adoption of a national language, the use of native languages in the household, or the acceptance of bilingualism or multilingualism in society.

(NOTE: Suggestions for essays requiring development by use of ARGUMENT follow.)

Writing Suggestions for Chapter 13

ARGUMENT

Choose one of the following topic areas, identify an issue (a conflict or problem) within it, and prepare an essay that tries to convince readers to share your opinion about the issue and to take any appropriate action. Use a variety of evidence in your essay, and choose any pattern of development you consider proper for the topic, for your thesis, and for the intended audience.

1. Gun control
2. The quality of education in American elementary and secondary schools
3. Treatment of critically ill newborn babies
4. Hunting
5. Euthanasia
6. Censorship in public schools and libraries
7. College athletics
8. The problem of toxic waste or a similar environmental problem
9. Careers versus family responsibilities
10. The separation of church and state
11. Law on the drinking age or on drunk driving
12. Evolution versus creationism
13. Medical ethics
14. Government spending on social programs
15. The quality of television programming
16. The impact of divorce
17. The effects of television viewing on children
18. Professional sports
19. Violence in service of an ideal or belief
20. Scholarship and student loan policies
21. Low pay for public service and the "helping" professions
22. Cheating in college courses
23. Drug and alcohol abuse
24. Product safety and reliability
25. Government economic or social policy

COLLABORATIVE ACTIVITIES

As you prepare an essay on one of the given topics (1–25) or on some other topic, make a list of the evidence for your opinion. Share the list with one or more readers. Ask the reader to rank each piece of evidence for persuasiveness, using a scale of 1 (unpersuasive) to 5 (very persuasive).

14

Further Readings: Combining Patterns

MARGARET ATWOOD

MARGARET ATWOOD was born in Ottawa, Ontario, in 1939. After attending college in Canada, she went to graduate school at Harvard University. She has had a distinguished career as a novelist, poet, and essayist, and is generally considered to be one of the central figures in contemporary Canadian literature and culture. Atwood's international reputation as a writer rests on her novels, including *The Edible Woman* (1960), *Surfacing* (1972), *Life Before Man* (1979), *Bodily Harm* (1982), *The Handmaid's Tale* (1986), *Cat's Eye* (1989), *The Robber Bride* (1993), *Alias Grace* (1996), *The Blind Assassin* (2000), and her short stories, including *Bluebeard's Egg and Other Stories* (1986) and *Good Bones* (1992), though she has written poetry, television plays, and children's books as well. Her essays were collected in the volume *Second Words* (1982) and have continued to appear in newspapers and magazines such as *Ms., Harper's, Globe and Mail, The Nation, Maclean's, Washington Post, Harvard Educational Review, The Humanist, The New Republic,* and *Architectural Digest.* As an essayist, Atwood frequently writes about issues in contemporary culture and society, including the nature of Canadian culture and relationships between Canada and the United States.

Pornography

In the following essay, Atwood addresses the question of pornography with a directness and originality that are characteristic of her work. This essay originally appeared in *Chatelaine Magazine,* a mass-circulation women's magazine. As you read the selection, consider how well it addresses both the concerns of its original audience and the concerns about pornography a somewhat wider audience might have. Note also how she makes use of definition and a number of other expository patterns.

When I was in Finland a few years ago for an international writ-   1
ers' conference, I had occasion to say a few paragraphs in public on the subject of pornography. The context was a discussion of political repression, and I was suggesting the possibility of a link between the two. The immediate result was that a male journalist took several large bites out of me. Prudery and pornography are two halves of the same coin, said he, and I was clearly a prude. What could you expect from an Anglo-Canadian? Afterward, a couple of pleasant Scandinavian men asked me what I had been so worked up about. All "pornography" means, they said, is graphic depictions of whores, and what was the harm in that?

Not until then did it strike me that the male journalist and I had   2
two entirely different things in mind. By "pornography," he meant naked bodies and sex. I, on the other hand, had recently been doing the research for my novel *Bodily Harm,* and was still in a state of shock from some of the material I had seen, including the Ontario Board of Film Censors' "outtakes." By "pornography," I meant women getting their nipples snipped off with garden shears, having meat hooks stuck into their vaginas, being disemboweled; little girls being raped; men (yes, there are some men) being smashed to a pulp and forcibly sodomized. The cutting edge of pornography, as far as I could see, was no longer simple old copulation, hanging from the chandelier or otherwise: it was death, messy, explicit and highly sadistic. I explained this to the nice Scandinavian men. "Oh, but that's just the United States," they said. "Everyone knows they're sick." In their country, they said, violent "pornography" of that kind was not permitted on television or in movies; indeed, excessive violence of any kind was not permitted. They had drawn a clear line between erotica, which earlier studies had shown did not incite men to more aggressive and brutal behavior toward women, and violence, which later studies indicated did.

Some time after that I was in Saskatchewan, where, because of   3
the scenes in *Bodily Harm,* I found myself on an open-line radio show answering questions about "pornography." Almost no one who phoned in was in favor of it, but again they weren't talking about the same stuff I was, because they hadn't seen it. Some of them were all

set to stamp out bathing suits and negligees, and, if possible, any depictions of the female body whatsoever. God, it was implied, did not approve of female bodies, and sex of any kind, including that practiced by bumblebees, should be shoved back into the dark, where it belonged. I had more than a suspicion that *Lady Chatterley's Lover,* Margaret Laurence's *The Diviners,* and indeed most books by most serious modern authors would have ended up as confetti if left in the hands of these callers.

For me, these two experiences illustrate the two poles of the   4 emotionally heated debate that is now thundering around this issue. They also underline the desirability and even the necessity of defining the terms. "Pornography" is now one of those catchalls, like "Marxism" and "feminism," that have become so broad they can mean almost anything, ranging from certain verses in the Bible, ads for skin lotion and sex tests for children to the contents of *Penthouse,* Naughty '90s postcards and films with titles containing the word *Nazi* that show vicious scenes of torture and killing. It's easy to say that sensible people can tell the difference. Unfortunately, opinions on what constitutes a sensible person vary.

But even sensible people tend to lose their cool when they start   5 talking about this subject. They soon stop talking and start yelling, and the name-calling begins. Those in favor of censorship (which may include groups not noticeably in agreement on other issues, such as some feminists and religious fundamentalists) accuse the others of exploiting women through the use of degrading images, contributing to the corruption of children, and adding to the general climate of violence and threat in which both women and children live in this society; or, though they may not give much of a hoot about actual women and children, they invoke moral standards and God's supposed aversion to "filth," "smut" and deviated *perversion,* which may mean ankles.

The camp in favor of total "freedom of expression" often comes   6 out howling as loud as the Romans would have if told they could no longer have innocent fun watching the lions eat up Christians. It too may include segments of the population who are not natural bedfellows: those who proclaim their God-given right to freedom, including the freedom to tote guns, drive when drunk, drool over chicken porn and get off on videotapes of women being raped and beaten, may be waving the same anticensorship banner as responsible liberals who fear the return of Mrs. Grundy, or gay groups for whom sexual emancipation involves the concept of "sexual theater." *Whatever turns you on* is a handy motto, as is *A man's home is his castle* (and if it includes a dungeon with beautiful maidens strung up in chains and bleeding from every pore, that's his business).

Meanwhile, theoreticians theorize and speculators speculate. Is 7 today's pornography yet another indication of the hatred of the body, the deep mind-body split, which is supposed to pervade Western Christian society? Is it a backlash against the women's movement by men who are threatened by uppity female behavior in real life, so like to fantasize about women done up like outsize parcels, being turned into hamburger, kneeling at their feet in slave-like adoration or sucking off guns? Is it a sign of collective impotence, of a generation of men who can't relate to real women at all but have to make do with bits of celluloid and paper? Is the current flood just a result of smart marketing and aggressive promotion by the money men in what has now become a multibillion-dollar industry? If they were selling movies about men getting their testicles stuck full of knitting needles by women with swastikas on their sleeves, would they do as well, or is this penchant somehow peculiarly male? If so, why? Is pornography a power trip rather than a sex one? Some say that those ropes, chains, muzzles and other restraining devices are an argument for the immense power female sexuality still wields in the male imagination: you don't put these things on dogs unless you're afraid of them. Others, more literary, wonder about the shift from the 19th-century Magic Woman or Femme Fatale image to the lollipop-licker, airhead or turkey-carcass treatment of women in porn today. The proporners don't care much about theory; they merely demand product. The antiporners don't care about it in the final analysis either; there's dirt on the street, and they want it cleaned up, now.

It seems to me that this conversation, with its *You're-a-prude/* 8 *You're-a-pervert* dialectic, will never get anywhere as long as we continue to think of this material as just "entertainment." Possibly we're deluded by the packaging, the format: magazine, book, movie, theatrical presentation. We're used to thinking of these things as part of the "entertainment industry," and we're used to thinking of ourselves as free adult people who ought to be able to see any kind of "entertainment" we want to. That was what the First Choice pay-TV debate was all about. After all, it's only entertainment, right? Entertainment means fun, and only a killjoy would be antifun. What's the harm?

This is obviously the central question: *What's the harm?* If there 9 isn't any real harm to any real people, then the antiporners can tsk-tsk and/or throw up as much as they like, but they can't rightfully expect more legal controls or sanctions. However, the no-harm position is far from being proven.

(For instance, there's a clear-cut case for banning—as the federal government has proposed—movies, photos and videos that depict children engaging in sex with adults: real children are used to make the movies, and hardly anybody thinks this is ethical. The possibilities for coercion are too great.)   10

To shift the viewpoint, I'd like to suggest three other models for looking at "pornography"—and here I mean the violent kind.   11

Those who find the idea of regulating pornographic materials repugnant because they think it's Fascist or Communist or otherwise not in accordance with the principles of an open democratic society should consider that Canada has made it illegal to disseminate material that may lead to hatred toward any group because of race or religion. I suggest that if pornography of the violent kind depicted these acts being done predominantly to Chinese, to blacks, to Catholics, it would be off the market immediately, under the present laws. Why is hate literature illegal? Because whoever made the law thought that such material might incite real people to do real awful things to other real people. The human brain is to a certain extent a computer: garbage in, garbage out. We only hear about the extreme cases (like that of American multimurderer Ted Bundy) in which pornography has contributed to the death and/or mutilation of women and/or men. Although pornography is not the only factor involved in the creation of such deviance, it certainly has upped the ante by suggesting both a variety of techniques and the social acceptability of such actions. Nobody knows yet what effect this stuff is having on the less psychotic.   12

Studies have shown that a large part of the market for all kinds of porn, soft and hard, is drawn from the 16-to-21-year-old population of young men. Boys used to learn about sex on the street, or (in Italy, according to Fellini movies) from friendly whores, or, in more genteel surroundings, from girls, their parents, or, once upon a time, in school, more or less. Now porn has been added, and sex education in the schools is rapidly being phased out. The buck has been passed, and boys are being taught that all women secretly like to be raped and that real men get high on scooping out women's digestive tracts.   13

Boys learn their concept of masculinity from other men: is this what most men want them to be learning? If word gets around that rapists are "normal" and even admirable men, will boys feel that in order to be normal, admirable and masculine they will have to be   14 rapists? Human beings are enormously flexible, and how they turn out depends a lot on how they're educated, by the society in which they're immersed as well as by their teachers. In a society that advertises and glorifies rape or even implicitly condones it, more women get raped. It becomes socially acceptable. And at a time when men and the traditional male role have taken a lot of flak and men are confused and casting around for an acceptable way of being male (and, in some cases, not getting much comfort from women on that score), this must be at times a pleasing thought.

It would be naïve to think of violent pornography as just harm- 15
less entertainment. It's also an educational tool and a powerful propaganda device. What happens when boy educated on porn meets girl brought up on Harlequin romances? The clash of expectations can be heard around the block. She wants him to get down on his knees with a ring, he wants her to get down on all fours with a ring in her nose. Can this marriage be saved?

Pornography has certain things in common with such addictive 16
substances as alcohol and drugs: for some, though by no means for all, it induces chemical changes in the body, which the user finds exciting and pleasurable. It also appears to attract a "hard core" of habitual users and a penumbra of those who use it occasionally but aren't dependent on it in any way. There are also significant numbers of men who aren't much interested in it, not because they're undersexed but because real life is satisfying their needs, which may not require as many appliances as those of users.

For the "hard core," pornography may function as alcohol does 17
for the alcoholic: tolerance develops, and a little is no longer enough. This may account for the short viewing time and fast turnover in porn theaters. Mary Brown, chairwoman of the Ontario Board of Film Censors, estimates that for every one mainstream movie requesting entrance to Ontario, there is one porno flick. Not only the quantity consumed but the quality of explicitness must escalate, which may account for the growing violence: once the big deal was breasts, then it was genitals, then copulation, then that was no longer enough and the hard users had to have more. The ultimate kick is death, and after that, as the Marquis de Sade so boringly demonstrated, multiple death.

The existence of alcoholism has not led us to ban social drink- 18
ing. On the other hand, we do have laws about drinking and driving, excessive drunkenness and other abuses of alcohol that may result in injury or death to others.

This leads us back to the key question: what's the harm?   19
Nobody knows, but this society should find out fast, before the saturation point is reached. The Scandinavian studies that showed a connection between depictions of sexual violence and increased impulse toward it on the part of male viewers would be a starting point, but many more questions remain to be raised as well as answered. What, for instance, is the crucial difference between men who are users and men who are not? Does using affect a man's relationship with actual women, and, if so, adversely? Is there a clear line between erotica and violent pornography, or are they on an escalating continuum? Is this a "men versus women" issue, with all men secretly siding with the proporners and all women secretly siding against? (I think not; there *are* lots of men who don't think that running their true love through the Cuisinart is the best way they can think of to spend a Saturday night, and they're just as nauseated by films of someone else doing it as women are.) Is pornography merely an expression of the sexual confusion of this age or an active contributor to it?

Nobody wants to go back to the age of official repression, when   20
even piano legs were referred to as "limbs" and had to wear pantaloons to be decent. Neither do we want to end up in George Orwell's *1984,* in which pornography is turned out by the State to keep the proles in a state of torpor, sex itself is considered dirty and the approved practice it only for reproduction. But Rome under the emperors isn't such a good model either.

If all men and women respected each other, if sex were considered joyful and life-enhancing instead of a wallow in germ-filled glop, if everyone were in love all the time, if, in other words, many people's lives were more satisfactory for them than they appear to be now, pornography might just go away on its own. But since this is obviously not happening, we as a society are going to have to make some informed and responsible decisions about how to deal with it.   21

LESLIE MARMON SILKO

> Leslie Marmon Silko was born in 1948 in Albuquerque, New
> Mexico. She was raised on the Laguna Pueblo Reservation and at-
> tended the University of New Mexico (B.A., 1969). Formerly on the
> English faculty of the University of Arizona, Silko now focuses full-
> time on her writing, for which she has received many awards, in-
> cluding a MacArthur Foundation grant. Much of Silko's writing
> draws on Native American traditions and myths and on the inter-
> actions of Native American cultures and perspectives with the con-
> temporary world. Her novels include the much-praised *Ceremony*
> (1977), *Almanac of the Dead* (1991), and *Gardens in the Dunes*
> (1999). She has also published a volume of poetry, *Laguna Woman*
> (1974); a collection of short stories, *Storyteller* (1981); an autobi-
> ography, *Sacred Water* (1993); and a collection of essays, *Yellow
> Woman and a Beauty of the Spirit* (1996).

Yellow Woman and a Beauty of the Spirit

> "Yellow Woman and a Beauty of the Spirit" comes from the book
> with the same title. In this essay, Silko recalls her differences in ap-
> pearance from other Laguna Pueblo children, the result of her
> mixed ancestry, and uses this memory as a springboard to an ex-
> planation of the traditional Pueblo disregard of physical appear-
> ance and emphasis instead on individual qualities of spirit as the
> basis of true beauty. She also discusses the Pueblo disregard of
> fixed gender, work, and family roles, but a correspondingly strong
> emphasis is on the quality of relationships among people, animals,
> and the land. As in much of her work, Silko's perspective lies at the
> center of the intersection between cultures.

From the time I was a small child, I was aware that I was different.   1
I looked different from my playmates. My two sisters looked different too. We didn't look quite like the other Laguna Pueblo children, but we didn't look quite white either. In the 1880s, my
great-grandfather had followed his older brother west from Ohio to
the New Mexico Territory to survey the land for the U.S. government. The two Marmon brothers came to the Laguna Pueblo reservation because they had an Ohio cousin who already lived there.
The Ohio cousin was involved in sending Indian children thousands
of miles away from their families to the War Department's big
Indian boarding school in Carlisle, Pennsylvania. Both brothers
married full-blood Laguna Pueblo women. My great-grandfather

had first married my great-grandmother's older sister, but she died in childbirth and left two small children. My great-grandmother was fifteen or twenty years younger than my great-grandfather. She had attended Carlisle Indian School and spoke and wrote English beautifully.

I called her Grandma A'mooh because that's what I heard her say whenever she saw me. *A'mooh* means "granddaughter" in the Laguna language. I remember this word because her love and her acceptance of me as a small child were so important. I had sensed immediately that something about my appearance was not acceptable to some people, white and Indian. But I did not see any signs of that strain or anxiety in the face of my beloved Grandma A'mooh.

Younger people, people my parents' age, seemed to look at the world in a more modern way. The modern way included racism. My physical appearance seemed not to matter to the old-time people. They looked at the world very differently; a person's appearance and possessions did not matter nearly as much as a person's behavior. For them, a person's value lies in how that person interacts with other people, how that person behaves toward the animals and the earth. That is what matters most to the old-time people. The Pueblo people believed this long before the Puritans arrived with their notions of sin and damnation, and racism. The old-time beliefs persist today; thus I will refer to the old-time people in the present tense as well as the past. Many worlds may coexist here.

I spent a great deal of time with my great-grandmother. Her house was next to our house, and I used to wake up at dawn, hours before my parents or younger sisters, and I'd go wait on the porch swing or on the back steps by her kitchen door. She got up at dawn, but she was more than eighty years old, so she needed a little while to get dressed and to get the fire going in the cookstove. I had been carefully instructed by my parents not to bother her and to behave, and to try to help her any way I could. I always loved the early mornings when the air was so cool with a hint of rain smell in the breeze. In the dry New Mexico air, the least hint of dampness smells sweet.

My great-grandmother's yard was planted with lilac bushes and iris; there were four o'clocks, cosmos, morning glories, and hollyhocks, and old-fashioned rosebushes that I helped her water. If the garden hose got stuck on one of the big rocks that lined the path in the yard, I ran and pulled it free. That's what I came to do early every morning: to help Grandma water the plants before the heat of the day arrived.

Grandma A'mooh would tell about the old days, family stories   6
about relatives who had been killed by Apache raiders who stole the
sheep our relatives had been herding near Swahnee. Sometimes she
read Bible stories that we kids liked because of the illustrations of
Jonah in the mouth of a whale and Daniel surrounded by lions.
Grandma A'mooh would send me home when she took her nap, but
when the sun got low and the afternoon began to cool off, I would be
back on the porch swing, waiting for her to come out to water the
plants and to haul in firewood for the evening. When Grandma was
eighty-five, she still chopped her own kindling. She used to let me
carry in the coal bucket for her, but she would not allow me to use
the ax. I carried armloads of kindling too, and I learned to be proud
of my strength.

I was allowed to listen quietly when Aunt Susie or Aunt Alice   7
came to visit Grandma. When I got old enough to cross the road
alone, I went and visited them almost daily. They were vigorous
women who valued books and writing. They were usually busy
chopping wood or cooking but never hesitated to take time to answer my questions. Best of all they told me the *hummah-hah* stories,
about an earlier time when animals and humans shared a common
language. In the old days, the Pueblo people had educated their children in this manner; adults took time out to talk to and teach young
people. Everyone was a teacher, and every activity had the potential
to teach the child.

But as soon as I started kindergarten at the Bureau of Indian   8
Affairs day school, I began to learn more about the differences between the Laguna Pueblo world and the outside world. It was at
school that I learned just how different I looked from my classmates.
Sometimes tourists driving past on Route 66 would stop by Laguna
Day School at recess time to take photographs of us kids. One day,
when I was in the first grade, we all crowded around the smiling
white tourists, who peered at our faces. We all wanted to be in the
picture because afterward the tourists sometimes gave us each a
penny. Just as we were all posed and ready to have our picture
taken, the tourist man looked at me. "Not you," he said and mo-
tioned for me to step away from my classmates. I felt so embarrassed that I wanted to disappear. My classmates were puzzled by
the tourists' behavior, but I knew the tourists didn't want me in their
snapshot because I looked different, because I was part white.

In the view of the old-time people, we are all sisters and broth-   9
ers because the Mother Creator made all of us—all colors and all
sizes. We are sisters and brothers, clanspeople of all the living be-

ings around us. The plants, the birds, fish, clouds, water, even the clay—they all are related to us. The old-time people believe that all things, even rocks and water, have spirit and being. They understood that all things want only to continue being as they are; they need only to be left as they are. Thus the old folks used to tell us kids not to disturb the earth unnecessarily. All things as they were created exist already in harmony with one another as long as we do not disturb them.

As the old story tells us, Tse'itsi'nako, Thought Woman, the 10 Spider, thought of her three sisters, and as she thought of them, they came into being. Together with Thought Woman, they thought of the sun and the stars and the moon. The Mother Creators imagined the earth and the oceans, the animals and the people, and the *ka'tsina* spirits that reside in the mountains. The Mother Creators imagined all the plants that flower and the trees that bear fruit. As Thought Woman and her sisters thought of it, the whole universe came into being. In this universe, there is no absolute good or absolute bad; they are only balances and harmonies that ebb and flow. Some years the desert receives abundant rain, other years there is too little rain, and sometimes there is so much rain that floods cause destruction. But rain itself is neither innocent nor guilty. The rain is simply itself.

My great-grandmother was dark and handsome. Her expres- 11 sion in photographs is one of confidence and strength. I do not know if white people then or now would consider her beautiful. I do not know if the old-time Laguna Pueblo people considered her beautiful or if the old-time people even thought in those terms. To the Pueblo way of thinking, the act of comparing one living being with another was silly, because each being or thing is unique and therefore incomparably valuable because it is the only one of its kind. The old-time people thought it was crazy to attach such importance to a person's appearance. I understood very early that there were two distinct ways of interpreting the world. There was the white people's way and there was the Laguna way. In the Laguna way, it was bad manners to make comparisons that might hurt another person's feelings.

In everyday Pueblo life, not much attention was paid to one's 12 physical appearance or clothing. Ceremonial clothing was quite elaborate but was used only for the sacred dances. The traditional Pueblo societies were communal and strictly egalitarian, which means that no matter how well or how poorly one might have dressed, there was no social ladder to fall from. All food and other resources were strictly shared so that no one person or group had more than another. I mention social status because it seems to me that most of the definitions of beauty in contemporary Western culture are really codes for determining social status. People no longer hide their face-lifts and they discuss their liposuctions because the point of the procedures isn't just cosmetic, it is social. It says to the world, "I have enough spare cash that I can afford surgery for cosmetic purposes."

In the old-time Pueblo world, beauty was manifested in behavior and in one's relationships with other living beings. Beauty was as much a feeling of harmony as it was a visual, aural, or sensual effect. The whole person had to be beautiful, not just the face or the body; faces and bodies could not be separated from hearts and souls. Health was foremost in achieving this sense of well-being and harmony; in the old-time Pueblo world, a person who did not look healthy inspired feelings of worry and anxiety, not feelings of well-being. A healthy person, of course, is in harmony with the world around her; she is at peace with herself too. Thus an unhappy person or spiteful person would not be considered beautiful. 13

In the old days, strong, sturdy women were most admired. One of my most vivid preschool memories is of the crew of Laguna women, in their forties and fifties, who came to cover our house with adobe plaster. They handled the ladders with great ease, and while two women ground the adobe mud on stones and added straw, another woman loaded the hod with mud and passed it up to the two women on ladders, who were smoothing the plaster on the wall with their hands. Since women owned the houses, they did the plastering. At Laguna, men did the basket making and the weaving of fine textiles; men helped a great deal with the child care too. Because the Creator is female, there is no stigma on being female; gender is not used to control behavior. No job was a man's job or a woman's job; the most able person did the work. 14

My Grandma Lily had been a Ford Model A mechanic when she was a teenager. I remember when I was young, she was always fixing broken lamps and appliances. She was small and wiry, but she could lift her weight in rolled roofing or boxes of nails. When she was seventy-five, she was still repairing washing machines in my uncle's coin-operated laundry. 15

The old-time people paid no attention to birthdays. When a person was ready to do something, she did it. When she no longer was able, she stopped. Thus the traditional Pueblo people did not worry about aging or about looking old because there were no social boundaries drawn by the passage of years. It was not remarkable for 16 young men to marry women as old as their mothers. I never heard anyone talk about "women's work" until after I left Laguna for college. Work was there to be done by any able-bodied person who wanted to do it. At the same time, in the old-time Pueblo world, identity was acknowledged to be always in a flux; in the old stories, one minute Spider Woman is a little spider under a yucca plant, and the next instant she is a sprightly grandmother walking down the road.

When I was growing up, there was a young man from a nearby   17
village who wore nail polish and women's blouses and permed his hair. People paid little attention to his appearance; he was always part of a group of other young men from his village. No one ever made fun of him. Pueblo communities were and still are very interdependent, but they also have to be tolerant of individual eccentricities because survival of the group means everyone has to cooperate.

In the old Pueblo world, differences were celebrated as signs of   18
the Mother Creator's grace. Persons born with exceptional physical or sexual differences were highly respected and honored because their physical differences gave them special positions as mediators between this world and the spirit world. The great Navajo medicine man of the 1920s, the Crawler, had a hunchback and could not walk upright, but he was able to heal even the most difficult cases.

Before the arrival of Christian missionaries, a man could dress   19
as a woman and work with the women and even marry a man without any fanfare. Likewise, a woman was free to dress like a man, to hunt and go to war with the men, and to marry a woman. In the old Pueblo worldview, we are all a mixture of male and female, and this sexual identity is changing constantly. Sexual inhibition did not begin until the Christian missionaries arrived. For the old-time people, marriage was about teamwork and social relationships, not about sexual excitement. In the days before the Puritans came, marriage did not mean an end to sex with people other than your spouse. Women were just as likely as men to have a *si'ash,* or lover.

New life was so precious that pregnancy was always appropri-   20
ate, and pregnancy before marriage was celebrated as a good sign. Since the children belonged to the mother and her clan, and women owned and bequeathed the houses and farmland, the exact determination of paternity wasn't critical. Although fertility was prized, infertility was no problem because mothers with unplanned pregnancies gave their babies to childless couples within the clan in open adoption arrangements. Children called their mother's sisters "mother" as well, and a child became attached to a number of parent figures.

In the sacred kiva ceremonies, men mask and dress as women   21
to pay homage and to be possessed by the female energies of the
spirit beings. Because differences in physical appearance were so
highly valued, surgery to change one's face and body to resemble a
model's face and body would be unimaginable. To be different, to
be unique was blessed and was best of all.

THE TRADITIONAL CLOTHING of Pueblo women emphasized a   22
woman's sturdiness. Buckskin leggings wrapped around the legs pro-
tected her from scratches and injuries while she worked. The more
layers of buckskin, the better. All those layers gave her legs the appearance of strength, like sturdy tree trunks. To demonstrate sister-
hood and brotherhood with the plants and animals, the old-time
people make masks and costumes that transform the human figures of
the dancers into the animal beings they portray. Dancers paint their
exposed skin; their postures and motions are adapted from their observations. But the motions are stylized. The observer sees not an actual eagle or actual deer dancing, but witnesses a human being, a
dancer, gradually changing into a woman/buffalo or a man/deer.
Every impulse is to reaffirm the urgent relationships that human beings have with the plant and animal world.

In the high desert plateau country, all vegetation, even weeds   23
and thorns, becomes special, and all life is precious and beautiful because without the plants, the insects, and the animals, human beings
living here cannot survive. Perhaps human beings long ago noticed
the devastating impact human activity can have on the plants and
animals; maybe this is why tribal cultures devised the stories about
humans and animals intermarrying, and the clans that bind humans
to animals and plants through a whole complex of duties.

We children were always warned not to harm frogs or toads,   24
the beloved children of the rain clouds, because terrible floods
would occur. I remember in the summer the old folks used to stick
big bolls of cotton on the outside of their screen doors as bait to keep
the flies from going in the house when the door was opened. The old
folks staunchly resisted the killing of flies because once, long, long
ago, when human beings were in a great deal of trouble, a Green
Bottle Fly carried the desperate messages of human beings to the
Mother Creator in the Fourth World, below this one. Human beings
had outraged the Mother Creator by neglecting the Mother Corn al-
tar while they dabbled with sorcery and magic. The Mother Creator
disappeared, and with her disappeared the rain clouds, and the
plants and the animals too. The people began to starve, and they had
no way of reaching the Mother Creator down below. Green Bottle

Fly took the message to the Mother Creator, and the people were saved. To show their gratitude, the old folks refused to kill any flies.

THE OLD STORIES demonstrate the interrelationships that the 25
Pueblo people have maintained with their plant and animal clans-people. Kochininako, Yellow Woman, represents all women in the old stories. Her deeds span the spectrum of human behavior and are mostly heroic acts, though in at least one story, she chooses to join the secret Destroyer Clan, which worships destruction and death. Because Laguna Pueblo cosmology features a female Creator, the status of women is equal with the status of men, and women appear as often as men in the old stories as hero figures. Yellow Woman is my favorite because she dares to cross traditional boundaries of ordinary behavior during times of crisis in order to save the Pueblo; her power lies in her courage and in her uninhibited sexuality, which the old-time Pueblo stories celebrate again and again because fertility was so highly valued.

The old stories always say that Yellow Woman was beautiful, 26
but remember that the old-time people were not so much thinking about physical appearances. In each story, the beauty that Yellow Woman possesses is the beauty of her passion, her daring, and her sheer strength to act when catastrophe is imminent.

In one story, the people are suffering during a great drought 27
and accompanying famine. Each day, Kochininako has to walk farther and farther from the village to find fresh water for her husband and children. One day she travels far, far to the east, to the plains, and she finally locates a freshwater spring. But when she reaches the pool, the water is churning violently as if something large had just gotten out of the pool. Kochininako does not want to see what huge creature had been at the pool, but just as she fills her water jar and turns to hurry away, a strong, sexy man in buffalo skin leggings appears by the pool. Little drops of water glisten on his chest. She cannot help but look at him because he is so strong and so good to look at. Able to transform himself from human to buffalo in the wink of an eye, Buffalo Man gallops away with her on his back. Kochininako falls in love with Buffalo Man, and because of this liaison, the Buffalo People agree to give their bodies to the hunters to feed the starving Pueblo. Thus Kochininako's fearless sensuality results in the salvation of the people of her village, who are saved by the meat the Buffalo People "give" to them.

My father taught me and my sisters to shoot .22 rifles when we 28
were seven; I went hunting with my father when I was eight, and I killed my first mule deer buck when I was thirteen. The Kochininako

stories were always my favorite because Yellow Woman had so many adventures. In one story, as she hunts rabbits to feed her family, a giant monster pursues her, but she has the courage and presence of mind to outwit it.

In another story, Kochininako has a fling with Whirlwind Man   29
and returns to her husband ten months later with twin baby boys. The twin boys grow up to be great heroes of the people. Once again, Kochininako's vibrant sexuality benefits her people.

The stories about Kochininako made me aware that sometimes   30
an individual must act despite disapproval, or concern for appearances or what others may say. From Yellow Woman's adventures, I learned to be comfortable with my differences. I even imagined that Yellow Woman had yellow skin, brown hair, and green eyes like mine, although her name does not refer to her color, but rather to the ritual color of the east.

There have been many other moments like the one with the   31
camera-toting tourist in the schoolyard. But the old-time people always say, remember the stories, the stories will help you be strong. So all these years I have depended on Kochininako and the stories of her adventures.

Kochininako is beautiful because she has the courage to act in   32
times of great peril, and her triumph is achieved by her sensuality, not through violence and destruction. For these qualities of the spirit, Yellow Woman and all women are beautiful.

MARTIN LUTHER KING JR.

MARTIN LUTHER KING JR. (1929–1968), was a Baptist minister, the president of the Southern Christian Leadership Conference, and a respected leader in the nationwide movement for equal rights for blacks. He was born in Atlanta, Georgia, and earned degrees from Morehouse College (A.B., 1948), Crozer Theological Seminary (B.D., 1951), Boston University (Ph.D., 1955), and Chicago Theological Seminary (D.D., 1957). He held honorary degrees from numerous other colleges and universities and was awarded the Nobel Peace Prize in 1964. Some of his books are *Stride Toward Freedom* (1958), *Strength to Love* (1963), and *Why We Can't Wait* (1964). King was assassinated April 4, 1968, in Memphis, Tennessee.

Letter from Birmingham Jail[1]

This letter, written to King's colleagues in the ministry, is a rea-soned explanation for his actions during the civil rights protests in Birmingham. It is a good example of both persuasion and logical argument. Here the two are completely compatible, balancing each other in rather intricate but convincing and effective patterns.

M y Dear Fellow Clergymen: 1

While confined here in the Birmingham city jail, I came across   2
your recent statement calling my present activities "unwise and untimely." Seldom do I pause to answer criticism of my work and
ideas. If I sought to answer all the criticisms that cross my desk, my
secretaries would have little time for anything other than such correspondence in the course of the day, and I would have no time for
constructive work. But since I feel that you are men of genuine good
will and that your criticisms are sincerely set forth, I want to try to

[1]This response to a published statement by eight fellow clergymen from Alabama (Bishop C. C. J. Carpenter, Bishop Joseph A. Durick, Rabbi Hilton L. Grafman, Bishop Paul Hardin, Bishop Holan B. Harmon, the Reverend George M. Murray, the Reverend Edward V. Ramage, and the Reverend Earl Stallings) was composed under somewhat constricting circumstances. Begun on the margins of the newspaper in which the statement appeared while I was in jail, the letter was continued on scraps of writing paper supplied by a friendly Negro trusty, and concluded on a pad my attorneys were eventually permitted to leave me. Although the text remains in substance unaltered, I have indulged in the author's prerogative of polishing it for publication.—King's note.

answer your statement in what I hope will be patient and reasonable terms.

I think I should indicate why I am here in Birmingham, since   3
you have been influenced by the view which argues against "outsiders coming in." I have the honor of serving as president of the
Southern Christian Leadership Conference, an organization operating in every southern state, with headquarters in Atlanta, Georgia.
We have some eighty-five affiliated organizations across the South,
and one of them is the Alabama Christian Movement for Human
Rights. Frequently we share staff, educational, and financial resources with our affiliates. Several months ago the affiliate here in
Birmingham asked us to be on call to engage in a nonviolent direct-
action program if such were deemed necessary. We readily con-
sented, and when the hour came, we lived up to our promise. So I,
along with several members of my staff, am here because I was invited here. I am here because I have organizational ties here.

But more basically, I am in Birmingham because injustice is   4
here. Just as the prophets of the eighth century B.C. left their villages
and carried their "thus saith the Lord" far beyond the boundaries of
their home towns, and just as the Apostle Paul left his village of
Tarsus and carried the gospel of Jesus Christ to the far corners of the
Greco-Roman world, so am I compelled to carry the gospel of freedom beyond my own home town. Like Paul, I must constantly respond to the Macedonian call for aid.

Moreover, I am cognizant of the interrelatedness of all commu-   5
nities and states. I cannot sit idly by in Atlanta and not be concerned
about what happens in Birmingham. Injustice anywhere is a threat
to justice everywhere. We are caught in an inescapable network of
mutuality, tied in a single garment of destiny. Whatever affects one
directly, affects all indirectly. Never again can we afford to live with
the narrow, provincial "outside agitator" idea. Anyone who lives inside the United States can never be considered an outsider within its
bounds.

You deplore the demonstrations taking place in Birmingham.   6
But your statement, I am sorry to say, fails to express a similar concern for the conditions that brought about the demonstrations. I am
sure that none of you would want to rest content with the superficial
kind of social analysis that deals merely with effects and does not
grapple with underlying causes. It is unfortunate that demonstrations are taking place in Birmingham, but it is even more unfortunate that the city's white power structure left the Negro community
with no alternative.

In any nonviolent campaign there are four basic steps: collec- 7
tion of the facts to determine whether injustices exist; negotiation;
self-purification; and direct action. We have gone through all these
steps in Birmingham. There can be no gainsaying the fact that racial
injustice engulfs this community. Birmingham is probably the most
thoroughly segregated city in the United States. Its ugly record of
brutality is widely known. Negroes have experienced grossly unjust
treatment in the courts. There have been more unsolved bombings
of Negro homes and churches in Birmingham than in any other city
in the nation. These are the hard, brutal facts of the case. On the basis of these conditions, Negro leaders sought to negotiate with the
city fathers. But the latter consistently refused to engage in good-
faith negotiation.

Then, last September, came the opportunity to talk with leaders 8
of Birmingham's economic community. In the course of the negotia-
tions, certain promises were made by the merchants—for example,
to remove the stores' humiliating racial signs. On the basis of these
promises, the Reverend Fred Shuttlesworth and the leaders of the
Alabama Christian Movement for Human Rights agreed to a mora-
torium on all demonstrations. As the weeks and months went by,
we realized that we were the victims of a broken promise. A few
signs, briefly removed, returned; the others remained.

As in so many past experiences, our hopes had been blasted, 9
and the shadow of deep disappointment settled upon us. We had
no alternative except to prepare for direct action, whereby we
would present our very bodies as a means of laying our case before the conscience of the local and the national community.
Mindful of the difficulties involved, we decided to undertake a
process of self-purification. We began a series of workshops on
nonviolence, and we repeatedly asked ourselves: "Are you able to
accept blows without retaliating?" "Are you able to endure the or-
deal of jail?" We decided to schedule our direct-action program for
the Easter season, realizing that except for Christmas, this is the
main shopping period of the year. Knowing that a strong economic-
withdrawal program would be the by-product of direct action, we
felt that this would be the best time to bring pressure to bear on the
merchants for the needed change.

Then it occurred to us that Birmingham's mayoral election was 10
coming up in March, and we speedily decided to postpone action
until after election day. When we discovered that the Commissioner
of Public Safety, Eugene "Bull" Connor, had piled up enough votes
to be in the run-off, we decided again to postpone action until the

day after the run-off so that the demonstrations could not be used to cloud the issues. Like many others, we waited to see Mr. Connor defeated, and to this end we endured postponement after postponement. Having aided in this community need, we felt that our direct-action program could be delayed no longer.

You may well ask, "Why direct action? Why sit-ins, marches, and so forth? Isn't negotiation a better path?" You are quite right in calling for negotiation. Indeed, this is the very purpose of direct action. Nonviolent direct action seeks to create such a crisis and foster such a tension that a community which has constantly refused to negotiate is forced to confront the issue. It seeks so to dramatize the issue that it can no longer be ignored. My citing the creation of tension as part of the work of the nonviolent-resister may sound rather shocking. But I must confess that I am not afraid of the word "tension." I have earnestly opposed violent tension, but there is a type of constructive, nonviolent tension which is necessary for growth. Just as Socrates felt that it was necessary to create a tension in the mind so that individuals could rise from the bondage of myths and half-truths to the unfettered realm of creative analysis and objective appraisal, so must we see the need for nonviolent gadflies to create the kind of tension in society that will help men rise from the dark depths of prejudice and racism to the majestic heights of understanding and brotherhood.

The purpose of our direct-action program is to create a situation so crisis-packed that it will inevitably open the door to negotiation. I therefore concur with you in your call for negotiation. Too long has our beloved Southland been bogged down in a tragic effort to live in monologue rather than dialogue.

One of the basic points in your statement is that the action that I and my associates have taken in Birmingham is untimely. Some have asked: "Why didn't you give the new city administration time to act?" The only answer that I can give to this query is that the new Birmingham administration must be prodded about as much as the outgoing one, before it will act. We are sadly mistaken if we feel that the election of Albert Boutwell as mayor will bring the millennium to Birmingham. While Mr. Boutwell is a much more gentle person that Mr. Connor, they are both segregationists, dedicated to maintenance of the status quo. I have hoped that Mr. Boutwell will be reasonable enough to see the futility of massive resistance to desegregation. But he will not see this without pressure from devotees of civil rights. My friends, I must say to you that we have not made a single gain in civil rights without determined legal and nonviolent pressure. Lamentably, it is an historical fact that privileged groups seldom give up their privileges voluntarily. Individuals may see the moral light and voluntarily give up their unjust posture; but, as Reinhold Niebuhr has reminded us, groups tend to be more immoral than individuals.

We know through painful experience that freedom is never voluntarily given by the oppressor; it must be demanded by the oppressed. Frankly, I have yet to engage in a direct-action campaign that was "well timed" in the view of those who have not suffered unduly from the disease of segregation. For years now I have heard the word "Wait!" It rings in the ear of every Negro with piercing familiarity. This "Wait" has almost always meant "Never." We must come to see, with one of our distinguished jurists, that "justice too long delayed is justice denied." 14

We have waited for more than 340 years for our constitutional and God-given rights. The nations of Asia and Africa are moving with jetlike speed toward gaining political independence, but we still creep at horse-and-buggy pace toward gaining a cup of coffee at a lunch counter. Perhaps it is easy for those who have never felt the stinging darts of segregation to say, "Wait." But when you have seen vicious mobs lynch your mothers and fathers at will and drown your sisters and brothers at whim; when you have seen hate-filled policemen curse, kick, and even kill your black brothers and sisters; when you see the vast majority of your twenty million Negro brothers smothering in an airtight cage of poverty in the midst of an affluent society; when you suddenly find your tongue twisted and your speech stammering as you seek to explain to your six-year-old daughter why she can't go to the public amusement park that has just been advertised on television, and see tears welling up in her eyes when she is told that Funtown is closed to colored children, and see ominous clouds of inferiority beginning to form in her little mental sky, and see her beginning to distort her personality by developing an unconscious bitterness toward white people; when you have to concoct an answer for a five-year-old son who is asking, "Daddy, why do white people treat colored people so mean?"; when you take a cross-country drive and find it necessary to sleep night after night in the uncomfortable corners of your automobile because no motel will accept you; when you are humiliated day in and day out by nagging signs reading "white" and "colored"; when your first name becomes "nigger," your middle name becomes "boy" (however old you are) and your last name becomes "John," and your wife and mother are never given the respected title "Mrs."; when you are 15 harried by day and haunted by night by the fact that you are a Negro, living constantly at tiptoe stance, never quite knowing what to expect next, and are plagued with inner fears and outer resentments; when you are forever fighting a degenerating sense of "nobodiness"—then you will understand why we find it difficult to wait. There comes a time when the cup of endurance runs over, and men are no longer willing to be plunged into the abyss of despair. I hope, sirs, you can understand our legitimate and unavoidable impatience.

You express a great deal of anxiety over our willingness to break   16
laws. This is certainly a legitimate concern. Since we so diligently urge people to obey the Supreme Court's decision of 1954 outlawing segregation in the public schools, at first glance it may seem rather paradoxical for us consciously to break laws. One may well ask: "How can you advocate breaking some laws and obeying others?" The answer lies in the fact that there are two types of laws: just and unjust. I would be the first to advocate obeying just laws. One has not only a legal but a moral responsibility to obey just laws. Conversely, one has a moral responsibility to disobey unjust laws. I would agree with St. Augustine that "an unjust law is no law at all."

Now, what is the difference between the two? How does one   17
determine whether a law is just or unjust? A just law is a man-made code that squares with the moral law or the law of God. An unjust law is a code that is out of harmony with the moral law. To put it in the terms of St. Thomas Aquinas: An unjust law is a human law that is not rooted in eternal law and natural law. Any law that uplifts human personality is just. Any law that degrades human personality is unjust. All segregation statutes are unjust because segregation distorts the soul and damages the personality. It gives the segregator a false sense of superiority and the segregated a false sense of inferiority. Segregation, to use the terminology of the Jewish philosopher Martin Buber, substitutes an "I-it" relationship for an "I-thou" relationship and ends up relegating persons to the status of things. Hence segregation is not only politically, economically, and sociologically unsound, it is morally wrong and sinful. Paul Tillich has said that sin is separation. Is not segregation an existential expression of man's tragic separation, his awful estrangement, his terrible sinfulness? Thus it is that I can urge men to obey the 1954 decision of the Supreme Court, for it is morally right; and I can urge them to disobey segregation ordinances, for they are morally wrong.

Let us consider a more concrete example of just and unjust   18
laws. An unjust law is a code that a numerical or power majority

group compels a minority group to obey but does not make binding on itself. This is *difference* made legal. By the same token, a just law is a code that a majority compels a minority to follow and that it is willing to follow itself. This is *sameness* made legal.

Let me give another explanation. A law is unjust if it is inflicted   19
on a minority that, as a result of being denied the right to vote, had no part in enacting or devising the law. Who can say that the legislature of Alabama which set up that state's segregation laws was democratically elected? Throughout Alabama all sorts of devious methods are used to prevent Negroes from becoming registered voters, and there are some counties in which, even though Negroes constitute a majority of the population, not a single Negro is registered. Can any law enacted under such circumstances be considered democratically structured?

Sometimes a law is just on its face and unjust in its application.   20
For instance, I have been arrested on a charge of parading without a permit. Now, there is nothing wrong in having an ordinance which requires a permit for a parade. But such an ordinance becomes unjust when it is used to maintain segregation and to deny citizens the First Amendment privilege of peaceful assembly and protest.

I hope you are able to see the distinction I am trying to point   21
out. In no sense do I advocate evading or defying the law, as would the rabid segregationist. That would lead to anarchy. One who breaks an unjust law must do so openly, lovingly, and with a willingness to accept the penalty. I submit that an individual who breaks a law that conscience tells him is unjust, and who willingly accepts the penalty of imprisonment in order to arouse the conscience of the community over its injustice, is in reality expressing the highest respect for the law.

Of course, there is nothing new about this kind of civil disobe-   22
dience. It was evidenced sublimely in the refusal of Shadrach, Meshach, and Abednego to obey the laws of Nebuchadnezzar, on the ground that a higher moral law was at stake. It was practiced superbly by the early Christians, who were willing to face hungry lions and the excruciating pain of chopping blocks rather than submit to certain unjust laws of the Roman Empire. To a degree, academic freedom is a reality today because Socrates practiced civil disobedience. In our own nation, the Boston Tea Party represented a massive act of civil disobedience.

We should never forget that everything Adolf Hitler did in   23
Germany was "legal" and everything the Hungarian freedom fighters did in Hungary was "illegal." It was "illegal" to aid and comfort

a Jew in Hitler's Germany. Even so, I am sure that, had I lived in Germany at the time, I would have aided and comforted my Jewish brothers. If today I lived in a Communist country where certain principles dear to the Christian faith are suppressed, I would openly advocate disobeying that country's anti-religious laws.

I must make two honest confessions to you, my Christian and   24
Jewish brothers. First, I must confess that over the past few years I have been gravely disappointed with the white moderate. I have almost reached the regrettable conclusion that the Negro's great stumbling block in his stride toward freedom is not the White Citizen's Counciler or the Ku Klux Klanner, but the white moderate, who is more devoted to "order" than to justice; who prefers a negative peace which is the absence of tension to a positive peace which is the presence of justice; who constantly says, "I agree with you in the goal you seek, but I cannot agree with your methods of direct action"; who paternalistically believes he can set the timetable for another man's freedom; who lives by a mythical concept of time and who constantly advises the Negro to wait for a "more convenient season." Shallow understanding from people of good will is more frustrating than absolute misunderstanding from people of ill will. Lukewarm acceptance is much more bewildering than outright rejection.

I had hoped that the white moderate would understand that law   25
and order exist for the purpose of establishing justice and that when they fail in this purpose they become the dangerously structured dams that block the flow of social progress. I had hoped that the white moderate would understand that the present tension in the South is a necessary phase of the transition from an obnoxious negative peace, in which the Negro passively accepted his unjust plight, to a substantive and positive peace, in which all men will respect the dignity and worth of human personality. Actually, we who engage in nonviolent direct action are not the creators of tension. We merely bring to the surface the hidden tension that is already alive. We bring it out in the open, where it can be seen and dealt with. Like a boil that can never be cured so long as it is covered up but must be opened with all its ugliness to the natural medicines of air and light, injustice must be exposed, with all the tension its exposure creates, to the light of human conscience and the air of national opinion, before it can be cured.

In your statement you assert that our actions, even though   26
peaceful, must be condemned because they precipitate violence. But is this a logical assertion? Isn't this like condemning a robbed man because his possession of money precipitated the evil act of robbery?

Isn't this like condemning Socrates because his unswerving commitment to truth and his philosophical inquiries precipitated the act by the misguided populace in which they made him drink hemlock? Isn't this like condemning Jesus because his unique God-consciousness and never-ceasing devotion to God's will precipitated the evil act of crucifixion? We must come to see that, as the federal courts have consistently affirmed, it is wrong to urge an individual to cease his efforts to gain his basic constitutional rights because the quest may precipitate violence. Society must protect the robbed and punish the robber.

I had also hoped that the white moderate would reject the myth   27
concerning time in relation to the struggle for freedom. I have just received a letter from a white brother in Texas. He writes: "All Christians know that the colored people will receive equal rights eventually, but it is possible that you are in too great a religious hurry. It has taken Christianity almost two thousand years to accomplish what it has. The teachings of Christ take time to come to earth." Such an attitude stems from a tragic misconception of time, from the strangely irrational notion that there is something in the very flow of time that will inevitably cure all ills. Actually, time itself is neutral; it can be used either destructively or constructively. More and more I feel that the people of ill will have used time much more effectively than have the people of good will. We will have to repent in this generation not merely for the hateful words and actions of the bad people, but for the appalling silence of the good people. Human progress never rolls in on wheels of inevitability; it comes through the tireless efforts of men willing to be co-workers with God, and without this hard work, time itself becomes an ally of the forces of social stagnation. We must use time creatively, in the knowledge that the time is always ripe to do right. Now is the time to make real the promise of democracy and transform our pending national elegy into a creative psalm of brotherhood. Now is the time to lift our national policy from the quicksand of racial injustice to the solid rock of human dignity.

You speak of our activity in Birmingham as extreme. At first I   28
was rather disappointed that fellow clergymen would see my nonviolent efforts as those of an extremist. I began thinking about the fact that I stand in the middle of two opposing forces in the Negro community. One is a force of complacency, made up in part of Negroes who, as a result of long years of oppression, are so drained of self-respect and a sense of "somebodiness" that they have adjusted to segregation; and in part of a few middle-class Negroes who, because of

a degree of academic and economic security and because in some ways they profit by segregation, have become insensitive to the problems of the masses. The other force is one of bitterness and hatred, and it comes perilously close to advocating violence. It is expressed in the various black nationalist groups that are springing up across the nation, the largest and best-known being Elijah Muhammad's Muslim movement. Nourished by the Negro's frustration over the continued existence of racial discrimination, this movement is made up of people who have lost faith in America, who have absolutely repudiated Christianity, and who have concluded that the white man is an incorrigible "devil."

I have tried to stand between these two forces, saying that we need emulate neither the "do-nothingism" of the complacent nor the hatred and despair of the black nationalist. For there is the more excellent way of love and nonviolent protest. I am grateful to God that, through the influence of the Negro church, the way of nonviolence became an integral part of our struggle. 29

If this philosophy had not emerged, by now many streets of the South would, I am convinced, be flowing with blood. And I am further convinced that if our white brothers dismiss as "rabble-rousers" and "outside agitators" those of us who employ nonviolent direct action, and if they refuse to support our nonviolent efforts, millions of Negroes will, out of frustration and despair, seek solace and security in black-nationalist ideologies—a development that would inevitably lead to a frightening racial nightmare. 30

Oppressed people cannot remain oppressed forever. The yearning for freedom eventually manifests itself, and that is what has happened to the American Negro. Something within has reminded him of his birthright of freedom, and something without has reminded him that it can be gained. Consciously or unconsciously, he has been caught up by the *Zeitgeist,* and with his black brothers of Africa and his brown and yellow brothers of Asia, South America, and the Caribbean, the United States Negro is moving with a sense of great urgency toward the promised land of racial justice. If one recognizes this vital urge that has engulfed the Negro community, one should readily understand why public demonstrations are taking place. The Negro has many pent-up resentments and latent frustrations, and he must release them. So let him march; let him make prayer pilgrimages to the city hall; let him go on freedom rides—and try to understand why he must do so. If his repressed emotions are not released in nonviolent ways, they will seek expression through violence; this is not a threat but a fact of history. So I have not said to my 31 people, "Get rid of your discontent." Rather, I have tried to say that this normal and healthy discontent can be channeled into the creative outlet of nonviolent direct action. And now this approach is being termed extremist.

But though I was initially disappointed at being categorized as 32 an extremist, as I continued to think about the matter I gradually gained a measure of satisfaction from the label. Was not Jesus an extremist for love: "Love your enemies, bless them that curse you, do good to them that hate you, and pray for them which despitefully use you, and persecute you." Was not Amos an extremist for justice: "Let justice roll down like waters and righteousness like an ever-flowing stream." Was not Paul an extremist for the Christian gospel: "I bear in my body the marks of the Lord Jesus." Was not Martin Luther an extremist: "Here I stand; I cannot do otherwise, so help me God." And John Bunyan: "I will stay in jail to the end of my days before I make a butchery of my conscience." And Abraham Lincoln: "This nation cannot survive half slave and half free." And Thomas Jefferson: "We hold these truths to be self-evident, that all men are created equal . . .". So the question is not whether we will be extremists, but what kind of extremists we will be. Will we be extremists for hate or for love? Will we be extremists for the preservation of injustice or for the extension of justice? In that dramatic scene on Calvary's hill three men were crucified. We must never forget that all three were crucified for the same crime—the crime of extremism. Two were extremists for immorality, and thus fell below their environment. The other, Jesus Christ, was an extremist for love, truth, and goodness, and thereby rose above his environment. Perhaps the South, the nation, and the world are in dire need of creative extremists.

I had hoped that the white moderate would see this need. 33 Perhaps I was too optimistic; perhaps I expected too much. I suppose I should have realized that few members of the oppressor race can understand the deep groans and passionate yearnings of the oppressed race, and still fewer have the vision to see that injustice must be rooted out by strong, persistent, and determined action. I am thankful, however, that some of our white brothers in the South have grasped the meaning of this social revolution and committed themselves to it. They are still all too few in quantity, but they are big in quality. Some—such as Ralph McGill, Lillian Smith, Harry Golden, James McBride Dabbs, Anne Braden, and Sarah Patton Boyle—have written about our struggle in eloquent and prophetic terms. Others have marched with us down nameless streets of the South. They have languished in filthy, roach-infested jails, suffering the abuse and brutality of policemen who view them as "dirty nigger-lovers." Unlike so many of their moderate brothers and sisters, they have recognized the urgency of the moment and sensed the need for powerful "action" antidotes to combat the disease of segregation.

Let me take note of my other major disappointment. I have been so greatly disappointed with the white church and its leadership. Of course, there are some notable exceptions. I am not unmindful of the fact that each of you have taken some significant stands on this issue. I commend you, Reverend Stallings, for your Christian stand on this past Sunday, in welcoming Negroes to your worship service on a nonsegregated basis. I commend the Catholic leaders of this state for integrating Spring Hill College several years ago.   34

But despite these notable exceptions, I must honestly reiterate that I have been disappointed with the church. I do not say this as one of those negative critics who can always find something wrong with the church. I say this as a minister of the gospel, who loves the church; who has nurtured in its bosom; who has been sustained by its spiritual blessings and who will remain true to it as long as the cord of life shall lengthen.   35

When I was suddenly catapulted into the leadership of the bus protest in Montgomery, Alabama, a few years ago, I felt we would be supported by the white church. I felt that the white ministers, priests, and rabbis of the South would be among our strongest allies. Instead, some have been outright opponents, refusing to understand the freedom movement and misrepresenting its leaders; all too many others have been more cautious than courageous and have remained silent behind the anesthetizing security of stained glass windows.   36

In spite of my shattered dreams, I came to Birmingham with the hope that the white religious leadership of this community would see the justice of our cause and, with deep moral concern, would serve as the channel through which our just grievances could reach the power structure. I had hoped that each of you would understand. But again I have been disappointed.   37

I have heard numerous southern religious leaders admonish their worshipers to comply with a desegregation decision because it is the law, but I have longed to hear white ministers declare: "Follow this decree because integration is morally right and because the Negro is your brother." In the midst of blatant injustices inflicted upon the Negro, I have watched white churchmen stand on the sideline and mouth pious relevancies and sanctimonious trivialities. In   38 the midst of a mighty struggle to rid our nation of racial and economic injustice I have heard many ministers say: "Those are social issues, with which the gospel has no real concern." And I have watched many churches commit themselves to a completely otherworldly religion which makes a strange, un-Biblical distinction between body and soul, between the sacred and the secular.

I have traveled the length and breadth of Alabama, Mississippi,   39
and all the other southern states. On sweltering summer days and crisp autumn mornings I have looked at the South's beautiful churches with their lofty spires pointing heavenward. I have beheld the impressive outlines of her massive religious-education buildings. Over and over I have found myself asking: "What kind of people worship here? Who is their God? Where were their voices when the lips of Governor Barnett dripped with words of interposition and nullification? Where were they when Governor Wallace gave a clarion call for defiance and hatred? Where were their voices of support when bruised and weary Negro men and women decided to rise from the dark dungeons of complacency to the bright hills of creative protest?"

Yes, these questions are still in my mind. In deep disappoint-   40
ment I have wept over the laxity of the church. But be assured that my tears have been tears of love. There can be no deep disappointment where there is not deep love. Yes, I love the church. How could I do otherwise? I am in the rather unique position of being the son, the grandson, and the great-grandson of preachers. Yes, I see the church as the body of Christ. But, oh! How we have blemished and scarred that body through social neglect and through fear of being nonconformists.

There was a time when the church was very powerful—in the   41
time when the early Christians rejoiced at being deemed worthy to suffer for what they believed. In those days the church was not merely a thermometer that recorded the ideas and principles of popular opinion; it was a thermostat that transformed the mores of society. Whenever the early Christians entered a town, the people in power became disturbed and immediately sought to convict the Christians for being "disturbers of the peace" and "outside agitators." But the Christians pressed on, in the conviction that they were "a colony of heaven," called to obey God rather than man. Small in number, they were big in commitment. They were too God-intoxicated to be "astronomically intimidated." By their effort and example they brought an end to such ancient evils as infanticide and gladiatorial contests.

Things are different now. So often the contemporary church is 42
a weak, ineffectual voice with an uncertain sound. So often it is an
archdefender of the status quo. Far from being disturbed by the
presence of the church, the power structure of the average community is consoled by the church's silent—and often even vocal—
sanction of things as they are.

But the judgment of God is upon the church as never before. If 43
today's church does not recapture the sacrificial spirit of the early
church, it will lose its authenticity, forfeit the loyalty of millions, and
be dismissed as an irrelevant social club with no meaning for the
twentieth century. Every day I meet young people whose disappointment with the church has turned into outright disgust.

Perhaps I have once again been too optimistic. Is organized reli- 44
gion too inextricably bound to the status quo to save our nation and
the world? Perhaps I must turn my faith to the inner spiritual
church, the church within the church, as the true *ekklesia*[2] and the
hope of the world. But again I am thankful to God that some noble
souls from the ranks of organized religion have broken loose from
the paralyzing chains of conformity and joined us as active partners
in the struggle for freedom. They have left their secure congrega-
tions and walked the streets of Albany, Georgia, with us. They have
gone down the highways of the South on tortuous rides for freedom.
Yes, they have gone to jail with us. Some have been dismissed from
their churches, have lost the support of their bishops and fellow
ministers. But they have acted in the faith that right defeated is
stronger than evil triumphant. Their witness has been the spiritual
salt that has preserved the true meaning of the gospel in these troubled times. They have carved a tunnel of hope through the dark
mountain of disappointment.

I hope the church as a whole will meet the challenge of this de- 45
cisive hour. But even if the church does not come to the aid of justice,
I have no despair about the future. I have no fear about the outcome
of our struggle in Birmingham, even if our motives are at present
misunderstood. We will reach the goal of freedom in Birmingham
and all over the nation, because the goal of America is freedom.
Abused and scorned though we may be, our destiny is tied up with
America's destiny. Before the pilgrims landed at Plymouth, we were
here. Before the pen of Jefferson etched the majestic words of the
Declaration of Independence across the pages of history, we were

[2]The Greek New Testament word for the early Christian church. (Editor's note.)

here. For more than two centuries, our forbears labored in this country without wages; they made cotton king; they built the homes of their masters while suffering gross injustice and shameful humiliation— and yet out of a bottomless vitality they continued to thrive and develop. If the inexpressible cruelties of slavery could not stop us, the opposition we now face will surely fail. We will win our freedom because the sacred heritage of our nation and the eternal will of God are embodied in our echoing demands.

Before closing I feel impelled to mention one other point in   46 your statement that has troubled me profoundly. You warmly commended the Birmingham police force for keeping "order" and "preventing violence." I doubt that you would have so warmly commended the police force if you had seen its dogs sinking their teeth into unarmed, nonviolent Negroes. I doubt that you would so quickly commend the policemen if you were to observe their ugly and inhumane treatment of Negroes here in the city jail; if you were to watch them push and curse old Negro women and young Negro girls; if you were to see them slap and kick old Negro men and young boys; if you were to observe them, as they did on two occasions, refuse to give us food because we wanted to sing our grace together. I cannot join you in your praise of the Birmingham police department.

It is true that the police have exercised a degree of discipline in   47 handling the demonstrators. In this sense they have conducted themselves rather "nonviolently" in public. But for what purpose? To preserve the evil system of segregation. Over the past few years I have consistently preached that nonviolence demands that the means we use must be as pure as the ends we seek. I have tried to make clear that it is wrong to use immoral means to attain moral ends. But now I must affirm that it is just as wrong, or perhaps even more so, to use moral means to preserve immoral ends. Perhaps Mr. Connor and his policemen have been rather nonviolent in public, as was Chief Pritchett in Albany, Georgia, but they have used the moral means of nonviolence to maintain the immoral end of racial injustice. As T.S. Eliot has said, "The last temptation is the greatest treason: To do the right deed for the wrong reason."

I wish you had commended the Negro sit-inners and demon-   48 strators of Birmingham for their sublime courage, their willingness to suffer, and their amazing discipline in the midst of great provocation. One day the South will recognize its real heroes. They will be the James Merediths, with the noble sense of purpose that enables them to face jeering and hostile mobs, and with the agonizing loneliness that characterizes the life of the pioneer. They will be old, oppressed, battered Negro women, symbolized in a seventy-two-year-old woman in Montgomery, Alabama, who rose up with a sense of dignity and with her people decided not to ride segregated buses, and who responded with ungrammatical profundity to one who inquired about her weariness: "My feets is tired, but my soul is at rest." They will be the young high school and college students, and young ministers of the gospel and a host of their elders, courageously and nonviolently sitting in at lunch counters and willingly going to jail for conscience' sake. One day the South will know that when these disinherited children of God sat down at lunch counters, they were in reality standing up for what is best in the American dream and for the most sacred values in our Judaeo-Christian heritage, thereby bringing our nation back to those great wells of democracy which were dug deep by the founding fathers in their formulation of the Constitution and the Declaration of Independence.

Never before have I written so long a letter. I'm afraid it is much   49
too long to take your precious time. I can assure you that it would have been much shorter if I had been writing from a comfortable desk, but what else can one do when he is alone in a narrow jail cell, other than write long letters, think long thoughts, and pray long prayers?

If I have said anything in this letter that overstates the truth and   50
indicates an unreasonable impatience, I beg you to forgive me. If I have said anything that understates the truth and indicates my having a patience that allows me to settle for anything less than brotherhood, I beg God to forgive me.

I hope this letter finds you strong in the faith. I also hope that   51
circumstances will soon make it possible for me to meet each of you, not as an integrationist or a civil-rights leader but as a fellow clergyman and a Christian brother. Let us all hope that the dark clouds of racial prejudice will soon pass away and the deep fog of misunderstanding will be lifted from our fear-drenched communities, and in some not too distant tomorrow the radiant stars of love and brotherhood will shine over our great nation with all their scintillating beauty.

Yours for the cause of Peace and Brotherhood,   52
MARTIN LUTHER KING JR.   53

A Guide to Terms

Abstract (See *Concrete/Abstract.*)

Allusion (See *Figures of Speech.*)

Analogy (See Chapter 6.)

Argument is writing that uses factual evidence and supporting ideas to convince readers to share the author's opinion on an issue or to take some action the writer considers appropriate or necessary. Like exposition, argument conveys information; however, it does so not to explain but to induce readers to favor one side in a conflict or to choose a particular course of action.

Some arguments appeal primarily to reason, others primarily to emotion. Most, however, mix reason and emotion in whatever way is appropriate for the issue and the audience. (See Chapter 13.)

Support for an argument can take a number of forms:

1. *Examples*—Real-life examples or hypothetical examples (used sparingly) can be convincing evidence if they are typical and if the author provides enough of them to illustrate all the major points in the argument or combines them with other kinds of evidence. (See Daly, Mills, Quammen, and Lynn.) Some examples are *specific,* referring to particular people or events. (See Daly.) Others are *general,* referring to kinds of events or people, usually corresponding in some way to the reader's experiences. (See Lynn.)

2. *Facts and figures*—Detailed information about a subject, particularly if presented in statistical form, can help convince readers by showing that the author's perspective on an issue is consistent with what is known about the subject. (See Lynn, Linn, and Quindlen.) But facts whose accuracy is questionable or statistics that are confusing can undermine an argument.

3. *Authority*—Supporting an argument with the ideas or the actual words of someone who is recognized as an expert can be an effective strategy as long as the author can show that the expert is a reliable witness and can combine the expert's opinion with other kinds of evidence that point in the same direction.

4. *Personal experience*—Examples drawn from personal experience or the experience of friends can be more detailed and vivid (and hence

more convincing) than other kinds of evidence, but a writer should use this kind of evidence sparingly because readers may sometimes suspect that it represents no more than one person's way of looking at events. When combined with other kinds of evidence, however, examples drawn from personal experience can be an effective technique for persuasion. (See Daly, Tyler.)

In addition, all the basic expository patterns can be used to support an argument. (See Chapter 13.)

Cause (See Chapter 8.)

Central Theme (See *Unity.*)

Classification (See Chapter 4.)

Clichés are tired expressions, perhaps once fresh and colorful, that have been overused until they have lost most of their effectiveness and become trite or hackneyed. The term is also applied, less commonly, to trite ideas or attitudes.

We may need to use clichés in conversation, of course, when the quick and economical phrase is an important and useful tool of expression—and when no one expects us to be constantly original. We are fortunate, in a way, to have a large accumulation of clichés from which to draw. To describe someone, without straining our originality very much, we can always declare that he is *as innocent as a lamb, as thin as a rail,* or *as fat as a pig;* that she is *as dumb as an ox, as sly as a fox,* or *as wise as an owl;* that he is *financially embarrassed* or *has a fly in the ointment* or that *her ship has come in;* or that, *last but not least, in this day and age,* the *Grim Reaper* has taken him to *his eternal reward.* There is indeed *a large stockpile* from which we can draw for ordinary conversation. But the trite expression, written down on paper, is a permanent reminder that the writer is either lazy or not aware of the dullness of stereotypes—or, even more damaging, it is a clue that the ideas themselves may be threadbare and therefore can be adequately expressed in threadbare language.

Occasionally, of course, a writer can use obvious clichés deliberately (see Lawrence, Par. 1; Tyler; and Stone). But usually to be fully effective, writing must be fresh and should seem to have been written specifically for the occasion. Clichés, however fresh and appropriate at one time, have lost these qualities.

Closings are almost as much of a problem as introductions, and they are equally important. The function of a closing is simply "to close," of course, but this implies somehow tying the entire writing into a neat package, giving the final sense of unity to the whole endeavor, and thus leaving the reader with a sense of satisfaction instead of an uneasy feeling that there ought to be another page.

There is no standard length for closings. A short composition may be effectively completed with one sentence—or even without any real closing at all, if the last point discussed is a strong or climactic one. A longer piece of writing, however, may end more slowly, perhaps through several paragraphs.

A few types of weak endings are so common that warnings are in order here. Careful writers will avoid these faults: (1) giving the effect of suddenly tiring and quitting; (2) ending on a minor detail or an apparent afterthought; (3) bringing up a new point in the closing; (4) using any new qualifying remark in the closing (if writers want their opinions to seem less dogmatic or generalized, they should go back to do their qualifying where the damage was done), and (5) ending with an apology of any kind (authors who are not interested enough to become at least minor experts in their subject should not be wasting the reader's time).

Of the several acceptable ways of giving the sense of finality to a paper, the easiest is the *summary,* but it is also the least desirable for most short papers. Readers who have read and understood something only a page or two before probably do not need to have it reviewed for them. Such a review is apt to seem merely repetitious. Longer writings, of course, such as research or term papers, may require thorough summaries.

Several other closing techniques are available to writers. The following ones which do not represent all the possibilities, are useful in many situations, and they can frequently be employed in combination:

1. *Using word signals*—for example, *finally, at last, thus, and so,* and *in conclusion,* as well as more original devices suggested by the subject itself. (See Simpson.)

2. *Changing the tempo*—usually a matter of sentence length or pace. This is a very subtle indication of finality, and it is difficult to achieve. (For examples of modified use, see Simpson, Gewande, and Walker.)

3. *Restating the central idea of the writing*—sometimes a "statement" so fully developed that it practically becomes a summary itself. (See Catton, Carter, and Buczynski.)

4. *Using climax*—a natural culmination of preceding points or, in some cases, the last major point itself. This is suitable, however, only if the materials have been so arranged that the last point is outstanding. (See Catton, Lawrence, Makihara, Walker, and Szalavitz.)

5. *Making suggestions,* perhaps mentioning a possible solution to the problem being discussed—a useful technique for exposition as well as for argument, and a natural signal of the end. (See Lynn.)

6. *Showing the topic's significance,* its effects, or the universality of its meaning—a commonly used technique that, if carefully handled, is an excellent indication of closing. (See Quindlen, Schwartz, and Lawrence.)

7. *Echoing the introduction*—a technique that has the virtue of improving the effect of unity by bringing the development around full circle, so to speak. The echo may be a reference to a problem posed or

a significant expression, quotation, analogy, or symbol used in the introduction or elsewhere early in the composition. (See Min and Berendt.)

8. *Using some rhetorical device*—a sort of catchall category, but a good supply source that includes several very effective techniques: pertinent quotations, anecdotes and brief dialogues, metaphors, allusions, ironic comments, and various kinds of witty or memorable remarks. All, however, run the risk of seeming forced and hence amateurish; but properly handled, they make for an effective closing. (See White, Lopate, Lawrence, Simpson, and King.)

Coherence is a quality of good writing that results from the presentation of all parts in logical and clear relations.

Coherence and unity are usually studied together and, indeed, are almost inseparable. But whereas unity refers to the relation of parts to the central theme (see *Unity*), coherence refers to their relations with each other. In a coherent piece of writing, each sentence, each paragraph, and each major division seem to grow out of those preceding them.

Several transitional devices (see *Transition*) help to make these relations clear, but far more fundamental to coherence is the sound organization of materials. From the first moment of visualizing the subject materials in pattern, the writer's goal must be clear and logical development. If it is, coherence is almost ensured.

Colloquial Expressions are characteristic of conversation and informal writing, and they are normally perfectly appropriate in those contexts. However, most writing done for college, business, or professional purposes is considered "formal" writing; for such usage, colloquialisms are too informal, too *folksy* (itself a word most dictionaries would label "colloq.").

Some of the expressions appropriate only for informal usage are *kid* (for child), *boss* (for employer), *flunk, buddy, snooze, gym, a lot of, phone, skin flicks,* and *porn.* In addition, contractions such as *can't* and *I'd* are usually regarded as colloquialisms and are never permissible in, for instance, a research or term paper.

Slang is defined as a low level of colloquialism, but it is sometimes placed "below" colloquialism in respectability; even standard dictionaries differ as to just what the distinction is. (Some of the examples in the preceding paragraph, if included in dictionaries at all, are identified both ways.) At any rate, slang generally comprises words either coined or given novel meanings in an attempt at colorful or humorous expression. Slang often becomes limp with overuse, however, losing whatever vigor it first had. In time, slang expressions either disappear completely or graduate to more acceptable colloquial status and thence, possibly, into standard usage. (This is one way in which our language is constantly changing.) But until their "graduations," slang and colloquialisms have an appropriate place in formal writing only if used sparingly and for special effect. Because dictionaries frequently differ in matters of usage, the student should be sure to use a standard edition approved by the instructor. (For further examples, see Tyler, Wolfe, and Simpson, Pars. 8, 16, and 17.)

Comparison (See Chapter 5.)

Conclusions (See *Closings.*)

Concrete and **Abstract** words are both indispensable to the language, but a good rule in most writing is to use the concrete whenever possible. This policy also applies, of course, to sentences that express only abstract ideas, which concrete examples can often make clearer and more effective. Many expository and argumentative paragraphs are constructed with an abstract topic sentence and its concrete support. (See *Unity.*)

A concrete word names something that exists as an entity in itself, something that can be perceived by the human senses. We can see, touch, hear, and smell a horse—hence *horse* is a concrete word. But a horse's *strength* is not. We have no reason to doubt that strength exists, but it does not have an independent existence: something else must *be* strong or there is no strength. Hence *strength* is an abstract word.

Purely abstract reading is difficult for average readers; with no concrete images provided, they are constantly forced to make their own. Concrete writing helps readers to visualize and is therefore easier and faster to read. (See *Specific/General* for further discussion.)

Connotation and **Denotation** both refer to the meanings of words. Denotation is the direct, literal meaning of a word as it would be found in a dictionary, whereas connotation refers to the response a word *really* arouses in the reader or listener. (See Wolfe, Par. 14; Daly; and Lawrence.)

There are two types of connotation: personal and general. Personal connotations vary widely, depending on the experiences and moods that an individual associates with the word. (This corresponds with personal symbolism; see *Symbol.*) *Waterfall* is not apt to have the same meaning for the happy young honeymooners at Yosemite as it has for the grieving mother whose child has just drowned in a waterfall. General connotations are those shared by many people. *Fireside,* far beyond its obvious dictionary definition, generally connotes warmth, security, and good companionship. *Mother,* which denotatively means simply "female parent," means much more connotatively.

A word or phrase considered less distasteful or offensive than a more direct expression is called a *euphemism,* and this is also a matter of connotation. (See Mitford.) The various expressions used instead of the more direct "four-letter words" referring to daily bathroom events are examples of euphemisms. (See Wolfe's "mounting," Pars. 16 and 17.) *Remains* is often used instead of *corpse,* and a few newspapers still report people *passing away* and being *laid to rest* rather than *dying* and being *buried.*

But a serious respect for the importance of connotations goes far beyond euphemistic practices. Young writers can hardly expect to know all the different meanings of words for all their potential readers, but they can at least be aware that words do *have* different meanings. Of course, this is most important in persuasive writing—in political speeches, in advertising copywriting, and in any endeavor where some sort of public image is being created. When President Franklin Roosevelt began his series of informal radio talks, he called them "fireside chats," thus putting connotation to work. An advertising copywriter trying to evoke the feeling of love and tenderness associated with motherhood is not seriously tempted to use *female parent* instead of *mother.*

In exposition, where the primary purpose is to explain, the writer ordinarily tries to avoid words that may have emotional overtones, unless these can somehow be used to increase understanding. In argument, however, a writer may on occasion wish to appeal to the emotions.

Contrast (See Chapter 5.)

Deduction (See Chapter 12.)

Denotation (See *Connotation/Denotation.*)

Description (See Chapter 10.)

Diction refers simply to "choice of words," but, not so simply, it involves many problems of usage, some of which are explained under several other headings in this guide, for example, *Clichés, Colloquial Expressions, Connotation/Denotation,* and *Concrete/Abstract*—anything, in fact, that pertains primarily to word choices. But the characteristics of good diction may be more generally classified as follows:

1. *Accuracy*—the choice of words that mean exactly what the author intends

2. *Economy*—the choice of the simplest and fewest words that will convey the exact meaning intended

3. *Emphasis*—the choice of fresh, strong words, avoiding clichés and unnecessarily vague or general terms

4. *Appropriateness*—the choice of words that suit the subject matter, the prospective reader-audience, and the purpose of the writing

(For contrasts of diction see Stone, Welsch, Walker, King, Twitchell, Murphy, Tyler, and Carter.)

Division (See Chapter 4.)

Effect (See Chapter 8.)

Emphasis is almost certain to fall *somewhere,* and the author should be the one to decide where. A major point, not some minor detail, should be emphasized.

Following are the most common ways of achieving emphasis. Most of them apply to the sentence, the paragraph, or the overall writing—all of which can be seriously weakened by emphasis in the wrong places.

1. By *position*—The most emphatic position is usually at the end, the second most emphatic at the beginning. (There are a few exceptions, including news stories and certain kinds of scientific reports.) The middle, therefore, should be used for materials that do not deserve special emphasis. (See Gewande, for saving until last a statement that undercuts many of the sentiments expressed or reported in the essay; Catton, Par. 16; Savage, for the long-withheld revelation of the real central theme.)

A sentence in which the main point is held until the last is called a *periodic sentence,* for example, "After a long night of suspense and horror, the cavalry arrived." In a *loose sentence,* the main point is disposed of earlier and followed by dependencies, for example, "The cavalry arrived after a long night of suspense and horror."

2. By *proportion*—Ordinarily, but not necessarily, important elements are given the most attention and thus automatically achieve a certain emphasis.

3. By *repetition*—Words and ideas may sometimes be given emphasis by reuse, usually in a different manner. If not cautiously handled, however, this method can seem merely repetitious, not emphatic. (See Atwood, who repeats words to give them varied meanings and highlight their importance.)

4. By *flat statement*—Although an obvious way to achieve emphasis is simply to *tell* the reader what is most important, it is often least effective, at least when used as the only method. Readers have a way of ignoring such pointers as "most important" and "especially true." (See Catton, Par. 16.)

5. By *mechanical devices*—Emphasis can be achieved by using italics (underlining), capital letters, or exclamation points. But too often these devices are used, however unintentionally, to cover deficiencies of content or style. Their use can quickly be overdone and their impact lost.

6. By *distinctiveness of style*—The author can emphasize subtly with fresh and concrete words or figures of speech, crisp or unusual structures, and careful control of paragraph or sentence lengths. (These methods are used in many essays in this book: see Tyler; Seip; Twain, who changes style radically for the second half of his essay; Catton; Stone, who uses numerous puns; and Wolfe.) *Verbal irony* (see *Irony*), including *sarcasm* (see Seip and Atwood) and the rather specialized form known as *understatement,* is another valuable means of

achieving distinctiveness of style and increasing emphasis. (See Wolfe, Mitford, and Gewande.)

Essay refers to a brief prose composition on a single topic, usually, but not always, communicating the author's personal ideas and impressions. Beyond this, because of the wide and loose application of the term, no satisfactory definition has been universally accepted.

Classifications of essay types have also been widely varied and sometimes not very meaningful. One basic and useful distinction, however, is between *formal* and *informal* essays, although many defy classification even in such broad categories as these. It is best to regard the two types as opposite ends of a continuum, along which most essays may be placed.

The formal essay usually develops an important theme through a logical progression of ideas, with full attention to unity and coherence, and in a serious tone. Although the style is seldom completely impersonal, it is literary rather than colloquial. (For examples of essays that are somewhere near the "formal" end of the continuum, see Linn, Quart, Lynn, Catton, Kilbourne, and Lawrence.)

The informal, or personal, essay is less elaborately organized and more chatty in style. First-person pronouns, contractions, and other colloquial or even slang expressions are often freely used. Informal essays are less serious in apparent purpose than formal essays. Although most do contain a worthwhile message or observation of some kind, an important purpose of many is to entertain. (See Stone, Seip, and Wolf.)

The more personal and intimate informal essays may be classifiable as *familiar* essays, although, again, there is no well-established boundary. Familiar essays pertain to the author's own experience, ideas, or prejudices, frequently in a light and humorous style. (See Buczynski, Tyler, White, Straight, and Murphy.)

Evaluation of a literary piece, as for any other creative endeavor, is meaningful only when based on the answers to three questions: (1) What was the author's purpose? (2) How successfully was it fulfilled? and (3) How worthwhile was it?

An architect could hardly be blamed for designing a poor gymnasium if the commission had been to design a library. Similarly, an author who is trying to explain for us why women are paid less than men cannot be faulted for failing to make the reader laugh. An author whose purpose is simply to amuse (a worthy goal) should not be condemned for teaching little about trichobothria. (Nothing prevents the author from trying to explain pornography through the use of humor, or trying to amuse by comparing two Civil War generals, but in these situations the purpose has changed—and grown almost unbearably harder to achieve.)

An architect who was commissioned to design a gymnasium, and who, in fact, designed one, however, could be justifiably criticized on whether the building is successful and attractive *as a gymnasium.* If an author is examining matters of cognition and personality, the reader has a right to expect sound reasoning and clear expository prose; and varied, detailed support ought to be expected in an essay that looks at the physical basis of human behavior (see Perry and Dawson).

Many things are written and published that succeed very well in carrying out the author's intent—but simply are not worthwhile. Although this is certainly justifiable grounds for unfavorable criticism, readers should first make full allowance for their own limitations and perhaps their narrow range of interests, and they should evaluate the work as nearly as possible from the standpoint of the average reader for whom the writing was intended.

Figures of Speech are short, vivid comparisons, either stated or implied, but they are not literal comparisons (e.g., "Your car is like my car," which is presumably a plain statement of fact). Figures of speech are more imaginative. They imply analogy but, unlike analogy, are used less to inform than to make quick and forceful impressions. All figurative language is a comparison of unlikes, but the unlikes do have some interesting point of likeness, perhaps one never noticed before.

A *metaphor* merely suggests the comparison and is worded as if the two unlikes are the same thing—for example, "the language of the river" and "was turned to blood" (Twain, Par. 1) and "a great chapter in American life" (Catton, Par. 1). (For another example in this book, see King.)

A *simile* (which is sometimes classified as a special kind of metaphor) expresses a similarity directly, usually with the word *like* or *as* (Lopate, Par. 12).

A *personification*, which is actually a special type of either metaphor or simile, is usually classified as a "figure" in its own right. In personification, inanimate things are treated as if they had the qualities or powers of a person. Some people would also label as personification any characterization of inanimate objects as animals or of animals as humans.

An *allusion* is literally any casual reference, any alluding, to something, but rhetorically it is limited to a figurative reference to a famous or literary person, event, or quotation, and it should be distinguished from the casual reference that has a literal function in the subject matter. Hence casual mention of Judas Iscariot's betrayal of Jesus is merely a reference, but calling a modern traitor a "Judas" is an allusion. A rooster might be referred to as "the Hitler of the barnyard," or a lover as a "Romeo." Many allusions refer to mythological or biblical persons or places. (See Wolfe, title and Par. 1; Simpson, Par. 2, for a discussion of some commonly employed allusions.)

Irony and paradox (both discussed under their own headings) and analogy (see Chapter 6) are also frequently classed as figures of speech, and there are several other less common types that are really subclassifications of those already discussed.

General (See *Specific/General*.)

Illustration (See Chapter 3.)

Impressionistic Description (See Chapter 10.)

Induction (See Chapter 12.)

Introductions give readers their first impressions, which often turn out to be the lasting ones. In fact, unless an introduction succeeds in somehow attracting a reader's interest, he or she probably will read no further. The importance of the introduction is one reason that writing it is nearly always difficult.

When the writer remains at a loss for how to begin, it may be a good idea to forget about the introduction for a while and go ahead with the main body of the writing. Later the writer may find that a suitable introduction has suggested itself or even that the way the piece begins is actually introduction enough.

Introductions may vary in length from one sentence in a short composition to several paragraphs or even several pages in longer and more complex expositions and arguments, such as research papers and reports of various kinds.

Good introductions in expository writing have at least three and sometimes four functions.

1. *To identify the subject and set its limitations,* thus building a solid foundation for unity. This function usually includes some indication of the central theme, letting the reader know what point is to be made about the subject. Unlike the other forms of prose, which can often benefit by some degree of mystery, exposition has the primary purpose of explaining, so the reader has a right to know from the beginning just *what* is being explained.

2. *To interest the readers,* and thus ensure their attention. To be sure of doing this, writers must analyze their prospective readers and the readers' interest in their subject. The account of a new X-ray technique would need an entirely different kind of introduction if written for doctors than if written for the campus newspaper.

3. *To set the tone* of the rest of the writing. (See *Style/Tone.*) Tone varies greatly in writing, just as the tone of a person's voice varies with the person's mood. One function of the introduction is to let the reader know the author's attitude since it may have a subtle but important bearing on the communication.

4. *Frequently,* but not always, *to indicate the plan of organization.* Although seldom important in short, relatively simple compositions and essay examinations, this function of introductions can be especially valuable in more complex papers.

These are the necessary functions of an introduction. For best results, keep these guidelines in mind: (1) Avoid referring to the title or even assuming that the reader has seen it. Make the introduction do all the introducing. (2) Avoid crude and uninteresting beginnings, such as "This paper is about . . . ." (3) Avoid going too abruptly into the main body—a smooth transition is at least as important here as anywhere else. (4) Avoid overdoing the introduction, either in length or in extremes of style.

Fortunately, there are many good ways to introduce expository writing (and argumentative writing), and several of the most useful are illustrated by the selections in this book. Many writings, of course, combine two or more of the following techniques for interesting introductions.

1. *Stating the central theme,* which is sometimes fully enough explained in the introduction to become almost a preview summary of the exposition or argument to come. (See Quart.)

2. *Showing the significance of the subject,* or stressing its importance. (See Catton, Wolfe, and Simpson.)

3. *Giving the background of the subject,* usually in brief form, in order to bring the reader up-to-date as early as possible for a better understanding of the matter at hand. (See Stone and Lynn.)

4. *"Focusing down"* to one aspect of the subject, a technique similar to that used in some movies, showing first a broad scope (of subject area, such as a landscape) and then progressively narrowing views until the focus is on one specific thing (perhaps the name "O'Grady O'Connor" on a mailbox by a gate—or the "young hungry people" in Tyler's office (par. 3)). (See also Rooney.)

5. *Using a pertinent rhetorical device* that will attract interest as it leads into the main exposition—for example, an anecdote, analogy, allusion, quotation, or paradox. (See Welsch and Simpson.)

6. *Using a short but vivid comparison or contrast* to emphasize the central idea. (See Lynn.)

7. *Posing a challenging question,* the answering of which the reader will assume to be the purpose of the writing. (See Lawrence and Buczynski.)

8. *Referring to the writer's experience with the subject,* perhaps even giving a detailed account of that experience. Some writings are simply continuations of experience so introduced, perhaps with the expository purpose of making the telling entirely evident only at the end or slowly unfolding it as the account progresses. (See White and Daly.)

9. *Presenting a startling statistic or other fact* that will indicate the nature of the subject to be discussed.

10. *Making an unusual statement* that can intrigue as well as introduce. (See Wolfe and Gansberg.)

11. *Making a commonplace remark* that can draw interest because of its very commonness in sound or meaning.

Irony, in its verbal form sometimes classed as a figure of speech, consists of saying one thing on the surface but meaning exactly (or nearly) the opposite—for example, "this beautiful neighborhood of ours" may mean that it is a dump. (For other illustrations, see Stone, Wolfe, Mitford, and Walker.)

Verbal irony has a wide range of tones, from the gentle, gay, or affectionate to the sharpness of outright *sarcasm* (see Seip), which is always intended to cut. It may consist of only a word or phrase, it may be a simple *understatement* (see Mitford), or it may be sustained as one of the major components of satire.

Irony can be an effective tool of exposition if its tone is consistent with the overall tone and if the writer is sure that the audience is bright enough to recognize it. In speech, a person usually indicates by voice or eye expression that he or she is not to be taken literally; in writing, the words on the page have to speak for themselves. (See Stone for the use of parentheses to indicate ironic or humorous statements.)

In addition to verbal irony, there is also an *irony of situation*, in which there is a sharp contradiction between what is logically expected to happen and what does happen—for example, a man sets a trap for an obnoxious neighbor and then gets caught in it himself. Or the ironic situation may simply be some discrepancy that an outsider can see while those involved cannot. (See Lawrence, Pars. 11–12 or Gewande, Pars. 13–16)

Logical Argument (See Chapter 13.)

Loose Sentence (See *Emphasis.*)

Metaphor (See *Figures of Speech.*)

Narration (See Chapter 11.)

Objective writing and **Subjective** writing are distinguishable by the extent to which they reflect the author's personal attitudes or emotions. The difference is usually one of degree, as few writing endeavors can be completely objective or subjective.

Objective writing, seldom used in its pure form except in business or scientific reports, is impersonal and concerned almost entirely with straight narration, with logical analysis, or with the description of external appearances. (For somewhat objective writing, see Simpson; and Staples, Par. 1.)

Subjective writing (in description called "impressionistic"—see Chapter 10) is more personalized, more expressive of the beliefs, ideals, or impressions of the author. Whereas in objective writing the emphasis is on the object being written about, in subjective writing the emphasis is on the way the author sees and interprets the object. (For some of the many examples in this book, see Twain; Lopate; Wolfe; Mitford; Welsch; Lawrence; and Staples, after Par. 1.)

Paradox is a statement or remark that, although seeming to be contradictory or absurd, actually contains some truth. Many paradoxical statements are also ironic.

Paragraph Unity (See *Unity.*)

Parallel Structure refers in principle to the same kind of "parallelism" that is studied in grammar: the principle that coordinate elements should have coordinate presentation, as in a pair or a series of verbs, prepositional phrases, or gerunds. It is often as much a matter of "balance" as it is of parallelism.

But the principle of parallel structure, far from being just a negative "don't mix" set of rules, is also a positive rhetorical device. Many writers use it as an effective means of stressing variety of profusion in a group of nouns or modifiers, or of emphasizing parallel ideas in sentence parts, in two or more sentences, or even in two or more paragraphs. At times it can also be useful stylistically to give a subtle poetic quality to the prose.

(For illustrations of parallel parts within a sentence, see Wolfe, Pars. 1 and 4; of parallel sentences themselves, see Catton, Par. 14; of both parallel parts and parallel sentences, see Twain.)

Periodic Sentence (See *Emphasis.*)

Persona refers to a character created as the speaker in an essay or the narrator of a story. The attitudes and character of a persona often differ from those of the author, and their persona may be created as a way of submitting certain values or perspectives to examination and criticism.

Personification (See *Figures of Speech.*)

Point of View in *argument* means the author's opinion on an issue or the thesis being advanced in an essay. In *exposition,* however, point of view is simply the position of the author in relation to the subject matter. Rhetorical point of view in exposition has little in common with the grammatical sort, and it differs somewhat from point of view in fiction.

A ranch in a mountain valley is seen differently by the ranch hand working at the corral, by the gardener deciding where to plant the petunias, by the artist or poet viewing the ranch from the mountainside, and by the geographer in a plane above, map-sketching the valley in relation to the entire range. It is the same ranch, but the positions and attitudes of the viewers are different.

So it is with expository prose. The position and attitude of the author are the important lens through which the reader sees the subject. Consistency is important, because if the lens is changed without sufficient cause and explanation, the reader will become disconcerted, if not annoyed.

Obviously, since the point of view is partially a matter of attitude, the tone and often the style of writing are closely linked to it. (See *Style/ Tone.*)

The expository selections in this book provide examples of numerous points of view. Twain's are those of an authority in his own fields of experience, Mitford's is as the debunking prober, and Makihara's is that of the participant with a limited perspective. In each of these (and the list could be extended to include all the selections in the book), the subject would seem vastly different if seen from some other point of view.

Process Analysis (See Chapter 7.)

Purpose that is clearly understood by the author before beginning to write is essential to both unity and coherence. A worthwhile practice, certainly in the training stages, is to write down the controlling purpose before even beginning to outline. Some instructors require both a statement of purpose and a statement of central theme, or thesis. (See *Unity; Thesis.*)

  The most basic element of a statement of purpose is the commitment to "explain" or, in some assignments, to "convince" (argument). But the statement of purpose, whether written down or only decided upon, goes further—for example, "to argue that 'dirty words' are logically offensive because of the sources and connotations of the words themselves" (Lawrence).

Qualification is the tempering of broad statements to make them more valid and acceptable, the authors themselves admitting the probability of exceptions. This qualifying can be done inconspicuously, to whatever degree needed, by the use of *possibly, nearly always, most often, usually, frequently, sometimes,* or *occasionally.* Instead of saying, "Chemistry is the most valuable field of study," it would probably be more accurate and defensible to say that it is for *some* people or that it *can* be the most valuable.

Refutation of opposing arguments is an important element in most argumentative essays, especially when the opposition is strong enough or reasonable enough to provide a real alternative to the author's opinion. A refutation consists of a brief summary of the opposing point of view along with a discussion of its inadequacies, a discussion that often helps support the author's own thesis.

  Here are three commonly used strategies for refutation:

  1. *Pointing out weaknesses in evidence*—If an opposing argument is based on inaccurate, incomplete, or misleading evidence, or if the argument does not take into account some new evidence that contradicts it, then the refutation should point out these weaknesses. (See Baumeister.)

  2. *Pointing out errors in logic*—If an opposing argument is loosely reasoned or contains major flaws in logic, then the refutation should point these problems out to the reader.

  3. *Questioning the relevance of an argument*—If an opposing argument does not directly address the issue under consideration, then the refutation should point out that even though the argument may well be correct, it is not worth considering because it is not relevant.

  Refutations should always be moderate in tone and accurate in representing opposing arguments; otherwise, readers may feel that the writer has treated the opposition unfairly and as a result judge the author's own argument more harshly.

Rhetorical Questions are posed with no expectation of receiving an answer; they are merely structural devices for launching or furthering a discussion or for achieving emphasis. (See Lawrence.)

Sarcasm (See *Irony.*)

Satire, sometimes called "extended irony," is a literary form that brings wit and humor to the serious task of pointing out frailties or evils of human institutions. It has thrived in Western literature since the time of the ancient Greeks, and English literature of the eighteenth century was particularly noteworthy for the extent and quality of its satire. Broadly, two types are recognized: *Horatian satire,* which is gentle and smiling, and which aims to correct by invoking laughter and sympathy; and *Juvenalian satire,* which is sharper and points with anger, contempt, and/or moral indignation to corruption and evil.

Sentimentality, also called *sentimentalism,* is an exaggerated show of emotion, whether intentional or caused by lack of restraint. An author can sentimentalize almost any situation, but the trap is most dangerous when writing of timeworn emotional symbols or scenes—for example, a broken heart, mother love, a lonely death, or the conversion of a sinner. However sincere the author may be, if readers are not fully oriented to the worth and uniqueness of the situation described, they may be either resentful or amused at any attempt to play on their emotions. Sentimentality is, of course, one of the chief characteristics of melodrama. (For examples of writing that, less adeptly handled, could easily have slipped into sentimentality, see Buczynski, Twain, Catton, Angelou, Staples, Straight, Simpson, and Gansberg.)

Simile (See *Figures of Speech.*)

Slang (See *Colloquial Expressions.*)

Specific and **General** terms, and the distinctions between the two, are similar to concrete and abstract terms (as discussed under their own heading), and for our purpose there is no real need to keep the two sets of categories separated. Whether *corporation* is thought of as "abstract" and *Ajax Motor Company* as "concrete," or whether they are assigned to "general" and "specific" categories, the principle is the same: in most writing, *Ajax Motor Company* is better.

But "specific" and "general" are relative terms. For instance, the word *apple* is more specific than *fruit* but less so than *Winesap.* And *fruit,* as general as it certainly is in one respect, is still more specific than *food.* Such relationships are shown more clearly in a series, progressing from general to specific: *food, fruit, apple, Winesap;* or *vehicle, automobile, Ford, Mustang.* Modifiers and verbs can also have degrees of specificity: *bright, red, scarlet;* or *moved, sped, careened.* It is not difficult to see the advantages to the reader—and, of course, to the writer who needs to communicate an idea clearly—in "the scarlet Mustang careened through the pass" instead of "the bright-colored vehicle moved through the pass."

Obviously, however, there are times when the general or the abstract term or statement is essential—for example, "A balanced diet includes some fruit" or "There was no vehicle in sight." But the use of specific language whenever possible is one of the best ways to improve diction and thus clarity and forcefulness in writing.

(Another important way of strengthening general, abstract writing is, of course, to use examples or other illustrations. See Chapter 3.)

Style and **Tone** are so closely linked and so often even elements of each other that it is best to consider them together.

But there is a difference. Think of two young men, each with his girlfriend on separate moonlit dates, whispering in nearly identical tender and loving tones of voice. One young man says, "Your eyes, dearest, reflect a thousand sparkling candles of heaven," and the other says, "Them eyes of yours—in this light—they sure do turn me on." Their *tones* were the same; their *styles* were considerably different.

The same distinction exists in writing. But, naturally, with more complex subjects than the effect of moonlight on a lover's eyes, there are more complications in separating the two qualities, even for the purpose of study.

The tone is determined by the *attitude* of writers toward their subject and toward their audience. Writers, too, may be tender and loving, but they may be indignant, solemn, playful, enthusiastic, belligerent, contemptuous—the list could be as long as a list of the many "tones of voice." (In fact, wide ranges of tone may be illustrated by essays in this book. Compare, for example, those of the two parts of Twain; Tyler and Lynn; and Staples and Seip.)

Style, on the other hand, expresses the author's individuality through choices of words (see *Diction*), sentence patterns (see *Syntax*), and selection and arrangement of details and basic materials. (All these elements of style are illustrated in the contrasting statements of the moonstruck lads.) These matters of style are partially prescribed, of course, by the adopted tone, but they are still bound to reflect the writer's personality, mood, education, and general background.

(Some of the more distinctive styles—partially affected by and affecting tone—represented by selections in this book are those of Viorst, Wolfe, Seip, White, Stone, Silko, Murphy, Staples, Tyler, and Walker.)

Subjective Writing (See *Objective/Subjective.*)

Symbol refers to anything that although real itself also suggests something broader or more significant—not just in greater numbers, however. A person would not symbolize a group or even humankind itself, although a person might be typical or representative in one or more abstract qualities. On the most elementary level, even words are symbols—for example, *bear* brings to mind the furry beast itself. But more important is that things, persons, or even acts may also be symbolic if they invoke abstract concepts, values, or qualities apart from themselves or their own kind. Such symbols, in everyday life as well as in literature and the other arts, are generally classifiable according to three types, which, although terminology differs, we may label *natural, personal,* and *conventional.*

In a natural symbol, the symbolic meaning is inherent in the thing itself. The sunrise naturally suggests new beginnings to most people, an island is almost synonymous with isolation, and a cannon automatically suggests war; hence these are natural symbols. It does not matter that some things, by their nature, can suggest more than one concept. Although a valley may symbolize security to one person and captivity to another, both meanings, contradictory as they might seem, are inherent, and in both respects the valley is a natural symbol.

The personal symbol, depending as it does on private experience or perception, is meaningless to others unless they are told about it or allowed to see its significance in context (as in literature). Although the color green may symbolize the outdoor life to the farm boy trapped in the gray city (in this respect perhaps a natural symbol), it can also symbolize romance to the young woman proposed to while wearing her green blouse, or dismal poverty to the woman who grew up in a weathered green shanty; neither of these meanings is suggested by something *inherent* in the color green, so they are personal symbols. Anything at all could take on private symbolic meaning, even the odor of marigolds or the sound of a lawnmower. The sunrise itself could mean utter despair, instead of fresh opportunities, to the man who has long despised his daily job and cannot find another.

Conventional symbols usually started as personal symbols, but continued usage in life or art permits them to be generally recognized for their broader meanings, which depend on custom rather than any inherent quality—for example, the olive branch for peace, the flag for love of country, the cross for Christianity, and the raised fist for revolutionary power.

Symbols are used less in expository and argumentative writing than in fiction and poetry, but a few authors represented in this book have either referred to the subtle symbolism of others or made use of it in developing their own ideas.

Syntax is a very broad term—too broad, perhaps, to be very useful—referring to the arrangement of words in a sentence. Good syntax implies the use not only of correct grammar but also of effective patterns. These patterns depend on sentences with good unity, coherence, and emphasis; on the use of subordination and parallel construction as appropriate; on economy; and on a consistent and interesting point of view. A pleasing variety of sentence patterns is also important in achieving effective syntax.

Theme (See *Unity.*)

Thesis In an argumentative essay, the central theme is often referred to as the thesis, and to make sure that readers recognize it, the thesis is often summed up briefly in a *thesis statement.* In a very important sense, the thesis is the center of an argument because the whole essay is designed to make the reader agree with it and, hence, with the author's opinion. (See *Unity.*)

Tone (See *Style/Tone.*)

Transition is the relating of one topic to the next, and smooth transition is an important aid to the coherence of a sentence, a paragraph, or an entire piece of writing. (See *Coherence.*)

The most effective coherence, of course, comes about naturally with sound development of ideas, one growing logically into the next—and that depends on sound organization. But sometimes beneficial even in this situation, particularly in going from one paragraph to the next, is the use of appropriate transitional devices.

Readers are apt to be sensitive creatures, easy to lose. (And, of course, the writers are the real losers since they are the ones who presumably have something they want to communicate.) If the readers get into a new paragraph and the territory seems familiar, chances are that they will continue. But if there are no identifying landmarks, they will often begin to feel uneasy and will either start worrying about their slow comprehension or take a dislike to the author and the subject matter. Either way, a communication block arises, and very likely the author will soon have fewer readers.

A good policy, then, unless the progression of ideas is exceptionally smooth and obvious, is to provide some kind of familiar identification early in the new paragraph to keep the reader feeling at ease with the different ideas. The effect is subtle but important. These familiar landmarks or transitional devices are sometimes applied deliberately but more often come naturally, especially when the prospective reader is kept constantly in mind at the time of writing.

An equally important reason for using some kinds of transitional devices, however, is a logical one: while functioning as bridges between ideas, they also assist the basic organization by pointing out the *relationship* of the ideas—and thus contributing still further to readability.

Transitional devices useful for bridging paragraph changes (and, some of them, to improve transitional flow within paragraphs) may be roughly classified as follows:

1. *Providing an "echo"* from the preceding paragraph. This may be the repetition of a key phrase or word, a pronoun referring back to such a word, or a casual reference to an idea. (See Lopate, last two paragraphs; Wolfe, especially from Pars. 1 to 2 and 4 to 5; and Mitford.) Such an echo cannot be superimposed on new ideas, but must, by careful planning, be made an organic part of them.

2. *Devising a whole sentence or paragraph* to bridge other important paragraphs or major divisions. (See Lynn, Pars. 11, 20, and 21.)

3. *Using parallel structure* in an important sentence of one paragraph and the first sentence of the next. This is a subtle means of making the reader feel at ease in the new surroundings, but it is seldom used because it is much more limited in its potential than the other methods of transition. (See Lawrence, Pars. 1 to 2.)

4. *Using standard transitional expressions,* most of which have the additional advantage of indicating relationship of ideas. Only a few of those available are classified below, but nearly all the selections in this book amply illustrate such transitional expressions:

Time—soon, immediately, afterward, later, meanwhile, after a while
Place—nearby, here, beyond, opposite
Result—as a result, therefore, thus, consequently, hence
Comparison—likewise, similarly, in such a manner
Contrast—however, nevertheless, still, but, yet, on the other hand, after all, otherwise
Addition—also, too, and, and then, furthermore, moreover, finally, first, second, third
Miscellaneous—for example, for instance, in fact, indeed, on the whole, in other words

Trite (See *Clichés.*)

Unity in writing is the same as unity in anything else—in a picture, a musical arrangement, or a campus organization—and that is a *one*-ness in which all parts contribute to an overall effect.

Many elements of good writing contribute in varying degrees to the effect of unity. Some of these are properly designed introductions and closings; consistency in point of view, tone, and style; sometimes the recurring use of analogy or thread of symbolism; and occasionally the natural time boundaries of an experience or event, as in the selections of Mitford, Simpson, Gansberg, and Orwell.

But in most expository and argumentative writing the only dependable unifying force is the *central theme,* which every sentence and every word must somehow help to support. (The central theme is also called the *central idea* or the *thesis* when pertaining to the entire writing, and it is almost always called the *thesis* in argument. In an expository or argumentative paragraph it is the same as the *topic sentence,* which may be implied or, if stated, may be located anywhere in the paragraph but is usually placed first.) As soon as anything appears that is not related to the central idea, there are *two* units instead of one. Hence unity is basic to all other virtues of good writing, even to coherence and emphasis, the other two organic essentials. (See *Coherence; Emphasis.*)

An example of unity may be found in a single river system (for a practical use of analogy), with all its tributaries, big or little, meandering or straight, flowing into the main stream and making it bigger—or at least flowing into another tributary that finds its way to the main stream. This is *one* river system, an example of unity. Now picture another stream nearby that does not empty into the river but goes off in some other direction. There are now two systems, not one, and there is no longer unity.

It is the same way with writing. The central theme is the main river, flowing along from the first capital letter to the last period. Every drop of information or evidence must find its way into this theme-river, or it is not a part of the system. It matters not even slightly if the water is good, the idea-stream perhaps deeper and finer than any of the others: if it is not a tributary, it has no business pretending to be relevant to *this* theme of writing.

And that is why most students are required to state their central idea or thesis, usually in solid sentence form, before even starting to organize their ideas. If the writer can use only tributaries, it is very important to know from the start just what the river is.

Credits

Index